Young People and Alcohol

Young People and Alcohol

Impact, Policy, Prevention, Treatment

Edited by

John B. Saunders MD, FRACP

Centre for Youth Substance Abuse Research,
Faculty of Health Sciences, University of Queensland,
Brisbane and Faculty of Medicine, University of Sydney,
Australia

Joseph M. Rey MD, PhD, FRANZCP

Head of Psychiatry, Notre Dame University Medical School,
Sydney and Honorary Professor, University of Sydney Medical
School, Sydney, Australia

WILEY-BLACKWELL

A John Wiley & Sons, Ltd., Publication

Library of Congress Cataloging-in-Publication Data

Young people and alcohol : impact, policy, prevention, treatment / Edited by John B. Saunders MD, FRACP, Centre for Youth Substance Abuse Research, Faculty of Health Sciences, University of Queensland, Brisbane and Faculty of Medicine, University of Sydney, Australia, Joseph M. Rey MD, PhD, FRANZCP Head of Psychiatry, Notre Dame University Medical School Sydney and Honorary Professor, University of Sydney Medical School, Sydney, Australia.
       p. ; cm.
  Includes bibliographical references and index.
  ISBN 978-1-4443-3598-9 (paperback : alk. paper)
  1. Youth–Alcohol use.   2. Teenagers–Alcohol use.   I. Saunders, John B. (John Barrington), 1949- editor.   II. Rey, Joseph M., editor.
    [DNLM: 1. Alcohol-Related Disorders.   2. Adolescent.   3. Alcohol Drinking.   WM 274]
    HV5135.Y673 2011
    618.92'861–dc22

                                                        2010049554

A catalogue record for this book is available from the British Library.

Set in 10/12.5 pt Times by Aptara® Inc., New Delhi, India

Printed and bound in Malaysia by Vivar Printing Sdn Bhd

1   2011

Contents

Contributors

Arpana Agrawal, PhD
Assistant Professor of Psychiatry, Department of Psychiatry, Washington University School of Medicine, St Louis, MO, USA

Peter Anderson, MD, MPH, PhD, FRCP
Professor of Alcohol and Health, Faculty of Health, Medicine and Life Sciences, Maastricht University, Maastricht, The Netherlands

Andrew Baillie, MPsychol, PhD, MAPS
Senior Lecturer and Director of Clinical Psychology, Training Centre for Emotional Health and Department of Psychology, Macquarie University, Sydney, Australia

Bridgette M. Bewick, BA, MA(Hons), PhD
Senior Lecturer in Health Research, Leeds Institute of Health Sciences, School of Medicine, University of Leeds, Leeds, UK

Joseph M. Boden, PhD
Senior Research Fellow and Principal Investigator, Christchurch Health and Development Study, Department of Psychological Medicine, University of Otago, Christchurch, New Zealand

Yvonne Bonomo, MBBS, FRACP, PhD, FAChAM
Clinical Associate Professor and Physician in Addiction Medicine and Adolescent Medicine, Department of Medicine, St Vincent's Hospital, University of Melbourne, Australia

Linda Bosma, PhD
President Bosma Consulting, LLC, Minneapolis, MN, USA

Andrew Clark, MD
Department of Psychiatry, Medical University of South Carolina, Charleston, SC, USA

Deborah Deas, MD, MPH
Professor, Centre for Drug and Alcohol Programs (CDAP), Department of Psychiatry, Medical University of South Carolina, Charleston, SC, USA

David M. Fergusson, PhD, FRSNZ, FNZPS(Hon), FRACP(Hon)
Professor and Executive Director, Christchurch Health and Development Study,
Department of Psychological Medicine, University of Otago, Christchurch, New Zealand

Norman Giesbrecht, PhD
Senior Scientist, Public Health and Regulatory Policy Section, and Social, Prevention
and Health Policy Research Department, Centre for Addiction and Mental Health,
Toronto, Ontario, Canada

Deborah S. Hasin, PhD
Professor of Clinical Epidemiology (in Psychiatry), New York State Psychiatric
Institute, New York, NY, USA; Department of Epidemiology, Mailman School of Public
Health, Columbia University, New York, NY, USA; Department of Psychiatry, College
of Physicians and Surgeons, Columbia University, New York, NY, USA

Bankole A. Johnson, DSc, MD, PhD, MPhil, FRCPsych
Alumni Professor and Chairman, Professor of Neuroscience, and Professor of Medicine,
Department of Psychiatry and Neurobehavioral Sciences, University of Virginia,
Charlottesville, VA, USA

Rose A. Juhasz, PhD
Department of Psychiatry, Addiction Research Center, University of Michigan, Ann
Arbor, MI, USA

Eileen F. S. Kaner, BSc(Hons), MSc, PhD
Professor of Public Health, Institute of Health and Society, Newcastle University,
Newcastle upon Tyne, UK

John F. Kelly, PhD
Associate Professor in Psychiatry, Harvard Medical School, Boston, MA, USA;
Associate Director, MGH-Harvard Center for Addiction Medicine, Massachusetts
General Hospital, Boston, MA, USA; Program Director, Addiction Recovery
Management Service, Massachusetts General Hospital, Boston, MA, USA

Katherine M. Keyes, MPH, MPhil
New York State Psychiatric Institute, New York, NY, USA; Department of
Epidemiology, Mailman School of Public Health, Columbia University, New York, NY,
USA

Michael T. Lynskey, PhD
Associate Professor, Department of Psychiatry, Washington University School of
Medicine, St. Louis, MO, USA

Fiona Measham, BA, MA, PhD
Senior Lecturer in Criminology, Lancaster University, Bailrigg, Lancaster, UK

Sonja Memedovic, BPsychol(Hons)
Research Officer, National Drug and Alcohol Research Centre, University of New South Wales, Sydney, Australia

Louise Mewton, BA (Psychol)(Hons)
Doctoral Candidate, National Drug and Alcohol Research Centre, University of New South Wales, Sydney, Australia

Jeanette Østergaard, PhD
SFI – The Danish National Centre for Social Research, Copenhagen, Denmark

Robert F. Saltz, PhD
Senior Scientist, Pacific Institute for Research and Evaluation, Prevention Research Center, Berkeley, CA, USA

Shauncie M. Skidmore, PhD
Department of Psychiatry, Addiction Research Center, University of Michigan, Ann Arbor, MI, USA

Linda Patia Spear, PhD
Distinguished Professor, Department of Psychology and Developmental Exposure Alcohol Research Center (DEARC), Binghamton University, Binghamton, NY, USA

Rockan Sayegh, MA
Center for Trauma and Injury Prevention Research, University of California Irvine, School of Medicine, Orange, CA, USA

Tim Slade, BSc (Psychol), PhD
Senior Research Fellow, National Drug and Alcohol Research Centre, University of New South Wales, Sydney, Australia

Maree Rose Teesson, PhD
Professor and NHMRC Senior Research Fellow, Assistant Director, National Drug and Alcohol Research Centre, University of New South Wales, Sydney, Australia

Lorna Templeton, MSc, BSc
Research Manager, Mental Health Research and Development Unit, Avon & Wiltshire Mental Health Partnership NHS Trust and the University of Bath, Bath, UK; Independent Research Consultant, Bristol, UK

Federico E. Vaca, MD, MPH
Professor of Emergency Medicine, Department of Emergency Medicine, Yale University School of Medicine, New Haven, CT, USA

Julie D. Yeterian, BA
MGH-Harvard Center for Addiction Medicine, Massachusetts General Hospital, Boston, MA, USA

Robert A. Zucker, PhD
Professor of Psychology, Departments of Psychiatry and Psychology; Director, University of Michigan Addiction Research Center; Director, Substance Abuse Section, Department of Psychiatry, University of Michigan, Ann Arbor, MI, USA

Preface

In the United States in 2008, 8 million adolescents—almost one-third of all people aged 12–17—drank alcohol. On an average day, 205 adolescents presented to hospital emergency departments as a result of their alcohol consumption, often because of alcohol poisoning. Each day, 76 sought substance abuse treatment.[1] Ian Gilmore, President of the Royal College of Physicians, London, UK, said, "The nation's growing addiction to alcohol is putting an immense strain on health services, especially in hospitals, costing the NHS [National Health Service] over £2.7 billion each year. " He added, "This burden is no longer sustainable"—costs had doubled in less than 5 years.[2] A specialist clinic for children with problems related to alcohol misuse was to be launched in the Netherlands following a marked increase in admissions to hospital of children younger than 16 years because of alcohol poisoning.[3] In Thailand, formerly a low alcohol consuming country, consumption of alcohol increased 32-fold between 1961 and 2001 (from 0.26 to 8.47 L per capita, respectively), with a consequent rise in health and social problems, particularly among young women.[4] These events and data draw attention to the fact that youth alcohol use is a growing concern worldwide.

Although consumption varies between countries and among cultural and ethnic groups, patterns of use among the young seem to be converging due to the influence of the mass media, marketing, growing affluence, and globalization. The *Surgeon General's Call to Action to Prevent and Reduce Underage Drinking*[5] highlights that the highest prevalence of alcohol abuse and dependence in any age group is among people aged 18 to 20. The report goes on to stress that adolescents use alcohol differently from adults, that they react uniquely to it, and that alcohol has a powerful attraction for adolescents, with often unpredictable and potentially devastating outcomes.[5] The medical costs of underage drinking (below 21 years of age) in the United States are estimated to be in excess of $5 billion a year. Notwithstanding all this, alcohol problems in the young are often ignored or minimized. For example, Australian data[6]—similar to data elsewhere—show that parents are the most common source of alcohol among school students.

The latest research demonstrates a compelling need to address alcohol use early, in the context of human development, and using a systematic approach that spans childhood through adolescence and into adulthood. The coming tide of medium- to long-term health consequences of increased youth alcohol use is tragically illustrated by Gary Reinbach, a 22-year-old Englishman from Dagenham, Essex, UK. This young man died in hospital after he was refused a liver transplant because he could not prove he had not drunk alcohol for at least 6 months—one of the requirements for liver transplant in the United Kingdom.

Mr. Reinbach had been admitted to hospital 10 weeks earlier with cirrhosis of the liver. His family said he had started drinking at 11 years of age and drank heavily after the age of 13.[7] Most physicians, educators, policymakers, youth workers, teachers, and parents underestimate this problem and are poorly equipped to deal with it. This book aims to fill this gap by providing workers from a range of professional backgrounds working with people aged 12–25 years with authoritative and up to date information about the effects of alcohol use in the young and, particularly, its management, with an emphasis on interventions whose effectiveness is supported by evidence.

The first three chapters deal with the sociological and developmental aspects of alcohol use. Chapter 1 examines the phenomenon of youth drinking in the context of youth culture in the twenty-first century, highlighting recent changes in drinking patterns, a convergence between wine-, beer-, and spirit-drinking cultures, and the novel phenomenon of drinking specifically to become intoxicated as quickly as possible. While Chapter 2 considers the factors associated with early onset drinking and its consequences, Chapter 3 reviews the research on the short- and long-term consequences of adolescent alcohol use; in particular, how much of these outcomes can be actually attributed to alcohol use and how much to other confounding factors.

The next three chapters focus on the biological aspects of alcohol use. Chapter 4 describes how alcohol is handled by the body, its effects on consciousness and behavior, and summarizes the neurobiological mechanisms by which alcohol exerts its acute effects and leads to dependence. Chapter 5 examines a considerable body of new research showing that alcohol has specific effects on the developing adolescent brain. Chapter 6 discusses advances in our understanding of the genetic contributions to alcohol use across the life span but with a focus on adolescence and early adulthood.

Chapters 7–10 describe in some detail prevention and early intervention strategies. Chapter 7 focuses on universal preventive measures such as alcohol policies, legislation, and their effect on youth drinking and on preventing harms such as motor vehicle accidents. There is currently much discussion in the literature and in several countries' media about minimum pricing policies, thus far rejected by legislators on the incorrect belief that they unfairly penalize moderate drinkers. Chapter 8 describes the practicalities of how to mobilize community resources to develop and implement prevention policies and programs in a specific community. Chapter 9 deals with brief alcohol interventions in young people and their effectiveness, with a particular focus on those that can be delivered using new technologies such as the Internet and cell phones. Finally, Chapter 10 examines preventative interventions in schools, colleges, and military, which are receiving considerable attention in the clinical and policy domains. For example, there is a widespread belief that college life encourages heavy drinking.

The next two chapters deal with the assessment and diagnosis of alcohol use disorders in youth, including diagnostic concepts and the classification of alcohol use disorders in the international diagnostic systems (Chapter 12). This chapter also describes the use of scales, diagnostic interviews and biological markers. Chapter 11 outlines the clinical interview of young people who misuse alcohol and emphasizes the importance of empathy and understanding of the young person's experiences with alcohol.

The final 6 chapters address various aspects of treatment, with an emphasis on those that have demonstrated effectiveness or show promise. Chapter 13 deals with the acute management of alcohol intoxication and withdrawal, highlighting the early signs of alcohol poisoning. Chapter 14 draws attention to the importance and issues involved in working with families of adolescents who misuse alcohol. Chapter 15 reviews the large body of literature on the psychological approaches to the treatment of adolescents who misuse alcohol that are the current mainstay of treatment, and offers practical advice on the implementation of these interventions in youth.

The last 10 years have witnessed a dramatic renewal of interest on the pharmacological approaches to the management of alcohol use disorders, resulting in a burgeoning literature. Although research targeting adolescents and young adults is still limited, these efforts are presented in Chapter 16. Chapter 17 describes the evidence for using 12-step programs such as Alcoholics Anonymous and advises clinicians on how to make them more attractive for adolescents and youth. Finally, Chapter 18 gives an excellent picture of the problems managing alcohol use disorders comorbid with other conditions, a very common occurrence in clinical practice.

At the beginning of each chapter, there is a list of "key points" that summarize the thrust of the chapter. At the end, when appropriate, there is a list of sound resources for practitioners, patients, and families, mostly available in the Internet free of charge. We also provide a glossary explaining the abbreviations and some of the technical terms used in this very broad field.

We would like to finish by thanking the contributors very much; they generously agreed to share their wisdom, knowledge, and clinical experience and adhered to a demanding and tight schedule. We are in their debt.

John B. Saunders
Joseph M. Rey

References

1. The OAS Report. *A Day in the Life of American Adolescents: Substance Use Facts Update.* Rockville, MD: Substance Abuse and Mental Health Services Administration; April 29, 2010. http://oas.samhsa.gov.
2. Anonymous. Rising alcohol addiction costs 'could cripple the NHS'. *BBC News* January 1, 2010.
3. Sheldon T. Dutch paediatrician launches clinic for children with alcohol problems. *BMJ* 2006; 333:720.
4. Casswell S, Thamarangsi T. Reducing harm from alcohol: Call to action. *Lancet* 2009; 373:2247–2257.
5. US Department of Health and Human Services. *The Surgeon General's Call to Action To Prevent and Reduce Underage Drinking.* Office of the Surgeon General, Department of Health and Human Services: Washindton, DC, 2007.
6. White V, Hayman J. *Australian Secondary School Students' Use of Alcohol in 2005.* Melbourne: The Cancer Council Victoria; 2006.
7. Rouse B. Alcoholic, denied liver transplant, dies at age of 22. *Irish Examiner* July 21, 2009.

Glossary and abbreviations

Joseph M. Rey

Acamprosate: A drug used in the treatment of alcohol dependence that blocks glutamatergic *N*-methyl-D-aspartate (NMDA) receptors and activates gamma-aminobutyric acid (GABA) type A receptors. Acamprosate's main effect in alcohol dependence seems to be suppression of glutamatergic hyperactivity, resulting in a dampening of craving.

Acetaldehyde: A toxic by-product of alcohol metabolism.

Acetate: A salt or ester of acetic acid; produced from the metabolism of acetaldehyde.

ADH: Alcohol dehydrogenase.

ADHD: Attention-deficit hyperactivity disorder.

Alcohol abuse: The term alcohol abuse is a DSM-IV diagnosis, but is not in the ICD 10. In DSM-IV, it is defined as a maladaptive pattern of alcohol use leading to clinically significant impairment or distress and social consequences, with at least one of the following occurring within a 12-month period:

- Recurrent alcohol use resulting in a failure to fulfill major role obligations at work, school, home (e.g., alcohol-related absences, suspensions, or expulsions from school).
- Recurrent alcohol use in situations in which it is physically hazardous (e.g., when driving an automobile or operating a machine).
- Recurrent alcohol-related legal problems.
- Continued use of alcohol despite having persistent or recurrent social or interpersonal problems caused or exacerbated by the effects of the alcohol.

Alcohol dehydrogenase (ADH): An enzyme that breaks down alcohol by oxidation, converting it to acetaldehyde.

Alcohol dependence: Alcohol dependence is a diagnostic entity in both ICD 10 and DSM-IV, and is described in essentially similar terms in the two systems. In ICD 10, it is defined as a cluster of behavioral, cognitive, and physiological phenomena that develop after repeated alcohol use and that typically include a strong desire to consume alcohol, difficulties in controlling its use, persisting in its use despite harmful consequences, a higher priority given to its use than to other activities and obligations, increased tolerance, and sometimes a physical withdrawal state.

Alcohol intoxication: See intoxication.

Alcohol misuse: Alcohol misuse is the use of alcohol in a way that is not consistent with legal or medical guidelines. It is not a diagnostic term in either ICD 10 or DSM-IV. It tends to be used as an umbrella term encompassing a range of drinking patterns leading to disorders, harm, and social problems.

Alcohol Use Disorders Identification Test (AUDIT): A screening and brief assessment instrument for alcohol misuse approved by the World Health Organization.

Alcohol withdrawal: It is defined by the American Psychiatric Association (DSM-IV) as the cessation of heavy or prolonged alcohol use resulting in two or more of the following: autonomic hyperactivity, increased hand tremor, insomnia, nausea or vomiting, hallucinations, psychomotor agitation, anxiety, and seizures.

Alcoholics Anonymous (AA): AA is a self-help group "of men and women who share their experience, strength and hope with each other that they may solve their common problem and help others to recover from alcoholism." The only requirement for membership is a desire to stop drinking. AA is an informal society of more than 2 million recovering alcoholics throughout the world and is not allied with any religion, political organization or institution. AA is nonprofessional—it does not have clinics, doctors, counselors or psychologists and there is no central authority controlling how groups operate. The "12 steps" provide a framework for self-examination and a road to recovery.

Alcoholism Type A: See Type A alcoholism.

Alcoholism Type B: See Type B alcoholism.

Allele: One of two or more variants of a certain gene.

Amino acids: The principal building blocks of proteins and enzymes.

Andersen model of health services utilization: A model developed by Andersen and Laake to determine the use of health services whereby medical contacts are determined by three factors: Predisposing (gender, age, and socioeconomic status), enabling (conditions that facilitate or inhibit the use of physician services—for example, the distance to the health center, the type of municipality, working hours, and family size) and need (such as chronic diseases, disability, new illnesses, and psychological well-being).

AODs: Alcohol and other drug use disorders.

Attention-deficit hyperactivity disorder: A common childhood condition characterized by developmentally inappropriate inattention, impulsivity and hyperactivity that causes significant functional impairment.

AUD: Alcohol use disorder.

AUDIT: The Alcohol Use Disorders Identification Test.

BAC: Blood alcohol concentration.

Baclofen: A $GABA_B$ receptor agonist which is typically used as muscle relaxant for the treatment of spasticity, and which is under investigation as a treatment for alcohol dependence.

BAL: Blood alcohol level.

BASICS: Brief Alcohol Screening and Intervention for College Students.

Behavioral inhibition: A temperament or style of reacting displayed by some infants and children when confronted with novel situations or unfamiliar adults or peers. Behavioral inhibition is characterized by withdrawal, avoidance, fear of the unfamiliar and overarousal of the sympathetic nervous system. These children tend to be fearful, cautious, quiet, introverted, and shy in unfamiliar situations.

Behavioral undercontrol: The inability, unwillingness or failure to inhibit behavior even in the face of anticipated or already received negative consequences. Behavioural undercontrol is considered a risk factor for alcohol misuse.

Binge drinking: The term "binge drinking" or "binge" has no generally accepted definition. Traditionally, a "binge" was used to describe an episode of heavy drinking occurring over a prolonged period set aside for the purpose. Recent use of the term "binge" refers to a single drinking session intended to achieve, or actually leading to, intoxication. The World Health Organization has defined it as consumption of six 10 g drinks (60 g alcohol) in a single session, an amount that would be expected to lead to perceptible impairment. The United States has recently introduced a definition of binge drinking meaning the consumption of five or more US standard drinks in a single session for males (65 g alcohol) and four for females (52 g alcohol). This is also called the "five/four" measure.

Blood alcohol concentration: It is the concentration of alcohol in a person's blood; it is measured either as mass per volume, or as a percentage of mass by mass. Several measurement units are used:

- Mass per volume of blood in the body (e.g., 80 mg/100 mL).
- Mass of alcohol per mass of blood (e.g., 0.08 g/kg).

Because 1 mL of blood is equivalent to 1.06 g of blood, units by volume are similar but not identical to units by mass. In anglophone countries, the mass per volume of blood (e.g., 80 mg/100 mL) is typically used. In many countries, BAC is measured and reported as grams of alcohol per 1,000 mL (1 L) of blood (g/L). For purposes of law enforcement, BAC is used to define intoxication and provides a rough measure of impairment.

Buspirone: A serotonin-1A partial agonist drug that is typically used for the treatment of anxiety, and is being investigated in the treatment of alcohol dependence.

CA: Cocaine Anonymous.

CD: Conduct disorder.

CDC: Centers for Disease Control and Prevention.

C57BL/6 mouse: An inbred mouse resulting from no less than 20 consecutive generations of brother–sister matings. This allows the offspring to possess both genetic and phenotypic uniformity. C57BL/6 mice show a high alcohol and morphine preference.

CHDS: Christchurch Health and Development Study.

Cocaine Anonymous: A 12-step self-help program for recovering cocaine users.

Conduct disorder: A common childhood and adolescent disorder characterized by a persistent pattern of breaking rules or age-appropriate societal norms (stealing, truancy, running away from home overnight . . .).

Cosegregate: The tendency for closely linked genes and genetic markers to be inherited (segregate) together.

COT: Children of twins design in genetic studies.

Cotinine: An alkaloid found in tobacco and a metabolite of nicotine. Serum and urinary levels of cotinine are used as a biomarker for exposure to tobacco smoke.

CPR: Cardiopulmonary resuscitation.

Cytochrome P450: A family of cytochromes, one of which (CYP2E1) can oxidize alcohol to form acetaldehyde; high alcohol levels stimulate CYP2E1 activity.

DA: Dopamine.

Disulfiram: A drug that inhibits the enzyme aldehyde dehydrogenase and prevents the metabolism of alcohol's primary metabolite, acetaldehyde. The accumulation of acetaldehyde in the blood causes unpleasant effects when alcohol is ingested: Sweating, headache, dyspnoea, lowered blood pressure, flushing, palpitations, nausea, and vomiting.

Dizygotic (twins): Also called "fraternal" twins, develop from two separate eggs (zygotes) that are fertilized by two separate sperm. Like other brothers and sisters, they share about half of their genetic material.

Dominance: In genetics, it is the phenomenon by which one of a pair of genes (alleles) exerts a greater influence that affects the expression of an inherited character. "Dominant" is the opposite of "recessive." However, a dominant trait does not mean higher potency, and recessive does not mean weak; the terms simply refer to the visible trait, the phenotype, seen in a heterozygote. If only two phenotypes are possible, and a heterozygote exhibits one phenotype, by definition the phenotype exhibited by the heterozygote is called "dominant" and the "hidden" phenotype is called "recessive."

Dopamine: A neurotransmitter that plays important functions in many brain systems such as those controlling motility, motivation and cognition. Dopamine has a key role in the reward systems of the brain, providing feelings of enjoyment and reinforcement to motivate a person to proactively perform certain activities, thus essential in the mechanisms underlying addiction.

Driving under the influence: A legal term that describes individuals found driving a motor vehicle while having a blood alcohol concentration above a determined level that varies between legislatures, for example, 0.05% (g/100 mL) in Australia.

"Dry" pattern of drinking: Refers to a pattern of drinking leading to intoxication, usually in nonfamily oriented social events. This pattern is common in Northern European countries.

DSM: The *Diagnostic and Statistical Manual of Mental Disorders* of the American Psychiatric Association, currently in its fourth edition (DSM-IV). The fifth edition is in preparation.

DUI: Driving under the influence (of alcohol).

DZ: Dizygotic or fraternal (twins).

Early onset drinking: Usually, but not universally, understood as alcohol use which starts before age 14.

Earned media: Also called "free media" (as opposed to paid media—publicity obtained through paid advertising) refers to publicity achieved through promotional efforts other than advertising.

Effect size: A measure of the strength of the relationship between two variables in a population. The most commonly used measure of effect size in the biomedical sciences is Cohen's *d*, which is defined as the difference between two means (e.g., mean days abstinent among a treated sample minus mean days abstinent among those treated with placebo) divided by the standard deviation for the whole group. An effect size of

0.2–0.3 is usually considered "small," around 0.5 "medium," and above 0.8 "large"; *d* can be larger than one.

Emerging adults: Young adults aged 18–25 years.

EMS: Emergency medical service.

Endophenotypes: Measurable biomarkers that are not directly observable or components of a disorder. An endophenotype may be neurophysiologic, biochemic, endocrine, neuroanatomic, cognitive, or neuropsychologic in nature. Endophenotypes represent more easily understood and measurable variables than the disorder itself.

EOD: Early onset drinking.

Epigenetics: The study of heritable changes in gene function that occur without a change in the DNA sequence.

Epistasis: The interaction between two or more genes (modifier genes) to control a single phenotype. The gene whose phenotype is expressed is said to be epistatic, while the phenotype altered or suppressed is said to be hypostatic.

ESPAD: European School Survey Project on Alcohol and Other Drugs

Event related potential (ERP): Any stereotyped electrophysiological response to an internal or external stimulus. ERPs are obtained by recording the electrical brain currents detected on the scalp through an electroencephalogram (EEG).

Executive functions: Term used to describe a set of higher level cognitive abilities that control other cognitive processes. They include the ability to initiate and stop actions, to monitor and change behavior as needed, and to plan when faced with novel tasks and situations. Executive functions allow individuals to anticipate outcomes and adapt to changing situations.

Externalizing disorders: A broad category of childhood behavior disorders that manifest in children's outward behavior rather than their internal thoughts and feelings (internalizing disorders). These conditions include conduct disorder, oppositional defiant disorder, and attention-deficit hyperactivity disorder. This term is not used to describe adult conditions.

FAS: Fetal alcohol syndrome.

FASD: Fetal alcohol spectrum disorder.

FDA: U.S. Food and Drug Administration.

Fetal alcohol spectrum disorder: A variety of alcohol-induced problems that include fetal alcohol syndrome and other alcohol-induced abnormalities that do not meet criteria for fetal alcohol syndrome. Fetal alcohol syndrome does not represent the full spectrum of alcohol teratogenesis, but a subset of individuals exposed to alcohol during pregnancy that have a recognizable pattern of malformation.

Fetal alcohol syndrome: Fetal alcohol syndrome is a set of malformations occurring in children exposed to alcohol during pregnancy. It is characterized by physical abnormalities in the face and reduced size of the newborn, as well as behavioral and cognitive problems. The facial abnormalities include short palpebral fissures and abnormalities in the premaxillary zone (e.g., flat upper lip, flattened *philtrum*, and flat midface); evidence of growth retardation (e.g., low birth weight for gestational age, disproportionally low weight to height); and evidence of neurodevelopmental anomalies (e.g., decreased cranial size at birth, microcephaly, partial or complete agenesis of the *corpus callosum*, and cerebellar hypoplasia).

5-HT: 5-Hydroxytryptamine or serotonin.

Fluoxetine: A selective serotonin reuptake inhibitor drug, typically used for the treatment of depression.

Fluvoxamine: A selective serotonin reuptake inhibitor drug, typically used for the treatment of depression.

fMRI: Functional magnetic resonance imaging.

Functional family therapy (FFT): A multisystemic treatment that focuses on the multiple domains and systems within which adolescents and their families live. In this context, FFT seeks to develop family members' inner strengths and sense of being able to improve their situation, providing the family with a platform for change and future functioning. FFT follows three phases: "engagement and motivation" (e.g., reattribution —reframing, developing positive themes); "behavior change" (e.g., therapists provide concrete behavioral interventions to guide and model specific behavior changes such as parenting, communication, and conflict management); and "generalization" (e.g., helping to generalize positive family change to other problem areas or situations, and to maintain change and prevent relapse).

Functional magnetic resonance imaging: Detects changes in blood flow in regions of the brain when performing a task; increases in blood flow reflecting increased neural activity.

GABA: Gamma-aminobutyric acid.

Gamma-aminobutyric acid: The main inhibitory neurotransmitter in the central nervous system, playing a key role in regulating neuronal excitability. GABA is also responsible for the regulation of muscle tone.

Gamma-glutamyl transferase: (Also known as gamma-glutamyl transpeptidase, gamma-glutamyltransferase, GGT, GGTP, and gamma-GT) is an enzyme present in cell membranes in many tissues and particularly the liver. Elevated serum GGT activity can be found in diseases of the liver, biliary system, and pancreas. GGT is used as a biomarker for abuse and dependence (elevated in about 50%) and to monitor for alcohol use in people receiving treatment for alcohol dependence.

Gene–environment interaction (GxE): It is the phenotypic effect of interactions between genes and the environment. Practically all human diseases result from the interaction of genetic susceptibility and modifiable environmental factors (infectious, chemical, physical, nutritional, and behavioral). Many people tend to classify the cause of disease as either genetic or environmental when practically all the common illnesses are a result of the complex interplay between genes and the environment. Often, what is inherited is sensitivity to the effects of various environmental risk factors. For example, sunlight exposure has a much stronger influence on skin cancer risk in fair-skinned humans than in individuals with an inherited tendency to darker skin.

Genotype: The complete genetic makeup of an organism determined by the particular combination of alleles for all genes.

GGT: Gamma-glutamyl transferase.

Health Beliefs Model: It is a psychological model that seeks to explain and predict health behaviors. It was developed in the 1950s by the US social psychologists Hochbaum, Rosenstock, and Kegels in response to the failure of a free tuberculosis health screening program. Since then, this model has been adapted to explore a variety of health behaviors, including sexual risk behaviors and the transmission of HIV/AIDS. The Health Beliefs Model is based on the understanding that individuals will take a health-related action (e.g., use condoms) if they: (a) feel that a negative health condition (e.g., HIV) can be avoided; (b) have a positive expectation that, by taking a recommended action, they will avoid a negative health outcome (e.g., using condoms will prevent HIV); and (c) believe that they can successfully take a recommended action (e.g., they can use condoms comfortably and with confidence).

Hepatocytes: The principal cells of the liver, which carry out most of the liver's metabolic activities.

Hippocampus: A pair of brain structures, one in each hemisphere, similar in shape to a seahorse, which are located beneath the cortical surface, inside the medial temporal lobe. The hippocampus is part of the limbic system and plays an important role in long-term memory.

ICD: International Classification of Diseases.

Ignition interlock: A mechanical device that does not allow a car to be driven by a driver who is over the legal alcohol limit.

Internalizing disorders: A group of psychiatric conditions characterized mostly by problematic internal thoughts and feelings such as depressive and anxiety symptoms (e.g., major depressive disorder, generalized anxiety, separation anxiety)—in contrast with "externalizing disorders." This term is chiefly used to describe child and adolescent disorders but not to adult conditions.

International Classification of Diseases: ICD is the World Health Organization's taxonomy of diseases, currently in its tenth revision (ICD 10). The eleventh revision is currently in preparation.

Intoxication (alcohol): A short-term state that occurs following ingestion of alcohol and has features compatible with the known physiological effects of alcohol (e.g., at increasing doses: euphoria, disinhibition, talkativeness, slurred speech, incoordination, memory impairment, stupor, and coma). Alcohol intoxication as clinical diagnosis (DSM or ICD) is a condition that follows consumption of alcohol to the extent that it causes significant disturbances in consciousness, cognition, perception, affect, behavior, or psychosocial functioning.

Lean body mass: The mass of the body minus the fat (i.e., bones, muscles, and organs).

Licensed (premise): When alcohol can be consumed in the premises (e.g., bars, pubs, and restaurants).

Linkage analysis (genetics): A statistical method used to associate functionality of genes to their location on chromosomes. When genes occur on the same chromosome, they are usually inherited as a single unit, that is, have a tendency to stick together when passed on to offspring. Genes inherited in this way are said to be linked, and are referred to as "linkage groups." For example, in fruit flies the genes affecting eye color and wing length are inherited together because they appear on the same chromosome. Thus, if some disease is often passed to offspring along with specific markers, then it can be concluded that the genes that are responsible for the disease are located close on the chromosome to these markers.

Mandated students/patients: Individuals who have violated alcohol policies or laws and are ordered by the appropriate authority or court to undergo treatment.

Mating, assortative: When individuals choose to mate with individuals that are similar (positive assortative mating) or dissimilar (negative assortative mating) to themselves in some specific manner. Assortative mating have the effect of reducing (positive) or increasing (negative) the range of variation (trait variance), when the assorting is cued on heritable traits.

Mating, random: When individuals choose a mate regardless of any physical, genetic, or social preference, that is, mating is not influenced by any environmental, hereditary, or social interaction (i.e., potential mates have an equal chance of being selected).

Minimum pricing: When the minimum price paid for gram of alcohol in beverages is set by legislation. Minimum pricing circumvents discounting or other measures to reduce the price of alcohol.

Monozygotic (twins): Also called "identical," develop from one single egg (zygote) that splits and forms two embryos. They share about 100% of their genetic material. The degree of separation of monozygotic twins in the uterus depends on when they split into two zygotes, which determines the chorionicity (the number of placentas) and amniocity (the number of amniotic sacs) and how much they share the uterine environment. Dichorionic twins divided within the first 4 days. Monoamnionic twins divide after the first week.

Motivational enhancement therapy: A form of therapy that follows motivational interviewing principles.

Motivational interviewing: Motivational interviewing is a directive, client-centered counseling style for eliciting behavior change by helping clients to explore and resolve ambivalence. Compared with nondirective counseling, it is more focused and goal directed. The examination and resolution of ambivalence is its central purpose, and the counselor is intentionally directive in pursuing this goal. Motivational enhancement strategies are based on the theory that individuals alone are responsible for changing their drinking behavior.

MST: Multisystemic therapy.

Multisystemic therapy (MST): An intensive family- and community-based treatment that focuses on the entire world of the young person. MST targets chronic and violent juvenile offenders—often with concurrent alcohol or drug problems—their homes and families, schools, and teachers, neighborhoods and friends. MST does not take place in a clinic but clinicians go to where the child is (home, school, and neighborhood) and are on call 24 hours a day, 7 days a week, supported by a skilled team. They work intensively with parents and caregivers to put them in control, to keep the adolescent focused on school and on gaining job skills; and the therapist and caregivers introduce the youth to sports and recreational activities as an alternative to "hanging out." MST is resource intensive.

MZ: Monozygotic (twins).

NA: Narcotics Anonymous.

Naltrexone: An opioid receptor antagonist (i.e., it blocks the opioid receptors in the brain and therefore blocks the effects of heroin and other opioids). Naltrexone and its active metabolite 6-β-naltrexol are competitive antagonists at μ (mu)- and κ (kappa)-opioid receptors, and to a lesser extent at δ (delta)-opioid receptors. Naltrexone is used primarily in the treatment of alcohol dependence and, to a lesser extent, opioid dependence (e.g., for the controversial rapid detoxification of opioid dependent individuals).

Neocortex: It is the top layer of the cerebral hemispheres. It is involved in higher functions such as sensory perception, complex motor activities, spatial reasoning and, in humans, conscious thought and language. It is called "neo" because it is the most recently evolved part of the brain.

NIAAA: National Institute on Alcohol Abuse and Alcoholism.

NMDA: *N*-Methyl-D-aspartate, an amino acid derivative that acts as a specific agonist at the NMDA receptor, and therefore mimics the action of the neurotransmitter glutamate on that receptor. In contrast to glutamate, NMDA binds to and regulates the NMDA receptor only, with no effect on other glutamate receptors. Ethanol has an NMDA antagonist effect.

NNT: Number needed to treat.

Nonshared environment: A term used in behavioral genetics to represent the effect of nongenetic factors other than those shared by siblings (i.e., those that uniquely affect individuals, making siblings different). An event is nonshared if it is experienced by only one sibling in a family regardless of the consequences it produces, this includes unsystematic, idiosyncratic, or serendipitous events such as accidents, illnesses, or traumas. In general, genetic and shared environmental factors explain about 50% of the differences between siblings; the other 50% is unexplained and is attributed to "nonshared" environmental factors.

Nucleus accumbens: It is a bilateral collection of neurons within the striatum, located where the head of the caudate and the anterior portion of the putamen meet, just lateral to the septum pellucidum. The nucleus accumbens maintains close links with the ventral tegmental area and the prefrontal cortex. Its operation chiefly involves two neurotransmitters: dopamine and serotonin. There is evidence the nucleus accumbens plays an important role in reward, pleasure, addiction, aggression, and fear.

Number needed to treat (NNT): The number of individuals who need to be treated in order to prevent one additional case or bad outcome (i.e., relapse in drinking). Data from randomized controlled trials are required to compute NNT, which is equal to one divided by the rate or response in the control group minus the rate of response in the treatment group (this is also called "absolute risk reduction"). For example, in the acamprosate meta-analysis of Mann and colleagues (see reference 205 in Chapter 16), 36.1% of participants achieved abstinence at 6 months compared with 23.4% of those on placebo. In this case, NNT $= 1/(0.234–0.361) = 7.9$. That is, eight patients (it is customary to round to the next whole number) will need to be treated with acamprosate for one additional patient to abstain from alcohol at 6 months. The lower the NNT the more effective the intervention.

Odds ratio: The ratio of the odds of an event occurring in one group to the odds of it occurring in another group. The odds ratio is a statistic that quantifies the strength of association or nonindependence between two variables. An odds ratio of 1 implies that the event is equally likely in both groups. An odds ratio greater than one implies that the event is *more likely* in the first group. An odds ratio less than one implies that the event is *less likely* in the first group.

Off-license: When alcohol can be purchased but not consumed in the premises (e.g., bottle shops and supermarkets)

Ondansetron: A serotonin 5-HT$_3$ receptor antagonist drug used mainly as antiemetic to treat chemotherapy-related nausea and vomiting.

One-on-ones: A term used in both clinical practice and health service organization and human resource management. In clinical practice, it is typically employed to describe an assessment or therapy session involving a patient or client and a health professional. In the organizational context, when they may also be known as "relational meetings," they are face-to-face discussion between two people (organizer and potential leader or leader and potential leader) for the purpose of exploring a relationship between a potential leader and an organization. Relational meetings are often used as recruitment and teaching tools. They are the building blocks of community organizing in community prevention initiatives. In this case, it is a conversation with individual community members to learn about their concerns in relation to the project's goals, level of interest and commitment for the project, and the resources they might bring to the project.

Opioid receptors: A group of receptors that bind with opioids (e.g., morphine and methadone) resulting in a wide array of cellular and physiological responses such as analgesia. The endogenous opioids include enkephalins and endorphins, among others. There are four major subtypes of opioid receptors: μ (mu), κ (kappa), δ (delta) and the nociceptin receptor.

OPRM1 gene: A gene that encodes the mu-opioid receptor—the primary site of action for the most commonly used opioids, including morphine, heroin, and methadone. It is also the primary receptor for endogenous opioid peptides such as beta-endorphin and the enkephalins.

OR: Odds ratio.

Oxidation: A chemical reaction that results in a loss of electrons by a substance and that usually involves removing a hydrogen atom from a molecule or adding oxygen to it, or both.

P300: The P300 (P3) wave is an event related potential elicited by infrequent, task-relevant stimuli. It is considered to reflect a person's reaction to the stimulus rather than to the stimulus itself.

Paroxetine: A selective serotonin reuptake inhibitor drug, typically used for the treatment of depression.

Phenotype: Represents the observable characteristics or traits of an organism, which are the joint product of both genetic *and* environmental influences (morphology, development, behavior, etc.).

Pleiotropy: When a single gene influences multiple phenotypic traits.

Polymorphism: Existence of a gene in several allelic forms.

Preference paradigms: The conditioned place preference paradigm is a behavioral model used to study the rewarding and aversive effects of drugs. The basic characteristics of this task involve the association of a particular environment with administration of a drug treatment, followed by the association of a different environment with the absence of the drug (i.e., the drug's vehicle). A conditioned place preference is found if the animals spend significantly more time in the drug-paired compartment *versus* the vehicle-paired compartment.

Prefrontal cortex: It is the very front of the brain, the anterior region of the frontal lobes, located immediately beneath the forehead. The prefrontal cortex is responsible for executive functions, complex cognitive behaviors, personality expression, decision making, and moderating correct social behavior.

Prevention:

- **Primary:** Primary prevention seeks to lower the incidence of new cases of a disorder in individuals who have not had the disorder.
- **Secondary:** Secondary prevention seeks to intervene following the first episode of a disorder or when the disorder is in its early stages, and prevent recurrence or progression of the disorder to a more severe stage.
- **Tertiary:** Tertiary prevention seeks through treatment of a disorder to ensure that the person affected recovers from its consequences and to prevent its continuing in a chronic phase.
- **Universal:** When preventive interventions are administered to a whole population; that is, do not select participants based on risk.
- **Selective:** When interventions are given to subgroups whose risk for the target factor is deemed to be above average.
- **Indicated:** When interventions are provided to people who have detectable, sub-threshold level of signs or symptoms, but who do not yet meet diagnostic criteria for the condition. Indicated prevention is a form of early intervention.

PTSD: Posttraumatic stress disorder.

Randomized controlled trial: A controlled study using an experimental condition design in which participants are randomly allocated to receive an intervention (the "active condition") or a placebo (e.g., an inactive substance or what would be regarded as standard existing treatment). The term "double blind" in this context means that neither researchers nor participants are aware of the group allocation.

RBS: Responsible beverage server training.

RCT: Randomized controlled trial.

Receptor: A protein on the surface of a cell that recognizes and binds to chemical messengers.

Relational meetings: See "one-on-ones."

Responsible beverage server training: Also known as "server training," refers to educating owners, managers, servers, and sellers at alcohol establishments about strategies to avoid illegally selling alcohol to underage youth or to intoxicated patrons.

Ritanserin: A serotonin-2 receptor antagonist with potential therapeutic effects.

Selective serotonin reuptake inhibitors: A group of drugs that block the reabsorption (reuptake) of serotonin in the synaptic cleft of certain neurons, increasing the amount of serotonin available in the brain. Increased serotonin enhances neurotransmission—the sending of nerve impulses—and improves mood. They are called selective because they seem to affect serotonin and not other neurotransmitters. They are mostly used for the treatment of depression and anxiety disorders. Examples include fluoxetine, sertraline, and cytalopram.

Serotonin: Is a neurotransmitter that activates serotonin or 5-hydroxytryptamine (5-HT) receptors. These are a group of receptors (more than seven have been identified— e.g.,

5-HT$_1$, 5-HT$_2$...) found in the central and peripheral nervous systems. They are involved in both excitatory and inhibitory neurotransmission—the sending of nerve impulses. The serotonin receptors modulate the release of many neurotransmitters, including glutamate, GABA, dopamine, epinephrine and acetylcholine, as well as hormones, including oxytocin, prolactin, and vasopressin. The serotonin receptors influence various biological and psychological processes such as mood, aggression, anxiety, and appetite.

Sertraline: A selective serotonin reuptake inhibitor drug, typically used for the treatment of depression.

Shared environment: A term used in behavioral genetics to represent the effects of shared factors, those shared by siblings growing up in the same family making them more similar.

Single-nucleotide polymorphism (SNP): A sequence variation in the DNA in which a single nucleotide in the genome (or other shared sequence) differs between members of a species or an individual's paired chromosomes. SNPs are important because they allow for comparisons in regions of the genome between cohorts (e.g., matched groups with and without a disease) in regions of the genome.

SNP: (Pronounced snip) single-nucleotide polymorphism.

Sprague-Dawley rat: A breed of albino rat, calm and easy to handle, that is used extensively in medical research.

SSRIs: Selective serotonin reuptake inhibitors.

Standard drink: A standard drink is a drink that contains a specified amount of pure alcohol. One standard drink (see Figure G.1) always contains the same amount of alcohol regardless of container size or type of alcoholic beverage. The "standard drink" is used in many countries to quantify alcohol intake, although there is no international agreement ("standard") on what constitutes a standard drink, varying substantially from country to country—from 6 g of alcohol in Austria to 19.75 g in Japan. For example, a standard drink is 7.0 g of alcohol in the United Kingdom, 10 g in Australia, 12 g in France, and 14 g in Canada and the United States.

SUD: Substance use disorder.

Taste perversion: Distorted sense of taste, often as a side effect of a medication.

Therapeutic community: A treatment in which the community itself, through self-help and mutual support, is the principal means for promoting personal change. Therapeutic communities (TCs) for the treatment of drug abuse and addiction have existed for more than 40 years. In general, TCs are drug-free residential settings where clients/patients and therapists live together and include group psychotherapy as well as practical activities. Peer influence, mediated through a variety of group processes, is used to help individuals learn and assimilate social norms and develop more effective social skills. TCs differ from other treatment approaches principally in their use of the community— comprising treatment staff and those in recovery—as key agents of change. Treatment usually follows three stages. *Induction and early treatment* typically occurs during the first 30 days to assimilate the individual into the TC. The new resident learns TC policies and procedures; establishes trust with staff and other residents; initiates an assisted personal assessment of self, circumstances, and needs; begins to understand the nature of addiction; and should begin to commit to the recovery process. *Primary treatment*

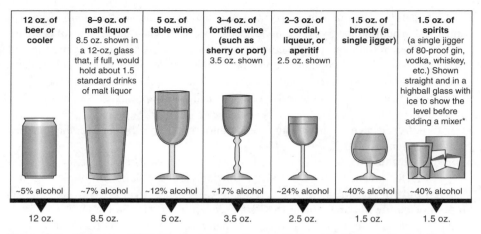

12 oz. of beer or cooler	8–9 oz. of malt liquor 8.5 oz. shown in a 12-oz, glass that, if full, would hold about 1.5 standard drinks of malt liquor	5 oz. of table wine	3–4 oz. of fortified wine (such as sherry or port) 3.5 oz. shown	2–3 oz. of cordial, liqueur, or aperitif 2.5 oz. shown	1.5 oz. of brandy (a single jigger)	1.5 oz. of spirits (a single jigger of 80-proof gin, vodka, whiskey, etc.) Shown straight and in a highball glass with ice to show the level before adding a mixer*
~5% alcohol	~7% alcohol	~12% alcohol	~17% alcohol	~24% alcohol	~40% alcohol	~40% alcohol
12 oz.	8.5 oz.	5 oz.	3.5 oz.	2.5 oz.	1.5 oz.	1.5 oz.

Figure G.1   Examples of US standard drinks. *Source*: National Institute on Alcohol Abuse and Alcoholism.

often uses a structured model of progression through increasing levels of prosocial attitudes, behaviors, and responsibilities. The TC may use interventions to change the individual's attitudes, perceptions, and behaviors related to drug use and to address the social, educational, vocational, familial, and psychological needs of the individual. *Reentry* is intended to facilitate the individual's separation from the TC and successful transition to the larger society. A TC graduate leaves the program drug-free and employed or attending school. Postresidential care may include individual and family counseling and vocational and educational guidance. Self-help groups such as AA are often incorporated into TC treatment, and TC residents are encouraged to participate in such groups after treatment.

Topiramate: A drug with multiple effects (such as blocking voltage-dependent sodium channels, augmenting the activity of some GABA receptors) that is typically used for treatment-resistant epilepsy and to prevent migraine, and is currently under investigation for the treatment of alcohol dependence.

Transfection: The process of deliberately introducing nucleic acids into cells (transfected cells), particularly if nonviral methods are used. This process is also called "transformation."

Twelve-step (12-step) groups/programs: Programs that follow the 12-step recovery model. The "12-steps" is a set of guiding principles outlining a course of action for recovery from addiction and other behavioral problems. The 12 steps were originally proposed by Alcoholics Anonymous but were later adapted to other problems in Narcotics Anonymous, Cocaine Anonymous, and Overeaters Anonymous.

Twelve-step (12-step) meetings: Meetings that have the same general format, content, and traditions of the "12-steps" recovery model.

Type A alcoholism: One of the two subtypes of alcoholism according to Babor and similar to Cloninger's classification. Type A is characterized by later onset (typically after the age of 25 years), fewer childhood risk factors, less severe dependence, fewer alcohol-related problems, and less psychopathological dysfunction.

Type B alcoholism: One of the two subtypes of alcoholism according to Babor and similar to Cloninger's classification. Type B is characterized by childhood risk factors, familial alcoholism, early onset of alcohol-related problems (typically before the age of 25 years), greater severity of dependence, polydrug use, a more chronic treatment history (despite their younger age), greater psychopathological dysfunction, and more life stress.

UK: United Kingdom (England, Northern Ireland, Scotland, and Wales).

Underage drinking: Consuming alcohol below the age in which the purchase of alcohol is legally allowed in a specific country (e.g., 21 years in the United States, 18 years in Australia, Canada, and the United Kingdom).

US: United States of America.

Vivitrol: Trade name of an extended-release (depot) formulation of naltrexone. It was formerly known as "vivitrex."

"Wet" pattern of drinking: It describes when small amounts of alcohol are consumed more frequently (e.g., at meal times) but consumption is less heavy. This pattern is more common in Southern European countries.

Wistar rat: It is an outbred (i.e., generated from breeding two genetically dissimilar strains of the same species) strain of albino rats. The Wistar rat is one of the most popular rat strains used for laboratory research. Wistar rats are more active than other strains like Sprague Dawley rats, which were developed from Wistar rats.

Withdrawal: See alcohol withdrawal.

Part I

The Phenomenon and Impact of Youth Drinking

Chapter 1

The phenomenon of youth drinking

Fiona Measham[1] and Jeanette Østergaard[2]
[1]Lancaster University, Lancaster, UK
[2]SFI – The Danish National Centre for Social Research, Copenhagen, Denmark

---

Key points

- Wide variations exist in young people's drinking and attitudes to alcohol around the world, influenced by family, peers, schools, ethnic and religious upbringing, media, advertising, and national and cultural contexts.
- Uptake of alcohol consumption in early adolescence can mark both a rite of passage between childhood and adulthood and a phase of limit-testing, transgression, or deviance from adult social constraints.
- Cross-national studies have noted the emergence of heavy sessional consumption or 'binge drinking' for both young women and young men, in higher and lower income groups, with drunkenness in some youth cultures seen as an intended and desirable consequence rather than negative side effect of heavy drinking.
- It has been suggested that the reason for the growth in young people's heavy sessional consumption is the globalization of cheap and high-strength alcoholic beverages across the world, associated with the expansion of an increasingly alcohol-oriented night-time economy appealing to youth and young adults.
- Evidence of convergence in drinking patterns between young women and young men in some developed countries has been linked to young women's growing educational and employment opportunities. However, gender remains significant to aspects of consumption, such as beverage choice and attitudes to public drunkenness.

For young people, alcohol is a potent symbol both of socialization into adult society and of transgression and rule breaking. In many societies, the uptake of alcohol is a developmental rite of passage, a period of adolescent experimentation that forms part of a broader phase of transgression that precedes individual consolidation of the cultural and social norms for that society. Drinking is sometimes one of a cluster of teenage risk-taking or deviant activities associated with rebellion, including smoking, risky sexual activities, and experimentation with illicit drugs. This chapter explores the themes of socialization and transgression, looking at both continuity and change in patterns of youthful alcohol consumption, following young people from early adolescence through to young adulthood, and from underage to legal purchase age and beyond. Drawing on examples from across the

---

Young People and Alcohol: Impact, Policy, Prevention, Treatment, First Edition.
Edited by John B. Saunders and Joseph M. Rey.
© 2011 Blackwell Publishing Ltd. Published 2011 by Blackwell Publishing Ltd.

globe, these changes include increased binge drinking, determined drunkenness, gender convergence, global branding, and the acute and chronic health and social problems associated with such drinking patterns. While particular reference is made to the European and the North American literature, the authors would also like to note the challenge of making meaningful generalizations both within countries and across continents.

Childhood influences

Certain aspects of young people's alcohol consumption and the concerns it invokes transcend the boundaries of countries, cultures, and classes. In countries where alcohol consumption is legal and socially sanctioned, the uptake of alcohol is interwoven with the transition to adulthood: surveys show that the first drink is often around the start of puberty, at the beginning of the teens. In Europe, for example, the first drink is at the age of 13 on average. About one in ten youth are already established weekly drinkers in many European countries and also in North America by the age of 13 (Table 1.2).[1] Surveys show that drinking is a significant feature of relaxing and partying with friends for teenagers, as well as helping to boost confidence in social and sexual situations.[2] Yet, even before young people start to drink, they already have developed certain attitudes and expectations around alcohol as a result of the influence of key socialization vehicles such as their families, peers, schools, local communities, and the media.

In terms of our understanding of these influences from childhood onward, reviews have noted a globalization of young people's alcohol-related attitudes and behaviors alongside a multiplicity of factors that influence their future drinking.[3] Regarding the role of ethnic and religious factors in socialization into alcohol, both in the United Kingdom[4-8] and in the United States,[9-11] a significant proportion of non-White young people drink less frequently, less heavily, and hold less positive attitudes to alcohol than

Table 1.1   Legal drinking age in selected countries.

	Age: on premise[a]	**Age: off premise**[b]
France	18	18
Italy	16	16
Portugal	16	16
Spain	18/16	18/16
England	18 (16)[c]	18
Ireland[a]	18	18
Denmark	18	16
Finland	18	18
Norway	18/20	18/20
Latvia	18	18
Canada	18/19	18/19
United States	21	21

[a]ICAP list (2010): *On-premise sales* refer to consumption on site; e.g., bars, pubs and restaurants.
[b]ICAP list (2010): *Off-premise retail sales* refer to sales of alcohol for consumption elsewhere; e.g., wine shops and supermarkets.
[c]In the United Kingdom, 16 for drinking with meals, accompanied with an adult.

their White counterparts. "Nonintact" family structures such as those with stepparents or without biological parents are significantly related to adolescent heavy drinking and even more so in societies where alcohol is more freely available to teenagers.[12] Children of alcohol-dependent parents are also at higher risk of developing alcohol-related problems themselves in later life.[13] Other reviews suggest that alcohol advertising and indirect marketing both play a significant role in both increased consumption by young people and brand preferences in Europe[14–16] and North America.[17,18] A major systematic review of the relationship between children, socioeconomic status and alcohol, by contrast, found a lack of evidence to support an association between children's socioeconomic background and later alcohol problems.[19]

Early teen drinking in "wet" and "dry" countries: transgression or rite of passage?

The most extensive surveys for cross-national comparison of underage drinking are the Health Behaviour in School-Aged Children (HBSC) studies, collected about every 4 years in 41 countries among school pupils aged 11, 13, and 15 years, and the European School Survey Project on Alcohol and Other Drugs (ESPAD), also collected every 4 years in 35 countries among 15–16-year-old school pupils.

In Europe, a number of drinking typologies have been developed in order to map cross-national differences. A key one is the "wet" versus "dry" distinction.[20] This does not refer to whether alcohol consumption is prohibited or not, but to how alcohol is integrated into everyday life and meal times. A "wet" pattern of consumption is common in Southern European countries, where small amounts of alcohol are consumed more frequently (e.g., at meal times), but consumption is less heavy. By contrast, the "dry" pattern of drinking, for example, in Northern European countries, places a greater emphasis on drinking to intoxication at less family-oriented social events. A second, related typology links traditional beverage preferences with specific geographical regions:[21] Southern European wine cultures are contrasted with central European beer drinking cultures and Northern European spirit drinking cultures. In relation to young people, however, there is growing evidence that these traditional distinctions that associate specific alcoholic beverage types with specific regions are weakening; beer is increasingly the preferred drink among young people across most of Europe, with declining wine consumption in Europe's traditional wine drinking countries.[22] Nevertheless, as this chapter will illustrate, such cultural distinctions still have some value when mapping specific differences in young people's drinking onto various countries.

This chapter considers young people's drinking by comparing European countries representative of the traditional Southern wine drinking culture (France, Italy, Spain, and Portugal), Central European beer drinking culture (England, Ireland, and Denmark), and Northern European (former) spirit drinking culture (Finland, Norway, and Latvia), alongside young people in the United States, Canada, and China. In countries representative of the Southern wine culture, underage drinking is more prevalent since alcohol is consumed traditionally in small quantities at family meals on an everyday basis; yet, intoxication among adolescents is less common. In contrast, in Central and Northern European beer cultures, alcohol is less integrated into meal times; drinking occurs during leisure time socializing and festivities and therefore it is not to the same extent considered an "ordinary commodity."[23] In these countries, daily alcohol consumption is less prevalent among adolescents, but once they start to drink, they are more likely to drink to intoxication. In Northern European spirit countries, alcohol has been considered a rare and exceptional commodity traditionally, and therefore, it is a symbol marking the rite of passage from adolescence to adulthood.[24]

Table 1.1 compares the legal drinking age for alcohol in both licensed premises and off-licensed premises for the selected countries mentioned above. Table 1.2 compares various rates of adolescent drinking patterns according to two recent international comparable surveys.[1,25] The legal drinking age—18 years—for buying and drinking alcohol in licensed premises is the same for all European countries listed in the table excluding Norway, and for many other countries around the world including China, Australia, and New Zealand. In some countries, including the United Kingdom, Germany, the Netherlands, Portugal, Denmark, and part of Spain, and in some Canadian states, the law also allows the purchase of alcohol and/or underage drinking under parental supervision in some circumstances in licensed and/or off-licensed premises. (This does not mean that alcohol cannot be consumed legally elsewhere. For instance, in the United Kingdom, alcohol can be consumed legally under parental supervision within the home from the age of 5. However, there has been a shift away from the continental European model of children learning moderate consumption under parental supervision within the home. For example, the British government recently introduced guidelines for the first time advising parents that "an alcohol-free childhood is the healthiest option," to avoid giving children alcohol until at least the age of 15 and between the ages of 15 and 17 only a small amount, infrequently and under parental supervision, not more than once a week). In the United States, the National Minimum Drinking Age Act 1984 operates across all the states and establishes one of the highest legal drinking ages in the world at 21 years. In some Middle Eastern and South East Asian countries of predominantly Muslim religious conviction (e.g., Afghanistan, Bangladesh, Iran, Pakistan, Saudi Arabia and Yemen), it is illegal to drink alcohol at any age, although some of these countries allow expatriate non-Muslim residents to drink.

The early teen years are a key period for young people in many developed countries to start experimenting with alcohol. In Table 1.2, the first column refers to HBSC data on the percentage of 13-year-olds who report drinking alcohol at least once a week. We see how Italian and French boys are more likely to be weekly drinkers by the age of 13 than adolescents in Denmark, Finland, Norway, the United States, and Canada. England and Latvia are notable for the large proportion of girls who are weekly drinkers by the age of 13. In contrast, Spain and Portugal appear similar to the Nordic countries, as the proportion of weekly drinkers in their early teens is low. Considerably fewer 13-year-old teens in the United States and Canada report drinking alcohol on a weekly basis.

In terms of drunkenness, the second column in Table 1.2, HBSC data show that the proportion of adolescents who experience intoxication aged 13 or younger is much higher in the Central European beer and Nordic (former) spirit countries compared to the Southern wine drinking countries. Among the Nordic countries, Norway stands out because of both

Table 1.2   Age of onset and youth drinking patterns in selected countries.

	13-year-old teens drink weekly (%)[a]	First drunk at 13 years of age or younger (%)[b]	Drunk at least twice (%)[c]	Drunk in last 30 days (%)[d]	5+ drinks in last 30 days (%)[e]
Males					
France	11	11	19	20	47
Italy	26	6	22	14	45
Portugal	6	10	25	12	58
Spain	6	8	33	24[a]	32[a]
England (UK: ESPAD)	20	24	50	31	52
Ireland	7	20	32	24	–
Denmark	7	21	59	51[a]	63[a]
Finland	4	23	47	19	35
Norway	1	10	32	17	35
Latvia	13	25	50	22	60
Canada	8	18	36	–	–
United States	7	13	20	19[a]	–
Females					
France	8	6	18	16	39
Italy	14	3	18	11	32
Portugal	3	8	18	10	53
Spain	7	9	29	25[f]	27[f]
England (UK: ESPAD)	17	23	44	34	55
Ireland	4	15	31	28	–
Denmark	3	19	56	47[f]	57[f]
Finland	3	22	44	23	33
Norway	0	8	25	22	42
Latvia	10	18	39	14	48
Canada	6	16	35	–	–
United States	6	9	20	17[f]	–

[a]HBSC 2006: The percentage of 13-year-old teens who report drinking alcohol at least once a week.
[b]HBSC 2006: The percentage of 15-year-old teens who report first intoxication at 13 years of age or younger.
[c]HBSC 2006: The percentage of 15-year-old teens who report intoxication at least twice in their lifetime.
[d]ESPAD 2007: The percentage of 15-year-old teens who report (subjective) drunkenness during the previous month.
[e]ESPAD 2007: The percentage of 15-year-old teens who report drinking five or more drinks on one occasion during the previous month.
[f]Denmark, Spain and the United States: Limited comparability – due to a low response rate; caution should be taken when interpreting the numbers from the ESPAD data from Denmark. Likewise, the data from Spain and the United States have been collected in different country-specific surveys, though using the same measurements as in the ESPAD study.

its very strict alcohol policy (with a legal drinking age for spirits of 20) and its much lower levels of adolescent drunkenness. In North America, the number of adolescents drinking to intoxication in the United States appears similar to the Mediterranean wine drinking countries, whereas Canada seems to have a youth drinking pattern more similar to Central and Northern Europe.

When we compare the differences in the number of times 15-year-olds have experienced intoxication (Table 1.2, third column, HBSC data), the percentages fit well with the drinking typologies outlined above. More adolescents in the central European beer drinking countries have been intoxicated than in other countries, including the United States and Canada, where adolescent drinking patterns again seem very similar to those of Southern Europe. If we compare all 41 countries participating in the HBSC study, we find that young Danes take the lead, with 59% of boys and 56% of girls having been intoxicated twice. England is fifth, very closely behind Lithuania, Wales and Estonia, with 50% of boys and 44% of girls having been intoxicated at least twice in their lifetime. The same pattern is revealed when we compare these data with the ESPAD survey. Adolescents in Denmark and England lead in terms of both heavy episodic drinking (i.e., five or more drinks on one occasion) and subjective drunkenness. Danish and English adolescents together appear to have set the stage for increased heavy episodic drinking since ESPAD data were first collected in 1995, increasingly emulated by other European countries, leading some to suggest that Denmark and the United Kingdom are the binge drinking capitals of Europe.[26] Others have noted that in the recent national and international surveys, English and Danish adolescent heavy drinking appears to be in decline.[27]

As expected, more adolescents in the Nordic countries drink to intoxication compared to adolescents in Southern European countries, but fewer do so compared to adolescents in Central Europe. In the Southern wine drinking cultures, however, there is a much larger discrepancy between "objective" measurements of intoxication and "subjective" perceptions of drunkenness than in Central and Northern European countries. For instance, in Portugal, more than half of girls and boys report heavy episodic drinking whereas only one in ten reports having been intoxicated in the last 30 days. This illustrates the cultural differences regarding perceptions of intoxication and acceptability of public drunkenness among young people across Europe.

These cultural differences have also been identified with older cohorts. For example, in a focus group study of 16–25-year-old people,[28] all the young Italian respondents strongly criticized drunkenness, stating that intoxication was an undesirable and unintended negative consequence of consumption. In contrast, for young people from the United Kingdom (Scotland), drunkenness was one of the main goals of social drinking. Attitudes to drunkenness in the Chinese focus group in the same study reflected rapid socioeconomic change in the country with a shift from drinking and toasting at traditional celebrations and banquets to a more Westernized pattern with students and work colleagues drinking together in the new bars and clubs, which have sprouted in urban areas in recent years. Ethnic and cultural differences are also evident in North America where traditional Anglo-Celtic, Afro-American, Hispanic, and Asian alcohol-related attitudes and behaviors are merging with newer influences and an enduring concern with college campus binge drinking.

Learning underage drinking in the company of friends

When studying underage drinking, the general assumption is that adolescent drinking patterns mirror those of their national country and, as revealed in Table 1.2, this is mostly true. There may be, however, more similarities between cross-national youth drinking than differences and therefore new drinking typologies such as the "damp" model have been suggested, as a refinement of the "wet" versus "dry" dichotomy.[29] A "damp" youth drinking model captures how the traditional drinking cultures are merging, as young people not only drink to intoxication but also do so regularly. Furthermore, a consistent finding in youth alcohol studies is that intoxication is not simply an individual's choice, but a learned behavior, socially and culturally context specific. As Douglas noted: "drinking is essentially a social act, performed in a recognised social context."[30] Research suggests that in many countries friendships are more influential than family, and it is among friends at parties rather than with parents at home that adolescents and young people learn to become alcohol users.[31-34] Three examples of this are discussed here: The Spanish *botellón*, the Norwegian *russefeiring*, and the Danish "house party. "

El botellón

In Spain, a Southern European country known for a "wet" drinking culture and for a low tolerance of public drunkenness, the phenomenon of the *botellón* has become widespread among young Spaniards.[35] *El botellón*, which translates in English as "the big bottle," began in Madrid in the late 1970s.[36,*] Today, however, it is increasingly popular among young adults[36] and adolescents as young as 12 years across Spain,[37] where cheap alcohol is obtained from the supermarkets and the young people gather in public streets and squares to socialize, listen to music and to drink large quantities of cheap alcohol. This scenario supports the notion of a new "culture of intoxication" relating to alcohol and illegal drugs, emerging among young people in an increasing number of countries and beyond the central European beer drinking countries where it was previously characteristic.[38]

Russefeiring

In Norway, a phenomenon known as *russefeiring*—an annual event of consecutive graduation parties taking place from the beginning of May—has elements similar to the Spanish phenomenon of *el botellón*. A distinction, however, is that *russefeiring* is more like a traditional rite of passage to adulthood, where alcohol along with other acts such as skinny-dipping, kissing police officers, and sexual experiments are the key symbols in distinguishing the period between youth and adulthood.[24] A similar pattern, called "schoolies week," is evolving in Australia in which high-school graduates have week-long celebrations following the end of their final high-school examinations.[39]

Danish "house party"

In Denmark, while prolonged graduation parties are also popular among high-school students, house parties tend to be where Danish adolescents learn to drink.[40] A house party is a gathering held for invited friends, usually in a private home or rented premises.

---

*When elected Mayor of Madrid, the elderly university professor Enrique Tierno Galvan encouraged indulgence in relaxant substances when he told a crowd 'el que no esté colocado, que se coloque . . . y al loro!' One translation of which is 'get stoned and do what's cool'. His comment in Madrid prompted young people from across Europe to visit the city, and the movida madrileña—whose literal translation is 'the Madrid scene'—was born.

Here, the collective consumption of alcohol (specifically getting drunk at the same speed as friends) is vital in transforming the (usually parents') lounge into a space for teenage partying. The collective drinking marks that something different will happen; for instance, that it is now socially acceptable and expected that the adolescents take part in gender games, sexualized dancing, and flirting.[41] One's refusal to drink could be seen as a refusal to participate in the process of what is considered integral to the creation of a coherent group in their friendship network. Danish house parties therefore play a crucial role not only in young Danes learning to drink but also in reaffirming their social networks and close friendships. In this regard, partying and drinking to intoxication is more part of a leisure "time out" from the structured and restrained everyday life associated with school and work than a traditional rite of passage celebration (as is the case with the Norwegian *russefeiring*). The integral role of intoxication in Danish partying is illustrated in that 48% of Danish 15–16-year-olds attend parties at least once a month and 44% report having been drunk in the last month, whereas although half of French 15–16-year-olds attend parties at least once a month only 9% report having been drunk in the last month.

Is the gender gap closing?

One recurrent theme in cross-national comparisons of young people's alcohol consumption is that men drink more than women across the world. More recently, however, in some developed countries, there is evidence that women are drinking in ways that increasingly resemble men's patterns of consumption.[42] A key explanation for this convergence is that women are becoming emancipated from traditional female roles and increasingly equal to men in terms of their aspirations and achievements both in higher education and their position in the labor market. In this process, it is argued that as women's lifestyle increasingly resembles men's lifestyle in all sorts of ways, it is to be expected that their consumption habits—including alcohol—also increasingly emulate men's.[43–45] The gender gap in youth drinking has been studied using this reasoning[46] and it is argued that in countries with greater gender equality (such as Nordic countries), girls' drinking patterns are increasingly resembling boys' and vice versa in countries with less gender equality.

This point is illustrated in Table 1.2, which shows that in Southern wine drinking countries more boys than girls consume five drinks on one occasion. Hence, in countries where public drunkenness is less acceptable,[28] girls are also less likely to be heavy drinkers, although girls in Portugal do stand out. By contrast, in countries characterized by extensive drunkenness—such as the United Kingdom, Norway, and Finland—the gender gap is closing.[47–50]

"Girls drinking like boys" calls for new interpretations of the meaning of alcohol in relationship to gender.[51,52] However, testing the convergence theory only by comparing gender differences in quantity and frequency of consumption limits our understanding of how drinking among both boys and girls is governed and constrained by different norms and ways of being together (i.e., collectiveness). Learning to become an alcohol user can be a much more risky process for young girls compared to boys.[53] Teenage girls, similar to boys, experiment with alcohol-related risky behavior. But the boundaries surrounding girls' alcohol-related attitudes and behaviors can be more constrained. For instance, while parties can still be seen as fun even having drank alcohol to the point of blacking out for teenage boys, this is less the case for girls.[41] Such gender differences in attitudes to intoxication can carry through into young adulthood.[52,54]

Late teen drinking: binge drinking and integration into the adult night-time economy

As young people reach their mid and late teens, a key debate relates to recent changes in sessional drinking, the harms associated with this pattern of consumption and the wider cultural context to this change. The term "binge" was originally applied in clinical practice to refer to a pattern of alcohol consumption where the key feature was an extended period of consumption to the point that the drinker's usual daily activities and obligations were subsumed or until the drinker lost consciousness.[55] In the early 1990s, a group of American researchers attempted to quantify the amount of alcohol consumed in a drinking session, which could lead to a significantly increased risk of physical harm: five standard drinks for men and four standard drinks for women.[56,57] This so-called "five/four" measure of binge drinking has led to an increasing tendency among social and medical researchers and practitioners toward quantifying binge drinking in terms of standard drinks or units of alcohol consumed in a drinking session, rather than the clinical definition of prolonged drinking beyond the boundaries of "normal" life.

Extreme drinking

Studies have noted that drunkenness is both an aim and an outcome of heavy sessional drinking for many young people, with the twenty-first century marked by increased "determined drunkenness" in a range of different societies.[58,59] For example, a series of studies across four continents noted that young people were drinking excessively, purposefully, as part of a risk-taking, pleasure-seeking leisure time where drinking resembled extreme sports. This led researchers to characterize this style of consumption as "extreme drinking."[28]

It appears not only that some young people are drinking greater quantities of alcohol during a drinking session but also the changes relate to who is drinking, where they are drinking, and what they are drinking. Thus, a key reason cited for this increased binge drinking, or extreme drinking, has been the emergence of high-strength spirit mixers and beverages appealing to young people ("alcopops"), along with a growing diversity, sophisticated design, and niche branding of the leisure venues supplying alcoholic beverages, appealing to "new" demographics of consumers.[38] The design of the recent generation of café bars, with advanced sound and light systems, modern designs, and DJs, is seen as having enticed a broader demographic of young people than was previously the case in traditional bars and pubs that had been associated with a lower income and predominantly male customer base.[60]

The perception is that not only are young women and young people from higher income and professional groups drinking more per session but also the restraints or inhibitions surrounding public intoxication previously identified in these groups are also being eroded.

Comparisons of male and female, higher and lower income groups, and different age clusters suggest that youth drunkenness and associated public order concerns are more than just an adolescent limit-testing phase. Such behavior is increasingly extending into young adulthood at a time when adolescence itself is lengthening due to the increasing need to acquire greater education skills, as well as delayed marriage, parenthood and other key life stage responsibilities.[61] At the international level, WHO reports suggest that this recent trend toward increased sessional consumption and drunkenness by young people could be partly linked to global branding, advertising and marketing, the funding for which outpaces economic growth around the world.[62]

Night-time economy

Furthermore, such heavy sessional consumption is seen by some commentators as linked to the broader economic regeneration in both developed and developing countries, with a proliferation of alcohol-oriented leisure venues in the growth of what has been termed in the research literature as the "night-time economy."[63] The expansion of the urban night-time economy and young people's alcohol-related attitudes and behaviors within it has led to a growing body of research on the management and regulation of the night-time economy.[64,65] In part, as discussed earlier in this chapter, there has been a conscious effort to remodel Northern European cities on the Mediterranean "café bar culture" to encourage more moderate and sociable alcohol consumption rather than frenzied binge drinking. The extent to which this cultural transplant has been successful, has been questioned by some researchers who have suggested that in countries such as the United Kingdom and Denmark this has led to "the worst of both worlds" in terms of stimulating more frequent consumption later into the evening while perpetuating "binge and brawl" cultural traditions.[27,66]

The costs of consumption: young people, alcohol, and harm

Young people are particularly vulnerable to the impact of alcohol. The consequences of young people's drinking and drunkenness can be broadly characterized as health-related or social, as well as acute and longer term or chronic, discussed further in later chapters. In terms of health consequences, young people risk problems such as alcohol poisoning, liver damage and some cancers, with teenage frequent and heavy consumption reflected in the increased diagnosis of liver disease earlier in adulthood, despite improvements in diagnosis and treatment. In France, for example, the number of young people aged 15–24 hospitalized for alcohol poisoning has doubled between 2004 and 2007. In the United Kingdom, hospital admissions for any alcohol-related condition have increased by 69% in the 5-year period from 2002–2003 to 2007–2008.[67]

The acute social consequences of young people's consumption inflict a heavy burden on society through the associations between consumption and road traffic accidents, public disorder, antisocial behavior, violent crime, and so forth. The longer term impact of drinking in adolescence and young adulthood also can be seen in the association identified, for example between alcohol consumption, educational and labor market outcomes.[68],[69] In the United States, a 40-year review of the evidence concluded that raising the minimum legal drinking age and enforcing this action appears to have reduced the harm to young people from alcohol, particularly the number of fatal road traffic accidents involving drink drivers across the 50 states.[70] This saves an estimated 1,000 lives each year.[71],[72] Consideration is now being given to whether the successful attitudinal shift in the acceptability of drink driving, smoking, and speeding could also be translated into a shift in young people's attitudes to public drunkenness and alcohol-related disorderly behavior.[73]

Such concerns are counterbalanced by evidence that the millennial increase in sessional consumption has now peaked in Europe[1],[74] and North America,[75] particularly in the regions that witnessed the greatest increases a decade earlier. Indeed, one of the interesting and as yet underresearched areas regarding young people and alcohol relates to the increase in teenage light drinkers and abstainers in some developed countries, which may relate not only to ethnic and religious influences but also to an anticonsumption stance by some.[76]

Conclusion

Wide variations exist in young people's drinking and attitudes to alcohol around the world, influenced by family, peers, schools, ethnic and religious upbringing, media and advertising, and national and cultural contexts. Starting to drink in adolescence has been seen both as a traditional rite of passage between childhood and adulthood, and also a phase of limit-testing, transgression, or deviance from adult social norms. This phase appears to be both intensifying and extending, with cross-national studies identifying the emergence of heavy sessional consumption or "binge drinking" for both young women and men, in higher and lower income groups, and extending into young adulthood. Furthermore, there is evidence of a convergence in drinking patterns between young women and young men in some developed countries, possibly linked to young women's growing equality and education and employment opportunities. There is also a convergence between "wet" and "dry," wine drinking and beer/spirit drinking cultures. The switch to drunkenness as an intended and desirable consequence rather than a negative side effect of heavy drinking in many countries has led some researchers to suggest that this behavior might better be understood as "extreme drinking." The reasons for this growth in young people's heavy sessional consumption have been postulated as influenced by the globalization of increasingly cheap and high-strength alcoholic beverages across the world, associated with the expansion of an increasingly alcohol-oriented night-time economy. Thus adolescents, at the symbolic crossroads between childhood and adulthood, themselves face a crossroads regarding cultural and commercial influences on youthful alcohol consumption.

References

1. Hibell B, Guttormsson U, Ahlström S *et al.* The 2007 ESPAD Report: Substance Use among Students in 35 European Countries. Stockholm: The Swedish Council for Information on Alcohol and Other Drugs, 2009.

2. Coleman L, Cater S. *Underage 'Risky' Drinking: Motivations and Outcomes*. York: Joseph Rowntree Foundation; 2005.
3. Velleman R. Influences on how children and young people learn about and behave towards alcohol: A review of the literature for the Joseph Rowntree Foundation (part one). York: Joseph Rowntree Foundation; 2009. Available at: www.jrf.org.uk.
4. Best D, Rawaf S, Rowley J, Floyd K, Manning V, Strang J. Ethnic and gender differences in drinking and smoking among London adolescents. *Ethn Health* 2001; 6:51–57.
5. Denscombe. M. Ethnic group and alcohol consumption: The case of 15–16-year-olds in Leicestershire. *Public Health* 1995; 109:133–142.
6. Foxcroft D, Lowe G. Adolescent drinking behaviour and family socialisation factors: A meta-analysis. *J Adolesc* 1991; 14:255–273.
7. Purser B, Davis P, Johnson M, Orford J. *Drinking in Second and Subsequent Generation Black and Asian Communities in the English Midlands*. London: Alcohol Concern; 2001.
8. Stillwell G, Boys A, Marsden J. Alcohol use by young people from different ethnic groups: Consumption, intoxication and negative consequences. *Ethn Health* 2003; 9:171–187.
9. Heath A, Madden P, Grant J, McLaughlin T, Todorov A, Bucholz K. Resiliency factors protecting against teenage alcohol use and smoking: Influences of religion, religious involvement and values, and ethnicity in the Missouri Adolescent Female Twin Study. *Twin Res* 1999; 2:145–155.
10. Li X, Feigelman S, Stanton B. Perceived parental monitoring and health risk behaviors among urban low-income African-American children and adolescents. *J Adolesc Health* 2000; 27:43–48.
11. Sale E, Sambrano S, Springer J, Pena C, Pan W, Kasim, R. Family protection and prevention of alcohol use among Hispanic youth at high risk. *Am J Community Psychol* 2005; 36:195–205.
12. Bjarnason T, Andersson B, Choquet M, Elekes Z, Morgan M, Rapinett G. Alcohol culture, family structure and adolescent alcohol use: Multilevel modelling of frequency of heavy drinking among 15–16 year old students in 11 European countries. *J Stud Alcohol Drugs* 2003; 64:200–208.
13. Cloninger. C. Genetics of substance abuse. In: Galanter M, Kleber H, eds. *Textbook of Substance Abuse Treatment*. 2nd edn. Washington: American Psychiatric Press, 1999, pp. 59–66.
14. Anderson P, Baumberg B. *Alcohol in Europe, A Public Health Perspective: A Report for the European Commission*. London: Institute of Alcohol Studies; 2006.
15. Hastings G, Anderson S, Cooke E, Gordon R. Alcohol marketing and young people's drinking: A review of the research. *J Public Health Policy* 2005; 26:296–311.
16. Hastings G. *Social Marketing: Why should the Devil have All the Best Tunes?* London: Butterworth-Heinemann; 2007.
17. Grube. J. Alcohol portrayals and alcohol advertising on television. *Alcohol Health Res World* 1993; 17:6166.
18. Grube J, Waiters E. Alcohol in the media: Content and effects on drinking beliefs and behaviors among youth. *Adolesc Med Clin* 2005; 16:327–243.
19. Wiles N, Lingford-Hughes A, Daniel J, Hickman M, Farrell M, Macleod J, Haynes J, Skapinakis P, Araya R, Lewis G. Socioeconomic status in childhood and later alcohol use: A systematic review. *Addiction* 2007; 102:1546–1563.
20. Room R, Mäkelä K. Typologies of the cultural position of drinking. *J Stud Alcohol* 2000; 61:475–483.
21. Sulkunen. P. Drinking patterns and the level of alcohol consumption: An international overview. In: Gibbins R *et al.*, eds. *Research Advances in Alcohol and Drug Problems*. Vol. 3. New York: John Wiley & Sons; 1976, pp. 223–281.

22. WHO. Global Overview. *Alcohol Consumption and Beverage Preferences. Global Status Report on Alcohol 2004.* World Health Organization: Department of Mental Health and Substance Abuse, 2004. Available at: http://www.who.int/substance_abuse/publications/globalstatus reportalcoholchapters/en/index.html.

23. Babor TF, Caetano R, Casswell S, Edwards G, Giesbrecht N, Graham K, Grube J, Gruenewald P, Hill L, Holder H, Homel R, Österberg E, Rehm J, Room R, Rossow I. *Alcohol: No Ordinary Commodity—Research and Public Policy.* Oxford and London: Oxford University Press; 2003.

24. Sande A. Intoxication and rite of passage to adulthood in Norway. *Contemp Drug Probl* 2002; 29:277–303.

25. Currie C, Gabhainn S, Godeau E, Roberts C, Smith R, Currie D, Picket W, Richter M, Morgan A, Barnekow V. *Inequality in Young People's Health. HBSC International Report 2005/2006.* World Health Organization: Department of Mental Health and Substance Abuse; 2008.

26. Palmer A. Binge drinking: Does Britain need to look to Italy to solve booze problem? *Daily Mirror.* 18 August 2009. Available at: www.mirror.co.uk/news/top-stories/2009/08/18.

27. Measham F, Østergaard J. The public face of binge drinking: British and Danish young women, recent trends in alcohol consumption and the European binge drinking debate. *Probation J* 2009; 56:415–434.

28. Martinic. M, Measham. F, eds. *Swimming With Crocodiles: The Culture of Extreme Drinking.* New York and Abingdon: Routledge; 2008.

29. Beccaria F, Sande A. Drinking games and rite of life projects: A social comparison of the meaning and functions of young people's use of alcohol during the rite of passage to adulthood in Italy and Norway. *Young Nordic J Youth Res* 2003; 11:99–119.

30. Douglas. M. A distinctive anthropological perspective. In: Douglas M, ed. *Constructive Drinking: Perspectives on Drink from Anthropology.* Abingdon: Routledge; 2003, p. 4.

31. Engels R, Knibbe R, Drop M. Visiting public drinking places: An explorative study into the functions of pub-going for late adolescents. *Subst Use Misuse* 1999; 34:1261–1280.

32. Demers A, Kairouz S, Adlaf E, Gliksman L, Newton-Taylor B, Marchand A. Multilevel analysis of situational drinking among Canadian undergraduates. *Soc Sci Med* 2002; 55:415–424.

33. Pavis S, Cunningham-Burley S, Amos A. Alcohol consumption and young people: Exploring meaning and social context. *Health Educ Res* 1997; 12:311–322.

34. Stoduto G, Adlaf E, Mann R. Adolescents, bush parties and drinking–driving. *J Stud Alcohol* 1998; 59:544–548.

35. Pérez-Fragero A. Case study: Botellón in Spain. In: Martinic M, Measham F, eds. *Swimming With Crocodiles: The Culture of Extreme Drinking.* New York and Abingdon: Routledge; 2008, pp. 193–197.

36. Gómez R, Rateb F, Rowe J, Merelo J. *The Botellón: A Social Event Modelled with MAS.* 2007. Available at: www.irit.fr/COSI/project/results/wt3/botwt3.pdf.

37. Keeley G. In Spain, drinkers as young as 12 are joining an outdoor bender. *The Times,* London, 17 March 2006: p. 43.

38. Measham F, Brain K. 'Binge' drinking, British alcohol policy and the new culture of intoxication. *Crime Media Culture Int J,* 2005; 1(3):263–284.

39. Winchester PM, McGuirk PM, Everett K. Schoolies week as a rite of passage. A study of celebration and control. In: Teather EK, eds. *Embodied Geographies: Spaces, Bodies and Rites of Passage.* London: Routledge, 1999, pp. 59–76.

40. Demant J, Østergaard J. Partying as everyday life: Investigations of teenagers' leisure life. *J Youth Stud* 2007; 10:517–537.

41. Østergaard J. Mind the gender gap? When boys and girls get drunk at a party. *Nordic Stud Alcohol Drugs* 2007; 24 (2): 127–148.

42. Bloomfield K, Allamani A, Beck F, Bergmark KH, Csemy L, Eisenbach-Stangi I, Elekes Z, Gmel G, Kerr-Correa, Knibb R, Mäkelä P, Monteiro M, Mora MEM, Nordlund S, Obut I, Plant M, Rahav G, Mendoza MR. *Gender, Culture and Alcohol Problems: A Multinational Study.* Berlin: Institute for Medical Informatics, Biometrics and Epidemiology, Charité Universitätsmedizin; 2005. Available at: http://www.genacis.org/Divers/report_final_040205.zip.

43. Mäkelä P, Gmel G, Grittner U, Kuendig H, Kuntsche S, Bloomfield K, Room, R. Drinking patterns and their gender differences in Europe. *Alcohol Alcohol* 2006; 41(Suppl.) S1i8–S1i18.

44. Bloomfield K, Gmel G, Neve R, Mustonen H. Investigating gender convergence in alcohol consumption in Finland, Germany, The Netherlands, and Switzerland: A repeated survey analysis. *Subst Abuse* 2001; 22:39–53.

45. Bloomfield K, Gmel G, Wilsnack S. Introduction to special issue 'gender, culture and alcohol problems: A multi-national study'. *AlcoholAlcohol* 2006; 41:I3–I7.

46. Ahlström S. Gender difference in youth drinking cultures. In: Järvinen M, Room R, eds. *Youth Drinking Cultures: European Experiences.* Hampshire: Ashgate; 2007.

47. Gill J. Reported levels of alcohol consumption and binge drinking within the UK undergraduate student population over the last 25 years. *Alcohol Alcohol* 2002; 37:109–120.

48. Lintonen T, Rimpela M, Ahlström S, Rimpela A, Vikat A. Trends in drinking habits among Finnish adolescents from 1977 to 1999. *Addiction* 2000; 95:1255–1263.

49. Ahlstrom S, Osterberg E. International perspectives on adolescent and young adult drinking. *Alcohol Res Health* 2004; 28:258–268.

50. Sweeting H, West P. Young people's leisure and risk-taking behaviours: Changes in gender patterning in the West of Scotland during the 1990s. *J Youth Stud* 2003; 6:391–412.

51. Sulkunen P. Between culture and nature: Intoxication in cultural studies of alcohol and drug use. *Contemp Drug Probl* 2002; 29:253–276.

52. Measham F. 'Doing gender'–'doing drugs': Conceptualising the gendering of drugs cultures. *Contemp Drug Probl* 2002; 29:335–373.

53. Østergaard J. Learning to become an alcohol user: Adolescents taking risks and parents living with uncertainty. *Addict Res Theory* 2009; 17:30–53.

54. Ettorre E. *Revisioning Women and Drug Use: Gender, Power and the Body.* Basingstoke: Palgrave Macmillan; 2007.

55. Newburn T, Shiner M. *Teenage Kicks? Young People and Alcohol: A Review of the Literature.* York: Joseph Rowntree Foundation; 2001.

56. Wechsler H, Austin S. Binge drinking: The five/four measure. *J Stud Alcohol.* 1998; 59:122–123.

57. Wechsler H, Davenport A, Dowdall G, Moeykens B, Castillo S. Health and behavioral consequences of binge drinking in college: A national survey of students at 140 campuses. *JAMA* 1994; 272:1672–1677.

58. Szmigin I, Griffin C, Mistral W, Bengry-Howell A, Weale L, Hackley C. Reframing 'Binge Drinking' as calculated hedonism: Empirical evidence from the UK. *Int J Drug Policy* 2008; 19:359–366.

59. Griffin C, Bengry-Howell A, Hackley C, Mistral W, Szmigin I. 'Every time I do it I absolutely annihilate myself': Loss of (self-) consciousness and loss of memory in young people's drinking narratives. *Sociology* 2009; 43:457–476.

60. Chatterton P, Hollands R. *Urban Nightscapes: Youth Cultures, Pleasure Spaces and Corporate Power.* London: Routledge; 2003.

61. The NHS Information Centre. *Statistics on Alcohol: England, 2009.* Leeds: The NHS Information Centre; 2009. Available at: www.ic.nhs.uk.

62. Jernigan D. *Global Status Report: Alcohol and Young People*. Geneva: World Health Organisation; 2001.
63. Hobbs D, Hadfield P, Lister S, Winlow S. *Bouncers: Violence and Governance in the Night-time Economy*. Oxford: Oxford University Press; 2003.
64. Newton A, Hirschfield A. Violence and the night-time economy: A multi-professional perspective. *Crime Prev Community Saf* 2009; 11:147–152.
65. Hadfield P. *Bar Wars: Contesting the Night in Contemporary British Cities*. Oxford: OUP; 2006.
66. Jayne M, Valentine G, Holloway S. Fluid boundaries: British binge drinking and European civility: Alcohol and the production and consumption of public space. *Space Polity* 2008; 12 (1): 81–100.
67. The NHS Information Centre. *Statistics on Alcohol: England, 2009*. The Health and Social Care Information Centre; 2009. Available at: www.ic.nhs.uk.
68. MacDonald Z, Shields M. The impact of alcohol consumption on occupational attainment in England. *Economica* 2001; 68:427–453.
69. Plant M, Miller P, Plant M, Gmel G, Kuntsche S, Bergmark K, Bloomfield K, Csémy L, Ozenturk T., Vidal A. The social consequences of binge drinking among 24 to 32 year olds in six European countries. *Subst Use Misuse* 2010; 45:528–542.
70. Wagenaar A, Toomey T. Effects of minimum drinking age laws: Review and analyses of the literature from 1960 to 2000. *J Stud Alcoho.Suppl* 2002; 14:206–225.
71. Jones N, Pieper C, Robertson L. The effect of legal drinking age on fatal injuries of adolescents and young adults. *Am J Public Health* 1992; 82:112–115.
72. Voas R, Scott Tippetts A, Fell, J. Assessing the effectiveness of minimum legal drinking age and zero tolerance laws in the United States. *Accid Anal Prev* 2003; 35:579–587.
73. Stead M, Gordon R, Holme I, Moodie C, Hastings G, Angus K. *Changing Attitudes, Knowledge and Behaviour: A Review of Successful Initiatives*. York: Joseph Rowntree Foundation, 2009. Available at: www.jrf.org.uk.
74. Measham F. The turning tides of intoxication: Young people's drinking in Britain in the 2000s. *Health Educ* 2008; 108:207–222.
75. Johnston L, O'Malley P, Bachman J. *Monitoring the Future: National Results on Adolescent Drug Use*. Rockville: NIDA; 2002.
76. Lee M, Fernandez K, Hyman M. Anti-consumption: An overview and research agenda. *J Bus Res* 2009; 62:145–147.

Chapter 2

Early onset drinking

Shauncie M. Skidmore, Rose A. Juhasz, and Robert A. Zucker

Department of Psychiatry, Addiction Research Center, University of Michigan, Ann Arbor, MI, USA

Key points

- For the purposes of this chapter, "early onset drinking" is used for drinking behavior that begins before age 14.
- Early onset drinking is an indicator for future alcohol abuse and dependency and covaries with a multitude of other problems during adolescence. Earlier onset of drinking is associated with a more rapid progression to, and a longer duration of alcoholism, greater difficulty achieving abstinence, and diagnostic profiles that include more symptoms and characteristics of alcoholism.
- Behavioral undercontrol—a vulnerability of disinhibitory processes that involves the inability or unwillingness or failure to inhibit behavior even in the face of anticipated or already received negative consequences—is a very early predictor of alcohol and other drug misuse.
- Links between attention deficit hyperactivity disorder (ADHD) and early onset drinking have been harder to establish, with inconsistent findings across studies. However, recent evidence strongly suggests a link between ADHD and early onset drinking, primarily when ADHD coexists with an externalizing disorder (conduct disorder or oppositional defiant disorder).
- Anxiety, depression, low resiliency, sleep difficulties, and social inhibition/shyness have all been noted in the research literature as risk factors for early onset drinking.
- Nonspecific environmental factors that may influence risk for early onset drinking include abuse, family conflict, poor parenting, poor monitoring, family socioeconomic status, and even neighborhood social disorganization.
- Alcohol-specific factors that influence risk for early onset drinking include, but are not limited to, fetal alcohol exposure, mass media portrayal of acceptance of drinking behavior, geographic clustering of alcohol outlets, parental modeling of drinking, and peer influences.
- Nurturing and supportive parenting, parental monitoring, behavioral control, and affiliation with well-functioning peers decrease the likelihood of early onset drinking.

In an era of increasing globalization, expanding cross-cultural research, and varying ages for legal access to alcohol, defining "early onset drinking" (EOD) is to some degree

---

Young People and Alcohol: Impact, Policy, Prevention, Treatment, First Edition.

Edited by John B. Saunders and Joseph M. Rey.

© 2011 Blackwell Publishing Ltd. Published 2011 by Blackwell Publishing Ltd.

arbitrary. Depending on the source, early onset drinking may be in reference to anyone considered underage,[1] to adolescents specifically,[2] or to those engaging in drinking behavior prior to some cutoff age, such as 14 years[3] where the criterion of "early" is based on a particular parameter of interest, such as less than the median age of first real drink or first sip (e.g., less than 11 years).[4]

Regardless of the population specifics, EOD has been a significant predictor of adolescent, young adult, and older adult problem drinking behavior.[3–7] Thus, EOD is not simply a behavioral anomaly that children and adolescents will outgrow with few consequences. Rather, early drinking is at the least a risk marker, and at best, a behavioral step that serves as a springboard to alcohol abuse, dependence, and a host of other problems for individuals and society.[8]

In this chapter, we briefly review the EOD construct and its empirical variations, explore why alcohol use/abuse during this development period is of special interest, delineate the risk factors associated with this developmental period as they relate to subsequent abuse and disorder, outline a possible causal model for early drinking, and describe the protective factors that may delay the initiation of this risky behavior.

A working definition of early onset drinking

Although this book focuses on the life course interval involving both the adolescence and the transition to young adulthood (operationally defined as 12–25 years of age), most research on early onset drinking focuses either on adolescents at the younger end of this age range or on preadolescence. Alcohol use in these youngsters is commonplace, and appears to be, if not worldwide, at the least international in scope (see Chapter 1). Epidemiological studies have shown that greater than 95% of 12–17-year-old youth in Denmark, Greece, the Czech Republic, and the Slovak Republic have used alcohol to some extent[9] (see Chapter 1 and Table 2.1). Even in Malaysia, a heavily Muslim and therefore largely prohibitionist society, the rate is 8%. Moreover, recent studies have identified substantial alcohol use in children under the age of 12[10,11] and even as young as 8.[4,12] Donovan[4] found that, in the United States, nearly 10% of 10-year-old group, 16% of 11-year-old group, and nearly 30% of 12-year-old group have consumed more than just a sip of alcohol. Likewise, Picherot and colleagues,[13] utilizing data from two European school surveys conducted in 2005–2006 and in 2007 reported that 59% of 11-year-old group, 72% of 13-year-old group, and 84% of 15-year-old group admitted to consuming alcohol in their lifetime.

In the United States, where the bulk of EOD research has been carried out, median age of first use is 14 years.[3] Most researchers have targeted that point as a differentiator, and have defined EOD as alcohol consumption that begins prior to that age. Following that custom, for the purposes of this discourse the term "early onset drinking" will be used for drinking behavior that begins before age 14, and "really early onset drinking" will be used in reference to drinking behavior that begins at or before age 10.

At the same time, despite the preponderant use of this marker, as research has probed its correlates, focus has increasingly turned to understanding what the active ingredient(s) are that make this indicator such a powerful predictor. A substantial literature on this issue

Table 2.1 Risk factors for early onset drinking.

Domain	Nonspecific risks	Alcohol-specific risks
Individual differences in temperament and behavior	– Aggressiveness – Delinquent, conduct disordered, and antisocial behavior – Behavioral undercontrol/ disinhibition – Impulsivity/risk Taking – Sensation seeking – Reward responsivity – Anxiety/depression – Deficits in attention – Low resiliency – Sleep difficulties – Social inhibition/shyness	– Positive beliefs and expectancies about alcohol
Environmental factors	– Abuse – Family conflict – Selected minority group affiliations (some are protective) – Poor parental monitoring – Poor/neglectful parenting – Low socioeconomic status	– Fetal alcohol exposure – Mass media – Modeling of heavy drinking by parents and/or peers – Geographic clustering of heavy drinkers – Easy alcohol availability
Genetics	Heritable pathways for – behavioral undercontrol/ disinhibition – delayed aversion/reward response – negative affect expression – aggressiveness	– Ethanol metabolism – Sensitivity of response to ETOH

is emerging. Given existing space constraints, we only note two such studies. An early one by DeWit *et al.*[5] investigated whether "time since first use of alcohol" rather than "age at first use of alcohol" would be the more important predictor of progression to alcoholism. The premise for the distinction was that the critical issue was length of time of exposure to alcohol, not the developmental aspect of age of onset. Their results, however, did not confirm the prediction; time since first use of alcohol was not an important predictor of progression to alcoholism. Rather, age of onset was the significant predictor of both risk for alcohol abuse and alcohol dependence, with those in the 11–14-year-old group having the highest vulnerability to risk, followed by those younger than age 11. The other more recent work, by Sartor and colleagues,[14] was able to demonstrate that a two-step differentiated model involving *both* age of onset *and* speed of progression, provided a better empirical fit in predicting dependence. Each of these factors was predicted by different antecedents, and each contributed variance to the dependence outcome. This is an early version of a cascade model (see below) suggesting that early onset brings exposure to a different universe of factors, which in turn mediate the appearance of the problem outcome.

Early onset drinking: a differentiator for pathways of use and abuse

In a 2009 report released by the SAMHSA Center for Substance Abuse Prevention,[15] it was estimated that in 1999 alcohol abuse cost the US $191.6 billion, with alcohol abuse and dependence ranking second in a list of national estimates of the cost of illness for 33 diseases and conditions. Likewise, a report[16] by two British health professional bodies revealed that during 2006–2007 alone alcohol abuse was estimated to have cost the British National Health System £2.7 billion ($4.38 billion); most nations are reporting similar high costs associated with alcohol abuse issues.

As is true of all chronic illnesses and conditions, patterns of abuse and disorder emerge gradually over time and developmental events that occur prior to the disorder are sometimes both a harbinger of the later outcome and a mediator. EOD is such a developmental marker. It is an indicator for future alcohol abuse and dependence in adolescence and adulthood and covaries with a multitude of other problems during adolescence. In adulthood, EOD has been found to predict clinical outcomes. Adult alcohol and drug abuse and antisocial behavior have all been associated with alcohol use prior to the age of 15.[17,18] Earlier onset of drinking is associated with a more rapid progression to and a longer duration of alcoholism, greater difficulty achieving abstinence, and diagnostic profiles that include more symptoms and characteristics of alcoholism.[19] Furthermore, early alcohol use has been found to precede the use of illicit drugs.[20,21]

However, there are more immediate consequences for adolescents who start to consume alcohol at an early age; these youngsters are more likely to experience health problems, injuries, academic difficulties, and problems with peers, as well as cognitive and behavioral control deficits, than their less precocious schoolmates. Students who report drinking before age 13 tend to perform worse academically and display more delinquent behaviors than peers who do not begin drinking this early.[10] Alcohol and drug abuse and alcohol related problems, such as driving under the influence, are more prevalent in adolescents who began drinking before age 12 than in those who initiated alcohol use later or not at all.[3,20] Moreover, Swahn and colleagues[22] found that early onset drinkers reported engaging in more violent behavior and suicide attempts than their later initiating peers.

The significance of EOD as a developmental marker has also been stimulated by questions about the physiological effects of early alcohol exposure on developing adolescents (see Chapter 5). Adolescent animals given alcohol are less apt to develop severe negative effects of intoxication such as sedation, hangover, and poor muscle coordination. However, adolescent animals' social behaviors and cognitive skills do seem to be more sensitive to alcohol exposure.[23,24] In human studies, adolescent drinking has been found to be associated with reduced prefrontal cortex size and disruptions in medial prefrontal function.[25] Taken together, studies linking EOD to behavioral and clinical outcomes throughout the lifespan, indicate that drinking in early adolescence has broad impact on both individuals and society.

Risk factors

Certain subgroups are known to be high-risk for EOD. Risks are in three domains: (a) Individual differences in temperament and behavior, (b) environmental influences, and (c) genetic influences. Together, these three domains interact and, in concert, predict alcohol use initiation at an early age. For each of these domains, Table 2.1 provides an abbreviated list of risk factors that are associated with EOD. (For extensive reviews covering most of these factors, see Zucker[26] and Zucker *et al.*[27]) Some are not themselves alcohol related, and also are predictive of other nonalcohol related behavior. We call these nonspecific risks. For each domain, the table also lists factors that are either alcohol-consumption behaviors in their own right or very closely tied to the use of alcohol. We call these alcohol-specific risks.

Nonspecific temperament and behavioral risks

As noted in Table 2.1, a substantial number of temperament and behavioral factors may place a child at risk for EOD. A significant subset can be characterized by the superordinate construct of *behavioral undercontrol*. Another subset can be characterized as subdomains of a *negative affectivity* construct. A third subset involves *delay aversion* and *high reward response*.

Behavioral undercontrol

Zucker and colleagues[27–29] have reviewed the extensive research evidence documenting the importance of behavioral undercontrol/disinhibition as a very early predictor of alcohol and other drug misuse. They define the construct as "a vulnerability of disinhibitory processes that involves the inability or unwillingness or failure to inhibit behavior even in the face of anticipated or already received negative consequences."[28] Antisocial behavior, conduct-disordered behavior, and sensation seeking are the core observable behaviors associated with behavioral undercontrol; while impulsivity and disinhibition are components that are more inferential in nature.

Research support for the individual component behaviors of this risk factor includes a study conducted by Clark *et al.*[30] in which early onset alcohol use from 11 through 15 years of age was predicted by conduct, oppositional defiant, and antisocial disorders, with 25% of the sample using alcohol prior to 13-years of age. Likewise, Boyle and colleagues[31] reported that children aged 8–12 rated by teachers as having conduct disorder were more likely to regularly use alcohol 4 years later.

With regard to impulsivity, sensation seeking, and risk taking, Potenza and de Wit[32] have noted that both sensation seeking and risk taking are manifestations of an impulsivity trait that developmentally precedes alcohol use and alcohol use escalation. This proposition is supported by a number of other studies. For example, Macpherson and colleages[33] investigated this relationship between alcohol use, sensation seeking, and risk-taking behavior in children initially in late childhood (ages 9–12) and followed yearly over a 3-year period. Although increases in both sensation seeking and risk taking are normative to adolescence, children who showed larger increases in change in sensation seeking and in risk-taking propensity were across time more likely to use alcohol in early adolescence.

In another study by Wong and colleagues,[34] children with lower initial levels of behavior control in early childhood were more likely to start drinking in early adolescence. The effects of behavioral (under) control were evaluated for their contribution above and beyond whatever effects might be present from ability to regulate emotion and level of rule breaking/antisocial behavior. When these factors were entered into the analysis, behavioral control continued to have a significant effect on EOD.

Attention deficit hyperactivity disorder

Driven by the observation that many abusive drinkers in adolescence show attentional deficits, this other area of (under) control, pertaining to attentional processes, has also received a considerable attention as a possible precursive risk factor for EOD. However, links between attention deficit hyperactivity disorder (ADHD) and EOD have been somewhat harder to establish, with inconsistent findings across studies. One subset of studies evaluating ADHD's contribution to alcohol use in conjunction with conduct disorder have found that childhood ADHD did not predict alcohol use in young adulthood once the effects of conduct disorder were controlled.[31,35,36]

Other work probing this connection suggests that the key issue in establishing the relationship is how well other potential comorbid factors are controlled. Thus, using parallel process latent growth modeling in a study of high risk youngsters from the time of school entry to middle adolescence, Jester and colleagues[37] were able to control for the effects of undercontrol (aggressiveness) when evaluating effects of attention/hyperactivity problems, and the effects of attention/activity problems when evaluating undercontrol effects. Growth mixture modeling indicated that there were two trajectory classes of inattention (one comorbid with aggression, the other not) and two for aggressive behavior, (one comorbid with attention/hyperactivity problems, the other not). Children with inattention/hyperactivity but lacking comorbid aggression were at an intermediate risk of EOD. Those comorbid for both attention problems and aggressiveness were at greatest risk; and those high in aggression but lacking the inattention/hyperactivity were intermediate between the other two. These results indicate that the risk for EOD contributed by inattention/hyperactivity is moderate, but when titrated by comorbid aggression (i.e., an indicator in the conduct disorder/behavioral disinhibition spectrum) risk increases. A more clinically differentiated study of subtypes of ADHD, as related to drinking behavior in early adulthood, reinforces the conclusions of the Jester *et al.*[37] findings. Elkins and colleagues[38] showed in a twin study that the hyperactive/impulsive type of ADHD was the most closely related to alcohol and other substance use at age 18.

Both studies indicate that preventing or reducing EOD in adolescence needs to involve a sophisticated, multicomponent process. Simple assessment of ADHD alone is not sufficient. Molina and colleagues[39] work reinforces this conclusion, showing that the relationship is also age dependent, and is more potent as a precursive risk factor in mid-adolescence than in other times.

Other nonspecific temperament and behavioral risks

Anxiety and depression, low resiliency, sleep difficulties, and social inhibition/shyness have all been noted in the research literature as risk factors for EOD. For instance, Kaplow and colleagues[40] found that youngsters assessed at 9, 11, and 13 years of age who were higher in depression and generalized anxiety were more likely to initiate alcohol use within 4 years. In other work, Wills and Ainette[41] found that early onset alcohol use in 11–15-year group was associated with poor self control, which in turn fostered low resiliency. In another extensive and long-term longitudinal study evaluating children at multiple points between ages 4–5 and 14, Baumrind[42] observed that less social assertiveness was associated with EOD for both sexes. More recently, a series of studies by Wong and colleagues[43] have shown that not all risks are immediately discernable behaviorally. This work shows that sleep difficulties in the preschool years (identified trouble sleeping, being overtired) are a robust predictor of EOD even when other, more obvious risk factors such as anxiety/depression and attention problems are controlled. These studies have implicated a level of systemic regulation not directly captured by behavioral risk, which indirectly leads to earlier use of alcohol. Mechanistically, the work raises the possibility of a central nervous system regulatory deficit that is disruptive of those physiological systems responsible for homeostasis and activity, which in turn has long-term consequences far removed from night-time functioning.

Nonspecific environmental factors

Nonspecific environmental factors that may influence risk for EOD include, but are not limited to, abuse, family conflict, poor parenting, and poor monitoring. More distal environmental factors, including minority group affiliation,[44] socioeconomic status, and even neighborhood social disorganization,[45] have also been shown to have a muted but direct role in elevating the risk for EOD. As noted above, behavioral undercontrol/disinhibition is one key risk pathway to early alcohol involvement. A number of environmental risks have been shown to exacerbate this system. At the proximal interpersonal level, family factors including coercive parenting and lack of parent concern, expressed through low levels of parental monitoring, have direct effects on drinking onset. (See for example, the work of Reid and colleagues[46] as one elaborated theory at the family social environmental level.) Other, more system-guided research has shown that a multilayered, multicomponent system of environmental influences have direct as well as interactive effects with individual-level risk. The work of Buu and colleagues[45] dramatically shows such a multilayered structure of risk—involving effects of parental psychopathology, family socioeconomic status, as well as neighborhood residential (in)stability—operating independently in the development of alcohol and other drug abuse and disorder. Some of these influences operate over time intervals as long as 10–15 years. Although not yet demonstrated longitudinally, one plausible hypothesis is that sociocultural/ethnic influences operate over such long time spans as well.

Alcohol-specific behavioral risks

Although alcohol consumption among the age group 8–12 is unusual, it should not be particularly surprising given that 8- and 9-year-old children are regularly tasked with processing and deciding how to react to and participate in scenarios involving alcohol use.[47] Thus, children's decisions to ingest alcohol do not just materialize spontaneously; they are influenced by the opportunities and environment that they encounter. In addition, beliefs and expectancies about alcohol that form in early development appear to play a significant role in risk for EOD.

In the preschool years, children establish schemas and norms about alcohol use that match the cultural and familial norms of the social environment in which they are being raised. The level of development of these schemas, for example, is predicted by the frequency of alcohol use in the child's home. In children of alcoholics, alcohol-related schemas and knowledge are more evident than in children of nonalcoholic parents.[47,48] Even after controlling for familial environment, having detailed knowledge and beliefs about alcohol use appear to influence children's decisions to begin using alcohol.[23] Precocious knowledge about alcohol appears to be part of a matrix of early childhood risk that leads to the development of precocious alcohol use, but that also is relevant in understanding the developmental course of drinking and alcohol abuse in adolescence and thereafter.

Alcohol-specific environmental risks

Alcohol-specific environmental factors that have been shown to influence risk for EOD include, but are not limited to, fetal alcohol exposure, mass media portrayal of acceptance/normalcy of drinking behavior, geographic clustering of alcohol outlets, as well as parental modeling of drinking (see above) and peer influences. It is beyond the scope of this chapter to detail these effects, but extensive discussion of them may be found in a review prepared by a select committee appointed by the US National Institute on Alcohol Abuse and Alcoholism to summarize this evidence.[27]

Genetic risk

Genetic influences on alcohol use and alcohol problems occur at multiple developmental points and involve complex interactions between the individual susceptibility and the physiological and social environment. Genetic studies relevant to EOD have largely focused on the importance of the undercontrol/disinhibition pathway as the mediator of genetic influences on behavior, that in turn leads to increased likelihood of involvement with deviant peers (social selection), and a greater likelihood that the risks and putative negative consequences of early, almost always surreptitious, drinking will be dismissed or not even considered. Evidence to date suggests that shared environmental influences play a greater role toward influencing EOD behavior than do direct genetic effects, but this behavior, which is only modestly heritable, may facilitate the expression of genes associated with vulnerability for problem drinking.[8] A review of this evidence by Dick[49] provides a good entry into this literature, as do the papers by Kendler and colleagues[50] and McGue and colleagues.[18] Chapter 6 in this volume provides an in-depth discussion of the role of genetics in adolescent problem drinking behavior.

The cascade of risk influences leading to early onset drinking

"While such factors as early antisocial behavior or genetic susceptibility to substance use increase one's vulnerability to negative outcomes, they do not necessarily doom a child to a life of substance abuse problems."[51] Risk factors are not static over the life course, nor do they act similarly for all people at all times.[11,51,52] As suggested by this review, preadolescent risk factors, or combinations thereof, may overshadow others with regard to influencing whether or not drinking initiation begins early or is deferred. Although a risk cumulation model[27]—that the additive impact of multiple risk factors greatly increases the likelihood of early drinking—is the most common conceptual framework for the field,[53] recent theoretical and empirical work suggests that this may be an overly simplistic and ultimately nondevelopmental model of how risk aggregates. The alternative is a developmental cascade framework.[54,55] The cascade model allows for risk dilution as well as risk aggregation, and for the possibility of time-dependent effects in the epigenesis of risk. It prompts for the specification of multiple risk factors, potentially operating sequentially across levels of influence. It also allows for the likelihood that effects may not individually be sufficient to generate the outcome, but the cascade model structure explicitly accommodates this, at the same time allowing heterogeneity of outcome.

Protective and promotive factors

Factors that predict fewer problems (i.e., level of risk) are promotive; factors that moderate the effects of risk are protective.[27,53] Nurturing and supportive parenting would be regarded as both a promotive and a protective factor for realizing better outcomes for youngsters, including a later initiation of drinking. When alcohol use occurs in childhood and early adolescence, the child is generally introduced to the substance by an adult, typically a parent or close family member.[43] In this context, responsible parental behavior would be operating as a protective factor; and parental monitoring would be operating as a promotive factor.

Child resilience, defined as positive adjustment in the face of adversity,[56] may also be considered a protective factor, as would good behavioral control. However, research on childhood resilience in the context of substance use, although statistically significant in terms of magnitude of effect size, has often shown that resilience plays a small role.[57] Resiliency, the ability to flexibly adapt one's level of control in response to the environment, also does not predict onset of drunkenness or level of alcohol problems in adolescence. Behavioral control, on the other hand, has consistently shown itself to be a strong protective factor.[27] Peer group affiliation also has a strong protective effect, but here too, the pathway of the relationship appears to be through reduction of disinhibitory behavior, either through lower cueing for early use or by way of modeling of nonuse.

Given this small menu of possible protectors/promoters, the field appears to still be in its infancy. Whether other modalities, either at the individual level or through manipulation of the social environment will be effective, is a task for the future, and a much needed one.

Summary

Early onset drinking can be conceptualized as a waypoint in a development trajectory, in which poor outcomes at earlier points tend to be antecedents for poor outcomes at later points in development. This problematic alcohol use is embedded in a multilevel matrix of influences, some of which are directly related to learning about, and encouraging the use of alcohol; and some of which are nonspecific to drinking, but very much related to the development of a disinhibitory behavioral style. Some influences are proximal to the drinking onset event, but many are substantially precursive. Although the specific risks we have identified are important to address in their own right, it is also essential to underscore the developmental nature of the drinking phenomenon. The existing literature is clear; harbingers of problem outcome are present well before the outcome is manifest. The potential preventive significance of this fact is still largely unappreciated by the treatment community, and to a lesser extent even by the prevention community, whose efforts tend to be focused on age periods relatively close to the early onset event.

Given the ubiquity of drinking by late adolescence in drinking cultures, and the evidence that early drinking tends to be more dangerous in consequences to both the drinkers and their peers, a better understanding of early starting, and how to delay and inhibit onset, is also likely to have substantial public health impact. Although there is some policy-level research that suggests population-based interventions that affect delay of drinking onset have longer term impact on prevalence and amount of adult drinking patterns,[58] both the general public and the psychiatric research establishment remain unaware of it. Given the ubiquity of underage drinking, this would appear to be a fertile ground for effecting social change.

Acknowledgments

Preparation of this chapter was supported in part by a grant to Robert A. Zucker from the US National Institute on Alcohol Abuse and Alcoholism (R37 AA07065).

References

1. Reboussin BA, Preisser JS, Song EY, Wolfson M. Geographic clustering of underage drinking and the influence of community characteristics. *Drug Alcohol Depend* 2010; 106:38–47.
2. York JL. Clinical significance of alcohol intake parameter at initiation of drinking. *Alcohol* 1999; 19:97–99.
3. Gruber E, DiClemente RJ, Anderson MM, Lodico M. Early drinking onset and its association with alcohol use and problem behavior in late adolescence. *Prev Med* 1996; 25:293–300.
4. Donovan JE. Really underage drinkers: The epidemiology of children's alcohol use in the United States. *Prev Sci* 2007; 8:192–205.
5. DeWit DJ, Adlaf EM, Offord DR, Ogborne AC. Age at first alcohol use: A risk factor for the development of alcohol disorders. *Am J Psychiatry* 2000; 157:745–750.
6. Chou SP, Pickering RP. Early-onset of drinking as a risk factor for lifetime alcohol-related problems. *Br J Addict* 1992; 87:1199–1204.
7. Hawkins JD, Graham JW, Maguin E, Abbott R, Hill KG, Catalano RF. Exploring the effects of age of alcohol use initiation and psychosocial risk factors on subsequent alcohol misuse. *J Stud Alcohol* 1997; 58:280–290.
8. Agrawal A, Sartor CE, Lynskey MT, Grant JD, Pergadia ML, Grucza R, Bucholz KK, Nelson EC, Madden PA, Martin NG, Heath AC. Evidence for an interaction between age at first drink and genetic influences on DSM-IV alcohol dependence symptoms. *Alcohol Clin Exp Res* 2009; 33:2047–2056.
9. Grant M, Choquet M, Spear LP, Araoz G, Higuchi S, Lee J, Robson G. *What Drives Underage Drinking? An International Analysis.* Report commissioned by the International Center for Alcohol Policies; 2004, pp. 1–62.
10. Peleg-Oren N, Saint-Jean G, Cardenas G, Tammara H, Pierre C. Drinking alcohol before age 13 and negative outcomes in late adolescence. *Alcohol Clin Exp Res* 2009; 33:1966–1972.
11. Zucker RA, Fitzgerald HE, Refior SK, Puttler L, Pallas DM, Ellis, DA. The clinical and social ecology of childhood for children of alcoholics: Description of a study and implications for a differentiated social policy. In: Fitzgerald HE, Lester BM, Zuckerman BS, eds. *Children of Addiction: Research, Health and Policy Issues.* New York: Routledge Falmer, 2000, pp. 109–141.
12. Donovan JE, Leech SL, Zucker RA, Loveland-Cherry CJ, Jester JJ, Fitzgerald HE, Puttler LI, Wong MM, Looman WS. Really underage drinking: Alcohol use among elementary students. *Alcohol Clin Exp Res* 2004; 28:341–349.
13. Picherot G, Urbain J, Dreno L, Caldagues E, Caquard M, Pernel AS, Amar M. Teenagers and age of first drinking: A disturbing precocity? *Arch Pediatr* 2010; 17:583–587 [in French].
14. Sartor CE, Lynskey MT, Heath AC, Jacob T, True W. The role of childhood risk factors in initiation of alcohol use and progression to alcohol dependence. *Addiction* 2007; 102:216–225.
15. Miller T, Hendrie D. *Substance Abuse Prevention Dollars and Cents: A Cost–Benefit Analysis.* Rockville, MD: Center for Substance Abuse Prevention, Substance Abuse and Mental Health Services Administration; 2009. DHHS Pub. No. (SMA) 07-4298.
16. The NHS Confederation. *Too much of the hard stuff: What alcohol costs the NHS.* Briefing January 2010; Issue 193.
17. Krueger RF, Hicks BM, Patrick CJ, Carlson SR, Iacono WG, McGue M. Etiologic connections among substance dependence, antisocial behavior, and personality: Modeling the externalizing spectrum. *J Abnorm Psychol* 2002; 11:411–424.
18. McGue M, Iacono WG, Legrand LN, Elkins I. Origins and consequences of age at first drink II. Familial risk and heritability. *Alcohol Clin Exp Res* 2001; 25:1166–1173.

19. Hingson RW, Heeren T, Winter MR. Age at drinking onset and alcohol dependence: Age at onset, duration, and severity. *Arch Pediatr Adolesc Med* 2006; 160:739–746.
20. Hingson RW, Heeren T, Edwards EM. Age at drinking onset, alcohol dependence, and their relation to drug use and dependence, driving under the influence of drugs, and motor-vehicle crash involvement because of drugs. *J Stud Alcohol Drugs* 2008; 69:192–201.
21. Kandel DB, Yamaguchi K, Chen K. Stages of progression in drug involvement from adolescence to adulthood: further evidence for gateway theory. *J Stud Alcohol* 1992; 53:447–457.
22. Swahn MH, Bossarte RM, Sullivent III EE. Age of alcohol use initiation, suicidal behavior, and peer and dating violence victimization and perpetration among high-risk, seventh-grade adolescents. *Pediatrics* 2008; 121:297–305.
23. Spear LP, Varlinskaya EI. Adolescence: Alcohol sensitivity, tolerance, and intake. *Recent Dev Alcohol* 2005; 17:143–159.
24. Windle M, Spear LP, Fuligni AJ *et al.* Transition into underage and problem drinking: Developmental processes and mechanisms between 10 and 15 years of age. *Pediatrics* 2008; 121 (Suppl. 4): 273–289.
25. Heitzeg MM, Nigg JT, Yau W-Y, Zucker, RA, Zubieta, J-K. Striatal dysfunction marks pre-existing risk and medial prefrontal dysfunction is related to problem drinking in children of alcoholics. *Biol Psychiatry* 2010; 68:287–295.
26. Zucker RA. The developmental behavior genetics of drug involvement: Overview and comments. *Behav Genet* 2006; 36:616–625.
27. Zucker RA, Donovan JE, Masten AS, Mattson ME, Moss HB. Early developmental processes and the continuity of risk for underage drinking and problem drinking. *Pediatrics* 2008; 121 (Suppl. 4): S252–S272.
28. Zucker RA, Nigg JT, Heitzeg MM. Parsing the undercontrol/disinhibition pathway to substance use disorders: A multilevel developmental problem. *Child Dev Perspect* 2011, in press.
29. Zucker RA, Donovan JE, Masten AS, Mattson ME, Moss HB. Developmental processes and mechanisms: Ages 0–10. *Alcohol Res Health* 2009; 32:16–29.
30. Clark DB, Parker AM, Lynch KG. Psychopathology and substance-related problems during early adolescence: A survival analysis. *J Clin Child Psychol* 1999; 28:333–341.
31. Boyle MH, Offord DR, Racine YA, Fleming JE, Szatmari P, Links PS. Predicting substance use in early adolescence based on parent and teacher assessments of childhood psychiatric disorder: Results from the Ontario Child Health Study follow-up. *J Child Psychol Psychiatry* 1993; 34:535–544.
32. Potenza MN, de Wit H. Control yourself: Alcohol and impulsivity. *Alcohol Clin Exp Res* 2010; 34:1303–1305.
33. Macpherson L, Magidson JF, Reynolds EK, Kahler CW, Lejuez CW. Changes in sensation seeking and risk-taking propensity predict increases in alcohol use among early adolescents. *Alcohol Clin Exp Res* 2010; 34:1400–1408.
34. Wong MM, Nigg JT, Zucker RA, Puttler LI, Fitzgerald HE, Jester JM, Glass JM, Adams K. Behavioral control and resiliency in the onset of alcohol and illicit drug use: A prospective study from preschool to adolescence. *Child Dev* 2006; 77:1016–1033.
35. Fergusson DM, Horwood LJ, Ridder EM. Conduct and attentional problems in childhood and adolescence and later substance use, abuse, and dependence: Results of a 25-year longitudinal study. *Drug Alcohol Depend* 2007; 88(Suppl. 1): S14–S26.
36. Pardini D, White HR, Stouthamer-Loeber M. Early adolescent psychopathology as a predictor of alcohol use disorders by young adulthood. *Drug Alcohol Depend* 2007; 88:S38–S49.
37. Jester JM, Nigg JT, Buu A, Puttler LI, Glass JM, Heitzeg MM, Fitzgerald HE, Zucker RA. Trajectories of childhood aggression and inattention/hyperactivity: Differential effects on substance abuse in adolescence. *J Am Acad Child Adolesc Psychiatry* 2008; 47:1158–1165.

38. Elkins IJ, McGue M, Iacono WG. Prospective effects of attention-deficit/hyperactivity disorder, conduct disorder, and sex on adolescent substance use and abuse. *Arch Gen Psychiatry* 2007; 64:1145–1152.

39. Molina BS, Pelham WE, Gnagy EM, Thompson AL, Marshal MP. Attention-deficit/hyperactivity disorder risk for heavy drinking and alcohol use disorder is age specific. *Alcohol Clin Exp Res* 2007; 31:643–654.

40. Kaplow JB, Curran PJ, Angold A, Costello EJ. The prospective relation between dimensions of anxiety and the initiation of adolescent alcohol use. *J Clin Child Psychol* 2002; 30:199–216.

41. Wills TA, Ainette MG. Good self-control as a buffering agent for adolescent substance use: An investigation in early adolescence with time-varying covariates. *Psychol Addict Behav* 2008; 22:459–471.

42. Baumrind D. Familial antecedents of adolescent drug use: A developmental perspective. In: Jones CL, Battjes RJ, eds. *Etiology of Drug Abuse: Implications for Prevention*. NIDA Research Monograph 56. Rockville MD: NIDA, 1985, pp. 13–44.

43. Wong MM, Brower KJ, Fitzgerald HE, Zucker RA. Sleep problems in early childhood and early onset of alcohol and other drug use in adolescence. *Alcohol Clin Exp Res* 2004; 28:578–587.

44. Walls ML, Whitbeck LB, Hoyt DR, Johnson KD. Early-onset alcohol use among Native American youth: Examining female caretaker influence. *J Marriage Fam* 2007; 69:451–464.

45. Buu A, DiPiazza C, Wang J, Puttler LI, Fitzgerald HE, Zucker RA. Parent, family, and neighborhood effects on the development of child substance use and other psychopathology from preschool to the start of adulthood. *J Stud Alcohol Drugs* 2009; 70:489–498.

46. Reid JB, Patterson GR, Snyder J. *Antisocial Behavior in Children and Adolescents: A Developmental Analysis and Model for Intervention*. Washington, DC: American Psychological Association, 2002.

47. Dalton MA, Bernhardt AM, Gibson JA *et al.* Use of cigarettes and alcohol by preschoolers while role-playing as adults. *Arch Pediatr Adolesc Med* 2005; 159:854–859.

48. Zucker RA, Kincaid SB, Fitzgerald HE, Bingham CR. Alcohol schema acquisition in preschoolers: Differences between children of alcoholics and children of nonalcoholics. *Alcohol Clin Exp Res* 1995; 19:1011–1017.

49. Dick DM. Developmental changes in genetic influences on alcohol use and dependence. *Child Dev Perspect* 2011, in press.

50. Kendler KS, Prescott CA, Myers J, Neale MC. The structure of genetic and environmental risk factors for common psychiatric and substance use disorders in men and women. *Arch Gen Psychiatry* 2003; 60:929–937.

51. Maggs JL, Schulenberg JE. Initiation and course of alcohol consumption among adolescents and young adults. In: Galanter M, ed. *Alcohol Problems in Adolescents and Young Adults: Epidemiology, Neurobiology, Prevention, and Treatment*. New York, NY, US: Springer Science + Business Media, 2006, pp. 29–47.

52. Zucker RA, Fitzgerald HE. Early developmental factors and risk for alcohol problems and alcoholism. *Alcohol Health Res World* 1991; 15:18–24.

53. Sameroff AJ. Developmental systems and psychopathology. *Dev Psychopathol* 2000; 12:297–312.

54. Dodge KA, Malone PS, Lansford JE, Miller S, Pettit GS, Bates JE. A dynamic cascade model of the development of substance-use onset. *Monogr Soc Res Child Dev* 2009; 74:1–120.

55. Masten AS, Roisman GI, Long JD *et al.* Developmental cascades: Linking academic achievement, externalizing and internalizing symptoms over 20 years. *Dev Psychol* 2005; 41:733–746.

56. Masten AS, Hubbard JJ, Gest SD, Tellegen A, Garmezy N, Ramirez M. Competence in the context of adversity: Pathways to resilience and maladaptation from childhood to late adolescence. *Dev Psychopathol* 1999; 11:143–169.

57. Lee HH, Cranford JA. Does resilience moderate the associations between parental problem drinking and adolescents' internalizing and externalizing behaviors? A study of Korean adolescents. *Drug Alcohol Depend* 2008; 96:213–221.
58. O'Malley PM, Wagenaar AC. Effects of minimum drinking age laws on alcohol use, related behaviors and traffic crash involvement among American youth: 1976–1987. *J Stud Alcohol* 1991; 52:478–491.

Chapter 3

The short- and long-term consequences of adolescent alcohol use

Joseph M. Boden and David M. Fergusson
Christchurch Health and Development Study, Department of Psychological Medicine,
University of Otago, Christchurch School of Medicine and Health Sciences,
Christchurch, New Zealand

Key points

- Adolescent alcohol use is associated with a wide range of adverse short- and long-term outcomes, including increased likelihood of accidents, risky sexual behavior, sexually transmitted infections and pregnancy, sexual assault and violence victimization and perpetration, obesity, and use of other substances.
- Higher levels of alcohol use or alcohol abuse/dependence in adolescence are associated with more unfavorable outcomes.
- Earlier onset of alcohol use is associated with increased risk of both short- and long-term adverse outcomes than later onset.
- Several methodological considerations arise in the study of alcohol use in adolescence, including: ascertaining the extent to which alcohol use *per se* plays a causal role in outcomes; the accuracy of measurements concerning timing of onset of alcohol use; and characteristics of the sample being studied.

In recent years, there has been increasing concern about the short- and long-term effects of alcohol use among adolescents. In particular, there has been an increased focus on the effects of problematic drinking patterns, including binge drinking, among young people.[1,2] Studies have suggested that problematic drinking patterns such as binge drinking have been steadily increasing over a number of years in Western countries, and governments and health authorities in many locations have taken a variety of steps to address the public health threats posed by excessive alcohol intake[1,2] (see Chapter 1).

One particular aspect of this issue is the extent to which problematic drinking has special consequences for adolescents and young adults. It is clear that excessive alcohol use is a feature of adolescent and young adult behavior in many Western societies,[3] and it has been argued that the consequences of excessive alcohol intake may be particularly severe when onset occurs during adolescence.[4] For example, chronic excessive alcohol intake

---

Young People and Alcohol: Impact, Policy, Prevention, Treatment, First Edition.
Edited by John B. Saunders and Joseph M. Rey.
© 2011 Blackwell Publishing Ltd. Published 2011 by Blackwell Publishing Ltd.

may have greater effects on the brain development of adolescents, leading to increased risks of subsequent health and behavioral problems[5] (see Chapter 5).

A further feature is that adolescence is generally associated with increased risk-taking behavior across a range of domains, irrespective of the effects of alcohol.[6] While excessive alcohol use may be viewed as one of the several forms of risk-taking behavior, it could also be argued that the normative increased risk-taking of adolescents is further exacerbated by the disinhibiting effects of alcohol.[7]

The purpose of this chapter is to summarize the findings on alcohol use, particularly the effects of excessive or problematic alcohol use, on psychosocial outcomes among adolescents. This will be done through a review of the literature and by examining the data from the Christchurch Health and Development Study (CHDS). The CHDS is a longitudinal study of a birth cohort of 1265 New Zealanders born in Christchurch in mid-1977.[8,9] Data from the CHDS is of particular interest not only because of the prospective nature of the study but also because the cohort is drawn from a Western country that is frequently considered to have a "drinking culture," which encourages early and excessive alcohol consumption among young people.[10] Finally, we will also examine methodological issues and briefly explore directions for future research.

Accidents

One of the primary dangers of alcohol use for adolescents is the risk of accidents. For example, in Australia between 2003 and 2006, of all alcohol-related deaths among 13–25-year-old people, 60% were unintentional. Of these, 79% were due to motor vehicle accidents, and 9% due to alcohol poisoning.[11] Numerous studies have shown that alcohol use, abuse, and dependence among adolescents is associated with increased risk of a variety of accidents, including pedestrian accidents[12]; falls[13]; drownings[14]; burns[15]; crush injuries[15,16]; injuries sustained as a result of fights[17]; and other miscellaneous accidents.[16] However, the vast majority of research on alcohol-related accidents among adolescents concerns motor vehicle accidents[18–20]; estimates have suggested that alcohol can be attributed as a cause of such accidents in as many as 50% of cases.[21]

Data from self-reports and simulation studies suggest that adolescent drivers are at greater risk of motor vehicle accidents than are drivers in any other age group[22] for several reasons, including the following:

- Greater risk-taking associated with the adolescent period of development.[22]
- Insufficient levels of driving experience and skills.[22,23]
- Insufficiently developed cognitive skills specific to driving.[24,25]

These risks are compounded when adolescent drivers are under the influence of alcohol.[19,25,26] Additionally, morbidity and mortality due to adolescent alcohol-impaired driving is greater than what would be predicted by an additive effect of alcohol-impaired driving and adolescent driving ability and behavior.[27]

Data from the CHDS also suggest that alcohol played a key role in increasing the risks of adolescents being involved in motor vehicle accidents. For example, Horwood and Fergusson[28] found that by age 21, rates of active motor vehicle collisions in which the driver could be held at fault were 2.5 times higher among those who scored in the highest 6% on a measure of alcohol-impaired driving than among those who reported no alcohol-impaired driving. Control for potentially confounding factors, including driver behavior, attitudes toward driving, and a range of factors related to family background and individual characteristics and behavior reduced the magnitude of the association, but it remained statistically significant. However, a further study of the same cohort[29] that focused in part on alcohol-impaired driving behavior during the period 21–25 years found that while those who reported driving under the influence of alcohol more than 21 times were 1.94 times more likely to be involved in an active motor vehicle collision. Unlike the data from age 21, this association was not statistically significant, suggesting that the strength of the statistical link between self-reported driving under the influence of alcohol and active motor vehicle collisions was too weak to be considered reliable. The reasons for this relatively weak finding may have been that: (a) the overall rate of self-reported alcohol-impaired driving had decreased during the period between 21—and 25 years of age, in comparison to the period prior to age 21; for example, 53% of the sample reported no alcohol-impaired driving prior to age 21, whereas nearly 73% of the sample reported no alcohol-impaired driving during the period 21–25 years; and (b) the overall rate of active motor vehicle collisions also decreased during the period 21–25 years, relative to the period prior to age 21. These data suggest that links between alcohol-impaired driving and active motor vehicle collisions may weaken as drivers become more mature and experienced, and in particular highlight the dangers faced by adolescent drivers who are alcohol impaired.

Risky sexual behavior, sexually transmitted infections, and pregnancy

An important issue is the extent to which alcohol use may be associated with increased rates of risky sexual behavior, exposure to sexually transmitted infections (STI), and pregnancy.[30,31] Research suggests that higher frequencies of alcohol consumption are associated with the following:

- Increased risk of unprotected sex[32];
- Increased numbers of sexual partners[33,34];
- Increased rates of self-reported and medically verified STI[33,34];
- Increased risk of pregnancy[33,35];
- Increased risk of abortion among adolescent females.[36]

There are two main explanations for the links between increasing levels of alcohol use and increased rates of risky sexual behavior and consequences of risky sexual behavior. First, the acute intoxicating effects of alcohol may increase impulsivity and cause disinhibition, altering normal patterns of sexual behavior and contraceptive use.[37] Alternatively, both higher alcohol intake and higher rates of risky sexual behavior reflect a general underlying predisposition to engage in reckless, impulsive behavior,[31] and it may be possible that a more general predisposition to recklessness explains the links between alcohol intake and risky sexual behavior.

What is somewhat less clear, however, is the extent to which increasing levels of alcohol use may be causally related to the consequences of risky sexual behavior among adolescents, and in particular pregnancy. While several studies have shown links between increasing alcohol use and increased risk of pregnancy, other studies have found that increasing alcohol use was associated with decreased risk of pregnancy, possibly due to alcohol's interference with fertility.[38] This issue was examined recently using data from the CHDS, in order to determine the extent to which patterns of alcohol consumption were related to increased risks of pregnancy among female cohort members.

The CHDS has collected extensive data on sexual behavior and pregnancy among female cohort members, and has examined the associations between alcohol consumption and rates of pregnancy.[39] During the period 15–18 years, adolescent females reporting five or more symptoms of alcohol abuse/dependence had relative risks of pregnancy that were approximately 1.45 times higher than females who reported no symptoms of alcohol abuse/dependence, although this association was not statistically significant. One possible reason for this finding, however, is that contemporaneous measures of alcohol abuse/dependence symptoms and pregnancy may be sensitive to the fact that pregnancy tends to reduce or eliminate alcohol consumption by females, which could attenuate the observed associations. Indeed, using the same data on alcohol abuse/dependence symptoms in women, but instead using a lagged modeling approach in which alcohol problems in one time period were linked to pregnancy in the subsequent period, there was a significant ($p < 0.01$) association between alcohol abuse/dependence symptoms during the period 15–18 years and risk of pregnancy during the period 18–21 years. Those women reporting five or more symptoms of alcohol abuse/dependence during the period 15–18 years had relative risks of pregnancy during the period 18–21 years that were approximately 2.55 times higher than women who reported no symptoms of alcohol abuse. The discrepancies between the contemporaneous and the time-lagged findings for women in the CHDS cohort highlight the importance of methodological issues, and in particular the accurate modeling of the time-dynamic association between alcohol consumption and pregnancy, in the study of the associations between alcohol consumption and risky sexual behavior/pregnancy.

Violence and sexual assault

Alcohol is commonly believed to play a major role in violent assault. For example, in England and Wales, it was reported that over half of the victims of violence perpetrated by a stranger judged the attacker to be under the influence of alcohol.[40] There is a very large literature on the links between alcohol and aggressive and violent behavior, one strand of which shows that adolescents who report higher levels of drinking are also more likely to have been involved in an incident of violence.[3]

Among adolescents, at least 30% of violent assaults,[41] and approximately 15–20% of sexual assaults[42,43] occur under the influence of alcohol, although, as noted below, the accurate assessment of these figures is difficult.[44] Evidence suggests that risks of violent and sexual assault victimization and perpetration increase as the level of alcohol intake increases.[43,45] Furthermore, adolescents may be at particular risk not only due to a lower level of experience with alcohol intoxication (that is, adolescents may become more intoxicated more quickly than intended) but also due to their exposure to situations in which binge drinking is more common.[45,46]

Evidence also suggests that the nature of the violent or sexual assault tends to vary with the extent of intoxication, perhaps due to the disinhibiting effects of alcohol.[47] For example, adolescent females are at particular risk for date rape, in which unwanted sexual contact occurs in the context of a date or other social activity and by a perpetrator known to the victim; again, alcohol use by both the victim and the perpetrator has been implicated as a causal factor in a large percentage of cases of date rape.[48] McCauley and Calhoun suggest that female adolescents who binge drink may underestimate their general risk of sexual assault while overestimating the extent to which they may be able to fend off a sexual assault while intoxicated.[49]

Having suffered a violent assault or sexual assault has been shown to have pervasive effects on psychosocial adjustment among adolescents and young adults.[50] In particular, sexual assault has been shown to have pervasive and lingering negative effects on mental health and sexual functioning,[51,52] including increased risk of depression, anxiety disorders, eating disorders, and PTSD, and being at increased risk of intimate partner violence and relationship instability. In addition, alcohol use moderates the relationship between sexual assault victimization and later revictimization.[53] The experience of guilt that sometimes accompanies sexual assault victimization[54] may be stronger or more salient for those individuals who were intoxicated with alcohol at the time the sexual assault took place.[55]

Despite these links, however, ascertaining the magnitude of the relationship between alcohol use among adolescents and increased risk of violent and sexual assault is a complex issue for a number of reasons. First, while it is clear that alcohol is associated with increased risk of violent and sexual assault perpetration, it is very difficult to determine accurately the magnitude of this risk, due to underreporting,[55] particularly so in the case of sexual assault. Second, it appears to be common that both the perpetrator and the victim in violent and sexual assault incidents have drunk alcohol prior to the assault,[56] making it difficult to determine the effects of alcohol on the behavior of the perpetrator and the victim, respectively.

Obesity

The study of the links between alcohol and obesity in adolescents has been motivated by the fact that adolescent obesity in Western societies has increased significantly in recent years,[57] a period that has also seen a concomitant increase in binge drinking among adolescents.[58] Also, longitudinal studies of adults have shown that long-term high levels of alcohol use are associated with increased risks of overweight and obesity.[59]

Adolescents who report higher levels of alcohol consumption, including binge drinking, are at greater risk of being overweight or obese,[60–62] although there may be gender differences—in terms of the extent to which alcohol consumption is associated with obesity among adolescents—with males being at greater risk.[63] In addition, links between alcohol consumption and obesity may be long-lasting; those who report higher levels of alcohol consumption and binge drinking in adolescence were found to be at greater risk of obesity and related health problems in early adulthood.[64]

It should also be noted, however, that some studies have shown the opposite effect, with obese adolescents, and in particular females, reporting lower alcohol consumption.[65] This may be due to the fact that obese adolescents may have fewer friendships and social contacts, partly as a result of social withdrawal associated with obesity, which may afford fewer opportunities for peer interaction and less exposure to situations in which alcohol is consumed. When interpreting these data it is important to note that many studies linking alcohol consumption to obesity in adolescents have not taken into account the wide range of potentially confounding factors, such as socioeconomic status, impulsivity, and mental health disorders, that may be related to both alcohol use and obesity.

Alcohol as a gateway substance

Is alcohol a "gateway" drug in relation to other substances, including tobacco, cannabis, and other illicit drugs[66]? Briefly put, the gateway hypothesis supports the existence of a developmental sequence of substance use in which the initiation of a particular substance increases the risk that an individual will go on to use other substances.[67]

In the case of alcohol, several studies have examined whether alcohol consumption increases the risk that adolescents will go on to use other substances. In general, there has been some empirical support for the linkages between alcohol use and later cannabis and other illicit drug use, with a range of studies finding evidence that alcohol precedes the use of other substances and increases the risk of the use of other substances, particularly cannabis and other illicit drugs.[66,68,69] However, the extent to which alcohol is the substance that is most likely to initiate the gateway transitions is unclear. Some studies have suggested that either alcohol or tobacco might serve as the initiating substance in the gateway progression,[68,70] while others have asserted that tobacco plays a stronger role than alcohol.[71,72] Attempts to model the links between alcohol use and tobacco use, in order to determine which substance plays a stronger role in initiating the gateway sequence, have produced equivocal results, suggesting that alcohol and tobacco use may arise as a result of common, underlying factors associated with both forms of substance use.[73]

One important methodological issue arising from gateway drug studies is the fact that it is difficult to accurately ascertain the timing of onset of the use of various substances.[67] In general, prospectively collected longitudinal data provide the most reliable measurement concerning the timing of onset of various forms of substance use, provided that participants are followed up frequently enough to ensure that data concerning onset and frequency of use are accurate.

Age of onset of use and consequences

A further issue of interest is the extent to which consequences of alcohol use vary by the age at which the individual begins using alcohol, such that the initiation of alcohol use at earlier ages, or heavier levels of use during adolescence, may increase the risk of negative consequences (see also Chapter 2). The accumulated evidence suggests that there is indeed a strong link between the age of onset of use and the later consequences; earlier use of alcohol has been linked to an increased risk of a range of adverse outcomes, the most prominent being subsequent alcohol abuse/dependence. Numerous studies have shown that individuals who begin using alcohol earlier are at increased risk of alcohol abuse/dependence in adolescence and early adulthood, and of lifetime alcohol abuse/dependence.[4,74,75] Furthermore, heavier levels of alcohol use at an earlier age are associated with more severe levels of alcohol problems in late adolescence and early adulthood.[76,77] Earlier initiation of use is also associated with increased risk of other adverse outcomes, including unintentional injury, alcohol-impaired driving, illicit drug use, mental health disorders, and convictions.[78,79]

One question that arises in examining the links between early onset of alcohol use and subsequent problems is the extent to which the adverse outcomes are causally related to the consumption of alcohol at an early age, or are more generally related to impulsive or reckless behavior related to both early alcohol consumption and later adverse life outcomes. Indeed, there has been some evidence that the links between early alcohol use and later outcomes may be attributable at least in part to an underlying "problem behaviors" factor.[80,81] However, a number of studies have shown that the links between early alcohol use and later adverse consequences persist even after controlling for a range of confounding factors, suggesting that the early use of alcohol may play a specific causal role in later problems.[4,77,79]

Data from the CHDS have been used to examine the links between age of onset of alcohol use and patterns of alcohol consumption in earlier adolescence.[82] In late childhood and early adolescence (ages 11–13), cohort members were asked to indicate the age at which they had first consumed alcohol. Among those who reported having used alcohol, the majority (67%) reported first using alcohol during the period 6–10 years of age. The findings suggested that, after adjustment for confounding factors related to family background and functioning, those who first consumed alcohol during the preschool years (up to age 6) had odds of heavy, frequent, or problem drinking by age 15 that were 1.9–2.4 times higher than those who did not drink alcohol before the age of 13. The findings suggest that those who were raised in home environments with more permissive attitudes toward alcohol use, and who were exposed to alcohol at an earlier age, were at greater risk of developing problematic alcohol consumption patterns in mid-adolescence.

Discussion and conclusions

While many questions remain, there are growing data showing that alcohol use in adolescence and early adulthood has considerable health and social consequences over and above those that would be expected. These can be summarized as follows:

1. Adolescent alcohol use is associated with a wide range of adverse outcomes, including motor vehicle and other accidents; risky sexual behavior, pregnancy, and STIs;

victimization by and perpetration of violent and sexual assault; obesity; and increased risk of the use of other substances.

2. There is a dose–response relationship between alcohol use and outcomes, such that higher levels of use are associated with greater severity of outcomes.
3. The increased risk of adverse outcomes is not limited to adolescence, but continues into adulthood.
4. Earlier onset of alcohol use is associated with greater levels of subsequent problems associated with alcohol use.

The weight of the evidence clearly shows that adolescent alcohol use is associated with a wide range of adverse outcomes in both the short- and the long-term, and underscores the urgent need for the development and implementation of programs designed to reduce adolescent alcohol use.[83]

One of the difficulties in program development and implementation is having a sufficient evidence base to underpin recommendations.[84] In general, in order to develop appropriate and cost effective interventions, it is necessary to have a good understanding of the causal mechanisms underlying the associations between exposures and outcomes. Unfortunately, the literature concerning alcohol use in adolescence, including some of the literature cited previously, is subject to a number of threats to validity that create difficulties in ascertaining the strength and direction of causal mechanisms. One key threat to validity is determining the extent to which the associations between alcohol use and outcomes can be accounted for by third or confounding factors. Some studies have, for example, provided evidence that at least some of the associations between adolescent alcohol use and later outcomes can be accounted for by common underlying factors, such as a general predisposition to problem behavior. However, there has also been evidence to suggest that, after controlling for these factors, there remain persistent statistically significant links between adolescent alcohol use and later adverse outcomes. A second threat to validity is ascertaining the direction of causality. It could be argued that alcohol use and outcomes are linked in a reciprocal manner, such that alcohol use among adolescents increases the risk of adverse outcomes, and that increasing levels of adverse outcomes increase the level of alcohol use. A third threat to validity pertains to the timing of measurements in longitudinal studies. As noted above, evidence from the CHDS concerning the link between alcohol use and pregnancy, for example, suggests that the timing of questions regarding exposure and outcome, particularly when measured contemporaneously, may play a critical role in the estimation and interpretation of the associations between alcohol use and outcomes. Similarly, studies examining the gateway theory in regard to alcohol use may show inconclusive results due to the difficulty of measuring alcohol and tobacco use in children and adolescents, particularly in terms of determining the timing at which the use of each substance began. A final threat to validity is that many of the existing findings concerning alcohol use in adolescents have been derived from data obtained from clinical samples or special populations. Each of these threats to validity can be addressed via the use of prospective longitudinal data, obtained from representative birth cohorts, that includes repeated measures of exposure (alcohol use and related problems) and outcomes over time.

In addition, while the links between alcohol use in adolescence and later alcohol disorders has been extensively studied, the link between alcohol use in adolescence and other long-term outcomes is less well understood. In particular, it is unclear whether the links between adolescent alcohol consumption and later outcomes reflects processes in which these links may be mediated by the effect of early alcohol use on later alcohol use/alcohol disorders. Again, further research using prospective longitudinal data is required to ascertain the nature of these links.

While additional research is needed to elucidate the links between alcohol use and adverse outcomes among adolescents, it is clear that public policy concerning alcohol use by young people requires further development. In order to reduce the level of adolescent alcohol use, and to weaken the links between alcohol use and adverse outcomes, policies and programs are required that will reduce the overall level of exposure to alcohol among adolescents, and that will reduce the level of harm among those adolescents already exposed to alcohol. While a number of different initiatives have been developed and implemented,[1,85–87] the high rates of alcohol use and associated adverse consequences among young people in western societies such as Australia, New Zealand and the United States suggest that a great deal of additional work is needed.

Future research on alcohol use among adolescents will need to focus on several key themes. These themes include the following:

- Strengthening the knowledge base concerning the casual links between alcohol use and adverse outcomes.
- Ascertaining the extent to which long-term risks of adverse outcomes are due to processes that link early alcohol use to increased risks of subsequent alcohol misuse.
- Empirical examination of the effects of various programs and interventions that may be implemented to reduce adolescent alcohol use.

In summary, it is clear that adolescent alcohol use and its effects are a significant public health problem for western societies in the twenty-first century, with adverse effects occurring across a wide range of outcomes, and ranging from short to long term. Although there is already a considerable knowledge base concerning these issues, more focused efforts are required in order to reduce the overall level of alcohol-related harm to the population that stems from adolescent alcohol use.

References

1. Stolle M, Sack PM, Thomasius R. Binge drinking in childhood and adolescence: Epidemiology, consequences, and interventions. *Dtsch Arztebl Int* 2009; 106:323–328.
2. Courtney KE, Polich J. Binge drinking in young adults: Data, definitions, and determinants. *Psychol Bull* 2009; 135:142–156.
3. Jernigan DH. *Global Status Report: Alcohol and Youth*. Geneva: World Health Organization, 2001.
4. Grant BF, Stinson FS, Harford TC. Age at onset of alcohol use and DSM-IV alcohol abuse and dependence: A 12-year follow-up. *J Subst Abuse* 2001; 13:493–504.

5. De Bellis MD, Clark DB, Beers SR *et al.* Hippocampal volume in adolescent-onset alcohol use disorders. *Am J Psychiatry* 2000; 157:737–744.

·6. Steinberg L. Risk taking in adolescence: What changes, and why? *Ann NY Acad Sci* 2004; 1021:51–58.

7. Spirito A, Jelalian E, Rasile D, Rohrbeck C, Vinnick L. Adolescent risk taking and self-reported injuries associated with substance use. *Am J Drug Alcohol Abuse* 2000; 26:113–123.

8. Fergusson DM, Horwood LJ. The Christchurch Health and Development Study: Review of findings on child and adolescent mental health. *Aust NZ J Psychiatry* 2001; 35:287–296.

9. Fergusson DM, Horwood LJ, Shannon FT, Lawton JM. The Christchurch Child Development Study: A review of epidemiological findings. *Paediatr Perinat Epidemiol* 1989; 3:278–301.

10. Alcohol Action NZ. *Alcohol Action NZ.* Available at: http://www.alcoholaction.co.nz/Default.aspx. Accessed August 10, 2010.

11. National Coroners Information System (NCIS). *Deaths of Persons Aged 13 to 25 Years in Australia (excluding QLD & SA) Which Involved Alcohol (Reported to a Coroner Between 2003 and 2006).* Southbank, Victoria, 2008.

12. Istre GR, McCoy M, Stowe M, Barnard JJ, Moore BJ, Anderson RJ. The "unintended pedestrian" on expressways. *Traffic Inj Prev* 2007; 8(4):398–402.

13. Lee KH. Epidemiology of mandibular fractures in a tertiary trauma centre. *Emerg Med J* 2008; 25:565–568.

14. Heninger M, Hanzlick R. Nonnatural deaths of adolescents and teenagers: Fulton County, Georgia, 1985–2004. *Am J Forensic Med Pathol* 2008; 29:208–213.

15. Miller TR, Levy DT, Spicer RS, Taylor DM. Societal costs of underage drinking. *J Stud Alcohol* 2006; 67:519–528.

16. Heather N. Alcohol, accidents, and aggression. *BMJ* 1994; 308:1254.

17. Lee K. Trend of alcohol involvement in maxillofacial trauma. *Oral Surg Oral Med Oral Pathol Oral Radiol Endod* 2009; 107:e9–e13.

18. Roudsari B, Ramisetty-Mikler S, Rodriguez LA. Ethnicity, age, and trends in alcohol-related driver fatalities in the United States. *Traffic Inj Prev* 2009; 10:410–414.

19. Bingham CR, Shope JT, Parow JE, Raghunathan TE. Crash types: Markers of increased risk of alcohol-involved crashes among teen drivers. *J Stud Alcohol Drugs* 2009; 70:528–535.

20. Hingson RW, Zha W. Age of drinking onset, alcohol use disorders, frequent heavy drinking, and unintentionally injuring oneself and others after drinking. *Pediatrics* 2009; 123:1477–1484.

21. Hingson R, Hereen T, Winter M, Wechsler H. Magnitude of alcohol-related mortality and morbidity among U.S. college students ages 18–24: Changes from 1998 to 2001. *Annu Rev Public Health* 2005; 26:259–279.

22. Clarke DD, Ward P, Truman W. Voluntary risk taking and skill deficits in young driver accidents in the UK. *Accid Anal Prev* 2005; 37:523–529.

23. Ferguson SA, Teoh ER, McCartt AT. Progress in teenage crash risk during the last decade. *J Safety Res* 2007; 38:137–145.

24. National Research Council Institute of Medicine and Transportation Research Board. *Preventing Teen Motor Crashes: Contributions from the Behavioral and Social Sciences, Workshop Report.* Washington, DC: The National Acadamies Press; 2007.

25. Dahl RE. Biological, developmental, and neurobehavioral factors relevant to adolescent driving risks. *Am J Prev Med* 2008; 35(Suppl. 3):S278–S284.

26. Zakletskaia LI, Mundt MP, Balousek SL, Wilson EL, Fleming MF. Alcohol-impaired driving behavior and sensation-seeking disposition in a college population receiving routine care at campus health services centers. *Accid Anal Prev* 2009; 41:380–386.

27. Peck RC, Gebers MA, Voas RB, Romano E. The relationship between blood alcohol concentration (BAC), age, and crash risk. *J Safety Res* 2008; 39:311–319.

28. Horwood LJ, Fergusson DM. Drink driving and traffic accidents in young people. *Accid Anal Prev* 2000; 32:805–814.
29. Fergusson DM, Horwood LJ, Boden JM. Is driving under the influence of cannabis becoming a greater risk to driver safety than drink driving? Findings from a 25 year longitudinal study. *Accid Anal Prev* 2008; 40:1345–1350.
30. Cooper ML. Alcohol use and risky sexual behavior among college students and youth: Evaluating the evidence. *J Stud Alcohol* 2002; (Suppl. 14):101–117.
31. Halpern-Felsher BL, Millstein SG, Ellen JM. Relationship of alcohol use and risky sexual behavior: A review and analysis of findings. *J Adolesc Health* 1996; 19:331–336.
32. Graves KL. Risky sexual behavior and alcohol use among young adults: Results from a national survey. *Am J Health Promot* 1995; 10:27–36.
33. Gillmore MR, Butler SS, Lohr MJ, Gilchrist L. Substance use and other factors associated with risky sexual behavior among pregnant adolescents. *Fam Plann Perspect* 1992; 24:255–261, 268.
34. Santelli JS, Brener ND, Lowry R, Bhatt A, Zabin LS. Multiple sexual partners among US adolescents and young adults. *Fam Plann Perspect* 1998; 30:271–275.
35. Naimi TS, Lipscomb LE, Brewer RD, Gilbert BC. Binge drinking in the preconception period and the risk of unintended pregnancy: Implications for women and their children. *Pediatrics* 2003; 111(5 Part 2):1136–1141.
36. Prager SW, Steinauer JE, Foster DG, Darney PD, Drey EA. Risk factors for repeat elective abortion. *Am J Obstet Gynecol* 2007; 197:575.e571–575.e576.
37. Parks KA, Hsieh YP, Collins RL, Levonyan-Radloff K, King LP. Predictors of risky sexual behavior with new and regular partners in a sample of women bar drinkers. *J Stud Alcohol Drugs* 2009; 70:197–205.
38. Jensen TK, Hjollund NH, Henriksen TB *et al*. Does moderate alcohol consumption affect fertility? Follow up study among couples planning first pregnancy. *BMJ* 1998; 317:505–510.
39. Fergusson DM, Boden JM, Horwood LJ. *Alcohol Misuse, Sexual Risk Taking, and Pregnancy in a Birth Cohort of Young Women. Unpublished Report*. University of Otago, Christchurch School of Medicine and Health Sciences; 2009.
40. United Kingdom Home Office. *Home Office Statistical Bulletin, Crime in England and Wales. HM Government*. Available at: http://www.crimereduction.homeoffice.gov.uk/statistics/statistics074.htm. Accessed February 24, 2010.
41. Bureau of Justice Statistics. Crime characteristics. *United States Department of Justice*. Available at: http://www.ojp.gov/bjs/cvict_c.htm#alcohol. Accessed November 16, 2009.
42. McCauley JL, Conoscenti LM, Ruggiero KJ, Resnick HS, Saunders BE, Kilpatrick DG. Prevalence and correlates of drug/alcohol-facilitated and incapacitated sexual assault in a nationally representative sample of adolescent girls. *J Clin Child Adolesc Psychol* 2009; 38:295–300.
43. Howard DE, Griffin MA, Boekeloo BO. Prevalence and psychosocial correlates of alcohol-related sexual assault among university students. *Adolescence* 2008; 43:733–750.
44. Ingemann-Hansen O, Sabroe S, Brink O, Knudsen M, Charles AV. Characteristics of victims and assaults of sexual violence—improving inquiries and prevention. *J Forensic Leg Med* 2009; 16:182–188.
45. Mohler-Kuo M, Dowdall GW, Koss MP, Wechsler H. Correlates of rape while intoxicated in a national sample of college women. *J Stud Alcohol* 2004; 65:37–45.
46. Cashell-Smith ML, Connor JL, Kypri K. Harmful effects of alcohol on sexual behaviour in a New Zealand university community. *Drug Alcohol Rev* 2007; 26:645–651.
47. Abbey A, Clinton-Sherrod AM, McAuslan P, Zawacki T, Buck PO. The relationship between the quantity of alcohol consumed and the severity of sexual assaults committed by college men. *J Interpers Violence* 2003; 18:813–833.

48. Rickert VI, Wiemann CM. Date rape among adolescents and young adults. *J Pediatr Adolesc Gynecol* 1998; 11:167–175.
49. McCauley JL, Calhoun KS. Faulty perceptions? The impact of binge drinking history on college women's perceived rape resistance efficacy. *Addict Behav* 2008; 33:1540–1545.
50. Beckman LJ, Ackerman KT. Women, alcohol, and sexuality. *Recent Dev Alcohol* 1995; 12:267–285.
51. Waldrop AE, Hanson RF, Resnick HS, Kilpatrick DG, Naugle AE, Saunders BE. Risk factors for suicidal behavior among a national sample of adolescents: Implications for prevention. *J Trauma Stress* 2007; 20:869–879.
52. Plichta SB, Falik M. Prevalence of violence and its implications for women's health. *Womens Health Issues* 2001; 11:244–258.
53. Gidycz CA, Loh C, Lobo T, Rich C, Lynn SJ, Pashdag J. Reciprocal relationships among alcohol use, risk perception, and sexual victimization: A prospective analysis. *J Am Coll Health* 2007; 56:5–14.
54. Olasov Rothbaum B, Foa EB, Riggs DS, Murdock T, Walsh W. A prospective examination of post-traumatic stress disorder in rape victims. *J Trauma Stress* 1992; 5:455–475.
55. Abbey A. Alcohol-related sexual assault: A common problem among college students. *J Stud Alcohol* 2002; S14:118–128.
56. Connor J, You R, Casswell S. Alcohol-related harm to others: A survey of physical and sexual assault in New Zealand. *N Z Med J* 2009; 122(1303):10–20.
57. Hedley AA, Ogden CL, Johnson CL, Carroll MD, Curtin LR, Flegal KM. Prevalence of overweight and obesity among US children, adolescents, and adults, 1999–2002. *JAMA* 2004; 291:2847–2850.
58. Farke W, Anderson P. Binge drinking in Europe. *Adicciones* 2007; 19:333–339.
59. Rissanen AM, Heliovaara M, Knekt P, Reunanen A, Aromaa A. Determinants of weight gain and overweight in adult Finns. *Eur J Clin Nutr* 1991; 45:419–430.
60. Fonseca H, Matos MG, Guerra A, Pedro JG. Are overweight and obese adolescents different from their peers? *Int J Pediatr Obes* 2009; 4:166–174.
61. Must A, Bandini LG, Tybor DJ, Janssen I, Ross R, Dietz WH. Behavioral risk factors in relation to visceral adipose tissue deposition in adolescent females. *Int J Pediatr Obes* 2008; 3(Suppl. 1):28–36.
62. Croezen S, Visscher TL, Ter Bogt NC, Veling ML, Haveman-Nies A. Skipping breakfast, alcohol consumption and physical inactivity as risk factors for overweight and obesity in adolescents: Results of the E-MOVO project. *Eur J Clin Nutr* 2009; 63:405–412.
63. Barry D, Petry NM. Associations between body mass index and substance use disorders differ by gender: Results from the National Epidemiologic Survey on Alcohol and Related Conditions. *Addict Behav* 2009; 34:51–60.
64. Oesterle S, Hill KG, Hawkins JD, Guo J, Catalano RF, Abbott RD. Adolescent heavy episodic drinking trajectories and health in young adulthood. *J Stud Alcohol* 2004; 65:204–212.
65. Duncan AE, Grant JD, Bucholz KK, Madden PA, Heath AC. Relationship between body mass index, alcohol use, and alcohol misuse in a young adult female twin sample. *J Stud Alcohol Drugs* 2009; 70:458–466.
66. Wagner FA, Anthony JC. Into the world of illegal drug use: Exposure opportunity and other mechanisms linking the use of alcohol, tobacco, marijuana, and cocaine. *Am J Epidemiol* 2002; 155(10):918–925.
67. Kandel DB. *Stages and Pathways of Drug Involvement: Examining the Gate-way Hypothesis.* Cambridge, England: Cambridge University Press; 2002.
68. Kandel DB, Yamaguchi K, Chen K. Stages of progression in drug involvement from adolescence to adulthood: Further evidence for the gateway theory. *J Stud Alcohol* 1992; 53(5):447–457.

69. Willner P. A view through the gateway: Expectancies as a possible pathway from alcohol to cannabis. *Addiction* 2001; 96:691–703.

70. Yu J, Williford WR. The age of alcohol onset and alcohol, cigarette, and marijuana use patterns: An analysis of drug use progression of young adults in New York State. *Int J Addict* 1992; 27:1313–1323.

71. Parra-Medina DM, Talavera G, Elder JP, Woodruff SI. Role of cigarette smoking as a gateway drug to alcohol use in Hispanic junior high school students. *J Natl Cancer Inst Monogr* 1995; (18):83–86.

72. Blaze-Temple D, Lo SK. Stages of drug use: A community survey of Perth teenagers. *Br J Addict* 1992; 87:215–225.

73. Ritchey PN, Reid GS, Hasse LA. The relative influence of smoking on drinking and drinking on smoking among high school students in a rural tobacco-growing county. *J Adolesc Health* 2001; 29:386–394.

74. Guo J, Collins LM, Hill KG, Hawkins JD. Developmental pathways to alcohol abuse and dependence in young adulthood. *J Stud Alcohol* 2000; 61:799–808.

75. Gruber E, DiClemente RJ, Anderson MM, Lodico M. Early drinking onset and its association with alcohol use and problem behavior in late adolescence. *Prev Med* 1996; 25:293–300.

76. McCarty CA, Ebel BE, Garrison MM, DiGiuseppe DL, Christakis DA, Rivara FP. Continuity of binge and harmful drinking from late adolescence to early adulthood. *Pediatrics* 2004; 114:714–719.

77. Bonomo YA, Bowes G, Coffey C, Carlin JB, Patton GC. Teenage drinking and the onset of alcohol dependence: A cohort study over seven years. *Addiction* 2004; 99:1520–1528.

78. Zakrajsek JS, Shope JT. Longitudinal examination of underage drinking and subsequent drinking and risky driving. *J Safety Res* 2006; 37:443–451.

79. Viner RM, Taylor B. Adult outcomes of binge drinking in adolescence: Findings from a UK national birth cohort. *J Epidemiol Community Health* 2007; 61:902–907.

80. Warner LA, White HR. Longitudinal effects of age at onset and first drinking situations on problem drinking. *Subst Use Misuse* 2003; 38(14):1983–2016.

81. Dubow EF, Boxer P, Huesmann LR. Childhood and adolescent predictors of early and middle adulthood alcohol use and problem drinking: The Columbia County Longitudinal Study. *Addiction* 2008; 103(Suppl. 1):36–47.

82. Fergusson DM, Lynskey MT, Horwood LJ. Childhood exposure to alcohol and adolescent drinking patterns. *Addiction* 1994; 89:1007–1016.

83. Hingson RW, Assailly JP, Williams AF. Underage drinking: Frequency, consequences, and interventions. *Traffic Inj Prev* 2004; 5:228–236.

84. Room R, Graham K, Rehm J, Jernigan D, Monteiro M. Drinking and its burden in a global perspective: Policy considerations and options. *Eur Addict Res* 2003; 9:165–175.

85. Wenzel V, Weichold K, Silbereisen RK. The life skills program IPSY: Positive influences on school bonding and prevention of substance misuse. *J Adolesc* 2009; 32:1391–1401.

86. Vogl L, Teesson M, Andrews G, Bird K, Steadman B, Dillon P. A computerized harm minimization prevention program for alcohol misuse and related harms: Randomized controlled trial. *Addiction* 2009; 104:564–575.

87. Newton NC, Vogl LE, Teesson M, Andrews G. CLIMATE Schools: Alcohol module: Cross-validation of a school-based prevention programme for alcohol misuse. *Aust NZ J Psychiatry* 2009; 43:201–207.

Part II

Neurobiology

Chapter 4

The biology of alcohol and alcohol misuse

John B. Saunders[1,2]

[1]Centre for Youth Substance Abuse Research, Faculty of Health Sciences, University of Queensland, Brisbane, Queensland, Australia
[2]Faculty of Medicine, University of Sydney, New South Wales, Australia

---

Key points

- Alcohol is a natural substance produced by fermentation and commonly taken in amounts that exceed the body's natural defense mechanisms.
- Alcohol is rapidly absorbed and is distributed throughout the lean body mass. It is cleared largely through metabolism in the liver, at an essentially fixed rate, which means that repeated doses result in disproportionately higher blood alcohol concentrations.
- Alcohol is a depressant, which acts at various sites in the brain, resulting in disinhibition, impaired memory and decision making, and incoordination. The toxic effects can progress to stupor and coma and death from respiratory depression.
- Other acute biological consequences of alcohol consumption include nausea, vomiting (and aspiration of vomit leading to asphyxiation), "hangover," amnesic episodes ("blackouts"), and diseases such as acute gastritis.
- Repeated consumption of alcohol leads to the development of alcohol dependence, a psychophysiological disorder that constitutes a "driving force" to drink more and is characterized by alcohol taking a more central role in the person's life, impaired control over its use, and sometimes withdrawal symptoms.
- Dependence on alcohol occurs because of the resetting of neurochemical systems concerned with reward, stress and behavioral control, and these changes are long enduring.
- The longer term biological consequences of repeated alcohol consumption include chronic liver disease, chronic pancreatitis, alcohol-related brain damage, and a range of other neuropsychiatric diseases.

Alcohol, more properly termed ethyl alcohol, is a natural product of fermentation and occurs widely in nature. It has been known to human beings for at least 10,000 years and has been consumed in most societies for much of this time. In evolutionary terms, human beings (and other animals) are designed to cope with only small amounts of alcohol. The quantities consumed by many people nowadays overwhelm the body's natural defense mechanisms and lead to dependence (addiction), a range of physical and mental disorders, and serious individual, interpersonal, and societal problems.

Young People and Alcohol: Impact, Policy, Prevention, Treatment, First Edition.
Edited by John B. Saunders and Joseph M. Rey.
© 2011 Blackwell Publishing Ltd. Published 2011 by Blackwell Publishing Ltd.

Absorption, distribution, and clearance

After ingestion, alcohol is absorbed rapidly from the gastrointestinal tract. Absorption occurs in two places, firstly in the stomach—but this is relatively slow and only about 20% of the total amount is absorbed here. Most, around 80%, is absorbed through the duodenum, the most proximal part of the small bowel, and absorption here is much more rapid.[1–3] From these sites of absorption, alcohol enters the liver via the portal venous system before it enters the systemic blood circulation. Some alcohol (~5%) is metabolized (broken down) in the stomach mucosa, more is metabolized in the liver, with the proportion ranging from 5% to 40% initially depending on the rate of absorption and other circumstances.[4–6] Alcohol can be detected in the systemic circulation within approximately 5 minutes of ingestion. The peak blood alcohol concentration (BAC) after a single amount of alcohol is reached 30–45 minutes after ingestion, again depending on the rate of absorption and whether food has been taken as well.

Alcohol is a highly water-soluble compound, which rapidly distributes into the total body water, which corresponds to the lean body mass (1 kg body mass is equivalent to ~750 mL water). Lean body mass amounts to approximately 45–55% in women and 55–65% in men. The remainder comprises fat in the subcutaneous tissues and elsewhere, and alcohol distributes little into this. The concentration of alcohol in the major organs (excluding fat) is essentially the same as in blood, with some variation according to the respective fat content of various organs. The concentration of alcohol reached throughout the body depends, naturally, on the amount consumed.

After the BAC peaks (at 45–60 minutes), there is a phase of fairly rapid decline (assuming no more alcohol is taken), which is due to distribution of alcohol throughout the lean body mass (Figure 4.1). After approximately 1.5 hours, the decline in BAC continues at a slower rate, and this decline is largely due to metabolism, predominantly in the liver. The BAC is typically measured in milligrams of alcohol per 100 mL of blood (g/mL), though units of measurement vary from country to country (e.g., in Australia it is measured as grams per 100 mL (g%)).

A person's BAC will generally increase by 10–20 mg/100 mL for each 10 g of alcohol consumed. This amount is that contained in approximately one "standard drink" of alcohol, though what is considered a "standard drink" varies from 8 g (in the United Kingdom), 10 g (Australia), 12 g (several Western European countries), 13 g (United States), and 14 g (Canada). It is important to note that there can be a fourfold interindividual variation in the BAC reached after consumption of alcohol, and even within an individual (at different times) the range can be two to three times. It is therefore very difficult to predict the BAC that a given person will reach after consumption of alcohol even when this is a measured amount, the person is of known weight, and variables affecting absorption have been eliminated (e.g., alcohol has been taken on an empty stomach). Some of the interindividual variation reflects genetic differences in the rate of absorption and metabolism of alcohol.[7]

Alcohol is removed from the systemic blood circulation (and the body more generally) by a combination of metabolism (90–95%), excretion in urine and sweat (2–3%), and evaporation in breath (1–3%). Metabolism occurs primarily by oxidation of alcohol in the liver (80–90%) and the stomach (10–20%) via the enzymes alcohol dehydrogenase (ADH) and aldehyde dehydrogenase (ALDH)[4,8] (Figure 4.2). A small proportion of metabolism

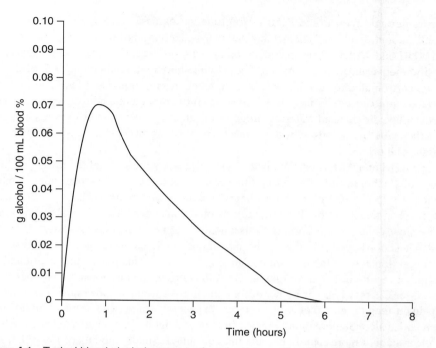

Figure 4.1   Typical blood alcohol concentration–time curve after consumption of 40 g of alcohol in a man weighing 70 kg. Blood alcohol concentration is measured in grams per 100 mL blood.

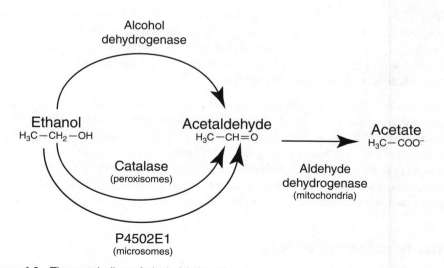

Figure 4.2   The metabolism of alcohol (ethanol).

occurs through cytochrome P450 mixed function oxidases (specifically cytP450 2E1). Small amounts of alcohol are metabolized in the pancreas, the lungs, and the brain, mostly via ADH and ALDH. The immediate breakdown product of alcohol is acetaldehyde, a highly reactive and toxic compound. The enzymes have kinetic (functional) characteristics designed to maintain acetaldehyde at very low concentrations, and facilitate its further metabolism to acetate. This in turn undergoes further metabolic conversion ultimately to form carbon dioxide and water. Hydrogen equivalents are generated from these reactions, and these fuel numerous subsidiary reactions resulting in the formation of fatty acids, lactate, and uric acid.

The ADH and ALDH enzyme pathways are capacity limited and the metabolic break-down of alcohol occurs at a constant rate equivalent to only 7–10 g per hour or approximately 10–15 mg/100 mL blood per hour. The rate of metabolism is hardly influenced by the BAC or, therefore, by the amount of alcohol consumed. Alcohol is also metabolized more slowly than it is absorbed. Consequently, the more alcohol is consumed, and the faster it is consumed, the higher the maximum BAC achieved. Indeed, the BAC rises disproportionately as the amount consumed increases.[9] This means that continued consumption results in larger and larger BACs leading to unconsciousness and potentially death (see Chapter 13). The higher the maximum BAC achieved, the higher the concentration in the major organs including the brain. In general, a larger and heavier individual will metabolize alcohol more rapidly than a smaller and lighter individual and hence will tend to clear alcohol more rapidly per amount consumed. Small amounts of alcohol are also removed by interacting with fatty acids to form compounds called fatty acid ethyl esters.

Both the distribution of alcohol and its metabolism—and therefore blood alcohol concentrations—are influenced by the sex and age of the person. The major difference is between men and women, and this is accounted for by the following two main influences:

- Differences in lean body mass, with women having a lower average body weight and proportionately smaller body mass because of the higher proportion of a woman's body comprising fatty tissue (into which alcohol distributes little).[10]
- Differences in the rate of metabolism, including (i) lower gastric metabolism and (ii) lower first-pass metabolism in the liver in men.[11]

Age-related differences in the handling of alcohol are known but there are many factors that influence both distribution and metabolism, and therefore act as confounders. Another crucial issue is that systematic investigation of the handling of alcohol in the body is ruled out because of ethical constraints against administering alcohol to young people under the legal age. Such age-related differences as are reported typically reflect differences in body composition or the effects of intercurrent or chronic disease (including liver disease) on the metabolism of alcohol[12,13] (see also Chapter 5).

Pharmacological effects

Alcohol is a pharmacological intoxicant that suppresses the brain and the rest of the central nervous system. Its effects in causing impairment of function and intoxication vary according to the BAC (and therefore concentration in the lean body mass), and thus on the amount consumed. In low concentrations alcohol has effects that are considered desirable by many individuals and societies, but in higher concentrations it produces increasingly serious behavioral abnormalities, impairment of alertness and coordination, suppression of vital functions, and death.

Table 4.1 illustrates the expected effects of various blood alcohol concentrations on behavior, functioning, and vital signs. Note that the material in this table is illustrative of what may be expected in an adult male of average weight (70 kg) in good health and without a history of hazardous or risky alcohol consumption. Note the caveats expressed earlier, that the BAC achieved can vary fourfold between individuals and that there is also interindividual variation in the effects of alcohol on the central nervous system.

Box 4.1   Therapeutic implications of alcohol metabolism.

Alcohol has numerous interactions with therapeutic drugs (medications) and also with illicit drugs. Some of these occur in the brain because alcohol and many psychoactive drugs are depressants. Other interactions occur in the liver (the main site of alcohol and drug metabolism). Alcohol, when ingested, acutely inhibits the metabolism of many drugs. In contrast, repeated alcohol consumption enhances the metabolism of many drugs. For example, interactions can occur between alcohol and other substances (such as anesthetics, analgesics, antibiotics, anticoagulants, antidepressants, antihistamines, and antidiabetic, antiepileptic, and antiulcer medications) because they compete for metabolism by the P450 2E1 enzyme pathway. If alcohol is preferentially metabolized by the P450 2E1 enzyme pathway, the blood concentration of the other substance will be increased and its effects will be increased. Alcohol suppresses the metabolism of the anticoagulant drug, warfarin. Alcohol that is consumed immediately prior to a dose of warfarin increases the blood concentration and availability of warfarin and its anticoagulant effects, which increases the patient's risk of uncontrolled hemorrhage. On the other hand, repeated alcohol consumption induces P450 2E1, which results in accelerated metabolism of warfarin, subtherapeutic blood levels, and the risk of thrombus (blood clot) formation and embolism, with potentially fatal consequences.

Alcohol intoxication

Acute intoxication is defined simply as a short-term state that occurs following ingestion of alcohol and has features that are compatible with the known physiological effects of alcohol. These include euphoria, disinhibition, talkativeness, slurred speech and, after higher doses, incoordination, unsteady gait, nystagmus, memory impairment, lack of attention, stupor, and coma (Table 4.1). Implicit in this definition is that other causes of these states have been excluded. The state of intoxication is time limited. When alcohol is no longer present, having been eliminated from the body, the person essentially returns to the state that existed prior to their consumption of alcohol. The exception to this is when a complication has occurred during the period of intoxication. This may include vomiting, hemorrhage from the stomach, aspiration of vomit and asphyxiation or pneumonia, hypoxia, head trauma, and other physical harm.

At a BAC of 20–50 mg/100 mL, a person in normal health generally experiences a sense of relaxation, well-being, and perhaps a loss of inhibition or shyness, which

Table 4.1 Effects of various blood alcohol concentrations on behavior, functioning, and vital signs.

Alcohol consumed in previous 4 hours[a] (g)	BAC range (mg/100 mL)	Signs of impairment/intoxication
10–30	20–50	• Sense of relaxation. • Increased self-confidence. • Greater talkativeness. • Reduced inhibition. • Impairment of ability to understand and process visual information and to perform divided attention tasks. • Reduction in psychomotor performance and simulated driving. • Increased risk of motor vehicle accident.
30–50	50–80	• Garrulousness, reduced inhibition, overconfidence. Sense of relaxation, loss of alertness. • Impaired processing of visual and auditory information. • Impaired psychomotor coordination. • Risk of accident increased twofold at BAC of 50 mg/100 mL.
50–90	80–150	Features observed at lower blood alcohol concentrations further heightened, together with: • Slurring of speech. • Impairment of coordination and unsteady balance. Understanding of auditory and visual information impaired. • Body sway increased—three to five times. • Exaggerated behaviors and emotional lability. • Risk of accident increased fourfold at BAC of 80 mg/100 mL.
90–160	150–250	• Reduced loss of consciousness with confusion, disorientation. • The person appears sedated and sleepy. • Typically, unable to stand up or move purposefully. Occasionally may be abusive and aggressive. • Eyes are glazed. • Major impairment on all tests of attention, understanding, and psychomotor function. • Physical symptoms such as nausea and vomiting are common. • Highly vulnerable to assault and injury. • Memory is extremely impaired for this period, resulting in an alcohol-induced amnesic episode ("blackout"), which is apparent on subsequent recovery from this state, the person having no recollection of what occurred during the period of intoxication.
160+	Above 250	• The person is typically unconscious and even comatose. • Breathing is suppressed, and the gag and cough reflexes are greatly diminished and may be paralyzed. • The person is unable to protect their airways and will be at risk of inhaling or choking on their vomit or other material aspirated into the respiratory tract. • Above 300 mg/100 mL, breathing slows and becomes increasingly irregular and may cease completely.

[a]This is an approximation and should not be taken as a guideline to consumption.

may be manifest in talkativeness and a sensation of light-headedness. The ability to understand and process information (e.g., motor response time to optical stimuli, as well as decision times) may become impaired.[14] Cognitive processes are affected and impaired by alcohol at a lower BAC than are motor processes or motor function (such as gross motor skills—larger movements of arms, legs, feet, or the entire body—and fine motor skills—small movements of the hands, wrists, fingers, feet, toes, lips, and tongue.[15]

The sense of relaxation and well-being combined with loss of inhibition of course makes it more likely that a person will continue drinking alcohol and reach higher BACs, that will produce serious impairments and lead to overt, clinically significant intoxication.

Clinical definitions of alcohol intoxication

Both the *International Classification of Diseases*[16] (ICD-10) and the *Diagnostic and Statistical Manual of Mental Disorders*,[17] fourth edition (DSM-IV TR) of the American Psychiatric Association include alcohol intoxication as a diagnostic entity. In both systems, there is a requirement for the intoxication to be "clinically significant"; in other words, for the person to be likely to require medical attention. In ICD-10, alcohol intoxication is defined as a condition that follows consumption of alcohol to the extent that there are significant disturbances in consciousness, cognition, perception, effect, behavior, or of other functions and responses. In DSM-IV, alcohol intoxication is characterized as a series of maladaptive behavioral or psychological changes, with examples being aggression, inappropriate sexual behavior, lability of mood, impaired judgment or impaired functioning in social settings or at work.

The disturbances resolve with the passage of time and there is complete recovery, except where complications such as hypoxia or tissue damage have arisen (see above). The level of disturbance correlates with the blood (or breath or tissue) alcohol concentration, but BAC is not a criterion for the diagnosis of intoxication.

In some cultures, alcohol intoxication has a broader definition than is indicated by these definitions. For example, it may refer to any degree of impairment due to the physiological effects of alcohol and these can be evident at a BAC as low as 20 mg/100 mL. In many situations in Western societies, impairment or intoxication for legal purposes is often defined by the BAC. For example, in Australia, it is illegal to drive a motor vehicle with a BAC of 50 mg/100 mL or more. In other countries, however, the term intoxication is equivalent to acute poisoning. Here, the state of intoxication is equivalent to an anesthetic or sedative overdose, which would likely require resuscitation.

The after effects of alcohol

Hangover

Alcohol has a biphasic effect on the body and brain. As described above, the initial effects are typically pleasant, though higher doses will produce toxic and undesirable effects such as nausea, vomiting, aggressive behavior, and incoordination. The later effects are usually unpleasant, especially after higher amounts have been consumed. Initially, the affected person will waken periodically from an alcohol-induced slumber or sleep. Sleep in the intoxicated state is not the normal physiological experience. In particular, rapid eye movement (REM) sleep (also known as "restorative sleep") is inhibited by alcohol intoxication.[18,19]

When the BAC declines further, the person may experience nausea and vomiting, headache and aching limbs, together with sweating and gooseflesh. Alcohol-induced diuresis (the increased formation of urine by the kidneys) causes dehydration, which contributes to headache and aching limbs, while nausea is a response to autonomic hyperactivity affecting the stomach and gastrointestinal tract. The "hangover" can continue even after the BAC has declined to zero.

However, the alcohol hangover is still a puzzling phenomenon whose causes are not well known. The common belief is that dehydration is one of the main culprits but that might not be the case. A multitude of changes take place after excessive drinking (such as endocrine, metabolic acidosis) and all may contribute. It has been hypothesized more recently that hangovers may be related to immune system activation.[20] Although the evidence is limited, adolescents also seem to be less sensitive to hangovers (see Chapter 5).

Alcohol-induced amnesic episodes ("blackouts")

Alcohol interferes with the ability to form new memories, particularly when it is taken in intoxicating amounts. A common consequence of clinically significant alcohol intoxication is memory loss for events that occurred while the person was intoxicated—a form of anterograde amnesia. A blackout may be partial (fragmentary), when there is patchy recollection of events, which may increase with the passage of time, and complete or *en bloc*, where there is complete loss of memory for the period with no subsequent recovery of memory.

Unlike alcohol-induced stupor or coma, blackouts do not involve a loss of consciousness, just a loss of memory. The typical blackout lasts approximately 2–6 hours, typically corresponding to the peak BAC. With increasing BAC during a bout of drinking, the likelihood of a blackout increases.[21] The BAC alone does not predict blackouts accurately; it is more the *rate* at which alcohol is consumed and the *rate of rise* of the BAC that is predictive.[22,23] However, even when the same BAC is reached by an individual, in only one-third of occurrences does that person experience the memory loss characteristic of a blackout.

Possible mechanisms for blackout include alcohol-induced hypoglycemia (low blood glucose level). However, there is no consistent relationship between the blood glucose level and the experience of a blackout. Mechanisms underlying alcohol-induced memory impairments include disruption of neurotransmission in the hippocampus, a brain region that plays a central role in the formation of new memories.[24] Consequently, brain and head injury and resulting concussion may also be a mechanism for some blackouts. There is no evidence for blackouts being epileptiform phenomena.

Alcohol and neurotransmission

Alcohol has many effects on the brain at cellular and subcellular levels, and these may be general (e.g., affecting all membranes) or specific (affecting a particular neurotransmitter only). The effects also depend on the concentration of alcohol to which the brain is exposed and the duration of exposure.

Alcohol's general effects include those on the composition and microstructure of biological membranes, including brain neurons (nerve cells) that generate and conduct electrical impulses, which convey signals ("messages"). A general effect is that alcohol alters the configuration of fatty acid chains in neuronal membranes. Specifically, acute exposure to alcohol increases the fluidization of these membranes, while repeated or chronic exposure decreases the fluidization (i.e., "stiffens" the membranes).[25] It is uncertain that these effects are operative at concentrations of alcohol that are reached in humans. Alcohol also affects specific neurotransmitters (chemical messengers). These are released at the terminals of neurons, cross a synaptic gap between the neuron and the next one, and then bind to receptors on the latter's surface membrane. This in turn causes ion channels to open, thus transmitting the signal.

The neurotransmitters primarily affected by alcohol are as follows:

- Gamma-amino-butyric acid (GABA)
- Adenosine
- Glutamate
- Dopamine
- Serotonin (5-HT)
- Opioid peptides

These neurotransmitters fall into three categories: excitatory, which activate the postsynaptic cell; inhibitory, which depress the activity of the postsynaptic cell; and neuromodulators, which modify the postsynaptic cell's response to other neurotransmitters (see also Chapter 16).

GABA

Alcohol's sedative effects are mediated by GABA, the main inhibitory neurotransmitter in the brain, which acts by opening chloride ion channels. These GABA-mediated effects also suppress anxiety and can lead to stupor and coma. When the BAC exceeds 250 mg/100 mL, alcohol can open the chloride ion channel independently of GABA, allowing excessive chloride influx that can result in paralysis of the neurons responsible for respiration, leading to asphyxiation. Alcohol also inhibits the degradation of GABA, thereby increasing its concentration and perpetuating its effects. Thus, the antianxiolytic, sedating effects of alcohol are primarily mediated by increasing the concentration and function of GABA. In addition, alcohol increases the activity of adenosine, another inhibitory neurotransmitter, such that this increase also causes sedation.

Glutamate

Sedation is also caused by alcohol decreasing the activity or function of glutamate, the main excitatory neurotransmitter, at the *N*-methyl-D-aspartate (NMDA) glutamate receptor. These receptors control the influx of calcium ions into the cell, which cause cellular excitability. Acute exposure to alcohol inhibits binding of glutamate to the receptor. This closes the calcium ion channel and decreases excitatory signaling throughout the brain.[26] In turn, the altered excitatory signaling reduces the NMDA-mediated release of other neurotransmitters such as dopamine, noradrenaline (norepinephrine), and acetylcholine. Glutamate activity is related to cognition, learning, and memory, and its inhibition may be instrumental in causing alcohol-induced blackouts.

Dopamine

Alcohol increases the synthesis and release of dopamine in the nucleus accumbens situated in the forebrain. These dopaminergic pathways arise in the ventral tegmental area (VTA) situated in the midbrain. Alcohol increases the information relayed from the VTA to the nucleus accumbens through this mechanism. Dopamine is regarded as the "final common pathway" by which alcohol and other psychoactive substances cause euphoria and reinforcement of consumption of the substance. It seems to act principally by altering the sensitivity of its target neurons to other neurotransmitters, as well as altering the release of other neurotransmitters. Dopamine has a key role in the experiences of reward and motivation, and the ability to experience pleasure. Dopamine is involved in emotion and mood, and associated behaviors, as well as in cognition.

Serotonin

Serotonin (5-HT) is also involved in the regulation of behavior, emotion and mood, such as both euphoria and depression. It is also involved in arousal, sleep, thinking, and certain appetites and consumption behaviors. Alcohol increases the release of 5-HT from different 5-HT receptor subtypes, each of which has its own specific influence on subsequent behavior. 5-HT may alter the rate at which its target neurons produce electrical signals and/or may alter the release or other transmitters such as GABA and dopamine.

Endogenous opioids

Finally, alcohol increases the activity of neurons that are subserved by endogenous opioids. The extent to which alcohol's actions in causing euphoria are influenced by opioid peptides is controversial. It seems likely that the opioidergic neurons play a modulating effect on the release of dopamine, rather than having a primary role in interacting with a range of neurotransmitter systems.

Alcohol not only affects neurotransmitters individually but also influences their interactions when working together. For example, 5-HT may interact with neurons that synthesize and release GABA. If alcohol is present, the alcohol influenced 5-HT may affect the actions of GABA neurons in areas involving behavior such as the hippocampus, where cognitive decisions are made and may contribute to alcohol-induced memory loss and impaired judgment. Similarly, alcohol influenced 5-HT stimulates dopamine synthesis and release in the VTA,[27,28] and hence nucleus accumbens.

Alcohol and hormones

Although alcohol's actions are not mediated primarily by circulating hormones, alcohol stimulates the synthesis and release of hormones produced by the adrenal gland, which are part of hypothalamic pituitary axis. The hormones include those of the adrenal cortex such as cortisol and those of the adrenal medulla such as adrenaline and noradrenaline.

Cortisol is a component of the body's stress-response system. The release of cortisol can focus alertness and attention, and increase blood pressure. Cortisol can also suppress bone growth, digestion, reproduction, and wound repair. A high BAC may be interpreted by the body and brain as a "stress," as alcohol directly affects the chemicals that signal the adrenal glands to synthesize and release cortisol. An increased concentration of cortisol can, however, induce depression, impair cognitive functioning, and alter sleep patterns,[29] all of which are associated with, and potentially additive to, the effects of alcohol on neurotransmitters.

Synthesis and release of the steroid or sex hormone, testosterone, may be either stimulated or inhibited by alcohol either in the adrenal cortex or peripherally in both men (testes) and women (ovaries), depending on the amount and pattern of alcohol consumed and individual characteristics.[30,31] For example, in men, alcohol consumption causes an acute transient decrease in the blood concentration of testosterone as it inhibits the production of testosterone in the testis. In young, premenopausal women, however, alcohol consumption can also cause an acute transient increase in the blood concentration of testosterone.[32] The blood testosterone concentration following alcohol consumption is due to the net effect of an inhibited liver metabolism of testosterone and an inhibited synthesis of testosterone in the gonads. The blood testosterone concentration would, therefore, depend on different hormonal conditions as well as different amounts and patterns of alcohol consumption such that the inhibited synthesis of testosterone may predominate after large amounts of alcohol are consumed over a short period of time, and also when in the late, descending phase of alcohol elimination, when all the alcohol consumed has been completely metabolized.

In addition, alcohol inhibits the release of antidiuretic hormone (ADH) or arginine vasopressin from the posterior pituitary gland. The decreased concentration of ADH prevents the kidneys from reabsorbing water, thus promoting water loss, which increases the rate of urine formation. The concentration of blood electrolytes correspondingly increases. The result is dehydration.

The long-term effects of alcohol

Dependence (addiction)

Repeated alcohol consumption leads over time (typically some years) to alcohol dependence (addiction) in many people. The risk of developing dependence is related to

(1) the level of alcohol consumption, (2) the frequency of consumption, (3) the duration of consumption, and (4) individual susceptibility factors such as genetic predisposition. No one is immune from this possibility. Alcohol dependence is rare in adolescents but increasingly common in the late teens and in the twenties. Indeed, recent survey evidence indicates a peak in prevalence in the 20s.[33]

Alcohol dependence is defined in both DSM-IV and ICD-10 as a clinical syndrome in which a number of behavioral, cognitive, and physiological phenomena cluster together and do so repeatedly as long as alcohol consumption is maintained. This definition is not particularly illuminating. In essence, alcohol dependence represents a psychobiological *driving force* to consume alcohol, which develops as a result of the resetting in an enduring (long-term) way of a number of key neurotransmitter systems in the brain. The driving force means that alcohol is consumed (almost) irrespective of the person's circumstances or current situation and despite the harmful consequences that have or may occur. The disorder influences behavior such that the person's life becomes increasing focused on accessing alcohol, consuming it, experiencing and recovering from its effects, and it tends to be self-perpetuating. The diagnosis of alcohol dependence is based on six criteria in ICD-10 and seven in DSM-IV. Table 4.2 compares and contrasts the criteria in these two systems. In both ICD-10 and DSM-IV, three criteria need to be fulfilled repeatedly over a 12-month period for the diagnosis to be made.

The neurobiology of alcohol dependence

A schematic representation of the development and perpetuation of alcohol dependence is presented in Figure 4.3. Alcohol dependence represents a fundamental resetting of key neuronal pathways (neurocircuits) subserving (1) reward and incentive, (2) alertness and stress, and (3) inhibitory control.

The reward systems

The two main reward systems involve dopamine and endogenous opioid peptides in the mesocorticolimbic system of the midbrain and lower forebrain. The dopaminergic system is primarily concerned with "incentive salience."[34,35] As described above, it originates in the VTA and runs to the nucleus accumbens. The second, also in the mesolimbic area, is the opioid peptide "consummatory" system. This can act in series with the dopamine system or independently of it. These two systems mediate (or contribute to) the effects of natural rewards such as food and sex, and seem to be instrumental in the euphoric, rewarding and reinforcing effects of alcohol, and indeed nearly all commonly used addictive substances.[35]

Initially, consumption of alcohol causes activation of projections from the nucleus accumbens to the prefrontal cortex and result in reinforcement of consumption. However, with repeated consumption the dopaminergic system is compromised and the effect of the substance is diminished. The number of dopamine D2 receptors is reduced after chronic exposure to alcohol and this seems to be an important mechanism in the development of tolerance. Thus, there is a "resetting" of the reward system such that more of the

Table 4.2 Diagnostic criteria for alcohol dependence.

ICD-10[16]	DSM-IV[17]
A strong desire or sense of compulsion to take the psychoactive substance (*craving or compulsion*).	No equivalent criterion—mentioned in text.
No equivalent criterion but text states that the subjective awareness of compulsion is most commonly seen during attempts to stop or control substance use.	There is persistent desire or unsuccessful attempts to cut down or control substance use.
Difficulties in controlling substance-taking behavior in terms of its onset, termination, or levels of use (*loss of control*).	The substance is often taken in larger amounts or over a longer period of time than was intended.
Progressive neglect of alternative pleasures because of psychoactive substance use, increased amount of time necessary to obtain or take the substance or to recover from its effects.	Important social, occupational, or recreational activities are given up or reduced because of drinking or psychoactive substance use.
	A great deal of time is spent in activities necessary to obtain the substance, use the substance or recover from its effects.
Tolerance, such that increased doses of the psychoactive substances are required in order to achieve effects originally produced by lower doses.	Tolerance, as defined by either a need for markedly increased amounts of the substance to achieve the desired effects or markedly diminished effect with continued use of the same amount of the substance.
A physiological withdrawal state when substance use has ceased or been reduced, as evidenced by the characteristic withdrawal syndrome for the substance; or use of the same (or a closely related substance) with the intention of relieving or avoiding withdrawal symptoms.	Withdrawal as manifested by either the characteristic withdrawal syndrome for the substance or the same (or a closely related) substance is taken to relieve or avoid withdrawal symptoms.
Persisting with substance use despite clear evidence of overtly harmful consequences.	The substance use is continued despite knowledge of having a persistent or recurrent physical or psychological problem that is likely to have been caused or exacerbated by the substance.

substance needs to be taken to maintain normal dopaminergic activity. Similar changes in the opioid system are hypothesized to accompany chronic use. Given that natural rewards are mediated through the same neurochemical systems, this resetting means that they are also diminished in intensity, including such survival-determining and evolutionary imperatives as food and sexual drive.[36]

Pathways involving several other neurotransmitters interact with the reward systems. Inputs exist in the VTA and amygdala from GABAergic neurons. Alcohol enhances GABAergic transmission, which in turn influences the primary reward systems.

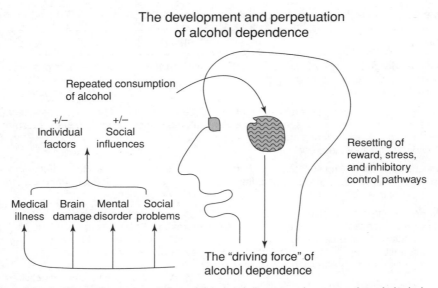

Figure 4.3   A schematic representation of the development and perpetuation of alcohol dependence.

The brain stress systems

A second major neurochemical mechanism of alcohol dependence is through the recruit-ment of the brain stress systems. These systems are responsible for maintaining levels of arousal appropriate to external circumstances. They comprise pairs of transmitters with opposite actions, which in normal circumstances allow a homeostatic balance. Mediators of arousal include glutamatergic pathways (the principal central nervous system excita-tory system),[37] noradrenergic pathways, and corticotropin releasing factor (CRF). These systems are counterbalanced by the inhibitory or antistress pathways involving GABA and neuropeptide Y.

Acute exposure to alcohol reduces the activity of the glutamatergic and noradren-ergic pathways that subserve stress, and enhances the activity of the antistress sys-tems GABA and neuropeptide Y. On the other hand, continued exposure leads to neuroadaptive responses, which include increases in NMDA glutamatergic, CRF and noradrenergic neurotransmission,[38] and, correspondingly, reduced GABA and NPY neurotransmission.[39] Again, these systems appear to be reset, the excitatory ones in an overactive ("supercharged") direction, and the inhibitory ones in an underactive direction.

Impaired inhibition

The brain's frontal regions exert a braking function on behaviors that are driven by the mesolimbic reward pathways. Pathways that originate in the prefrontal and orbitofrontal cortex course to the nucleus accumbens and override responses which would otherwise be initiated by the activated reward systems.

These inhibitory pathways exert imperfect control over reward-driven behaviors even in optimal circumstances. There is increasing evidence that inhibitory function is impaired in substance dependence to the extent that substance and cue-related behaviors are unfettered to an even greater extent.[40]

Summary

The principal mechanisms involved in the development of alcohol dependence are: (1) enhancement, followed by inhibition, of dopaminergic neurotransmission, leading to hedonic and medicinal drives to maintain high levels of substance use, (2) recruitment of central nervous system stress pathways, including those subserved by glutamate, and (3) impairment of inhibitory pathways from the frontal cortex that attempt to regulate these drives.

Details of the cellular and subcellular mechanism by which these neurocircuits are reset are being elucidated. However, it is clear the changes are persistent. In experimental animals, some changes last for the life of the animal even when alcohol exposure ceases. It suggests that in human beings, once the neurobiological changes underlying alcohol dependence have developed, they are persistent, lasting many years, possibly decades and, potentially, for the life of the individual.

Alcohol withdrawal

Alcohol withdrawal is a syndrome that occurs when alcohol consumption suddenly ceases (or there is a marked reduction in consumption) in an alcohol-dependent individual. Although some of the symptoms of alcohol withdrawal are similar to those of hangover, the experience is quantitatively different. The alcohol withdrawal syndrome typically lasts for 3–5 days, and is only diagnosed when it has been present for 24 hours or more. It consists of three main types. *Simple* alcohol withdrawal is a syndrome of central nervous system hyperactivity, where many of the features are the opposite of those of the acute pharmacological effects of alcohol. Common symptoms include tremor (most marked when the hands are outstretched), perspiration, anxiety, agitation, and gastrointestinal symptoms such as nausea and retching. In approximately 2–3% of cases, the syndrome is accompanied by seizures; these are tonic–clonic (grand mal) in type with sudden loss of consciousness and have no premonitory symptoms. They usually occur singly and recovery is typically prompt. In about 1% of cases, the alcohol withdrawal syndrome progresses to *delirium tremens*. This is a far more severe disorder than simple withdrawal. It consists of marked and progressive tremor and sweating, increasing agitation and distractibility, perceptual disturbances, visual hallucinations, paranoid ideation, confusion, and disorientation. Before adequate treatment it had a mortality of 30%.

The alcohol withdrawal syndrome is uncommon in young people under the age of 18 years (probably because of the predominant pattern of binge drinking rather than regular excessive daily drinking in this age range). However, from this age it becomes increasingly common, although the most severe form of delirium tremens remains uncommon until the early 30s. Concurrent physical disease, chemical (electrolyte) disturbances, and recent trauma aggravate the withdrawal syndrome.

The neurobiological mechanisms of alcohol withdrawal largely reflect the resetting of the brain stress system, which in the absence of alcohol, produces an unfettered syndrome of hyperactivity in all modalities. There are high levels of noradrenergic activity in particular, resulting in tremor and sweating, and other autonomic and gastrointestinal disturbance.[41]

Physical diseases

Although there is near-universal acceptance nowadays that most alcohol-related diseases are caused by the tissue toxic effects of alcohol and its metabolites, up to the 1970s there was a widespread view that malnutrition, vitamin deficiency, and trauma were the cause and alcohol an "innocent bystander." For example, alcoholic liver disease was considered to be a disorder of malnutrition (e.g., choline deficiency). In treatment, emphasis was placed on ensuring that the person had a nutritious diet and less attention was paid to their alcohol consumption.

A key figure in identifying the mechanisms by which alcohol led to tissue injury was Charles Lieber.[42] Over a period of more than 40 years, his group has amassed evidence that excessive alcohol consumption leads to fatty liver, fibrosis, alcoholic hepatitis, cirrhosis, acute and chronic pancreatitis, and acute and chronic myopathy. They have identified several of the key mechanisms including the generation of excessive hydrogen equivalents that fuel a number of subsidiary reactions leading to enhanced synthesis of fatty acids and also reduced degradation. Later work has emphasized the important role of generation of free oxygen species through alcohol metabolism and the formation of covalent bonds, which denature cellular proteins and impact on cellular microarchitecture.

Laboratory tests

Laboratory tests are necessary in the emergency situation to evaluate the young person who is intoxicated or whose conscious level is impaired. In this situation, the following tests should be undertaken:

- Breath or blood alcohol concentration
- Urine sampling for immediate assessment of the presence of other psychoactive substances (using benchtop or dip stick tests), or to be sent subsequently for laboratory analysis
- Relevant biochemical tests such as electrolytes, urea, creatinine, glucose, and liver function tests
- Relevant radiography
- Arterial blood gases (or oxygen saturation if less severely ill)

Outside the emergency situation, the value of laboratory tests (biological and markers of alcohol) in the young person is low. This is in contrast to the findings in older age groups where laboratory tests, although imperfect, have considerable utility.[43] Common laboratory markers such as gamma-glutamyl transferase (GGT) are raised in 25–60% of subjects aged 25 years and older, depending on duration and extent of alcohol consumption. The serum transaminases, AST and ALT, are abnormal in 25–40% and mean cell volume (MCV) is raised in a similar percentage.

The most sensitive test, albeit more expensive than the others, is carbohydrate-deficient transferrin (CDT), which is raised in approximately 40–70% of older people with alcohol use disorders. In young people, the percentage of hazardous drinkers who have laboratory abnormalities is under 10%. In routine practice, therefore, there is no indication to undertake laboratory tests. If there is a specific diagnostic issue, for example the possibility of an alcohol use disorder in a young person who denies significant consumption of alcohol, the most appropriate test would be the CDT.

Resources

- Alcohol Research & Health. Neuroscience: pathways to alcohol dependence. Part II. Neuroadaptation, risk, and recovery. *Alcohol Res Health* 2008; 31(4). Available at: http://pubs.niaaa.nih.gov/publications/arh314/toc31-4.htm.
- Alcohol Research & Health. Neuroscience: pathways to alcohol dependence. Part 1. Overview of the neurobiology of dependence. *Alcohol Res Health* 2008; 31(3). Available at: http://pubs.niaaa.nih.gov/publications/arh313/toc31-3.htm.
- Smart L (ed). *Alcohol and Human Health*. Oxford, UK: Oxford University Press; 2008.
- Sher L. *Research on the Neurobiology of Alcohol Use Disorders*. New York: Nova Science Publishers; 2008.

References

1. Halsted CH, Robles EA, Mezey E. Distribution of ethanol in the human gastrointestinal tract. *Am J Clin Nutr* 1973; 26:831–834.
2. Julkunen RJK, Tannembaum L, Baraona E, Lieber CS. 1st pass metabolism of ethanol: an important determinant of blood-levels after alcohol consumption. *Alcohol* 1985; 2:437–441.
3. Jian R, Cortot A, Ducrot F, Jobin G, Chayvialle JA, Modigliani R. Effect of ethanol ingestion on postprandial gastric-emptying and secretion, biliopancreatic secretions, and duodenal absorption in man. *Dig Dis Sci* 1986; 31:604–614.
4. Krebs HA, Perkins JR. The physiological role of liver alcohol dehydrogenase. *Biochem J* 1970; 118:635–644.
5. Pawan GLS. Metabolism of alcohol (ethanol) in man. *Proc Nutr Soc* 1972; 31:83–89.
6. Baraona E, Lieber CS. Effects of ethanol on lipid metabolism. *J Lipid Res* 1979; 20:289–315.
7. Whitfield JB, Nightingale BN, Bucholz KK, Madden PAF, Heath AC, Martin NG. ADH genotypes and alcohol use and dependence in Europeans. *Alcohol Clin Exp Res* 1998; 22:1463–1469.
8. Comporti M, Signorini C, Leoncini S , Gardi C, Ciccoli L, Giardini A, Vecchio D, Arezzini B. Ethanol-induced oxidative stress: Basic knowledge. *Genes Nutr* 2010; 5:101–109.
9. Wagner JG, Wilkinson PK, Sedman AJ, Kay DR, Weidler DJ. Elimination of alcohol from human blood. *J Pharm Sci* 1976; 65:152–154.
10. Saunders JB, Davis M, Williams R. Do women develop alcoholic liver disease more readily than men? *Br Med J (Clin Res Ed)* 1981; 282:1140–1143.
11. Lieber CS. Metabolism and metabolic effects of alcohol. *Med Clin North Am* 1984; 68:3–31.

12. Pozzato G, Moretti M, Franzin F, Croce LS, Lacchin T, Benedetti G, Sablich R, Stebel M, Campanacci L. Ethanol metabolism and aging: The role of first-pass metabolism and gastric alcohol dehydrogenase activity. *J Gerontol A Biol Sci Med Sci* 1995; 50:B135–B141.

13. Lamminpää A. Acute alcohol intoxication among children and adolescents. *Eur J Pediatr* 1994; 153:868–872.

14. Breitmeier D, Seeland-Schulze I, Hecker H, Schneider U. The influence of blood alcohol concentrations of around 0.03% on neuropsychological functions: A double-blind, placebo-controlled investigation. *Addict Biol* 2007; 12:183–189.

15. Moskowitz H, Fiorentino D. *A Review of the Literature on the Effects of Low Doses of Alcohol on Driving-Related Skills*. Washington, DC: National Highway Traffic Safety Administration (NHTSA); 2000.

16. World Health Organization. *International Classification of Diseases and Related Health Problems*. Geneva: World Health Organization; 1990.

17. American Psychiatric Association. *Diagnostic and Statistical Manual of Mental Disorders*. 4th edn, Text Revision: DSM-IV TR. Washington, DC: American Psychiatric Association; 2000.

18. Rohers T, Roth T. Sleep, sleepiness, sleep disorders and alcohol use and abuse. *Sleep Med Rev* 2001; 5:287–297.

19. Brower KJ. Alcohol's effects on sleep in alcoholics. *Alcohol Res Health* 2001; 25:110–125.

20. Verster JC. The alcohol hangover: A puzzling phenomenon. *Alcohol Alcohol* 2008; 43:124–126.

21. Perry PJ, Argo TR, Barnett MJ *et al*. The association of alcohol-induced blackouts and grayouts to blood alcohol concentrations. *J Forensic Sci* 2006; 51:896–899.

22. Ryback RS. Alcohol amnesia. *JAMA* 1970; 212:1524.

23. Ryback RS. Alcohol amnesia. Observations in seven drinking inpatient alcoholics. *Q J Stud Alcohol* 1970; 31:616–632.

24. White AM. What happened? Alcohol, memory blackouts, and the brain. *Alcohol Res Health* 2003; 27:186–196.

25. Chin JH, Goldstein DB. Drug tolerance in biomembranes: A spin label study of the effects of ethanol. *Science* 1977; 196:684–685.

26. Lovinger DM, White G, Weight FF. Ethanol inhibits NDMA-activated ion current in hippocampal neurons. *Science* 1989; 243: 1721.

27. Brodie MS, Trifunovic RD, Shefner SA. Serotonin potentiates ethanol-induced excitation of ventral tegmental area neurons in brain slices from three different rat strains. *J Pharmacol Exp Ther* 1995; 273:1139–1146.

28. Campbell AD, Kohl RR, McBride WJ. Serotonin-3 receptor and ethanol-stimulated somato-dendritic dopamine release. *Alcohol* 1996; 13:569–574.

29. Born J, DeKloet ER, Wenz H, Kern W, Fehm HL. Gluco- and antimineralocorticoid effects on human sleep: A role of central corticosteroid receptors. *Am J Physiol* 1991; 260:E183–E188.

30. Sarkola T, Eriksson CJ. Testosterone increases in men after a low dose of alcohol. *Alcohol Clin Exp Res* 2003; 27:682–685.

31. Sierksma A, Sarkola T, Eriksson CJ, van der Gaag MS, Grobbee DE, Hendriks HF. Effect of moderate alcohol consumption on plasma dehydroepiandrosterone sulfate, testosterone, and estradiol levels in middle-aged men and postmenopausal women: A diet-controlled intervention study. *Alcohol Clin Exp Res* 2004; 28:780–785.

32. Alomary AA, Vallee M, O'Dell LE , Koob GF, Purdy RH, Fitzgerald RL. Acutely administered ethanol participates in testosterone synthesis and increases testosterone in rat brain. *Alcohol Clin Exp Res* 2003; 27:38–43.

33. Grant BF, Goldstein RB, Chou SP *et al*. Sociodemographic and psychopathologic predictors of first incidence of DSM-IV substance use, mood and anxiety disorders: Results from the Wave

2 National Epidemiologic Survey on Alcohol and Related Conditions. *Mol Psychiatry* 2009; 14:1051–1066.

34. Koob GF. The neurobiology of addiction: A neuroadaptational view relevant for diagnosis. *Addiction* 2006; 101(Suppl. 1): 23–30.

35. Koob GF, Le Moal M. Drug addiction, dysregulation of reward, and allostasis. *Neuropsychopharmacology* 2001; 24:97–129.

36. Volkow ND, Fowler JS, Wang GJ. The addicted human brain viewed in the light of imaging studies: Brain circuits and treatment strategies. *Neuropharmacology* 2004; 47 (Suppl. 1): 3–13.

37. Johnson BA. Update on neuropharmacological treatments for alcoholism: Scientific basis and clinical findings. *Biochem Pharmacol* 2008; 75:34–56.

38. Davidson M, Shanley B, Wilce P. Increased NMDA-induced excitability during ethanol withdrawal: A behavioural and histological study. *Brain Res* 1995; 674:91–96.

39. Roy A, Pandey SC. The decreased cellular expression of neuropeptide Y protein in rat brain structures during ethanol withdrawal after chronic ethanol exposure. *Alcohol Clin Exp Res* 2002; 26:796–803.

40. Childress AR, Ehrman RN, Wang Z *et al.* Prelude to passion: Limbic activation by "unseen" drug and sexual cues. *PLoS One* 2008; 3:e1506.

41. Hall W, Zador D. The alcohol withdrawal syndrome. *Lancet* 1997; 349:1987–1900.

42. Lieber CS. Alcoholic fatty liver: Its pathogenesis and mechanism of progression to inflammation and fibrosis. *Alcohol* 2004; 34:9–19.

43. Conigrave KM, Saunders JB, Whitfield JB. Diagnostic tests for alcohol consumption. *Alcohol Alcohol* 1995; 30:13–26.

Chapter 5

Alcohol and the developing brain

Linda Patia Spear

Department of Psychology and Developmental Exposure Alcohol Research Center
(DEARC), Binghamton University, Binghamton, NY, USA

Key points

- There are two times during ontogeny when the developing brain is particularly likely to be exposed to alcohol—via maternal exposure during the fetal period, and via initiation of alcohol use during the rapid brain transformations of adolescence.
- Alcohol exposure during the fetal period is clearly teratogenic, that is, able to disturb growth and development, whereas less is known of the potential consequences of alcohol exposure during the rapid brain changes that characterize the adolescent period.
- There is substantial evidence that adolescents differ markedly from adults in their sensitivity to many of the acute effects of alcohol, being remarkably resistant to many of the intoxicating and aversive effects of alcohol that normally serve as cues to terminate intake, but more sensitive to the social facilitating and perhaps rewarding effects of alcohol. These adolescent-typical ethanol sensitivities may permit relatively high intakes during adolescence that may be exacerbated further via genetic or environmental factors, perhaps leading to long-term consequences.
- Cross-sectional neuropsychological and imaging studies in humans have revealed a number of cognitive and neural alterations in adolescents exhibiting problematic patterns of alcohol use, although it is difficult to determine conclusively from these studies whether such alterations are a result of early use and/or predate this use and represent risk factors for problematic alcohol involvement. There is emerging evidence in these studies and ongoing prospective, longitudinal studies to support both of these possibilities.
- In initial basic science studies with laboratory animals that permit direct empirical assessment of causality, a variety of lasting adverse neural and behavioral effects of adolescent alcohol exposure have been observed, although more work is needed to characterize these effects, determine the extent to which they are apparent at typical human exposure levels, and assess whether adolescence joins the fetal period as a critical period of developmental vulnerability to alcohol.

Alcohol exposure: vulnerable periods of brain development

Brain development is a life-long process. It begins with a rapid escalation in formation of neurons and their interconnections during fetal life, continues at a more moderate

---

Young People and Alcohol: Impact, Policy, Prevention, Treatment, First Edition.
Edited by John B. Saunders and Joseph M. Rey.
© 2011 Blackwell Publishing Ltd. Published 2011 by Blackwell Publishing Ltd.

maturational pace through infancy and childhood, and undergoes a series of sometimes dramatic transformations during adolescence to reach the relative (but still dynamic) stability of the mature brain. There are two intervals along this developmental trajectory during which the immature brain is particularly likely to be exposed to alcohol: (1) passive exposure during the fetal period when pregnant women use alcohol and (2) during adolescence when youth begin to experiment with alcohol.[1] These exposures may be interrelated, with children exposed prenatally to alcohol being particularly likely to use alcohol as young adolescents, and both exposures increasing the probability of developing persistent alcohol use disorders (AUD), thereby escalating the likelihood that the next generation will be exposed fetally to alcohol, and perpetuating the cycle.[1] Thus, alcohol abuse has its origins during development.

Developmental exposure to alcohol can do more, though, than increase the probability of later AUD. It has long been recognized that fetal exposure to alcohol can induce long-term neurotoxicity, with notable behavioral and cognitive ramifications that are often more pronounced than those seen with other drugs of abuse. Of more recent concern are possible consequences of alcohol exposure during adolescence, with its marked developmental transformations in the brain. In the sections to follow, well-established evidence for lasting effects of alcohol exposure during the fetal period of rapid brain growth will be briefly discussed before focusing on adolescence, some of the major neurobehavioral characteristics of this dynamic developmental period, and immediate and long-term effects of exposure to alcohol at this time.

Fetal alcohol exposure

Alcohol is a well-known fetal teratogen, with about 1% of all births estimated to exhibit the diversity of physical, hormonal, behavioral, and cognitive deficits associated with maternal abuse of alcohol during pregnancy, deficits that are collectively termed fetal alcohol spectrum disorder (FASD). A subset of these offspring that are most severely affected exhibit a stereotyped set of problems characterized by specific facial dysmorphologies, cognitive impairments, and growth retardation that define fetal alcohol syndrome (FAS). Over the past 30 years, cognitive, behavioral, and neural consequences of fetal alcohol exposure have been well characterized through research in clinical populations and in laboratory animals, with studies in the latter used to explore important issues of critical periods, dosing, underlying mechanisms, and potential therapeutic approaches. These well-established findings have been discussed extensively elsewhere (e.g., see references 2–4) and will be highlighted here only briefly to set the stage for discussion of recently emerging research focusing on the possible developmental toxicity of alcohol during adolescence.

Individuals with FASD characteristically show deficits in motor function, information processing, and attention, along with disruptions in working memory, behavioral inhibition, and other executive functions. Many of the same functional deficits have long been seen in studies using animal models of fetal alcohol exposure as well.[2] Basic science studies have shown that fetal alcohol exposure induces marked brain abnormalities that are particularly pronounced in areas such as the neocortex (including frontal and parietal regions critical for executive functioning, information processing, and attention), cerebellum and caudate (regions traditionally associated with motor functions, although more recently implicated in cognition as well), and hippocampus (thought to play a particularly important role in working memory).[3] Recent human imaging studies largely have found alterations in these same brain regions, including growth deficiencies in frontal and parietal regions and volume reductions in cerebellum and caudate, although findings in the hippocampus are more mixed.[4] Prominent alterations are also seen in offspring with FASD in the corpus callosum, a large mass of nerve fibers (axons) that crosses the midline of the brain to transfer information from one side of the cortex to the other. A number of studies have reported regional reductions in size or shape of portions of the corpus callosum, with these signs of altered connections across the left and right sides of the cortex correlated with a variety of cognitive and behavioral deficits.[4]

Basic science studies have confirmed that these characteristic neural alterations associated with FASD and FAS are causally related to alcohol exposure per se, and have also revealed factors influencing susceptibility to these effects of alcohol. The magnitude of damage is critically dependent on dose, with binge levels of consumption or repeated alcohol abuse producing blood alcohol levels among pregnant women similar to those inducing marked neurobehavioral toxicity in animal models of FASD.[2] Timing of fetal exposure is also crucial. For example, the cardinal feature of FAS, facial dysmorphologies, is seen in both human and animal studies and is associated with high levels of alcohol exposure during an early stage of embryogenesis—*gastrulation*, a stage that corresponds to the third week of gestation in humans (before some women may realize that they are pregnant). In contrast, formation and migration of cells destined for the neocortex and various other brain regions are perturbed by alcohol exposure during a later fetal stage (corresponding to 7–20 weeks of human gestation), whereas even later alcohol exposure (during the "brain growth spurt" of roughly the third human trimester) disrupts development in regions such as the hippocampus and cerebellum.[3] Thus, the amount and timing of exposure likely impacts the specific pattern of neural, cognitive, and behavioral alterations seen following fetal alcohol exposure. Other factors are probably influential as well, including maternal age and nutrition, and genetic background of both the mother and the fetus.

Basic science studies in laboratory animals also have proved useful for revealing candidate mechanisms underlying these dysfunctions. Fetal alcohol exposure disrupts substances critical for regulating gene expression, mediating interactions between cells, and producing and controlling growth factors that coordinate formation, migration, and differentiation of nerve cells (neurons) and their critical support cells (glia).[3] With this information in hand, current basic research is beginning to focus on development of strategies for strengthening fetal resiliency of potentially vulnerable individuals, and toward development of environmental or drug-based therapeutic approaches to improve outcome following fetal alcohol exposures, with the ultimate goal of decreasing the incidence of FASD and improving functioning in young individuals with this disorder.

Alcohol use during adolescence

The second time during development when alcohol exposure is likely to occur is via voluntary use during adolescence, with at least some experimental use of alcohol one of the number of other age-typical behavioral proclivities associated with this developmental period. By about 14 years of age, a majority of adolescents in the US report that they have had tried alcohol.[5] And when adolescents drink, they drink on average more than twice as much per drinking episode than do adults.[6] Indeed, the drinking of a significant number of these youth reaches high levels, with 10% of 8th graders, 22% of 10th graders, and 26% of high school seniors reporting consumption of five or more drinks in a row within the past 2 weeks.[5] Although high, these binge-use percentages are two- to threefold lower than those reported among adolescents in some European countries[7] (see Chapter 1).

During this time when youth begin to experiment with alcohol (sometimes excessively), the adolescent brain undergoes considerable transformation, including alterations in many alcohol-sensitive neural systems. One consequence of these neural transformations may be age-related differences between adolescents and adults in their sensitivity to alcohol. Indeed, adolescents have been found in basic science studies to differ notably from adults in their sensitivity to a variety of alcohol effects—in ways that may permit or even promote relatively high levels of alcohol consumption during adolescence. Yet, at the same time, this period of rapid brain transformation may represent a vulnerable period for lasting consequences of alcohol exposure. It is to these issues that we now turn.

The adolescent brain and alcohol

Efforts to systematically examine acute alcohol sensitivity in underage youth are limited by ethical constraints, as are the use of empirical studies to determine the lasting effects of such exposure. However, adolescence appears to be a highly evolutionarily conserved developmental stage with similar underlying biology across species, raising the possibility that simple animal models of adolescence may be of some use for exploring acute and lasting consequences of adolescent alcohol exposure. In the sections to follow, adolescence will be briefly considered from an evolutionary perspective as rationale for the judicious use of animal models of adolescence in studies of adolescent neurobehavioral development.

Evolutionary roots of adolescence and the use of animal models

Adolescence is characterized by a number of biological transformations, including puberty, a growth spurt, and a variety of other hormonal and physiological changes, along with prominent, regionally specific developmental transformations in the brain. Many of these hormonal alterations and transformations in the brain are also evident during the transition from immaturity to maturity in other mammalian species as well.[8,9] Human adolescents as well as adolescents from a variety of other mammalian species exhibit certain similar age-typical ways of responding to their environment, including an increased focus on peer-directed social interactions, increases in risk-taking and novelty seeking, and increases in consummatory behaviors (including greater per occasion use of alcohol than seen in adulthood).[8–10] These behavioral similarities presumably are commonly expressed across species because of their ultimate adaptive significance. For instance, an increasing emphasis on social interactions with peers is thought to guide choice behavior and develop social skills necessary for independence, whereas elevations in risk-taking/novelty-seeking are posited to serve as a means for increasing the probability of reproductive success in males, gaining additional resources, and avoiding the adverse consequences of genetic inbreeding by encouraging emigration away from the home territory around sexual maturation.[8,9]

These fundamental similarities in biology and behavior of adolescents across species suggest that the biological roots of adolescence are deeply embedded in our evolutionary past. Such similarities also provide reasonable face and construct validity to support the use of basic animal models to explore certain aspects of adolescent neurobehavioral function.[8] Of course, the rich complexity of human brain and behavioral function seen during adolescence (or at any other age, for that matter) is not evident in other species, and hence the appropriateness of animal models must be carefully considered from the perspective of what is to be modeled. Nevertheless, animal models have been used to explore manipulations and levels of analysis that provide ethical or technical challenges for study among human adolescents.

Transformations in the adolescent brain

Unlike the proliferation of neurons and their interconnections (synapses) that characterize the formation of the brain during the fetal period, later phases of neural development emphasize a refinement of that connectivity. Such refinement is commonly seen across species during adolescence and involves adjustments in gene expression and in molecular, cellular, and functional activity to ultimately reach the levels characteristic of the mature brain.[9] During adolescence, there is a substantial culling of the number of synaptic connections, with almost half of the synapses eliminated in some cortical regions at this time.[11] This pruning is highly selective within and across brain areas, and likely contributes to the fine-tuning of connectivity necessary for the emergence of adult-typical networks of functionally interconnected brain areas.[12] Emergence of networks that interconnect distant portions of the brain is seemingly aided by speeding information flow across these distant regions via myelination of the neural processes (axons) that interconnect these regions. Myelination is a process by which axons are wrapped with a white, fatty sheathing material (myelin) that serves to insulate them, speeding the rate at which they are able to transmit nerve impulses along their length.

The prevalence and relative timing of these and other neural changes during adolescence are regionally specific. For instance, in animal experiments and human imaging studies, regionally specific developmental timing can be roughly indexed via assessment of relative size (volume) of different brain areas across age, as well as via regional assessment of age-related changes in the ratio of gray matter (areas enriched in cell bodies, synaptic connections, and nonneuronal support cells) to white matter (areas enriched in myelinated axons). For instance, gray matter volumes, and gray/white matter ratios in the neocortex typically rise to a gentle plateau and decline thereafter, with this decline generally occurring earlier (prior to adolescence) in sensory and motor areas than the decline seen during adolescence in the prefrontal cortex and other cortical association areas thought to be critical for more advanced cognitive functions.[13] Indeed, protracted development in frontal regions such as the prefrontal cortex has been suggested to reflect immaturities in "top–down" cognitive control and other executive functions whose capacities continue to develop through adolescence, perhaps contributing to the greater propensity of adolescents to engage in risky behaviors, including illegal ones such as underage drinking, relative to adults.[14] Adolescent-associated decreases as well as increases in gray matter volumes are seen in some subcortical regions, including brain regions such as the nucleus accumbens, amygdala, and hippocampus,[15] that are critical for responding to, learning about, and motivating behavior toward emotional and/or rewarding stimuli, including alcohol and other drugs of abuse.

Alcohol alters chemical communication at the synaptic level through action on a number of the most prominent chemical communication systems (neurotransmitters) in the brain, many of which undergo marked developmental change during adolescence. The prototypic neurotransmitter in the reward system, the dopamine system, undergoes complex remodeling during adolescence, including apparent developmental shifts in the balance of activity of dopamine projections to the nucleus accumbens versus the prefrontal cortex.[8] The major inhibitory neurotransmitter system in the brain, the gamma-amino-butyric acid (GABA) system, is still developmentally immature during adolescence, whereas portions of the major excitatory neurotransmitter system, the glutamate neurotransmitter system—and its N-methyl-D-aspartate (NMDA) receptor system—exhibit greater functional activity in adolescence than at maturity.[16,17] These developmental alterations could easily exert a major impact on responsiveness to alcohol, given that many of alcohol's intoxicating effects are associated with disruption of NMDA receptor action as well as stimulation of the GABA system.[18] Given the differences between adolescents and adults in these alcohol-sensitive brain regions, it might be expected that alcohol would induce notably different effects in adolescents than in adults. Indeed, there is substantial evidence from basic science studies showing this to be the case.

Adolescent-typical shifts in alcohol sensitivity

Many stimuli, including alcohol, have multiple consequences, some of which are typically viewed positively and others negatively. In the case of alcohol, this mixed profile includes positive rewarding, relaxing, anxiety-reducing, social stimulatory, and pleasurably tasting effects that contrast with unsteadiness, slurred speech, and other signs of motor impairment, sedation, nausea, and general aversive effects of alcohol intoxication, along with later "hangover" effects. Acute alcohol exposure also influences cognitive functions, including well-studied disruptions in memory. Intriguingly, studies conducted primarily in laboratory animals have shown adolescents to often differ from adults in their sensitivity to many of these effects, although the direction varies markedly with the alcohol effect examined, as discussed in the sections to follow.

Alcohol effects on memory, cognition, and executive functions

Performance on executive function tasks is disrupted at doses producing blood alcohol levels in the "binge" drinking range (e.g., $\geq$90–100 mg%), including disruption in planning and spatial working memory.[19] Alcohol primarily disrupts the ability to form new explicit memories when in an intoxicated state, while leaving intact the ability to retrieve information learned prior to intoxication. Studies using laboratory animals provide evidence that adolescents may be more sensitive to alcohol-related disruptions in learning and retention, and in brain plasticity than their adult counterparts. For instance, adolescent and preadolescent animals are more vulnerable than adults to alcohol-induced disruptions in a form of brain synaptic plasticity termed "long-term potentiation" in the hippocampus, a brain region important for memory formation. Likewise, on a spatial memory task where rats were trained to learn the position of a hidden platform in a large vat of water, impaired performance was seen in adolescents at only about half the alcohol exposure levels that were necessary to see impairment on this task in adults.[20] Although ethical issues have precluded conducting similar alcohol challenge studies in underage youth, analogous age-related vulnerabilities were seen in a study examining individuals across a late adolescent to young adult range (i.e., early vs. late twenties). On both verbal and nonverbal memory tasks, individuals in their early twenties (21–24-years of age) showed notably more memory disruption in response to the alcohol challenge than those in their late twenties (from 25–29-years).[21] Thus, even though the individuals in this study were at the outer fringes of adolescence, an enhanced vulnerability to alcohol-induced memory disruption was still evident among these older adolescents relative to their more mature counterparts, findings reminiscent of those in basic science studies with laboratory animals.

Social facilitation and other rewarding alcohol effects

The rewarding and social facilitatory effects of alcohol are the only other consequences of alcohol consumption to which adolescents have been shown to be more sensitive than adults. Place conditioning is a classical conditioning paradigm in which animals, typically rats or mice, learn to associate the effects of a drug or other discrete treatment with a particular environment. Second-order conditioning or higher order conditioning is a classical conditioning term that refers to a form of learning in which a stimulus that was previously neutral (e.g., a bell) is associated with food (first-order conditioning), and then that association is transferred to another stimulus (e.g., light) (second-order conditioning). Using measures such as place conditioning, second-order conditioning, and heart-rate as an index of positive effect, several studies have found adolescent animals to be unusually sensitive to the rewarding effects of alcohol, although work in this area is still at its initial stages and findings are mixed.[22,23] A better characterized effect is the greater sensitivity of adolescents to the social facilitatory effects of alcohol, with adolescent rats showing an increase in social interactions following exposure to low doses of alcohol in familiar (low anxiety producing) situations; increases in social behavior are not seen under these circumstances in adults.[22] Reminiscent of these basic science studies, human adolescents report that one of their main motives for drinking is the ability of alcohol to facilitate social interactions, with drinking rates highest among adolescents with the strongest social motives for drinking.[24]

Intoxicating and aversive effects

While animal studies have shown adolescents to be more sensitive to alcohol-induced disruptions in memory and brain plasticity, as well as to the social facilitatory and possibly other positive rewarding effects of alcohol, adolescents are often less sensitive to other alcohol effects, especially those produced by moderate or higher levels of intoxication that may normally serve as cues to limit intake. These include motor impairment (e.g., ataxia), social impairment (e.g., disinhibition), sedation, and general aversive effects such as nausea, as well as hangover-related elevations in anxiety.[22] For instance, when rats are given a sufficiently high dose of alcohol that they lose consciousness, adolescent rats awake in about one-half the time as adult rats.[25] Moreover, when they regain consciousness, adolescent rats have significantly higher levels of alcohol in their brains than adults, supporting the conclusion that this age-related difference in the sedative properties of alcohol is related to an attenuated sensitivity of the adolescent brain to this effect of alcohol. Similar age differences were seen when using conditioned taste aversion to assess the aversive properties of alcohol. During *taste aversion conditioning*, rats are given the opportunity to ingest a novel, highly palatable fluid followed by an injection of one of the variety of doses of alcohol or a control solution; to the extent that they find the consequences of the alcohol exposure aversive, they will later reduce their consumption of the novel fluid. Using this procedure, adolescent rats require about twice as much alcohol than adults to exhibit a conditioned taste aversion,[26] suggesting that adolescents are notably less sensitive to the aversive properties of alcohol than adults.

Of course, as noted above, studies to determine whether human adolescents might exhibit a similar insensitivity to these aversive and intoxicating effects of alcohol are limited due to ethical constraints. There is, however, one rare study by Behar and colleagues[27] that examined 8–15-year-old boys following administration of a dose of alcohol known to be intoxicating to adults. After giving them a battery of objective and subjective tests of intoxication, the researchers noted that they "were impressed by how little gross behavioral change occurred in the children . . . after a dose of alcohol which had been intoxicating in an adult population" (see reference 27, p. 407). Thus, although the data are very limited, these findings hint that the relative insensitivity of adolescents to the intoxicating and aversive effects of alcohol that has been systematically documented in laboratory animals may be seen in humans as well.

Contributors to adolescent-typical alcohol sensitivities: tolerance development

Multiple factors may contribute to these alcohol sensitivities observed in adolescents. As discussed earlier, developmental changes in activity in several critical neurotransmitter systems upon which alcohol exerts its effects, including NMDA excitatory receptor systems and GABA inhibitory systems as well as dopamine input to reward-relevant regions, are likely to play major roles in these differential sensitivities to alcohol during adolescence.[20,22,23] Another important contributor to the greater resistance that adolescents show to many of the intoxicating (e.g., motor impairing, sedating, dysphoric) effects of alcohol relative to adults may be the greater propensity of the young brain to rapidly adapt to the presence of alcohol—a phenomenon termed "acute tolerance,"

Acute tolerance is defined as the attenuated sensitivity to alcohol that develops within a single episode of alcohol exposure. Acute tolerance can be indexed in a number of ways that generally reflect a more rapid decline in alcohol impairment than the decline seen in blood or brain alcohol levels, that is, recovery occurs more rapidly than expected relative to the amount of alcohol still in the body. In basic science studies, adolescents have been shown to exhibit notably greater acute tolerance than adults to the sedative properties of alcohol[25] and to the social inhibition that emerges at moderate or higher doses of alcohol.[28] For instance, whereas adolescents and adults showed equivalent ethanol-induced social inhibition 5 minutes following challenge with a 1 g/kg dose of alcohol, when tested at 30 minutes following an alcohol challenge, adults were still quite impaired, whereas little sign of social impairment was seen among the adolescents.[28] This behavioral recovery was seen in adolescents despite rising blood alcohol levels across this time interval—a finding consistent with the rapid emergence of acute tolerance during adolescence. In this study, animals were tested at a variety of points during adolescence, with the most pronounced acute tolerance effect evident early in adolescence and declining gradually throughout adolescence and into adulthood.

The insensitivity that adolescents show to many of alcohol's intoxicating effects could be enhanced further following a history of prior alcohol use. Indeed emergence of chronic tolerance following repeated exposure to alcohol has been reported in surveys of adolescents,[29] although findings from basic science are mixed as to the circumstances under which adolescents express chronic tolerance, and whether this longer term adaptation is more or less pronounced than the chronic tolerance to alcohol that emerges in adults.[22] The story is likely to be nuanced by the specific effect of alcohol under investigation, and the frequency, amount, and timing of chronic exposure. It is also likely that alcohol exposure during the brain transformations of adolescence may not only trigger long-term compensations normally expressed as chronic functional tolerance but also disrupt ongoing processes of brain development, with possible long-term consequences as discussed later.

Potential impact of adolescent: typical shifts in alcohol sensitivity for the emergence of alcohol use disorders

Differential sensitivity to the various effects of alcohol could influence in a number of ways the propensity of adolescents to use alcohol and exhibit high levels of consumption. One age difference that may influence the propensity for adolescents to consume more alcohol per occasion than adults is their tendency to show alcohol-induced social facilitation, given evidence from basic science studies that alcohol notably facilitates social interactions among adolescents.[23] That is, given that adolescents drink largely in social groups (Chapter 1), a greater sensitivity of adolescents to alcohol-induced social facilitation may encourage them to continue drinking. Any age-related enhancement of adolescents' sensitivity to the positive rewarding effects of alcohol might also help to promote high levels of drinking at this time.

Adolescent-associated insensitivities to alcohol's aversive intoxicating effects may also influence their propensity to use alcohol. First, the likelihood of continued use after first experimentation could be affected. That is, individuals experimenting for the first time with a drug such as alcohol that experience notable negative consequences may be disinclined to use the substance again. To the extent that adolescents are insensitive to the dysphoric/

aversive effects of intoxication, they may be more likely to try it again. More broadly, a decreased sensitivity to alcohol's intoxicating effects has long been characterized as a major risk factor for problematic alcohol use, with "a lower sensitivity to moderate doses of alcohol associated with a significant increase in the risk of future alcoholism, perhaps through increasing the chances that a person will drink more heavily."[30] Likewise, studies of mice from different genetic backgrounds have revealed strong associations between enhanced alcohol intake and insensitivity to the aversive and sedating effects of alcohol.[31]

Thus, as individuals with genetically related insensitivities to alcohol enter adolescence and experiment with alcohol, their capacity for consuming alcohol would likely be relatively high, and might be enhanced even further with continued use and the emergence of chronic tolerance. Work in laboratory animals suggests that a history of prior exposure to stressors may further lower the sensitivity to alcohol's intoxicating properties.[32] Thus, adolescent-typical alcohol insensitivities may interact with a number of risk factors—family history of alcohol abuse; stressors; and tolerance associated with prior use—to promote higher levels of alcohol consumption during drinking episodes among vulnerable adolescents. Consequences of these high consumption levels during the rapid brain remodeling of adolescence have the potential to be pronounced and persistent, a topic to which we now turn.

Long-term consequences of adolescent alcohol exposure

As discussed earlier, alcohol exposure during gestation can result in the physiological and neurocognitive deficits characterized as FAS and FASD. Persistent exposure to high levels of alcohol among alcohol-dependent adults also results in cognitive deficits and neurotoxic effects. Given these findings, it would be surprising indeed if repeated exposure to alcohol during adolescence did not likewise induce neurocognitive effects under some circumstances. But, under what circumstances? Are the rapid brain changes of adolescence a time of particular vulnerability to alcohol neurotoxicity? And if so, what magnitude of use is sufficient to cause changes? These critical questions are being tackled in both human and basic science studies, with each approach having its particular strengths and challenges, as we shall see.

Effects on later alcohol consumption and propensity for alcohol use disorders and dependence

One particularly well-characterized finding in the human research literature is that the earlier one begins to drink alcohol, the more likely that individual is to develop a pattern of risky drinking and become dependent on alcohol[33] (see also Chapters 2 and 3). Although this early exposure effect is a strong predictor of later alcohol dependence, there are two potential, nonmutually exclusive, explanations for this association—that is, either early use may play a causal role in producing later problems with alcohol or/and some third variable may convey vulnerability for both early use and later alcohol problems. Data are beginning to emerge supporting both possibilities. For instance, a recent prospective, longitudinal study found not only that childhood conduct disorder increased the probability of developing early alcohol/substance use but also that early alcohol/substance use per se (i.e., independent of childhood characteristics) elevated the probability of later alcohol/substance dependence, along with a variety of other adverse outcomes.[34]

Exploring whether adolescent alcohol exposure is causal for influencing later levels of alcohol consumption has also been explored to some extent using animal models, although results are mixed. Generally speaking, the findings suggest that adult intake may not be elevated following typical levels of voluntary alcohol consumption during adolescence (although these intakes are often two- to threefold greater during adolescence than seen in adulthood). Instead, later consumption is more likely to be increased when adolescent exposure is elevated beyond these levels—via enhanced consumption due to genetic propensity (i.e., using genetic lines of animals that drink high levels of alcohol) or by using other means to elevate consumption or expose animals intermittently to relatively high doses of alcohol.[35] Impact of the timing of the onset of alcohol exposure within the adolescent period has received little attention to date in animal studies.

Neurocognitive alterations: human studies

Determining the neural consequences of alcohol use during adolescence is difficult using cross-sectional imaging studies due to challenges in disentangling whether observed neural alterations are a consequence of alcohol exposure or whether they predated alcohol use, and perhaps served as a risk factor for that use. Some success in partially disentangling these possibilities has been obtained through the assessment of correlations between neural findings and variables such as age of onset of use, duration of alcohol use disorders, or number of withdrawal episodes. The reasoning is that when age and other potential confounding variables are controlled, neural alterations significantly correlated with alcohol intake during adolescence would likely be a result of that consumption, whereas neural alterations not correlated with such consumption would more likely reflect predisposing neural characteristics.[36] Using this approach, De Bellis and colleagues observed that hippocampal volumes were correlated positively with age of onset of use and negatively with duration of AUDs, whereas prefrontal cortex volume was not significantly associated with these variables, leading to the hypothesis that the reductions in hippocampal volume seen in adolescent AUDs may reflect toxic effects of that alcohol exposure, whereas declines in prefrontal cortex white matter seen in these individuals may manifest "an inherent vulnerability that enhances the risk for poorer executive cognitive functioning and an adolescent-onset AUD" (see reference 36, p. 1597). Volume reductions have been reported in the amygdala, a region processing emotional and affective stimuli, among adolescents (and adults) with alcohol/substance use disorders, with a lack of correlation of these volumes with measures of use/abuse suggesting that this decline in amygdala volume may represent a predisposing factor rather than a consequence of use/abuse.[37] Thus, part of the risk for early onset and extensive use of alcohol during adolescence may be associated with preexisting delays or disruptions in development of key brain regions involved in cognitive control, emotional regulation, and behavioral inhibition.

As illustrated by the De Bellis study,[36] there has been substantial interest in white matter development and adolescent alcohol exposure, given the amount of myelination that normally occurs during the adolescent period. In addition to studying white matter volume, emphasis in a number of recent studies has turned to assessing white matter function in adolescent binge drinkers using diffuse tensor imaging. This imaging technique utilizes the property of water to diffuse more rapidly along myelinated axonal tracts than across them to index quality/integrity of white matter by measuring the speed and directionality of water diffusion ("fractional anisotropy"). In initial diffuse tensor imaging studies, binge-drinking adolescents were observed to have reduced fractional anisotropy in a variety of pathways interconnecting frontal regions with other regions in networks thought to be involved in modulating complex cognitive, motor, and sensory processes.[38] These changes were significantly greater with longer duration of heavy use, greater numbers of previous alcohol withdrawal symptoms, and elevated recent consumption levels – correlational evidence suggestive of possible causality, although not definitely so. The possibility remains that delays in myelination or decreases in the quality of myelination production in these pathways may begin prior to initiation of use and may constitute a risk factor for early use and emergence of adolescent AUDs.[39]

Youth and young adults with a history of adolescent alcohol use have shown a variety of cognitive alterations, including subtle deficits in memory retrieval, attention and information processing, and language functioning.[38] In a manner reminiscent of earlier discussions, at least some of these differences may be evident prior to initiation of alcohol use, potentially reflecting predisposing neurobiological delays or developmental disruptions in brain regions critical for these cognitive functions. In a recent prospective study where neuropsychological functioning, alcohol initiation, and use patterns were examined across a 3-year follow-up period during the early teen years, drinking during the last year was found to predict poorer visuospatial task performance in girls, whereas number of hangovers over the year tended to be correlated with poorer sustained attention in boys. The authors noted that these findings, although preliminary, are "concerning as the severity of alcohol use is relatively low (mean drinks/month = 7.4) and most drinking is subclinical" (see reference 38, p. 720).

Signs of neurocognitive disruption among alcohol-using adolescents are also evident when examining neural activity during performance of cognitive tasks using functional magnetic resonance imaging (fMRI). fMRI measures changes in blood flow in particular brain regions when performing a target cognitive task relative to baseline conditions, with increases in blood flow to a region used as an index of neural activity in that region during the performance of the task. Using cognitive tasks modified to allow performance within the movement and space constraints of an MRI scanner, a number of studies have found alterations in which brain regions are activated ("recruited") during performance of cognitive tasks among adolescents with different histories of alcohol use/abuse. For instance, during verbal encoding as well as while performing a response inhibition ("go/no-go") task, adolescents with a history of binge drinking (i.e., consumption of four to five or more drinks on a given occasion) exhibited less activation than controls in some regions (e.g., certain specific frontal and parietal regions on the verbal encoding task;

cerebellum with the response inhibition task), while showing greater recruitment in other regions (e.g., occipital cortex during verbal encoding and frontal regions during response inhibition).[40] These differential activation patterns were suggested to reflect some degree of neural reorganization among adolescent binge drinkers, with increased task-related activation in some regions and attenuated activation in others. Likewise, when comparing adolescents drinking heavily for 1–2 years with light drinkers on a working memory task on which both groups performed similarly, areas of both increased (parietal cortex) and decreased (occipital cortex; cerebellum) activation were seen in the heavy drinkers. Yet, when young adults with 4–5 years of heavy drinking were assessed on the same working memory task, they displayed both decreased performance and reduced recruitment in parietal and frontal regions, findings interpreted to suggest that continued heavy alcohol exposure during development may strain and override the capacity of the brain to compensate for alcohol-related neural deficits.[40] Of course, as discussed above, data from such cross-sectional studies cannot be definitely interpreted to suggest causal relationships, leading a recent review to conclude that "while adolescent alcohol consumption has been asserted to adversely alter brain development, research in human adolescents has not yet provided us with sufficient evidence to support or refute this position" (see reference 39, p. 1).

Neurobehavioral alterations: studies using animal models

The issue of causality can be empirically determined in experimental studies using animal models of adolescence. Data available to date in this emerging field provide evidence that adolescent exposure to high levels of alcohol can exert long-term effects in a variety of brain regions, altering activity in dopamine reward-relevant systems,[41] inducing neural toxicity, and disrupting the formation of new neurons (neurogenesis) in hippocampal and neocortical regions, with evidence for greater damage in some frontal cortical regions than seen following comparable levels of alcohol exposure in adulthood.[42,43] A variety of behavioral alterations are also evident, including deficits in working memory that are reminiscent of those seen in human adolescents with a history of heavy alcohol use.[22,44] There is also emerging evidence in these experiments in laboratory animals that repeated exposure to alcohol during adolescence may induce tolerance to the aversive and impairing effects of alcohol that lasts well into adulthood,[45,46] maintaining the adolescent insensitivity to these ethanol effects that normally serve as feedback cues to limit intake, thereby perhaps contributing to the enhanced alcohol consumption often seen in adulthood following a history of heavy adolescent alcohol exposure. Work in this area is at its beginning stages, however, and large gaps still exist in determining the extent of lasting neural and behavioral consequences of adolescent alcohol exposure. Moreover, while the basic science data to date have shown that adolescent alcohol exposure *can* produce toxicity, the relevance of these findings for human adolescents remains to be established. Critical issues that need to be resolved include establishing whether adolescence is a sensitive period for alcohol neurobehavioral toxicity, and the degree to which alcohol burdens producing these effects are comparable to those seen among human youth drinking heavily.

Summary and conclusions

There are two times during ontogeny when the developing brain is particularly likely to be exposed to alcohol—via maternal exposure during the fetal period, and via initiation of alcohol use during the rapid brain transformations of adolescence. Alcohol exposure during the fetal period is clearly teratogenic—that is, able to disturb growth and development—inducing dose-dependent and timing-critical neurotoxicity with adverse cognitive and behavioral ramifications that have been well characterized clinically and in more mechanistically focused basic science studies using animal models.

Less is known of the potential consequences of alcohol exposure during the rapid brain changes that characterize the adolescent period. There is substantial evidence that adolescents differ markedly from adults in their sensitivity to many of the acute effects of alcohol, being remarkably resistant to many of the intoxicating and aversive effects that normally serve as cues to terminate intake, but more sensitive to the social facilitating and perhaps rewarding effects. These adolescent-typical ethanol sensitivities may not only permit relatively high intake during adolescence that may be exacerbated further via genetic or environmental factors, but may also reflect marked age differences in the functional impact of acute alcohol exposure on the brain—differential alcohol effects that might well lead to markedly different neural consequences of repeated alcohol perturbation on the adolescent brain than on the mature brain.

Cross-sectional neuropsychological and imaging studies in humans have revealed a number of cognitive and neural alterations in adolescents exhibiting potentially problematic patterns of alcohol use, including early initiation of drinking, binge drinking, or other patterns of heavy exposure to alcohol during adolescence. These neural alterations are highly regionally specific and evident in terms of changes in regional volumes and in white matter integrity. Both increases and decreases in regional brain activation patterns during performance of cognitive tasks are also seen, suggesting that different brain regions are recruited during performance of these tasks in these adolescents than in adolescents without a history or early alcohol use or alcohol abuse. From such cross-sectional studies it is difficult, however, to determine whether neural and functional alterations associated with early use and/or extensive alcohol consumption predate this use and represent risk factors for problematic alcohol intake, and/or whether these alterations are a consequence of that use. Using correlational approaches based on the strategy that functional or neural alterations correlated with use are more likely to reflect consequences of that use than preexisting vulnerabilities, some evidence is provided from cross-sectional studies to support both possibilities. Similar conclusions have been reached in prospective, longitudinal studies, where issues of causality can be somewhat more directly examined by assessing youth beginning prior to the onset of drinking. In initial experiments with laboratory animals that permit direct empirical assessment of causality, a variety of lasting adverse neural and behavioral effects of adolescent alcohol exposure have been observed. More work remains to be done, however, to characterize these alterations, determine the extent to which they are apparent at blood alcohol levels consistent with alcohol-abusing adolescents, and whether they are more pronounced than those seen with comparable levels of exposure in adulthood. Together, these approaches, ranging from cross-sectional and prospective longitudinal studies in humans to basic research with animal models, will help determine whether adolescence represents a period of heightened vulnerability to the neurotoxic effects of alcohol—information that ultimately will be critical for guiding public health policy and prevention efforts.

Acknowledgements

This work was supported in part by NIH grants R01 AA18026, R01 AA17355, R01 AA16887, R37 AA12525, and R01 DA19071.

References

1. Miller MW, Spear LP. The alcoholism generator. *Alcohol Clin Exp Res* 2006; 30:1466–1469.
2. Driscoll CD, Streissguth AP, Riley EP. Prenatal alcohol exposure: Comparability of effects in humans and animal models. *Neurotoxicol Teratol* 1990; 12:231–237.
3. Guerri C, Bazinet A, Riley EP. Foetal alcohol spectrum disorders and alterations in brain and behaviour. *Alcohol Alcohol* 2009; 44:108–114.
4. Spadoni AD, McGee CL, Fryer SL, Riley EP. Neuroimaging and fetal alcohol spectrum disorders. *Neurosci Biobehav Rev* 2007; 31:289–245.
5. Johnston LD, O'Malley PM, Bachman JG, Schulenberg JE. *Monitoring the Future; National Results on Adolescent Drug Use. Overview of Key Findings, 2007*. NIH Publication No. 08–6418, 2008; pp. 1–70.
6. SAMHSA. *Results from the 2005 National Survey on Drug Use and Health: National Findings*. National Survey on Drug Use and Health Series H-30, DHHS Publication No. SMA 06–4194. Rockville, MD; 2006.
7. Ahlström SK, Österberg EL. International perspectives on adolescent and young adult drinking. *Alcohol Res Health* 2004; 28:258–268.
8. Spear LP. The adolescent brain and age-related behavioral manifestations. *Neurosci Biobehav Rev* 2000; 24:417–463.
9. Spear L. *The Behavioral Neuroscience of Adolescence*. New York: Norton; 2010.
10. Steinberg L. A social neuroscience perspective on adolescent risk-taking. *Dev Rev* 2008; 28:78–106.
11. Rakic P, Bourgeois JP, Goldman-Rakic PS. Synaptic development of the cerebral cortex: Implications for learning, memory, and mental illness. In: van Pelt J, Corner MA, Uylings HBM, eds. *The Self-Organizing Brain: From Growth Cones to Functional Networks*. Amsterdam: Elsevier Science; 1994, pp. 227–243.
12. Rubia K, Smith AB, Taylor E *et al.* Linear age-correlated functional development of right inferior fronto–striato–cerebellar networks during response inhibition and anterior cingulate during error-related processes. *Hum Brain Mapp* 2007; 28:1163–1177.
13. Gogtay N, Giedd JN, Lusk L *et al.* Dynamic mapping of human cortical development during childhood through early adulthood. *Proc Natl Acad Sci USA* 2004; 101:8174–8179.
14. Casey BJ, Getz S, Galvan A. The adolescent brain. *Dev Rev* 2008; 28:62–77.
15. Østby Y, Tamnes CK, Fjell AM *et al.* Heterogeneity in subcortical brain development: A structural magnetic resonance imaging study of brain maturation from 8 to 30 years. *J Neurosci* 2009; 29:11772–11782.
16. Vallano M. Developmental aspects of NMDA receptor function. *Crit Rev Neurobiol* 1998; 12:177–204.

17. Brooks-Kayal AR, Shumate MD, Jin H, Rikhter TY, Kelly ME, Coulter DA. y-Aminobutyric acid(A) receptor subunit expression predicts functional changes in hippocampal dentate granule cells during postnatal development. *J Neurochem* 2001; 77:1266–1278.

18. Eckardt MJ, File SE, Gessa GL, Grant KA, Guerri C, Hoffman PL, Kalant H, Koob GF, Li T-K, Tabakoff B. Effects of moderate alcohol consumption on the central nervous system. *Alcohol Clin Exp Res* 1998; 22:998–1040.

19. Weissenborn R, Duka T. Acute alcohol effects on cognitive function in social drinkers: Their relationship to drinking habits. *Psychopharmacology* 2003; 165:306–312.

20. White AM, Swartzwelder HS. Age-related effects of alcohol on memory and memory-related brain function in adolescents and adults. In: Galanter M, ed. *Recent Developments in Alcoholism, Volume 17: Alcohol Problems in Adolescents and Young Adults.* New York: Kluwer Academic/Plenum Publishers; 2005, pp. 161–176.

21. Acheson SK, Stein RM, Swartzwelder HS. Impairment of semantic and figural memory by acute ethanol: Age-dependent effects. *Alcohol Clin Exp Res* 1998; 22:1437–1442.

22. Spear LP, Varlinskaya EI. Adolescence: Alcohol sensitivity, tolerance, and intake. In: Galanter M, ed. *Recent Developments in Alcoholism, Volume 17: Alcohol Problems in Adolescents and Young Adults.* New York: Kluwer Academic/Plenum Publishers; 2005, pp. 143–159.

23. Doremus-Fitzwater TL, Varlinskaya EI, Spear LP. Motivational systems in adolescence: Possible implications for age differences in substance abuse and other risk-taking behaviors. *Brain Cogn* 2010; 72:114–123.

24. Mohr CD, Armeli S, Tennen H *et al.* Moving beyond the keg party: A daily process study of college student drinking motivations. *Psychol Addict Behav* 2005; 19:392–403.

25. Silveri MM, Spear LP. Decreased sensitivity to the hypnotic effects of ethanol early in ontogeny. *Alcohol Clin Exp Res* 1998; 22:670–676.

26. Vetter-O'Hagen C, Varlinskaya EI, Spear L. Sex differences in ethanol intake and sensitivity to aversive effects during adolescence and adulthood. *Alcohol Alcohol* 2009; 44:547–554.

27. Behar D, Berg CJ, Rapoport JL, Nelson W, Linnoila M, Cohen M, Bozevich C, Marshall T. Behavioral and physiological effects of ethanol in high-risk and control children: A pilot study. *Alcohol Clin Exp Res* 1983; 7:404–410.

28. Varlinskaya EI, Spear LP. Ontogeny of acute tolerance to ethanol-induced social inhibition in Sprague-Dawley rats. *Alcohol Clinl Exp Res* 2006; 30:1833–1844.

29. Grant BF, Harford TC, Muthén BO, Yi H, Hasin DS, Stinson FS. DSM-IV alcohol dependence and abuse: Further evidence of validity in the general population. *Drug Alcohol Depend* 2007; 86:154–166.

30. Schuckit MA. Low level of response to alcohol as a predictor of future alcoholism. *Am J Psychiatry* 1994; 151:184–189.

31. Green AS, Grahame NJ. Ethanol drinking in rodents: Is free-choice drinking related to the reinforcing effects of ethanol? *Alcohol* 2008; 42:1–11.

32. Varlinskaya EI, Doremus-Fitzwater TL, Spear LP. Repeated restraint stress alters sensitivity to the social consequences of ethanol in adolescent and adult rats. *Pharmacol Biochem Behav* 2010; 96:228–235.

33. Ehlers CL, Slutske WS, Gilder DA, Lau P, Wilhelmsen KC. Age at first intoxication and alcohol use disorders in Southwest California Indians. *Alcohol Clin Exp Res* 2006; 30:1856–1865.

34. Odgers CL, Caspi A, Nagin DS *et al.* Is it important to prevent early exposure to drugs and alcohol among adolescents? *Psychol Sci* 2008; 19:1037–1044.

35. Vetter CS, Doremus-Fitzwater TL, Spear LP. Time-course of elevated ethanol intake in adolescent relative to adult rats under continuous, voluntary-access conditions. *Alcohol Clin Exp Res* 2007; 31:1159–1168.

36. De Bellis MD, Narasimhan A, Thatcher DL, Keshavan MS, Soloff P, Clark DB. Prefrontal cortex, thalamus, and cerebellar volumes in adolescents and young adults with adolescent-onset alcohol use disorders and comorbid mental disorders. *Alcohol Clin Exp Res* 2005; 29(9):1590–1600.

37. Hill SY, De Bellis MD, Keshavan MS, Lowers L, Shen S, Hall J, Pitts T. Right amygdala volume in adolescent and young adult offspring from families at high risk for developing alcoholism. *Biol Psychiatry* 2001; 49:894–905.

38. Squeglia LM, Spadoni AD, Infante MA. Initiating moderate to heavy alcohol use predicts changes in neuropsychological functioning for adolescent girls and boys. *Psychol Addict Behav* 2009; 23:715–722.

39. Clark DB, Thatcher DL, Tapert SF. Alcohol, psychological dysregulation, and adolescent brain development. *Alcohol Clin Exp Res* 2008; 32:375–385.

40. Squeglia LM, Jacobus J, Tapert SF. The influence of substance use on adolescent brain development. *Clin EEG Neurosci* 2009; 40:31–38.

41. Pascual, M., Boix J, Felipo V, Guerri C. Repeated alcohol administration during adolescence causes changes in the mesolimbic dopaminergic and glutamatergic systems and promotes alcohol intake in the adult rat. *J Neurochem* 2008; 108:920–931.

42. Crews FT, Braun CJ, Hoplight B, Switzer III RC, Knapp DJ. Binge ethanol consumption causes differential brain damage in young adolescent rats compared with adult rats. *Alcohol Clin Exp Res* 2000; 24:1712–1723.

43. Crews FT, Mdzinarishvili A, Kim D, He J, Nixon K. Neurogenesis in adolescent brain is potently inhibited by ethanol. *Neuroscience* 2006; 137:437–445.

44. Schulteis G, Archer C, Tapert SF, Frank LR. Intermittent binge alcohol exposure during the periadolescent period induces spatial working memory deficits in young adult rats. *Alcohol* 2008; 42:459–467.

45. Diaz-Granados JL, Graham D. The effects of continuous and intermittent ethanol exposure in adolescence on the aversive properties of ethanol during adulthood. *Alcohol Clin Exp Res* 2007; 31:2020–2027.

46. Matthews DB, Tinsley KL, Diaz-Granados JL, Tokunaga S, Silvers JM. Chronic intermittent exposure to ethanol during adolescence produces tolerance to the hypnotic effects of ethanol in male rats: A dose-dependent analysis. *Alcohol* 2008; 42:617–621.

Chapter 6

Genetic influences on alcohol use and alcohol use disorders

Michael T. Lynskey and Arpana Agrawal

Department of Psychiatry, Washington University School of Medicine, St Louis, MO, USA

Key points

- Results from adoption, twin, and extended family studies have demonstrated moderate to strong genetic components to the liability to use alcohol and to develop alcohol use disorders.
- Twin and related designs provide important and innovative methodologies for addressing numerous unresolved issues including the extent to which the salience of genetic and environmental factors vary across the lifespan, the extent to which similar or different genetic factors are salient at each stage of the development of alcohol problems, and the extent to which alcohol use disorders, as well as both externalizing and internalizing psychiatric disorders, are influenced by similar or different genetic and environmental factors.
- Whether associations between early onset drinking and subsequent dependence potentially reflect causal mechanisms remains controversial, but it is clear that genetic factors make substantial contributions to these observed associations.
- A shared predisposition plays a role in trajectories of alcohol use and misuse. Thus, genetic factors identified in adolescents who use alcohol occasionally may be involved in the development of dependence.
- Alcohol use, drug use, and externalizing behaviors may be influenced by overlapping genetic and shared environmental factors.
- Heritable influences on alcohol use and misuse are more pronounced in those exposed to less restrictive environments.
- Loci on chromosomes 1, 2, 4, and 7, and genes such as GABRA2 and those comprising the ADH cluster may influence liability to alcohol misuse. The effects of these genes on alcohol use may also be modified via environmental exposure to low parental monitoring.

First use of alcohol typically occurs during adolescence and frequent, heavy, or symptomatic alcohol use is common among teenagers. While many youth who use alcohol do so only infrequently and without experiencing any apparent adverse consequences, adolescent alcohol use is an important area for research: The acute effects of intoxication increase the risk of motor vehicle and other unintentional injuries; a substantial proportion of

---

Young People and Alcohol: Impact, Policy, Prevention, Treatment, First Edition.
Edited by John B. Saunders and Joseph M. Rey.
© 2011 Blackwell Publishing Ltd. Published 2011 by Blackwell Publishing Ltd.

adolescents report meeting criteria for alcohol abuse and/ or dependence; and age of onset of alcohol use is prognostic of subsequent risks for the development of abuse/dependence and other measures of alcohol-related harm. Despite numerous challenges in assessing alcohol misuse—and particularly concerns about the diagnostic criteria for alcohol abuse and dependence in youth—there have been considerable advances in our understanding of the mechanisms by which heritable influences contribute to risks for alcohol misuse. This chapter describes genetically informative research designs and reviews key findings related to the heritability of alcohol misuse and the comorbidity between alcohol misuse and psychiatric disorders and describes emerging findings concerning the importance of gene by environmental interplay in the development of alcohol misuse.

Genetically informative research designs

Family studies

Studies of the aggregation of alcohol misuse in youth with a family history of alcohol-related problems suggested that alcohol misuse runs in families (Figure 6.1).[1] While

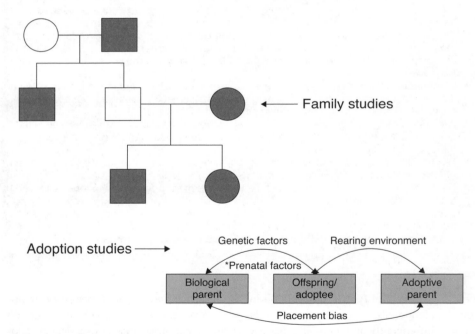

Figure 6.1   Family and adoption designs. The upper panel "family studies" shows a family/pedigree densely affected for alcoholism (shaded probands). While alcoholism *runs* in this family, it cannot be determined whether the correlations between individuals are due to genetic or familial environmental factors. The lower panel "adoption studies" shows correlations between the adoptee and his/her biological and adoptive parent for alcoholism. If the correlation with the biological parent is significant, then genetic influences contribute to the observed correlation. *However, correlations between the biological mother and offspring or adoptee may also be due to intrauterine/prenatal factors and age at adoption.

parent–offspring correlations from these studies were high, this design does not afford the ability to distinguish genetic influences from those attributable to family environment.

Adoption studies

Some of the earliest findings suggesting heritable influences on alcohol use came from adoption studies in which offspring outcomes were compared with analogous measures in both the biological and the adoptive parents (Figure 6.1). Strong associations between biological parent and offspring behavior are interpreted as suggesting heritable influences, while strong associations between adoptive parent and offspring behavior suggest environmental influences. While the seminal Iowa[2] and Swedish[3] adoption studies established strong heritable components on alcohol and drug use disorders, they were based on adult samples.

The adoption design has important limitations: adoption studies have typically relied on official records to characterize biological parent psychopathology (e.g., arrest, hospitalization) and are likely to identify only severe cases. Additionally, due to both adoption agency screening and self-selection by adoptive parents, the number of adopted individuals raised in high-risk environments is likely to be limited: Compared with the general population, adoptive parents are likely to be older, more affluent and less likely to show high rates of psychopathology. Furthermore, while links between biological parent and offspring behavior are presumed to exclude shared environment, exposure to maternal intrauterine environment (Figure 6.1) as well as age at adoption can result in sharing of environmental factors between biological mothers and their offspring.[4]

Twin studies

The majority of twin studies is based on samples of twins reared together and compares concordance rates between monozygotic/identical (MZ) and dizygotic/fraternal (DZ) twin pairs for a trait or disorder. A higher degree of similarity in MZ (who share 100% of their genes) than in DZ twins (who, on average share 50% of their segregating genes) provides evidence for heritable influences on the behavior being studied. Standard twin modeling decomposes observed correlations within twin pairs into three components: Additive genetic (A), shared environmental (C), and nonshared environmental (E) influences (Figure 6.2). Heritability is the proportion of total variance in behavior that is attributed to additive (and, in the case of broad heritability, nonadditive, when they play a role) genetic factors. Several assumptions and potential limitations underlying the analysis of twin data that need to be considered including the following:

- Whether the equal environment assumption (which assumes that the shared environmental correlation (C) is 1.0 in both MZ and DZ twin pairs) is justified.
- The assumption of random mating, the violation of which can inflate estimates of shared environment.
- If some of the genetic variation in outcome is due to nonadditive genetic effects (dominance or epistasis), the importance of shared family environmental influences may be underestimated.

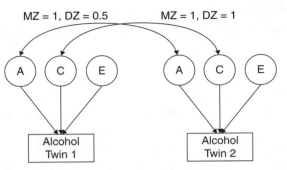

Figure 6.2   Univariate twin (ACE) model. A, additive genetic influences; C, shared environmental influences; E, nonshared environmental influences + measurement error.

- Genetic effects and gene by shared environment effects are confounded. However, it is possible to explicitly model this gene–environment interplay by obtaining estimates of heritability that are conditioned on, or vary as a continuous function of environmental exposure.

The "children of twins" and other extended family designs

An extension of the classical twin study is the "children-of-twins" (COT) design that compares outcomes in offspring of twins. As shown in Figure 6.3, using data on children of affected and unaffected MZ and DZ pairs, the following four groups can be defined:

- High genetic risk and high environmental risk (parent is affected).
- High genetic risk but reduced environmental risk (parent is unaffected but parent's MZ twin is affected).

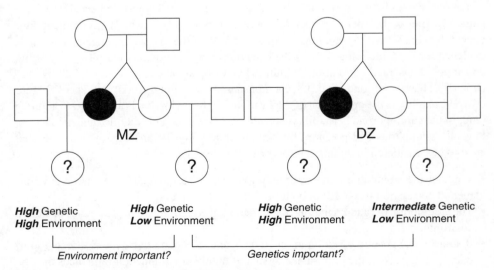

Figure 6.3   Children of twins model. Affected twin is in black.

- Intermediate genetic risk but reduced environmental risk (parent is unaffected but parent's DZ twin is affected).
- Children at low genetic and low environmental risk (parent and cotwin are both unaffected).

This design can detect both genetic transmission and the environmental consequences of parental substance use disorders that may depend upon offspring's genetic vulnerability or be masked by genetic nonadditivity, and therefore remain undetected in the traditional twin study design. Additionally, COT studies can determine whether genetic transmission accounts for associations between an apparent environmental risk-factor and offspring outcomes.[5] Utilizing this design Jacob *et al.*[6] reported that offspring of an unaffected (i.e., no history of abuse or dependence) MZ twin whose cotwin had alcohol dependence were no more likely to exhibit alcohol abuse or dependence than were offspring of nonalcoholic twins, therefore suggesting that a low risk environment (no exposure to paternal alcohol dependence) can ameliorate the influence of a high-risk genetic background.

In addition to COT, extended twin designs that incorporate information on spouses of twins (i.e., to test for the assumption of random mating, or whether spousal correlations for behaviors like drinking are attributable to shared genes and environments) as well as parents and nontwin siblings have been employed to enhance informativeness.[7]

Heritability of alcohol initiation and use

Heritability is that proportion of individual differences (or variation) in a behavior (or trait) that is attributable to genetic influences. There are several large-scale twin studies examining the heritability of alcohol consumption in adolescents and youth. For example, in a study of over 1,200 Dutch twin pairs Koopmans and Boomsma[8] reported that 34% of variation in alcohol use among 15–16-year-old teens could be attributed to heritable influences while this increased to 43% among 17-year-old teens. Similarly, in a study of Finnish twins, Viken *et al.*[9] reported that the heritability of alcohol use increased with age (from 14% in 16-year-old group to 26% in 17-year-old group). Measures of frequency of drinking, intoxication, and frequency of intoxication showed overall higher levels of heritable influences, with the magnitude of these influences also increasing with age. While not based on adolescent samples, several studies of adult twins have also found that retrospective reports of age of onset of alcohol use are influenced by heritable factors.

Heritability of alcohol use disorders

There is now considerable evidence of substantial genetic influences on lifetime alcohol abuse and dependence in adults. Goldman *et al.*[10] pooled information from five independent studies of alcohol dependence in a large sample of adult twins and concluded that 56% of the variation in liability to alcohol dependence could be attributed to genetic factors. Furthermore, despite earlier suggestions that heritable influences on alcohol dependence may be stronger in males than in females, more recent research has concluded that the strength of heritable influences on alcohol dependence is equal in males and females.[11]

Similarly, one of the relatively few studies of adolescents estimated that 78% of variation in liability to problem alcohol use (defined as meeting criteria for at least one symptom of alcohol abuse or dependence) could be attributed to additive genetic factors.[12]

Early onset alcohol use and risks for subsequent dependence

Genes influencing initiation of alcohol use may also impact the transitions to problem use or alcohol use disorders. Recognizing the conditional nature of these disorders (development of an alcohol use disorder is self-evidently conditional on initiation of alcohol use), several genetically informative studies have modeled the genetic and environmental overlap across alcohol use and subsequent abuse/dependence and concluded that 80–90% of the heritable influences on DSM-IV alcohol abuse/dependence overlap with indices of alcohol consumption,[13,14] while shared environment also facilitates escalation of use. A study of Finnish adolescent twins[15] examining the genetic overlap across alcohol use, frequency of consumption, and problem drinking found that while drinking frequency and problem drinking shared over 50% of their genetic influences, the link between initiation and problem drinking was largely due to shared environment.

Given considerable overlap in both the genetic and the environmental factors associated with alcohol use and subsequent misuse, there has been ongoing interest in applying genetically informative methodologies to examine whether the frequently observed—yet controversial—association between earlier age of alcohol onset and increased risk of subsequent dependence can be attributed to shared genetic and environmental influences on these behaviors. An early examination of this issue was reported by Prescott and Kendler[16] who used multivariate genetic modeling and concluded that the observed associations between early onset alcohol use and subsequent risks of dependence were likely noncausal, arising instead from the influence of shared genetic factors both on age of onset of alcohol use and on alcohol dependence. In contrast, Grant and colleagues[17] reported that, although contributions to early regular drinking were significantly correlated with those on alcohol dependence (and other measures of substance use/ dependence), the association was not entirely explained by genetic or shared family environmental factors. More recently, analyzing data from a large sample of Australian twins, we reported that heritable influences on symptoms of alcohol dependence were considerably larger in those who reported early onset alcohol use, while variance in alcohol dependence among later onset drinkers was largely attributable to nonshared environmental variance (and measurement error), suggesting that age at first drink may facilitate the expression of genes associated with vulnerability to alcohol dependence symptoms.

Comorbidity

Comorbidity—the occurrence of multiple psychiatric disorders in a single individual—is highly prevalent and has strong implications for prognosis and course of both treated and untreated conditions.[18,19] Multiple epidemiological studies have established that alcohol use and alcohol use disorders are frequently associated both with other measures of problem behavior (e.g., illicit drug use) and with a range of psychiatric disorders. In a comprehensive review of studies examining the psychiatric comorbidity of adolescent substance use and abuse/dependence in community samples, Armstrong and Costello[20] reported that alcohol use, abuse, and dependence were associated with significantly elevated risks of depressive disorders, anxiety disorders and post-traumatic stress disorder (PTSD), associations being particularly strong for disruptive behavior disorders.

While the extent and importance of comorbidity is now well established, there are ongoing debates concerning the mechanisms underlying these observed associations: distinctions have been drawn between *true* comorbidity and *artifactual* comorbidity (which may arise because of methodological issues such as item contamination or sample selection).[19] At a very basic level, explanations proposed to explain "true" comorbidity vary from one disorder inducing or causing the other (e.g., depression increases substance use through self medication) to no causal association between the disorders. In the latter explanation, comorbidity would be the result of common risk factors—both genetic and environmental—that may increase the risk for each disorder. While a useful heuristic, the comparison between causal and noncausal explanations of comorbidity is an oversimplification of the complex processes that may underlie any observed comorbidity and there have been at least 13 separate models of comorbidity described.[21] Multivariate twin studies can be used to model the extent to which the same genetic factors influence vulnerability across substances and psychopathology and can thus be used to inform the debate about the mechanisms underlying observed comorbidity.[22]

Comorbidity between alcohol and other drug use/abuse/dependence

Evidence from twin studies supports the role of overlapping genetic influences on the use of alcohol and other drugs—as well as smoking—although to a lesser extent. For example, Young *et al.*[23] report a genetic correlation of 0.15 between alcohol use and tobacco use, and a genetic correlation of 0.14 between alcohol use and cannabis use, while the shared environmental correlations were 0.22 and 0.33, respectively. Similarly, Koopmans *et al.*[24] reported that the genetic correlation between alcohol use and tobacco use was negligible during adolescence but increased during adulthood. There is also evidence that genetic influences on alcohol dependence are shared with those on nicotine and illicit drug dependence. Kendler *et al.*[25] concluded that there are two genetic factors—one predisposing largely to licit drug dependence (alcohol, nicotine, and caffeine) and one to illicit drug dependence (cannabis, cocaine)—underlying dependence on these substances, although there was also evidence of quite large specific genetic influences on both nicotine and caffeine.

In adolescents, problem use of alcohol, tobacco, and cannabis is influenced by overlapping genetic—but not shared environmental—factors. Rhee *et al.*[26] examined several mechanisms of genetic comorbidity between alcohol and illicit drug dependence in an adolescent sample and demonstrated that alcohol and illicit drug dependence may be manifestations of a single common and heritable liability. In contrast, utilizing a COT design, Volk *et al.*[27] reported that after accounting for the correlation among the offspring between alcohol and nicotine dependence, there was evidence for the specificity of genetic transmission of vulnerability to alcohol and nicotine dependence.

Comorbidity with psychiatric disorders

There is growing evidence of substantial genetic overlap of alcohol use disorders with both externalizing[28-30] and internalizing disorders[31] with inconsistent evidence for gender differences.[32,33] For example, in a study of retrospectively reported childhood conduct disorder and lifetime alcohol dependence in a sample of young adult twins, Slutske *et al.*[34] reported that 76% and 71% of the phenotypic association between conduct disorder and alcohol dependence in men and women, respectively, could be attributed to common genetic risk factors for the two disorders. Using COT data, Knopik *et al.*[35] demonstrated that intergenerational links between maternal alcohol dependence and offspring with ADHD may be mediated by pleiotropic genetic effects—when a single genetic factor influences multiple seemingly unrelated traits—again supporting the important role of genetic influences on both within individual comorbidity and familial aggregation.

In contrast, multiple studies of adolescents suggest that associations between alcohol use and externalizing problems are largely attributable to shared environmental influences,[36,37] while Malone and colleagues[38,39] have demonstrated that maternal and paternal alcohol consumption are strong and independent predictors of both externalizing disorders and substance use in offspring. Twin studies imply that parental alcohol use may link offspring alcohol involvement to other psychopathology via familial environmental mechanisms.

Evidence for genes influencing both alcohol involvement and internalizing disorders is less consistent. Nonetheless, Kendler *et al.*[40] reported substantial overlap between genetic influences on alcohol dependence and those on major depressive disorder in a sample of adult female twins.

Gene by environment interaction

There has been increasing recognition of the importance of gene–environment interplay in the etiology of alcohol use and other psychiatric disorders.[41] There are two related mechanisms by which genes work in concert with environmental exposures: Gene–environment correlation and gene–environment interaction. *Gene–environment correlation* refers to genetic predispositions that influence the likelihood of being exposed to a certain environment. For example, heritable influences have been found to influence deviant peer affiliations suggesting that vulnerability to substance use is partly responsible for exposure to deviant peer groups that may, in turn, act to influence substance use. *Gene–environment interaction* refers to a moderation of genetic predisposition as a consequence of environmental exposure. For example, studies of Finnish adolescent twins suggested that the importance of genetic influences on alcohol use increased in less stable neighborhoods.[43] Conversely, in more supervised and restricted environments genetic predispositions were less influential while environmental effects were more pronounced.[42,43] However, it appears that these effects may be age specific: These findings were reported for a sample of 16–18-year–old teens but the authors were unable to replicate the findings in a younger sample of 12–14-year-old group.[44] Likewise, low levels of parental monitoring[45] as well as increased affiliations with substance using peers,[46] have been found to augment the importance of genetic influences of substance use.

Endophenotypes

There is increasing interest in studying *endophenotypes*—defined by Gottesman and Gould[47] as a measurable index of liability to a phenotype that is often assumed to be more proximal to the biological underpinnings of the behavior. Endophenotypes are not only associated with disease (or behavior) but also transmitted in families (i.e., heritable) of affected individuals and while they may cosegregate with disease, they are never a consequence of it. A wide variety of endophenotypes have been identified as indices of alcohol use and other externalizing behavior in youth, including behavioral sensitivity (for alcohol, measured using measures of balance or subjective measures of intoxication),[48] event-related potential (such as P300) and electroencephalogram (EEG) activity (e.g., beta wave patterns).[49] The evoked potential P300, for example, reflects human cognitive ability to respond to "oddball" stimuli. In a study of adolescent twins, reduced P300 was noted in the unaffected cotwins of twins who developed alcohol dependence during early adulthood.[50] However, while P300 is a potential link between alcohol problems and externalizing psychopathology, it does not sufficiently explain the association across these disorders.

Genomics

Thus far, in discussing genetic influences, we have referred to *latent* genetic factors, that is, the aggregate effects of all segregating genes that contribute to similarity in MZ and DZ twin pairs. With rapid technological advances, research is moving from delineation of these latent genetic influences (see Box 6.1) to the identification of specific gene variants that may confer vulnerability to various aspects of alcohol involvement. Several large family-based samples of densely affected alcoholic families have provided unique avenues for the discovery of genomic regions and, subsequently, genes (see Box 6.2) involved in alcoholism. However, these studies have largely focused on adult populations to capitalize on an age group where genetic vulnerability to alcoholism has had the full

---

Box 6.1   Latent genetic influences.

- Latent genetic factors represent the unmeasured and aggregate effects of all genetic variation influencing liability to alcohol use and misuse.
- The effects of latent genetic influences can be studied using family, adoption, twin, and children-of-twin studies.
- Alcohol use and misuse, and alcohol use disorders run in families.
- Adult adoptee alcohol misuse is highly correlated with alcohol misuse in biological (but not adoptive) parents suggesting genetic influences.
- Twin studies demonstrate moderate heritability (20–40%) for alcohol use and substantially higher heritability (50–60%) for alcohol use disorders.
- Heritability of alcohol use and consumption are lower during adolescence—shared environmental factors are more relevant during this phase.
- Nearly 80–90% of the genetic influences on alcohol use disorders overlap with those on earlier stages of use and alcohol consumption.

Box 6.2   Genetic material in humans.

- Human genetic material is comprised of 46 chromosomes: 22 pairs of autosomes and a pair (XX, XY) of sex chromosomes.
- Within chromosomes, genetic material is present as the double-helical deoxy-ribonucleic acid (DNA).
  - DNA is comprised of a backbone of basepairs, A (adenine), G (guanine), C (cytosine), and T (thymine). A pairs with T while G pairs with C.
  - Human DNA is broadly classified into genes and intergenic DNA (DNA sequences located between gene clusters).
  - Genes are comprised of strings of basepairs that form exons and introns. Exons are transcribed into ribonucleic acid (RNA) and then translated into protein while introns are not.
  - Variation in human DNA occurs as short tandem repeats (STRs) or SNPs.
    - STRs refer to a set of basepairs, in a sequence, repeated a variable number of times (AGGCAGGC vs. AGGCAGGCAGGCAGGC).
    - SNPs refer to single base pair changes (AA**G**TGTC to AA**T**TGTC).
    - SNPs and STRs may or may not have known function.
- All cells contain two copies of genetic variation (maternal and paternal alleles).

---

opportunity to express itself. Summarized below are key genomic findings for alcohol involvement.

The earliest genomic efforts utilized a linkage approach (see Box 6.3). The advantage of linkage analysis is that it allows for a scan of the entire genome, which can, if well powered, lead to discovery of novel genetic regions. Several such large-scale linkage studies, which rely on sibling pairs or multiplex families (families with multiple affected relatives, particularly siblings, who meet criteria for alcoholism), have shown promising results.[51] Most notably, the Collaborative Study on the Genetics of Alcoholism[52] provided some of the earliest evidence for linkage to alcohol dependence on chromosomes 1, 2, 4, and 7, as well as others (e.g., chromosome 16 for an alcohol dependence severity phenotype[53] and chromosomes 6 and 21 for endophenotypes of event-related potentials[54]

Box 6.3   Measured genetic or genomic influences.

- Genetic and genomic influences can be broadly classified as "linkage" and "association."
- The earliest approach was to study linkages that use allele sharing across pairs of affective relatives to identify genomic regions harboring genes of interest.
- Regions on chromosomes 1, 2, 4, and 7 were identified.
- "Association" targets markers (SNPs, STRs) in genes that may have biological plausibility or may be encompassed by a linkage region.
- Association studies show that SNPs in GABRA2 and genes comprising the alcohol dehydrogenase cluster are associated with aspects of alcohol misuse.
- Genome-wide association studies (GWAS) is a new method of interrogating the entire human genome for association.
- No replicated promising leads have emerged from GWAS.

SNPs, single nucleotide polymorphisms; STRs, short tandem repeats; GABRA2, gene involved in the encoding of gamma-aminobutyric acid receptor subunits.

and subjective reactions to alcohol[55]). Of these, the linkage findings on chromosomes 1 and 4 have been most widely replicated. Both regions, particularly the two linkage regions on chromosome 4, where pairs of siblings affected with alcoholism show a very high degree of allele sharing, have offered critical insights into potential genes involved in the etiology of alcohol dependence. Two clusters of genes on chromosome 4, the gamma-amino butyric acid genes (GABRB1, GABRA2, GABRA4, and GABRB2) and the alcohol dehydrogenase cluster (ADH1A, ADH1B, and ADH1C as well as ADH4, ADH5, and ADH7), have been identified in the neighborhood of the markers that showed elevated allele sharing.

A disadvantage with linkage is that with respect to homing in on the genome, it is a fairly low-resolution technique. For example, 1 centiMorgan (cM)—the measure of genetic distance used to cover the area of the genome that shows excess allele sharing—is equivalent to one million bases of DNA, and linkage regions often span 10–50 cM. Hence, with the clues provided by linkage analyses and by selecting candidate genes that may, a priori, have putative biological relevance to alcoholism, genomic inquiry shifted rapidly to an association framework.

At its simplest, while linkage examines allele sharing within affected relatives, *association* compares the prevalence of the risk allele of a single-nucleotide polymorphism (SNP) in those who are affected and unaffected. These individuals may be related or unrelated (individuals from the population where case subjects are affected and control subjects are not). There have been several gene association studies of alcoholism and alcohol misuse. Most notably, subsequent to its identification using linkage methods, SNPs in ADH1B, ADH1C, and GABRA2 have been found to be highly associated with susceptibility to alcohol misuse.[56] Particularly in ADH1B and ADH1C, SNPs that have key functional relevance in regulating the speed and efficiency of alcohol metabolism have been implicated.[57] While the association with SNPs in GABRA2 have been equally well replicated, these SNPs currently have no known functional relevance and hence, the robust association between GABRA2 and alcohol misuse remains provocative.

While linkage studies led investigators to the now well-documented association between alcohol misuse and GABRA2, the protective influence of the aldehyde dehydrogenase genotype (ALDH2*2) on susceptibility to alcoholism is largely attributed to its biological plausibility. The ALDH2*2 polymorphism, which is observed in select Asian populations, is responsible (along with ADH1B) for the flushing response, whereby an individual upon consumption of alcohol experiences nausea, dizziness, and a discernable facial reddening (or flush). Individuals with one or two copies of this polymorphism are less efficient at metabolizing acetaldehyde, hence this polymorphism confers protection against subsequent development of alcoholism.[58]

Several other genes have been implicated in the etiology of alcoholism. These include genes on chromosome 7 (CHRM2[59] and hTAS2R16[60]) that are in the vicinity of linkage regions and DRD2 and ANKK1[61] on chromosome 11. However, the principal limitations of the candidate gene association method are the rather short list of candidate genomic regions and genes and the fairly modest effect sizes of these gene variants. While these studies allow the investigator to focus on a specific gene with high resolution, they preclude the possibility of gene discovery. Genome-wide association studies, where SNPs are used to map the entire genome, combine the resolution of gene association studies with the exploratory capabilities of linkage.

There are currently three published genome-wide association studies of alcohol dependence.[62–64] The number of SNPs used to cover the genome across these studies ranged from 370,000 to 1 million and while this incredible wealth of genomic data would suggest an increased likelihood of identifying multiple causal variants associated with risk for alcoholism, results across these studies have been of modest effect sizes (i.e., explaining very little of the heritability associated with alcoholism) and, disappointingly, have failed to yield viable and replicated signals. Some genes worth noting include PKNOX2 and PECR. PKNOX2 has been implicated in animal models of addiction, while PECR is involved in the catalysis of certain fatty acids for mitochondrial energy regulation. Despite the potential links between these genes and alcoholism, the precise mechanism underlying the association remains elusive.

A majority of the genomic findings enumerated above emerged from studies of adult populations. There are caveats to genomic studies of adolescents. First, twin studies suggest that genetic influences on alcohol involvement gain prominence during early adulthood and that twin similarity in vulnerability to alcohol use is attributable to shared environmental factors during adolescence. Second, due to the developmental course of alcohol abuse and dependence, onset during adolescence is uncommon, particularly in the general population. When taken together, these factors dramatically reduce statistical power and influence the methodology for genomic studies.

Do genes explain comorbidity?

Alcohol misuse often occurs against a background of other internalizing and externalizing psychopathology. To some extent, shared genomic influences may be responsible for this co-occurrence (see Box 6.4).

Externalizing disorders and alcohol

GABRA2 has emerged as an important link between externalizing behaviors, such as antisocial personality disorder, conduct disorder, impulsivity, other substance use disorders, and alcohol misuse. Of particular interest to the adolescent literature, Dick and

---

Box 6.4   Genetics and comorbidity.

- Twin studies suggest that shared latent genetic influences are partly responsible for the comorbidity between use and misuse of alcohol and other drugs.
- Common genetic influences also link alcohol misuse to externalizing behaviors, such as conduct disorder.
- GABRA2 is one gene that has been found to contribute to the common genetic influences on alcohol misuse, drug use/misuse and other externalizing problems.
- GABRA2 is also associated with endophenotypes, such as P300, which represent risk for alcohol misuse and general central nervous system disinhibition.

GABRA2, gene involved in the encoding of gamma-aminobutyric acid receptor subunits.

colleagues[65] have found that rs279871 (an intronic SNP in this gene associated with alcohol dependence in adults) was also associated with childhood conduct disorder symptoms (however, this finding was not replicated by Sakai *et al.*[66]). Additionally, SNPs in GABRA2 have also been linked to EEG endophenotypes of brain oscillations that indicate central nervous system disinhibition.[67]

Internalizing disorders and alcohol

Internalizing problems during adolescence are associated with an increased risk of subsequent alcohol use disorders. A recent review of the literature implicated multiple genes as contributors to this association.[68] The most notable, albeit controversial, effects have been noted for the long/short alleles of the 5-HTTLPR (SLC6A4) gene. The short (S) allele is associated with reduced trascriptional efficiency resulting in an overabundance of synaptic serotonin, the major neurotransmitter associated with mood management. Carriers of the S-allele have been found to be more likely to report alcoholism marked by onset during youth and with general disinhibition. The S-allele has also been linked to higher neuroticism scores and to major depressive disorder, particularly via an interaction with exposure to stressful life events. While recent meta-analyses[68,69] cast doubt on the hypothesis of a genotype × stressful life events interaction, it is possible that modulations in serotonin levels may impact on the comorbidity between mood and alcohol misuse, even as early as during adolescence.

Measured genotype by environmental (G × E) interaction

As heritability can be moderated by changing environmental exposure, genotype may also influence behavior in certain environmental milieus (Box 6.5). For example, the

---

Box 6.5   Gene–environment interplay.

- Gene–environment correlation (rGE) refers to genetic influences on alcohol misuse also modifying likelihood of environmental exposure.
- Gene × environment (G × E) interaction refers to modification of the genetic susceptibility to alcohol misuse upon environmental exposure.
- Twin studies report G × E: heritability of alcohol use is greater in less restrictive (urban, low parental monitoring) environments.
- GABRA2 effects on alcohol misuse may also be more pronounced in those receiving low parental monitoring.
- One of the most potent environmental risk factors for alcohol misuse is early age at first drink.
- There is evidence for rGE—nearly 35% of the genetic influences on age at first drink are shared with alcohol dependence.
- There is also evidence for G × E—heritability of alcohol use disorders in those with early age at first drink is markedly higher than in those with later age at first drink.

GABRA2, gene involved in the encoding of gamma-aminobutyric acid receptor subunits.

association between GABRA2 (SNP rs279871) and alcohol dependence was found to be moderated by marital status.[70] Those with the "high-risk" genotype were more likely to be alcohol dependent if they were never married or divorced. However, these results were complicated by an association between the high-risk genotype and marital status—a gene/environment correlation. Thus, the same genotype that was associated with risk for alcohol misuse was also associated with a lower likelihood of being stably married (presumably due to disinhibitory characteristics).

G × E likely plays an important role during youth—as discussed previously, the influential role played by peer deviance and parental monitoring may also modify the effects of risk genotypes. For example, Dick and colleagues[71] reported that the effect of GABRA2 on externalizing behaviors was more pronounced in those who received low parental monitoring; however, this hypothesis was not tested specifically for adolescent alcohol misuse.

Does environment modify gene expression?

Epigenetics refers to heritable and de novo changes in gene expression that do not involve changes in DNA sequence. Thus, individuals with the same genotype may demonstrate variations in gene expression in response to exogenous (e.g., prolonged exposure to stress) or endogenous (e.g., elevated cortisol levels in response to stress) environments. Mechanisms inducing epigenetic modification include gene methylation, chromatin remodeling, and imprinting.

Does epigenetic modification contribute to the etiology of adolescent alcohol misuse and, if so, is it a cause or consequence of it? Change in the methylation status of certain clusters of CpG (C-phosphate-G) sites in promoter regions of genes such as DAT, HERP, POMC, N2RB, and in the atrial natriuretic peptide and vasopressin precursor genes have been implicated in alcohol dependence, alcohol craving and withdrawal.[72–74] The addition of a methyl group to cytosine of a CpG site leads to gene silencing and lower expression; however, both hypo- and hypermethylation have been implicated in disruption of gene activity.

While DNA methylation is associated with later stages of alcohol misuse, chronic exposure to alcohol, particularly during early embryogenesis, has been demonstrated to contribute to epigenetic modification in neuronal growth,[75] Some argue that such epigenetic change may be associated with the consequences of fetal alcohol exposure. This leads to speculation surrounding the effects of early onset alcohol exposure as well. As discussed in Chapter 2, early onset alcohol use is among the leading risk factors for subsequent alcohol misuse; to what extent the effects of chronic early alcohol exposure induce epigenetic change in gene expression, remains to be explored.

There are limitations to epigenetic studies of alcohol misuse in humans. The methylation profile of genes is posited to be tissue specific. Hence, methylation status of genes expressed in leukocytes (i.e., extracted from peripheral blood) may not completely correlate with gene expression in the brain. While several initiatives are underway to establish intertissue similarities and differences, epigenetic studies in the human paradigm do hint at the role of epigenetic change as both a contributor to and a consequence of alcohol misuse.

Conclusions

Results from a substantial number of adoption, twin and extended family studies have demonstrated moderate to strong genetic components to the liability to develop substance use disorders. Twin and related designs provide important and innovative methodologies for addressing numerous unresolved issues including: whether the salience of genetic and environmental factors vary across the lifespan, whether similar or different genetic factors are relevant at each stage of the development of substance use problems; the extent to which the spectrum of substance use disorders, as well as both externalizing and internalizing psychiatric disorders, are influenced by similar or different genetic and environmental factors. Rapid technological advances have made the search for specific gene variants influencing substance use disorders feasible and future work is likely to elucidate not only the precise genetic variants that confer risk for a disorder but also the environmental conditions that interact with these variants to confer risk or resilience.

Resources

- A comprehensive overview of human molecular genetics is provided by Strachan T, Read AP. *Human Molecular Genetics*, 4th ed. New York: Garland Science, 2010.
- An overview of behavioral genetic methodologies and findings can be found in Plomin R, DeFries JC, McClearn GE, McGuffin P. *Behavioral Genetics*, 5th ed. New York: Worth Publishers, 2008.
- For an overview of the interplay between genetic and environmental influences on behavior, see Rutter M. *Genes and Environment: Nature–Nurture Interplay Explained*. Malden, MA: Wiley-Blackwell, 2006.
- For further information on the web, including links to other sites, see the Web site for the Human Genome Project: http://www.ornl.gov/sci/techresources/Human_Genome/home.shtml.

References

1. Bierut LJ, Dinwiddie SH, Begleiter H *et al.* Familial transmission of substance dependence: Alcohol, marijuana, cocaine, and habitual smoking: A report from the Collaborative Study on the Genetics of Alcoholism. *Arch Gen Psychiatry* 1998; 55:982–988.
2. Cadoret RJ, Troughton E, O'Gorman TW, Heywood E. An adoption study of genetic and environmental factors in drug abuse. *Arch Gen Psychiatry* 1986; 43:1131–1136.
3. Cloninger CR, Bohman M, Sigvardsson S, von Knorring AL. Psychopathology in adopted-out children of alcoholics. The Stockholm Adoption Study. *Recent Dev Alcohol* 1985; 3: 37–51.
4. Bouchard TJ Jr, Lykken DT, McGue M, Segal NL, Tellegen A. Sources of human psychological differences: The Minnesota Study of Twins Reared Apart. *Science* 1990; 250:223–228.

5. Heath AC, Todorov AA, Nelson EC, Madden PA, Bucholz KK, Martin NG. Gene–environment interaction effects on behavioral variation and risk of complex disorders: The example of alcoholism and other psychiatric disorders. *Twin Res* 2002; 5:30–37.

6. Jacob T, Waterman B, Heath A *et al.* Genetic and environmental effects on offspring alcoholism: New insights using an offspring-of-twins design. *Arch Gen Psychiatry* 2003; 60:1265–1272.

7. Maes HH, Neale MC, Kendler KS, Martin NG, Heath AC, Eaves LJ. Genetic and Cultural Transmission of Smoking Initiation: An Extended Twin Kinship Model. *Behav Genet* 2006; 36:795–808.

8. Koopmans JR, Boomsma DI. Familial resemblances in alcohol use: Genetic or cultural transmission? *J Stud Alcohol* 1996; 57:19–28.

9. Viken RJ, Kaprio J, Koskenvuo M, Rose RJ. Longitudinal analyses of the determinants of drinking and of drinking to intoxication in adolescent twins. *Behav Genet* 1999; 29:455–461.

10. Goldman D, Oroszi G, Ducci F. The genetics of addictions: Uncovering the genes. *Nat Rev Genet* 2005; 6:521–532.

11. Heath AC, Bucholz KK, Madden PA *et al.* Genetic and environmental contributions to alcohol dependence risk in a national twin sample: Consistency of findings in women and men. *Psychol Med* 1997; 27:1381–1396.

12. Rhee SH, Hewitt JK, Young SE, Corley RP, Crowley TJ, Stallings MC. Genetic and environmental influences on substance initiation, use, and problem use in adolescents. *Arch Gen Psychiatry* 2003; 60:1256–1264.

13. Kendler KS, Myers J, Dick D, Prescott CA. The relationship between genetic influences on alcohol dependence and on patterns of alcohol consumption. *Alcohol Clin Exp Res* 2010; 34:1058–1065.

14. Grant JD, Agrawal A, Bucholz KK *et al.* Alcohol consumption indices of genetic risk for alcohol dependence. *Biol Psychiatry* 2009; 66:795–800.

15. Pagan JL, Rose RJ, Viken RJ, Pulkkinen L, Kaprio J, Dick DM. Genetic and environmental influences on stages of alcohol use across adolescence and into young adulthood. *Behav Genet* 2006; 36:483–497.

16. Prescott CA, Kendler KS. Age at first drink and risk for alcoholism: A noncausal association. *Alcohol Clin Exp Res* 1999; 23:101–107.

17. Grant JD, Scherrer JF, Lynskey MT *et al.* Adolescent alcohol use is a risk factor for adult alcohol and drug dependence: Evidence from a twin design. *Psychol Med* 2006; 36: 109–118.

18. Caron C, Rutter M. Comorbidity in child psychopathology: Concepts, issues and research strategies. *J Child Psychol Psychiatry* 1991; 32:1063–1080.

19. Angold A, Costello EJ, Erkanli A. Comorbidity. *J Child Psychol Psychiatry* 1999; 40:57–87.

20. Armstrong TD, Costello EJ. Community studies on adolescent substance use, abuse, or dependence and psychiatric comorbidity. *J Consult Clin Psychol* 2002; 70:1224–1239.

21. Kendler KS, Heath AC, Neale MC, Kessler RC, Eaves LJ. Alcoholism and major depression in women. A twin study of the causes of comorbidity. *Arch Gen Psychiatry* 1993; 50:690–698.

22. Waldman ID, Slutske WS. Antisocial behavior and alcoholism: A behavioral genetic perspective on comorbidity. *Clin Psychol Rev* 2000; 20:255–287.

23. Young SE, Rhee SH, Stallings MC, Corley RP, Hewitt JK. Genetic and environmental vulnerabilities underlying adolescent substance use and problem use: General or specific? *Behav Genet* 2006; 36:603–615.

24. Koopmans JR, van Doornen LJ, Boomsma DI. Association between alcohol use and smoking in adolescent and young adult twins: A bivariate genetic analysis. *Alcohol Clin Exp Res* 1997; 21:537–546.

25. Kendler KS, Myers J, Prescott CA. Specificity of genetic and environmental risk factors for symptoms of cannabis, cocaine, alcohol, caffeine, and nicotine dependence. *Arch Gen Psychiatry* 2007; 64:1313–1320.

26. Rhee SH, Hewitt JK, Young SE *et al*. Comorbidity between alcohol dependence and illicit drug dependence in adolescents with antisocial behavior and matched controls. *Drug Alcohol Depend* 2006; 84:85–92.

27. Volk HE, Scherrer JF, Bucholz KK *et al*. Evidence for specificity of transmission of alcohol and nicotine dependence in an offspring of twins design. *Drug Alcohol Depend* 2007; 87:225–232.

28. Haber JR, Jacob T, Heath AC. Paternal alcoholism and offspring conduct disorder: Evidence for the 'common genes' hypothesis. *Twin Res Hum Genet* 2005; 8:120–131.

29. Hicks BM, Krueger RF, Iacono WG, McGue M, Patrick CJ. Family transmission and heritability of externalizing disorders: A twin-family study. *Arch Gen Psychiatry* 2004; 61:922–928.

30. Slutske WS, Heath AC, Dinwiddie SH *et al*. Modeling genetic and environmental influences in the etiology of conduct disorder: A study of 2,682 adult twin pairs. *J Abnorm Psychol* 1997; 106:266–279.

31. Saraceno L, Munafo M, Heron J, Craddock N, van den Bree MB. Genetic and non-genetic influences on the development of co-occurring alcohol problem use and internalizing symptomatology in adolescence: A review. *Addiction* 2009; 104:1100–1121.

32. Fu Q, Heath AC, Bucholz KK *et al*. Shared genetic risk of major depression, alcohol dependence, and marijuana dependence: Contribution of antisocial personality disorder in men. *Arch Gen Psychiatry* 2002; 59:1125–1132.

33. Miles DR, van den Bree MB, Gupman AE, Newlin DB, Glantz MD, Pickens RW. A twin study on sensation seeking, risk taking behavior and marijuana use. *Drug Alcohol Depend* 2001; 62:57–68.

34. Slutske WS, Heath AC, Dinwiddie SH *et al*. Common genetic risk factors for conduct disorder and alcohol dependence. *J Abnorm Psychol* 1998; 107:363–374.

35. Knopik VS, Heath AC, Jacob T *et al*. Maternal alcohol use disorder and offspring ADHD: Disentangling genetic and environmental effects using a children-of-twins design. *Psychol Med* 2006; 36:1461–1471.

36. Knopik VS, Jacob T, Haber JR, Swenson LP, Howell DN. Paternal alcoholism and offspring ADHD problems: A children of twins design. *Twin Res Hum Genet* 2009; 12:53–62.

37. Rose RJ, Dick DM, Viken RJ, Pulkkinen L, Kaprio J. Genetic and environmental effects on conduct disorder and alcohol dependence symptoms and their covariation at age 14. *Alcohol Clin Exp Res* 2004; 28:1541–1548.

38. Malone SM, Iacono WG, McGue M. Drinks of the father: Father's maximum number of drinks consumed predicts externalizing disorders, substance use, and substance use disorders in preadolescent and adolescent offspring. *Alcohol Clin Exp Res* 2002; 26:1823–1832.

39. Malone SM, McGue M, Iacono WG. Mothers' maximum drinks ever consumed in 24 hours predicts mental health problems in adolescent offspring. *J Child Psychol Psychiatry* 2010; 51:1067–1075.

40. Kendler KS, Heath AC, Neale MC, Kessler RC, Eaves LJ. Alcoholism and major depression in women. A twin study of the causes of comorbidity. *Arch Gen Psychiatry* 1993; 50:690–698.

41. Moffitt TE, Caspi A, Rutter M. Strategy for investigating interactions between measured genes and measured environments. *Arch Gen Psychiatry* 2005; 62:473–481.

42. Dick DM, Rose RJ, Viken RJ, Kaprio J, Koskenvuo M. Exploring gene–environment interactions: Socioregional moderation of alcohol use. *J Abnorm Psychol* 2001; 110:625–632.

43. Rose RJ, Dick DM, Viken RJ, Kaprio J. Gene–environment interaction in patterns of adolescent drinking: Regional residency moderates longitudinal influences on alcohol use. *Alcohol Clin Exp Res* 2001; 25:637–643.

44. Dick DM, Bernard M, Aliev F *et al.* The role of socioregional factors in moderating genetic influences on early adolescent behavior problems and alcohol use. *Alcohol Clin Exp Res* 2009; 33:1739–1748.
45. Dick DM, Pagan JL, Viken R *et al.* Changing environmental influences on substance use across development. *Twin Res Hum Genet* 2007; 10:315–326.
46. Agrawal A, Balasubramanian S, Smith EK, Madden PAF, Bucholz KK, Heath AC, Lynskey MT. Peer substance involvement modifies genetic influences on regular substance involvement in young women. *Addiction* 2010; 105:1844–1853.
47. Gottesman II, Gould TD. The endophenotype concept in psychiatry: Etymology and strategic intentions. *Am J Psychiatry* 2003; 160:636–645.
48. Schuckit MA. An overview of genetic influences in alcoholism. *J Subst Abuse Treat* 2009; 36:S5–S14.
49. Begleiter H, Porjesz B. Genetics of human brain oscillations. *Int J Psychophysiol* 2006; 60:162–171.
50. Carlson SR, Iacono WG, McGue M. P300 amplitude in nonalcoholic adolescent twin pairs who become discordant for alcoholism as adults. *Psychophysiology* 2004; 41:841–844.
51. Dick DM, Bierut LJ. The genetics of alcohol dependence. *Curr Psychiatry Rep* 2006; 8:151–157.
52. Reich T, Edenberg HJ, Goate A *et al.* Genome-wide search for genes affecting the risk for alcohol dependence. *Am J Med Genet* 1998; 81:207–215.
53. Foroud T, Edenberg HJ, Goate A *et al.* Alcoholism susceptibility loci: Confirmation studies in a replicate sample and further mapping. *Alcohol Clin Exp Res* 2000; 24:933–945.
54. Porjesz B, Begleiter H, Wang K *et al.* Linkage and linkage disequilibrium mapping of ERP and EEG phenotypes. *Biol Psychol* 2002; 61:229–248.
55. Schuckit MA, Edenberg HJ, Kalmijn J *et al.* A genome-wide search for genes that relate to a low level of response to alcohol. *Alcohol Clin Exp Res* 2001; 25:323–329.
56. Edenberg HJ, Foroud T. The genetics of alcoholism: Identifying specific genes through family studies. *Addict Biol* 2006; 11:386–396.
57. Edenberg HJ. The genetics of alcohol metabolism: Role of alcohol dehydrogenase and aldehyde dehydrogenase variants. *Alcohol Res Health* 2007; 30:5–13.
58. Thomasson HR, Crabb DW, Edenberg HJ, Li TK. Alcohol and aldehyde dehydrogenase polymorphisms and alcoholism. *Behav Genet* 1993; 23:131–136.
59. Jones KA, Porjesz B, Almasy L *et al.* A cholinergic receptor gene (CHRM2) affects event-related oscillations. *Behav Genet* 2006; 36:627–639.
60. Hinrichs AL, Wang JC, Bufe B *et al.* Functional variant in a bitter-taste receptor (hTAS2R16) influences risk of alcohol dependence. *Am J Hum Genet* 2006; 78:103–111.
61. Munafo MR, Matheson IJ, Flint J. Association of the DRD2 gene Taq1 A polymorphism and alcoholism: A meta-analysis of case–control studies and evidence of publication bias. *Mol Psychiatry* 2007; 12:454–461.
62. Treutlein J, Cichon S, Ridinger M *et al.* Genome-wide association study of alcohol dependence. *Arch Gen Psychiatry* 2009; 66:773–784.
63. Bierut L, Agrawal A, Bucholz K *et al.* A Genome-wide association study of alcohol dependence. *Proc Natl Acad Sci USA* 2010; 107:5082–5087.
64. Edenberg HJ, Koller DL, Xuei X *et al.* Genome-wide association study of alcohol dependence implicates a region on chromosome 11. *Alcohol Clin Exp Res* 2010; 34:840–852.
65. Dick DM, Bierut LJ, Hinrichs AL *et al.* The role of GABRA2 in risk for conduct disorder and alcohol and drug dependence across different developmental stages. *Behav Genet* 2006; 36:577–590.

66. Sakai JT, Stallings MC, Crowley TJ, Gelhorn HL, McQueen MB, Ehringer MA. Test of association between GABRA2 (SNP rs279871) and adolescent conduct/alcohol use disorders utilizing a sample of clinic referred youth with serious substance and conduct problems, controls and available first degree relatives. *Drug Alcohol Depend* 2010; 106:199–203.

67. Rangaswamy M, Porjesz B. Uncovering genes for cognitive (dys)function and predisposition for alcoholism spectrum disorders: A review of human brain oscillations as effective endophenotypes. *Brain Res* 2008; 1235:153–171.

68. Munafo MR, Durrant C, Lewis G, Flint J. Gene X environment interactions at the serotonin transporter locus. *Biol Psychiatry* 2009; 65:211–219.

69. Risch N, Herrell R, Lehner T *et al.* Interaction between the serotonin transporter gene (5-HTTLPR), stressful life events, and risk of depression: A meta-analysis. *JAMA* 2009; 301:2462–2471.

70. Dick DM, Agrawal A, Schuckit MA *et al.* Marital status, alcohol dependence, and GABRA2: Evidence for gene–environment correlation and interaction. *J Stud Alcohol* 2006; 67:185–194.

71. Dick DM, Latendresse SJ, Lansford JE *et al.* Role of GABRA2 in trajectories of externalizing behavior across development and evidence of moderation by parental monitoring. *Arch Gen Psychiatry* 2009; 66:649–657.

72. Qiang M, Denny A, Chen J, Ticku MK, Yan B, Henderson G. The site specific demethylation in the 5′-regulatory area of NMDA receptor 2B subunit gene associated with CIE-induced up-regulation of transcription. *PLoS One* 2010; 5:e8798.

73. Biermann T, Reulbach U, Lenz B *et al.* N-Methyl-D-aspartate 2b receptor subtype (NR2B) promoter methylation in patients during alcohol withdrawal. *J Neural Transm* 2009; 116:615–622.

74. Hillemacher T, Frieling H, Luber K *et al.* Epigenetic regulation and gene expression of vasopressin and atrial natriuretic peptide in alcohol withdrawal. *Psychoneuroendocrinology* 2009; 34:555–560.

75. Liu Y, Balaraman Y, Wang G, Nephew KP, Zhou FC. Alcohol exposure alters DNA methylation profiles in mouse embryos at early neurulation. *Epigenetics* 2009; 4:500–511.

Part III

Prevention and Early Intervention

Chapter 7

Alcohol policy and the prevention of harm in young people

John B. Saunders[1,2], Peter Anderson[3], and Joseph M. Rey[2,4]

[1]Centre for Youth Substance Abuse Research, Faculty of Health Sciences, University of Queensland, Brisbane, Australia
[2]Faculty of Medicine, University of Sydney, NSW, Australia
[3]Faculty of Health, Medicine and Life Sciences, Maastricht University, Maastricht, The Netherlands
[4]Notre Dame Medical School, Sydney, NSW, Australia

Key points

- The amount of alcohol-related harm in a society and the proportion of people who drink harmfully are closely related to the overall or per capita level of alcohol consumption.
- Whether it is better to concentrate on universal interventions to reduce alcohol-related harm or to target subgroups of the population at particularly high risk of harm remains a contentious issue. The two approaches can, however, be usefully combined.
- Most alcohol-related harm in a community occurs not in the heaviest drinkers, but in those whose consumption is at lesser levels.
- The arguments in favor of universal measures are scientifically compelling.
- Increasing the price of alcohol through taxation—particularly minimum pricing (when the minimum price paid per gram of alcohol in beverages is set by legislation)—is the most effective means of reducing alcohol consumption and alcohol-related harm in youth.
- Price rises delay the age when young people start to drink, reduce the number of drinking bouts and binge drinking, reduce the amount of alcohol consumed on each occasion, and slow progression toward drinking larger amounts.
- Most countries have passed laws regulating the minimum age at which alcohol can be consumed in licensed premises, the most common being 18 years (21 years in the United States). The implementation of these laws leads to clear reductions in drink–driving casualties and other alcohol-related harms. However, the full benefit of a higher drinking age is only realized if the law is enforced.
- The greater the number of alcohol outlets and the wider the hours of trade, the greater the alcohol consumption among young people, with increased levels of assault, homicide, child abuse and neglect, and self-inflicted injury.
- Almost all countries outlaw driving a motor vehicle with a blood alcohol concentration (BAC) above specified levels, which vary according to country (usually 50 mg/100 mL or

(continued)

Young People and Alcohol: Impact, Policy, Prevention, Treatment, First Edition.
Edited by John B. Saunders and Joseph M. Rey.
© 2011 Blackwell Publishing Ltd. Published 2011 by Blackwell Publishing Ltd.

(Continued)

80 mg/100 mL). At all levels of BAC, the risk of being involved in a crash is greater for younger people and can be reduced by enforcement of the law via random breath testing.
- The appropriateness of bans on alcohol advertising has been the subject of public and political debate for years. Based on growing evidence, public health advocates generally argue that advertising increases total alcohol consumption and misuse and that children, at least, should be protected from exposure to advertising and marketing of alcoholic beverages.

Alcohol has been part of human culture from the dawn of civilization. It is indeed "no ordinary commodity,"[1] and it is an attractive one for young people. It is valued in most cultures for its relaxing effects and facilitation of social interactions; consumption is often regarded as a "right of passage" into the adult world. However, the negative aspects of alcohol consumption in young people are increasingly recognized. In recent decades, there has been a worldwide increase in alcohol consumption due in part to industrialization of the developing world and the effects of globalization. "Across England, half a million children between the ages of 11 and 15 will have been drunk in the past four weeks, and young people under 18 will have consumed the equivalent of 2 million bottles of wine in the past week alone [. . .] since 1990 the amount of alcohol consumed by 11 to 15 year olds who drink has doubled".[2] It was estimated that in the United States in 2007, 8 million children aged 12–17 drank alcohol. On an average day, 7,540 of them drank alcohol for the first time.[3] Alcohol consumption is a leading cause of accidents, trauma, and overall mortality. Excessive consumption retards brain development (so crucial in this age group), while fetal alcohol syndrome is one of the two commonest causes of mental retardation in many countries (see Chapter 5).

This chapter will outline some of the health impacts of alcohol, and will examine the societal influences on consumption of alcohol among young people. This chapter will also review the societal responses that can limit alcohol consumption and harm in this age group. It acts as an introduction to and complements the review of community-based prevention approaches discussed in Chapter 8 and the chapter on prevention in schools, colleges, and the military (Chapter 10).

Alcohol and harm

Alcohol is a causal factor for accidents, injuries, and harm to both drinkers and people around them, no matter whether they are family members, friends, or simply persons who happen to be in their proximity. It is a cause of reduced school, college, and job performance, absenteeism, family problems, suicide, homicide, and crime. It is a leading cause of injuries and deaths from motor vehicle accidents. It is also a contributory factor for risky sexual behavior, sexually transmitted diseases, and HIV infection (see Chapter 3). Alcohol is a potent teratogen with a range of negative outcomes to the fetus, including low birth weight, cognitive deficiencies, and fetal alcohol disorders. Alcohol is neurotoxic to brain development, which is manifested in mental retardation in children with fetal alcohol syndrome, and it inhibits brain maturation, especially the development of the frontal lobes and consequent adaptive decision making (described in Chapter 5 in detail). Alcohol is also a major cause of acquired brain damage in later years.

Alcohol is a dependence-producing drug through its reinforcing properties and neuroadaptation in the brain. It is an immunosuppressant, increasing the risk of communicable diseases, including tuberculosis. Alcoholic beverages are classified as carcinogenic by the International Agency for Research on Cancer, increasing the risk of cancers of the oral cavity and pharynx, esophagus, stomach, colon, rectum, and breast in a linear dose–response relation.[4] Alcohol has a bimodal association with coronary heart disease. In low and apparently regular doses (as little as 10 g every other day), alcohol is cardio protective, although doubt remains about the effect of confounders.[5] At high doses, especially when consumed irregularly, it is cardiotoxic.

Alcohol's overall public health impact can be readily quantified. It is the fifth most important cause of the global burden of disease, accounting for an estimated net harm of 4.4%, as measured by disability-adjusted life years (DALYs). On a global basis, alcohol-related unintentional injury and neuropsychiatric disorders head the list, while cirrhosis contributes up to 10% of the burden of disease.[6] Overall, approximately 4% of deaths worldwide are caused by alcohol. Poorer people and lower income countries suffer a greater burden per liter of alcohol consumed than wealthier ones.[7] Its impact, in particular as a cause of fatal injuries, is greater in younger age groups—of both sexes. For example, in the United States, underage (below 21 years) alcohol intoxication was estimated to have contributed to or caused 24% of fatal motor vehicle accidents, 30% of drownings, 30% of fatal burns, 41% of homicides, 43% of sexual assaults, and 24% of property crimes among the young.[8] In Australia, of all deaths among 13–25-year-old people reported to a coroner from 2003 to 2006, 13% showed an alcohol level of 0.05% or above.[9]

Alcohol-attributable costs amount to more than 1% of GDP in most nations, the United States having the largest (2.7%) of the high-income countries and South Korea the highest (3.3%) among middle-income nations for which reliable data are available.[7] The total annual cost to the US economy was estimated in 1998 to be $184 billion,[10] and £20 billion in the United Kingdom in 2001.[11] In Australia, the estimated costs of alcohol-related harm are AU$15 billion each year, when crime ($1.6 billion), health ($1.9 billion), productivity in the workplace ($3.5 billion), and road traffic accidents ($2.2 billion) are taken into account.[12]

Level and pattern of consumption and the nature of harm

The risk of death from a chronic alcohol-related disease increases linearly from zero consumption in a dose–response manner with the volume of alcohol consumed; death from an acute alcohol-related disease increases from zero consumption in a dose–response manner with frequency of drinking, and rises exponentially with the amount drunk in one session.[13] Noncommercial alcohol can bring extra health risks from high ethanol concentrations and toxic contaminants, compounded by social marginalization.

There is a very close link between a country's total alcohol per head consumption and its prevalence of alcohol-related harm and alcohol dependence. This implies that when alcohol consumption increases, so does alcohol-related harm, the proportion of people with alcohol dependence, and vice versa.[13] The European Union (EU) is the heaviest drinking region of the world, with over one-fifth of the population older than 14 years reporting heavy episodic drinking.[14] Thus, it is not surprising that European countries have the highest proportion in the world of total ill health and premature death due to alcohol.[14] Heavy episodic drinking patterns are more common in poorer than in richer drinking communities, and are largely responsible, for example, for alcohol's contribution to the differences in life expectancy between Eastern and Western Europe. In Russia, alcohol has been a cause in more than half of all deaths in people aged 15–54 in recent years.[15]

Societal influences on alcohol consumption

Alcohol consumption tends to start in the teen years, with the actual age being influenced by the legal minimum age for drinking. Alcohol consumption in most societies is a socially influenced phenomenon (see Chapter 1). Indeed, it has been described as "socially infectious." In the early 1950s, Ledermann, a French mathematician, proposed that alcohol intake occurred as a *single distribution*, with no clear distinction between the groups of *normal drinkers* and *heavy drinkers*. He and others provided empirical support for this distribution.[16] The following are the implications of this theory:

- There is no group of people within a population whose alcohol consumption is entirely separate from that of the general population (if this were the case the distribution would be bimodal).
- If overall alcohol consumption increases in a society, the number of people drinking the highest amount also rises and the increase, because of the log–normal curve, is proportionately greater than the average increase in the number of drinkers.
- Factors that influence the level of alcohol consumption overall in a society will therefore increase the number of the heaviest drinkers.

Thus, a key influence on alcohol-related harm, and on the proportion of people who drink harmfully, is the overall level of consumption in that society. There is consistent data showing a strong correlation between per capita alcohol intake and the occurrence of alcohol-related harm and mortality.[13] Likewise, when consumption increases or decreases, the occurrence of harm increases or decreases correspondingly.[7]

Skog[17] developed the notion of *social contagion*. This states that a person's drinking has a societal impact and vice versa. In Skog's words "if a person increases his alcohol consumption, the likelihood that he will offer his friends alcohol will increase. Their consumption increases and it is more likely that they will also offer their friends alcohol. And so it continues, with the semblance of a passing wave."[17]

The Ledermann model[16] has been an extremely influential one and has underpinned alcohol control measures that seek to reduce the overall consumption of alcohol. Although the single distribution theory has been criticized,[17] the essential implication of the model—when alcohol consumption changes overall in a society so does the proportion of people who drink in a harmful way—remains valid. This has resulted in a groundswell of opinion that the primary approach to the prevention of alcohol-related harm should be to reduce the overall level of use.

Prevention: universal versus targeted interventions

Universal preventive interventions apply to a whole population; they do not select participants based on risk. Examples are taxation measures, media campaigns, and legislation about wearing seat belts. *Selective* interventions apply to subgroups among which the prevalence of a risk factor is above average (e.g., pregnant women, juvenile delinquents, native populations). *Targeted* interventions are provided to people who have detectable, subthreshold level of signs or symptoms (e.g., individuals found driving while intoxicated), but who do not yet meet diagnostic criteria for the condition. An example of these is early intervention for people misusing alcohol.

Approaches to prevention can also be considered *population level* when they are delivered to large groups (including selective interventions) and *individual* when they are delivered one-to-one, often in clinic settings. Population-level approaches are essential because they can help reduce the overall level of alcohol consumed and therefore lower the risk of alcohol-related harm in that population, and are usually more cost effective because many individuals are targeted at the same time. Individual interventions can help make people aware of the potential risks they are taking (or harm they may be doing) at an early stage but are more expensive.

A constant theme in the debate about effective measures of reducing alcohol-related harm is whether it is better to concentrate on universal population measures to reduce per capita consumption, or to target subgroups of the population at particular risk of harm. This debate is fuelled not only by the scientific evidence but also by the cultural and political views of those participating. To what extent should individual behavior—in this case alcohol consumption—be controlled by the (presumably benevolent) state?

The arguments in favor of universal measures are scientifically compelling. There is a wealth of data gathered over more than 100 years—and historical data dating over several centuries—which demonstrates that control measures affecting consumption of the whole population significantly reduce indices of alcohol use, alcohol misuse, alcohol-related harm, medical morbidity, and mortality.

Although controlling per capita alcohol intake reduces consumption in the heaviest drinkers, alcohol-related harm is also prevalent among those with lower consumption. The *preventive paradox*, a term originally coined by Kreitman,[18] states that the majority of alcohol-related harm occurs not in the heaviest drinkers but in those whose consumption is at lesser levels. The reason for the paradox is that there are many more people with lower level alcohol consumption. Even though harm is less frequent in them, their much greater number means they account for a larger proportion of the total harm. Reducing the consumption of the entire population will lessen alcohol-related harm in the community to a greater extent than measures that target only those with alcohol dependence and others with high consumption levels.

Recent analyses have caused a reinterpretation of the preventive paradox. Stockwell and colleagues[19] have shown the need to analyze particular patterns of alcohol consumption with regard to the consequences. Episodic heavy drinking is strongly associated with accidents, trauma, aggressive behavior, and domestic violence. The overall alcohol consumption of this particular group may not be especially high because of the episodic nature of their drinking. Therefore, when expressed as average daily alcohol intake, their consumption might be in the middle range. In reality, this pattern of drinking is not moderate but high risk and only considered middle range by the somewhat artificial measure of average daily intake. Nonetheless, reducing overall alcohol intake would have beneficial effects by reducing consumption across the range of patterns and levels of consumption.

Targeted interventions are logical in that it is the consumption patterns of particular subgroups or individuals that are identified as the goal of prevention. For example, an important target group would be drivers operating motor vehicles. Random breath testing has been shown to reduce drink–driving and alcohol-related motor vehicle deaths. Other target groups could be (1) workers using industrial machinery, (2) young people gathering in particular drinking environments, and (3) patients attending doctors or in a range of heath care settings. This has led to the development of approaches for screening for hazardous or harmful drinking patterns[20] and individualized intervention of those identified with such alcohol use.[21] There is considerable evidence for the benefits of brief, structured interventions aimed at reducing alcohol intake in people with hazardous or harmful consumption. The key issue that has emerged in recent years is whether these individualized interventions can be delivered systematically through health care and other providers so that the promise of reduced alcohol-related harm becomes a reality.

Alcohol policies

Alcohol policies are sets of measures seeking to minimize the health and social harm caused by the use of alcohol. Additionally, policies can try to deter minors from using alcohol, protect people other than drinkers from the harm done by alcohol, and inform consumers about the negative effects of alcohol.[14] As highlighted, there is now a growing body of research about the effectiveness of a variety of alcohol policies. Also, the reasons why alcohol policies work are quite well understood and can often be applied across cultures. For example, measures to counter drink–driving are based on a deterrent effect, while taxes on alcoholic beverages seek to reduce consumer demand by decreasing the affordability of alcohol.[13] Yet, the complexity of the alcohol world needs to be acknowledged; it includes not only social and cultural mores but also many people whose livelihood depends on alcohol—primary producers, small and large businesses—as well as the multinational alcohol beverage industry. All have become increasingly involved in the policy arena in order to protect their interests, which may not coincide with the greater good, and this can create tensions. What has happened in Thailand, formerly a low alcohol consumption country, in the last half century illustrates the consequences of government policy inaction: Per head consumption of alcohol increased 32-fold, from 0.26 L in 1961 to 8.47 L in 2001, with the consequent rise in health and social problems, particularly among young women.[22]

Setting policy is the ultimate responsibility of governments and understanding and managing these factors as well as public opinion is essential to achieve the best possible outcomes. How to optimally achieve this is described in Chapter 8.

Pricing policies

Consumers of alcohol respond to changes in the price of alcohol as consumers respond to the price of products generally. When other factors are held constant, such as income and the price of other goods, a rise in alcohol prices leads to less alcohol consumption and less alcohol-related harm, and vice versa. As an example, France had the highest per capita alcohol consumption in the world for most of the twentieth century. This has been attributed to the very low cost of alcoholic beverages, its protected agrarian economy, the prominence of wine production, and the free allocation of wine for soldiers after the World War I. Per capita alcohol intake remained high by world standards through to the early 1990s. Not surprisingly, France has had exceptionally high rates of alcohol-related disorders, such as cirrhosis of the liver. Other countries in Europe, such as Portugal and Luxembourg, have recently overtaken France, and per capita intake is now rapidly increasing in the United Kingdom and some Nordic countries, with the attendant increases in cirrhosis deaths.[14]

Because of the close relationship between the cost of alcoholic drinks and consumption, several countries have employed taxation as a means of reducing alcohol-related harm. In particular, the Nordic countries have a long tradition of imposing high taxes on alcoholic drinks, such that they are regarded as luxury commodities. In recent years this traditional approach has been challenged by cross-European legislation, consequent on the formation of the European Union, and the dominance of the single European market. This has resulted in deregulation of markets in counties joining the European Union, through so-called "harmonization" of legislation. In Finland, alcohol sales have increased threefold since that country joined the European Union and was therefore subjected to EU legislation.[23]

In contrast to the increase in per capita alcohol intake in many Northern European counties, alcohol intake overall has declined in some Mediterranean countries, notably France and Italy, and alcohol-related deaths have fallen. The extent to which this was a response to policy initiatives is uncertain.[24] Many consider the decreases to be due to urbanization, shifts to factory and service work, to changes in family structure and "de-structuring" of meals, supported in more recent years by increased health consciousness and alcohol policies (see also Chapter 1).

Price elasticity

Alcohol consumption is described as *price elastic* when the percent change in the amount of alcohol consumed is *greater* than the percent change in price, and *price inelastic* if the percent change in the amount of alcohol consumed is *less* than the percent change in price. For example, an elasticity of –2 would mean that a 10% rise in the price of alcohol would lead to a 20% fall in consumption, and would be described as "price elastic." Price inelastic does *not mean* that the consumption is not responsive to the price; it only means that the proportional change is smaller.[6]

A meta-analysis of 132 studies found a median price elasticity for all beverage types of –0.52 in the short term and –0.82 in the long term, elasticity being lower for beer than for wine or spirits.[25] An elasticity of –0.52 means that for every 10% increase in price, consumption would fall by 5.2%. Another meta-analysis of 112 studies found mean price elasticity for beer of –0.46, for wine of –0.69, and for spirits of –0.80.[26] That is, reduction in consumption varies according to beverage type (less price sensitivity for beer than for wine or spirits, the last having the highest sensitivity), country, shorter or longer term, and type of consumer (occasional or heavy drinker).

If prices are raised,[14] the following will occur:

- Consumers reduce their overall drinking and shift to cheaper beverages.
- Heavier drinkers tend to buy the cheaper products within their preferred beverage type.
- Impact is stronger in the longer rather than the shorter term.
- Increasing the price of the cheapest drinks has a larger impact on total consumption than increasing the price of more expensive ones.

The opposite is also true: Decreasing the price of alcohol results in higher consumption. For example, in 2004, a one-third decrease in alcohol tax led to a significant drop in the price of alcoholic beverages in Finland—total alcohol consumption grew by 10%.[23]

Affordability

Increasing taxes not only reduces alcohol consumption and related harm but also increases government revenue. This is important because the revenue collected is usually well below the actual social costs of alcohol. In spite of increased taxation, alcoholic beverages have become more affordable in many countries (e.g., in Northern European nations) due to cheaper production, illegal manufacture, cross-border trade, globalization, inflation, and growing affluence.

The optimal approach is a taxation policy scaled according to the alcohol content of beverages (the higher the alcohol content the higher the tax), regularly adjusted for inflation and for changes in affluence (income). Young people in particular reduce consumption of alcohol to a greater extent when alcohol becomes less affordable (more expensive).

Minimum pricing

In the United Kingdom, women purchase a higher proportion (54%) of their alcohol from supermarkets and off-licenses than do men (29%), while those aged 18–24 years purchase alcohol mainly in pubs, bars, and clubs. Beverage preferences also vary, 59% of the alcohol consumed by men is as beer, while 60% of that consumed by women is as wine and, for women aged 18–24 years, 20% is from ready-to-drink beverages ("alcopops").[27] Young people who drink and those who drink harmful amounts tend to choose cheaper beverages and purchase alcohol mainly in licensed establishments. Establishing a minimum price per unit of alcohol would limit the ability of these groups to *trade down* to cheaper products.

Minimum pricing means that suppliers cannot sell alcoholic beverages for less than a set amount (e.g., 50 cents) per unit of alcohol contained. This type of legislation should also outlaw discounting or marketing using *loss leaders* below the minimum pricing.

Minimum pricing would also encourage producers to reduce the alcohol content of their products—they would be cheaper.

In the United Kingdom, alcohol is currently sold at less than £0.05 per gram in 59% of off-license trade and 14% of licensed trade. *Off-license* means that alcohol cannot be consumed in the premises (e.g., bottle shops, supermarkets) while *licensed* means that alcohol can be consumed in the premises (e.g., bars, pubs, restaurants). "A £0.50 per unit minimum price would probably reduce mean consumption by 6.9%, save 2930 lives per year, and offer cumulative health savings (including valuation of quality-adjusted life years) of £6.2 billion over 10 years."[28] The cost impact of the policy on consumers would vary substantially between types of drinkers. The overall estimate was £22 per drinker per annum, £106 per annum for harmful drinkers, and £6 per annum for moderate drinkers. If drinkers did not change their alcohol consumption, the effect on their pockets would be £138 per annum for harmful drinkers and £6 per annum for moderate drinkers. As a result, both England's Chief Health Officer[2] and the National Institute for Health and Clinical Excellence[29] recommended the introduction of minimum price legislation in the United Kingdom. This was rejected by the government on the grounds that it would harm the interests of the "sensible majority of moderate drinkers."[30]

Price and younger drinkers

Younger drinkers are responsive to price increases as already highlighted. Price rises[29] instigate the following:

- Delay the age when young people start to drink.
- Reduce the number of drinking bouts.
- Reduce the amount of alcohol consumed on each occasion.
- Slow progression toward drinking larger amounts.

Moreover, as in adults, due to the addictive nature of alcohol, this effect is more marked in the longer than shorter term. Although alcoholic beverages appear to behave in the market similar to most other consumer goods, the demand for alcoholic drinks among some individuals may differ from the demand for other products because of the addictive nature of alcohol. This implies that an increase in past consumption would raise current consumption, so that price elasticity in the short term, which holds past consumption constant, would be smaller in absolute value than price elasticity in the long term, which allows past consumption to vary. For example, a price increase in 2004 would reduce consumption in 2004, with consumption in previous years held constant. Because of the addictive nature of alcohol, it would be expected that consumption in 2005 and in all future years would also fall. Consequently, the reduction in consumption observed over several years (i.e., in the long term) after the price increase would exceed the reduction observed in 2004 (i.e., in the short term). A study of the relationship between price and alcohol consumption by young adults aged 17–29 years has found this to be the case.[31] Ignoring previous years' consumption (and thus the addictive aspects of alcohol), the price elasticity of demand for alcohol was –0.29 (i.e., a reduction of 2.9%). When previous years' consumption (and thus the addictive aspects of alcohol) was taken into account, the estimated long-term price elasticity of demand was more than twice as high at –0.65

(i.e., a reduction of 6.5%), indicating that price had a much greater influence on alcohol consumption. This also means that about half of the reason that young adults who drink heavily do not reduce their consumption is the difficulty (cost) of overcoming the addictive nature of alcohol.

Binge drinking by young people—a growing problem (see Chapter 1)—is also highly responsive to price. For example, it was shown that in the United States, a 5% increase in the price of alcohol decreased an individual's probability of heavy binge drinking by 2.2%.[32]

Minimum drinking age laws

Drinking age laws deal with a variety of behaviors relating to where, when and under what circumstances alcoholic beverages can be purchased or consumed. The minimum legal drinking age typically refers to the minimum age at which alcohol can be consumed in licensed premises, which may be different from the minimum age at which alcohol can be purchased. Laws generally apply to venues outside the home, such as bars or restaurants. Most laws make no reference to alcohol consumption in the home, the exception being the United Kingdom, where alcohol may be consumed from the age of 5 years with parental consent. Selected countries and their minimum drinking ages are listed in Tables 1.1 and 1.2 of Chapter 1. For religious reasons, many Muslim countries have more restrictive laws that in some extend to total prohibition. England's Chief Medical Officer has called for an alcohol-free childhood up to the age of 15.[2] As highlighted in Chapters 2 and 5, because young people are still developing both physically and emotionally, they are particularly vulnerable to alcohol. They may also be drinking in unsupervised situations and in *unsafe* environments (parks and street corners) where problems are more likely to occur.[29]

The most common minimum drinking age is 18 years; the United States being one of the few countries with minimum drinking age of 21 years. The National Minimum Drinking Age Act of 1984 states that revenue will be withheld from states that allow the purchase of alcohol by anyone under the age of 21. However, some states are more specific about the prohibitions than others, and some municipalities actually have no legislation specifically related to drinking age. What is and is not allowed varies much according to state but all states have enacted some type of minimum drinking age legislation—with exceptions in at least 31 states (e.g., for parents providing alcohol, for entering establishments, and for work purposes). For example, in Texas, people must be 21 to consume alcohol, but many bars allow entering the premises if aged 18 although one is not allowed to drink alcohol while there.

Implementation of laws setting a minimum age for the purchase of alcohol shows subsequent reductions in drink–driving casualties and other alcohol-related harms. A review of 132 studies published between 1960 and 1999 found very strong evidence that changes in minimum drinking-age laws can have substantial effects on drinking among young people and on alcohol-related harm, particularly road traffic accidents, often for well after young people reach the legal drinking age.[33] A systematic review of drinking age laws in the United States found that among 14 studies looking at the effects of raising the minimum legal drinking age, crash-related outcomes declined by a median of 16% for the targeted age groups, and that among 9 studies looking at the effects of lowering the minimum legal drinking age, crash-related outcomes increased by a median of 10% within the targeted age groups. The effects were stable over follow-up times ranging from 7 months to 9 years.

The full benefit of a higher drinking age is only realized if the law is enforced. Despite higher minimum drinking age laws, young people do succeed in purchasing alcohol (or obtaining it in other ways—often from parents[34]). Among the 35 European Union countries participating in the European School Survey Project on Alcohol and other Drugs, students aged 15–16 years thought that getting any type of alcoholic beverage was fairly or very easy, rising to 78% for beer (range: 50–95%) and 70% for wine (range: 54–85%).[35] This results from low and inconsistent enforcement, especially where there is little community support for enforcement of the law regarding alcohol sales to underage drinkers. Even moderate increases in enforcement can reduce sales to underage drinkers by as much as 35% to 40%, especially when combined with media and other community campaigns. The most effective means of enforcement is through sellers, who have a vested interest in retaining the right to sell alcohol.

Availability of alcohol

While there are total bans on the sale of alcohol in several countries with majority Muslim populations, as well as at community level in a number of indigenous communities (e.g., in Australia), there are frequent bans on the use of alcohol in particular locations and circumstances, such as drinking in parks or streets, hospitals or at the workplace. A licensing system for the sale of alcohol allows for control, since infringement of the laws can be punished by revocation of the license. On the other hand, a licensing system with fees generated from licenses can lead to a proliferation of licensed establishments as an income-generating mechanism for jurisdictions. Government monopolies on the sale of alcohol can reduce alcohol-related harm. Such systems tend to have fewer outlets open for shorter hours than private retailers.

Outlets

In general, the number of alcohol outlets is associated with the level of alcohol-related harm, which is strongest when there are major changes in the number or type of such outlets. A greater density of alcohol outlets is associated with higher alcohol consumption among young people, with increased levels of assault and with other harms such as homicide, child abuse and neglect, self-inflicted injury and, with less consistent evidence, road traffic accidents.[36]

Strict restrictions on availability can create an opportunity for a parallel illicit market, although in the absence of substantial home or illicit production, this can in most circumstances be managed with enforcement. Where a large illicit market exists, license-enforced restrictions may increase the competitiveness of the alternative market, and this will need to be taken into account in policymaking.

Days and hours of sale

A number of studies have indicated that although changing either hours or days of alcohol sale can redistribute the times at which many alcohol-related crashes and violent events related to alcohol take place, it does so at the cost of an overall increase in problems. Around-the-clock opening in Reykjavik, for instance, produced net increases in police work, emergency room admissions and drink–driving cases.[37] The police work was spread more evenly throughout the night, but a change in police shifts was necessitated to accommodate the extra work. A series of studies in Sweden found a net 3.6% increase in alcohol sales when government alcohol stores opened on Saturdays, although the changes in harm were not big enough to be significant.[38] Following the 2003 Licensing Act in the United Kingdom, which recommended in general that shops and supermarkets be allowed to sell alcohol at any time they choose to open (24 hours opening), pubs stayed open on average only an extra 27 minutes. No real change in alcohol-related crimes was found until 03:00 AM, but a 22% increase in crimes occurred between 03:00 AM and 06:00 AM. In other words, alcohol-related crimes were shifted to later in the night.[39] A further study in Newcastle (Australia)[40] showed that reducing licensed premises closing time from 06:00 AM to 03:00 AM, resulted in a 37% reduction in assaults compared with a control suburb where closing times remained unchanged.

Homicide is a leading cause of death in Brazil, with one of the highest murder rates occurring in the city of Diadema. To respond to this situation, measures were introduced which included a new licensing law in 2002 prohibiting on-premises alcohol sales after 23:00 hours. This resulted in a 44% decline in the number of murders.[41]

Drink–driving laws

In the United States, 11,773 people were killed in 2008 in alcohol impaired driving crashes, accounting for nearly one-third of all traffic related deaths. Every day, 32 people in the United States die in motor vehicle accidents that involve an alcohol-impaired driver; this amounts to one death every 45 minutes. The annual cost of alcohol-related crashes totals more than $51 billion.[42]

Practically all the measures that reduce alcohol consumption contribute to a greater or lesser extent to reduce alcohol-related road traffic accidents, but there are policies specifically aimed at this goal. Road safety measures are often not described as alcohol policies since they are not specifically implemented to reduce harm as a primary aim. Yet, they are particularly important for young people. At all levels of blood alcohol concentration (BAC), the risk of being involved in a crash is greater for younger people. Among the US drivers with BAC levels of 0.08% or higher involved in fatal accidents in 2008, more than one-third were between 21 and 24 years of age.[42]

In 1936, Norway passed the world's first law making an offense to drive with more than a specified amount of alcohol in the body. Nowadays almost all countries outlaw driving a motor vehicle with a BAC above specified levels, which vary according to country (e.g., 0.08/100 mL in the United States, Canada, and the United Kingdom; 0.05/100 mL in Australia, France, and Germany; 0.04/100 mL in Lithuania; 0.03/100 mL in Russia; 0.02/100 mL in China, Norway, and Sweden; 0.0/100 mL in Brazil, Iran, Saudi Arabia, and Slovakia). Lower blood alcohol limits apply in some countries for novice drivers or operators of heavy vehicles.

A European Union study of the impact of reducing BAC levels from 0.08/100 mL to 0.05/100 mL found that this did not have an effect unless the regulation was enforced by random checks. When the two measures were implemented together the fatality rate per kilometer driven fell by 6.1%.[14]

In summary, there is considerable evidence that drink–driving accidents and fatalities can be reduced by[13]:

- Establishing (or lowering) the legal concentration of alcohol in the blood while driving.
- Systematic random breath testing (when police regularly stop drivers at random to check BAC through breath testing).
- Setting up sobriety checkpoints (all vehicles are stopped and drivers breath tested).
- For repeat drink drivers, mandatory treatment and the use of an ignition interlock (mechanical device that does not allow a car to be driven by a driver who is over the limit).

Designated driver programs, heavily promoted among young people in many countries, seek to reduce alcohol-related accidents by facilitating a safe means of transport for those who have been drinking. Although current evidence suggests that designated driver campaigns can increase the use of designated drivers, it is unclear whether they also lead to a reduction in drink–driving or alcohol-related crashes.[43]

Marketing

In the United States alone, the alcohol industry spent $2 billion on advertising in measured media (television, radio, print, outdoor, and newspapers) in 2005, while it was estimated that expenditure to promote alcohol (sponsorships, Internet advertising, point-of-sale materials, product placement, brand-logoed items and other means) was three times higher, approximately $6 billion. Between 2001 and 2005, youth exposure to alcohol advertising on television in the United States increased by 41%. Much of this increase resulted from the rise in advertising of distilled spirits.

Marketing and advertising of alcoholic beverages in mainstream media has become increasingly sophisticated. It often targets young people through linking alcohol brands to sports and cultural activities, sponsorships and product placement, and using the Internet, podcasting, and mobile telephones.

The appropriateness of bans on alcohol advertising has been the subject of public and political debate for many years. The fundamental question has been whether alcohol advertising increases total alcohol consumption or whether it simply influences brand choice. Public health advocates generally argue that advertising increases total alcohol consumption and misuse. The alcohol industry's position has consistently been that advertising merely affects the market share of the various brands, leaving total consumption unchanged. Evidence is mounting that alcohol advertising influences children and young people.[44] Longitudinal studies have shown an effect of various forms of alcohol marketing—including alcohol advertising in traditional media and promotion in the form of movie content and alcohol-branded merchandise—on the initiation of dinking and on riskier patterns of drinking in youth, and the effects seem to be cumulative.[44]

The data suggest that children and young people should be protected as much as possible from alcohol marketing and advertising.[29] Thus restrictions placed on marketing (e.g., sports sponsorship) and advertising (e.g., bans on television advertisements at certain times when children and young people are more likely to watch or during children's programs) are likely to minimize this effect. There is evidence that self-regulation of commercial marketing of alcohol does not prevent the kind of marketing that has an impact on younger people.[13]

Harm reduction

The environment in which drinking takes place (licensed premises) can also contribute to, or reduce the likelihood of alcohol-related harm.[13] Interventions to reduce harm in licensed premises are important, since the problems potentially averted more often than not harm people other than the drinker (e.g., fights). This includes the design of licensed premises, security arrangements, and the attitude and skills of staff serving alcohol. For example, serving practices that promote intoxication, the inability of bar staff to manage problem behavior, or continuing to serve alcohol to intoxicated individuals contribute to harm and result in some licensed premises being associated with a disproportionately high number of assaults, antisocial behavior and other harms. Training bar staff on responsible beverage service would appear to be useful but evidence is scant in this regard. There has been increasing interest in the use of toughened or plastic drinking glasses, which cannot be used as a weapon, though evidence about its effectiveness is still lacking.

Resources

- Anderson P, Baumberg B. *Alcohol in Europe. A public health perspective*. London: Institute of Alcohol Studies; 2006.
- http://ec.europa.eu/health/ph_determinants/life_style/alcohol/documents/alcohol_europe.pdf.
- WHO. *Handbook for Action to Reduce Alcohol-Related Harm*. WHO Regional Office for Europe. Copenhagen: Denmark, 2009. Available at: http://www.euro.who.int/en/what-we-do/health-topics/disease-prevention/alcohol-use/publications/2009/handbook-for-action-to-reduce-alcohol-related-harm. Accessed August 13, 2010.
- WHO. *Evidence for the Effectiveness and Cost–Effectiveness of Interventions to Reduce Alcohol-Related Harm*. WHO Regional Office for Europe. Copenhagen: Denmark, 2009. Available at: http://www.euro.who.int/en/what-we-do/health-topics/disease-prevention/alcohol-use/publications/2009/evidence-for-the-effectiveness-and-costeffectiveness-of-interventions-to-reduce-alcohol-related-harm. Accessed August 13, 2010.

References

1. Babor TF, Caetano R, Casswell S *et al. Alcohol: no Ordinary Commodity. Research and Public Policy*. Oxford: Oxford University Press; 2003.
2. Donaldson L. *Guidance on the Consumption of Alcohol by Children and Young People*. London, UK: Department of Health; 2009.
3. Office of Applied Studies. *The OAS Report: A Day in the Life of American Adolescents: Substance Use Facts Update*. Rockville, MD: Substance Abuse and Mental Health Services Administration; 2010.
4. Lewis S, Campbell S, Proudfoot E, Weston A, Cotter T, Bishop J. *Alcohol as a Cause of Cancer*. Sydney: Cancer Institute NSW; 2008.
5. Corrao G, Rubbiati L, Bagnardi V, Zambon A, Poikolainen K. Alcohol and coronary heart disease: A meta-analysis. *Addiction* 2000; 95:1505–1523.
6. Anderson P, Baumberg B. *Alcohol in Europe. A Public Health Perspective*. London: Institute of Alcohol Studies; 2006.
7. Rehm J, Mathers C, Popova S, Thavorncharoensap M, Teerawattananon Y, Patra J. Global burden of disease and injury and economic cost attributable to alcohol use and alcohol-use disorders. *Lancet* 2009; 373:2223–2233.
8. Miller TR, Levy DT, Spicer RS, Taylor DM. Societal costs of underage drinking. *J Stud Alcohol* 2006; 67:519–528.
9. National Coroners' Information System (NCIS). *Deaths of Persons Aged 13 to 25 Years in Australia (Excluding Qld & SA) which Involved Alcohol* (Reported to a Coroner Between 2003 and 2006). Available at: http://www.ncis.org.au/Alcohol%20deaths%20and%20young%20people%20FINAL%20for%20web.pdf. Accessed June 2, 2010.
10. Harwood H. *Updating Estimates of the Economic Costs of Alcohol Abuse in the United States: Estimates, Update Methods and Data*. Report prepared by The Lewin Group for the National Institute on Alcohol Abuse and Alcoholism (NIAAA), 2000.
11. Leontaridi R. *Alcohol Misuse: How Much Does it Cost?* London: Cabinet Office; 2003.
12. Collins DJ, Lapsley HM. *The Costs of Tobacco, Alcohol and Illicit Drug Abuse to Australian Society in 2004/05*. Canberra: Commonwealth of Australia; 2008.
13. Anderson P, Chisholm D, Fuhr DC. Effectiveness and cost–effectiveness of policies and programmes to reduce the harm caused by alcohol. *Lancet* 2009; 373:2234–2246.
14. World Health Organisation. *Evidence for the Effectiveness and Cost–Effectiveness of Interventions to Reduce Alcohol-Related Harm*. Copenhagen, Denmark: WHO Regional Office for Europe; 2009.
15. Zaridze D, Brennan P, Boreham J, Boroda A, Karpov R, Lazarev A, Konobeevskaya I, Igitov W, Terechova T, Boffetta P, Peto R. Alcohol and cause-specific mortality in Russia: A retrospective case–control study of 48 557 adult deaths. *Lancet* 2009; 373:2201–2214.
16. Ledermann S. *Alcool, Alcoolisme, Alcoolisation*. Paris: Presses Universitaires de France; 1956.
17. Skog O-J. The collectivity of drinking cultures: A theory of the distribution of alcohol consumption. *Br J Addict* 1985; 80:83–99.
18. Kreitman N. Alcohol consumption and the preventive paradox. *Br J Addict* 1986; 81:353–363.
19. Stockwell T, Hawks D, Lang E, Rydon P. Unravelling the preventive paradox for acute alcohol problems. *Drug Alcohol Rev* 1996; 15:7–15.
20. Saunders JB, Aasland OG, Babor TF *et al.* Development of the Alcohol Use Disorders Identification Test (AUDIT): WHO collaborative project on early detection of persons with harmful alcohol consumption II. *Addiction* 1993; 88:791–804.

21. Kaner EFS, Dickinson HO, Beyer F *et al.* The effectiveness of brief alcohol interventions in primary care settings: A systematic review. *Drug Alcohol Rev* 2009; 28:301–323.
22. Casswell S, Thamarangsi T. Reducing harm from alcohol: Call to action. *Lancet* 2009; 373:2247–2257.
23. Helakorpi S, Mäkelä P, Uutela A. Alcohol Consumption before and after a significant reduction of alcohol prices in 2004 in Finland: Were the effects different across population subgroups? *Alcohol Alcohol* 2010; 45:286–292.
24. Allamani A, Prina F. Why the decrease in consumption of alcoholic beverages in Italy between the 1970s and the 2000s? Shedding light on an Italian mystery. *Contemp Drug Probl* 2007; 34:187–198.
25. Gallet CA. The demand for alcohol: A meta-analysis of elasticities. *Aust J Agric Resour Econ* 2007; 51:121–135.
26. Wagenaar AC, Salois MJ, Komro KA. Effects of beverage alcohol price and tax levels on drinking: A meta-analysis of 1003 estimates from 112 studies. *Addiction* 2009; 104:179–190.
27. Purshouse RC, Meier PS, Brennan A, Taylor KB, Rafia R. Estimated effect of alcohol pricing policies on health and health economic outcomes in England: An epidemiological model. *Lancet* 2010; 375:1355–1364.
28. Gilmore IT, Atkinson S. Evidence to drive policy on alcohol pricing. *Lancet* 2010; 375:1322–1324.
29. National Institute for Health and Clinical Excellence. *Alcohol-Use Disorders: Preventing the Development of Hazardous and Harmful Drinking.* NICE public health guidance 24. London: National Institute for Health and Clinical Excellence, 2010. http://www.nice.org.uk/nicemedia/live/13001/48984/48984.pdf. Accessed June 4, 2010.
30. Hencke D, Sparrow A. Gordon Brown rejects call to set minimum prices for alcohol. *The Guardian*, March 16, 2009.
31. Grossman M, Coate D, Arluck GM. Price sensitivity of alcoholic beverages in the United States: Youth, alcohol consumption. In: HD Holder, ed. *Advances in Substance Abuse: Behavioral and Biological Research. Control Issues in Alcohol Abuse Prevention: Strategies for States and Communities.* Greenwich, CT: JAI; 1987, pp. 169–198.
32. Keng S-H, Huffman W. Binge drinking and labor market success: A longitudinal study on young people. *J Popul Econ* 2007; 20:35–54.
33. Wagenaar AC, Toomey TL. Alcohol policy: Gaps between legislative action and current research. *Contemp Drug Probl* 2000; 27:681–733.
34. White V, Hayman J. *Australian Secondary School Students' Use of Alcohol in 2005.* Melbourne: The Cancer Council Victoria; 2006.
35. Hibell B, Guttormsson U, Ahlström S, Balakireva O, Bjarnason T, Kokkevi A, Kraus L. *Substance Use among Students in 35 European Countries. The 2007 ESPAD Report.* Stockholm: The Swedish Council for Information on Alcohol and Other Drugs; 2009.
36. Livingston M, Chikritzhs T, Room R. Changing the density of alcohol outlets to reduce alcohol-related problems. *Drug Alcohol Rev* 2007; 26:557–566.
37. Ragnarsdottir T, Kjartansdottir A, Davidsdottir S. Effect of extended alcohol serving hours in Reykjavik, Iceland. In: Room R, ed. *The Effects of Nordic Alcohol Policies.* Helsinki: Nordic Council for Alcohol and Drug Research; 2002, pp. 145–154.
38. Norstöm T, Skog OJ. Saturday opening of alcohol retail shops in Sweden: An experiment in two phases. *Addiction* 2005; 100:767–776.
39. Hough M, Hunter G, Jacobson J, Cossalter S. *The Impact of the Licensing Act 2003 on Levels of Crime and Disorder: An Evaluation.* London, Home Office, 2008 (Research Report 04) Available at: http://rds.homeoffice.gov.uk/rds/pdfs08/horr04c.pdf. Accessed August 13, 2010.

40. Kypri K, Jones C, McElduff P, Barker D. Effects of restricting pub closing times on night-time assaults in an Australian city. *Addiction*, in press. Available at http://onlinelibrary.wiley.com/doi/10.1111/j.1360-0443.2010.03086.x/full.
41. Duailibi S, Ponicki W, Grube J, Pinsky I, Laranjeira R, Raw M. The effect of restricting opening hours on alcohol-related violence. *Am J Public Health* 2007; 97:2276–280.
42. Dept of Transportation (US), National Highway Traffic Safety Administration (NHTSA). *Traffic Safety Facts 2008: Alcohol-Impaired Driving*. Washington, DC: NHTSA; 2009. Available at http://www-nrd.nhtsa.dot.gov/Pubs/811155.PDF. Accessed August 1, 2010.
43. Ditter SM, Elder RW, Shults RA, Sleet DA, Compton R, Nichols JL. Effectiveness of designated driver programs for reducing alcohol-impaired driving a systematic review. *Am J Prev Med* 2005; 28:280–287.
44. Anderson P, de Bruijn A, Angus K, Gordon R, Hastings G. Impact of alcohol advertising and media exposure on adolescent alcohol use: A systematic review of longitudinal studies. *Alcohol Alcohol* 2009; 44:229–432.

Chapter 8

Community-based approaches to prevention: reducing high-risk drinking and alcohol-related damage among youth and young adults

Norman Giesbrecht[1] and Linda Bosma[2]
[1]Centre for Addiction and Mental Health, Toronto, Ontario, Canada
[2]Bosma Consulting, LLC, Minneapolis, MN, USA

Key points

- Give priority to community-based efforts as a necessary component of comprehensive prevention efforts to reduce and prevent youth alcohol use and misuse.
- Focus on environmental strategies that impact population-based change, rather than programs that target individual change.
- Mobilize the community to gain support for efforts.
- Hire a professional community organizer with the skill set necessary to mobilize the community.
- Avoid "one time only" events that are not part of an ongoing coherent action that creates change.
- Reducing the availability and access to alcohol leads to reduced youth drinking and related problems.
- Focus on efforts that reduce commercial access to alcohol (compliance checks, merchant training, product placement restrictions, reduced outlet density, efforts that reduce young people's ability to obtain alcohol in stores, restaurants, pubs, and bars).
- Focus on efforts that reduce social access to alcohol (restrictions at community festivals/events, family celebrations, home parties, and tolerance of adults who provide alcohol).
- Focus on efforts that target risky drinking by young people (restrictions on cheap drink promotions, happy hours, drinking games and contests, and training of servers and sellers).
- Institutionalize efforts by passing policies and regulations and insuring that resources are provided to enforce them.

The negative health impact of alcohol is among the top ranking risk factors for the global burden of disease and disability.[1] A major study by the World Health Organization

---

Young People and Alcohol: Impact, Policy, Prevention, Treatment, First Edition.
Edited by John B. Saunders and Joseph M. Rey.
© 2011 Blackwell Publishing Ltd. Published 2011 by Blackwell Publishing Ltd.

(WHO)[2] examined 26 risk factors according to their contributions to disability-adjusted life years (DALYs) using 2004 data. The results indicated that the global burden from alcohol use (4.5% of total DALYs) was just below that from unsafe sex (4.6%).[2] In some low mortality countries in South America, the burden is even greater than that of tobacco.[3] Both at the global level and in the established economies such as Australia, Canada, and the United States, the estimated burden from alcohol use in 2004 was greater than the effects of each of the following: overweight and obesity, high blood pressure, high blook glucose, physical inactivity, high cholesterol, and illicit drug use.[2]

In high income economies, the rank order of the *top three* causes of disease and disability were: tobacco (10.7% of DALYs), alcohol (6.7%), and overweight and obesity (6.5%).[2] As reported by Rehm *et. al.*[1] the global damage from alcohol has increased between 2000 and 2004. Alcohol is considered one of the largest avoidable risk factors—even after adjusting for beneficial health effects attributable to alcohol as related to low volume consumption.[1]

Furthermore, in many countries, there has been an increase in recent decades in overall consumption and in the proportion of people drinking in a high-risk manner—such as five or more drinks in one session at least monthly.[1,4] Therefore, unless there is a substantial increase in the scope, intensity and effectiveness of policies and interventions, it is very likely that the burden from alcohol will increase in the coming years.

High-risk drinking negatively impacts all sections of the population; however, this chapter focuses on youth and young adults. While young people may not yet experience high rates of chronic problems related to alcohol use, they do have elevated rates of high-risk drinking, trauma and social problems related to drinking (see Chapters 1 and 2). In many cultures, adolescence is a period of exploration and experimentation, combined with perceptions of invincibility as well as inexperience handling high-risk situations or the physical effects of alcohol.

The focus of this chapter is community-based initiatives that include youth as a focus population. As will be noted, a number of policies and strategies that have been or might be implemented in a community context are outlined and analyzed below. However, some of the interventions that are feasible at a higher jurisdictional level—province, state, or nation—such as control of consumption through alcohol taxes or prices, are not our primary focus (see Chapter 7). Thus, the range of interventions referred to is not comprehensive vis-à-vis youth or young adults. Nevertheless, it is noteworthy that local initiatives can have implications for the alcohol policies at the state/provincial or national levels. The recent history of alcohol control provides a useful context and is dramatically different than tobacco control. Given the legacy of alcohol control's temperance movement's salami tactics of "local option" as a major strategy, the alcohol industry has subsequently striven to keep whatever control there was as centralized as possible.[5] Therefore, it is not surprising that some of the most potent levers for reducing alcohol-related harm[6] are ultimately not determined by local decision makers in many countries but at provincial/state or national levels—these include taxes on alcohol, ceilings on outlet density, type of retailing system, and controls on mass media advertising, especially electronic advertising. In contrast, tobacco control had to start from the ground up, and numerous local initiatives strongly influenced developments at higher jurisdictions.[5]

While there are examples of local initiatives bearing on alcohol policies at the next levels, in many cases there have not been systematic evaluations. The reasons for this are not fully clear, but two might be hypothesized: advocates working at the local level may not be oriented, expected or rewarded for seeking peer-reviewed publications; and in some cases, there is a long lag time between the local efforts and outcomes at the central levels. Although it is easier to find examples of the state restricting the scope of local action rather than local action enhancing the prevention of alcohol problems at a more central level, the extensive impact of advocacy organizations, such as *Mothers Against Drunk Driving*, illustrate how what may start as a local initiative can eventually have substantial impact nationally and internationally.[7] Several other examples illustrate how local initiatives have a bearing on what happens in the larger context or responds to secular change at the national or regional levels.

Since the late 1990s state level tools in Sweden have been crippled since it has joined the European Union, and now it is up to the community level to use what tools it can to reduce alcohol-related problems.[5,8] One such example is the STAD project that started in Stockholm.[9] Communities in Australia and the United Kingdom find themselves hindered by central governments that frequently preempt local ability to restrict alcohol establishments, and the alcohol industry is able to exert significant influence over central governments through lobbying and campaign contributions.[5] Recent developments in Scotland also illustrate how local initiatives have had a bearing on a central campaign to control alcohol-related problems through implementing effective policies.[10]

While centralized controls may preempt local initiatives in some settings, local efforts have proved effective in numerous settings where they have been attempted. Two of these US-based efforts have been rigorously evaluated and been placed on the US government's Substance Abuse and Mental Health Services Administration's National Registry of Evidence-based Programs and Practices. In *Communities Mobilizing for Change on Alcohol*,[11] local policy initiatives resulted in reductions in youth access to alcohol from both commercial and social sources and drunk driving among 18–20-year-old youth. *The Community Trials Intervention*[12] employed zoning and environmental strategies, including reducing outlet density and responsible beverage server trainings, leading to reduced consumption and related problems, including alcohol-related crashes and assaults.

The research by Wagenaar *et al.*[11] and Holder *et al.*[12] has supported local level policy efforts in numerous settings in the United States. Many local jurisdictions have increased efforts to reduce underage alcohol sales through greater enforcement, training servers and sellers of alcohol, and enacting more restrictive local ordinances and regulations.[13] To reduce problems around establishments, local level nuisance and neighborhood livability laws, such as in Puerto Rico, are contributing to reductions in alcohol-related crime. Alcohol restrictions in public places, such as parks or beaches, reduce opportunities for youth to engage in public drinking and parties. Social host laws, which hold adult homeowners accountable for underage drinking parties on their property, are being passed in many cities and counties in the United States, although rigorous study of such laws is still needed.

Furthermore, local initiatives in California employed the planning and zoning and general business licensing authority to build a local alcohol control system and thus evade the limits of the centralized alcohol control laws or regulations that are less restrictive.[5,14] Another US-based example comes from the *Minnesota Join Together Coalition to Reduce Underage Drinking* (MJT), funded by the Robert Wood Johnson Foundation.[15] This statewide policy coalition distributed 82 mini grants over 5 years to local groups including law enforcement and advocacy, youth, and public health groups, encouraging policy efforts at the local level, which also helped build support for MJT's state policy efforts, including passage of a statewide social host law.

Finally, a Canadian example of recurring relevance relates to the repeated initiatives to privatize alcohol retailing in Ontario, as well as other provinces. In 1995, when this proposal was floated in Ontario there was a vocal response from the local boards of health, including letters from municipal medical officers of health drawing attention to the risks of increasing access to alcohol.[16] Subsequent proposals have also faced critiques from Toronto Public Health[17] and other local jurisdictions. Despite numerous initiatives to seek to privatize alcohol retailing, so far the Ontario provincial government still has a large role in day-to-day retailing of alcohol in that province. This may be largely due to a combination of alcohol industry support for the current system, effective union-funded media campaigns against privatized alcohol sales, public opposition to the plan and financial considerations. Nevertheless, the impact of the local public health interventions cannot be considered as inconsequential.[16]

This chapter will discuss community-based policies or prevention strategies focusing on youth and young adults. Several points are noted to frame the material that follows.

- It examines a range of interventions, not just educational programs—which are very popular but typically with no strong evidence of effectiveness.[18] This range includes so-called environmental strategies that focus on broad population level context and social factors that impact drinking by youth and young adults—such as drinking contexts and norms, availability of alcohol, alcohol promotion and marketing and policies that impact distribution, sale and use of alcohol.
- Efforts that reduce commercial access to alcohol (compliance checks, merchant training, product placement, efforts that reduce young people's ability to obtain alcohol in stores, restaurants or bars) are another central theme of this chapter.
- A parallel focus involves efforts that reduce social access to alcohol (at community festivals/events, family celebrations, home parties, tolerance of adults who provide alcohol to youth).
- It will discuss efforts that mobilize the community in supporting these strategies, enforcement of laws and regulations and implementation of policies that are on the books.
- Furthermore the long-term changes in norms with regard to drinking will be an additional foci.
- Looking more broadly, it will comment on avoiding "one time only" events that are not part of an ongoing coherent action that creates change.

In short, the focus is on community-based efforts that curtail inappropriate alcohol use and high-risk drinking among youth and young adults and thus reduce the alcohol-related damage in the jurisdiction.

Evidence

There is an extensive research and evaluation literature on community-based alcohol policies and prevention interventions.[6,19–21] While youth and young adults are not the only
foci, they are central to many projects with their orientation to curtailing high-risk drinking, drinking-related trauma and accidents. In this section, first, we note several secular
developments that have influenced this field. Second, the scope and main designs of this
literature are summarized. Third, we provide examples of community-based interventions
that have reduced high-risk drinking or alcohol-related harm—drawing on experiences in
Europe, North America, South America, and Oceania. Finally, the central features of an
effective intervention are outlined.

Sources of influence

Several secular developments have influenced the emergence in the 1970s and beyond
of community-based interventions focusing on alcohol. Three are highlighted below. The
large-scale prevention programs focusing on reducing smoking and cardiovascular disease
provide a background context.[22] These projects consisted of a combination of public media
and information strategies, and individually focused interventions by health professionals
but, typically, they differed from the alcohol-related programs that followed on several
aspects; while they were conducted in the community, they did not include alcohol as a
risk factor—even though there is substantial evidence that alcohol use is a noteworthy
contributor to cardiovascular disease[23] and interacts with smoking and other risk factors.[24]
Another is the application of randomized control trial designs to the community arena.
Finally, community-based interventions also drew inspiration and techniques from a
range of policy advocacy and community organizing traditions, including the temperance
movement and others.

In the past three decades there has been extensive activity under the general umbrella
of community-based prevention and policies focusing on reducing alcohol-related harm.
Examples are found in Australia, Brazil, Canada, Finland, New Zealand, Norway, Sweden,
the United States, and elsewhere. A series of reports, based on international symposia
on this topic, provide a useful overview of how the field evolved[19,25–29]—including
Larsson and Hanson's[29] report on the proceedings of the first European symposium on
this topic.

While youth or young adults were not the primary focus in all these initiatives, we
know of none where they were excluded, and a number where they were the main or
one of the central foci. Given the relatively short timeframe of these projects—typically
3–5 years—they are likely to focus on outcome variables such as high volume or binge
drinking, trauma or accidents, rather than chronic problems related to alcohol. The former
are more common among younger drinkers than the latter. High-risk drinking and alcohol-
related harm is evident across the lifespan, including damage to innocent children from
drinking by others. However, the prevalence of acute problems tends to be higher in young
adults than older adults.

Context

Community-based prevention initiatives do not operate in a social and cultural vacuum. Their targets, scope and potential influence are enhanced or curtailed by drinking levels and patterns in each jurisdiction, and the alcohol marketing, retailing and control strategies. For the most part, these projects emerged and were implemented when access to alcohol and promotion of alcoholic beverages was on the increase, thus creating unique challenges in reducing alcohol-related harm at the community level, and future projects will likely face comparable challenges.[30] While there have been isolated examples of reduced availability of alcohol or more intensive controls in a host jurisdiction, the dominant pattern worldwide is one of increased availability, reduction in controls, and more extensive and intensive promotion of alcohol products.[6,21] These include structural changes such as higher density of outlets, longer hours of sale, increased diversification of outlets, and decline in the "real price" of alcohol.[4] Deregulation of controls on advertising and monitoring systems is evident,[31] combined with extensive alcohol sponsorship (e.g., of sports) and other types of promotion, extensive internet advertising and flaunting of self-imposed voluntary guidelines set by the alcohol industry. Controlling the *per capita* rate of overall consumption is not a priority of many retailing systems. Furthermore, many government-run retailing systems (such as the Liquor Control Board of Ontario[32]) are oriented to generating more revenue rather than reducing high-risk drinking by controlling overall per capita consumption.[33] In contrast to the epidemiological evidence that alcohol is a major contributor to disease and disability—second behind tobacco in high income countries[1,2]—the most effective levers to manage alcohol problems, typically controlled by central governments, have been devalued or eroded during these decades when community-based prevention initiatives emerged. These contextual developments have proven to be important challenges for community-based projects already completed, and are expected to create strong challenges for future initiatives.

Targets, goals, and interventions

Considered together, these projects have a wide range of targets, goals, and interventions, often involving many sectors of the community and not only medical staff, other health providers or health educators. Given that the most effective interventions involve controlling access to alcohol,[6] the officials who make policy, regulate alcohol sales and distribution, and enforce legislation have key roles to play in these projects. Table 8.1 provides an overview of *foci*, goals, and interventions.

Foci

There are two main types. The first column (far left) of Table 8.1 provides examples of interventions that have the potential for facilitating change in the community on alcohol issues and youth. The second column of Table 8.1 lists those sectors of the community whose drinking behavior or orientation to alcohol is relevant for a successful intervention.

With regard to the targets in the first column, several points need to be emphasized. First, unlike with treatment of those dependent on alcohol, or treatment of injury or disease

Table 8.1 Community-based prevention projects: overview of potential foci, goals, and interventions.

	Foci	Goals–interim	Goals–outcome	Interventions	
Legislators	General population	Raise local awareness of problems	Reduce access to alcohol	Community mobilization	Changes response protocol to alcohol issues
Police/law enforcement	Youth, drinking drivers, public drinkers, violent drinkers	Raise local awareness of response options	Reduce access by youth	Media advocacy	Realign players and local leadership on alcohol issues
Alcohol servers and retailers	Young adults, underage drinkers	Increase effective management	Reduce overall consumption	Capacity development	Policy changes
Social workers	Heavy drinkers	Increase monitoring of retail practices	Reduce high-risk drinking	Information dissemination	Regulatory modifications
Prevention and health promotion specialists	Drinking drivers, heavy drinkers, early experimenters	Increase enforcement of laws	Reduce social problems related to drinking	Education	Change delivery of prevention services
ER personnel; MDs, and other health care staff	Violent drinkers; heavy drinkers who experience injury/complications	Increase prevention activities	Reduce trauma and violence related to drinking	Training	Increase/change law enforcement
Teachers	Adolescents, early experimenters	Develop local alcohol policies	Reduce chronic problems related to drinking	Offer alternatives to drinking or high-risk drinking	
Parents	Victims of alcohol-related problems, adolescent drinkers	Promote institutionalization of prevention strategies and interventions			

related to alcohol use, a successful outcome of prevention programs does not rest solely with one profession or type of expertise. If a measurable positive outcome is to be achieved it is very likely that more than one of the "players" listed in the first column needs to be involved. Prevention and health promotion specialists provide evidence and the rationale for legislators to move forward on harm reduction measures, and law enforcement is required if the legislation is to produce the desired impact. In short, a team approach is signaled by the list in the first column. Not all those listed need to be involved in all interventions, but several are needed, as well as coordination if there are several concurrent efforts. Second, it is desirable that the "team" includes a cross section of those who control alcohol and manage its sale and those who deal more directly with prevention and health promotion issues. Third, the relative importance of the different players is not something that can be determined without reference to the specifics of the community-based effort. For example, physicians may have a pivotal role for some projects, but not for all.

The second column of Table 8.1 illustrates that community-based projects can focus on one or more partially overlapping groups: A general population, heavy or high-risk drinkers, those who have experienced harm from alcohol, and victims of alcohol-related problems. There is a temptation to focus a project too broadly—the general population—or too narrowly—high-risk drinking youth. Given that drinking experiences and problems in a community are influenced by both broad social forces and cultural dimensions, as well as by the behavior of individuals, a combination of broad and narrow population targets is optimal.

Goals

The third column of Table 8.1 labeled "goals-interim" serves two purposes. The list signals what changes are needed to move toward reducing alcohol-related harm and concurrently, if there is progress, noting that some interim positive milestones have been achieved. Note that the goals are a combination of activities designed to raise awareness, program development and implementation, policy development, monitoring and institutional transformation, with considerable variation in the level of difficulty and resources required to implement them.

With regard to the "goals-outcomes" column of Table 8.1, all are important. However, the last four are the *bottom line*: reducing social problems, trauma, violence, and/or chronic problems related to alcohol use. These are the ultimate proof that a community-based project has been successful. Most projects do not achieve these goals during their relatively short time span, although some have demonstrated desired outcomes with regard to the other goals in this list.

Community-based projects face many challenges; three are worth highlighting: (1) Too much is taken on—either there are too many goals, too wide a focus, or trying to involve everyone who has even a passing interest in the issues. This means that limited resources are devoted to a wide range of issues with many diverse interests at the table and a great deal of time is spent on processes that are not outcome oriented; (2) The complexity of the tasks and resources required is underestimated. Staffing may be insufficient or lack appropriate expertise to address the problem, or proposed solutions and strategies may be inadequate for the scope of the problem; (3) Resistance to change may be stronger than expected and may come from unexpected quarters. While it is reasonable to expect opposition to community-based prevention from alcohol suppliers and retailers, some sectors of the treatment community are also know to be either lukewarm or overtly opposed to community-based prevention initiatives.

Interventions

The two far right columns of Table 8.1 list potential interventions. Community mobilization is a core dimension that impacts on the others. Unlike individually oriented approaches, community-based efforts promote population level changes across the community, requiring an engaged citizenry to make those changes. Policy work involves influencing elected officials to take action, but this necessitates public support and public action. A mobilized community also helps ensure follow through and sustainability.

Scope and main designs

There is substantial variation in the scope of community-based projects. Some target specific behaviors, such as drinking and driving, overserving in bars/restaurants, heavy drinking among youth, and so on. This is also evident in the scope of intervention, ranging from single-dimension strategies, to those involving a combination of media advocacy, legislative change, enforcement, community mobilization and institutional change. Some projects run for a few years, others have a longer timeframe with follow-up some years after funding ended. In short, there is no one community-based model that typifies the majority of such initiatives.

There is also considerable variation in the research design. A case study approach that involves primarily anecdotal evaluation is not uncommon. Other projects involve a temporal comparison: Data are gathered at two points in time, or tracked over several years and compared with another community.[34] Several projects have involved matched pairs of communities, including the three matched pairs in the *Community Trials Project* in California and South Carolina,[35] and three pairs in New Zealand.[36] Relatively few have a randomized design. This was the case in *Communities Mobilizing for Change against Alcohol* (CMCA) by Wagenaar and colleagues[11] in this project a total of 15 small communities from Wisconsin and Minnesota were randomly assigned to either the intervention or the comparison group.

Each design has its own unique opportunities and challenges. Documentation of the intervention and how it actually unfolded is often a devalued or neglected aspect. At the end of the day, the evaluators and project managers may know in general terms whether or not the intervention had an impact, but will likely not be able to say which aspects of the intervention were particularly potent, and how this worked.

Another challenge relates to ownership and management of the project, both the overall initiative and the specific aspects. As Robin Room has indicated,[37] these projects involve the convergence of several interests, including research and evaluation, community-based advocacy, policy analysis, and law enforcement. The individuals that represent these interests may have quite different views about what the project is about and how to achieve the perceived aims. In many cases, those conducting the evaluation are also the project managers with vested interest in seeing a positive impact from the intervention.

In other cases, there is an "arms length" arrangement whereby those doing the evaluation are not beholden to the project managers.

Examples of community-based interventions

There have been numerous community-based interventions focused on alcohol.[19,25–29,38–41] In this section, we summarize a few completed projects in several countries (see Table 8.2), that illustrate a range of goals, designs, interventions, and outcomes. A common theme is that they are youth oriented, by design or default. By focusing on violence, drinking and driving, or controlling service of alcohol, these projects are especially relevant to youth and young adults. No standard design is evident. Designs range from a community compared over time to itself—as is evident in a project based in Sao Paulo, Brazil[42]—to random assignment of towns into intervention and control communities.[11] Most have a comparative site or jurisdiction.

All projects used more than one intervention; community organizing is a dominant theme, responsible beverage service and controls on access to alcohol are also noted frequently. In all of these illustrations, the authors conclude that there are some benefits related to the intervention. These benefits range from a dramatic reduction in homicides and assaults in the Brazil-based project,[42] to a perceived reduction in problems in an Ontario-based project.[43] Typically, there are multiple outcomes, with some desired results for some dimensions and equivocal or no impact findings on others.

The projects summarized in Table 8.2 show promise in that there is change in the desired direction; yet, one wonders about the stability of the changes reported. The importance of institutionalizing a project's overall strategy, and its most potent features, is a recurring theme in this literature.[40] For example, after a few years the safety benefits of the Surfer's Paradise project in Australia had been eroded and alcohol management practices went back to preproject levels.[44,45] Maintaining the initial positive impacts is a challenge that can only be addressed through sustained attention and designation of resources required to build local capacity.

Central features of effective interventions

Before turning to a discussion of how to implement community-based approaches, a checklist is provided of 12 central features of an effective community-based intervention drawing on the literature cited, summarized in the tables, and listed in the resources at the end of this chapter:

1. Have clear and attainable goals and objectives—based on knowledge of the community and its resources.
2. Have measurable action steps and operational milestones as agreed upon by the key participants.
3. Focus on frequent and high-risk behavior as compared to infrequent and low-risk behavior.
4. Use research evidence and local monitoring to support the overall prevention plan and specific strategies that are part of this plan.
5. Have an intervention that is of sufficient scope, intensity, capacity, and duration to achieve the desired change, and devote resources to capacity development as needed.

Table 8.2 Examples of community-based intervention projects.

Country and Project ↓	Time	Goals and Focus Areas	Design	Main interventions	Outcomes
Australia[44,45]: *Surfers Paradise Safety Action Project*	Early 1990s	To reduce violence in and around licensed venues Alcohol service and drinking practices in a tourist district.	Intervention community and comparison jurisdiction.	Partnership with university research team, police, health, and government agencies, community, and business groups. Three main strategies: (1) Creation of a community forum including the development of task groups and a safety audit; (2) The implementation of risk assessments, model house policies and a code of practice; (3) Regulation of licensed premises by police and liquor licensing inspectors.	Significant decrease in violence and crime in events that enhanced risky alcohol consumption. Improvements in operation of drinking establishments and treatment of patrons. However, by summer of 1996 (how many years later?) observational data indicated that violence had returned to the preproject levels and compliance with the code of practice had almost ceased.
Brazil[42]:	2000–2005	To reduce homicides and assaults in section of São Paulo.	Time series analysis of monthly data before and after the intervention.	Community mobilization; new restrictions on hours of sale; increase in law enforcement.	A 46% reduction in homicides over 4 years—estimated 528 lives saved. A 26% reduction in assaults over 4 years—estimated 432 assaults prevented.

Canada[43,49]: *Municipal Alcohol Policy (MAP)*	1980 ongoing	To reduce overserving, service to minors, and alcohol-related problems in venues that are owned or managed by a municipality, including special occasion permit events.	Between 1980 and 1996, 177 Ontario communities adopted a MAP and a further 72 had MAPs in development. Evaluation included three types of communities with a matched "control" community for each.	Formation of a policy committee. Committee develops terms of reference and reviews situation. Feedback with community. Policy adopted by municipality. Social marketing to inform community and users of facility.	A survey of 107 communities that had adopted formal policies, 44% reported a reduction in problems, and 7% no reduction. More communities reported a reduction in problems once policies were in place for more than 6 months.
Finland[50,51]: *Lahti project*	1992–1994	Reflexive problem prevention approach.	Comparison of community to self over time and to comparison site qualitative process evaluation and quantitative outcome evaluation.	Educational events, analysis of local key persons' ideas, brief intervention in primary health care, youth work, social surveillance, and responsible service of alcohol.	Heaviest drinking group in Lahti reduced its drinking more than the comparison site. However, overall level of alcohol use did not reduced more than in the comparison site. Public's awareness of alcohol problems increased. People's level of knowledge increased. Prevention message reached its target groups, and were well known. Increase in media articles on prevention. Project created new permanent methods of prevention work in several sectors.

(Continued)

Table 8.2 Examples of community-based intervention projects. (*Continued*)

Country and Project ↓	Time	Goals and Focus Areas	Design	Main interventions	Outcomes
New Zealand[36,52]:	1982–1985 Period of increasing access to alcohol	Alcohol availability and advertising.	Three pairs of cities; one reference pair. Before and after surveys.	Community organizing re policies; counter-advertising campaigns.	No change in support for age restrictions or supermarket sales. No change in avoidance of drinking & drinking to reduce tension, boredom or worries. Increase in support for restrictions on alcohol advertising and price controls. Impact of mass-media campaign plus community action was slightly greater than mass media alone.
Sweden[9]: *STAD project*	1996–2000	To improve server intervention, law enforcement, and reduce violence in entertainment district. Server training, law enforcement.	Compared Stockholm Central with Södermalm, a district with similar characteristics re outlet density and entertainment profile.	Multicomponent: Community mobilizing; responsible beverage service promotion and training; increased law enforcement.	During the intervention period violent crimes decreased in the intervention area. Effect most likely due to a combination of various policy changes initiated by the project.
United States[34]: *Saving Lives Project*	1984–1993	To reduce drinking and driving and increase safety drinking and driving, speeding and pedestrian safety	Six communities with special funding. Five not funded, rest of Massachusetts.	Multicomponent intervention.	Alcohol-related fatal crashes declined in the six intervention communities. Reduced drinking and driving among teenagers.

United States[12,35]: *Preventing Alcohol Trauma: Community Trial*	1993–1998	To reduce alcohol access, drinking and driving, and trauma.	Three intervention and three matched comparison medium sized cities.	Community mobilization; responsible beverage service; reduced alcohol retail availability to minors; alcohol access using local zoning powers; media advocacy.	Self-reported volume consumption per occasion declined, as did "having too much to drink." Self-reported driving "over the legal limit" declined. Nighttime crashes declined and crashes where a driver had been drinking declined. Assaults observed in ER declined and all hospitalized assault injuries also declined.
United States[11,53]: *Communities Mobilizing for Change on Alcohol (CMCA)*	1991–1995	To reduce social and commercial access to alcohol by youth. Reduce alcohol use by 18–20-year-old youth. To reduce arrests and car crashes.	Seven intervention and eight control communities, randomly assigned.	Community organizers worked with local officials, media, schools to reduce youth access to alcohol.	Merchants: more care in sales (check ID more often, decrease in selling to "confederate" buyers). Higher perceived likelihood of being cited by law enforcement agents if selling to minors. Youth (18–20 years of age): less purchasing and consumption of alcohol. Significant decrease in driving while under the influence (DUI) arrests.

6. Use or develop a conceptual model that seeks to explain the linkages between the intervention, the intervening variables, and the desired outcomes.
7. Have a logic model or similar schema that shows the linkages between activities, intervening goals, and final outcomes.
8. Use a combination of interventions focusing on at least two among the three following levels—individual, small group, and the community as a whole.
9. Consider an overall prevention plan that includes a combination of legislative measures—such as policies, regulations, law enforcement—and voluntary measures—such as media advocacy, persuasion, and mobilization.
10. Involve local personnel who have a strong commitment to the harm reduction outcomes of the project.
11. Have a community-based leadership capable of tackling the issues and dealing with vested interests opposed to the goals and vision of the project.
12. Develop a model for project management that is respectful and cognizant of the key vested interests involved, without losing sight of the prevention goals of the project.

Implementing community-based prevention approaches

Effective prevention programming should be comprehensive in nature, and focus on the community as well as the individual. Young people do not make decisions and choices about alcohol use in a vacuum. Community attitudes, tolerance, and acceptance of alcohol use, media, and laws all combine to influence young people's alcohol use. Many endeavors that seek to prevent young people from using or abusing alcohol focus on the individual: educational efforts focus on increasing knowledge of alcohol's risks and harms, treatment and counseling interventions address problem drinking, enforcement strategies target an individual's violation of a the law, such as drinking and driving. Young people's decisions to begin drinking are influenced by the world around them, including families, friends, school, and the larger community and society. While strategies targeting the individual are laudable, they are insufficient unless they are combined with community-based approaches that focus on population-level change.

The reach of strategies that focus on individual change is limited by the resources available and are costly, for example, by requiring continual restocking of curricula and ongoing counseling services for each patient served. Only a handful of classroom-based approaches have data demonstrating sustained behavioral changes as young people enter adulthood[46] (see Chapter 10). Most limiting is the fact that individual strategies must be continually reapplied—teaching a curriculum to one class does nothing to increase knowledge in other classes, and individual counseling and treatment address only the patients who receive these services. Thus, individual approaches can be prohibitively costly while doing nothing to achieve systemic, long-lasting changes across a population.

Community-based approaches focus on change in the larger community, using environmental, policy, and community mobilization strategies to alter the community's norms about youth drinking. Community-based approaches are locally led efforts that engage stakeholders to undertake initiatives that will effect change in their community, for instance, by modifying the overall attitude and norms around alcohol use by young people, and by supporting and encouraging non-use and non-risky use. While laws at provincial, state, of national government level may set limitations for youth drinking, they may be far removed from local conditions. Community-based efforts take the local context into account and seek solutions that are applicable at the local level.

Typically, community-based approaches include the following:

- *Community mobilization:* a professionally trained community organizer who conducts outreach, forms a leadership body, and mobilizes broad support for community level change.
- *Environmental strategies:* Strategies are population based and aim to change the *community* rather than the *individual*. These include reducing outlet density, restricting availability and access, restricting areas where drinking is allowed in public spaces (such as parks), accountability measures aimed at those who serve and sell alcohol, as well as those who provide alcohol.
- *Policy change:* Enactment and enforcement of community level policies, including laws, ordinances and zoning requirements, that regulate drinking behavior and hold adults *and* youth responsible for youth drinking.
- *Media strategies, including media advocacy and social marketing campaigns:* Community efforts are supported by media advocacy such as editorials, letters to the editor, press releases, and earned media (i.e., when coverage of policy work moves into the editorial news cycle of the media, rather than just reprinting press releases or public service announcement) on efforts to increase awareness of alcohol-related problems and support for policy change.
- *Focus on access and availability of alcohol (supply) rather than demand:* reducing easy availability, rather than reducing young people's desire to consume alcohol.
- Increase the cost of alcohol through taxation and set limits on specials and promotions.

To be most effective, community-based approaches should engage a community's citizens and be tailored for the problems specific to that community. While all communities experience problems related to youth drinking, the underlying causes and manifestations vary from one community to another. In one, youth drinking at house parties may be a common source of problems; in another alcohol outlets selling to underage persons or an overconcentration of alcohol outlets in a university area may be the main issues; yet another may face problems associated with a local festival. Thus, communities should start by identifying their local youth drinking problems, and the specific local issues that contribute to youth drinking.

Mobilizing the community

Community problems cannot be solved by an individual or agency alone—they require the engagement of that community. Thus a community organizing approach is essential. A professional community organizer should be hired for this purpose. Efforts without sufficiently skilled community organizing staff will have little success. (Some community resources that offer training in this area are listed in the resources section at the end of the chapter.)

Table 8.3 illustrates a model for implementation of community based prevention programs using a community organizing approach. This table shows the progression from

Table 8.3 A logic model for community based Interventions using community mobilization.

Problems related to youth alcohol use	Underlying causes (why is it a problem?)	Community assessment: identify local causes of youth alcohol use/misuse	Mobilize community	Implementation	Evaluation and adjustments	Long-term outcomes and evaluation
Youth drinking: Early onset, frequency of use, attitudes toward use (e.g., not seen as risky/harmful)	Easy availability	Examine local data	Community outreach (one-on-ones, focus groups, presentations)	Policy passage	Process evaluation to assess levels of community action, policy efforts	Reduction in alcohol-related crime/offenses
Risky drinking behaviors: binge drinking, drinking and driving	→ Community tolerance/acceptance of youth alcohol use	→ Assessment and outreach in community to learn community concerns/resources/issues	→ Create group of committed stakeholders to lead efforts (action team, coalition, etc.)	→ Policy enforcement	→ Monitor enforcement (level to which new laws are being enforced)	→ Reduced availability of alcohol (e.g., young people report that alcohol is less readily available from commercial and social sources)

Alcohol-related harms: violence, assaults, date rape, victim of violence	→	Adult provision of alcohol (parents, other adults, older sibling, and friends provide alcohol)	→	Assess local community for outlet density, advertising saturation, alcohol placement and promotions	→	Develop action plan of environmental and policy approaches	→	Policy monitoring to ensure enforcement is occurring	→	Ongoing policy analysis	→	Age of onset of drinking is older
		Commercial sales to underage persons and overservice in bars/restaurants		Identify local sources of alcohol		Media advocacy		Media advocacy		Media content analysis		Reduced frequency of youth drinking
		Insufficient alcohol control policies and insufficient enforcement of existing policies		Assess existing policies		Advocate with decision makers (elected officials, police chiefs, etc.)						Reduced binge drinking and related problems by youth

problem identification through successful policy passage and implementation, and the typical outcomes.

While there are several models of community organizing, all employ several basic steps (such as this basic model described by Bosma *et al.*)[47]:

- *Step one—assessment*. Identify community members' concerns about alcohol problems, including their self-interest (what motivates them to be worried about the issue); learn what resources exist and the history of past attempts. Keep in mind that different stakeholders will be impacted differently, so it is important to talk with many people to learn how they view youth drinking problems. Talk to a broad range of people in the community, by setting up face-to-face meetings—often called "one-on-ones" (see Box 8.1). For example, a concentration of alcohol outlets near a university campus may contribute to high rates of binge drinking. For youth, this may create a difficult environment for study and peer pressure to engage in risky drinking. For neighbors, it may mean property damage, loitering, and disruptive behavior. Alcohol outlet owners may resent what they see as interference by the community. Nonalcohol businesses may find it difficult to attract customers who are deterred by the area's reputation as a drinking spot. Lecturers may be frustrated by students missing classes, attending with hangovers, and performing poorly on their coursework. The university administration may be concerned that their school has gained a reputation for heavy drinking and be anxious about liability. Local police may feel overburdened by excessive police calls to the area. All parties may feel they are the only ones concerned about the problem.

Box 8.1   "One-on-ones"—the building blocks of community organizing.

"One-on-ones" help community organizers know people's level of support and concern, and build the relationships that undergird community mobilization efforts. "The one-on-one is an essential part of community organizing that begins the necessary relationship building and lays the foundation for the work that follows. A one-on-one is a personal, face-to-face conversation with an individual community member to learn about his/her self-interest and concerns relative to the project's goals, level of interest and commitment for project issues, and the resources they might bring to a project. During the one-on-one, the organizer asks probing questions to learn the community members' concern and level of interest, and introduces the project to get reactions to it. It is important to note that the one-on-one is not a survey, but rather an interactive dialogue."[47] (See reference 47, p. 10.)

The Midwest Academy, which trains community organizers in the United States, stresses the value of building these relationships through individual contacts: "The personal is political: Organizing is overwhelmingly about personal relationships. It is about changing the world and changing how individuals act together. The relationships organizers develop are their most important resource and most important talent."[48] (See reference 48, p. 6.)

In addition, local data should be assessed where available. Identify and obtain existing information on alcohol-related problems. This may include student survey data to learn more about the prevalence of use, crime statistics, drink driving statistics, and existing policies. Other information should include reviewing City Council actions regarding alcohol policy to learn about local government's receptivity to regulation and zoning related to alcohol outlets, becoming familiar with local media sources and the stories they cover, and identifying key groups and stakeholders.

- *Step two—creating an "action team"*. Form a group of committed citizens/stakeholders who are committed to the issue and to a systems approach that will lead efforts (this group may be called a coalition, task force, action team, or committee). Members should be willing to devote time, be committed to pursuing a community approach, and able to contribute to the process. This group may not necessarily have much knowledge about alcohol prevention or addiction. Rather, these are people who are concerned about the issue as a *community problem* and want to change the environment that promotes and tolerates youth alcohol use and problems. People who want to work on individual approaches may not be well suited for the group, as even if they have a strong concern about youth drinking, they may only be interested in pursuing options that address individual behaviors.

- *Step three—make an action plan*. The leadership group should brainstorm and research possible strategies to address their community's problems. Identify the environmental and policy changes that can address these problems. Is a new or stronger law needed? Will a zoning change be necessary? Do people serving alcohol need training on preventing underage sales or about serving intoxicated patrons? Are policies needed for owners of establishments that sell liquor? Are existing laws sufficiently enforced? Does the community need more information on its role and what it can do to reduce youth drinking? Are there problem alcohol outlets that need to be encouraged to run their establishments more responsibly, or even be closed? Can special events restrict sale and consumption of alcohol to a limited area and limit amount of sales?

  Environmental approaches require thoughtful methods and strategic application. The leadership group creates an action plan of concrete steps to move the issue forward, with efforts focused on action not just activities, with each step strategically building on the previous step and contributing to the ultimate goal. This requires the leadership group to think beyond its next meeting, about its long-term goals, and what steps will need to be taken to achieve them. In the previous example, the group might decide what is needed to address overconsumption by youth at bars near the college: Is it a city ordinance that mandates Responsible Beverage Server training for all workers at alcohol outlets? A change in the city's zoning requirements to reduce the overconcentration of bars in a small area? A campus policy that has consequences for alcohol-related problems? A special entertainment tax on the campus area bars to pay for added police enforcement of minimum age of sale laws and address problems? Environmental changes take substantial effort and time to implement, and your goals will need to be long term.

- *Step four—mobilization and action*. Additional "one-on-ones" and outreach to introduce and frame the issue to the broader public, increase awareness, meeting with decision makers and elected officials, targeted actions and tactics to influence public opinion and leaders, media advocacy. Once the action plan is created, the group begins mobilizing support in the community, increasing awareness of the problems and its proposed solutions, and garnering support from decision makers. Group members meet with individual community members, including citizens, decision makers, influential persons, community leaders, and elected officials to garner support. Presentations are made to groups and organizations. The group uses media advocacy to promote efforts, writes letters to the editor, and holds meetings with editorial staff. Direct actions may be taken by holding events that promote awareness and hold decision makers accountable. Key meetings are held with elected officials, to introduce the topic and identify support.

- *Step five—implementation.* Strategic implementation of the action plan and policies, including monitoring and adjustments of goals as needed when successes and challenges are encountered, holding decision makers accountable.
- *Step six—evaluation.* Successful groups evaluate their progress. It is important to evaluate *community* outcomes, not just *individual* outcomes. Policy work takes substantial time; changes in individual drinking rates and prevalence should not be expected until other successes are realized. Thus, it is important to track policy *progress* such as increased involvement and support, changes in practices, and changes in the community's environment.

The importance of policy

Environmental approaches should be supported and institutionalized by policy. While voluntary efforts may be an initial way to move forward, they are dependent on supportive individuals and the current political climate; normal turnover in a police department or city council can bring a voluntary effort to an abrupt end. Thus, many environmental approaches need to be enacted into public policy to be most effective. In order to be effective, policy must be passed, publicized, and enforced.

Table 8.4 summarizes policy approaches that can lead to reductions in youth alcohol consumption and related problems. This list is not exhaustive, and local groups are encouraged to explore sites listed in the resources section of this chapter for additional ideas. The key issue is to look at policies that will address the concerns specific to your community.

Key points on how to proceed

- *Identify youth alcohol problems that are specific to your community.* It is essential to identify the issues that are most problematic in *your* community in order to identify the best solutions. A community should identify the local circumstances that enable young people to obtain and drink alcohol. Every community has its unique problems related to youth drinking—focusing on a policy that does not address a problem in your community will garner limited support and have little or no impact.
- *Identify approaches that address your community's specific youth drinking issues.* Be sure that the community-based approaches you promote apply to your community's problems.
- *Hire a professional community organizer.* Mobilizing the community requires a unique skill set; many groups struggle because they do not hire someone with the necessary mobilizing skills to engage the community. Resist the temptation to move an existing staff person into this position; seek out an experienced community organizer with demonstrated skills at mobilizing communities and successfully working on policy and

Table 8.4 Policies that address youth alcohol consumption and related problems.

Policy	Problems addressed	Capacity/enforcement need	Outcome/result
Restrict alcohol possession and consumption in public spaces	Public intoxication/drinking and related noise/litter/violence in public spaces	Police regularly patrol park (public area) to enforce policy; post signs prohibiting alcohol and encourage reporting, neighboring residents and businesses monitor and call police	Youth alcohol use and accompanying noise, litter, and violence problems no longer tolerated by community. Park is restored to original use
Place restrictions on alcohol licensees regarding over service, enforce public intoxication laws, require RBS and outlets to enact policies for employees	Bar/pub over serves young adult drinkers to the point of intoxication; rowdy behavior in nearby neighborhood	Police work with owner regarding enforcement issues, patrol bar at closing times, neighbors track and report problems, servers/sellers must learn signs of intoxication/over service	Bar is cited when violations occur, leading to either compliance to avoid future sanctions or eventual loss of license due to refusal to cooperate and comply
Conduct compliance checks to monitor compliance with minimum age of sale laws and procedures for checking age identification	Service to underage persons and problems related to youth alcohol consumption in and around establishments that sell/serve alcohol	Police resources and staffing necessary to conduct compliance checks, support from elected officials and community	Outlets operate more responsibly and underage access to alcohol is reduced
Restrict sales of alcohol at events, including amount of alcohol sold and end service well before end of event (sixth inning, third quarter, etc.); train servers, increase patrols, create family only seating sections where no alcohol is allowed	Crowds of over intoxicated patrons at sporting events, disruptive behavior, fighting, and related problems in neighborhoods around stadiums where sporting events are held	Training stadium servers, enforcement of sales	Reduced overintoxication at events and reduced related violence

(Continued)

Table 8.4 Policies that address youth alcohol consumption and related problems. (*Continued*)

Policy	Problems addressed	Capacity/enforcement need	Outcome/result
Limit drink specials, enforce age of sale laws, train servers, decrease outlet density near campus, conditional use permits; restrictions on promotions (drink specials, happy hours, etc.) and advertising	Bars surrounding college campus serve underage persons and over serve patrons	Police and license enforcement, compliance checks, additional patrols, license monitoring	Reduced service to underage persons and reductions in overintoxication, decreased density, less availability, less promotion of alcohol
Increase taxes on alcohol	Alcohol costs make it easily accessible for young people and encourage overdrinking; alcohol's societal costs exceed public revenue raised through taxation	Knowledge of tax codes, public support for tax increases, political will to raise taxes	Revenues are increased, allowing for greater enforcement and prevention activities; increased price of alcohol leads to reduced demand and consumption
Limit and reduce outlet density	Overconcentration of alcohol outlets is associated with violence and other problems	Knowledge of zoning and municipal codes, public support, political support from elected officials	Fewer outlets reduce availability of alcohol which leads to lower consumption and reduction in alcohol-related crime and violence
Limits hours of sale and operation for alcohol establishments	Alcohol outlets are open for long hours, making it easy to obtain alcohol	Knowledge of zoning and municipal codes, public support, political support from elected officials	Outlets are open fewer hours, reducing consumption and alcohol-related problems
Require warning labels and signage at establishments that sell/serve alcohol	General public lacks awareness of risk and harm related to alcohol use; servers/sellers need additional support and reminders of laws related to sales and service of alcohol	Knowledge of existing laws to determine appropriate method for enactment and application, public support, political support from elected officials	Limits alcohol consumption in places such as parks, parking lots, malls, and other public areas where alcohol consumption may occur and where young people may be at risk for obtaining and consuming alcohol; prohibits all consumption or possession in public spaces

Low risk drinking guidelines	Public misperception about the "beneficial" effects and/or lack of risk to consuming small amounts of alcohol	Understanding of research on risks and harms of alcohol use, political will of regulatory bodies, counter-marketing to alcohol industry promotions	Increases public awareness of the risks of consuming even small amounts of alcohol
Minimum legal drinking age	Public misperception that young people need to "learn" to drink and lack of awareness of the damage and risks related to use at younger ages	Political will at state, provincial, or national levels to pass minimum age of sale laws, strong public support, and advocacy	Reduces consumption by young adults and youth and leads to reduced alcohol-related problems, including car crashes
Controls on advertising	Marketing targets young people and promotes high-risk drinking behaviors such as drinking and driving, engaging in recreational activities while drinking, or excessive consumption	Political will of regulatory bodies and public support	Prohibits alcohol industry advertising that targets young people and minimizes risks of alcohol consumption
Social host ordinances	Parents and adults host parties where young people are allowed to consume alcohol in homes with limited or no supervision	Public support for passage, political support at local levels to pass policy	Hold parents/home owners responsible for underage drinking on their property, reducing the likelihood that parents will host underage drinking parties

systems-change efforts. If your agency does not have the option of hiring someone new with experience, sufficient community organizing training should be provided.

- *Mobilize and engage the community.* The support and participation of the community is essential for successful community based approaches. Sufficient community support is necessary to convince decision makers to implement changes, whether it is passage of laws by elected officials, law enforcement, or changing practices within alcohol outlets. Initiatives without sufficient community support and engagement are unlikely to be sustained over time.
- *Be strategic: action (not activities).* Policy work is a concerted, ongoing action—not merely a collection of activities. Efforts should strategically target specific interim goals that build toward and lead to eventual policy adoption. Any action the group takes should build on a previous action and be a step that contributes toward ultimate enactment of the group's policy goals.
- *Policy Passage—do not stop now!* Once your policy is passed, monitor and support its implementation. There are often challenges in the initial implementation stage. It is important to stay involved to ensure the policy gets implemented, and to support the agencies responsible for the changes. Law enforcement may need additional resources, education, support, or encouragement, or there may be shortcomings in the law that need to be modified. Do not assume your group's work is done when the policy is adopted.
- *Evaluation and adjustments.* Use evaluation measures that assess the environment, *not* individual outcomes. While environmental approaches will eventually lead to reductions in individual alcohol use, initial evaluation measures should focus more on the policy's implementation success. This includes measures such as how many individuals are trained, specific changes in practices at an establishment or festival, reduced sales to underage persons, reductions in police calls to parties, and fewer emergency department admissions by youth with alcohol poisoning.

In conclusion, we might point to several interrelated themes for future consideration in community-based prevention projects focusing on young people and alcohol. First, while many community-based interventions are evaluated, not all, and possibly not even the majority of these are published. Therefore, those who manage these projects and secure the funds need to place high priority to have the outcomes published so that the available literature better reflects the range of processes and outcomes and therefore provides an enhanced resource for new initiatives.

Second, as related to the first point, the published evaluations or projects with the most thorough evaluation may not reflect the most potent interventions. Projects that have considerable success in achieving interim and outcome goals may be very time consuming to the team and getting the results in peer-reviewed publications may not be a high priority unless this is part of the work expectations as in academic settings.

Third, to our knowledge there is no central repository or tracking system whereby one can get a handle on current or recent projects. The basic information might be structured and have space limitations so as not be a burden for the reader. It might include the following summary information: Project principal investigator and contact person, timeframe, location, source of funding, main goals and foci, social context of the project, main intervention strategies and focus populations, interim results and outcomes (if available), policy implications, web site (if available), and date that this information was posted or updated. This would allow institutions or organizations starting new projects to determine similar or comparative initiatives, and, combined with the published literature, obtain a "state-of-the-art" overview of the most relevant projects. Encouraging information exchange across jurisdictions is expected to promote more effective interventions.

Acknowledgments

This chapter has benefited from access to slide presentation by Harold Holder at the Folkhälsostämman, Stockholm, Sweden, March 12–14, 2003. It is based, in part, on a plenary presentation by N. Giesbrecht at the Australian Professional Society on Alcohol and Other Drug Conference, Cairns, November 5–8, 2006, and a 2003 publication by N. Giesbrecht in *Nordisk Alkohol & Narkotikatidskrift* [41]. With regard to Norman Giesbrecht's contribution, we acknowledge that support to the Centre for Addiction and Mental Health for the salary of scientists and infrastructure has been provided by the Ontario Ministry of Health and Long Term Care.

We thank the editors of this volume for their suggestions. Robert Nash Parker and Robin Room provided insightful comments and directed us to resource material. The views and opinions expressed in this chapter are those of the authors and do not necessarily reflect those of the persons acknowledged.

Resources

- Bonnie RJ, O'Connell ME, eds. *Reducing Underage Drinking: A Collective Responsibility.* Washington, DC: The National Academies Press; 2004.
- Bobo K, Kendall J, Max S. *Organizing for Social Change: Midwest Academy Manual for Activists.* Santa Ana, CA, Minneapolis, MN, Washington, DC: Seven Locks Press; 2001.
- Casswell S, Thamarangsi T. Alcohol and Global Health 3: Reducing harm from alcohol: Call to action. *Lancet* 2009; 373:2247–2257.
- Giesbrecht N, Rankin J. Reducing alcohol problems through community action research projects: Contexts, strategies, implications and challenges. *Subst Use Abuse* 2000; 35 (1&2):31–53.
- Giesbrecht N. Alcohol, tobacco and local control: A comparison of several community-based prevention trials. *Nordic Stud Alcohol Drugs* 2003; (English supplement) 20:25–40.
- Kahn S. *Organizing: A Guide for Grassroots Leaders.* Washington, DC: National Association of Social Workers; 1991.
- United States Department of Health and Human Services. *The Surgeon General's Call to Action to Prevent and Reduce Underage Drinking.* Washington, DC: US Department of Health and Human Services, Office of the Surgeon General; 2007. http://www.surgeongeneral.gov/topics/underagedrinking/.

Internet resources

Two programs in the United States are listed on the Substance Abuse and Mental Health Services (SAMHSA) National Registry of Evidence-Based Programs and Practices (NREPP): Communities Mobilizing for Change on Alcohol and the Community Trials Intervention to Reduce High Risk Drinking. Both have information available online and offer training to community groups. Programs from other countries are also listed below.

- *Communities Mobilizing for Change on Alcohol (CMCA).* Description of research and outcomes: http://www.epi.umn.edu/alcohol/cmca/index.shtm and http://www.nrepp.samhsa.gov/programfulldetails.asp?PROGRAM_ID = 116 . CMCA training is provided by the Youth Leadership Institute: http://yli.org/cmca/index.php. CMCA is a community organizing approach to reduce youth access to alcohol from commercial and social sources by enacting and enforcing local policies. The original research was conducted by Alexander Wagenaar and colleagues at the University of Minnesota.
- *Community Trials Intervention to Reduce High Risk Drinking.* Description of research and outcomes: http://www.nrepp.samhsa.gov/programfulldetails.asp?PROGRAM_ID = 161. Information on the original research, environmental prevention strategies, and training is available through the Pacific Institute for Research and Evaluation (PIRE) at: http://www.pire.org/communitytrials/index.htm. The Community Trials Intervention uses a "coalition" model to implement environmental interventions to enact and enforce policies and regulations to restrict alcohol access and outlet density to reduce underage and high-risk drinking. The original research was conducted by Harold Holder and colleagues at the Prevention Research Center.
- *OJJDP Model Programs Guide.* Provides descriptions of and rates evidence for youth-oriented interventions, many of which are relevant to the prevention of substance use and abuse. http://www.dsgonline.com/mpg2.5/mpg_htm; http://www2.dsgonline.com/mpg/program_types_description.aspx?program_type = Community%20Awareness%20/%20Mobilization&continuum = prevention.
- *The AERC Alcohol Academy.* Established by the Alcohol Education and Research Council in the United Kingdom, the Alcohol Academy provides information on resources, research and training to prevent harms related to alcohol use. http://www.alcoholacademy.net/.
- *The Alcohol Policy Network.* Provides information on resources and strategies in Ontario, Canada, including information packs for community members, current legislation efforts, and workshops and forums. http://www.apolnet.ca/Index.html.
- *The AER Center for Alcohol Policy Research.* Research on alcohol policy, outlet density, and alcohol harms in Australia. http://www.turningpoint.org.au/research/alcohol_policy_research/alcohol_policy_research_about.htm.
- *The Alcohol Epidemiology Program (AEP) at the University of Minnesota.* This site includes information for practitioners and researchers. It includes current research conducted by the AEP, including PDF files of peer-reviewed articles on community based environmental and policy approaches, and many practitioner tools such as sample

policy components, a compliance checks manual, fact sheets, and tips on approaches with different community sectors. http://www.epi.umn.edu/alcohol/.

- *Underage Drinking Enforcement Training Center (UDETC).* UDETC has resources on research and strategies aimed at enforcing underage drinking laws. The site offers publications, research, and success stories of community efforts. UDETC also offers regular free electronic seminars on underage drinking prevention topics that feature successful community examples. http://www.udetc.org/.
- *Center for Alcohol Marketing to Youth (CAMY).* Alcohol marketing and influence on youth, including information on research, fact sheets, and action that communities can take. http://camy.org/.
- *FACE*®. An online action guide for community members is featured on the site. FACE® also offers training and has numerous resources available for purchase that focus on community based environmental prevention. http://www.faceproject.org/.
- *Social Host.org.* Social host ordinances are increasingly used to hold adults accountable for underage alcohol use in home setting where an adult should reasonable be able to prevent underage drinking. This site includes information about social host ordinances, how they work, and implementation information for the state of California. http://socialhost.org/.
- *Preventing Binge Drinking.* A project of the Center for Applied Research Solutions (CARS), practitioners can find resources and strategies for work with communities, parents, agencies, and schools to prevent and reduce high-risk (binge) drinking. http://www.youthbingedrinking.org/index.php.
- *The Power of Parents.* This site focuses on parents and what they can do to prevent underage drinking. The site is hosted by MADD (Mothers Against Drunk Drivers) and allows parents to ask researchers questions about teen drinking issues. http://www.thepowerofparents.org/.

References

1. Rehm J, Mathers C, Popova S, Thavorncharoensap M, Teerawattananon Y, Patra J. Alcohol and Global Health 1: Global burden of disease and injury and economic cost attributable to alcohol use and alcohol-use disorders. *Lancet* 2009; 373:2223–2233.
2. World Health Organization. *Global health risks. Mortality and burden of disease attributable to selected major risks.* Geneva: World Health Organization; 2009. Available at: www.who.int/healthinfo/global_burden_disease/GlobalHealthRisks_reportfull.pdf. Accessed January 25, 2011.
3. Monteiro M.G. *Alcohol and Public Health in the Americas: A Case for Action.* Washington, DC: Pan American Health Organization; 2007.
4. Anderson P, Chisholm D, Fuhr D. Alcohol and Global Health 2: Effectiveness and cost–effectiveness of policies and programmes to reduce the harm caused by alcohol. *Lancet* 2009; 373:2234–2246.
5. Room R. Personal communication, April 28, 2010.
6. Babor T, Caetano R, Casswell S, Edwards G, Giesbrecht N, Grube J, Hill L, Holder H, Homel R, Livingstone M, Österberg E, Rehm J, Room R, Rossow I. *Alcohol: No ordinary commodity—research and public policy—Second edition.* Oxford: Oxford University Press; 2010.

7. Fell JC, Voas RB. Mothers Against Drunk Driving [MADD]: The first 25 years. *Traffic Inj Prev* 2006; 7:195–212.
8. Holder HD, ed. *Sweden and the European Union: Changes in National Alcohol Policy and Their Consequences.* Stockholm: Almqvist & Wiksell International; 2000.
9. Wallin E, Gripenberg J, Andréasson S. Over-serving at licensed premises in Stockholm: Effects of a community action program. *J Stud Alcohol* 2005; 66:806–814.
10. Brown S. *Response to the call for evidence for the Alcohol Commission.* Prepared for Alcohol Focus Scotland, 2010. Available at: http://www.alcohol-focus-scotland.org.uk/pdfs/Response to the Alcohol Commission 20 Feb 2010.pdf.
11. Wagenaar AC, Murray DM, Toomey TL. Communities Mobilizing for Change on Alcohol (CMCA): Effects of a randomized trial on arrests and traffic crashes. *Addiction* 2000; 95:209–217.
12. Holder HD, Gruenewald PJ, Ponicki WR, Treno AJ, Grube JW, Saltz RF, Voas RB, Reynolds R, Davis J, Sanchez L, Gaumont G, Roeper P. Effects of community-based interventions on high-risk drinking and alcohol-related injuries. *JAMA* 2000; 284:2341–2347.
13. Stewart K, Pacific Institute of Research and Evaluation. First printing 1999, revised for fourth printing. *Strategies to Reduce Underage Alcohol Use: Typology and Brief Overview.* Calverton, MD; 2009.
14. Wittman F. *Prevention by Design: Community Planning for Safe and Healthy Environments.* Community Prevention Planning Program at the Institute for the Study of Social Change, University of California at Berkeley; 2007. Available at: http://socrates.berkeley.edu/~pbd/planning_guide.html.
15. Bosma LM, Nachbar J. Using mini-grants as a method to encourage alcohol policy activity: Five years of experience from the Minnesota Join Together Mini Grants Program. Presented at the American Public Health Association, Annual Meeting, November 2005.
16. Giesbrecht N, Stoduto G, Kavanagh L. Privatization postponed? Ontario's experience with convergent interests and extensive alcohol marketing. In: Giesbrecht N, Demers A, Ogborne A, Room R, Stoduto G, Lindquist E, eds. *Sober Reflections: Commerce, Public Health, and the Evolution of Alcohol Policy in Canada. 1980–2000.* Montreal: McGill-Queen's University Press; 2006, pp. 175–200.
17. Toronto Public Health. *A Public Health Response to the Proposed LCBO Franchise System.* Toronto Public Health; 2002.
18. Giesbrecht N. Reducing alcohol-related damage in populations: Rethinking the roles of education and persuasion interventions. *Addiction* 2007; 101:1345–1349.
19. Giesbrecht N, Conley P, Denniston R, Gliksman L, Holder H, Pederson A, Room R, Shain M, eds. *Research, Action, and the Community: Experiences in the Prevention of Alcohol and Other Drug Problems.* Rockville, MD: Office for Substance Abuse Prevention; 1990.
20. Edwards G, Anderson P, Babor TF, Casswell S, Ferrence R, Giesbrecht N, Godfrey C, Holder HD, Lemmens P, Mäkelä K, Midanik LT, Norström T, Österberg E, Romelsjö A, Room R, Simpura J, Skog O-J. *Alcohol Policy and the Public Good.* Oxford: Oxford University Press; 1994.
21. Babor T, Caetano R, Casswell S, Edwards G, Giesbrecht N, Graham K, Grube J, Gruenewald P, Hill L, Holder H, Romel R, Österberg E, Rehm J, Room R, Rossow R. *Alcohol, no Ordinary Commodity: Research and Public Policy.* Oxford: Oxford University Press; 2003.
22. Holder HD, Howard J, eds. *Methodological Issues in Community Prevention Trials for Alcohol Problems.* Westport, CT: Praeger; 1992, pp. 97–112.
23. Puddey IB, Rakic V, Dimmitt SB, Beilin LJ. Influence of pattern of drinking on cardiovascular disease and cardiovascular risk factors: A review. *Addiction* 1999; 94:649–663.

24. Zeka A, Gore R, Kriebel, D. Effects of alcohol and tobacco on aerodigestive cancer risks: A meta-regression analysis. *Cancer Causes Control* 2003; 14:897–906.

25. Greenfield TK, Zimmerman R, eds. *CSAP Prevention Monograph—14: Second International Research Symposium on Experiences with Community Action Projects for the Prevention of Alcohol and Other Drug Problems*. Washington, US: Department of Health and Human Services; 1993.

26. World Health Organization. *Community Action to Prevent Alcohol Problems*. Papers presented at the Third Symposium on Community Action Research, Greve, Chianti, Italy, September 25–29, 1995. Copenhagen: World Health Organization; 1998.

27. Casswell S, Holder H, Holmila H, Larsson S, Midford R, Moewaka Barnes H, Nygaard P, Stewart L, eds. *Kettil Bruun Society Thematic Meeting Fourth Symposium on Community Action Research and the Prevention of Alcohol and Other Drug Problems*. Auckland, New Zealand: Alcohol and Public Health Research Unit, University of Auckland; 1999.

28. Allamani A, Casswell S, Graham K, Holder HD, Holmila M, Larsson S, Nygaard P. Introduction: Community action research and the prevention of alcohol problems at the local level. *Subst Use Misuse* 2000; 35:1–10.

29. Larrsson S, Hanson BS, eds. *Community-based Alcohol Prevention in Europe—Research and Evaluations*. Lund: Lunds Universitet; 1999.

30. Holmila M. The Finnish case: Community prevention in a time of rapid change in national and international trade. *Subst Use Misuse* 2000; 35:111–123.

31. Ogborne A, Stoduto G. Changes in federal regulation of broadcast advertisements for alcoholic beverages. In: Giesbrecht N, Demers A, Ogborne A, Room R, Stoduto G, Lindquist E, eds. *Sober Reflections: Commerce, Public Health, and the Evolution of Alcohol Policy in Canada, 1980–2000*. Montreal: McGill-Queen's University Press; 2006, pp. 237–259.

32. Liquor Control Board of Ontario. *Annual Report: Our Eight Straight Record Year*. Toronto: LCBO Corporate Communications; 2002–2003.

33. Giesbrecht N. Roles of commercial interests in alcohol policies: Recent developments in North America. *Addiction* 2000; 95(Suppl. 4): S581–S595.

34. Hingson R, McGovern T, Howland J, Heeren T, Winter M, Zxakoes R. Reducing alcohol-impaired driving in Massachusetts: The Saving Lives Program. *Am J Public Health* 1996; 86:791–797.

35. Holder HD, Saltz RF, Grube JW, Treno AJ, Reynolds RI, Voas RB, Gruenewald PJ. Summing up: Lessons from a comprehensive community prevention trial. *Addiction* 1997; 92 (sup 2): S293–S301.

36. Casswell S, Gilmore L. An evaluated community action project on alcohol. *J Stud Alcohol* 1989; 50:339–346.

37. Room R. Introduction: Community action and alcohol problems: The demonstration project as an unstable mixture. In: Giesbrecht N, Conley P, Denniston R, Gliksman L, Holder H, Pederson A, Room R, Shain M., eds. *Research, Action, and the Community: Experiences in the Prevention of Alcohol and Other Drug Problems*. Rockville, MD: Office for Substance Abuse Prevention; 1990, pp. 1–25.

38. Hydman B, Giesbrecht N, Bernardi DR, Coston N, Douglas RR, Ferrence RG, Gliksman L, Goodstadt MS, Graham DG, Loranger PD. Preventing substance abuse through multi-component community action research projects: Lessons from past experiences and challenges for future initiatives. *Contemp Drug Probl* 1992; (19): 133–164.

39. Giesbrcht N, Ferris J. Community-based research initiatives in prevention. *Addiction* 1993; 88 (Suppl.):83S–93S.

40. Giesbrecht N, Rankin J. Reducing alcohol problems through community action research projects: Contexts, strategies, implications & challenges. *Subst Use Misuse* 2000; 35:31–53

41. Giesbrecht N. Alcohol, tobacco and local control: A comparison of several community-based prevention trials. *Nordic Stud Alcohol Drugs* 2003; (English supplement) 20:25–40.

42. Duailibi S, Ponicki W, Grube J, Pinsky I, Laranjeira R, Raw M. The effect of restricting opening hours on alcohol-related violence. *Am J Public Health* 2007; 97:2276–2280.

43. Gliksman L, Douglas RR, Rylett M, Narbonne-Fortin C. Reducing problems through municipal alcohol policies: The Canadian experience in Ontario. *Drugs Educ Prev Policy* 1995; 2:105–118.

44. Homel R, Burrows T, Gross J, Herd B, Ramsden D, Teague R. *Preventing Violence: A review of the literature on violence and violence prevention*. A report prepared for the Crime Prevention Division of the NSW Attorney General's Department; 1999.

45. Homel R, Carvolth R, Hauritz M, McIllwain G, Teague R. Making licensed venues safer for patrons: What environmental factors should be the focus of interventions? *Drug Alcohol Rev* 2004; 23:19–29.

46. Komro KA, Toomey TL. Strategies to prevent underage drinking. *Alcohol Res Health* 2002; 26:5–14.

47. Bosma LM, Komro KA, Perry CL, Veblen-Mortenson S, Farbakhsh K. Community organizing to prevent youth drug use and violence: The D.A.R.E. Plus Project. *J Community Pract* 2005; 13; 5–19.

48. Bobo K, Kendall J, Max S. *Organizing for Social Change: Midwest Academy Manual for Activists*. Santa Ana, CA, Minneapolis, MN, Washington, DC: Seven Locks Press; 2001.

49. Gliksman L, Douglas R, Rylett M. Two decades of municipal alcohol policy development: Challenges, solutions and findings in a Canadian province. In: Casswell S, Holder H, Holmila H, Larsson S, Midford R, Moewaka Barnes H, Nygaard P, Stewart L, eds. *Kettil Bruun Society Thematic Meeting Fourth Symposium on Community Action Research and the Prevention of Alcohol and Other Drug Problems*. Auckland, New Zealand: Alcohol and Public Health Research Unit, University of Auckland; 1999.

50. Holmila M. *Community Prevention of Alcohol Problems*. London: Macmillan; 1997.

51. Holmila M. Community-based prevention of alcohol problems: A case study from Lahti, and its lessons for future prevention research in Finland. In: Larsson S, Hanson BS, eds. *Community-based Alcohol Prevention in Europe—Research and Evaluations*. Lund: Lunds Universitet; 1999.

52. Casswell S, Ransom R, Gilmore L. Evaluation of a mass-media campaign for the primary prevention of alcohol-related problems. *Health Promot Int* 1990; 5:9–17.

53. Wagenaar AC, Gehan JP, Jones-Webb R, Toomey TL, Forser JL. Communities Mobilizing for Change on Alcohol: Lessons and results from a 15-community randomized trial. *J Community Psychol* 1999; 27:315–326.

Chapter 9

Brief alcohol intervention in young people

Eileen F.S. Kaner[1] and Bridgette M. Bewick[2]

[1]Institute of Health and Society, Newcastle University, Newcastle upon Tyne, UK
[2]Leeds Institute of Health Sciences, School of Medicine, University of Leeds, Leeds, UK

Key points

- Brief interventions are aimed at individuals who are drinking excessively or in a pattern that is likely to be harmful to their health or well-being. Young people who drink alcohol are particularly vulnerable to its adverse effects.
- Brief interventions generally consist of structured advice or counseling of short duration aimed at reducing alcohol consumption or decreasing the number or severity of problems associated with drinking.
- Most of the work on brief interventions with young people has focused on older adolescents attending educational establishments. However, there is a rapidly growing body of work on brief intervention delivery using information technology and the Internet.
- Brief interventions focused on young people tend to follow motivational interviewing principles and produce positive changes in drinking behavior. Relatively few of the reduced drinking effects seem to persist beyond 6 months following the intervention. Booster or repeat sessions may be needed to sustain changes.
- There is much interest in the use of the Internet and mobile phone technology to deliver brief interventions to young people. Initial results are conflicting, though mostly promising. Much work remains to be done to clarify what intervention works with which group of young people.

Excessive drinking is a significant public health problem worldwide and the third greatest risk to health as measured in Disability Adjusted Life Years.[1] Health risks due to excessive drinking are particularly evident in developed countries and in young people.[1] While alcohol is responsible for 3.6% of worldwide deaths, the proportion in young people is 5%.[2] Indeed in young people, the adverse impact of alcohol exceeds that from tobacco largely because alcohol problems tend to take their toll earlier in life.[2] This disease burden is costly, in the United Kingdom the recent estimates indicated that alcohol-related problems costs the national health service between £2.7[3] and £3 billion[4] per annum.

Young People and Alcohol: Impact, Policy, Prevention, Treatment, First Edition.
Edited by John B. Saunders and Joseph M. Rey.
© 2011 Blackwell Publishing Ltd. Published 2011 by Blackwell Publishing Ltd.

The impact of alcohol on the development and behavior of young people has been well characterized in early,[5] middle,[6] and late adolescence.[7] It is now well known that young people are much more vulnerable than adults to the adverse effects of alcohol due to a range of physical and psychosocial factors that often interact.[8] These adverse affects include (1) physiological factors resulting from a typically lower body mass and less efficient metabolism of alcohol,[5,6] (2) neurological factors due to changes that occur in the developing adolescent brain after alcohol exposure,[6,9,10] (3) cognitive factors due to psychoactive effects of alcohol, which impair judgment and increase the likelihood of accidents and trauma,[11] and (4) social factors that arise from a typically high-intensity drinking pattern that leads to intoxication and risk-taking behavior. The latter are compounded by the fact that young people have less experience at dealing with the effects of alcohol than adults[12] and they have fewer financial resources to help buffer the social and environmental risks that result from drinking alcohol[7] (see Chapter 5).

As a result of the above risk factors, the list of negative consequences that result from heavy drinking in young people is extensive and includes physical, psychological, and social problems in both the shorter and the longer term. Immediate problems result from accidents and trauma, physical and sexual assault including rape in young people, criminal behavior including driving while intoxicated, and riding as a passenger with an intoxicated driver and early onset of sexual intercourse and sexual risk taking.[8,13] Longer-term problems include the development or exacerbation of mental health problems,[14] self-harm, and/or suicidal behavior.[15] Moreover, individuals who begin drinking in early life have an significantly increased risk of developing alcohol use disorders including dependence later in life.[16,17] As a result of this extensive array of damage, the prevention of excessive drinking in young people is a global public health priority.[2]

Brief alcohol intervention and young people

A recent review of interventions to reduce the harm associated with adolescent substance use outlined the positive potential of brief alcohol intervention.[18] Brief intervention is a secondary (or selective) preventive activity, aimed at individuals who are drinking excessively or in a drinking pattern that is likely to be harmful to their health or well-being.[19] Brief intervention generally consist of structured advice or counseling of short duration that is aimed at reducing alcohol consumption or decreasing the number or severity of problems associated with drinking.[20] Although there has been a great deal of evidence on primary prevention, which aims to delay the age that drinking begins and which uses general health education to prevent underage drinking, this body of work has been reported to be methodologically weak[21] and only a relatively small number of programs have reported clearly positive outcomes.[22] Thus, targeting interventions at young people who are already drinking excessively may be a more effective strategy, since the intervention will have more salience for the individuals receiving them.

Brief intervention theory and practice

Brief interventions are grounded in psychological theory that is concerned with understanding, predicting, and changing human behavior. Brief interventions are broadly based on social cognitive theory that is drawn from the concept of social learning.[23] Here, behavior is regarded to be the result of a dynamic interaction between individual, behavioral, and environmental factors that include both physical (structural) and social aspects. It is assumed that each individual has cognitive (thinking) and affective (feeling) attributes that affect not only how they behave but also how their behavior is influenced and/or reinforced by aspects of the external world. Thus brief interventions generally include a focus on individuals' beliefs and attitudes about a behavior, their self-efficacy or sense of personal confidence about changing it, and a focus on how an individual's behavior sits in relation to other people's actions (normative comparison).

In terms of practical application, early brief interventions were based on the principles of cognitive–behavioral therapy (CBT) that focused on promoting positive changes in how individuals think (cognitive) and act (behavior). CBT addresses immediate problems and difficulties instead of focusing on causes or symptoms in the past.[24] CBT-based brief interventions tend to apply a condensed version of *behavioral self-control training*.[25] Recently, brief interventions have moved away from condensed CBT toward adaptations of motivational interviewing (MI).[26] MI is a person-centered approach, which aims to resolve conflicts regarding the pros and cons of behavior change and thus enhance motivation. MI is characterized by empathy and an avoidance of direct confrontation. Elicited statements associated with positive behavior change are encouraged so as to support self-efficacy and a commitment to take action. Since the time available for delivering brief intervention often does not allow for MI in its full form,[27] the general ethos and some of the techniques of MI have been distilled into a more directive format called *behavior change counseling* (BCC).[28]

There is wide variation in the duration and frequency of brief alcohol sessions.[29] In the adult literature, brief alcohol intervention is often described as consisting of five or fewer sessions.[20,30] A key feature of brief intervention is that it is designed to be delivered by generalist practitioners (not addiction specialists) and targeted at individuals who are generally not alcohol dependent, and who may not be aware that they are experiencing alcohol-related problems. Thus the goal is usually a reduction in drinking or alcohol-related problems rather than abstinence.[31] Despite the heterogeneity in published descriptions of brief alcohol intervention there are six essential elements summarized by the acronym FRAMES[32]:

Feedback	provides feedback on the client's risk for alcohol problems
Responsibility	the individual is responsible for change
Advice	advises reduction or gives explicit direction to change
Menu	provides a variety of options for change
Empathy	emphasizes a warm, reflective, and understanding approach
Self-efficacy	encourages optimism about changing behavior

Thus, brief intervention is not traditional psychological counseling done in a shorter time frame; there is a clear structure on top of which may be added various components (e.g., self-help manuals, behavioral skills training, and motivational interviewing).

Technological developments in brief interventions for young people

There are a number of challenges inherent in delivering brief interventions to young people who drink and these relate to both the setting in which intervention can occur and its traditional face-to-face format. Brief interventions with adults have primarily been delivered in health settings; thus, this approach often misses individuals who tend not to engage with health services such as young people.[33] Moreover, some young people are reluctant to seek traditional services for alcohol problems; in part due to skepticism of the benefit of discussing their alcohol concerns directly with health practitioners. Thus, it has been suggested that young people may prefer self-directed or minimal-contact methods of alcohol intervention.[34–36]

The technological advances of the 1980s offered the potential to develop electronic forms of brief intervention.[37,38] Initially, it was anticipated that computer software loaded onto stand alone computers and/or distributed via CD-ROMS (and later DVDs) would be ideal. Such predictions were based on the limitations of the Internet (penetration, reliability, speed, etc.) and security concerns. While interventions have been developed using CD-ROM or DVD technologies, increasingly the focus has shifted toward interventions delivered via the Internet and other mobile technologies.[39] This has been possible due to the steady increase in the number of individuals who have access to the Internet and the increased availability of broadband services.[40] Indeed, electronically delivered brief interventions have been reported in North America,[41–44] Australasia,[45,46] and Europe.[47,48]

The evidence base for brief intervention in young people

Numerous reviews have been published, which have focused on brief alcohol interventions in young people. These broadly fall into studies where brief interventions are directly delivered in educational or health settings and indirectly delivered via electronic media.

The evidence base for directly delivered brief interventions is most substantial in educational settings where there have now been around 16 controlled trials, the majority involving brief motivational interviewing.[49–54] In contrast to the large amount of work in education settings, just one systematic review has focused on health care settings alone and this identified eight controlled trials.[55] Although four reviews have covered both types of settings in which directly delivered brief interventions occur.[56–59]

Regarding indirectly delivered brief interventions, three reviews have focused on computer or web-based interventions in young people including students.[60–62] An additional four reviews have focused on interventions aimed at young people but have not exclusively looked at computer/web-based interventions.[53,54,63,64] An additional three reviews included computer or web-based interventions but not exclusively in young people.[65–67]

Brief interventions in educational settings

Two recent systematic reviews have focused on individual-level alcohol interventions delivered to students attending colleges.[53,54] Across these reviews, 62 unique studies were identified, of which a subset of around 16 trials included were directly delivered brief interventions. Brief interventions were delivered directly to students by a range of physicians, nurses, counselors, or psychologists. Most studies evaluated a single brief intervention session, although a couple of studies included two or more sessions. The duration of the interventions ranged from 30 minutes to around 2 hours. The modal duration of the brief intervention session was 1 hour. The number of participants in the trials ranged from around 60[68] to over 500 students.[69] The methodological quality of the studies appears to have improved over time with larger samples and clearer random assignment to study conditions.[53] Nevertheless, subjects in these trials have tended to be a relatively selective group of young people aged between 18 and 21[58] who were mostly white American college students and highly motivated to participate in an alcohol intervention program. In an increasing number of studies, the participants were mandated students who had been involved in alcohol-related disorder and who were impelled to attend the brief intervention session. In some studies, participants received a financial or educational incentive to participate.

Nevertheless, meta-analyses have consistently reported that students who received brief interventions subsequently reduced their drinking behavior compared to control conditions—who typically received assessment only.[53,54] The key elements of the brief interventions were motivational interviewing approaches and/or personalized feedback on alcohol consumption typically with a normative component.[53] Such brief interventions typically achieved small to medium effect sizes[70] across multiple measures of alcohol consumption including quantity, frequency, and intensity of drinking. The effects of brief interventions seemed to peak in the shorter term and then diminish over time. Indeed, it has been noted that relatively few of the reduced drinking effects seem to persist beyond 6 months following the intervention.[54] Thus it is clear that booster or repeated brief intervention sessions may be needed in college populations to help sustain positive changes in drinking behavior. However, while reductions in alcohol-related problems often took longer to emerge, they were reported in longer-term follow-up of 1 year to 18 months.

Brief interventions in health settings

A recent systematic review of brief alcohol interventions in young people attending health settings identified eight randomized controlled trials between 1999 and 2008.[55] Seven were based in the United States,[71–77] and one in Australia.[78] In addition, a further trial based in a student health center was published in 2009.[79] Thus, there have been nine trials in total. These studies appear to be of a relatively high methodological quality although two trials had weak or unclear methods of randomization and allocation concealment.[72,78] Study population sizes ranged from 34 to 655 young people and their ages ranged from 12 to 24 years. Three trials targeted brief intervention at socioeconomically disadvantaged groups.[72,76,78] Four trials were based in an emergency departments,[73–75,77] two in primary care settings[71,72] and one in a university health center.[79] The remaining trials targeted homeless youth[76] and those attending a youth center which delivered health services.[78] These brief interventions tended to be one to two sessions of MI that lasted between 20 and 45 minutes,[72,74–77,79] although one trial included four MI sessions during a 1-month period.[78] Delivery was carried out by a range of trained professionals including physicians, nurse practitioners, psychologists, clinicians, and youth workers. Two studies used information technology within the health setting to help deliver brief intervention; one involved an audio program in primary care clinics[71] and the other involved an interactive laptop in a minor injury unit.[73]

Five trials reported significant positive effects of brief intervention on a range of alcohol consumption measures.[74,75,77–79] Two trials also reported a reduction in alcohol-related risk-taking behavior.[74,79] However, three trials reported reduced drinking in both intervention and control conditions.[74,75,77] In addition, three trials reported null effects after brief intervention.[72,73,76] Lastly, one trial that included 12–17-year-old adolescents reported an increase in alcohol use and binge drinking among the brief intervention subjects, representing a possible adverse effect of this brief intervention.[71] No other trials reported adverse outcomes associated with brief intervention delivered in health settings.

Electronic forms of brief interventions

The recent systematic reviews of electronically delivered brief alcohol intervention have identified 17 controlled trials in young people.[61,67] Over time, there appears to have been a marked increase in the quality of studies investigating the effectiveness of electronic forms of brief intervention. In particular, there has been an increase in the number of studies using a randomized controlled design and well-validated measures of alcohol consumption.[80]

A recent meta-analysis concluded that single sessions of personalized feedback, including those delivered electronically (without therapist input) can be effective in reducing problem drinking in the short term (with follow-up up to 9 months postintervention), although further evidence is needed on the long-term impact.[65] Riper *et al.* reported that electronic forms of brief intervention tend to produce small to modest effect sizes.[80] However, while electronic forms of brief intervention can modify behavior compared to controls, who generally receive screening or assessment only,[54,66,67] this approach might not be effective for all young people. It has been reported that electronic forms of brief intervention may be less effective in (1) young women compared to young men,[44] (2) young people who have already considered changing their alcohol consumption compared to those who have not considered change,[48] (3) individuals who report higher intention to become intoxicated through drinking,[81] and (4) those who report drinking for social reasons.[82]

It is not clear whether electronic forms of brief intervention are as effective as those delivered by therapists since there are conflicting accounts across different trials.[47] One potential source of conflicting findings could be the heterogeneous nature of interventions that often contain multiple components.[54] Hence, it is difficult to ascertain which components are effective. Within the published literature, it is common for electronic forms of brief intervention to include (1) alcohol education, (2) feedback on drinking behavior and/or negative consequences, and (3) normative comparisons.[41,44,45,47,48,83–86] A recent review of social norms interventions concluded that personalized feedback, delivered either face to face or electronically, appeared to reduce excessive drinking and alcohol-related problems.[87] However, there was less convincing evidence for interventions that did not personalize feedback.[87] The benefits of personalized feedback have recently been supported by additional research reporting significantly greater reductions in alcohol consumption in mandated students receiving personalized web-based brief intervention compared to those receiving web-based education without personalisation.[88]

Finally, not all studies support the effectiveness of electronic forms of brief intervention and those reporting null findings may provide insight into potential reasons for the behavior change when it occurs. Where null effects have been reported, the authors point out that the studies have included a high proportion of nondrinkers, light drinkers or infrequent drinkers.[46,73,89] Indeed, some studies report reduced alcohol consumption in at-risk students but not among abstainers and light drinkers.[41,44,84] Thus, electronic forms of brief alcohol interventions may be most helpful for more heavily drinking young people or those who have experienced alcohol-related problems. Hence, it is not clear whether it is the brief intervention that produces reductions in drinking or if this is due to an increased motivation for change following an adverse experience that causes the young person to go looking for help.

Discussion

There is a large and growing body of research on brief alcohol interventions in young people. This literature is highly concentrated on educational settings and there is much less work with young people attending health settings. In addition, there is a rapidly expanding body of work on electronic forms of brief intervention. Taking the field of work as a whole, it is clear that brief interventions generally have positive effects on young people's drinking behavior and their experience of alcohol-related problems. It has been reported that effects on consumption emerge earlier then decay over time while effects on alcohol-related problems have a delayed appearance but are sustained for longer.[54] Brief motivational interviewing and interventions with personalized feedback, often with a normative component, appear to have the most benefit in young people.

There is a need, however, to be cautious about brief interventions delivered in health settings since this smaller body of work reported mixed outcomes. One explanation might be that brief intervention trials that have occurred in health settings have included younger adolescents (or adolescents with more severe problems?) while brief interventions in educational and web-based contexts have targeted older adolescents (more motivated?), often attending higher education colleges and universities. The one trial that reported an adverse effect of brief intervention used an audio-tape program to deliver brief intervention to adolescents as young as 12 years.[71] Thus, it is necessary to be conservative when considering the use of brief interventions in young people below the age of 18 and particularly in using electronic forms of brief intervention with younger adolescents.

The brief intervention literature that has focused on young people is strongly dominated by studies conducted in the United States. Moreover, the participants in most of the brief intervention trials were highly selective, especially in the educational settings where participants tended to be more affluent, well-educated, and primarily Caucasian.[58] Thus, it is difficult to know how far to generalize this literature. Since electronic forms of brief intervention are likely to require moderately high levels of reading and computer literacy, it is important to establish if such brief interventions are appropriate for young people with low levels of educational attainment.

In many studies, reductions in alcohol consumption were reported in both brief intervention and control groups. Changes in both controls and brief intervention conditions can mask the relatively small effect sizes expected from brief intervention. This tendency to find changes in both the experimental and the controls groups of brief intervention trials is well known in the broader brief intervention field.[29] Reported changes in both intervention and control conditions might be due to a "Hawthorn effect" in which the process of observing or studying a population tends to produce behavior change.[90] Alternatively, it could be the result of a "regression to the mean" in which extreme measures of behavior tend to shift toward a less-extreme position from one time point to another,[91] which is likely in studies where excessive drinking is an inclusion criterion. Some of the electronic brief intervention trials have reported *within-group* effects, where heavier drinkers reduced their consumption but lighter drinkers did not. However, recent brief intervention trials have reported reductions in alcohol consumption as a specific response to screening[92] or assessment procedures.[93] Thus, it is not clear if it is brief intervention per se or screening/assessment reactivity[92,93] that produces the behavior changes. It has been suggested that, for adolescents, a visit to an emergency department or primary care clinic for an alcohol-related event may provide sufficient motivation for behavior change rather than the brief intervention.[77]

It is clear that electronic forms of brief interventions may enable more rapid and widespread distribution of alcohol-related prevention work to young people.[39] Young people appear willing to engage with remotely delivered brief interventions[94–96] and they report finding this form of intervention acceptable.[97] Since young people are often reluctant to seek advice for alcohol-related problems, this new media provides them with an opportunity to access interventions anonymously, in an environment that affords complete confidentially. In addition, access to electronic forms of brief intervention can occur at a time and place of convenience to young people. Moreover, young people do not appear to be deterred by invitations to engage with web-based brief interventions that specifically mention alcohol[98] and there is evidence to suggests that young people access electronic brief intervention services even when they have not been specifically targeted as the population of interest.[99] Thus, Internet-based brief interventions offer a very promising opportunity for alcohol risk reduction work in young people.

Nevertheless, there are a number of challenges that need to be overcome in order to realize the full potential of electronic forms of brief intervention with young people. Internet-based trials report low follow-up rates and there may be attrition bias in these evaluations.[100] Evidence suggests that heavier drinkers and those reporting higher levels of alcohol-related problems maybe most likely to be lost from Internet brief intervention trials,[43,47] although this finding is not consistently found across studies.[81,101] In addition, the unregulated nature of the Internet means that there are currently no guarantees regarding the quality of brief interventions delivered on Internet sites.[102,103] Furthermore, although researchers are beginning to explore how individuals engage with Internet-based brief interventions, monitoring and understanding this engagement continues to present a challenge. Lastly, current evidence has largely focused on fixed-site Internet technologies. However, new wireless technologies and text messaging are constantly emerging.[104,105] The extent to which brief intervention development can capitalize on new technologies, including visual forms of communication, may dictate if brief interventions can be made available to individuals who are uncomfortable with text based material or those who do not have access to broadband services.

Conclusion

Brief alcohol intervention in young people seems to be moderately successful for selected individuals, in certain settings. In particular, the current available evidence relates primarily to white, US-based subjects most often in educational settings and at the older end of the youth spectrum. The evidence is inconsistent in terms of outcome effectiveness in health settings. Moreover, it is currently not clear if electronic forms of brief intervention are more effective than those delivered by therapists. The newer technologies are, however, likely to have less costs associated with brief intervention delivery; thus, they may be more efficient in the long run.

However, there is currently insufficient evidence to be confident about the use of brief intervention to reduce excessive drinking and/or alcohol-related harm in younger adolescents. Given one report of an adverse effect of an indirectly delivered brief intervention in such young people, it is wise to remain cautious about using electronic media in young people under the age of 18. Nevertheless, there is a large and growing literature on the use of brief alcohol intervention to reduce heavy drinking in young people. Taken as a whole this work indicates that brief interventions can be effective at reducing excessive drinking and alcohol-related risk in young drinkers. The current evidence-based suggests that the most effective forms of brief intervention are those containing motivational interviewing approaches and elements of personalized feedback about a young person's drinking behavior and level of alcohol-related risk.

Resources for youth, parents, and practitioners

Given the inconclusive nature of the evidence base, the authors of this chapter are not in a position to recommend or endorse specific resources for use. However, the following may be of interest to those wishing to find out more about brief interventions approaches that are being developed for young people attending health settings and accessing alcohol advice via the Internet.

- The *How Much is Too Much* is a brief intervention protocol aimed at adults. This is available at http://www.ncl.ac.uk/ihs/enterprise/index.htm. A youth focused version has recently been developed after consultation and extensive field work with young people (see Appendix 9.1).
- For an Internet-based brief intervention site, see http://www.downyourdrink.org.uk/. An explanation of the development process can be found in Linke S, McCambridge J, Khadjesari Z, Wallace P, Murray E. Development of a psychologically enhanced interactive online intervention for hazardous drinking. *Alcohol Alcohol* 2008; 43:669–674.
- For an Internet-based brief intervention site that provides personalised feedback and social norms information see www.unitcheck.co.uk. An explanation of the development and evaluation can be found in: Bewick BM, Trusler K, Mulhern B, Barkham M, Hill AJ. The feasibility and effectiveness of a web-based personalised feedback and social norms alcohol intervention in UK university students: A randomised control trial. *Addictive Behaviors* 2008;33: 1192–1198; and in Bewick BM, West R, Gill J, O'May F, Mulhern B, Barkham M, Hill AJ. Providing web-based feedback and social norms information to reduce student alcohol intake: A multisite investigation. *Journal of Medical Internet Research* 2010; 12:e59 p.1.

Appendix 9.1

North Tyneside NHS
Primary Care Trust

ALCOHOL

How much is too much?

Why should I cut down?

I might avoid the big disasters such as sexual assault, unwanted pregnancy police record, accidents and injuries (to me or by me) but also I might:

- Sleep better
- Lose weight and feel fitter
- Skip the hangover
- Hang on to brain cells – and my dignity!
- Have an improved mood and more energy
- Get less hassle from family and friends
- Avoid accidents, injuries, fights and STIs
- Save money
- Stop having memory blackouts
- Be more attractive to hang out with
- Be in control
- Stop feeling guilty

And in the long term prevent future health problems.

Look out for your friends and make sure they look out for you.

Having a great night out, and feeling good about it the next day

People find these things may help...

- Eat before you go out, or eat during the evening
- Drink water regularly - rehydration will help prevent a hangover the next morning
- Use soft drinks to pace yourself - a tonic looks just like vodka
- Avoid salty snacks - they make you thirsty and you will drink more
- Remember, alcohol will do nothing for your looks - you're drop dead gorgeous until you drop down drunk
- Don't accept drinks from strangers, never leave your drink unattended
- Avoid shooters - they are designed to get you drunk faster
- Carry a condom, if you plan to possibly do more than kiss.

Remember

It is possible to have a good time with out getting completely off your head!

Up for changing things a bit? What steps could I take?

....
....
....

-
-
-
-

Where to go for help:

Your GP surgery or public health nurse at your school or college.

Useful websites:
www.units.nhs.uk/
www.drinkaware.co.uk/

Designed and produced by Dr Dave Tomson and Clare Butler,
North Tyneside and Kirklees PCTs

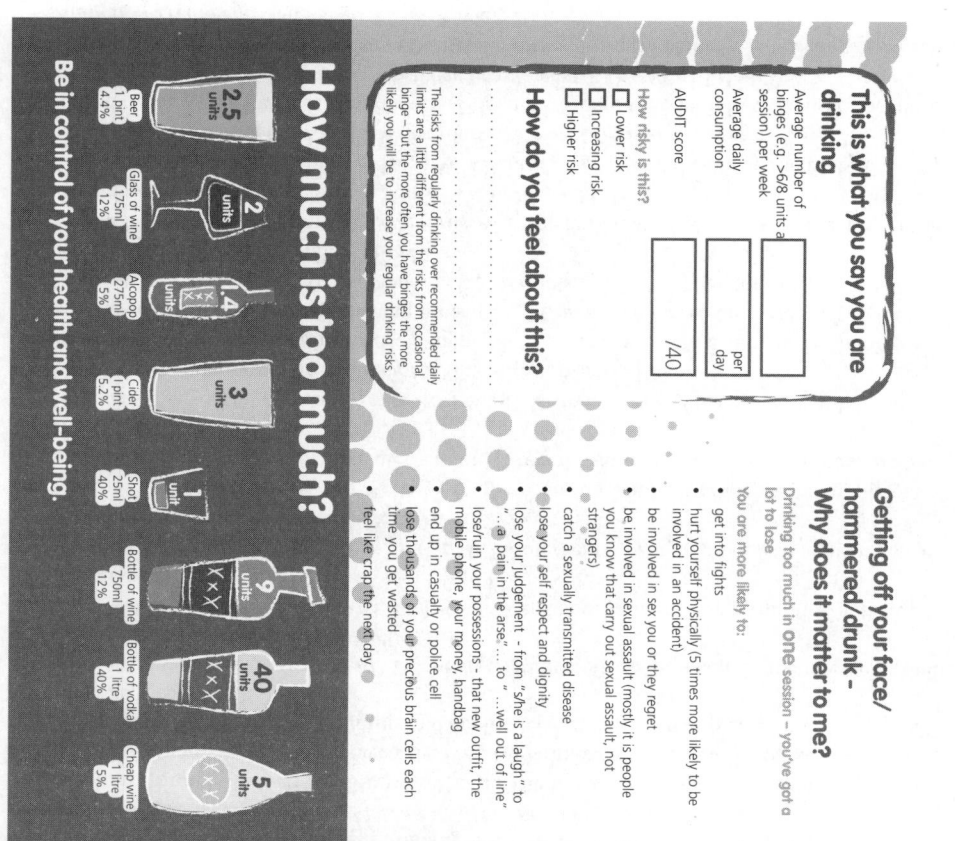

This is what you say you are drinking

Average number of binges (e.g. >6/8 units a session) per week

Average daily consumption

Average daily consumption [per day]

AUDIT score [/40]

How risky is this?
☐ Lower risk
☐ Increasing risk
☐ Higher risk

How do you feel about this?

The risks from regularly drinking over recommended daily limits are a little different from the risks from occasional binge – but the more often you have binges the more likely you will be to increase your regular drinking risks.

Getting off your face/hammered/drunk - Why does it matter to me?

Drinking too much in ONE session – you've got a lot to lose

You are more likely to:

- get into fights
- hurt yourself physically (5 times more likely to be involved in an accident)
- be involved in sex you or they regret
- be involved in sexual assault (mostly it is people you know that carry out sexual assault, not strangers)
- catch a sexually transmitted disease
- lose your self respect and dignity
- lose your judgement - from "she is a laugh" to "...a pain in the arse"... to "...well out of line"
- lose/ruin your posessions - that new outfit, the mobile phone, your money, handbag end up in casualty or police cell
- lose thousands of your precious brain cells each time you get wasted
- feel like crap the next day

How much is too much?

Beer 1 pint 4.4%	Glass of wine 175ml 12%	Alcopop 275ml 5%	Cider 1 pint 5.2%	Shot 25ml 40%	Bottle of wine 750ml 12%	Bottle of vodka 1 litre 40%	Cheap wine 1 litre 5%
2.5 units	2 units	1.4 units	3 units	1 unit	9 units	40 units	5 units

Be in control of your health and well-being.

Regularly drinking too much – what can I expect? (NB Regularly = all or most days of the week)

drinking level	AUDIT score	young men	young women	common effects if this is how you usually drink over a few months or more	
Lower risk	0-7	No more than 3-4 units per day on a regular basis	No more than 2-3 units per day on a regular basis	• relaxed • sociable • feeling good, having a laugh!	
Increasing risk	8-15	More than 3-4 units per day on a regular basis	More than 2-3 units per day on a regular basis	The more you drink over lower risk levels, the greater the risk of: • regular hangovers • depression and increased stress • insomnia and less energy • sexual difficulties • all those calories make you fat	• relationship difficulties, work problems and family problems • dangerous with street drugs and mucks up prescription drugs • judgement affected, getting into risky situations
Higher risk	16-19	More than 8 units per day on a regular basis or more than 50 units per week	More than 6 units per day on a regular basis or more than 35 units per week	• age quicker • skin looks rubbish • gut problems and poor diet • memory loss, blackouts • alcohol dependence	• breast cancer in women and other cancers in everyone • liver disease • high blood pressure • alcohol just ruins your life when you go on drinking really heavily

References

1. World Health Organization. *Global Health Risks: Mortality and Burden of Disease Related to Selected Major Risks*. Geneva: World Health Organization; 2009.
2. Jernigan D. *Global Status Report: Alcohol and Young People*. Geneva: World Health Organisation; 2001.
3. Health Improvement Analytical Team, Department of Health. *The Cost of Alcohol Harm to the NHS in England: An Update to the Cabinet Office (2003) Study*. London: Department of Health; 2008.
4. Balakrishnan R, Allender S, Scarborough P, Webster P, Rayner M. The burden of alcohol-related ill health in the United Kingdom. *J Public Health* 2009; 31:366–373
5. Zucker R, Donovan J, Masten A, Mattison M, Moss H. Developmental perspective on underage alcohol use. Developmental processes and mechanisms 0–10. *Alcohol Res Health* 2009; 32:16–29.
6. Windle M, Spear L, Fuligni A *et al*. Transitions into underage and problem drinking summary of developmental processes and mechanisms: Ages 10–15. *Alcohol Res Health* 2009; 32: 30–40.
7. Brown S, McGue M, Maggs J *et al*. Underage alcohol use summary of developmental processes and mechanisms: Ages 16–20. *Alcohol Res Health* 2009; 32:41–52.
8. Newbury-Birch D, Gilvarry E, McArdle P *et al*. The impact of alcohol consumption on young people: A review of reviews. Newcastle, UK: Department of Children Schools and Families; 2009. Available at: http://www.drugsandalcohol.ie/12292/3/Review_of_existing_reviews.pdf. Accessed August 13, 2010.
9. Zeigler D, Wang C, Yoast R *et al*. The neurocognitive effects of alcohol on adolescents and college students. *Prev Med* 2005; 40:23–32.
10. Witt E. Research on alcohol and adolescent brain development: Opportunities and future directions. *Alcohol Alcohol* 2010; 44:119–124.
11. Rodham K, Brewer H, Mistral W, Stallard P. Adolescents' perception of risk and challenge: A qualitative study. *J Adolesc* 2006; 29:261–272.
12. Murgraff V, Parrott A, Bennett P. Risky single-occasion drinking amongst young people – definition, correlates, policy, and intervention: A board overview of research findings. *Alcohol Alcohol* 1999; 34:3–14.
13. Perkins W. Surveying the damage: A Review of research on consequences of alcohol misuse in college populations. *J Stud Alcohol* 2002; 14 (Suppl.):91–100.
14. Barnes G, Mitic W, Leadbeater B, Dhami M. Risk and protective factors for adolescent substance use and mental health symptoms. *Can J Commun Ment Health* 2009; 28:1–15.
15. Carpenter C. Heavy alcohol use and suicide: Evidence from tougher drunk driving laws. *J Policy Anal Manage* 2004; 23:831–842.
16. DeWit DJ, Adlaf EM, Offord DR, Ogborne AC. Age at first alcohol use: A risk factor for the development of alcohol disorders. *Am J Psychiatry* 2000; 157:745–750.
17. Dawson D, Goldstein R, Chou P, Ruan W, Grant B. Age at first drink and the first incidence of adult-onset DSM-IV alcohol use disorders. *Alcohol Clin Exp Res* 2008; 32:1–12.
18. Toumbourou J, Stockwell T, Neighbors C, Marlatt G, Sturge J, Rehm J. Interventions to reduce harm associated with adolescent substance use. *Lancet* 2007; 369:1391–1401.
19. Kaner E, Newbury-Birch D, Heather N. Brief interventions. In: Miller P, ed. *Evidence-Based Addiction Treatment*. San Diego, CA: Elsevier; 2009.
20. Kaner E, Dickinson H, Beyer F *et al*. The effectiveness of brief alcohol interventions in primary care settings: A comprehensive review. *Drug Alcohol Rev* 2009; 28:301–323.

21. Foxcroft DR, Lister-Sharp D, Lowe G. Alcohol misuse prevention for young people: A systematic review reveals methodological concerns and lack of reliable evidence of effectiveness. *Addiction* 1997; 92:531–537.

22. Foxcroft DR, Ireland D, Lister-Sharp DJ, Lowe G, Breen R. Longer-term primary prevention for alcohol misuse in young people: A systematic review. *Addiction* 2003; 98:397–411.

23. Bandura A. *Social Learning Theory.* Englewood Cliffs, NJ: Prentice-Hall; 1997.

24. Heather N, Campion PD, Neville RG, MacCabe D. Evaluation of a controlled drinking minimal intervention for problem drinkers in general practice (The DRAMS Scheme). *J R Coll Gen Pract* 1987; 37:358–363.

25. Hester R. Behavioural self-control training. In: Hester R, Miller W, eds. *Handbook of Alcoholism Treatment Approaches: Effective Alternatives.* 2nd edn. Massachusetts: Needham Heights; 1995, pp. 148–159.

26. Miller W, Rollnick S. *Motivational Interviewing: Preparing People for Change.* New York: Guilford; 2002.

27. Rollnick S, Heather N, Bell A. Negotiating behaviour change in medical settings: The development of brief motivational interviewing. *J Ment Health* 1992; 1:25–37.

28. Rollnick S, Mason P, Butler C. *Health Behaviour Change: A Guide for Practitioners.* Edinburgh: Churchill Livingstone; 1999.

29. Kaner E, Beyer F, Dickinson H *et al.* Effectiveness of brief alcohol interventions in primary care populations. *Cochrane Database Syst Rev* 2007; (2):CD004148. DOI: 10.1002/14651858.CD4148.pub3.

30. Babor TF. Avoiding the horrid and beastly sin of drunkenness: Does dissuasion make a difference? *J Consult Clin Psychol* 1994; 62:1127–1140.

31. Bien TH, Miller WR, Tonigan JS. Brief interventions for alcohol problems: A review. *Addiction* 1993; 88:315–335.

32. Miller W, Sanchez V. *Motivating Young Adults for Treatment and Lifestyle Change.* Notre Dame, IN: University of Notre Dame Press; 1993.

33. Roche AM, Freeman T. Brief interventions: Good theory but weak in practice. *Drug Alcohol Rev* 2004; 23:11–18.

34. Paperny DM, Aona JY, Lehman RM, Hammar SL, Risser J. Computer-assisted detection and intervention in adolescent high-risk health behaviours. *J Pediatr* 1990; 116:456–462.

35. Kypri K, Saunders JB, Gallagher SJ. Acceptability of various brief intervention approaches for hazardous drinking among university students. *Alcohol Alcohol* 2003; 38:626–628.

36. Saunders JB, Kypri K, Walters ST, Laforge RG, Larimer ME. Approaches to brief interventions for hazardous drinking in young people. *Alcohol Clin Exp Res* 2004; 28:322–329.

37. Djikstra A, DeVries H. The development of computer generated tailored interventions. *Patient Educ Couns* 1999; 36:193–203.

38. Skinner HA, Allen BA, McIntosh MC, Palmer WH. Lifestyle assessment: Applying microcomputers in family practice. *Br Med J* 1985; 290:212–214.

39. Cassell MM, Jackson C, Cheuvront B. Health communication on the Internet: An effective channel for health behaviour change? *J Health Commun* 1998; 3:71–79.

40. Nilsen P. Brief alcohol intervention—where to from here? Challenges remain for research and practice. *Addiction* 2010; 105:954–959.

41. Doumas DM, Hannah E. Preventing high risk drinking in youth in the workplace: A web based normative feedback program. *J Subst Abuse Treat* 2008; 34:263–271.

42. Lewis MA, Neighbors C, Oster-Aaland LO, Kirkeby BS, Larimer ME. Indicated prevention for incoming freshmen: Personalised normative feedback and high risk drinking. *Addict Behav* 2007; 32:2495–2508.

43. Saitz R, Palfai T, Freedner N *et al.* Screening and brief intervention online for college students: The ihealth study. *Alcohol Alcohol* 2007; 42:28–36.
44. Chiauzzi E, Green T, Lord S, Thum C, Goldstein M. My student body: A high risk drinking prevention web site for college students. *J Am Coll Health* 2005; 53:263–274.
45. Kypri K, Saunders JB, Williams SM *et al.* Web-based screening and brief intervention for hazardous drinking: A double-blind randomized controlled trial. *Addiction* 2004; 99:1410–1417.
46. Kypri K, McAnnally HM. Randomised controlled trial of a web based primary care intervention for multiple health risk behaviours. *Prev Med* 2005; 41:761–766.
47. Bewick BM, Trusler K, Mulhern B, Barkham M, Hill AJ. The feasibilty and effectiveness of a web-based personalised feedback and social norms alcohol intervention in UK university students: A randomised control trial. *Addict Behav* 2008; 33:1192–1198.
48. Bendtsen P, Johansson K, Akerline I. Feasibility of an email based electronic screening and brief intervention (eSBI) to college students in Sweden. *Addict Behav* 2006; 31:777–787.
49. Hunter Fager J, Mazurek Melnyk B. The effectiveness of intervention studies to decrease alsohol use in college undergraduate students: An integrative analysis. *Worldviews Evid Based Nurs* 2004; 1:102–119.
50. Barnett NP, Read JP. Mandatory alcohol intervention for alcohol-abusing college students: A systematic review. *J Subst Abuse Treat* 2005; 29:147–158.
51. Walters ST, Neighbors C. Feedback interventions for college students: What, why and for whom? *Addict Behav* 2005; 30:1168–1182.
52. Larimer ME, Cronce JM, Lee CM, Kilmer JR. Brief intervention in college settings. *Alcohol Res Health* 2005; 28:94–104.
53. Larimer M, Cronce J. Identification, prevention, and treatment revisited: Individual-focused college drinking prevention strategies 1999–2006. *Addict Behav* 2007; 32:2439–2468.
54. Carey K, Scott-Sheldon L, Carey M, DeMartini K. Individual-level interventions to reduce college student drinking: A meta-analytic review. *Addict Behav* 2007; 32:2469–2494.
55. Jackson R, Johnson M, Campbell F *et al.* Screening and Brief Interventions: Effectiveness Review to the National Institute for Health & Clinical Excellence. Sheffield, UK: School of Health and Related Research (ScHARR), University of Sheffield; 2009.
56. Monti P, O'Leary Tevyaw T, Borsari B. Drinking among young adult: Screening, brief intervention, and outcome. *Alcohol Res Health* 2005; 28:236–244.
57. Neighbors C, Larimer ME, Lostutter TW, Woods BA. Harm reduction and individually focused alcohol prevention: A review. *Int J Drug Policy* 2006; 17:304–309.
58. Natarajan M, Kaner E. Brief alcohol interventions in young people: Evidence and applicability. In: Gilvarry E, McArdle P, eds. *Clinics in Developmental Medicine*. Vol. 172. London: McKeith Press; 2007.
59. Tait RJ, Hulse GK. A systematic review of the effectiveness of brief interventions with substance using adolescents by type of drug. *Drug Alcohol Rev* 2003; 22:337–346.
60. Bewick BM, Trustler K, Barkham M, Hill AJ. The effectiveness of web-based interventions designed to decrease alcohol consumption: a systematic review. *Prev Med* 2008; 47:17–26.
61. Elliott JC, Carey KB, Bolles JR. Computer based interventions for college drinking: A qualitative review. *Addict Behav* 2008; 33:994–1005.
62. Walters ST, Miller E, Chiauzzi E. Wired for wellness: E-interventions for addressing college drinking. *J Subst Abuse Treat* 2005; 29:139–145.
63. Zisserson RN, Palfai TP, Saitz R. " No-contact" interventions for unhealthy college drinking: Efficacy of alternatives to person-delivered intervention approaches. *Subst Abus* 2007; 28:119–131.
64. White HR. Reduction of alcohol-related harm on United States college campuses: The use of personal feedback interventions. *Int J Drug Policy* 2006; 17:310–319.

65. Riper H, van Straten A, Keuken M, Smit F, Schippers G, Cuijpers P. Curbing problem drinking with personalised feedback interventions: A meta-analysis. *Am J Prev Med* 2009; 36: 247–255.
66. Kypri K, Sitharthan T, Cunningham J, Kavanagh D, Dean J. Innovative approaches to intervention for problem drinking. *Curr Opin Psychiatry* 2005; 18:229–234.
67. Khadjesari Z, Murray E, Hewitt C, Hartley S, Godfrey C. Can stand-alone computer-based interventions reduce alcohol consumption? A systematic review. *Addiction* 2010; 106: 618–619.
68. Borsari B, Carey K. Two brief alcohol interventions for mandated college students. *Psychol Addict Behav* 2005; 19:296–302.
69. Carey KB, Carey MP, Maisto SA, Henson JM. Brief motivational interventions for heavy college drinkers: A randomized controlled trial. *J Consult Clin Psychol* 2006; 74:943–954.
70. Cohen J. *Statistical Power of Analysis for the Behavioural Sciences.* New York, NY: Academic Press; 1969.
71. Boekeloo BO, Jerry J, Lee-Ougo WI *et al.* Randomized trial of brief office-based interventions to reduce adolescent alcohol use. *Arch Pediatr Adolesc Med* 2004; 158:635–642.
72. D'Amico EJ, Miles JN, Stern SA, Meredith LS. Brief motivational interviewing for teens at risk of substance use consequences: A randomized pilot study in a primary care clinic. *J Subst Abuse Treat* 2008; 35:53–61.
73. Maio RF, Shope JT, Blow FC *et al.* A randomized controlled trial of an emergency department-based interactive computer program to prevent alcohol misuse among injured adolescents. *Ann Emerg Med* 2005; 45:420–429.
74. Monti PM, Spirito A, Myers M *et al.* Brief intervention for harm reduction with alcohol-positive older adolescents in a hospital emergency department. *J Consult Clin Psychol* 1999; 67:989–994.
75. Monti PM, Barnett NP, Colby SM *et al.* Motivational interviewing versus feedback only in emergency care for young adult problem drinking. *Addiction* 2007; 102:1234–1243.
76. Peterson PL, Baer JS, Wells EA, Ginzler JA, Garrett SB. Short-term effects of a brief motivational intervention to reduce alcohol and drug risk among homeless adolescents. *Psychol Addict Behav* 2006; 20:254–264.
77. Spirito A, Monti P, Barnett N *et al.* A randomized clinical trial of a brief motivational intervention for alcohol-positive adolescents treated in an emergency department. *J Pediatr* 2004; 145:396–402.
78. Bailey KA, Baker AL, Webster RA, Lewin TJ. Pilot randomized controlled trial of a brief alcohol intervention group for adolescents. *Drug Alcohol Rev* 2004; 23:157–166.
79. Schaus JF, Sole ML, McCoy TP, Mullett N, O'Brien MC. Alcohol screening and brief intervention in a college student health center: A randomized controlled trial. *J Stud Alcohol Drugs* 2009; 16 (Suppl.): 131–141.
80. Cunningham JA, Khadjesari Z, Bewick BM, Riper H. Internet-based interventions for problem drinkers: From efficacy trials to implementation. *Drug Alcohol Rev* 2010; 29(6):617–622.
81. Neighbors C, Lee CM, Lewis MA, Fossos N, Walter T. Internet based personalised feedback to reduce 21st birthday drinking: A randomised controlled trial of an event-specific prevention intervention. *J Consult Clin Psychol* 2009; 77:51–63.
82. Neighbors C, Larimer ME, Lewis MA. Targetting misperceptions of descriptive drinking norms: Efficacy of a computer delivered personalised normative feedback intervention. *J Consult Clin Psychol* 2004; 72:434–347.
83. Butler LH, Correia CJ. Brief alcohol intervention with college student drinkers: Face to face versus computerised feedback. *Psychol Addict Behav* 2009; 23:163–167.

84. Walters ST, Vader AM, Harris TR. A controlled trial of web-based feedback for heavy drinking college students. *Prev Sci* 2007; 8:83–88.

85. Neighbors C, Lewis MA, Bergstrom RL, Larimer ME. Being controlled by normative influences: Self determination as a moderator of a normative feedback alcohol intervention. *Health Psychol* 2006; 25:571–579.

86. Dimeff MA, McNeely M. Computer enhanced primary care practitioner advice for high risk college drinkers in a student primary health care setting. *Cogn Behav Pract* 2000; 7:82–100.

87. Moreira MT, Smith LA, Foxcroft D. Social norms interventions to reduce alcohol misuse in university or college students (review). *Cochrane Database Syst Rev* 2009; (3):CD006748.

88. Doumas DM, McKinley LL, Book P. Evaluation of two web based alcohol interventions for mandated college students. *J Subst Abuse Treat* 2009; 36:65–74.

89. Bersamin M, Paschall MJ, Fearnow-Kenney M, Wyrick D. Effectiveness of a web-based alcohol misuse and harm prevention course among high and low risk students. *J Am Coll Health* 2007; 55:247–254.

90. Mayo E. *The Human Problems of an Industrial Civilization*. New York: MacMillan; 1933.

91. Bland J, Altman D. Regression towards the mean. *Br Med J* 1994; 308:1499.

92. McCambridge J, Day M. Randomized controlled trial of the effects of completing the Alcohol Use Disorders Identification Test questionnaire on self-reported hazardous drinking. *Addiction* 2007; 103:241–248.

93. Kypri K, Langley JD, Saunders JB, Cashell-Smith ML. Assessment may conceal therapeutic benefit: Findings from a randomised controlled trial for hazardous drinking. *Addiction* 2006; 102:62–70.

94. Simon-Arndt CM, Hurtado SL, Patriarca-Troyk LA. Acceptance of web-based personalise feedback: User ratings of an alcohol misuse prevention program targeting US marines. *Health Commun* 2006; 20:13–22.

95. Moore MJ, Soderquist J, Werch C. Feasibility and efficacy of a binge drinking prevention intervention for college students delivered via the Internet versus postal mail. *J Am Coll Health* 2005; 54:38–44.

96. Rodriguez-Martos A, Castellano Y. Web based screening and advice for hazardous drinkers: Use of a Spanish site. *Drug Alcohol Rev* 2009; 28:54–59.

97. Copeland J, Martin G. Web-based interventions for substance use disorders: A qualitative review. *J Subst Abuse Treat* 2004; 26:109–116.

98. Saitz R, Svikis D, D'Onofrio G, Kraemer KL, Perl H. Challenges applying alcohol brief intervention in diverse practice settings: populations, outcomes, and costs. *Alcohol Clin Exp Res* 2006; 30:332–338.

99. Sinadinovic K, Berman AH, Hasson D, Wennbnberg P. Internet based assessment and self monitoring of problematic alcohol and drug use. *Addict Behav* 2010; 35:464–670.

100. McCoy TP, Ip EH, Blocker JN, Champion H, Rhodes SD, Wagoner KG, Mitra A, Wolfson M. Attrition bias in a US Internet survey of alcohol use among college freshmen. *J Stud Alcohol Drugs* 2009; 70:606–614.

101. Kypri K, Hallett J, Howat P *et al.* Randomised controlled trial of proactive web-based alcohol screening and brief intervention for university students. *Arch Intern Med* 2009; 169:1508–1514.

102. Boyer EW, Shannon M, Hibberd PL. Web sites with misinformation about illicit drugs. *N Engl J Med* 2001; 345:469–471.

103. Monahan G, Colthurst T. Internet based information on alcohol, tobacco and other drugs: Issues of ethics, quality and accountability. *Subst Use Misuse* 2001; 36:2171–2180.

104. LaBrie JW, Hummer JF, Huchting KK, Neighbors C. A brief live interactive normative group intervention using wireless keypads to reduce drinking and alcohol consequences in college student athletes. *Drug Alcohol Rev* 2009; 28:40–47.
105. Weitzel JA, Bernhardt JM, Usdan S, Mays D. Using wireless handheld computers and tailored text messaging to reduce negative consequences of drinking alcohol. *J Stud Alcohol Drugs* 2007; 68:534–537.

Chapter 10

Preventing and responding to alcohol misuse in specific contexts: schools, colleges, the military

Joseph M. Rey[1,2] and Robert F. Saltz[3]

[1]Notre Dame University Medical School, Sydney, NSW, Australia
[2]University of Sydney Medical School, Sydney, Australia
[3]Pacific Institute for Research and Evaluation, Prevention Research Centre, Berkeley, CA, USA

Key points

- Schools, colleges, and the armed forces not only face specific challenges dealing with alcohol use but also have unique opportunities for prevention, early detection, and intervention.
- Characteristics shared by school prevention programs that have been shown to be effective include the following: A sound theoretical base, sociocultural relevance, providing cognitive–behavioral skills, incorporating training of facilitators or staff, being multimodal, involving parents, providing opportunities for positive relationships, and having a larger number of sessions. Programs that only provide alcohol education are not efficacious.
- Evidence of effectiveness for the large majority of programs is lacking, or data show that participation does not reduce alcohol consumption, drunkenness or alcohol-related harm in the medium to long term. The Strengthening Families Program, Life Skills Training Program, School and Alcohol Harm Reduction Project, Seattle Social Development Project, and Linking the Interest of Families and Teachers are some of the programs with evidence of effectiveness.
- Factors that increase the likelihood of college drinking include the following: Living arrangements (highest among students living in fraternities and lowest in those living with their families), college characteristics, being a first-year student, price and availability of alcohol in the area surrounding the campus, and the institution's alcohol policies and their enforcement.
- Effective college prevention strategies need to target three constituencies: The student population, the college and its surrounding environment, and the students at risk or alcohol-dependent drinkers. Interventions for students found to misuse alcohol based on motivational enhancement principles have been shown to be effective, even if they are brief. They appear to also be effective for mandated students. There is growing evidence of efficacy for community and campus-level interventions as well as Internet-based programs that provide individualized feedback.

Young People and Alcohol: Impact, Policy, Prevention, Treatment, First Edition.
Edited by John B. Saunders and Joseph M. Rey.
© 2011 Blackwell Publishing Ltd. Published 2011 by Blackwell Publishing Ltd.

- The prevalence of heavy alcohol use among the young military personnel is substantially higher than among civilians of the same age. Young adult personnel are about three times more likely to drink heavily than older enlistees. Alcohol use is one of the strongest predictors of misconduct in the forces.
- The current US armed forces' policies emphasize that consumption of alcohol is a personal decision, but individuals who choose to drink alcohol must do so lawfully and responsibly.
- Since most alcohol use by the military occurs off duty and off base, it can be argued that programs are likely to fail unless nearby communities are engaged and there is an emphasis on reducing the supply of alcohol.

Alcohol use in school and university students is a worldwide problem. Although use varies between countries and among cultural and ethnic groups, patterns of use seem to be converging due to the influence of the mass media, marketing, and globalization (see Chapter 1). Governments and institutions across the globe struggle to deal with this problem. This chapter expands and builds on information and concepts mentioned in Chapters 7–9 focusing on prevention and intervention strategies in schools, colleges/universities, and the military. It is of note that most of the available research on prevention refers to substance use prevention (mostly including alcohol, tobacco, and cannabis) rather than to alcohol specifically. Policies to reduce alcohol availability and consumption, which are also relevant to school and college students, are described in Chapter 7.

Different cultures favor different approaches to alcohol education and prevention. While in the United States many programs seek to achieve abstinence among teenagers, some alcohol use in adolescents is accepted in a number of countries, which favor a *harm minimization* or *harm reduction* approach that aims to achieve sensible drinking. Sensible alcohol use can be defined as drinking in a way that is unlikely to cause the individual or others significant risk of harm. In some European countries, it is acceptable for children and young teenagers to occasionally have a small alcoholic drink during meals with the family (Chapter 1). Under UK law, children can consume different types of alcohol in different contexts, depending on their age. For instance, young people aged 16 or 17 may consume beer, cider, or wine with a meal when under adult supervision on licensed premises. In all other circumstances, it is illegal for anyone younger than 18 years to "knowingly" consume alcohol on licensed premises or to buy or attempt to buy alcohol.[1] Regrettably, there is no convincing data yet on what is the safe level of alcohol use in children and adolescents, if any.

The problem

School students

Alcohol use among adolescents in the United States is more widespread than use of any of the illicit drugs, although consuming alcohol is legally prohibited before the age of 21. In 2008, almost three out of every four twelfth-grade students (72%) had tried alcohol and almost half (43%) were current drinkers (i.e., used alcohol in the previous month).[2] Of

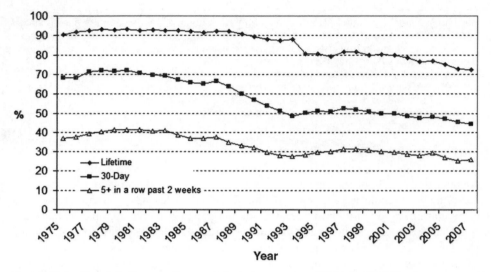

Figure 10.1 Trends in the prevalence of alcohol use among US high-school seniors. *Source*: Johnston LD, O'Malley PM, Bachman JG, Schulenberg JE. *Monitoring the Future National Results on Adolescent Drug Use: Overview of Key Findings, 2007*. Bethesda, MD: NIDA, NIH, Publication No. 08–6418; 2008.

greater concern is drinking to the point of inebriation; in this line 18% of eighth graders, 37% of tenth graders, and 55% of twelfth graders said they had been drunk at least once in their lifetime. The prevalence of drunkenness during the previous month was high: 5%, 14%, and 28% for grades 8, 10, and 12, respectively. Alcohol use is more common in males than in females. For example, among twelfth graders, daily drinking was reported by 4% of males compared with 2% of females. African-American students had the lowest rates of alcohol use.[2] Figure 10.1 shows changes in alcohol use among US teenagers from 1975 to 2007. Overall, there has been a gradual decline and this refers to the following:

- Having drunk alcohol ever—from 90% in 1975 to 72% in 2007.
- Having drunk in the last month (current drinkers)—from 68% in 1975 to 44% in 2007.
- Having had five or more drinks in the previous 2 weeks (binge drinkers)—from 37% in 1975 to 26% in 2007.

Almost 90% of 15-year-old teens in the United Kingdom have tried alcohol (Figure 10.2), but the overall proportion of those aged 11–15 who drink alcohol has fallen since 2001. However, those who do drink alcohol consume larger amounts and more often.[1] Binge drinking—defined as five or more drinks in a session on at least three occasions in the previous month—appears to be higher among European than the US school students. Binge drinking is particularly prevalent in Ireland (32%), the Netherlands (28%), and the United Kingdom (27%). Following an increase in the level of binge drinking in UK teenage boys between 1995 and 1999, rates fell slightly by 2003. On the contrary, binge drinking among teenage girls increased between 1995 and 2003 so that by 2003 teenage girls in the United Kingdom were more likely than boys to binge drink,[3] mirroring changes in young women's drinking patterns.[4]

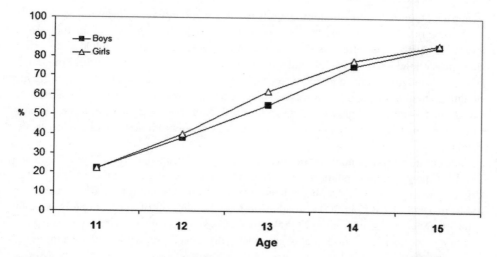

Figure 10.2   Percentage of 11–15 year olds in the UK in 2005 who had ever had an alcoholic drink. *Source*: Becker E, Blenkinsop S, Constantine R *et al*. *Drug Use, Smoking and Drinking Among Young People in England in 2005*. London: The Information Centre; 2006.

The proportion of Australian secondary school students drinking in the previous week (current drinkers) during the first years of the twenty-first century increased with age from 10% of 12-year-old teens to 49% of 17-year-old teens. As in the United States, prevalence of alcohol use among students aged 12 to 15 decreased between 1999 and 2005: 87% had ever tried alcohol in 1999 compared with 82% in 2005. A similar decrease was found for those drinking during the previous month (43% and 34%, respectively). However, this reduction in drinking was not observed among 16- and 17-year-olds.[5]

How do school students obtain alcohol?

Usually unable to lawfully purchase alcohol themselves, the methods used by students to obtain alcohol also have implications for prevention. The Australian data[5]—broadly comparable to data elsewhere—show that parents are the most common source of alcohol; with 37% of males and 38% of females indicating their parents gave them their last drink. Approximately 20% of students who were current drinkers had asked someone else to buy alcohol for them and this person was most likely to be a friend aged 18 years (the legal drinking age in Australia) or older. Spirits (e.g., vodka, scotch, and rum), in either the premixed (i.e., "alcopops") or the non-premixed form, were the most common type of drinks consumed.

College and university students

There is a widespread belief that college life encourages heavy drinking.[6] The prevalence of hazardous drinking in college and university students in Australasia, Europe, and South America is largely similar to that in the United States, but higher than in African and Asian countries.[7] Contrary to the belief that college life encourages heavy drinking, several US studies report that heavy alcohol use is quite pervasive among people in their early twenties, whether they attend college or not. In fact, college students drink less often than their noncollege peers (3.7% of students vs. 4.5% of nonstudents report drinking daily) but when students drink (e.g., at parties and on weekends), they tend to do it in greater quantities than nonstudents.[8] However, students seem to stop heavy drinking earlier than nonstudents—perhaps "growing out" of harmful alcohol use before it becomes a long-term problem but also because they leave a college environment conducive to heavy drinking.[9]

Rates of alcohol dependence are lower for college students than for 18- to 24-year-old youth in the general population. This does not mean that the consequences of college drinking are not serious. Alcohol-related deaths among US college students rose from 1,440 in 1998 to 1,825 in 2005, in addition to an annual toll of approximately 600,000 injuries, 690,000 assaults, and 97,000 cases of sexual assault or date rape each year. Further, more than one-fourth of college students drive each year while under the influence of alcohol.[10]

School prevention and intervention programs

Against a background of widespread school-age use, it is not surprising that governments and communities seek to prevent or reduce alcohol consumption among students. Schools are optimal settings for the delivery of alcohol prevention programs because (a) most individuals begin using alcohol during their school years, (b) schools provide an efficient way of reaching almost all young people, and (c) schools can implement a broad range of educational and disciplinary policies. As a result, schools often have programs in place to encourage children not to drink, to delay the age at which they start drinking, and to reduce the harm that alcohol may cause among those who do drink. In the United States, almost all the school districts have received support for drug prevention curricula from the Safe and Drug Free Schools Program of the Department of Education. Schools receiving these funds are required to deliver evidence-based interventions.

Schools are more likely to adopt programs that are perceived to be age appropriate, relevant to the specific student alcohol use problems in their locality (see Chapter 8), supported by evidence of effectiveness, less costly, and easier to implement. Schools also tend to adopt programs that directly seek to change student's knowledge, attitudes, and behaviors instead of changing the school environment. These interventions complement universal policies to restrict access to alcohol such as sale, price, and marketing controls—discussed in Chapter 7. The elements shared by programs likely to be effective are summarized in Table 10.1.

There are numerous school-based prevention programs. Some Web sites, such as http://nrepp.samhsa.gov/—The National Registry of Evidence-based Programs and Practices of the U.S. Substance Abuse and Mental Health Services Administration (SAMHSA)—maintain a database of interventions with description of their characteristics (e.g., target population, areas of interest, outcomes sought, implementation history,

Table 10.1   Characteristics shared by programs with evidence of effectiveness.

- Theory driven, with specific reference to social cognitive theory
- Socioculturally relevant (i.e., address cultural norms, beliefs, and influences)
- Address cognitive–behavioral skills (e.g., have skills-based components, active, and interactive format)
- Incorporate training of facilitators or staff
- Multimodal (e.g., include multiple components and settings)
- Involve parents
- Provide opportunities for positive relationships (e.g., parent–child communication, peer influences)
- Have a larger number of sessions (i.e., adequate dose)

Sources: Nation M, Crusto C, Wandersman A *et al*. What works in prevention: Principles of effective prevention programs. *Am Psychol* 2003; 58:449–456; Peters LWH, Kok G, Ten Dam GTM *et al*. Effective elements of school health promotion across behavioral domains: A systematic review of reviews. *BMC Public Health* 2009; 9:182.

replications, cost, quality of the evidence, and publications). Rather than repeating this information, we suggest interested readers to use that trustworthy free-access resource. In this chapter, we summarize the key aspects of these programs and provide some examples.

Interventions are often situation specific, that is, programs may not be transportable. For example, researchers from the University of Florida found that a 3-year, three-pronged prevention program that worked well in rural Minnesota did little to keep Chicago middle-school students from drinking or using drugs. In Minnesota, the program had reduced alcohol use to 20–30%. Also, interventions that may be useful or acceptable to one population (e.g., Native Americans, such as Project Venture[11]) may not be so to another. Cultural factors may play a role in this, so that programs that seek to achieve abstinence might be readily accepted and effective in the United States, but not in countries where sensible drinking in the young is socially acceptable.

Table 10.2 lists some of the programs according to whether they are delivered (e.g., in the classroom or outside), who delivers them (e.g., teachers and uniformed police officers), whether they target alcohol exclusively or not, etc. There are many more programs than those listed Table 10.2; these are listed only as examples.

In spite of considerable research:

- Evidence of effectiveness for the large majority of programs is lacking.
- The evidence indicates that in most cases participation *does not* reduce alcohol consumption, drunkenness, or alcohol-related harm in the medium to long term (>12 months).

A recent review[12] concluded that there was evidence for the longer term effectiveness of the *Strengthening Families Program*,[13] the *Life Skills Training program* (LST),[14] the *School and Alcohol Harm Reduction Project* (SHAHRP),[15] the *Seattle Social Development Project* (SSDP),[16] and the *Linking the Interest of Families and Teachers* (LIFT)[17] program. There is inconsistent and insufficient evidence to determine the cost-effectiveness of school-based interventions.

As discussed in Chapter 9 in section "Electronic forms of brief interventions" and later in this chapter (section on college drinking), there has also been a surge of interest

Table 10.2 Selected school prevention programs and their effectiveness.

Program	Evidence for longer term effectiveness[a]
Classroom-based programs led by teachers	
Specifically targeting alcohol use	
▪ School and Alcohol Harm Reduction Project (SHAHRP)[15]	√
▪ Alcohol Misuse Prevention Study (AMPS)[18]	×
▪ WHO Alcohol Education Program[19]	×
Targeting alcohol and other substances	
▪ The Life Skills Training program (LST)[14]	√√
Targeting general health behaviors	
▪ Gatehouse Project[20]	×
Classroom-based programs led by external contributors	
Specifically targeting alcohol use	
▪ Adolescent Alcohol Prevention Trial (AAPT)[21] (delivered by project staff)	×
Targeting alcohol and other substances	
▪ Project ALERT[22] (delivered by adult health educators)	√
▪ Project DARE (Drug Abuse Resistance Education)[23] (delivered by uniformed police officers)	×
Nonclassroom-based programs	
▪ Start Taking Alcohol Risks Seriously (STARS) for Families[24]	×
School-based peer support programs	
▪ Protecting You/Protecting Me (PY/PM)[25]	×
School-based counseling programs	
▪ It is your decision[26]	×
Multicomponent programs	
▪ Seattle Social Development Project (SSDP)[16]	√√
▪ Linking the Interest of Families and Teachers (LIFT)[17]	√
▪ Strengthening Families Program (SFP)[25]	√
▪ Healthy School and Drugs Project[27]	√

[a]12 or more months; many studies report short term gains; √√: good evidence; √: some evidence; ×: lack of evidence or evidence of no effect.

on individual interventions for school students using the Internet and cellular phones. Some of the interventions that include personalized feedback appear to reduce excessive drinking and alcohol-related problems. However, there is less convincing evidence for interventions that did not personalise feedback (see Chapter 9).

Examples of programs

School and Alcohol Harm Reduction Project[15]

This is a curriculum-based program that focuses on the identification of alcohol-related harm and the development of harm reduction strategies (i.e., it follows a harm minimization model). SHAHRP lessons are conducted in three phases with eight lessons in the first year of the program (phase 1), five booster lessons the following year (phase 2), and four booster lessons 2 years later (phase 3). Phase 1 targets students prior to the time when they start drinking (usually 12–13-year-old teens). This allows students to gain alcohol harm reduction skills and strategies immediately before the adoption of a new behavior (drinking). Phase 2 reinforces knowledge and skills during a time when most students are experimenting with alcohol, ensuring that information is immediately relevant. This period of experimentation often exposes teenagers to a higher level of risk due to the type of drinking generally undertaken (bingeing) and their relative inexperience in handling the changes brought about by alcohol in themselves and in others. The third and final phase of the intervention is conducted in later teenage years, when data indicates there is a steep rise in alcohol use. Drunk driving and drinking at licensed premises are additional issues for consideration at that age. (http://ndri.curtin.edu.au/research/shahrp/index.cfm).

Life Skills Training Program[14]

This is a universal, school-based, proprietary intervention that aims to prevent alcohol, tobacco, and marijuana use and violence by targeting the main social and psychological factors that promote the initiation of substance use and other risky behaviors. It was initially designed for seventh graders with the purpose of developing personal and social skills. It has been subsequently adapted for elementary-, middle-, and high-school students. For example, the middle-school program consists of 30 class sessions conducted over 3 years beginning at either grade 6 or grade 7 and followed by booster sessions. LST has three main components:

- *Drug resistance skills*: Helping students recognize and challenge common misconceptions about tobacco, alcohol, and other drug use. Students learn, through coaching and practice, information and skills for dealing with peer and media pressure.
- *Personal self-management skills* that focus on learning about self image and its effects on behavior, goal setting, keeping track of personal progress, identifying how everyday decisions may be influenced by others, analyzing difficult situations, and weighing the consequences of alternative options before making decisions.
- *General social skills*: Helping students develop skills to overcome shyness, communicate effectively, initiate and carry out conversations, and appropriately handle social requests.

Linking the Interests of Families and Teachers[17]

This is a selective intervention targeting school-age children at risk of conduct problems to decrease delinquent behaviors and promote healthy development. The three main components are: (a) classroom-based problem-solving and social skills training, (b) playground-based behavior modification, and (c) group-delivered parent training. LIFT instructors meet with all the participants in a classroom for 1 hour twice a week for 10 weeks.

Strengthening Families Program[13]

The SFP is also a selective intervention designed for high-risk families. It consists of 14 sessions that target parenting skills and children's and families' life skills. Parents and children participate in SFP separately and together. It can be administered to children from the ages of 3–14 years.

The SFP is not greatly different from other parenting programs. The parenting sessions review appropriate developmental expectations, teach parents to interact positively with children, such as showing enthusiasm and attention for good behavior and letting the child take the lead in play activities, increasing attention and praise for desirable children's behaviors, positive family communication (including active listening and reducing criticism and sarcasm), family meetings to improve order and organization, and effective and consistent discipline including consequences and time-outs. The children's skills training content includes: communication skills to improve relationships with parents, peers, and teachers; hopes and dreams; resilience skills; problem solving; peer resistance; identification of feelings; anger management; and coping skills. The family practice sessions allow parents and children time to practice what they learned in their individual sessions in experiential exercises (http://www.strengtheningfamiliesprogram.org/).

What can schools do?

To be successful schools need to adopt a sophisticated approach to prevention that includes universal, selective and indicated approaches (see Chapter 7). Leaving aside universal measures to reduce access and availability to alcohol (discussed in Chapter 7) an examination of the more effective interventions[12] suggests that alcohol prevention programs, apart from being tailored to the circumstances of the specific age group, should aim to encourage children not to drink, delay the age at which pupils start drinking, and reduce the harm it can cause among those who do drink. To achieve that, education programs need to: (a) increase knowledge of the harm alcohol use can cause, physically, mentally and socially (including legal consequences); (b) provide opportunities to explore attitudes to and perceptions of alcohol use; (c) help students develop decision-making, assertiveness, coping and expressive skills; (d) increase awareness of how the media, advertisements, role models as well as the views of parents, peers, and society can influence alcohol use; and (e) provide personalized feedback. A *whole school* approach (i.e., involving staff, parents, and pupils) to alcohol is likely to be the most successful. In addition, schools should offer parents information about where they can get help to develop their parenting skills.

Schools also need to have in place mechanisms to identify students who are drinking or drinking excessively to offer them brief, individual, evidence-based interventions by appropriately trained personnel (see Chapter 9) or referral to external services. Violations of school alcohol policies and driving while intoxicated often result in attending mandatory education or treatment programs; in the case of drink driving convictions, participation may result in reduced penalties. The effectiveness of mandated treatment is discussed in the college section below because more research is available for college students. Medical amnesty policies similar to those implemented by some colleges may also contribute to lessen the risk of harm in case of alcohol poisoning.

Preventing and dealing with college drinking

There has been much concern about drinking among college students especially in the United States where most of the available research originates. Indeed, US federal regulations require institutions of higher education to notify students and staff about the institution's standards of conduct that prohibit the unlawful possession, use, or distribution of alcohol and illicit drugs on college property or as part of any college-related activity. Alcohol use is the most frequent reason for emergency medical care and campus discipline. Research on this area was stimulated by the National Institute on Alcohol Abuse and Alcoholism (NIAAA) and its 2002 report A Call to Action: Changing the Culture of Drinking at US Colleges.[28] The fact that the United States is one of the few countries in which drinking is not legal until the age of 21 years may have also contributed. As already noted, heavy alcohol use is quite pervasive among people in their early twenties whether they attend college or not but fewer data are available for nonstudents. Severe drinking and binge drinking among young adults, which peaks at the age of 19, is the strongest predictor of abusing or being dependent on alcohol over the course of a lifetime.[29]

Risk factors in college drinking

It is important to know what factors, if any, specifically influence college drinking, which can then become the target for intervention. These include[28]:

(a) Living arrangements—rates are higher among students living in fraternities and sororities followed by on-campus housing (e.g., dormitories and residence halls), and living off-site (e.g., in apartments). Students who live with their families drink the least.
(b) College characteristics—excessive alcohol use is more likely in colleges where fraternities and sororities dominate or where athletic teams are prominent.
(c) Being a first-year student seems to also increase the risk—many students initiate heavy drinking during the early days of college life; the first 6 weeks seem to be critical. This is paradoxical because during their high-school years, those who actually go on to college tend to drink less than their peers who do not intend to progress to college.
(d) Other factors, such as pricing and availability of alcohol in the area surrounding a campus, the institution's alcohol policies and their enforcement.

As a result, effective prevention strategies should target simultaneously three constituencies: the student population as a whole, the college and its surrounding environment, and the students at risk or alcohol-dependent drinkers. These are no different from the interventions mentioned in other chapters of this book, but need to be tailored to the specific circumstances of college life. Interventions may also target specific groups such as freshmen, athletes, fraternity/sorority society members, and students that violate college alcohol policies.[30] The following interventions can be grouped on four levels[31]:

(a) community, (b) institutional, (c) group–interpersonal (i.e., strategies that draw on the influence of parents and peers), and (d) individual–interventions targeting students who drink heavily (indicated interventions).

Community and campus strategies

There is compelling evidence about the effectiveness of increased enforcement of laws about minimum drinking age and driving under the influence of alcohol, restrictions on alcohol retail outlet density near campuses, and of other policies discussed in Chapter 7.[28] There is no reason to believe that application or enforcement of these policies at colleges would not be efficacious although specific evidence is becoming available only in recent years.

Despite the limited number of studies on community and campus interventions, interest in population-level strategies has been spurred by several considerations. First, many of the individual-level interventions are ideally suited for students whose alcohol consumption is greater than that of their peers—thus, good candidates for receiving personalized normative feedback showing them how they compare to other students. However, alcohol-related harm is not limited to those whose drinking can be characterized as consistently heavy or risky.[32,33] At the population level, light and moderate drinkers so outnumber the heaviest drinkers that, even at their lower level of individual risk, they are responsible for the majority of alcohol-related problems[34] (see also Chapter 7). Therefore, interventions aimed at risky drinkers should be complemented by universal prevention strategies.

Second, there is the possibility that ignoring the broader campus/community environment may actually sabotage the effectiveness of other prevention efforts. In looking for an explanation as to why a social norms marketing campaign failed to replicate, DeJong *et al.*[31] concluded that the intervention was thwarted at campuses surrounded by a high density of alcohol outlets.

Finally, the prevalence and stability of college student drinking in many countries strongly suggests that reducing consumption and consequences will require a comprehensive set of effective strategies with the hope of achieving a synergistic impact.

There has been a small number of multicomponent community-based college interventions reported in the literature but, as summarized by Toomey *et al.*,[35] nearly all of them had a weak design (e.g., no comparison campuses). One of the better studies was an evaluation of the American Medical Association's "A Matter of Degree" program. Weitzman and her colleagues[36] compared a comprehensive environmental community intervention comprising strategies such as reduced alcohol availability, enhanced enforcement of serving laws, and restrictions on alcohol advertising at ten colleges with a high prevalence of heavy drinking with 32 similar campuses. Initially, they reported no significant reduction in drinking between the intervention and comparison colleges. However, when they examined a subset of five campuses that implemented the program with greater intensity they found significantly lower rates of heavy drinking and alcohol-related negative consequences in these campuses. The study did not employ random assignment to condition but rather selected the treatment sites partially based on the interest and willingness of the campus personnel to conduct the intervention.

Clapp and his colleagues[37] evaluated a driving under the influence (DUI) prevention program on one campus that included enhanced enforcement via roadside checkpoints and patrols accompanied by a media advocacy campaign and a social marketing effort. Self-reported DUI at that campus decreased (odds ratio of 0.55) while no change was reported among students at a comparison college. As the authors themselves note, the study was limited in its not being able to use random assignment and multiple campuses in a more rigorous design, but the results are suggestive of what might be possible in an enhanced replication.

Examples of programs

Neighborhoods Engaging with Students (NEST) Project[38]

The NEST project is an example of a multicomponent community intervention. The program consists of a combination of alcohol-control measures and an education campaign. Enforcement interventions included increased party/alcohol emphasis patrols and increased compliance checks at on-premise and off-premise establishments within 2 miles of the campus, supplemented by student-targeted publicity, such as advertisements in the student newspaper and articles in the local media. Neighborhood engagement interventions focused on educating students regarding the rights and responsibilities associated with living in that community, supplemented with interventions to integrate students into neighborhood organizations and activities. The Neighborhood Service Alternative Project required students who received minor "in-possession-of-alcohol" citations to complete community service in those neighborhoods. There was also an increase in late-night programming on campus that focused on first-year students. An evaluation of the implementation of this project in three public universities in Washington in 2005 and 2006 showed a reduction in heavy episodic drinking in the intervention schools compared with no intervention.[38]

Study to Prevent Alcohol-Related Consequences[39]

The Study to Prevent Alcohol-Related Consequences (SPARC) is a comprehensive intervention using a community organizing approach to implement environmental strategies in and around college campuses. The ultimate goal was to reduce high-risk drinking and alcohol-related consequences among college students. Eight public and two private universities in North Carolina were randomized to the intervention or comparison condition. A repeated cross-sectional design was used to assess impact of the intervention. Each intervention school was assigned a campus/community organizer. The organizer worked to form a campus-community coalition, which developed and implemented a unique strategic plan, which was implemented over a period of 3 years.

The researchers[39] found decreases in the intervention group compared to the control group in severe consequences due to students' own drinking and alcohol-related injuries caused to others. In secondary analyses, higher levels of implementation of the intervention were associated with reductions in interpersonal consequences due to others' drinking and alcohol-related injuries caused to others.

Safer California Universities[40]

The Safer California Universities study was designed to test the efficacy of a community-based environmental alcohol risk management prevention strategy applied to college campuses. The study used a control group and a randomized experimental design involving 14 public universities—half randomly assigned to the intervention condition. The comprehensive intervention included nuisance party enforcement operations ("party patrols"), minor decoy operations, DUI checkpoints, social host ordinances, and the use of campus and local media to increase the visibility of environmental strategies. Annual surveys of randomly selected undergraduates measured the proportion of drinking occasions in which students drank to intoxication at six different settings during the fall semester (residence hall party, campus event, fraternity or sorority party, party at off-campus apartment or house, bar/restaurant, outdoor setting), any intoxication at each setting during the semester, and whether students drank to intoxication the last time they went to each setting.

Significant reductions in the incidence and likelihood of intoxication at off-campus parties and bars/restaurants were observed for the intervention universities compared to controls. A lower likelihood of intoxication was also observed for intervention universities the last time students drank at an off-campus party (odds ratio 0.81), a bar or restaurant (0.76), or across all settings (0.80). No increase in intoxication (i.e., displacement) appeared in other settings. Furthermore, stronger intervention effects were achieved at universities with the highest intensity of implementation.[40]

Other strategies

There are a host of other policies and strategies that have been offered for prevention, although most of these measures have not been specifically evaluated. Strategies suggested to achieve this include: holding Friday classes and examinations to reduce Thursday night partying; expanding alcohol-free late night student activities; establishing alcohol-free dormitories; controlling or eliminating alcohol at sports events; refusing sponsorship gifts from the alcohol industry to avoid perceptions that underage drinking is acceptable; and banning alcohol on campus, including at faculty and *alumni* events.[28] Event-specific prevention strategies are another example. This intervention seeks to address student drinking associated with peak times and events such as orientation and beginning of the academic year, twenty-first birthday celebrations, spring break, and graduation.[41] Toomey *et al.*[35] provide additional examples in their review of more specific campus-level strategies.

Ineffective approaches

There is evidence also about strategies that are not effective. These chiefly include educational interventions (i.e., providing information about alcohol and alcohol-related harms). Although education is often one of the elements of effective multimodal interventions, educational programs in isolation have been repeatedly shown to be ineffective—yet they are often favored by institutions for they are cheap and easy to implement. Other strategies such as using breath-analysis tests to give students information on their blood alcohol concentration or "nominated driver" schemes have also been shown to be ineffective in reducing drinking, and the former may even encourage competition for achieving the highest blood alcohol concentration.

Electronic (online) interventions

Although traditional "information only" educational programs have been ineffective, there has been a great deal of interest in, and development of online, electronic educational interventions that bear a resemblance to information strategies but which incorporate features found in the effective cognitive–behavioral or brief motivational interventions. Those that have been evaluated in recent years include myStudentBody, CollegeAlc, Alcohol eCheckup to Go (e-Chug), and AlcoholEdu. Notably, they all incorporate personalized feedback based on the student having entered data on his or her drinking behavior. The student is then shown how their own drinking compares to those of their peers. These programs typically incorporate interactive components along with information about alcohol and its effects. Some also provide students with tips or skills for monitoring and limiting their drinking.

In a recent evaluation of e-Chug alongside AlcoholEdu, Hustad and his colleagues[42] provide a concise summary of the work done in this area. However, it is premature to draw definite conclusions given the few evaluations and the methodological weaknesses (some minor and some major) they contain. Programs are under constant development as well, so the current version may not be the same as the one evaluated just 2 or 3 years before. Application of the programs also vary: Some are being used as universal strategies—required of all students—while in others the intervention is used for students who have been mandated to take the course in light of their problematic drinking. Nevertheless, the evidence suggests that this strategy can reduce alcohol consumption and possibly also alcohol-related harms. In the evaluation cited,[42] incoming freshmen students from a small private university were randomly assigned to one of the intervention programs or to an assessment-only condition. The evaluation found that both programs reduced student alcohol consumption (several measures) at 1-month follow-up. This type of intervention shows promise and is likely to improve with further development. Among the issues to be considered are whether the program works equally well for all types of students and at what time the students should be exposed to it. Given the low marginal cost of delivering these programs, demand for them is likely to be high.

Individual and group strategies

These are particularly useful interventions for students found to misuse alcohol, for example, those who have violated college rules or become intoxicated. Most of the effective individual strategies to reduce drinking contain the following elements[28]:

- *Cognitive–behavioral skills training* that seeks to change the individual's dysfunctional beliefs and thinking about the use of alcohol through activities such as altering expectancies about alcohol's effects, documenting daily alcohol consumption, and learning to manage stress. For instruments to assess alcohol consumption, alcohol problems, and the symptoms of alcohol abuse and dependence, see Chapter 12.

- *Norms or values clarification*, which examines students' perceptions about the acceptability of drinking behavior, using data to refute beliefs about the tolerance for this behavior as well as beliefs about the number of students who drink excessively and the amounts of alcohol they consume. It should be noted that some of these beliefs are "implicit," that is, individuals may be unaware or barely aware of them. Some prevention programs do *not* assume that every choice a student makes has been carefully considered before acting on it. Personalized normative feedback—where a student's alcohol consumption is shown relative to his or her peers—appears to be an especially important component in these interventions.[30]

- *Motivational enhancement* tries to stimulate students' intrinsic desire or motivation to change their behavior. Motivational enhancement strategies are based on the theory that individuals alone are responsible for changing their drinking behavior. In motivational enhancement interventions, interviewers assess students' alcohol consumption using a formal screening instrument. Results are scored and students receive nonjudgmental feedback on their personal drinking habits in comparison with that of others, and its potential negative consequences. Students also receive suggestions to support their decisions to change.

Among the individual and group interventions, there are education and awareness programs (that provide information and or knowledge, clarification of values, or normative reeducation), CBT skills-based programs, motivational/feedback-based approaches, multimodal interventions, intensive treatment, and medication. By and large, research evidence suggests that the available education and awareness programs by themselves are not effective, while there is evidence of effectiveness for CBT skills-based programs, particularly the multicomponent ones, and for brief motivational interventions with personalized feedback, delivered individually or in groups.[30]

One of the main problems is that one-to-one interventions are both labor and time intensive. There is evidence, however, that alternative (and less expensive) modes of delivery may be equally, or even more effective.[30,42,43] Individual and group treatment and pharmacological interventions are described in detail in Chapters 15 and 16. The Brief Alcohol Screening and Intervention for College Students (BASICS) is an example of this type of intervention.

Brief Alcohol Screening and Intervention for College Students[44]

BASICS is a preventive, harm-minimization, individual intervention that follows motivational interviewing principles; it was initially developed for college students aged 18–24, but later extended to other groups. BASICS targets students who drink alcohol heavily and have experienced or are at risk for experiencing alcohol-related problems such as poor class attendance, missed assignments, accidents, sexual assault, and violence. BASICS seeks to reduce alcohol consumption (quantity and frequency) in heavy drinkers and the negative consequences of alcohol use.

The program is conducted over two interviews (i.e., it is brief). The first interview gathers information about the student's recent alcohol consumption, personal beliefs about alcohol, and drinking history, while providing instructions for self-monitoring any drinking between sessions and preparing the student for the online assessment survey. Information from the online assessment survey is used to develop a customized feedback profile for use in the second interview, which compares personal alcohol use with alcohol use norms, reviews individualized negative consequences and risk factors, clarifies per-ceived risks and benefits of drinking, and provides options to assist in making changes to decrease or abstain from alcohol use.

There are several studies supporting the effectiveness of BASICS.[30] For example, one study evaluated the impact of the intervention on students with high-risk drinking over a 4-year follow-up period. Compared with students in the no-treatment control group, students receiving BASICS had significantly greater reductions in drinking quantity that persisted over a 4-year period, with the intervention appearing to have its greatest impact during the first year. However, the effect size of the benefit after 2 years was small.[44] This intervention appears to be equally effective with mandated students.[45]

Amnesty policies

Colleges and universities in the United States do not allow drinking (illegal for those younger than 21) on or off campus; being intoxicated can attract serious penalties. In recent years, some institutions have implemented medical amnesty policies (also called Good Samaritan policies) to minimize the risk of death in cases of alcohol poisoning and to encourage students to seek medical help when severely intoxicated.

These policies are well meaning and have the potential to reduce harm. However, it is unclear whether students[46]:

(a) can identify the symptoms of alcohol poisoning (e.g., pale or bluish skin, vomiting, nausea, confusion, unconsciousness or cannot be roused, seizures, low body temper-ature, and slow or irregular breathing);
(b) understand the risks associated with the symptoms;
(c) are sober enough to judge the risk;
(d) are afraid to seek help because of fear of getting in trouble, either for themselves or their peers; and
(e) are more likely to call for help if an amnesty policy exists.

While there is evidence that students are able to identify symptoms of alcohol poisoning, they have more difficulty distinguishing alcohol-related symptoms that are not signs of alcohol poisoning.[46] Students who do not seek help usually state that the main reason is not fear of getting in trouble but not understanding the risks. Thus, identifying the symptoms of alcohol poisoning and understanding the risks while intoxicated are likely to be considerable barriers to seeking help. It follows that amnesty policies need to educate students in assessing alcohol poisoning to understand which symptoms require immediate action and what that action should be (i.e., call emergency services). Because students who consume more alcohol are the most likely to be in situations requiring help and in situations where they can actually help, prevention efforts regarding alcohol poisoning should focus on heavy drinkers.[46]

Mandated students

Most US colleges have sanctions or required interventions for students who violate alcohol policies or have undergone medical evaluation for intoxication (mandated students). There is some evidence that these students, who are at high risk for alcohol-related harm, benefit from brief interventions similarly to nonmandated students. An important question is whether these changes are due to the intervention or to having been caught, although both may play a role.[45,47]

The military

What'll we do with a drunken sailor,
Earl-aye in the morning?

(Traditional song)

Historically, alcohol use has been strongly linked with warfare and the military. One of the best-known associations is with the UK's Royal Navy. Prior to the seventeenth century, sailors drank beer or ale because drinking water on board ships quickly became stagnant. In 1740, instead of beer the Royal Navy began to issue half a pint of strong rum to each sailor daily (the "rum ration") and continued to do so—to all enlisted men, even those in nuclear submarines—until July 31, 1970 (Black Tot Day). Alcohol rations had been abolished in the US Navy 100 years earlier, in 1862.

Heavy alcohol use (drinking five or more drinks per occasion at least once a week in the last 30 days) increased among military personnel in the United States between 1980 and 1982, decreased between 1982 and 1988, remained relatively stable between 1988 and 1998, and increased again from 1998 (15%) to 2008 (20%).[48] Heavy alcohol use is higher among personnel deployed to an operational theater than among those not deployed.[48] Military men are more likely than women to be heavy or binge drinkers and to experience more alcohol-related problems. Similarly, enlisted men and women are more likely than male and female officers to be heavy or binge drinkers.[49] Alcohol abuse is the most common mental disorder in the UK military[50] (18%). While public attention focuses on combat fatalities, a Canadian study shows that most members of the Canadian military die from other causes, with 11% of deaths attributed to alcohol use compared with less than 5% combat-related deaths.[51] Alcohol use is also one of the strongest predictors of misconduct in the forces. Problems exist across the services. For example, an U.S. Air Force report indicated that 33% of suicides, 57% of sexual assaults, 29% of domestic violence incidents, and 44% of motor vehicle accidents were alcohol related.

In the United States, young males in the Marines have the highest rate of heavy alcohol use (39%)—compared 33% in the Army, 32% in the Navy, and 25% in the Air Force.[52] Rates of heavy drinking in all service branches are nearly four times higher among young men (32%) than women (8%).[52] Overall, prevalence of heavy alcohol use among the young military personnel is substantially higher than in civilians of the same age (15% for civilians, 27% for the military).[53] Young adults in the military are about three times more likely to drink heavily than older enlistees. In 2002, 27% of those aged 18–25 reported heavy drinking, compared with 9% of those aged 26–55.[52]

Prevention

When seeking to prevent and deal with alcohol misuse, the problems faced by the military are not too different from those confronted by enterprises, schools, colleges and the community at large, and the principles to deal with them are also similar, as described in Chapters 7 and 8. Nevertheless, effective programs will need to take into account the specific make up (e.g., conscripted vs. professional), problems, traditions, culture, and hierarchical structure of each country's armed forces.

Reasons for the high drinking rates in the military include a workplace culture that supports alcohol use (e.g., drinking rituals and traditional celebrations, expectations about heavy drinking after work and while on leave, drinking to cope and as a recreational activity), the increased availability of alcohol both in and around military bases, as well as the stress associated with deployment and the specific demands of military life. However, in many cases, heavy drinking predates entering the military. A study found that those who entered the US military were more likely than other young adults to have been heavy drinkers in high school.[54]

It is of note that the vast majority of drinking by military personnel takes place off duty. Yet, the division between work and leisure for the military is not as clear-cut as for other professions; it can be argued that all drinking by military personnel, whether on duty or off duty, is work related due to their need to be available at all times.

One aspect to consider when implementing prevention programs in military settings is that circumstances vary enormously from base to base and that interventions need to be adapted to the particular needs of each base, service or locality. The importance of this issue is illustrated by a report that a specific policy change designed to reduce off-base alcohol use among young marines stationed near the Mexican border resulted in a 78% reduction in the number of underage intoxicated marines returning across the Mexican border, while the number returning with blood alcohol concentration $\geq 0.08\%$ was reduced by 84%. Marines stationed at Camp Pendleton, California, 67 miles from the Mexican border, were attracted to the bars in Mexico by inexpensive alcohol and a minimum drinking age of 18, often returning to base intoxicated. In response, commanders at Camp Pendleton adopted a policy that required marines to obtain written permission to cross the border.[55]

While alcohol misuse is a problem for most armed forces around the world,[48,50,51] published information is limited. Thus, most data presented in this chapter refers to the US military. However, problems and solutions are likely to be similar in other jurisdictions.

Policies

The US military adopted strict policies in the early 1980s with the aim of reducing rates of alcohol, tobacco, and illicit drug use.[56] The current policy emphasizes that consumption of alcohol is a personal decision but individuals who choose to drink alcohol must do so lawfully and responsibly. The policy defines responsible drinking as "drinking in a way that does not adversely affect an individual's ability to fulfill their obligations and does not negatively impact the individual's job performance, health, or well-being, or the good order and discipline in a unit."[56] Underage (<21 years of age) drinking is prohibited. On-duty impairment due to alcohol consumption is not tolerated (impairment is defined as having a blood alcohol ≥0.05%). The policy also allows for random testing, disciplinary measures for violations, and include components for detection of problem drinkers and referral, treatment, rehabilitation, and prevention (educate about the harms of alcohol, deglamorize alcohol use and reduce availability).

Of course, policies are only effective if they are enforced. Implementation varies between the services and the locations. For example, the Air Force has a "zero-tolerance" policy toward underage drinking and problematic use of alcohol. It promotes a "culture of responsible choices," which emphasizes drinking as one of many lifestyle choices active-duty members make that can affect combat readiness. A component of this initiative is the "0–0–1–3 campaign": "0" underage drinking; "0" driving-under-the influence incidents; and if personnel are of legal drinking age and choose to drink alcohol, "1" drink per hour, with a maximum of "3" drinks per night.[57]

While this policy has been in place since the 1980s, it does not seem to have resulted in a reduction in alcohol consumption in the decade to 2008[48] and evaluation of the various programs is limited. As for schools and colleges, prevention programs that rely exclusively on information and education are unlikely to be effective. As in the case of colleges (see above), there has recently been an emphasis in the development of online educational interventions that not only include information but also incorporate personalized feedback and features found in the effective cognitive–behavioral or brief motivational individual interventions. These approaches are promising but need further evaluation.

Availability

Availability, be it easy access or low price, is a strong predictor of the level of alcohol use and alcohol-related harms (see Chapter 7). Thus, reducing availability is one of the most effective means of minimizing use. In general, alcohol is cheaper for military personnel because of pricing policies. For example, the U.S. Department of Defense allows alcoholic beverages sold in military stores to be discounted below prices in local civilian stores. Navy personnel report that alcohol and opportunities for drinking are easily available both in foreign ports (where the US minimum legal drinking age usually does not apply and alcohol is often inexpensive) and on the US bases. But this is far from universal; for example, alcohol consumption is not permitted aboard US Navy ships, with the rare exceptions of ceremonial drinks (e.g., to honor a visiting high-ranking officer) and tightly controlled beer distribution (two per crew member) during "steel beach picnics"—when vessels have been at sea for at least 45 consecutive days. Thus, availability of alcohol in these circumstances largely refers to drinking opportunities in port.[58]

Multimodal programs

Since most alcohol use by the military occurs off duty and off base, it can be argued that programs are likely to fail unless nearby communities are engaged, including media efforts targeted toward policy makers, joint community-level collaboration, and an emphasis on reducing the supply of alcohol (see Chapter 8). One project involved examining underage drinking in 18–25-year-old active-duty air force members in five demonstration and five comparison communities.[57] Each demonstration community implemented a set of strategies to reduce drinking by (a) reducing the social availability of alcohol; (b) compliance checks to ensure that establishments were not selling alcohol to underage active-duty members (using covert underage buyers); (c) impaired driving enforcement; (d) local policy development; (e) a community-based media campaign to reduce drinking; and (f) offering alternative activities that do not include drinking (e.g., sports activities). The early results showed that the percentage of junior enlisted personnel at risk for an alcohol problem dropped as much as 14% and 10% in the two Arizona demonstration communities that implemented the intervention.

Resources for practitioners

- Army Regulation 600–85. Available at: http://www.apd.army.mil/pdffiles/r600_85.pdf.
- Hantman I, Crosse C. *Progress in prevention: National study of local education activities under the Safe and Drug-free Schools and Communities Act*. Washington, DC: U.S. Department of Education, Office of the Under Secretary, Planning and Evaluation Service; 2000.
- Johnston LD, O'Malley PM, Bachman JG, Schulenberg JE. *Monitoring the Future: National Survey Results on Drug Use, 1975–2008: Volume I, Secondary School Students* (NIH Publication No. 09–7402). Bethesda, MD: National Institute on Drug Abuse; 2009. Available at: http://monitoringthefuture.org/pubs.html#monographs.
- National Institute for Health and Clinical Excellence. School-based interventions on alcohol. Available at: http://www.nice.org.uk/PH7.
- Peters LWH, Kok G, Ten Dam GTM *et al*. Effective elements of school health promotion across behavioral domains: A systematic review of reviews. *BMC Public Health* 2009; 9:182.
- Task Force of the National Advisory Council on Alcohol Abuse and Alcoholism. A Call to Action: Changing the Culture of Drinking at U.S. Colleges. Bethesda, MD: National Institute on Alcohol Abuse and Alcoholism; 2002. Available at: http://www. collegedrinkingprevention.gov/niaaacollegematerials/taskforce/taskforce_toc.aspx.
- The National Registry of Evidence-based Programs and Practices of the U.S. Substance Abuse and Mental Health Services Administration. Available at: http://nrepp. samhsa.gov/.

Resources for patients and families

- NIAAA college drinking, changing the culture: A variety of useful documents are available; among them What Colleges Need to Know Now: An Update on College Drinking Research is available at: http://www.collegedrinkingprevention. gov/NIAAACollegeMaterials/.

- Army Substance Abuse Programs' (ASAP) Web site: http://acsap.army.mil/sso/pages/index.jsp.
- Navy Alcohol and Drug Abuse Prevention Program Web site: http://www.npc.navy.mil/CommandSupport/NADAP/.

References

1. National Institute for Health and Clinical Excellence. *Interventions in Schools to Prevent and Reduce Alcohol Use Among Children and Young People.* NICE Public Health Guidance 7, London, UK: National Institute for Health and Clinical Excellence; 2007.
2. Johnston LD, O'Malley PM, Bachman JG, Schulenberg JE. *Monitoring the Future: National Survey Results on Drug Use, 1975–2008: Volume I, Secondary School Students* (NIH Publication No. 09–7402). Bethesda, MD: National Institute on Drug Abuse; 2009.
3. Hibell B, Andersson B, Bjarnasson T. *The 2003 ESPAD Report: Alcohol and Other Drugs Use Among Students in 35 European Countries.* Stockholm: Swedish Council for Information on Alcohol and Other Drugs; 2004.
4. British Medical Association. *Alcohol Misuse: Tackling the UK Epidemic.* BMA, 2008. Available at: http://www.bma.org.uk/health_promotion_ethics/alcohol/tacklingalcoholmisuse.jsp. Accessed September 1, 2010.
5. White V, Hayman J. *Australian Secondary School Students' Use of Alcohol in 2005.* Melbourne: The Cancer Council Victoria; 2006.
6. Toomey TL, Wagenaar AC. Environmental policies to reduce college drinking: Options and research findings. *J Stud Alcohol* 2002; (Suppl. 14): 193–205.
7. Karam E, Kypri K, Salamoun M. Alcohol use among college students: An international perspective. *Curr Opin Psychiatry* 2007; 20:213–221.
8. Johnston LD, O'Malley PM, Bachman JG, Schulenberg JE. *Monitoring the Future: National Survey Results on Drug Use, 1975–2004. Volume II: College Students and Adults Ages 19–45.* NIH Pub. No. 05–5728. Bethesda, MD: National Institute on Drug Abuse; 2005.
9. O'Neill SE, Parra GR, Sher KJ. Clinical relevance of heavy drinking during the college years: Cross-sectional and prospective perspectives. *Psychol Addict Behav* 2001; 15:350–359.
10. Hingson RW, Zha W, Weitzman ER. Magnitude of and trends in alcohol-related mortality and morbidity among US college students ages 18–24, 1998–2005. *J Stud Alcohol Drugs* 2009; (Suppl. 16): 12–20. Available at http://www.ncbi.nlm.nih.gov/pmc/articles/PMC2701090/.
11. Carter S, Straits KJE, Hall M. Project Venture: Evaluation of an experiential, culturally-based approach to substance abuse prevention with American Indian youth. *J Exp Educ* 2007; 29:397–400.
12. Jones L, James M, Jefferson T, Lushey C *et al. A Review of the Effectiveness and Cost-Effectiveness of Interventions Delivered in Primary and Secondary Schools to Prevent and/or Reduce Alcohol Use by Young People Under 18 Years Old.* London, UK: National Institute for Health and Clinical Excellence; 2007.
13. Foxcroft DR, Ireland D, Lister-Sharp DJ *et al.* Longer-term primary prevention for alcohol misuse in young people: A systematic review. *Addiction* 2003; 98:397–411.
14. Botvin GJ, Baker E, Dusenbury L *et al.* Long-term follow-up results of a randomized drug abuse prevention trial in a white middle-class population. *J Am Med Assoc* 1995; 273:1106–1112.
15. McBride N, Farringdon F, Midford R *et al.* Harm minimisation in school drug education. Final results of the School Health and Alcohol Harm Reduction Project (SHAHRP). *Addiction,* 2004; 99:278–291.

16. Hawkins JD, Catalano RF, Kosterman R *et al.* Preventing adolescent health-risk behaviors by strengthening protection during childhood. *Arch Pediatr Adolesc Med* 1999; 153:226–234.

17. Eddy JM, Reid JB, Stoolmiller M, Fetrow RA. Outcomes during middle school for an elementary school-based preventive intervention for conduct problems: Follow-up results from a randomized trial. *Behav Ther* 2003; 34:535–552.

18. Shope JT, Kloska DD, Dielman TE, Maharg R. Longitudinal evaluation of an enhanced Alcohol Misuse Prevention Study (AMPS) curriculum for grades six-eight. *J School Health* 2009; 64:160–166.

19. Perry CL, Grant M, Ernberg G, Florenzano RU *et al.* WHO collaborative study on alcohol education and young people: Outcomes of a four-country pilot study. *Subst Use Misuse* 1989; 24:1145–1171.

20. Bond L, Patton G, Glover S, Carlin JB *et al.* The Gatehouse Project: Can a multilevel school intervention affect emotional wellbeing and health risk behaviours? *J Epidemiol Commun Health* 2004; 58:997–1003.

21. Donaldson SI, Thomas CW, Graham JW, Au JG *et al.* Verifying drug abuse prevention program effects using reciprocal best friend reports. *J Behav Med* 2000; 23:585–601.

22. Ellickson PL, McCaffrey DF, Ghosh-Dastidar B, Longshore DL. New inroads in preventing adolescent drug use: Results from a large-scale trial of Project ALERT in middle schools. *Am J Public Health*, 2003; 93:1830–1836.

23. Lynam DR, Milich R, Zimmerman R *et al.* Project DARE: No effects at 10-year follow-up. *J Consul Clin Psychol* 1999; 67:590–593.

24. Werch CE, Owen DM, Carlson JM *et al.* One-year follow-up results of the STARS for Families alcohol prevention program. *Health Educ Res* 2003; 18:74–87.

25. Padget A, Bell ML, Shamblen SR, Ringwalt CL. Does learning about the effects of alcohol on the developing brain affect children's alcohol use? *Prev Sci* 2006; 7:293–302.

26. Bremberg S, Arborelius E. Effects on adolescent alcohol consumption of a school based student-centred health counselling programme. *Scand J Soc Med* 1994; 22:113–119.

27. Cuijpers P, Jonkers R, De Weerdt I, De Jong A. The effects of drug abuse prevention at school: The 'Healthy School and Drugs' project. *Addiction* 2002; 97:67–73.

28. Task Force of the National Advisory Council on Alcohol Abuse and Alcoholism. *A Call to Action: Changing the Culture of Drinking at U.S. Colleges.* Bethesda, MD: National Institute on Alcohol Abuse and Alcoholism; 2002.

29. Hasin DS, Stinson FS, Ogburn E, Grant BF. Prevalence, correlates, disability, and comorbidity of DSM-IV alcohol abuse and dependence in the United States: Results from the National Epidemiologic Survey on Alcohol and Related Conditions. *Arch Gen Psychiatry* 2007; 64:830–842.

30. Larimer M, Cronce J. Identification, prevention, and treatment revisited: Individual-focused college drinking prevention strategies 1999–2006. *Addict Behav* 2007; 32:2439–2468.

31. DeJong W, Schneider SK, Towvim LG *et al.* A multisite randomized trial of social norms marketing campaigns to reduce college student drinking: A replication failure. *Subst Abus* 2009; 30:127–140.

32. Gruenewald P, Johnson F, Light J, Lipton R, Saltz R. Understanding college drinking: Assessing dose response from survey self-reports. *J Stud Alcohol* 2003; 64:500–514.

33. Weitzman ER, Nelson TF. College student binge drinking and the "prevention paradox": Implications for prevention and harm reduction. *J Drug Educ* 2004; 34:247–266.

34. Kreitman N. Alcohol consumption and the preventive paradox. *Br J Addict* 1986; 81:353–363.

35. Toomey TL, Lenk KM, Wagenaar AC. Environmental policies to reduce college drinking: An update of research findings. *J Stud Alcohol Drugs* 2007; 68:208–219.

36. Weitzman ER, Nelson TF, Lee H, Wechsler H. Reducing drinking and related harms in college: Evaluation of the "A Matter of Degree" program. *Am J Prev Med* 2004; 27:187–196.
37. Clapp J, Johnson M, Voas RB *et al.* Reducing DUI among US college students: Results of an environmental prevention trial. *Addiction* 2005; 100:327–334.
38. Saltz RF, Welker LR, Paschall MJ *et al.* Evaluating a comprehensive campus—community prevention intervention to reduce alcohol-related problems in a college population. *J Stud Alcohol Drugs* 2009; (Suppl. 16): 21–27.
39. Wolfson M, DuRant RH, Champion H *et al.* Impact of a group-randomized trial to reduce high risk drinking by college students. *Alcohol Clin Exp Res* 2007; 31 (Suppl. 2):115A.
40. Saltz RF. Safer California Universities Project: Early findings. *Alcohol Clin Exp Res* 2007; 31:289A.
41. Neighbors C, Walters ST, Lee CM *et al.* Event-specific prevention: Addressing college student drinking during known windows of risk. *Addict Behav* 2007; 32:2667–2680.
42. Hustad JTP, Barnett NP, Borsari B, Jackson KM. Web-based alcohol prevention for incoming college students: A randomized controlled trial. *Addict Behav* 2010; 35:183–189.
43. Kypri K, Sitharthan T, Cunningham JA, Kavanagh DJ, Dean JI. Innovative approaches to intervention for problem drinking. *Curr Opin Psychiatry* 2005; 18:229–234.
44. Baer JS, Kivlahan DR, Blume AW *et al.* Brief intervention for heavy drinking college students: 4-year follow-up and natural history. *Am J Public Health* 2001; 91:1310–1316.
45. White HR, Mun EY, Pugh L, Morgan TJ. Long-term effects of brief substance use interventions for mandated college students: Sleeper effects of an in-person personal feedback intervention. *Alcohol Clin Exp Res* 2007; 31:1380–1391.
46. Oster-Aaland L, Lewis MA, Neighbors C, Vangsness J, Larimer ME. Alcohol poisoning among college students turning 21: Do they recognize the symptoms and how do they help? *J Stud Alcohol Drugs* 2009; (Suppl. 16):122–130. Available at http://www.ncbi.nlm.nih.gov/pmc/articles/PMC2701093/.
47. White HR, Mun EY, Morgan TJ. Do brief personalized feedback interventions work for mandated students or is it just getting caught that works? *Psychol Addict Behav* 2008; 22:107–116.
48. Bray RM, Pemberton MR, Lane ME *et al.* Substance use and mental health trends among US military active duty personnel: Key findings from the 2008 DoD Health Behavior Survey. *Mil Med* 2010; 175:390–400.
49. Brown JM, Bray RM, Hartzell MC. A Comparison of alcohol use and related problems among women and men in the military. *Mil Med* 2010; 175:101–107.
50. Iversen AC, van Staden L, Hughes JH *et al.* The prevalence of common mental disorders and PTSD in the UK military: Using data from a clinical interview-based study. *BMC Psychiatry* 2009; 9:68.
51. Tien HCN, Acharya S, Redelmeier DA. Preventing deaths in the Canadian military. *Am J Prev Med* 2010; 38:331–339.
52. Bray RM, Hourani LL, Rae KL et al. 2002 *Department of Defense Survey of Health-Related Behaviors among Military Personnel*. Research Triangle Park, NC: RTI International; 2003.
53. Ames G, Cunradi C. Alcohol use and preventing alcohol-related problems among young adults in the military. *Alcohol Res Health* 2004; 28:252–257.
54. Bachman JG, Freedman-Doan P, O'Malley PM *et al.* Changing patterns of drug use among U.S. military recruits before and after enlistment. *Am J Public Health* 1999; 89:672–677.
55. Voas RB, Johnson M, Lange J. Permission to cross the border: Effective policy reduces high-risk drinking by marines. *J Stud Alcohol* 2002; 63:645–648.
56. Army Regulation 600–85. Available at: http://www.apd.army.mil/pdffiles/r600_85.pdf. Accessed August 23, 2010.

57. Spera C, Franklin K, Uekawa K *et al.* Reducing drinking among junior enlisted air force members in five communities: Early findings of the EUDL program's influence on self-reported drinking behaviors. *J Stud Alcohol Drugs* 2010; 71:373–383.
58. Moore RS, Ames GM, Cunradi CB. Physical and social availability of alcohol for young enlisted naval personnel in and around home port. *Subst Abuse Treat Prev Policy* 2007; 2:17.

Part IV

Assessment and Diagnosis

Chapter 11

The clinical interview of young people about alcohol use

Yvonne Bonomo

Department of Medicine, St Vincent's Hospital, University of Melbourne, Melbourne, Australia

---

Key points

- Use a holistic approach in the clinical interview of youth, making a broad psychosocial assessment, rather than focusing only on alcohol use.
- Take into account developmental stage when working with young people and adjust your communication style accordingly.
- Keep in mind the risk and protective factor framework in the assessment of any young person.
- Enquire about age of onset, pattern of alcohol consumption, and alcohol-related consequences during the clinical interview.
- Screen for use of other drugs including tobacco and illicit substances, as it is common for young people to use more than one substance.
- Comprehensive evaluation by a mental health professional is indicated where screening reveals significant symptoms of depression, anxiety, or other mental health disorder.

Building rapport

As with any other clinical context, to work effectively with a young person experiencing difficulties with alcohol, rapport needs to be established. Key principles in establishing rapport are described below.

Opening the interview

Initial interactions can have a significant impact on establishing rapport with a young person. Ideally, address the young person first. Greet the individual by name and introduce yourself stating who you are. If the young person is accompanied by an adult, it is often helpful to get him/her to introduce the accompanying adult. In doing this, the young person is more likely to understand that he or she is the focus of the consultation, not the adult.[1]

Young People and Alcohol: Impact, Policy, Prevention, Treatment, First Edition.
Edited by John B. Saunders and Joseph M. Rey.
© 2011 Blackwell Publishing Ltd. Published 2011 by Blackwell Publishing Ltd.

A holistic approach

Young people often express frustration when the clinical interview, rather than being holistic, is focused on the alcohol "problem." This is because very often the alcohol misuse is not felt by the young person to be an issue. They are frequently more concerned about other aspects of their life. A broad medical and psychosocial assessment is therefore more likely to engage the young person and yield the information needed. The assessment should include information about the social, educational and vocational background of the adolescent. This is important because alcohol misuse can often contribute to problems such as poor performance at school or in sport, difficulty in relationships with parents and other significant adults, low employment prospects, and homelessness. A useful framework (in mnemonic form) that can be followed to assist the process of taking a psychosocial history will be described shortly.

Mental disorders often begin during adolescence and young adulthood[2,3] and it is important to screen for these, especially given that they are strongly associated with alcohol and drug use. Comprehensive evaluation by a mental health professional is indicated where screening reveals significant symptoms of depression, anxiety, psychotic disorder, etc., or where a diagnosis is unclear and an expert opinion will assist in the management plan.

A familial history of heavy alcohol or other drug use is an important risk factor to inquire of the young person. Familial mental health problems such as depression and anxiety are other important risk factors and should also be inquired about. However, one needs to bear in mind the limitations of some young people in knowing these details about members of their family.

Gathering useful information in the first minutes of the assessment

Much useful information can be gathered in the first minutes of the assessment. A mental note of who is present and how these individuals appear to be interacting with each other can give some indication of the underlying issues. For instance, it may be very clear from the body language that the young person does not want to be present at the appointment. Alternatively, there may be signs of considerable angst on the part of the accompanying parents or other adults. The context of the assessment is an important influence here. A routine visit to the family doctor in which alcohol is assessed as part of the adolescent health check will be quite different to the young teenager brought to the medical practitioner because of parental concern about their son/daughter's alcohol consumption. These situations also differ substantially from the teenager brought by ambulance to the emergency department as a result of alcohol-related trauma or the teenager who is being seen in the legal context because of having been charged for alcohol-related offences.

Additional potentially valuable information that can be obtained in these initial stages include how the young person presents in terms of mode of dress, evidence of self-care or grooming, etc. These observations can provide preliminary impressions of the character of the young person or their background. Sometimes they can be useful ways of engaging the young person.

> That's an interesting T-shirt you are wearing—do you have an interest in Grand Prix racing? What's your favorite team?

In cases where the young person appears particularly unkempt with a depressed demeanor, it is particularly important, as the clinical interview progresses, to screen for a number of mental health disorders including depression, psychosis, or other diagnoses.

A framework for psychosocial assessment

A useful framework to perform a comprehensive psychosocial assessment uses the "HEADSS" mnemonic. The framework comprises a set of questions designed to explore various psychosocial domains that impact on a young person's well-being. The mnemonic includes the following:

- Home
- Education/employment
- Activities
- Drugs (including alcohol)
- Sexuality
- Suicide and depression

Since its original description, it has been expanded to include Eating/exercise and Safety (HEEADSSS).[4]

Home includes exploring the type of accommodation where the young person lives, who lives with that young person, and whether there is alcohol readily available in the home. The latter is associated with.[5] Education/employment includes the highest educational achievement the young person has so far attained and what their aspirations for the future are. Activities includes hobbies, special interests, particular talents the young person may have, and what he/she most likes to spend time doing. Many adolescents will describe enjoying spending time with their friends; this needs further exploration to determine what the peer group does with their time together, in particular ascertaining to what extent alcohol plays a role in peer group activities. (Details to explore with regard to alcohol and other drugs are outlined later in this chapter.) When approaching the area of sexuality, it is particularly important to ascertain whether alcohol plays a role in unsafe sexual practices of the young person. In addition, given that adolescence is the key period for exploration of self-identity, including sexual identity, it is important not to assume heterosexual orientation of the individual and frame questions in an open-ended way. When talking about symptoms of depression and suicidal ideation or attempts, determining links with heavy alcohol consumption is relevant. Heavy alcohol consumption has been strongly associated with depressive symptoms[6] and frequently plays a role in suicide attempts.[7] A history of sexual or other abuse is frequently associated with alcohol or other drug use disorders and it is often, but not always, appropriate to ask about experiences of sexual abuse.

Sign posting the psychosocial screen before starting is useful to reassure the young person that there is an appropriate purpose for asking these questions. It can allay anxiety or uncertainty the young person may have about the questions and facilitates engagement of the individual.

> When doctors do checkups of young people they need to ask about a number of behaviors that can impact on a person's health. I'm now going to ask you about some of these things. This is something we do with all young people . . .

It is not essential to work through psychosocial screens such as the HEEADSSS in order; however, in practice, rapport with the young person is usually best achieved if the least sensitive areas (home, school, peers) are asked about before the more sensitive areas are discussed (sexuality, drug use). Reinforcing the principle of confidentiality and its caveats before broaching the sensitive areas of questioning is advisable.

> Now I need to ask you a few questions that you may find quite personal. If you don't want to answer them you don't have to, but the reason that I am asking you is that . . .

The HEEADSSS framework is useful not only for establishing rapport but also for making a psychosocial assessment of the young person. It can also provide a means of opportunistic health care in the form of health promotion and anticipatory counseling when potential health risks or issues are mentioned.

Confidentiality

Confidentiality is key to establishing good rapport. It has been documented that if a young person is concerned about breaches of confidentiality on the part of the professional offering assistance then the likelihood of reliable information being given, and therefore an accurate assessment of the young person being made, is substantially diminished.[8,9] Confidentiality is best addressed with the young person at the outset of the clinical interview. It is important to check that the young person understands what is meant by confidentiality. This includes making them aware of the ethical and legal limits on confidentiality, and those situations when there may be a need to break confidentiality. As a general rule, confidentiality may be broken in cases of the young person being at risk of harming themselves or others, or if they are at risk of abuse (physical or sexual). It is important, however, to note that laws pertaining to confidentiality vary between countries, and between states or provinces in a given country. They can also vary in relation to the age of the adolescent. Practitioners should therefore clarify the regulations in the jurisdiction in which the young person is being seen. An important aspect of maintaining confidentiality is to ascertain with the young person how they would like to be contacted if follow-up is required. This helps avoid accidental breaches of confidentiality.

Parents need to be aware about confidentiality. Specifically, they need to be aware that privacy is standard practice in adolescent health care. Note that awareness of cultural sensitivities is important as different cultures have different approaches to adolescence. In some cultures, the individual and their independence is the emphasis, while in other

Table 11.1 Developmental tasks of adolescence.

- Achievement of biological maturation.
- Establishment of independence and autonomy and peer relationships.
- Development of personal identity that is realistic, positive, and stable.
- Development of sexual self-identity and intimate relationships with appropriate peers.
- Consolidation of a moral/value system and establishment of educational/vocational goals.

Source: Modified from reference 12.

cultures greater importance is placed on family and cultural identity. It is often helpful to explain to parents that the purpose of confidentiality is not to exclude them as parents, rather to facilitate the young person's personal development. Research shows that young people often turn to their parents or adult caregivers with their health and well-being concerns first,[10,11] and young people should be encouraged and empowered to continue to talk with their parents or adult caregivers about important issues relating to their health and well-being.

Taking into account stage of adolescent development

Adolescent development is not just chronological age or the physical phenomenon of puberty. It involves a number of "tasks" (Table 11.1) and these are achieved in stages as the young brain develops and matures. Working with young people requires an understanding of the individual's developmental stage because it influences the nature of communication with the young person and what can be expected of them. Assessment of developmental stage in the clinical setting needs to bear in mind that cognitive, physical and psychosocial maturation may not necessarily be in synchrony with each other.

The age range included in the term "adolescence" can vary but from a practical perspective, adolescent development can usually be considered as fitting three main stages followed by young adulthood. The characteristic features of each stage are outlined in Table 11.2.

It is now known that the brain continues undergoing significant change during adolescence[14,15] (see Chapter 5). As the brain matures, there is substantial pruning of some neural connections while at the same time there is myelination of other neurons. The latter allows effective and efficient transmission of signals. The maturation process occurs from the brain toward the prefrontal cortex, which is responsible for executive function. Executive function includes the ability to determine between good and bad, suppress urges, determine the consequences of actions, discern between conflicting thoughts or concepts, etc. These processes are in their early stages at the commencement of adolescence and manifest as concrete thinking and little in the way of abstract reasoning or logical deductive thinking in young adolescents (approximately 12–14 years of age). Teenagers who drink alcohol at this age often fail to make optimal decisions around alcohol because they find it difficult to properly comprehend the negative consequences that can occur with excessive drinking. By mid-adolescence, young people are usually able to think in more abstract terms about their health and they are better at recognizing the

Table 11.2 Stages of adolescent development.

Stage	Key feature	Details
Early adolescence ~11–14 years of age	Physiological changes of puberty: "Am I normal?"	• Concrete thought. • Early adolescence is characterized by the physical and physiological changes of puberty. • Frequently concerned about whether their development is "normal" and in keeping with their peers. • In early adolescence, teenagers are usually still dependent on family but peers (usually of the same sex) become increasingly important.
Middle adolescence ~15–17 years of age	Peers and identity: "Who am I?" "With whom do I belong?"	• Abstract thought. • Striving to define identity; most young people in this age group become more experimental in their behavior. A certain amount of risk taking is necessary for healthy adolescent development but a sense of omnipotence and invincibility results in many young people engaging in behavior that places them at significant danger of physical and psychological harm (e.g., high-risk drinking). Risk taking may also be motivated by seeking peer acceptance or as a release from the pressures of everyday life. Experimentation with drugs, alcohol, and unsafe sex usually peaks in mid-adolescence but often the young person's cognitive skills are not yet sufficiently developed to evaluate their consequences. • Peer group exerts considerable influence in middle adolescence. Sexual identity emerges; dating becomes more frequent although relationships tend to have a self-centered quality.
Late adolescence ~18–20 years of age	Planning for the future: "What will I do with my life?"	• Young people in this age group will usually have more mature intellectual abilities. They have a sense of their own identity and place in society. They understand the consequences of their behavior and have a more developed ethical and moral value system. • The influence of peer group and family diminish at this stage in favor of one-to-one intimate relationships. With consolidation of personal identity, relationships become more mutually sharing in quality. Young people develop their educational and vocational capacities and move toward financial independence.
Young adulthood ~21–25 years of age and beyond	Establishing and consolidating adult roles	• Young adults are usually in continuing education and/or in employment and consolidating their career paths. Financial considerations and independence are now a priority and include plans for the future as well as the present. • Social circles are largely established and there is often a longer term view of intimate partnerships, and for some, children. Individuals generally have a clearer view about the relevance of friends and family, and these relationships take on a more mature aspect.

Source: Adapted from reference 13.

impact of drinking alcohol on their health and well-being and that of others, although they are often inconsistent in their thoughts and behavior. Peers are a very significant influence in middle adolescence and it is generally accepted that the role of peers in adolescent alcohol initiation is crucial.

Assessing a young person's capacity for formal operational thought can be performed by asking the young person to identify and weigh up the various options that exist in a situation relating to alcohol misuse. Asking the young person about their vocational goals is another means of assessing developmental stage. If the individual is still in the concrete thinking stage, they will provide relatively unrealistic options such as wanting to be a supermodel, celebrity, or astronaut without being able to describe how they might achieve these ambitions. By late adolescence (around 18 years and older), the young person's cognitive maturation has developed and they can more comprehensively understand the information they are given. They start to have a clearer idea of the future, be more capable of making decisions through deductive reasoning and systematic evaluation of the options, and also understand the implications of preventative health measures. It is at this time that young people comprehend how negatively excessive alcohol consumption can impact on their work/study performance, sporting performance, and future health.

It is important to note that adolescent development does not progress at the same rate in all individuals. Some young people are more capable of mature thinking than others, related to such factors as social interaction and cultural context. It is also important to note that a small proportion of young people progress into adulthood still unable to engage in complex abstract thinking. This is particularly relevant in long-term heavy drinkers.

Psychosocial risk

The holistic approach to interviewing the young person not only facilitates their engagement with the clinical interview but also enables the health professional to make an assessment of psychosocial risk. Psychosocial risk in an adolescent is a function of the balance of "risk factors" and "protective factors" (see Table 11.3 for some examples of risk and protective factors). Risk factors are those factors in a young person's life that make it more likely that the young individual will engage in behaviors that lead to negative outcomes in health and well-being.[5,16] Examples of risk factors include lack of engagement with school, being bullied, familial conflict, etc.

Protective factors are those factors that reduce the likelihood that the risks adolescents take will result in harm. Some examples of protective factors are strong parental guidance, good peer relationships, and participation in sporting or in creative activities.[5,16]

In the clinical interview, the health professional should actively seek risk and protective factors to make an assessment of the overall risk in that young person at the time of presentation. Despite the importance of psychosocial risk screening to effective adolescent health care, research indicates that it tends to be underperformed in many young people presenting to health professionals.[17]

Table 11.3 Some common risk and protective factors.

Domain	Risk factors	Protective factors
Individual	• Low self-esteem • Low intelligence • Chronic illness • Refugee experience • Hyperactivity	• High self-esteem and efficacy • Robust intelligence • Strong moral values • Creative and sporting pursuits • Participation in volunteer work
Family	• Family breakdown • Poor parenting • Poor relationship with parents • Parental psychopathology • Family history of risk behavior • Parental tolerance of risk-taking behavior • Low socioeconomic status	• Intact family • Effective parenting • Positive relationship with at least one parent or caregiving adult • Absence of parental psychopathology • Family rituals
Peer group and school	• Bullying • Peer participation in risk-taking behavior • Poor academic performance • Isolated at school • Low parental interest in education	• Positive peer relationships • Low peer participation in risk-taking behaviors • Scholastic achievement • Engaged in school activities • High parental interest in education
Community	• Poor community cohesion • Low employment rates • Racial discrimination • Easy availability of drugs and alcohol	• Stable, connected community • High employment rates • Culture of cooperation • Opportunities for contribution to community

Source: Reproduced from reference 13, p. 137.

Assessing a young person's alcohol use

The assessment of alcohol use requires gathering information that clarifies age of onset of drinking, when consumption became regular, frequency of consumption (monthly, weekly, daily), dose of alcohol typically consumed, and alcohol-related consequences (see Table 11.4 for a summary).

A young person's alcohol consumption may sometimes be a sensitive area, especially if that individual is not happy about attending the clinical interview. Sometimes it is helpful

Table 11.4 Summary of features to assess regarding a young person's alcohol use.

- Age of onset of alcohol consumption
- Patterns of drinking:
  - Recently
  - Heaviest
  - Context of drinking (alone, with peers, or both)
  - Attitudes to alcohol consumption (young person, their peers, their parents, or other adult caregivers)
- Alcohol-related consequences: Frequency of intoxication, hangover, accidents, sexual risk taking, or other
- Other substance use: Tobacco, cannabis, psychostimulants, or sedatives

to approach sensitive topics by using a "third person" approach, talking about adolescents in general terms before specifically focusing on the young person.

Some young people your age drink alcohol. What's happening in your friendship group?

Then . . .

Do you drink alcohol?

Additional information can be ascertained by noting the body language and the mood of the individual during the interview. For example, loss of eye contact, turning away from the clinician, and uncomfortable facial expressions can indicate tension related to the topic of discussion. On the other hand, a young person may appear at ease despite describing having experienced significant negative consequences of his or her drinking. In these situations, further exploration is needed to determine whether this is attributable to their developmental stage or whether there is another explanation.

Having ascertained that the person does drink alcohol, further important details are usually best obtained using a conversational style although some clinicians use questionnaires or scales. The latter can complement the information obtained in the interview and can be useful for monitoring outcomes of interventions (see Chapter 12). Whatever the method, maintaining rapport is important to continue working with the individual. It is important that the young person does not feel as if they are being "interrogated."

Age of onset of drinking

This is usually defined as *the age at which more than a sip of alcohol was consumed*. It is important to ascertain age of onset of drinking because early onset is associated with increased risk of alcohol dependence[18,19] (see Chapter 2). Establishing at what age (approximately) the individual began drinking regularly, the frequency of alcohol consumption, and amounts consumed also gives an indication of the degree of neuro-adaptation that may have occurred. Recalling amounts of alcohol consumed can be difficult for adults as well as for young people as they are unlikely to have been monitoring their consumption of alcohol during the course of a night of socializing. One technique to address this is to ask the young person to reflect on their last drinking occasion and try to recall the number of each type of drink according to its trade name, as it is often easier to remember this rather than the type of alcohol (beer, wine, or spirits) (e.g., 'Four and coke, three and two full strength beers,' etc.). This method of ascertaining self-reported alcohol consumption has been shown to result in more accurate reports of consumption than global questions (e.g., "How many beers did you have?").[20]

Patterns of drinking

Drinking patterns can vary quite substantially over time; therefore, obtaining patterns of drinking at different periods is useful. The periods best recounted by young people are the most recent (e.g., past week or last drinking occasion) and the heaviest drinking period. The latter may be the same as the most recent or may have occurred months previously. Establishing the nature of the heaviest drinking gives an indication of the extent of alcohol consumption in that particular young person. Inquiring about the context of drinking (alone, with peers, or both), attitudes of peers to alcohol and other drug use, perceived benefits of drinking as well as availability of alcohol in the home, and parental attitudes to drinking can also give the clinician valuable insight into the context of alcohol in the individual's life.

Sometimes young people are unable to describe the details of their drinking because they pay no attention to what they consume or because of blackouts on drinking occasions. In such circumstances, a discussion with the young person about the beverage types (beer, wine, spirits) and drink sizes can provide opportunities for health education. It should be noted that commercial products very often contain more than one "standard drink"—about 10 g alcohol, although what is considered a standard drink varies from country to country (see Chapter 4). This can be reviewed and monitored at future clinical interviews.

Alcohol-related consequences

This is a particularly important aspect of the clinical interview. Addressing alcohol misuse involves working through these consequences with the young person. In addition, alcohol-related consequences in adolescence may have prognostic implications as they have been shown to be associated with increased risk of alcohol use disorders in young adulthood.[20] For example, questions such as the following have to be asked:

> Have you ever been intoxicated?
> Many times? How often does this happen?
> Some young people plan deliberately to get drunk . . . do you?
> A few of the young people I see tell me that they have had blackouts and cannot remember the next day what happened the night before . . . They hear about the things they got up to from friends or see it in photos or on film on the Internet—has that ever happened to you?
> Some, particularly males, tell me that they have been involved in alcohol-related fights or assaults, have you ever been caught up in that sort of thing? Were you physically hurt or did you hurt someone else or both?

Other important alcohol-related consequences to ascertain are as follows:

- Hangover—does it occur after every/most occasions of drinking?

- Alcohol-related accidents (road trauma, machinery—particularly if in manual employment).
- Alcohol-related sexual risk taking (unprotected sex, sexual intercourse that is later regretted, unplanned pregnancies).
- Other alcohol-related consequences. After making the above inquiries, it is useful to ask the young person about any other problems they may have experienced that do not fall into the typically reported categories listed above.

Polysubstance use

It is very common for young people to use more than one psychoactive substance and it is therefore important to always screen for use of substances other than alcohol. Most young people do not consider tobacco to be a "drug," so cigarette smoking needs to be explicitly asked about. Each specific group of illicit substances should also be asked about including cannabis, ecstasy and other "party" drugs, amphetamines such as "speed," "ice" (methamphetamine) and cocaine, benzodiazepines, opiates including heroin and prescription opiates (long-acting morphine, etc.), as well as other prescription medications such as ibuprofen (with or without codeine) and others.

For any given substance, information to gather includes the duration of use (weeks, months, years), how often that particular substance is used and the amount used (e.g., how many cigarettes a day, how many times marijuana is used in a given week or on a given day, etc.), and route of administration (ingestion, inhalation, injection where relevant).

Seeking and integrating information from multiple sources

When dealing with adolescents, it is often helpful to obtain information from multiple sources. Parents or family provide a particularly important perspective. This includes not only the details relating to alcohol consumption but also the nature of the adolescent–family relationship. The importance of family has consistently been noted in the literature.[5,21] Further, family relations have been postulated to be important to the development of a healthy self-concept in the adolescent.[21]

Consent

Generally, consent of the young person should be sought prior to seeking this information. If the consultation has commenced with the parents and young person in attendance prior to seeing the young person alone, consent is implied—although it is good practice to address the issue when talking with the teenager alone. Reminding the young person that seeking this information will not compromise the confidentiality of what has been disclosed by the young person in the consultation is particularly important. Teenagers generally give consent readily, although they may seek reassurance regarding certain things they would not want revealed. It can be explained to the adolescent that obtaining information from relevant others is a common practice in (adolescent) health care and that the reason for seeking such information is not to "check on" the young person's honesty, rather that it can provide additional perspectives that are helpful to developing an intervention. Listing the sort of information that would be sought can help the adolescent understand this. Sometimes it is appropriate to have the young person present when the parents are interviewed while at other times it is better to discuss issues separately if there are sensitive matters that need to be addressed.

Areas to explore with parents/family

Apart from a generic history of the young persons' developmental milestones from birth and their school history, specific details to explore with regard to alcohol include patterns of alcohol consumption among family members, parental "rules" (if any) relating to drinking, consistency (if any) in parental approach to the young person's drinking, family history of alcohol or other drug use or abuse and of mental health disorders, patterns of alcohol consumption among peers, and alcohol and drug education (if any) that has occurred at school.

Reliability and validity of any information collected always needs consideration. Specifically, underlying motivations of individuals need thought. For instance, parents may have a strong emotional investment in the family and may be less objective in their responses to the clinician. Parents may also feel inclined to give socially desirable responses. Adolescents, on the other hand, given their growing autonomy and independence from the family, may be inclined to report a negative picture of the family. Information from multiple sources should therefore be taken on balance.

Information from other sources such as school or other professionals involved with the adolescent should follow similar principles. Discussion with the young person regarding the reasons for seeking this information, confirmation of confidentiality and consent from the young person are all required.

Physical examination

As part of the assessment of the young person, medical professionals may need to conduct a physical examination. Adolescents, especially young individuals, are usually very self-conscious about their bodies and even a routine examination can be quite confronting for them. Any physical examination must therefore be undertaken with care, respect, and sensitivity. Preliminary explanation of why the physical examination is needed, what it will involve and importantly, what it will not involve, usually help make the young person feel more comfortable. Attention to privacy and modesty at all times is important as well as awareness of cultural and gender issues. Generally, male doctors who need to examine a female adolescent arrange for a chaperone to be present. Providing feedback during the examination is helpful as it is a key opportunity to reassure young people about their development.

Physical examination should include measurement of height, weight, and blood pressure and mapping these against charts with normative data. Physical signs in young people who are experiencing problems with alcohol are not common. Rarely, a young person may have an enlarged liver if the drinking has been occurring at a high dose for a considerable length of time. Other signs of substance use (e.g., intravenous injection sites) may be evident and serve to confirm the history given or provide an opportunity to continue the comprehensive assessment.

Finishing the clinical interview

Finishing the clinical interview is as important as its opening. Young people generally appreciate feedback after they have engaged in the process of answering questions and sharing information about themselves. Summarizing the assessment and providing an initial opinion, or at least a framework of "where to from here" is therefore important.

Formulation

Gathering and integrating the information outlined above enables a formulation that includes several domains:

1. Diagnoses:
   - *Alcohol related*: Specifically, whether the misuse of alcohol by the young person is a manifestation of adolescent experimentation with alcohol or whether there is an alcohol use disorder (DSM-IV alcohol abuse or dependence).
   - *Mental health* diagnoses such as depression or anxiety.
   - *General health* diagnoses such as diabetes and asthma.
2. *Risk factors/protective factors*: An evaluation of risk and protective factors, identifying those that might be addressed as part of the intervention.

It is always useful to provide a balanced feedback, presenting not only those areas that are advisable to address and the reasons why but also the positive aspects of the young person who have emerged during the assessment. Sometimes, it can be difficult to come up with positive messages, especially if the interview has been challenging and the young person difficult to engage; at the very least the young person can be commended for having attended the assessment.

It is important to note that a comprehensive assessment of a young person frequently takes more time than usual, but it can often be conducted on more than one consultation. Subsequent interviews can yield further valuable information that develops the clinical picture of the young person and their alcohol consumption. This is not unusual, and reflects that it is rare to be able to ascertain the whole picture in one interview. It can also be due in part to the young person becoming more comfortable with attending the appointments.

Motivational interviewing

The health care of young people often needs to be opportunistic and the clinical interview of a young person is one such opportunity. An underlying principle of opportunistic health care of young people is that they are typically motivated by the "here and now" rather than by future benefits of changing current drinking patterns. The goals of adolescence (refer to Table 11.1) are generally more important to them than doing things to improve their health, especially long-term health. Notwithstanding this, treatment goals can be made relevant to them. For instance, during the course of the interview, young people can be made aware of levels of consumption (standard drinks in various containers or commercial products of alcohol, strength of beverages, etc.), how their drinking can affect their appearance and their ability to socialize. The effects of heavy alcohol consumption on brain function can be useful to mention, particularly with respect to what is important to them, be they recreational, educational or employment achievements. Many young people describe continuing to feel impaired beyond the "hangover." This may relate to the effects of alcohol, or sleep deprivation, or other reasons. Discussing these concepts with young people is valuable opportunistic health education. Sharing examples of when this has been observed is helpful; the young person may be able to reflect on someone they know (such as friend, relative, and colleague) who performs less well after heavy drinking.

Encouraging the young person to participate in the negotiation of treatment plans helps maintain engagement in treatment and empowers change.[22] Discussion with the young person that works toward developing concrete short-term goals (weeks to months) related to their drinking (or other issues that arise during the interview) also helps the young person stay motivated to address their health and well-being. Promotion of self-management skills is also of key importance when working with young people. They need to develop a sound knowledge of the triggers and the nature of excessive drinking that is specific to them. The clinical interview is an ideal opportunity to explore with the young person the symptoms and signs that trigger excessive drinking and the strategies that can be put in place to help them adopt a lifestyle that reduces complications. Talking about access and use of support services is also a critical component of self-management.

Above all, it is essential that these discussions are always delivered in a nonjudgmental or nonpatronizing way and at a level that is developmentally and cognitively appropriate, adapting as the young person matures.

Resources for practitioners, patients, and families

- The "ABC of Adolescence" series of 12 articles published by the *British Medical Journal* in 2005.
- Gilvarry E, McArdle P, eds. *Alcohol, Drugs and Young People: Clinical Approaches*. London: Mac Keith Press; 2007.
- Latt N, Conigrave K, Marshall J, Saunders J, Nutt D, eds. *Addiction Medicine: Oxford Specialist Handbooks*. Oxford: Oxford University Press; 2009
- Simmons M, Shalwitz S, Pollock S *et al. Adolescent Health Care 101: The Basics*. San Francisco, CA: Adolescent Health Working Group; 2003 Available at: http://www.ahwg.net/assets/library/74_adolescenthealthcare101.pdf. Accessed August 14, 2010.
- American Academy Pediatrics. Available at: www.aap.org. Accessed August 14, 2010.
- World Health Organisation. Child and adolescent health and development. Available at: www.who.int/child_adolescent_health/en/. Accessed August 14, 2010.

References

1. Sawyer S, Kennedy A. Care of the adolescent. In: Roberton D, South M, eds. *Practical Paediatrics*. 6th edn. London, UK: Churchill Livingstone; 2007.
2. Patton GC, Viner R. Pubertal transitions in health. *Lancet* 2007; 369:1130–1139.
3. Kessler R, Berglund P, Demler O *et al.* Lifetime prevalence and age-of-onset distributions of DSM IV disorders in the National Co-morbidity Survey Replication. *Arch Gen Psychiatry* 2005; 62:593–602.
4. Goldenring JM, Rosen DS. Getting into adolescent heads: an essential update. *Contemp Pediatr* 2004; 21:64–90.
5. Resnick MD, Bearman PS, Blum R et al. Protecting adolescents from harm. *JAMA* 1997; 278:823–832.
6. Sher L. Depression and alcoholism. *Q J Med* 2004; 97:237–240.
7. Hayward L, Zubrick SR, Silburn S. Blood alcohol levels in suicide cases. *J Epidemiol Community Health* 1992; 46:256–260.
8. Bukstein OG, Lutka-Fedor T. Principles of assessment for adolescents with substance use disorders. In: Gilvarry E, McCardle P, eds. *Alcohol, Drugs and Young People: Clinical Approaches*. London: Mac Keith Press; 2007.
9. Sanci L, Sawyer SM, Kang MS *et al.* Confidential health care for adolescents: reconciling clinical evidence with family values. *Med J Aust* 2005; 183:410–414.
10. Booth M, Bernard D, Quine S *et al.* Access to health care among Australian adolescents: young people's perspectives and their sociodemographic distribution. *J Adolesc Health* 2004; 34L:97–103.
11. American Academy of Pediatrics, Committee on Adolescence. The adolescent's rights to confidential health care when considering abortion. *Pediatrics* 1996; 97:746–751.
12. Christie D, Viner R. Adolescent development: ABC of adolescence. *BMJ* 2005; 330:1–4.
13. Joint Adolescent Health Committee. *Working with Young People: A Training Resource in Adolescent Health*. Sydney: Royal Australasian College of Physicians; 2008.
14. Gogtay N. Dynamic mapping of the human cortical development during childhood through early adulthood. *Proc Natl Acad Sci USA* 2004; 101:8174–8179.
15. Giedd JN. Brain development during childhood and adolescence: a longitudinal MRI study. *Nat Neurosci* 1992; 2:861–863.
16. Hawkins JD, Catalano RF, Miller JY. Risk and protective factors for alcohol and other drug problems in adolescence and early adulthood: implications for susbtance use prevention. *Psychol Bull* 1992; 112:64–105.
17. Yeo SM, Bond LM, Sawyer SM. Health risk screening in adolescents: room for improvement in a tertiary inpatient setting. *Med J Aust* 2005; 183:427–429.
18. Chou SP, Pickering RP. Early onset of drinking as a risk factor for lifetime alcohol-related problems. *Br J Addict* 1992; 87:1199–1204.
19. Grant BF, Dawson DA. Age at onset of alcohol use and its association with DMS IV alcohol abuse and dependence. Results from the National Longitudinal Alcohol Epidemiological Survey. *J Subst Abuse* 1997; 9:103–110.
20. Dawson DA. Measuring alcohol consumption: limitations and prospects for improvement. *Addiction* 1998; 93:965–968.
21. Hayes L, Smart D, John W, Sanson A. *Parental Influences on Adolescent Alcohol Use*. Australian Institute of Family Studies, 2004. Available at: http://www.aifs.gov.au/institute/pubs/resreport10/parentinginfluences.html. Accessed August 14, 2010.
22. Sawyer SM, Drew S, Yeo MS, Britto MT. Adolescents with a chronic condition: challenges living, challenges treating. *Lancet* 2007; 369:1481–1489.

Chapter 12

Detection, evaluation, and diagnosis of alcohol use disorders

Maree Teesson[1], Sonja Memedovic[1], Louise Mewton[1], Tim Slade[1], and Andrew Baillie[2]

[1]National Drug and Alcohol Research Centre, University of New South Wales, Sydney, Australia
[2]Centre for Emotional Health and Department of Psychology, Macquarie University, Sydney, Australia

---

Key points

- Two important roles of assessment are to provide feedback to the individual on their alcohol use and to develop a rapport between the therapist and the individual. A collaborative approach is recommended to build rapport and engage the young person in assessment.
- Assessment measures and biomarkers and their use in younger adults are a developing area. However, more information and development of measures directly addressing the patterns of use and problems for young adults are required.
- There are a number of valid and reliable measures that can aid the thorough assessment of alcohol use and associated problems in young adults.

Given the high prevalence of alcohol-related harms and alcohol use disorders in young adults, reliable, valid and early detection and assessment of problems is critical. The current chapter summarizes the literature on assessment including, the role of assessment in clinical practice, a review of reliable and valid measures and how to use them, and the challenges of assessment in young adults.

Assessment in practice

Clear, well-documented assessment is important for the understanding of alcohol-related problems and is the first stage in the identification of problems associated with alcohol use, and in treatment. Assessment should cover both a review of the quantity of alcohol used and its health and social consequences. In clinical practice, two important roles of assessment are to provide feedback to the individual on their alcohol use and to develop

---

Young People and Alcohol: Impact, Policy, Prevention, Treatment, First Edition.
Edited by John B. Saunders and Joseph M. Rey.
© 2011 Blackwell Publishing Ltd. Published 2011 by Blackwell Publishing Ltd.

a rapport between the therapist and the individual. Some of these aspects are dealt with in detail in Chapter 11.

The aim of assessment is to:

1. identify individuals who continue to drink alcohol despite the harms it is causing them,
2. quantify the amount of alcohol consumed,
3. ascertain the main diagnosis and comorbid disorders as well as harms (e.g., physical, psychological, familial, work related, and social) associated with alcohol misuse,
4. highlight the areas that require intervention (e.g., alcohol consumption) so that goals can be set and a management plan can be devised,
5. identify a baseline against which improvement or deterioration can be measured, and
6. build rapport—as assessment typically occurs at the beginning of a therapeutic relationship, it provides an opportunity to build rapport and to develop a common understanding of the reasons for treatment.

Assessment measures for alcohol misuse have proliferated and are useful in the systematic collection of the information required for a thorough assessment. Measures range from brief screening interviews by general health care workers, which may lead to early intervention, to in-depth assessment of psychosocial functioning including alcohol use disorder.[1]

The diagnosis of alcohol use disorder is a critical component of any comprehensive assessment. However, individuals with acute alcohol-related problems may be in contact with clinical services and should be considered in assessment even when diagnostic criteria are not met. For example, a person may present to a clinical emergency service after injuring him(her)self while drinking. Alternatively, an individual may have contact with emergency services after attempting suicide while intoxicated with alcohol following a relationship breakdown.

Table 12.1 lists the criteria for alcohol use disorders according to the American Psychiatric Association's *Diagnostic and Statistical Manual of Mental Disorders*, fourth edition (DSM-IV).[2] For a diagnosis of alcohol dependence, three of the seven dependence symptoms are required. For a diagnosis of alcohol abuse, at least one of the four abuse symptoms must be met. It should be noted that DSM-IV is currently being revised and one of the proposals is to do away with the distinction between abuse and dependence.

Assessment measures in young adults

Standardized methods of screening for excessive drinking and problems associated with drinking include clinical examination, questionnaires of use, harms and diagnosis, and testing for biological markers. The most reliable and valid of the measures available are reviewed in this chapter.

We identified assessment instruments for alcohol use and associated problems employed with young people through previous literature reviews[3–5] and database searches. We include only measures that have sound psychometric properties in younger populations. We also provide information on the number of citations each measure has generated thus far, based on listings in Scopus.

Table 12.1   DSM-IV criteria for alcohol abuse and alcohol dependence.

DSM-IV diagnosis	DSM-IV criterion	Description
Alcohol abuse	"Major role"	Recurrent use despite the inability to fulfill major role obligations at work, school, or home
	"Hazard"	Recurrent use in physically dangerous situations
	"Legal"	Recurrent use despite substance-related legal problems
	"Social"	Recurrent use despite substance-related social or interpersonal problems
Alcohol dependence	"Tolerance"	Need for greater amounts or diminishing effect
	"Withdrawal"	Withdrawal
	"Larger"	Using more alcohol or for longer than intended
	"Cut down"	Desire or unsuccessful efforts to cut down
	"Time spent"	A great deal of time obtaining, using, or recovering from the effects of alcohol
	"Give up"	Reduction in important activities because of alcohol use
	"Continue"	Continued use despite knowing alcohol is causing a significant problem

It should be noted that although this chapter focuses on alcohol, many of these measures assess problems with substances other than alcohol as well. Since other drug use is common amongst younger problem drinkers we are broad in the inclusion of measures.[3] In addition, while the focus of this chapter is the assessment of alcohol use disorders in young people (aged 12–25) many of the measures listed in Table 12.2 were specifically developed for use in adolescence. There are very few measures targeting young adults (18–24 years). Young adults over the age of 18 tend to be assessed using measures developed and standardized in adult populations, which have been applied to younger age groups with little empirical basis. The exception is college students in the United States for whom growing concerns over their problematic alcohol use has led to the development of specific measures.[4] These include the College Alcohol Problem Scale—Revised,[6] Young Adult Alcohol Consequences Questionnaire[7] and the Young Adult Alcohol Problem Screening Test.[8] It should be noted that the problems assessed with these instruments are likely to be specific to young adults attending US college campuses and may not apply to the young adult population in general.

The measures identified can be divided into the following five categories according to their purpose:

- Screening instruments
- Comprehensive measures of alcohol use and related problems
- Diagnostic interviews
- Expectancy and readiness for change
- Measures of quantity and frequency of use

Table 12.2 Assessment instruments for alcohol use problems in young adults.

Assessment instrument	Items	Time[a] (min)	Administration	Description	Citations[b]
Screening instruments					
Adolescent Alcohol Involvement Scale[43]	14	5	Self- or interviewer-rated questionnaire	Assesses the type and the frequency of alcohol use through questions on reasons for drinking, drinking context, last drinking episode, short- and long-term consequences, adolescent's/others' perception of drinking	46
Adolescent Drinking Index[44]	24	5	Self-rated questionnaire	Assesses the severity of drinking problems by measuring psychological, physical and social symptoms, and loss of control. Subscales measure self-medicating drinking and rebellious drinking	32
Adolescent Obsessive–Compulsive Drinking Scale[45]	14	5–10	Self-rated questionnaire	Measures obsessive thoughts about alcohol and the distress associated with them (interference scale), and inquires about compulsive drinking behaviors and efforts made to resist drinking (irresistibility scale)	8
Alcohol and Drug Problem Acknowledgement Scale[46]	13	5	Self-rated questionnaire	Scale from the Minnesota Multiphasic Personality Inventory for Adolescents. Assesses willingness to acknowledge substance use-related symptoms, attitudes, and beliefs	26
Alcohol and Drug Problem Proneness Scale[46]	36	10	Self-rated questionnaire	Scale from the Minnesota Multiphasic Personality Inventory for Adolescents. Assesses potential for developing substance use problems based on family and peer characteristics, academic interests, and antisocial behaviors and beliefs	26
Alcohol Use Disorders Identification Test[9]	10	2	Self- or interviewer-rated questionnaire	Assesses hazardous drinking and major physical and psychosocial consequences	881
College Alcohol Problem Scale—Revised[6]	8	3	Self- or interviewer-rated questionnaire	Assesses frequency of drinking-related personal and social problems. Personal problems relate to self-esteem and problems with appetite or sleeping; social problems address involvement in hazardous situations and legal problems	26

(continued)

Table 12.2 Assessment instruments for alcohol use problems in young adults. (*Continued*)

Assessment instrument	Items	Time[a] (min)	Administration	Description	Citations[b]
CRAFFT[47]	6	2	Self- or interviewer-rated questionnaire	CRAFFT is an acronym of the first letters of key words from the six items of the questionnaire, which assesses substance use and related problems	88
Drug Use Screening Inventory—Revised[48]	159	20	Self- or interviewer-rated questionnaire	Assesses substance-use severity and problems with behavior patterns, health, mental illness, social competency, peer and family relations, school, work, and leisure	124
Leeds Dependence Questionnaire[49]	10	2–5	Self- or interviewer-rated questionnaire	Assesses the pathophysiological components of substance dependence (tolerance and withdrawal) in psychological terms	65
Personal Experience Screening Questionnaire[50]	40	10	Self-rated questionnaire	Assesses the severity and history of substance use, psychosocial problems, and response distortion tendencies (faking good and faking bad)	54
Problem Oriented Screening Instrument for Teenagers[51]	139	20–25	Self-rated questionnaire	Assesses substance use, physical and mental health, family and peer relationships, educational and employment status, social skills, leisure and recreation, and aggressive and delinquent behavior	87
Rutgers Alcohol Problem Index[52]	23	10	Self- or interviewer-rated questionnaire	Assesses the consequence of alcohol use on family and social relations, psychological and neuropsychological functioning, delinquency, and physical problems	411
Substance Abuse Proclivity Scale[53]	36	10	Self-rated questionnaire	A scale derived from the Minnesota Multiphasic Personality Inventory designed to detect substance abuse tendencies in adolescent and young adult males	3
Substance Abuse Subtle Screening Inventory—Adolescents[54]	100	10–15	Self-rated questionnaire	Designed to identify individuals who have a high probability of having a substance use disorder; includes items seeking to identify those who are unwilling or unable to admit substance abuse	77
Young Adult Alcohol Problem Screening Test[8]	27	10	Self-rated questionnaire	Measures adverse consequences of drinking, including role failure, social/interpersonal problems, legal problems, hazardous situations, withdrawal, tolerance, acute effects of intoxication, damaged self-esteem	106

Comprehensive measures

Measure					
Adolescent Drug Abuse Diagnosis[55]	150	45–55	Structured interview	Assesses substance use, medical and psychological status, legal involvement, family background/problems, peer relations, social activities, and school/employment	56
Adolescent Problem Severity Index[56]	85	45	Structured interview	Addresses reason for assessment, referral source, and adolescent's understanding of reason for referral. Assesses substance use, family and personal relationships, school and work, legal, medical, and psychosocial adjustment	12
Adolescent Self-Assessment Profile[57]	225	25–50	Self-rated questionnaire	Assesses the frequency, benefits, and consequences of substance use, as well as risk factors associated with substance involvement	5
Comprehensive Addiction Severity Index[58]	Varies	45–90	Semistructured interview	Measures substance use, education, leisure and use of free time, peer relationships, family (including history and abuse), legal history, and psychiatric status	56
Global Appraisal of Individual Needs[59]	1606	60–120	Self- or interviewer-rated questionnaire	Measures the recency, breadth, and frequency of problems and service utilization related to substance use; physical and mental health, risk and protective factors, environment and employment situation	169
Personal Experience Inventory[60]	276	45–60	Self-rated questionnaire	Assesses the severity, frequency and onset of substance use, risk and protective factors, and response distortion tendencies. Includes screens for eating disorders, suicidality, trauma history, and parental history of substance use	103
Teen Addiction Severity Index[61]	154	20–45	Semistructured interview	Assesses substance use and functioning in the domains of school, employment, family and peer relationships, and legal and psychiatric status	42
Young Adult Alcohol Consequences Questionnaire[7]	48	n/a	Self-rated questionnaire	Assesses drinking-related problems in eight domains: social/interpersonal, impaired control, self-perception, self-care, risk behaviors, academic/occupational consequences, physical dependence, and blackout drinking	19

(continued)

Table 12.2 Assessment instruments for alcohol use problems in young adults. (*Continued*)

Assessment instrument	Items	Time[a] (min)	Administration	Description	Citations[b]
Diagnostic interviews					
Adolescent Diagnostic Interview[62]	213	45	Structured interview	Assesses lifetime DSM-IV disorders, as well as the level of functioning, severity of psychosocial stressors, and memory and orientation	49
Composite International Diagnostic Interview—Substance Abuse Module[63]	38	30–45	Structured interview	Assesses lifetime DSM-IV and ICD-10 substance use disorders, quantity and frequency of use, age of onset, impairment and treatment for reported symptoms	NA
Customary Drinking and Drug Use Record[64]	Varies	20–30	Structured interview	Assesses current and lifetime DSM-IV substance use disorders, level of substance involvement, psychological/behavioral dependence symptoms, and negative consequences	124
Diagnostic Interview Schedule for Children Version IV[65]	Varies	70–120	Structured interview	Assesses lifetime, past year and past month DSM-IV and ICD-10 psychiatric disorders. Also collects information about age of onset, impairment and treatment for reported symptoms. Separate forms exist for the child and parent	790
Structured Clinical Interview for DSM-IV—Adolescent Version[66]	Varies	60–90	Structured interview	Assesses current and lifetime psychiatric disorders and collects information regarding the onset and remission of reported symptoms	128
Expectancy and readiness for change measures					
Alcohol Expectancy Questionnaire—Adolescents[67]	90	20–30	Self-rated questionnaire	Measures individual's expected effects of alcohol use. Both positive and negative expectancies are assessed	248
Circumstances, Motivation, Readiness and Suitability[68]	42	5–10	Self-rated questionnaire	Aims to predict retention of treatment by assessing external and internal motivation, readiness for treatment, and perceived appropriateness of treatment modality	103
Drug Avoidance Self-Efficacy Scale[66]	16	5	Self-rated questionnaire	Assesses adolescent's ability to refrain from substance use in different high risk situations (e.g., boredom, interpersonal influence, availability of substances)	6

	[a]				[b]
Perceived Benefit of Drinking Scale[69]	5	2	Self-rated questionnaire	A nonthreatening problem severity screen that assesses beliefs about benefits received from substance use. Based on idea that the higher the perceived benefit, the higher the likelihood of substance use	11
Problem Recognition Questionnaire[70]	25	5	Self-rated questionnaire	Assesses adolescent's readiness for treatment and receptivity to substance use change	33
Quantity and frequency of alcohol use					
Alcohol Time Line Follow-Back[71]	Varies	10–30	Self- or interviewer-rated questionnaire	Estimates quantity/frequency of daily drinking up to 12 months from interview date, using calendar, and memory aids	909
Form 90[72]	58	40–60	Semistructured interview	Reconstructs substance use for the past 90 days	115

[a] Approximate time that it takes to complete.
[b] Number of citations in SCOPUS as on April 21, 2010.

Screening instruments

Screening measures are often the first step in the assessment of alcohol problems as they are designed to determine whether an alcohol problem might exist. There are range of screening instruments available for alcohol (Table 12.2). The most widely used is the Alcohol Use Disorders Identification Test (AUDIT).[9] In choosing a screening instrument it is important to consider the target problems you are screening for and the population on which the measure was developed. The time required to complete a screening instrument ranges from 2 to 25 minutes, so the setting in which screening is to take place (e.g., emergency room, clinical treatment program) is critical in the choice of measure.

Alcohol Use Disorders Identification Test

One of the most commonly used screening measures is the AUDIT.[9] The AUDIT was developed as a simple method of screening for excessive drinking and to assist in brief assessment. The AUDIT can assist in the identification of excessive drinking as the cause of the presenting problem. It also provides a framework for intervention to help risky drinkers reduce or cease alcohol consumption. The AUDIT helps to identify alcohol dependence and some specific consequences of harmful drinking. It is particularly designed for the use by health care practitioners, but can be self-administered. More recently, internet/mobile phone technology has been used with success in the administration of the AUDIT, particularly when young people are concerned.[10]

The scores on the AUDIT have been designed to reflect practical responses to the level of alcohol-related problems. Four levels of risk have been defined.[11] The first level refers to low-risk drinking or abstinence. The second level corresponds to alcohol use in excess of low-risk guidelines: AUDIT score between 8 and 15. A brief intervention using simple advice and education materials is recommended for people in this level. The third level is suggested by AUDIT scores in the range of 16–19 and represents harmful and hazardous drinking. This can be managed by a combination of simple advice, brief counseling and continued monitoring, with further diagnostic evaluation indicated if the individual fails to respond. The fourth risk level is suggested by AUDIT scores in excess of 20. These individuals require diagnostic evaluation and possible treatment for alcohol dependence.

Comprehensive measures of alcohol use and related problems

If the initial screen indicates presence of a problem, more comprehensive measures can be used to delineate the nature, history, and severity of alcohol problems, to assign an alcohol use disorder diagnosis, to assess the effects of drinking on multiple domains of functioning, and to determine the risk factors that predispose an individual to alcohol misuse. As younger problem drinkers are more likely to report history of trauma, suicidality, and comorbidity with other psychological conditions, such comprehensive assessments are important.[5] Comprehensive measures include problem-focused interviews and multiscale questionnaires. Reliable and valid examples of comprehensive measures have been included in Table 12.2.

Diagnostic interviews

Structured diagnostic interviews have been developed in order to reliably assess psychiatric disorders according to the major classification systems. Structured interviews assess mental disorders in a systematic and standardized way to increase the reliability of diagnosis. In structured interviews, questions are designed to be short and easily understood, with most requiring dichotomous yes/no responses, and only a few requiring an open-ended response. The reliability and validity of some of these measures have been established in younger age groups and these are presented in Table 12.2.

The applicability of current diagnostic criteria and instruments to younger age groups (12–25 years of age) is an issue of increasing interest and research focus. The current diagnostic criteria (see Table 12.1) and assessment instruments were largely developed and standardized using adult populations[12] and have been subsequently applied to younger age groups with little empirical basis.

When assessing problems with alcohol use among youth, it is necessary to distinguish between normative and clinically significant behaviors. For example, the prevalence of *tolerance* symptoms (Table 12.1) among younger age groups is particularly high. These high rates may be partially explained by a mild to moderate degree of *tolerance* symptoms reflecting normal developmental processes in youth[13] (see Chapter 5). Compared to older adults, adolescents and young adults also have higher levels of impulsivity and behavioral disinhibition,[14] characteristics that overlap substantially with diagnostic criteria that reflect use of alcohol in risky situations such as those represented in the *hazard* and *legal* criteria (Table 12.1).

There is some support for the reliability and validity of these diagnostic criteria and instruments when applied to young people. For example, a meta-analysis[15] found moderate agreement across studies in the prevalence of symptoms, the ratio of alcohol abuse to dependence diagnoses, and the prevalence of physiological dependence among adolescents. Alcohol use disorder diagnoses also show good discriminant validity in younger age groups, in that the prevalence of these disorders was considerably higher in clinical than in community samples.[16]

However, some of the alcohol use disorder criteria have been identified as problematic among young adults in that they are endorsed differentially by populations defined by various demographic variables. The *hazard* and *legal* criteria (Table 12.1) were found to be related to young adults that tended to be male, older, and predisposed to comorbid conduct disorder.[17] There were also significant gender differences. Males were more likely to endorse *social*, *hazard*, and *tolerance* symptoms, and less likely to endorse *major role* symptoms when compared with their female counterparts.[18] Recent studies have also shown that the *hazard*, *legal*, *cut down*, and *continue* criteria discriminate poorly between young people with and without an alcohol use disorder. These criteria seem also to provide somewhat redundant clinical information when applied to younger age groups.[16,19]

More recent analyses have shown that eight of the eleven DSM-IV alcohol use disorder criteria perform differently when applied to different age groups.[16,19] Younger adults were more likely to report the "tolerance," "time spent," "withdrawal," and "larger" criteria, when compared with their older counterparts.[20] In contrast, older adults were more likely to endorse "hazard," "give up," "major role," and "cut down" when compared with the younger age group. These analyses have also been replicated in the cannabis use disorder criteria.[21] These findings indicate that age-based differences in the reporting of alcohol use disorder criteria should be interpreted with caution.

Other measures

Measures of expectancy and readiness for change, and of quantity and frequency of use can be administered as needed, but may be particularly helpful in treatment planning and in the evaluation of treatment effects.

Validity of self-reports

One of the issues to be considered in assessment is that the information about young people's use of alcohol and the associated problems is primarily obtained through self-reports[5] whose validity is often questioned. Obtaining information from other sources has been used to verify assessment information but the effect of this on rapport should be weighed against the benefits. For example, while parents are a common source of information about young people's involvement with alcohol, research suggests that parents often do not know the extent of their child's alcohol use and related problems since parent-reported rates of alcohol use disorders and problems have repeatedly been found to be lower than those reported by the adolescents themselves.[22,23] Illustrating the consequences of parental under-reporting, in one study 67% of alcohol use disorder diagnoses would have been missed if parental report had been the only source of information. Conversely, only 8% of the diagnoses would have been missed if adolescent self-report data alone were relied upon.[23] Clearly, self-reports are crucial for assessing adolescents for alcohol use problems in spite of questions about their validity.

A long-standing concern over the use of self-reports is that respondents may intentionally minimize or exaggerate their alcohol use, depending on the perceived consequences of disclosure. Underreporting of alcohol use is thought to be particularly likely among individuals who have been coerced into treatment.[24] Since adolescents are more likely than adults to be forced into treatment, and since alcohol use by adolescents is illegal in some jurisdictions, the risk of underreporting may be especially pertinent in this age group. On the other hand, adolescents may also exaggerate their alcohol intake if alcohol use is associated with status in their social setting, or if portraying themselves as having an alcohol problem may help them avoid consequences such as incarceration.[25] In addition to intentionally distorting reports of alcohol use, developmental factors may also impact on the validity of adolescents' self-reports. Many adolescents are still maturing in terms of social and emotional functioning, which may affect their insight into problems and their willingness to report them. Similarly, various attitudes and behaviors that characterize adolescence, such as risk-taking and rebellion, may also impair adolescents' ability to recognize and report alcohol-related problems.[3]

Extant research on the validity of adolescent self-reports paints a mixed picture. Reliance on self-report has been found to be problematic in cases where alcohol use is infrequent.[26] It has also been noted that adolescents sometimes report higher pretreatment alcohol use at the completion of treatment than at entry into treatment.[27] Although it is not clear from this finding whether pretreatment alcohol use was underreported at entry to treatment, or overreported at treatment completion, other evidence indicates that under-reporting at onset of treatment does occur among adolescents who are referred through medical practitioners, social services, courts, or their parents.[28] On the other hand, several lines of evidence provide support for the validity of adolescent self-reports. First, in school and drug treatment settings, few adolescents appear to endorse questions that indicate "faking good" and "faking bad" tendencies.[25] Second, many studies indicate that adolescent self-reports of alcohol use tend to remain stable over time.[29,30] Third, correspondence between self-report and urinalysis has been found to be high among adolescents who have been accepted into treatment, presumably because once in treatment, disclosure of alcohol use carries no negative consequences.[31] Furthermore, a study on cannabis provides some indication that when adolescents are informed of the requirement to provide a urine sample prior to completing self-reports of use, accuracy of self-reports is quite high.[32]

Although some of the aforementioned findings suggest that in certain contexts the validity of adolescent self-reports is of concern, several factors have been found to increase their validity, such us using standardized measures[3]; building rapport[3]; assurances of confidentiality[33]; ability to verify responses through collateral informants[34]; and performing urine tests before obtaining self-report responses.[35] Thus, the research on the validity of adolescent self-reports of alcohol use illustrates that this is a complex issue, influenced by many factors, including the characteristics of the respondent and the setting where they are interviewed.

Biomarkers

Biological markers of alcohol consumption are often used in the assessment of adolescent alcohol problems and as a means of verifying self-report of alcohol use. Biomarkers can be considered in two groups: markers of acute alcohol consumption (Has the individual been drinking today?) and markers of long-term alcohol consumption (Does the individual have a chronic drinking problem?). They are considered in more detail below.

Acute biomarkers

The most commonly used biological measures are urinalysis and blood-alcohol content (BAC).[36] BAC is often measured using a breathalyzer. As these measures only detect recent alcohol use, a positive test finding provides no information about the history, patterns and severity of alcohol use. On the other hand, a negative test finding could be due to short detection periods, or to sample tampering (e.g., providing someone else's urine).[37] Thus, caution is required with the interpretation of findings from urinalysis and BAC tests. Despite the limitations of these biomarkers, it has been suggested that their use is still valuable as it indicates to the adolescent that their self-reports will be checked, which may promote reporting honesty. However, such checking can undermine rapport, which is of critical importance.

Longer term use biomarkers

A number of biomarkers have also been tested for their potential in the detection and monitoring of longer term problem drinking. These include carbohydrate deficient transferrin (CDT), the liver enzymes glutamyltransferase (GGT) and aspartate aminotransferase (AST), and the early detection of alcohol consumption (EDAC) test. These markers detect the degree of physical alcohol-related harm an individual has experienced. Most of the research on these biomarkers has been conducted with adult populations. Intuitively, it seems unlikely that these biomarkers would perform well at detecting harms in younger drinkers given that younger drinkers tend to consume alcohol in a sporadic manner, have short drinking histories, and have a liver function that is more resilient to alcohol-related damage.[38] Indeed, the few studies that have examined younger drinkers (generally college-age populations) indicate that these biomarkers have poor sensitivity and minimal association with self-reported alcohol consumption.[39–41] Findings for a new generation of biomarkers such as phosphatidylethanol (PEth) and fatty acid ethyl esters (FAEEs) are also not promising. A recent study of 16–19-year-old drinkers found that these markers had poor sensitivity, poor agreement with interviews and with each other.[42] Clearly, more information on the utility of these markers in young adults is required, and in particular on their utility in the 12–18-year-old age group, which has been underresearched thus far.

References

1. Teesson M, Dietrich U, Degenhardt L, Lynskey M, Beard J. Substance use disorders in an Australian community survey. *Drug Alcohol Rev* 2002; 21:275–280.
2. American Psychiatric Association. *Diagnostic and Statistical Manual of Mental Disorders*. 4th edn. (DSM-IV). Washington, DC: American Psychiatric Association; 1994.
3. Winters KC. Assessment of alcohol and other drug use behaviors among adolescents. In: Allen JP, Wilson VB, eds. *Assessing Alcohol Problems: A Guide for Clinicians and Researchers*. 2nd edn. Bethseda, MD: National Institute on Alcohol Abuse and Alcoholism; 2003, pp. 101–123.
4. Devos-Comby L, Lange JE. Standardized measures of alcohol-related problems: A review of their use among college students. *Psychol Addict Behav* 2008; 22:349–361.
5. Perepletchikova F, Krystal JH, Kaufman J. Practitioner review: Adolescent alcohol use disorders: assessment and treatment issues. *J Child Psychol Psychiatry* 2008; 49:1131–1154.
6. Maddock JE, Laforge RG, Rossi JS, O'Hare T. The College Alcohol Problems Scale. *Addict Behav* 2001; 26:385–398.
7. Read JP, Kahler CW, Strong DR, Colder CR. Development and preliminary validation of the young adult alcohol consequences questionnaire. *J Stud Alcohol* 2006; 67:169–177.
8. Hurlbut SC, Sher KJ. Assessing alcohol problems in college students. *J Am Coll Health* 1992; 41:49–58.
9. Saunders JB, Aasland OG, Babor TF, de la Fuente JR, Grant M. Development of the Alcohol Use Disorders Identification Test (AUDIT): WHO Collaborative Project on Early Detection of Persons with Harmful Alcohol Consumption-II. *Addiction* 1993; 88:791–804.

10. Kypri K, Langley JD, Saunders JB *et al.* Randomized controlled trial of web-based alcohol screening and brief intervention in primary care. *Arch Intern Med* 2008; 168:530–536.

11. Babor T, De La Fuente J, Saunders J, Grant M. *AUDIT: The Alcohol Use Disorders Identification Test: Guidelines for Use in Primary Health Care.* Geneva: WHO; 1992.

12. Deas D, Riggs P, Langenbucher J, Goldman M, Brown S. Adolescents are not adults: Developmental considerations in alcohol users. *Alcohol Clin Exp Res* 2000; 24:232–237.

13. Chung T, Martin CS. What were they thinking? Adolescents' interpretations of DSM-IV alcohol dependence symptom queries and implications for diagnostic validity. *Drug Alcohol Depend* 2005; 80:191–200.

14. Krueger RF, Hicks BM, Patrick CJ, Carlson SR, Iacono WG, McGue M. Etiologic connections among substance dependence, antisocial behavior, and personality: Modeling the externalizing spectrum. *J Abnorm Psychol* 2002; 111:411–424.

15. Chung T, Martin CS, Armstrong TD, Labouvie EW. Prevalence of DSM-IV alcohol diagnoses and symptoms in adolescent community and clinical samples. *J Am Acad Child Adolesc Psychiatry* 2002; 41:546–554.

16. Gelhorn H, Hartman CA, Sakai JT *et al.* Towards DSM-V: An item response theory analysis of the diagnostic process for DSM-IV alcohol abuse and dependence in adolescents. *J Am Acad Child Adolesc Psychiatry* 2008; 47:1329–1339.

17. Martin CS, Winters KC. Diagnosis and assessment of alcohol use disorders among adolescents. *Alcohol Health Res World* 1998; 22:95–105.

18. Young SE, Corley RP, Stallings MC, Rhee SH, Crowley TJ, Hewitt JK. Substance use, abuse and dependence in adolescence: Prevalence, symptom profiles and correlates. *Drug Alcohol Depend* 2002; 68:309–322.

19. Martin CS, Chung T, Kirisci L, Langenbucher JW. Item response theory analysis of diagnostic criteria for alcohol and cannabis use disorders in adolescents: Implications for DSM-V. *J Abnorm Psychol* 2006; 115:807–814.

20. Saha TD, Chou SP, Grant BF. Toward an alcohol use disorder continuum using item response theory: Results from the National Epidemiologic Survey on Alcohol and Related Conditions. *Psychol Med* 2006; 36:931–941.

21. Mewton L, Teesson, M., Slade, T. "Youthful epidemic" or diagnostic bias? Differential item functioning of the DSM-IV cannabis use criteria in an Australian general population survey. *Addict Behav* 2010; 35:408–413.

22. Chung T, Colby SM, O'Leary TA, Barnett NP, Monti PM. Screening for cannabis use disorders in an adolescent emergency department sample. *Drug Alcohol Depend* 2003; 70:177–186.

23. Fisher SL, Bucholz KK, Reich W *et al.* Teenagers are right: parents do not know much: An analysis of adolescent-parent agreement on reports of adolescent substance use, abuse, and dependence. *Alcohol Clin Exp Res* 2006; 30:1699–1710.

24. Hesselbrock M, Babor TF, Hesselbrock V. 'Never believe an alcoholic'? On the validity of self-report measures of alcohol dependence and related constructs. *Int J Addict* 1983; 18:593–609.

25. Winters KC, Stinchfield RD, Henly GA, Schwartz RH. Validity of adolescent self-report of alcohol and other drug involvement. *Int J Addict* 1990; 25:1379–1395.

26. Single E, Kandel D, Johnson BD. Reliability and validity of drug-use responses in a large-scale longitudinal survey. *J Drug Issues* 1975; 5:426–443.

27. Stinchfield R. Reliability of adolescent self-reported pretreatment alcohol and other drug use. *Subst Use Misuse* 1997; 32:425–434.

28. Williams RJ, Nowatzki N. Validity of adolescent self-report of substance use. *Subst Use Misuse* 2005; 40:299–311.

29. Percy A, McAlister S, Higgins K, McCrystal P, Thornton M. Response consistency in young adolescents' drug use self-reports: A recanting rate analysis. *Addiction* 2005; 100:189–196.

30. Shillington AM, Clapp JD. Self-report stability of adolescent substance use: Are there differences for gender, ethnicity and age? *Drug Alcohol Depend* 2000; 60:19–27.

31. Solbergsdottir E, Bjornsson G, Gudmundsson LS, Tyrfingsson T, Kristinsson J. Validity of self-reports and drug use among young people seeking treatment for substance abuse or dependence. *J Addict Dis* 2004; 23:29–38.

32. Buchan BJ, Dennis ML, Tims FM, Diamond GS. Cannabis use: Consistency and validity of self-report, on-site urine testing and laboratory testing. *Addiction* 2002; 97(Suppl. 1): 98–108.

33. Harrell AV. The validity of self-reported drug use data: The accuracy of responses on confidential self-administered answered sheets. *NIDA Res Monogr* 1997; 167:37–58.

34. Babor TF, Stephens RS, Marlatt GA. Verbal report methods in clinical research on alcoholism: Response bias and its minimization. *J Stud Alcohol* 1987; 48:410–424.

35. Hamid R, Deren S, Beardsley M, Tortu S. Agreement between urinalysis and self-reported drug use. *Subst Use Misuse* 1999; 34:1585–1592.

36. Meyers K, Hagan TA, Zanis D *et al.* Critical issues in adolescent substance use assessment. *Drug Alcohol Depend* 1999; 55:235–246.

37. Winters KC, Latimer WW, Stinchfield R. Clinical issues in the assessment of adolescent alcohol and other drug use. *Behav Res Ther* 2002; 40:1443–1456.

38. Reynaud M, Karila L, Chinet L, Allen JP, Streel E, Pelc I. Original strategies of screening, evaluation, and care of adolescent substance abuse. *Alcohol Clin Exp Res* 2005; 29:1264–1267.

39. Conigrave KM, Degenhardt LJ, Whitfield JB, Saunders JB, Helander A, Tabakoff B. CDT, GGT, and AST as markers of alcohol use: The WHO/ISBRA Collaborative Project. *Alcohol Clin Exp Res* 2002; 26:332–339.

40. Harasymiw J, Seaberg J, Bean P. Using routine laboratory tests to detect heavy drinking in the general population. *J Addict Dis* 2006; 25:59–63.

41. Nystrom M, Perasalo J, Salaspuro M. Screening for heavy drinking and alcohol-related problems in young university students: The CAGE, the Mm-MAST and the trauma score questionnaires. *J Stud Alcohol* 1993; 54:528–533.

42. Comasco E, Nordquist N, Leppert J *et al.* Adolescent alcohol consumption: Biomarkers PEth and FAEE in relation to interview and questionnaire data. *J Stud Alcohol Drugs* 2009; 70:797–804.

43. Mayer J, Filstead WJ. The adolescent alcohol involvement scale. An instrument for measuring adolescents' use and misuse of alcohol. *J Stud Alcohol* 1979; 40:291–300.

44. Harrell AV, Wirtz PW. Screening for adolescent problem drinking: Validation of a multidimensional instrument for case identification. *Psychol Assess* 1989; 1:61–63.

45. Deas D, Roberts JS, Randall CL, Anton RF. Adolescent Obsessive–Compulsive Drinking Scale: An assessment tool for problem drinking. *J Natl Med Assoc* 2001; 93:92–103.

46. Weed NC, Butcher JN, Williams CL. Development of MMPI-A alcohol/drug problem scales. *J Stud Alcohol* 1994; 55:296–302.

47. Knight JR, Shrier LA, Bravender TD, Farrell M, Bilt JV, Shaffer HJ. A new brief screen for adolescent substance abuse. *Arch Pediatr Adolesc Med* 1999; 153:591–596.

48. Tarter RE. Evaluation and treatment of adolescent substance abuse: A decision tree method. *Am J Drug Alcohol Abuse* 1990; 16:1–46.

49. Raistrick D, Bradshaw J, Tober G, Weiner J, Allison J, Healey C. Development of the Leeds Dependence Questionnaire (LDQ): A questionnaire to measure alcohol and opiate dependence in the context of a treatment evaluation package. *Addiction* 1994; 89:563–572.

50. Winters KC. Development of an adolescent alcohol and other drug abuse screening scale: Personal Experience Screening Questionnaire. *Addict Behav* 1992; 17:479–490.

51. Rahdert E, ed. *The Adolescent Assessment/Referral System Manual*. Rockville, MD: DHHS. Publication No. ADM 91–1735; 1991.

52. White H, Labouvie EW. Towards the assessment of adolescent problem drinking. *J Stud Alcohol* 1989; 50:30–37.

53. MacAndrew C. Toward the psychometric detection of substance misuse in young men: The SAP scale. *J Stud Alcohol* 1986; 47:161–166.

54. Miller G. *The Substance Abuse Subtle Screening Inventory: Adolescent Version*. Bloomington, IN: SASSI Institute; 1985.

55. Friedman AS, Utada A. A method for diagnosing and planning the treatment of adolescent drug abusers (the Adolescent Drug Abuse Diagnosis [ADAD] instrument). *J Drug Educ* 1989; 19:285–312.

56. Metzger D, Kushner H, McLellan AT. *Adolescent Problem Severity Index*. Philadelphia: University of Pennsylvania; 1991.

57. Wanberg KW. *Adolescent Self-Assessment Profile*. Arvada, CO: Center for Alcohol/Drug Abuse Research and Evaluation; 1992.

58. Meyers K, McLellan T, Jaeger JL, Pettinati HM. The development of the Comprehensive Addiction Severity Index for Adolescents (CASI-A): An interview for assessing multiple problems of adolescents. *J Subst Abuse Treat* 1995; 12:181–193.

59. Dennis M, Titus J, White M, Unsicker J, Hodgkins D. *Global Appraisal of Individual Needs (GAIN): Administration Guide for the GAIN and Related Measures*. Bloomington, IL: Chestnut Health Systems; 2002.

60. Winters KC, Henly GA. *Personal Experience Inventory Test and Manual*. Los Angeles, CA: Western Psychological Sciences; 1989.

61. Kaminer Y, Bukstein O, Tarter RE. The teen-addiction severity index: Rationale and reliability. *Int J Addict* 1991; 26:219–226.

62. Winters KC, Henly GA. *Adolescent Diagnostic Interview Schedule and Manual*. Los Angeles: Western Psychological Services; 1993.

63. Cottler L. *Composite International Diagnostic Interview: Substance Abuse Module*. St Louis, MO: Department of Psychiatry, Washington School of Medicine; 2000.

64. Brown SA, Myers MG, Lippke L, Tapert SF, Stewart DG, Vik PW. Psychometric evaluation of the Customary Drinking and Drug Use Record (CDDR): A measure of adolescent alcohol and drug involvement. *J Stud Alcohol* 1998; 59:427–438.

65. Shaffer D, Fisher P, Lucas CP, Dulcan MK, Schwab-Stone ME. NIMH Diagnostic Interview Schedule for Children Version IV (NIMH DISC-IV): Description, differences from previous versions, and reliability of some common diagnoses. *J Am Acad Child Adolesc Psychiatry* 2000; 39:28–38.

66. Martin CS, Kaczynski NA, Maisto SA, Bukstein OM, Moss HB. Patterns of DSM-IV alcohol abuse and dependence symptoms in adolescent drinkers. *J Stud Alcohol* 1995; 56:672–680.

67. Brown SA, Christiansen BA, Goldman MS. The alcohol expectancy questionnaire: An instrument for the assessment of adolescent and adult alcohol expectancies. *J Stud Alcohol* 1987; 48:483–491.

68. De Leon G, Melnick G, Kressel D, Jainchill N. Circumstances, motivation, readiness, and suitability (the CMRS scales): Predicting retention in therapeutic community treatment. *Am J Drug Alcohol Abuse* 1994; 20:495–515.

69. Petchers MK, Singer MI. Perceived-Benefit-of-Drinking Scale: Approach to screening for adolescent alcohol abuse. *J Pediatr* 1987; 110:977–981.

70. Cady ME, Winters KC, Jordan DA, Solberg KB, Stinchfield RD. Motivation to change as a predictor of treatment outcome for adolescent substance abusers. *J Child Adolesc Subst Abuse* 1996; 5:73–91.

71. Sobell LC, Sobell MB. Timeline Follow-back: A technique for assessing self-reported ethanol consumption. In: Allen J, Litten RZ, eds. *Measuring Alcohol Consumption: Psychosocial and Biological Methods*. Totowa, NJ: Humana Press; 1992, pp. 41–72.

72. Tonigan JS, Miller WR, Brown JM. The reliability of Form 90: An instrument for assessing alcohol treatment outcome. *J Stud Alcohol* 1997; 58:358–364.

Part V

Treatment

Chapter 13

Recognition and acute management of severe alcohol intoxication and withdrawal in youth

Federico E. Vaca[1] and Rockan Sayegh[2]

[1]Department of Emergency Medicine, Yale University School of Medicine, New Haven, CT, USA
[2]Center for Trauma and Injury Prevention Research, University of California Irvine, School of Medicine, Orange, CA, USA

On February 19, 1980, Bon Scott, lead singer of one of the most successful rock bands ever, AC/DC, passed out in a car on his way home after a night of heavy drinking. A friend left him to sleep in the car because he could not be awakened. A few hours later Bon Scott was found lifeless and was rushed to London's King's College Hospital where he was pronounced dead on arrival. At the coronial enquiry the cause of death was listed as "acute alcohol poisoning."

Key points

- Heavy episodic (binge) drinking in youth is a key contributor to alcohol poisoning.
- The clinical care goal in successful treatment of a youth with alcohol poisoning begins with out-of-hospital recognition.
- Although young persons may have stopped consuming alcohol some time before their presentation to the emergency department, blood alcohol level may continue rising through the initial medical assessment, resuscitation, and treatment phases.
- The mainstay emergency care treatment objective of alcohol poisoning is aggressive respiratory and cardiovascular supportive care.
- In youth who are intoxicated but awake with a secure airway at the initial presentation, the emergency treatment team should perform a thorough focused physical examination; the objective is to identify evidence of traumatic injury that may be masquerading as "intoxication" or coexisting with severe intoxication.
- Peers, parents, police, and EMS should work together in youth poisoning identification and start basic lifesaving measures infield treatment.
- Peers, parents, and police need to carefully monitor if the youth becomes unconscious and refrain from giving food or liquids as this may exacerbate nausea and vomiting.
- Strong consideration should be given to psychosocial and mental health evaluation of a youth with an alcohol poisoning event.

Young People and Alcohol: Impact, Policy, Prevention, Treatment, First Edition.
Edited by John B. Saunders and Joseph M. Rey.
© 2011 Blackwell Publishing Ltd. Published 2011 by Blackwell Publishing Ltd.

As children ultimately transition into adolescence and then into emerging adulthood, they are faced with a paradoxical life stage; one that imparts greater physical strength and capacity for decision making, yet has substantially greater risk of premature morbidity and mortality. Further, during this important transition, young people remain particularly vulnerable to substance abuse, of which alcohol (ethanol) is noted to be the drug of choice among adolescents in the United States.[1]

Globally, with relatively few exceptions in developed countries, the consumption of alcohol is a socially acceptable practice (see Chapter 1). The World Health Organization (WHO) estimates that throughout the world approximately 2 billion people consume alcohol.[2] Unfortunately, significant premature morbidity and mortality are frequently the result of episodic, regular, and chronic alcohol consumption in young people. While in most instances long-term health consequences of alcohol use include a constellation of serious liver diseases, increased risk of multiple types of cancer, and cardiovascular disease,[3–5] more acute consequences such as injury-related disability and death are more prevalent in adolescent and young adult populations. To make matters worse, the number of years of potential life lost in youth due to alcohol-related injury death is staggering, and the burden to societies and communities throughout the world remains overwhelming. In the United States alone, the Centers for Disease and Control and Prevention (CDC) report that between 2001 and 2005, nearly 5,000 deaths of young people younger than age 21 were associated with excessive alcohol consumption.[6]

Alcohol consumption patterns among youth

When adolescents and young adults throughout the world consume alcohol, *heavy episodic drinking* or *binge drinking* (consumption of five or more drinks in a single session[7]) is a common and prevalent pattern of drinking[8–10] (see also Chapter 1). Recent studies in the United States have shown that, in general, alcohol use begins at ages 12–14 and that there is a consistent rise in binge drinking in the ages of between 12 and 21 years.[11,12] Further, a national study showed that more than 7 million youth aged 12–21 in the United States reported an episode of binge drinking within a 30-day period prior to being surveyed.[13] In Canada, a 2009 study conducted by the Canadian Centre for Addiction and Mental Health showed that 1 in 4 Ontario teens surveyed screened in the binge-drinker category.[14] A recent English study showed that 17% out of nearly 7,800 students in the ages between 11 and 15 surveyed across schools in England reported being drunk at least once within a 30-day period in 2008.[15] Finally, a survey conducted by the European School Survey Project on Alcohol and Other Drugs (ESPAD) in 35 European countries found that 43% of 15–16-year-old teens reported drinking five drinks or more on one occasion during a 30-day period.[10] Unfortunately, no matter what the geographic location, the pattern of binge drinking among adolescents and young adults continues to pose serious health threats to themselves, their families, and their communities.

Alcohol consumption consequences

In the United States, alcohol consumption remains a formidable contributing factor to injury and fatal motor vehicle collisions, homicides, and suicides that encompasses the three leading causes of death among 15–24-year-old youth.[16,17] As a result, a considerable amount of morbidity is routinely encountered in emergency departments. Adolescents and young adults are regularly treated for excessive alcohol consumption-related events due to intentional and unintentional injury, sexual assault and abuse, and alcohol poisoning.

Beyond the United States, other countries encounter similar acute medical care and public health burdens with adolescents and emerging adults related to alcohol abuse. In 2000, the ESPAD report showed that 13% of 15–16-year-old teens surveyed had been involved in an accident or had been injured as a result of alcohol consumption.[18] Further, from 2000–2003, nearly 2,400 Canadians younger than 25 years were admitted to Canadian hospitals for an alcohol-associated injury.[19] Between 1997 and 2007, 40% of the 594 Croatian children ages 0–18 years had alcohol-attributable admissions to a pediatric hospital.[20] In 2007, the German Federal Commissioner for Narcotic Drugs reported that the number of alcohol poisoning hospitalizations had doubled since 2000.[21] Dutch youth hospital admissions due to alcoholic poisoning have also been noted to be on the rise. In 2008, 337 youth aged 11–17 years were admitted to hospital: A rise of 13% compared with 2007, while the average age of admission had dropped slightly to 15 years.[22] Finally, in the United Kingdom, nearly 1,000 youth younger than 15 years of age require emergency treatment for alcohol poisoning each year.[23] The global public health burden of alcohol abuse in adolescents and emerging adults has been and continues to be pernicious and pervasive with far reaching negative consequences at the individual as well as the societal level.

Clinical features of alcohol poisoning

Youth alcohol intoxication and alcohol poisoning are among the acute alcohol-related illnesses that require immediate medical attention. Nonclinically trained individuals such as parents, teachers, and peers may recognize and associate slurred speech, poor coordination, and acute broad mood swings with overt manifestations of intoxication. However, without recognition and medical attention, a young person that initially appears mildly intoxicated one moment may easily go unnoticed the next, only to become unresponsive with impending alcohol poisoning and potential death.

Acute alcohol poisoning in young people commonly occurs as a result of binge drinking. Unfortunately, poor alcohol tolerance along with excessive consumption of alcohol can turn the cliché "experimentation" by youth into a deadly outcome. Most commonly, severe depression of the central nervous system coupled with respiratory depression is associated with alcohol poisoning. This is also a final common pathway to alcohol poisoning-related coma and death. In acute alcohol poisoning, the narrow spectrum of moderate to severe intoxication leading to poisoning and coma should be taken into strong consideration.

When initially encountered, the intoxicated youth may be found to be slightly to profoundly somnolent and difficult to arouse. Table 13.1 lists several clinical features that are well-known hallmarks of alcohol intoxication. These manifestations are also well correlated (in nondrinkers and casual drinkers) to blood alcohol concentration (BAC) and reveal the levels at which poisoning, coma, and eventual death may result.

The effects of severe alcohol intoxication can eventually render the youth unresponsive, hypothermic, with heart rhythm disturbances and ineffective heart function, as well as with

Table 13.1   Clinical features of severe alcohol intoxication and poisoning.

- Outside of the hospital setting, it is difficult to predict which intoxicated youth may go on to alcohol poisoning.
- The severely intoxicated youth can be found to be unresponsive, cold (hypothermic), with a slow heart rate (bradycardic) and a low blood pressure (hypotensive).
- The clinical manifestations in a severely intoxicated youth known to have coingested other drugs may vary widely and depend on the pharmacological interaction between alcohol and the other drug(s) taken.
- A major life-threat to the severely intoxicated youth is obstruction of the airway due to loss of gag and cough reflex and ensuing aspiration of stomach contents.
- Alcohol is a potent central nervous system depressant that can lead to cardiopulmonary arrest in the setting of alcohol poisoning.

shallow and severely compromised respiratory effort. The latter effect will ultimately leave the youth's vitals organs in a critically oxygen-poor state with progression to irreparable end organ injury. In many cases, the progressive central nervous system depression alone can lead to the youth being unable to intentionally and effectively clear their respiratory airway (gag or cough) should the youth vomit. Not uncommonly, this can lead to an acute respiratory obstruction, cardiopulmonary arrest and death.

There are other important considerations associated with alcohol consumption that can accentuate its negative physiological effects. Excessive consumption of alcohol can lead to a diuretic effect that in turn can exacerbate loss of intravascular volume in the circulatory system, further stressing the cardiovascular system and making it difficult for the body to maintain a normal core body temperature. Coingestion of alcohol with other drugs (over the counter, prescription, illicit) can dangerously potentiate acute alcohol poisoning and bring on coma and death more rapidly than expected with alcohol ingestion alone. This can be seen when alcohol is consumed with the use of other central nervous system depressants such as barbiturates, benzodiazepines, and narcotics. In situations where the coingested agent is a central nervous system stimulant (e.g., cocaine and methamphetamine), the youth may initially present in a hyperalert, anxious, agitated, or combative state only to quickly decompensate clinically and without proper clinical care become obtunded and experience cardiopulmonary arrest.

Alcohol metabolism

Ingested alcohol is absorbed throughout the entire gastrointestinal tract. The greatest absorption (approximately 80%) occurs in the small intestine while the remaining 20% is absorbed in the stomach. Due to alcohol's high affinity for water, it is largely found in tissues with high water content such as circulating blood. More than 95% of alcohol consumed is metabolized in the liver. A much smaller proportion is removed from the body in urine, breath, tears, and saliva.[24]

In general, the rate of alcohol metabolism depends on a variety of important factors that include initial health status of the youth, gender, body–fat composition, and the individual's efficiency of alcohol metabolizing enzymes. Because adults are generally larger (greater body–fat composition) than adolescents, there is a larger volume of distribution for alcohol. As a result, BACs that may be well tolerated in some adults can easily be life-threatening in adolescents and young adults. Consequently, youth are at a significantly greater risk for alcohol poisoning because they are frequently unaware of safe drinking limits and their large volume consumption easily overwhelms their capacity to metabolize alcohol.[25,26]

Alcohol intoxication

Initial emergency department management

Initial management is summarized in Table 13.2. The overall goal in the acute treatment and management of an intoxicated youth is to rapidly assess their respiratory, cardiovascular, and neurological systems in order to provide lifesaving supportive and corrective care, if needed. This may include respiratory support, intravenous fluid resuscitation and electrolyte correction as well as identifying and addressing any coexisting life-threat.

Some of the signs and the symptoms that may be present upon emergency department arrival of a moderate to severely intoxicated youth include tachycardia, hypotension, hypothermia, hypoventilation, hypoxia, vomiting, dysarthria, muscular incoordination, ataxia, and altered level of consciousness.[24] In this setting, evolving acute alcohol poisoning must be considered and the collection of the key medical and event history can be lifesaving for the youth. Obtaining important historical features from friends and family as well as from emergency medical service (EMS) personnel or police can yield insights that can guide clinical treatment and help avert treatment error. This is of particular importance if traumatic injury to the head (intracranial) or spine (spinal cord) is being considered. In this context, considerable care and caution should be exercised by the treating physician and the team in the clinical evaluation phase so as to not worsen the youth's clinical condition. Moreover, with the suspicion of traumatic injury, targeted diagnostic tests, emergent consultations, and interventions can be initiated in coordination with acute alcohol poisoning treatment.

Table 13.2   Initial emergency management of severe alcohol intoxication and poisoning.

- Evolving acute alcohol poisoning must be considered and the collection of the key medical and event history from friends, family, emergency medical service, and law enforcement personnel can be lifesaving for the youth.
- The treating physician and acute care treatment team should give strong consideration to associated trauma and/or other toxic coingestion in the severely intoxicated youth.
- Stabilizing and securing a youth's airway, breathing and circulation, followed by intravenous fluid resuscitation and ruling out traumatic injury is mainstay treatment in the isolated severe alcohol intoxication.
- The clinical management of a severely intoxicated youth with toxic coingestion of other drugs can be complicated and may warrant the use of drug specific antidotes.
- Even in the setting of an isolated alcohol poisoning without toxic coingestion, mechanical ventilation may be warranted as a lifesaving measure.

It is important to know that although alcohol consumption by the youth may have stopped some time before their presentation to the emergency department, BAC can continue to rise through the initial medical assessment, resuscitation, and treatment phase. Toxic coingestion or trauma may be concomitant reasons for the youth to have an altered level of consciousness on presentation. Therefore, the clinical history taken should be detailed enough to include type and quantity of alcohol consumed, last known intake of alcohol, other coingestions, history of trauma, seizure activity, episodes of loss of consciousness, complaints of pain, and any significant past medical history. If the youth should arrive to the emergency department by way of private auto or ambulance, the friends/family and EMS personnel, respectively, should be a primary source of historical information. They should be thoroughly questioned by the definitive acute care treatment team and physician.

Along with obtaining relevant clinical history, a careful, thorough and rapid basic life support[27] assessment of the youth's airway, breathing, and circulation should take place by the treating physician. Ethanol interacts with a variety of neurotransmitters[28–32] leading to central nervous system depression. As a result, excessive alcohol consumption can compromise breathing, circulation, and the protective gag reflex.[24]

A critical action that must be established within the first few minutes of clinical assessment is assuring that the youth is alert and awake, with a stable blood pressure and respiratory effort and pattern. The youth should be able to spontaneously gag and cough in order to protect themselves from the threat of aspiration. If the youth is found to be unresponsive and the physician cannot assure maintenance of an open and secure airway, mechanical ventilation and admission to an intensive care unit may be warranted until the youth becomes more responsive as the BAC begins to decrease. While there is currently no pharmacologically proven antidote that is routinely used for alcohol poisoning that facilitates rapid alcohol elimination from the body, in rare and extreme instances hemodialysis has been employed as an additional supportive measure.[33,34]

Comparatively, given an awake yet intoxicated youth with a secure airway at the initial emergency department presentation, the physician and the emergency treatment team should similarly perform a thorough yet rapid focused physical examination of the youth. Here, the objective is to identify any evidence of traumatic injury that may be masquerading as "intoxication" or coexisting with severe intoxication. Any historical evidence that would otherwise suggest a traumatic injury to the head and spine, thorax, abdomen, or extremity long bones should prompt the physician to exercise the appropriate acute trauma care evaluation and intervention.[35] This may include both a primary and a secondary physical assessment (survey) of the intoxicated youth with accompanying diagnostic imaging and intervention or emergency referral with transfer to a hospital with higher level-of-care specialists and resources.

In a scenario were the intoxicated youth is fully conscious and conversant at presentation to the emergency department, the treating physician and emergency treatment team should conduct a complete and diligent history and physical examination. Further questioning of the youth regarding coingestions and trauma should be a core part of the initial assessment. Ultimately, the medical history coupled with the clinical examination routinely enables the physician to form an effective diagnostic and treatment plan for a youth presenting with suspected severe intoxication or alcohol poisoning.

If the youth is found to be free of traumatic injury, the treatment of suspected alcohol poisoning in adolescent and emerging adults is in most respects similar to that in adults. This involves supportive care until the alcohol is appreciably eliminated from the body. Only after a period of extended observation and assurance that the youth has become sober and potential life-threatening conditions have been ruled out can the treating emergency physician entertain discharging the youth to a safe and responsible environment. This final disposition of the youth can occur safely when they are clinically sober and under the care of a responsible sober adult. Finally, prior to discharge, while the youth is alert and awake, a social work and or psychiatric consultation should take place to facilitate alcohol-related health promotion, education, brief intervention and referral to alcohol treatment services (see Chapter 8).

Peers, parents, and police

Alcohol poisoning is a spectrum of disease and recognizing the difference between moderate to severe intoxication and poisoning can be difficult for peers, parents, police, and other medically untrained individuals. As a result, some experts have labeled alcohol poisoning a silent killer. While acute medical support for cardiovascular and respiratory systems is the mainstay of treatment in this context, many parts of the world lack the EMS personnel and infrastructure to provide infield medical care and transport of severely intoxicated youth to hospitals equipped with emergency care staff and resources. Therefore, the probability of survival from an alcohol-poisoning episode in these settings is dramatically reduced. However, when quick recognition and medical treatment are available, the prognosis for isolated acute alcohol poisoning in adolescents and emerging adults is relatively positive.

When peers, parents, and police encounter a youth who is intoxicated, there are several considerations and actions that should be undertaken to help avoid a detrimental outcome. Each of these groups should initially entertain the suspicion of impending alcohol poisoning in the intoxicated youth. They should also follow a systematic process (summarized in Figure 13.1) to provide simple, basic lifesaving measures and call for professional help by notifying EMS about the potential alcohol poisoning and the need for transport to an acute care facility.

As previously noted, excessive amounts of alcohol depress the central nervous system to the extent that the area that regulates involuntary actions such as breathing, heart rate, and gag reflex cease to function. Recognizing the initial signs and symptoms associated with acute alcohol poisoning and contacting EMS or taking the young person to an acute care facility is essential for youth's survival. Other signs and symptoms of acute alcohol poisoning include mental confusion, stupor, coma, vomiting, seizures, bradycardia, irregular breathing, hypoxia, and hypothermia. It is important that peers, parents, and police are familiar with and able to recognize these signs. This is of particular importance because most adolescents and young adults consume alcohol in a home[36] or college[37] setting where EMS may not be immediately available. Because there can be considerable variation in some of the clinical manifestations of life-threatening alcohol poisoning, peers and parents should not delay helping the youth seek medical attention nor should they assume that the intoxicated youth will "sleep it off." It is worth repeating that although the

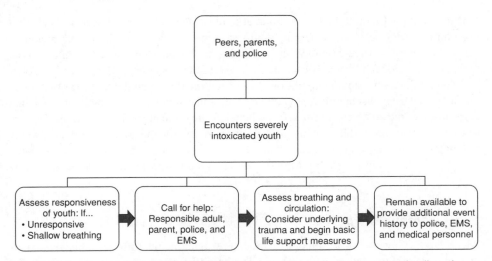

Figure 13.1 Assessment and treatment considerations for peers, parents, and police of severely intoxicated youth.

intoxicated youth may, at first encounter, appear to be mildly to moderately intoxicated and no longer actively consuming alcohol, without proper medical attention their BAC can continue to increase to life-threatening levels (Table 13.3).

In some settings, it is not EMS personnel but police that are called first to respond to the need for help of a severely intoxicated young person. As a result, it should be a mainstay of law enforcement training that they be familiar with the hallmark signs of the spectrum of alcohol intoxication to alcohol poisoning in youth. This basic training could help identify and direct medical care to the arrested youth with impending

Table 13.3 Blood alcohol concentration and physiological effects.

Blood alcohol level (mg/dL)	Physiological effects[a]
20–50	Subtle decrease in fine motor coordination, light sedation, and mildly impaired concentration.
50–100	More impaired judgment, greater decrease in sensory–motor coordination, euphoria, and worsening reaction time.
100–150	Gait limitations, increased difficulty with balance, memory, and speech.
150–300	Lethargy and decreased response to stimuli, incontinence.
300–400	Profoundly decreased consciousness or coma.
>400	Profoundly diminished respiratory effort and/or respiratory failure resulting in death.

[a]The particular blood alcohol concentration and physiological patterns above are associated with occasional or casual drinkers and may be different in chronic drinkers.

alcohol poisoning. Without proper training, such a youth might be placed in custody without adequate medical attention only to succumb to alcohol-induced coma and cardio-vascular arrest. The law enforcement agency that trains their personnel with such basic lifesaving recognition skills is not only able to keep the public's safety but also avoid preventable loss of life and needless litigation secondary to the death of a youth while in custody.

Once EMS is notified and en route to the scene, peers, parents, and police should be closely monitoring the intoxicated individual for any change in clinical status. Alcohol is a well-known gastric irritant that can cause vomiting and coupled with its effect as a central nervous system depressant, the intoxicated individual remains at considerable risk of death due to gastric content aspiration. Therefore, peers, parents, and police should closely monitor the youth for any signs of change in consciousness and refrain from giving the intoxicated youth food or liquid as this may exacerbate nausea and ultimately lead to vomiting without the ability to protect the airway. If the youth subsequently becomes unarousable, they should be put on their *right lateral side* to reduce the risk of aspiration (Figure 13.2). However, in the setting of *suspected traumatic injury* to the youth's head (intracranial) and or spine (spinal cord), caution should be exercised so as to not worsen the youth's clinical condition. Avoiding excessive movement of the youth's head and neck would be prudent until EMS arrives and is able to apply appropriate spinal immobilization prior to transporting to hospital. As soon as EMS personnel arrive on the scene, peers, parents, and police should be as complete and accurate as possible when answering questions regarding the drinking behavior (timing, quantity, and quality) and any related mechanism of injury (fall, assault, motor vehicle crash, etc.) of the intoxicated youth.

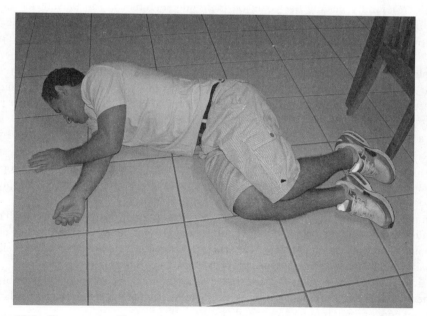

Figure 13.2   Recovery position.

Emergency medical personnel and ambulance officers

The main clinical priority for EMS and ambulance officers in acute alcohol poisoning of a youth is to initiate and facilitate stabilization of vital signs by monitoring or securing the airway, breathing, and circulation. As previously noted, the principal effect of acute alcohol poisoning is the depression of the central nervous system. Due to this effect, core body temperature, blood pressure, heart rate, and breathing can be decreased. EMS and ambulance officers should understand the basic pathophysiology associated with alcohol intoxication, to be more familiar with the clinical manifestations and hallmarks of alcohol poisoning. Having this fund of knowledge can help guide their initial assessment and intervention strategies in the out-of-hospital setting. Moreover, it can also aid them with infield disposition decisions so they might properly identify the youth with impending alcohol poisoning, subsequently transporting them to an acute care facility.

As with the acute assessment of the intoxicated youth by the emergency physician, EMS and ambulance officers should immediately obtain relevant contextual and clinical history, as well as assess the status of the youth's airway, cardiovascular, and neurological stability. In the uncontrolled field setting, this relatively simple procedure can be challenging and EMS personnel should remain focused on stabilizing and transporting the alcohol-poisoned youth to the emergency department despite this limitation.

Initial EMS interventions that might need to be undertaken on scene can include obtaining intravenous access and initiating fluid resuscitation, stabilizing the airway to protect from aspiration, and keeping the youth covered with blankets to mitigate alcohol induced hypothermia.[38] If the severely intoxicated youth is hemodynamically stable but unresponsive to stimuli with no history of trauma and proceeds to vomit, EMS should consider carefully placing the youth on their side (Figure 13.2) to prevent the aspiration of gastric contents. If the youth is unconscious upon EMS arrival to the scene or deteriorates during transport, basic and advanced (if the capability by the EMS or ambulance officers exists) life support[27] skills should be used. This could include delivery of supplemental oxygen and intravenous fluids, oral suctioning of emesis or oral secretions from the airway, oral tracheal intubation (or some other advanced airway technique), and cardiopulmonary resuscitation with the delivery of emergency cardiovascular pharmacotherapy if necessary. It is important to note that if traumatic injury to the head (intracranial) and or spine (spinal cord) is suspected, caution should be exercised by the EMS or ambulance officers so as to not worsen the youth's clinical condition. Careful airway assessment avoiding excessive cervical spine movement followed by appropriate spinal immobilization prior to transporting the youth into the ambulance and hospital is important.

Immediately upon delivery of the youth to the emergency department, a thorough relay of infield clinical assessment and intervention should be provided to the emergency physician and acute care treatment team. The EMS personnel or the ambulance officers should remain available for further event and treatment-related questioning by the emergency physician. This is important because it is not uncommon for event or clinical history gathered by the EMS personnel to significantly influence the management, particularly in cases of concomitant trauma or suicidal gesture.

Alcohol withdrawal in youth

The National Institute on Alcohol Abuse and Alcoholism has highlighted major differences between adolescent and adult alcohol abuse.[39] Adolescents are more likely to demonstrate episodic alcohol consumption and less likely to demonstrate chronic daily use and abuse.[40–42] Adolescents also tend to use a greater variety of substances, resulting in more complicated withdrawal and dependency patterns.

The American Psychiatric Association defines alcohol withdrawal as a cessation of heavy or prolonged alcohol use resulting in two or more of the following symptoms: Autonomic hyperactivity, increased hand tremor, insomnia, nausea or vomiting, hallucinations, psychomotor agitation, anxiety, and seizures.[24,43] These symptoms are associated with the effects of alcohol on neuronal pathways that regulate involuntary control. Chronic alcohol consumption results in both a downregulation of inhibitory GABA receptors[44,45] and upregulation of stimulatory NMDA receptors.[46]

Adult chronic alcohol users are mostly affected by alcohol withdrawal. However, to a considerably lesser extent teens and young adults can also suffer from alcohol withdrawal.[47–49] The literature regarding specific treatment regimens of alcohol withdrawal in youth is severely limited and to date there are no definitive randomized controlled trials on optimal pharmacological management or treatment protocols. However, despite this limitation and the rarity with which alcohol withdrawal is encountered in young adults in the emergency department, emergency physicians should generally treat acute withdrawal by managing psychomotor agitation and seizure activity using benzodiazepines, addressing abnormal vital signs and treating deficiencies in nutrients (vitamins and electrolytes) commonly found in chronic alcohol users.[24,50]

The most frequently occurring withdrawal symptoms reported by adolescents in one study were nausea, vomiting, depression or irritability, myalgias, and weakness.[51] Withdrawal symptoms usually occur within the first 24 hours after alcohol use cessation. Thereafter, symptoms can persist as long as up to 7 days depending on the extent to which medical attention is provided.[43]

Compared to adults, adolescents are more likely to present with co-occurring problems, such as depressive symptoms, social and academic problems, delinquent behavior, and other substance use[52] (see Chapter 18). Health professionals should be familiar with these important differences and adjust their methods of assessment and treatment for abuse and withdrawal patterns accordingly.

Ethical considerations

In the emergency department setting, once treatment is administered and the youth is in recovery, ethical considerations and moral obligations are important to take into account. Adolescents and emerging adults commonly drink alcohol for reasons beyond experimentation with their peers. Some youth will use alcohol as self-treatment of depression[53] and other serious emotional and negative mental health states.[54] Still others will drink heavily to the point of alcohol poisoning as an expression of self-harm and suicidal gesture.[55]

Peers, parents, police, and health professionals should be aware that alcohol intoxication or poisoning episodes might be the overt manifestation of an underlying serious mental health problem. Police called to a home for a suspected alcohol poisoning should query family and friends at he scene regarding similar episodes of intoxication by the youth. They should also notify parents, welfare agencies, or other mental health services as deemed appropriate in order that the youth might receive appropriate evaluation and treatment.

Emergency physicians are similarly obligated to consider coexisting mental health disorders when treating a youth for severe alcohol intoxication or poisoning. Once the youth has been stabilized clinically and either admitted to the hospital or there are plans to safely discharge the youth home, strong consideration to emergency department social work and psychiatric consultation should be given. Taking advantage of the index emergency department visit or hospitalization can potentially reveal more serious underlying substance abuse and mental health disorders. Furthermore, if the capacity exists, it can provide an opportunity to arrange more complete mental health evaluation and treatment in follow-up.

Finally, patient confidentiality and protection of privacy are important in both the adolescent and the emerging adult populations. However, healthcare agency, hospital, and state policies may be considerably different across geographic regions. For example, in the United States, many states have implemented laws to protect the confidentiality of minors with regard to substance abuse testing and detection.[56] Familiarity with confidentiality-related procedures and protocols particularly when dealing with adolescent minors and parents is important.

Acknowledgment

Dr. Vaca is supported, in part, by the Eunice Kennedy Shiver, National Institute for Child Health and Human Development (K23HD050630).

Web resources for youth, parents, health professionals, and researchers

Category	Organization	Web site
Youth and parents	The Cool Spot	http://drugs.homeoffice.gov.uk/index.html
Youth and parents	Tackling Drugs Changing Lives	http://www.thecoolspot.gov/
Parents	Monitoring the Future	http://monitoringthefuture.org/
Parents	The Antidrug	http://www.theantidrug.com/
Parents and health professionals	Surgeon General's Call to Action to Prevent and Reduce Underage Drinking	http://www.surgeongeneral.gov/topics/underagedrinking/index.html

Category	Organization	Web site
Parents and health professionals	Office of National Drug Control Policy (ONDCP)	http://www.whitehousedrugpolicy.gov/females/index.html
Parents and health professionals	National Clearinghouse for Alcohol and Drug Information, Substance Abuse and Mental Health Services Administration, US Department of Health and Human Services	http://ncadi.samhsa.gov/
Parents, health professionals, and researchers	National Institute on Alcohol Abuse and Alcoholism	http://www.niaaa.nih.gov/
Parents, health professionals, and researchers	World Health Organization	http://www.who.int/en/

References

1. Johnston LD, O'Malley PM, Bachman JG *et al. Monitoring the Future, National Survey Results on Drug Use, 1975–2005. Volume 1: Secondary School Students.* NIH Pub. No. 06–5883. Bethesda, MD: National Institute on Drug Abuse; 2006.
2. World Health Organization. *The World Health Report 2002—Reducing Risks, Promoting Healthy Life.* Geneva: World Health Organization; 2002.
3. Room R, Babor T, Rehm J. Alcohol and public health. *Lancet* 2005; 365:519–530.
4. Bellis MA, Hughes K, Tocque K, Hennell T, Humphrey G, Wyke S. Assessing and communicating the health and judicial impact of alcohol use. *Public Health* 2005; 119:253–261.
5. Hughes K, Tocque K, Humphrey G, Bellis MA. *Taking Measures: A Situational Analysis of Alcohol in the North West.* Liverpool: Centre for Public Health; 2004.
6. Centers for Disease and Control. *Alcohol-Related Disease Impact (ARDI).* Available at: https://apps.nccd.cdc.gov/ardi/Homepage.aspx.
7. Cahalan D, Cisin IH, Crossley HM. *American Drinking Practices. A National Study of Drinking Behavior and Attitudes.* New Brunswick, NJ: Rutgers Center of Alcohol Studies; 1969.
8. Goddard E, Higgins V. *Smoking, Drinking and Drug Use Among Young Teenagers in 1998.* London: Office for National Statistics; 1999.
9. Calculated Using the Substance Abuse and Mental Health Data Archive. Available at: http://www.icpsr.umich.edu/SAMHDA/.
10. Hibell B, Guttormsson U, Ahlström S *et al. The 2007 ESPAD Report. Substance Use among Students in 35 European Countries.* Stockholm, Sweden: The Swedish Council for Information on Alcohol and Other Drugs; 2009.
11. Faden VB. Trends in initiation of alcohol use in the United States 1975 to 2003. *Alcohol Clin Exp Res* 2006; 30:1011–1022.
12. Substance Abuse and Mental Health Services Administration (SAMHSA). *Results from the 2007 National Survey on Drug Use and Health: National Findings.* NSDUH Series H–30, DHHS Publication SMA 06–4194. Rockville, MD: Substance Abuse and Mental Health Services Administration; 2008.

13. Substance Abuse and Mental Health Services Administration. *Results from the 2004 National Survey on Drug Use and Health: National Findings*. Rockville, MD: Office of Applied Studies; 2005, p. 25.

14. Paglia-Boak A, Mann RE, Adlaf EM, Rehm J. *Drug Use Among Ontario Students, 1977–2009: OSDUHS Highlights*. CAMH Research Document Series No 28. Toronto, ON: Centre for Addiction and Mental Health; 2009.

15. Fuller E, ed. *Smoking, Drinking, and Drug Use among Young People in England in 2008*. London: National Centre for Social Research and National Foundation for Educational Research; 2009.

16. US Department of Health and Human Services. *The Surgeon General's Call to Action to Prevent and Reduce Underage Drinking*. HHS, Washington, DC: Office of the Surgeon General; 2007.

17. Tsai VW, Anderson CL, Vaca FE. Alcohol involvement among young female drivers in US fatal crashes: Unfavourable trends. *Inj Prev* 2010; 16:17–20.

18. Hibell B, Andersson B, Ahlstrom S *et al. The 1999 ESPAD Report: The European School Survey Project on Alcohol and Other Drugs*. Stockholm, Sweden: The Swedish Council for Information on Alcohol and Other Drugs and Council of Europe, Pompidou Group; 2000.

19. Black K, Asbridge M, Lea S. An overview of injuries to adolescents and young adults related to substance use: Data from Canadian emergency departments. *CJEM* 2009; 11:330–336.

20. Bitunjac K, Saraga M. Alcohol intoxication in pediatric age: Ten-year retrospective study. *Croat Med J* 2009; 50:151–156.

21. Stolle M, Sack P, Thomasius R. Binge drinking in childhood and adolescence: Epidemiology, consequences, and interventions. *Dtsch Arztebl Int* 2009; 106:323–328.

22. Anonymous. *BMJ* 2009; 338:b1633.

23. Department of Health. *Hospital Episode Statistics 2002–2000*. London: The Stationery Office; 2003.

24. Yip L. Ethanol. In: Flomenbaum NE, Goldfrank LR, Hoffman RS, Howland MA, Lewin NA, Nelson LS, eds. *Goldfrank's Toxicologic Emergencies*. 8th edn. New York: McGraw-Hill; 2006, pp. 1147–1161.

25. Spear LP. The adolescent brain and age-related behavioral manifestations. *Neurosci Biobehav Rev* 2000; 24:417–463.

26. Spear LP, Varlinskaya EI. Adolescence: Alcohol sensitivity, tolerance, and intake. In: Galanter M, ed. *Recent Developments in Alcoholism, Vol. 17: Alcohol Problems in Adolescents and Young Adults: Epidemiology, Neurobiology, Prevention, Treatment*. New York: Springer; 2005, pp. 143–159.

27. American Heart Association. 2005 American Heart Association Guidelines for Cardiopulmonary Resuscitation and Emergency Cardiovascular Care. Part 4. Adult Basic Life Support. *Circulation* 2005; 112:III-5-III-16.

28. Tsai GE, Ragan P, Chang R *et al.* Increased glutamatergic neurotransmission and oxidative stress after alcohol withdrawal. *Am J Psychiatry* 1998; 155:726–732.

29. Tsai GE, Coyle JT. The role of glutamatergic neurotransmission in the pathophysiology of alcoholism. *Annu Rev Med* 1998; 49:173–184.

30. Krystal JH, Petrakis IL, Krupitsky E *et al.* NMDA receptor antagonism and the ethanol intoxication signal: From alcoholism risk to pharmacotherapy. *Ann NY Acad Sci* 2003; 1003:176–184.

31. Krystal JH, Petrakis IL, Mason G *et al.* N-methyl-D-aspartate glutamate receptors and alcoholism: Reward, dependence, treatment, and vulnerability. *Pharmacol Ther* 2003; 99:79–94.

32. Ueno S, Harris RA, Messing RO *et al.* Alcohol actions on GABA(A) receptors: From protein structure to mouse behavior. *Alcohol Clin Exp Res* 2001; 25(5 Suppl. ISBRA):76S–81S.

33. Morgan DL, Durso MH, Rich BK, Kurt TL. Severe ethanol intoxication in an adolescent. *Am J Emerg Med* 1995; 13:416–418.
34. Elliott RW, Hunter PR. Acute ethanol poisoning treated by haemodialysis. *Postgrad Med J* 1974; 50:515–517.
35. American College of Surgeons Committee on Trauma. *Advanced Trauma Life Support for Doctors, Instructor Course Manual.* 8th edn. Chicago, IL: American College of Surgeons; 2008.
36. Substance Abuse and Mental Health Services Administration, Office of Applied Studies. *The NSDUH Report. Underage Alcohol Use: Where Do Young People Drink?* Rockville, MD: Substance Abuse and Mental Health Services Administration. 2008.
37. The National Center on Addiction and Substance Abuse at Columbia University. *Wasting the Best and the Brightest: Substance Abuse at America's Colleges and Universities.* New York: The National Center on Addiction and Substance Abuse at Columbia University; 2007.
38. Williams SR. Ethanol. In: Olson KR, ed. *Poisoning & Drug Overdose.* 5th edn. New York, NY: McGraw-Hill; 2007.
39. National Institute on Alcohol Abuse and Alcoholism. Alcohol and development in youth: A multi-disciplinary overview. *Alcohol Res Health* 2004/2005; 28:112–114, 167.
40. Langenbucher J, Martin C, Labouvie E *et al.* Toward the DSM-V: A withdrawal gate model of alcohol abuse and dependence. *J Consult Clin Psychol* 2000; 68:799–809.
41. Clark DB, Kirisci L, Tarter RE. Adolescent *vs* adult onset and the development of substance use disorders in males. *Drug Alcohol Depend* 1998; 49:115–121.
42. Deas D, Riggs P, Langenbucher J *et al.* Adolescents are not adults: Developmental considerations in alcohol users. *Alcohol Clin Exp Res* 2000; 24:232–237.
43. American Psychiatric Association. *Diagnostic and Statistical Manual of Mental Disorders.* 4th edn, Text Revision (DSM-IV-TR). Washington, DC: American Psychiatric Association; 2000.
44. Buck KJ, Hahner L, Sikela J, Harris RA. Chronic ethanol treatment alters brain levels of gamma-aminobutyric acid A receptor subunit mRNAs: Relationship to genetic differences in ethanol withdrawal seizure severity. *J Neurochem* 1991; 57:1452–1455.
45. Keir WJ, Morrow AL. Differential expression of $GABA_A$ receptor subunit mRNAs in ethanol-naive withdrawal seizure resistant (WSR) vs. withdrawal seizure prone (WSP) mouse brain. *Brain Res Mol Brain Res* 1994; 25:200–208.
46. Haugbol SR, Ebert B, Ulrichsen J. Upregulation of glutamate receptor subtypes during alcohol withdrawal in rats. *Alcohol* 2005; 40:89–95.
47. Martin CS, Kaczynski NA, Maisto SA, Bukstein OM, Moss HB. Patterns of DSM-IV alcohol abuse and dependence symptoms in adolescent drinkers. *J Stud Alcohol* 1995; 56:672–680.
48. Clark DB, Buckstein O, Cornelius J. Alcohol use disorders in adolescents: Epidemiology, diagnosis, psychosocial interventions, and pharmacological treatment. *Paediatr Drugs* 2002; 4:493–502.
49. Martin CS, Winters KC. Diagnosis and assessment of alcohol use disorders among adolescents. *Alcohol Res Health* 1998; 22:95–105.
50. Cravo ML, Gloria LM, Selhub J *et al.* Hyperhomocysteinemia in chronic alcoholism: Correlation with folate, vitamin B-12, and vitamin B-6 status. *Am J Clin Nutr* 1996; 63:220–224.
51. Stewart DG, Brown SA. Withdrawal and dependency symptoms among adolescent alcohol and drug abusers. *Addiction* 1995; 90:627–635.
52. National Institute on Alcohol Abuse and Alcoholism. Adolescents and treatment of alcohol use disorders. Module 10A. Social work education for the prevention and treatment of alcohol use disorders. Bethesda, MD: Author; 2004. Available at: http://pubs.niaaa.nih.gov/publications/Social/Module10AAdolescents/Module10A.pdf. Accessed August 24, 2010.

53. Marmorstein R. Longitudinal associations between alcohol problems and depressive symptoms: Early adolescence through early adulthood. *Alcohol Clin Exp Res* 2009; 33:49–59.

54. Kairouz S, Gliksman L, Demers A *et al.* For all these reasons, I do … drink: A multilevel analysis of contextual reasons for drinking among Canadian undergraduates. *J Stud Alcohol* 2002; 63:600–608.

55. Deykin EY, Buka SL. Suicidal ideation and attempts among chemically dependent adolescents. *Am J Public Health* 1994; 4:634–639.

56. American College of Obstetricians and Gynecologists At-risk drinking and illicit drug use: Ethical issues in obstetric and gynecologic practice. ACOG Committee Opinion No. 294. *Obstet Gynecol* 2004; 103:1021–1031.

Chapter 14

Working with families of adolescents who misuse alcohol

Lorna Templeton[1,2]

[1]Mental Health Research and Development Unit, Avon & Wiltshire Mental Health Partnership NHS Trust and the University of Bath, Bath, UK

[2]Independent Research Consultant, Bristol, UK

Young people are more likely to delay or avoid substance misuse when they talk openly with their parents. Research also shows that where young people develop serious problems with substances, the involvement and support of parents and families can contribute greatly to improved outcomes.

Sir Liam Donaldson, Chief Medical Officer, *Guidance on the Consumption of Alcohol by Children and Young People*. Department of Health, London, 2009, pp. 31–32.

Key points

- The family can be both a risk factor and a protective factor for young people in their use and misuse of alcohol and in their experience of a range of associated alcohol-related harms.
- Family-focused interventions are one of the most popular elements of the response to tackling alcohol misuse and related harms in young people, with strong empirical evidence to support their effectiveness across a range of individual and family domains.
- It is vital that family-focused interventions take the bigger picture into account, as the problematic use of alcohol usually coexists with a number of other problems. So, it is necessary to consider the wider needs of young people and their families.
- Research has identified that one of the most important things that parents can do to reduce the risk of their children using and misusing alcohol is to regularly sit down and eat dinner as a family.
- Family-focused interventions are a crucial component of a growing number of "multicomponent" programs that offer a multifaceted response to what are often overlapping and complex problems. If the development of these multicomponent initiatives is to persist then attention must continue to focus on targeting individual, familial, and environmental needs.

Alcohol misuse contributes a major proportion of global disease burden, yet the majority of alcohol-related harm is preventable.[1,2] The use and misuse of alcohol by young people, including in developed countries,[3,4] is an issue of global concern[5] and there is an

Young People and Alcohol: Impact, Policy, Prevention, Treatment, First Edition.
Edited by John B. Saunders and Joseph M. Rey.

impressive library of evidence that indicates how alcohol use and misuse can negatively affect all domains of young lives, both in the short term and the long term, including their physical and mental health, education, behavior, and relationships with family and others.[6–9] There is also a related set of research findings, which summarizes the "ripple effect" of how alcohol (and drug) misuse, including that by young people, can negatively affect families and other social networks.[10]

The role of the family

The family is the biggest influence for children and young people, particularly in their formative years. In the early years, when children spend most of their time at home, family-related characteristics, such as stability of care, consistency, safety, lack of conflict, and positive family harmony are important. Throughout their teenage years, young people spend less time at home, and hence other domains of influence, such as school, peers, the community, and the workplace, become equally or more important than that of the family.

It has been recognized that the "early roots of adolescent and adult alcohol use behaviors begin in childhood,"[11] and that "young people develop alcohol expectancies before ever having direct experience with alcohol."[9] Recent research reported by the Department for Children, Schools, and Families in England highlighted the extent to which parents' own drinking habits can influence their children.[12] It is logical, therefore, that the family is both a risk factor and a protective factor for young people developing, or avoiding, a range of harms, which includes the use and misuse of alcohol.[7–9,13,14] The focus of this chapter is on how the family can be manoeuvered and involved to support the reduction of alcohol misuse and related harm in young people. It is increasingly recognized that not everyone is at equal risk of experiencing alcohol-related harms as a result of alcohol consumption, the problematic alcohol consumption of others (e.g., parents), or as a consequence of other problems that often coexist alongside alcohol misuse. A clearer picture of the protective factors and processes—which are both general and specific to alcohol consumption and that operate at the individual, familial, or wider environmental levels to reduce impact of risk—is emerging. Separately or in combination, these protective factors and processes are believed to promote "resilience" and there are numerous indicators for resilience to alcohol misuse and alcohol-related problems.[15]

Table 14.1 summarizes the primary *familial* risk and protective factors in relation to the misuse of alcohol by young people. This list is not exhaustive and the factors are not listed in any particular order. There is consensus that family factors, combinations of supportive environments, family practices, and family resources, are particularly significant in influencing resilience to alcohol misuse and alcohol-related problems, including both the onset of consumption and the subsequent drinking behavior.[9,14] Seven familial domains of influence have been identified: family relations versus structure; family cohesion; family communication; modeling of behavior by parents; family management; parental supervision; and the influence of parents and peers.[14] Some research has suggested that some factors might be particularly influential. For example, Velleman[9] concludes from the available evidence that "relational aspects (e.g., cohesion, discipline, and communication) of families seem to have a much greater influence than structural aspects (e.g.,

Table 14.1 Familial risk and protective factors in relation to the misuse of alcohol by young people.

Familial risk factors	Familial protective factors
• Parenting style. For example, inconsistent, too controlling, ambivalent, neglectful, or unsupportive • Disruptive or conflictual family environment • Lack of closeness of parental relationships or support from the wider family/network • Family structure and breakdown (e.g., parental separation, divorce, or one-parent families) • Parental education/employment status • Parental substance use (particularly if both parents use, the problem is severe, or use takes place in the home) • Regular maternal alcohol consumption during childhood • Living with parental/familial alcohol misuse and other problems (e.g., domestic violence or mental health problems) • Sibling substance misuse • Being a foster child or in the social care system	• Family structure (e.g., presence of a stable/supportive adult figure, living in a small family, or living with one or both biological parents) • Family relationships and general family environment (e.g., good attachment, warmth, positive family communication, reduced family conflict, or time together as a family) • Parenting style (good care–control balance) (e.g., appropriate supervision and monitoring, discipline, or rules and control) • The presence of other, supportive, family members • Learning about alcohol, drinking alcohol healthily in the home and consequences of use/misuse • Parental modeling of positive behaviors, including moderate/sensible alcohol consumption, attitudes toward alcohol, supply of alcohol • Adaptive and appropriate sibling behavior

Source: Summarized from references 8 and 9.

single-parent families, family size, and birth order)" in how children learn about alcohol. More specifically, it has been suggested that the presence of a stable, consistent, and supportive adult, and regular family mealtimes are both very important.[9,15]

Involving families in the response

The family can therefore be a vital part of any response to reducing alcohol misuse and related harm among young people; the younger the adolescent, the more important the family. The role of parents in communicating appropriate messages about alcohol before children are introduced to it has been highlighted. For example, Van Der Vorst *et al.*'s[16] longitudinal study of nearly 430 families (including young people aged 13–16 years) reported the benefits of intervention as: "once adolescents have established a drinking pattern, the impact of parental alcohol-specific rules declined or even disappeared [...] Alcohol prevention programs should make parents aware that they play a role in preventing youth drinking by setting rules before their children have established a drinking pattern" (see reference 16, p. 1064). Building on evidence such as this, England's Chief Medical Officer published a guidance[6] in 2009, which recommends that an alcohol-free childhood is the healthiest and best option for children who should not be introduced to alcohol until they are at least 15 years old; when they are introduced to alcohol, it should be under parental or carer supervision (or in a supervised environment) and the amount and frequency of consumption should be carefully monitored. To support the implementation of this guidance, the Chief Medical Officer further recommended that, "the importance of parental influences on children's alcohol use should be communicated to parents, carers, and professionals. Parents and carers require advice on how to respond to alcohol use and misuse by children" so that the messages and boundaries that they set with their children are informed and can be confidently presented. However, many young people will misuse alcohol and develop problems requiring intervention as a result, and this chapter will now consider how the family can be involved.

It has been recognized that "family-based treatment is the most thoroughly studied behavioral treatment modality for adolescent substance abuse"[17,18] (although this probably relates particularly to the US context) and has substantial empirical support behind it[17,19–21] (see also Chapters 15 and 18). It has also been acknowledged that family-oriented interventions are a central component of "multicomponent" programs or initiatives to tackle alcohol misuse and related harms (e.g., see references 9 and 22). Family-focused initiatives have grown in popularity in recent years because of the clear conclusions from a wealth of research that has demonstrated the pivotal role that families can play as not only "a risk for" but also "a protective factor against" alcohol misuse and related problems, as outlined above. The involvement and role of the family in adolescent substance misuse treatment has also been highlighted,[6] with family involvement identified as one of the best scoring domains of quality in adolescent treatment services in the United States.[23] Furthermore, one of the characteristics of the top scoring programs was that they offered multidimensional family therapy (see below).

Family-focused interventions

In response to the knowledge of how families can potentially be involved in reducing alcohol misuse and related harms in young people, a large number of family-focused interventions and services have been developed. Consistent with the evidence about how the family can exert a positive influence over young people, some of the main areas where such interventions attempt to effect positive change are as follows:

- Delay the onset of alcohol consumption.
- Reduce alcohol consumption or alcohol-related harms.
- Enhance family factors, such as parent–child communication.
- Support the family in modeling sensible drinking or supervising alcohol consumption.
- Encourage parents to consider their own levels of alcohol consumption and their behavior when they are drinking, and how they might model the messages being communicated to their children.

The rationale behind this is that low levels of parental alcohol use, warm and supportive relationships between parents and children, and how parents manage children's behavior all reduce the use and misuse of alcohol by children and young people.[6] Ward and Snow[24] highlighted that "an important goal of contact with a young person and his/her family should be to facilitate and/or strengthen communication between the two parties so that potential alcohol-related harm contexts can be identified. Part of the role of practitioners is to help parents see some challenging behavior/risk taking as healthy and normal—that is, not to "pathologize" the normal developmental changes (see reference 24, p. 8.) There is evidence from a range of family-focused interventions of their effectiveness, in reducing alcohol-related risks, reducing intention to drink in the future, or actual consumption, or delaying the onset of use.[25–28] Hogue and Liddle's review[17] demonstrates that family-based treatment for adolescent substance misuse is promising in terms of "treatment engagement, outcomes, and durability and moderators of outcomes" (see reference 17, p. 131). A meta-analysis of the impact of general population family interventions on young people's drinking included 18 papers (summarizing the results of nine studies) and reported successes for family interventions in achieving their goal of curbing the initiation of alcohol use and frequency of consumption.[29] These findings were consistent across the included studies, with positive effects seen up to 48 months. Another review[20] concluded that results from studies of a range of family interventions have effect sizes — two to nine times greater than interventions that work with young people alone, with cognitive-behavioral approaches the most promising. The family-focused interventions reviewed included in-home family support, behavioral parent training, family skills training, family education, and family therapy, and the authors recommended that, "effective family strengthening prevention programs should be included in all comprehensive substance abuse prevention activities" (see reference 20, p. 1759).

Many of the research studies that have been conducted recruit young people when they are around 12–13-years of age, which has been identified as the "tipping point" for when young people are most likely to commence alcohol use or to start experiencing alcohol-related problems or harm.[30] Therefore, the evidence that some interventions can delay or reduce consumption at this time is significant. However, while there are strengths to many of these studies (e.g., their large sample sizes and lengths of follow-up), there are also some limitations, most notably that they are often oriented toward the school setting, often struggle to recruit, and retain families, and consider a narrow range of outcomes, often focusing primarily on alcohol (or other substance) use and related harms, ignoring the opportunity to collect data on other individual or family-related factors that could provide a broader understanding of how the interventions might operate or reduce risk in these areas.

Nonetheless, several leading reviews have demonstrated that there is consistent evidence of the effectiveness of family-based interventions in bringing about a range of positive outcomes through changes in individual and family functioning across several domains.[9,14,15,17–19,29,31] Key program components include, for example, parent training (such as guiding parental understanding of the impact of their own drinking on their children), facilitating good parent-child communication, modifying childhood behaviors, family skills training, children's activities, and promoting family time.[9,26,32] Hogue and Liddle's review[17] (see also reference 18) summarized the breadth and depth of family-based treatments for adolescent substance use, highlighting their superior substance use outcomes, superior outcomes in terms of reducing other behaviors (including educational performance, delinquency, and comorbidity), and positive family outcomes. This review

Table 14.2 Examples of family-focused interventions.

Program	Key points
Strengthening Families Programme (SFP—US and UK)[19–20,27,33,34]	7-session primary prevention program, usually delivered weekly to groups of families. SFP targets familial factors associated with substance use.
Multidimensional Family Therapy[21,25,35]	A manualized family-based treatment program for adolescent drug abuse and related behavior problems. Sessions are usually delivered weekly over a few months and can involve separate and/or combined work with a parent and/or adolescent.
STARS (Start Taking Alcohol Risks Seriously) programme[28]	Delivered over 2 years in the school setting. Program includes school-based intervention with the young people as well as materials for young people to take home (or that are mailed directly to parents) and work through with their families.
Resilient Families Programme (Australia)[1]	The program has five components that are delivered over the first 2 years of secondary school. Overall aim of the program is to support schools in developing partnerships with families to improve adolescent health and well-being.

also indicated that such positive outcomes were both maintained and sustained in the longer term. Another study[9] reported that the "single most important thing that parents needed to do was to regularly and frequently eat dinner with their children." Family-focused interventions can facilitate superior treatment engagement and retention rates for young people (e.g., see references 15 and 18).

Some of the research evidence has promoted certain approaches. Examples of the most well-known and widely implemented are listed in Table 14.2. (It should be highlighted that the bulk of the research in this area has taken place in Australia, the United Kingdom, the United States, and to a lesser extent elsewhere in Europe.) Development and testing have been carefully considered, with all the programs following a structured manualized format, consisting of several, regular sessions with young people and/or parents. The programs are a mix of prevention and intervention, and all target one or more of the domains believed to be most open to influence in terms of preventing or reducing alcohol use and misuse.

Delivery of family-focused interventions

The initial and one of the most important things that a practitioner will need to do is to offer a space to listen to a young person and/or their family, and consider what the problems are and how best to offer support and a targeted response. Depending on the circumstances, that response could be aimed at prevention, intervention, or the need for more specialist treatment. Ward and Snow's framework[24] for supporting parents suggests that practitioners should consider nine domains in working out the "line of best fit" (see reference 24, p. 3) in supporting families to tackle alcohol use and misuse among young people:

1. Family structure
2. Alcohol use in early childhood
3. Children's temperament
4. Alcohol use within the family
5. Parenting styles and rules
6. Communication
7. Supervision/monitoring
8. Settings
9. Supply

These nine domains can be seen as areas of assessment, which will allow a practitioner to develop the best package of support for the young person and their family.

In practice, a number of issues should be considered, and are summarized in Box 14.1. These guidelines can be applied to the delivery of a range of family-focused interventions or programs by professionals in different disciplines and sectors. It is the case that what a practitioner can do will be influenced by a number of factors, including the country where they work, the specifics of their job, and the sector where they work; within their job remit, what time, support, and other resources they have available. The ideas presented here are intended to be an introduction to the issues to consider and how to move forward. How to intervene will also be informed by whether a practitioner is involved with prevention, detection or treatment, or whether their role overlaps one or more of these spheres.

Discussion

The influence that the family has over young people, and the role that it can play in interventions targeting young people's alcohol misuse and related harms, is unquestioned. This chapter offers insight into the issue and guidance on how to establish support with young people and their families. There is evidence that family-focused interventions can delay the onset of alcohol use, can bring reductions in consumption and alcohol-related harm, and can bring positive individual and familial outcomes in other areas. Interventions that aim to strengthen family protective factors, by using approaches grounded in parent training (e.g., their own use of alcohol and how to communicate messages about alcohol consumptions and harms to their children), family skills training, or family therapy, appear to be among the most promising because they influence key protective factors and processes understood to facilitate resilience, thus strengthening families and reducing harm and risk.[20] Furthermore, there is evidence that family-focused approaches can be effective, not only if introduced before young people start to drink and before their alcohol-related expectancies are fully formed but also when young people have started to drink and where problems may be present. It seems to be the case that additional input might be needed where alcohol consumption or related harms are more advanced, or for young people and families in higher risk groups. Also, family-focused approaches

---

Box 14.1   Issues to consider when delivering family-focused services or interventions where a young person is misusing alcohol.

- Conduct a comprehensive assessment with each family and with individual family members. This will highlight particular issues such as safeguarding or domestic violence. A good assessment can improve retention with the service and maximize safe practice.
- "Think Family": Consider the needs of the wider family and how those could be met individually and collectively.
- Consider the bigger picture in terms of other coexisting problems that may be present for young people and their families.
- Consider what specific needs the young people might have not only related to their misuse of alcohol but also considering what other problems might be present.
- Consider what additional support could be useful to other family members (e.g., parents) in their own right.
- Work within the structure of interventions or programs, but be prepared to be flexible so that support can be tailored to meet specific needs.
- Consider specific supervision and management needs for those who will be delivering support to families.
- Consider training needs of staff. Within this, consider a minimum standard of basic training in key issues, such as child protection and safeguarding, and domestic violence and abuse. You could also consider training around working with more than one client at a time.
- Consider interventions with families in terms of not only the reduction of key risk factors but also how to promote protective factors and processes that can facilitate resilience and strengthen families and the individuals within them.
- Consider the practical issues of working with more than one member of the same family, such as record keeping and information sharing (within families and also with other organizations that you may be joint-working with). Remember that confidentiality is not a barrier; it can be used constructively to facilitate positive communication.
- You are not going to be able to offer a total solution to all families. Work within the parameters of your training and the remit of the service you are delivering. Develop good partnership working arrangements with other agencies so you can share information, seek advice or cross-refer where necessary.
- Be familiar with the research evidence of working with young people and families so that you can develop the intervention or service in line with the evidence. You can also consider how an intervention could be adapted or applied in a particular setting (e.g., transferability between countries, services, or population groups).
- Include research and evaluation in your work and use the findings to inform delivery and sustainability. Ask the families how the service or intervention is helping them and seek their views as to how things might be changed or improved.

---

could usefully assess the additional needs of "affected family members", such as parents and offer additional support where relevant. Interventions, such as the "5-step method", "behavioral couples therapy", "pressures to change", or the "community reinforcement approach" have all shown promise in this regard,[36] highlighting that such interventions can not only support adult family members in their own right but also have a positive knock-on effect on the problematic user, sometimes facilitating their engagement with treatment.

Given that alcohol misuse often coexists alongside other problems, for both young people and their families, it is vital that such interventions do not operate in a vacuum. Rather the response needs to be as multifaceted as the problems themselves. In other words, family-focused interventions are part of a larger response, a framework that needs to consider the needs not only of the family as a collective but also of the individuals within that family. For example, a young person may have additional needs that are best met by individual support from elsewhere, while a parent or sibling may well benefit from additional support that addresses their needs and concerns in their own right.

A further area where more research is needed is in the implementation of interventions and programs beyond the narrow parameters of empirical research.[17,37] Liddle has identified some of the barriers toward the widespread adoption and implementation of well-evidenced family treatments, including the lack of access to training, intervention manuals, supervision, and data collection.[18] As with the need to offer more to adult family members of alcohol (and drug) misusers, there is a need to take a more flexible approach to the broader implementation of interventions.[37] Related to this work, future research could also consider the transferability of interventions (e.g., between countries, services, or population groups).

Finally, in a climate quick to highlight problems and demonize young people, it is often ignored that there are large numbers of children and young people (about half of the samples surveyed) who do not drink, who have never got drunk or experienced any alcohol-related problems.[8] Moreover, many of these young people do not belong to cultural groups usually associated with moderate or no alcohol consumption. We do not yet know enough about the reasons these young people give for not drinking or the strategies they employ to avoid drinking or getting drunk, nor the influence that their families may exert. Further research in this area might inform the prevention and intervention agenda and the ongoing development and implementation of family-focused interventions in this domain. Related to this, any response to alcohol misuse and alcohol-related harms in young people must also involve the young people themselves by asking them what they would find helpful; this also allows ideas from national and international research and policy to be implemented at the local and community level to best meet the needs of that population. For example, the Youth Involvement Project consulted with around 60 young people aged 12–20 about substance misuse prevention (covering both alcohol and drugs) and reported 10 key messages of what young people thought needed to be part of the response to tackling alcohol-related harm.[38] One of those messages was, "We need to be able to talk to our parents and carers about drugs. They also need support because drugs also affect families."

References

1. Shortt A, Hutchinson D, Chapman R, Toumbourou J. Family, school, peer and individual influences on early adolescent alcohol use: First-year impact of the Resilient Families programme. *Drug Alcohol Rev* 2007; 26:625–634.
2. Toumbourou J, Stockwell T, Neighbors C, Marlatt G, Sturge J, Rehm J. Interventions to reduce harm associated with adolescent substance use. *Lancet* 2007; 369:1391–1401.
3. Hibell B, Andersson B, Bjarnason T, Ahlstrom S, Balakireva O, Kokkevi A, Morgan M. *The ESPAD Report 2003. Alcohol and Other Drugs Use Among Students in 35 European Countries.* Stockholm: Swedish Council on Information on Alcohol and Other Drugs; 2004.

4. Jernigan D. *Global Status Report: Alcohol and Young People*. Geneva: World Health Organisation; 2001.

5. World Health Organisation. *Global Status Report on Alcohol 2004*. Geneva: World Health Organisation, Department of Mental Health and Substance Abuse; 2004.

6. Chief Medical Officers of England, Wales and Northern Ireland. *Draft Guidance on the Consumption of Alcohol by Children and Young People from the Chief Medical Officers of England, Wales and Northern Ireland*. London: Department for Children, Schools and Families; 2009.

7. Newbury-Birch D, Walker J, Avery L *et al*. The Impact of Alcohol Consumption on Young People: A Systematic Review of Published Reviews. Research Report No DCSF–RR067. Newcastle, UK: Department for Children, Schools and Families; 2009.

8. Templeton L. *Alcohol-Related Problems Facing Young People in England: Risks, Harms and ProtectiveFactors. Paper Prepared for the Young People and Alcohol Project*. London: Thomas Coram Research Unit, Institute of Education University of London; 2009.

9. Velleman R. *How do Children Learn about Alcohol?* Review for the Joseph Rowntree Foundation. New York, UK: Joseph Rowntree Foundation; 2009.

10. Orford J, Natera G, Copello A, Atkinson C, Tiburcio M, Velleman R, Crundall I, Mora J, Templeton L, Walley G. *Coping with Alcohol and Drug Problems: The Experiences of Family Members in Three Contrasting Cultures*. London: Taylor and Francis; 2005.

11. Maggs J, Patrick M, Feinstein L. Childhood and adolescent predictors of alcohol use and problems in adolescence and adulthood in the National Child Development Study. *Addiction* 2008; 103(Suppl. 1):7–22.

12. Williams B, Davies L, Wright V. *Children, Young People and Alcohol*. Research Report for the DCSF–RR195. London: DCSF; 2010.

13. Scaife V, O'Brien M, McEune R, Notley C, Millings A, Biggart L. Vulnerable young people and substance misuse: Expanding on the risk and protection-focussed approach using social psychology. *Child Abuse Rev* 2009; 18:224–239.

14. Velleman R, Templeton L, Copello A. The role of the family in preventing and intervening with substance use and misuse: A comprehensive review of family interventions, with a focus on young people. *Drug Alcohol Rev* 2005; 24:93–109.

15. Velleman R, Templeton L. Substance misuse by children and young people: The role of the family and implications for intervention and prevention. *Paediatr Child Health* 2007; 17:25–30.

16. Van Der Vorst H, Engels R, Dekovic M, Meeus W, Vermulst A. Alcohol-specific rules, personality and adolescents' alcohol use: A longitudinal person–environment study. *Addiction* 2007; 102:1064–1075.

17. Hogue A, Liddle H. Family-based treatment for adolescent substance abuse: Controlled trials and new horizons in services research. *J Fam Ther* 2009; 31:126–154.

18. Liddle H. Family-based therapies for adolescent alcohol and drug use: research contributions and future research needs. *Addiction* 2004; 99 (Suppl. 2): 76–92.

19. Foxcroft D, Ireland D, Lister-Sharp D, Lowe G, Breen R. Longer-term primary prevention for alcohol misuse in young people: A systematic review. *Addiction* 2003; 98:397–411.

20. Kumpfer K, Alvarado R, Whiteside H. Family-based interventions for substance use and misuse prevention. *Subst Use Misuse* 2003; 38:1759–1787.

21. Vaughn M, Howard M. Adolescent substance abuse treatment: A synthesis of controlled evaluation. *Res Soc Work Pract* 2004; 14:325–335.

22. Thom B, Bayley M. *Multicomponent Programmes: An Approach to Prevent and Reduce Alcohol-Related Harm*. New York: Joseph Rowntree Foundation; 2007.

23. Brannigan R, Schackman B, Falco M, Millman R. The quality of highly regarded adolescent substance abuse treatment programs: Results of an in-depth national survey. *Arch Pediatr Adolesc Med* 2004; 158:904–909.

24. Ward B, Snow P. Supporting parents to reduce the misuse of alcohol by young people. *Drugs Educ Prev Policy* 2010; 17:718–731.
25. Liddle H, Rowe C, Dakof G, Henderson C, Greenbaum P. Multidimensional family therapy for young adolescent substance abuse: Twelve-month outcomes of a randomised controlled trial. *J Consult Clin Psychol* 2009; 77:12–25.
26. Loveland-Cherry C, Thomson Ross L, Kaufman S. Effects of a home-based family intervention on adolescent alcohol use and misuse. *J Stud Alcohol* 1999; 13:94–102.
27. Spoth R, Redmond C, Shin C, Azevedo K. Brief family intervention effects on adolescent substance initiation: School-level growth curve analyses 6 years following baseline. *J Consult Clin Psychol* 2004; 72:535–542.
28. Werch C, Owen D, Carlson J, Diclemente C, Edgemon P, Moore M. One-year follow-up results of the STARS for Families alcohol prevention program. *Health Educ Res* 2003; 18:74–87.
29. Smit E, Verdurmen J, Monshouwer K, Smit F. Family interventions and their effect on adolescent alcohol use in general populations: A meta-analysis of randomised controlled trials. *Drug Alcohol Depend* 2008; 97:195–206.
30. Talbot S, Crabbe T. *Binge-Drinking: Young People's Attitudes and Behaviour*. Crime Concern (Positive Futures) Final Report; 2008.
31. Foxcroft D. *Alcohol Misuse Prevention for Young People: A Rapid Review of Recent Evidence*. WHO Technical Report; 2006.
32. Elliott G, Morleo M, Cook P. *Identifying Effective Interventions for Preventing Under-Age Alcohol Consumption*. Final Report Prepared for Wirral Drug and Alcohol Action Team; 2009.
33. Coombes L, Allen D, Marsh M, Foxcroft D. The Strengthening Families Programme (SFP) 10–14 and substance misuse in Barnsley: The perspectives of facilitators and families. *Child Abuse Rev* 2009; 18:41–59.
34. Spoth R, Randall G, Trudeau L, Shin C, Redmond C. Substance use outcomes $5^1/_2$ years past baseline for partnership-based, family-school preventive interventions. *Drug Alcohol Depend* 2008; 96:57–68.
35. Liddle H, Dakof G, Turner R, Henderson C, Greenbaum P. Treating adolescent drug abuse: A randomized trial comparing multidimensional family therapy and cognitive behaviour therapy. *Addiction* 2008; 103:1660–1670.
36. Copello A, Velleman R, Templeton L. Family interventions in the treatment of alcohol and drug problems. *Drug Alcohol Rev* 2005; 24; 369–385.
37. Templeton L, Velleman R, Russell C. Psychological interventions with families of alcohol misusers: A systematic review. *Addict Res Theory* 2010; 18 (6), 616–648.
38. Mentor UK. *First Measures: A Guide to Alcohol Misuse Prevention Work with Children*. London: Mentor UK; 2008.

Chapter 15

Psychosocial treatment for adolescents with alcohol use disorders

Deborah Deas and Andrew Clark

Department of Psychiatry, Medical University of South Carolina, Charleston, SC, USA

> **Key points**
>
> - There has been much progress in the development and use of psychosocial treatments for the treatment of adolescents with alcohol and other drug use disorders over the past decade.
> - Clinicians and researchers have increasingly recognized that "adolescents are not adults" and they require treatments that are specifically tailored to their need and developmental stage.
> - Various types of family therapy are effective in reducing alcohol and other drug use among adolescents. When family therapy is combined with other effective treatments, family therapy appears to have an additive effect in reducing substance use.
> - Multisystemic therapy (MST), which has the key feature of intensively treating adolescents in their social environment, has been shown to be efficacious and cost–effective in multiproblem youth with substance use and juvenile justice system involvement.
> - Although data is limited, behavioral therapy and cognitive behavioral therapy (CBT) approaches appear to be effective and worthy of further exploration.
> - Brief interventions and motivational interviewing are widely used and seem to be effective at least in the short term. However, efficacy may decay with the passage of time suggesting that combined treatments might provide further enhancement of treatment effect. Effectiveness of brief interventions may also vary according to developmental stage (e.g., adolescents versus young adult). Nevertheless, they may be attractive to adolescents because of their client-centered approach and emphasis on empowering the patient.
> - Contingency management approaches (reinforcement of nonalcohol use by monetary rewards or prizes) are gaining acceptance. Contingency management is flexible, transportable to various settings and situations, empowers parents and adolescents, and takes advantage of the fact that young people prefer immediate rewards.
> - Taken together, these interventions represent tremendous progress and serve as a foundation for expansion and development of other psychosocial approaches for the treatment of adolescents and young adults with alcohol and other drug use disorders.

Alcohol use among adolescents remains a public health problem even though the prevalence rates have not increased substantially over the past few years. On the basis of data

Young People and Alcohol: Impact, Policy, Prevention, Treatment, First Edition.

Edited by John B. Saunders and Joseph M. Rey.

© 2011 Blackwell Publishing Ltd. Published 2011 by Blackwell Publishing Ltd.

from the Monitoring the Future program, alcohol is the most common substance of abuse among adolescents; in 2009, 22% of senior high school students reported drinking five or more drinks in a row within 2 weeks of the survey, while 14.4% and 27.6% of the twelfth graders reported drunkenness in the previous 30 days.[1]

Most adults with alcohol dependence began drinking during adolescence, although the majority of those who seek treatment do not usually engage in any type of formal treatment until adulthood. Until a decade ago, the adolescents who were treated for alcohol dependence received some form or combination of what was used for adults. Since that time, clinicians and researchers have recognized that "adolescents are not adults" and certain developmental characteristics, specific to adolescents, may influence treatment design, implementation, compliance, and outcomes.[2] The existing treatments for adolescents with alcohol use disorders are primarily psychosocial, and there is no U.S. Food and Drug Administration (FDA) approved medications for the treatment of adolescents with alcohol use disorders (see Chapter 16). Most of the psychosocial treatments presented in this chapter have been empirically tested in adolescents and have been shown to be effective in treating adolescent alcohol and other drug use disorders (AODs). Moreover, most of the psychosocial treatments presented are readily available, implementable, and skills taught in treatment are applicable to multiple areas of the adolescent's social and family life. This chapter will review the several psychosocial treatment modalities for adolescents with AODs. The following psychosocial treatments will be discussed:

- Family-based and multisystemic interventions.
- Behavioral therapy.
- Cognitive behavioral therapy.
- Brief interventions.
- Contingency management.

Family-based and multisystemic interventions

Unlike adults, adolescents rarely seek treatment on their own, but rather are often brought to the attention of treatment providers by parents, caretakers, and/or social agencies such as school and the juvenile justice system. Adolescents are therefore more often treated in the context of their families or social systems. The premise underlying family-based therapy for adolescents with AODs is that adolescents' behaviors are shaped in the context of existing relationships and social environments (e.g., family, peer, school, and community), which play a role in the development and execution of these behaviors. These social environments may have dual functions, one leading to dysfunctional behaviors resulting in AODs and other providing the necessary support to disrupt deviant behavioral patterns associated with AODs. Disruption or dysfunction within any of these social systems may lead to problem behaviors; therefore, treatment should involve individuals within these systems.[3] Family therapy is the most studied evidence-based treatment for adolescents with AODs, and its use should be assessed and implemented in the context of the dynamics of the family.

Family therapy

In a study conducted by Friedman,[4] which randomly assigned families of adolescents aged 14–21 years to outpatient family therapy or parent groups, adolescents reduced frequency and severity of substance use regardless of treatment assignment. Functional family therapy emphasizes establishing consistent and clear communications, positive reframing, and creating an environment that fosters trust, hope, self-esteem, and responsibility.[5] Families are empowered to have an impact on the adolescent's behavior and taught to function from a position of strength. Parents often learn better communication skills as well as assertiveness skills. Similarly, Lewis and colleagues[6] focused on imparting parenting skills and addressing family dynamics among 84 adolescents assigned to family therapy or family education interventions. The family therapy intervention was based on the Purdue Brief Family Therapy Program, which uses a variety of strategies to address the context of the adolescent's AOD use within the family unit. Some important features include: reducing the family's resistance to AOD treatment; reframing the AOD use as a family problem; interrupting dysfunctional family behaviors and reestablishing positive and appropriate parental influences; assessing the impact of AOD use on family relationships; providing assertiveness training to siblings to promote AOD refusal; and implementing strategies that promote positive changes. The family education arm of the study explored training in parenting skills and education of the family about AODs, the effects of these substances, and strategies to address use and overcome dependence. Adolescents assigned to the family therapy intervention were significantly more likely to decrease baseline levels of AOD use as well as its severity.

The aforementioned family-based treatment studies emphasize the importance of communication styles and addressing the dynamics of how family members relate to each other. The period of adolescence is marked by individuation, feelings of invulnerability and immortality. This transition period occurs during a time of hormonally induced physiological and psychological changes with fluctuating variability. While some adolescents make the transition smoothly, others have a tumultuous course. In the quest for independence, some adolescents become increasingly defiant with parental and other adult authority, as well as engaging in risk taking behaviors such as unprotected sex, alcohol and drug use, and illegal activities. The lack of understanding of the adolescents' maturational processes by parents and caregivers often complicates how these behaviors might be addressed and may further lead to disruption in the family system. Furthermore, parental denial of the challenges they face may lead to a perception of the adolescent as "the problem". Sometimes parents recognize the role they inadvertently play in perpetuating the adolescents' AOD use, at other times they are in denial. Family therapy addresses these issues in a safe environment for both the adolescent and the parents/caregivers.

Multisystemic therapy

Henggeler and colleagues[7] utilized MST to treat AOD use in adolescents with juvenile justice system involvement. The key features of MST include treating the adolescent in his/her social environment and developing a plan of action after thoroughly assessing the strengths and the weaknesses of the adolescent and their environment. The strengths are the bedrock for facilitating change and most of the therapy is conducted in the home environment. Resources are available to the parents for handling difficult situations and parents have access to the therapist or therapist designee on a 24-hour basis in case of emergencies. Although MST is time and resource intensive, it has been shown to be very cost–effective in these multiple problem populations (substance using youth with conduct disorders and often delinquency).[8] Juvenile justice-involved adolescents treated with MST versus individual counseling had significantly less AOD-related arrests. When MST was compared to community-based treatment of adolescents for AOD, the MST group had significantly less alcohol, marijuana, and other drug use.[9]

The powerful impact of family therapy approaches is demonstrated by Joanning and associates'[10] study comparing three approaches: Brief strategic family therapy, group therapy, and family drug education to treat AOD using adolescents. Despite lack of differences in family functioning among the groups, adolescents in the family therapy group were significantly more likely to be abstaining from AODs at the end of the study. Similar impact on adolescent AOD use has been found by other investigators using integrated family therapy with CBT—an approach that uses problem-focused family therapy (i.e., it emphasizes family communication, effective parenting skills, engaging in age appropriate roles, and promoting AOD abstinence while simultaneously teaching problem-solving skills to the adolescents[11]). Waldron and colleagues[12] also utilized CBT with the family therapy modality. In this case, they combined CBT with functional family therapy to treat AOD abusing adolescents. The adolescents were assigned to functional family therapy, CBT, functional family therapy plus CBT, or psychoeducation. Greatest reduction in AOD use was seen in the functional family therapy plus CBT and the psychoeducation at the end of the treatment phase (12 weeks) as well as follow-up (7 months).

Family therapy is a robust psychosocial treatment intervention, which has been shown to be successful in reducing AOD use among adolescents in various settings. Even when family therapy is combined with known effective treatments, family therapy appears to have an additive effect in reducing AOD use. The engagement of systems that are operational in the adolescents' growth and development is key to the success of family therapy. Sometimes, it is necessary to engage siblings regardless of age as long as the engagement is age and developmentally appropriate. Studies have shown that adolescents who have an AOD using sibling are at risk for developing AODs themselves.[13,14] Some of these issues may be addressed during the family therapy sessions. Family therapy empowers the individual members of the family as well as the unit.

Behavioral therapy

Behavioral therapy rests on the foundation of the principles of operant and classical conditioning. The primary goal of behavioral therapy in treating adolescents with AOD use disorders is to identify negative behaviors, which promote AOD use, and devise ways to disrupt the negative behaviors. The adolescents are taught skills specifically designed to disrupt AOD use-promoting behaviors and situations. Some of the skills taught in the behavioral therapy sessions include drug refusal skills, assertiveness skills, as well as relapse prevention skills.

There is a paucity of studies, which have explored behavioral therapy as an intervention for adolescents with AODs. In a study comparing behavioral therapy to supportive counseling for the treatment of adolescents with AOD use, Azrin and associates[15] employed the following behavioral therapy strategies: rehearsals of specific risky situations in which the therapist modeled for the adolescent positive ways of handling the situation; having the adolescent identify time spent in "risky" versus "safe" situations, while pointing out discrepancies and aiming toward increasing time in "safe" situations; identification of internal stimuli, such as craving for alcohol or drugs, and ways to disrupt these cravings; assigning written work and reviewing the assignments during the sessions. The adolescents assigned to the behavioral therapy group used alcohol or drugs less frequently at the end of treatment as well as at follow-up. Specifically, adolescents reported increased days of school attendance, less alcohol or drug use, and increased number of days worked.[15]

Cognitive behavioral therapy

CBT extends behavioral therapy to include the interplay between cognitive and behavioral factors and how they function to assist in the disruption of unwanted behaviors. The roles and interactions of developmental, social, and cognitive factors are emphasized, and the way these factors function to promote or maintain AOD use is emphasized. The assumption is that the alcohol or drug use plays a functional role in the individual's life; without recognition of this, it is difficult to disrupt the pattern of functioning. The therapist conducts a functional analysis by exploring how the alcohol or drug use operates in the context of the aforementioned factors. The CBT intervention targets social situations, thoughts, and behaviors identified through the functional analysis. While there are individually specific interventions, some general principles of CBT in treating individuals with AOD use are applied. Some common issues addressed in CBT include: coping skills training, AOD refusal skills, problem-solving skills, anger management, and dealing with emergencies and relapse.

As previously described, some studies[11,12] have shown significant reductions in adolescent AOD use when CBT was combined with family therapy. Kaminer and colleagues[16] found that CBT for adolescents with alcohol or drug use disorders plus a psychiatric disorder (dually diagnosed adolescents) showed significant reductions in the quantity and frequency of AOD use if they had a disruptive disorder (attention deficit hyperactivity disorder, oppositional defiant disorder, or conduct disorder), commonly referred to as externalizing disorders. This study was conducted in an outpatient setting and the components of CBT included: therapist modeling, role modeling by the adolescent, homework assignment as well as presentations. In a larger follow-up study,[17] CBT was compared with psychoeducational therapy in treating AOD using adolescents. There was a significant reduction in alcohol use among the psychoeducation group, while the CBT group showed greater reduction in illicit drug use. However, both groups improved from their use at the time of assessment to the 3-month and 9-month follow-up. The CBT study in the dually diagnosed sample indicates a more robust improvement in AOD use in the presence of disruptive disorder. The study showed improvement over time and at follow-up with CBT favoring a reduction in illicit drugs and psychoeducation favoring a reduction in alcohol use. The use of CBT as a stand-alone intervention for adolescent AOD use shows promise; however, more studies are needed to replicate the positive findings.

Brief interventions and motivational interviewing

Brief interventions, defined as one to four sessions, are a useful psychosocial treatment for alcohol use in adolescents. Brief interventions are considered most effective when alcohol-related consequences become most evident. Alcohol-related consequences such as driving while under the influence (DUI), suspension/expulsion from school, arrest for public drunkenness, and motor vehicle accidents resulting in injury offer an opportunity for intervention. Clinicians should take advantage of the motivation to change in the immediate setting where alcohol-related consequences are first realized such as in the emergency room after an alcohol-related injury. This *window of opportunity* to intervene may be greatest in emergency departments, schools, and primary care offices. The effectiveness of brief interventions is well supported for adults with alcohol use disorders as found by a review of 22 controlled brief interventions.[18] However, these interventions cannot be assumed to have equivalent efficacy among adolescents due to the stark developmental differences from adults. Clinically, adolescents are more difficult to engage in treatment, have more sporadic drinking patterns, perceive drinking as normative among peers, and often do not recognize problematic use.[2] Engagement is crucial for the success of psychosocial treatment for adolescent alcohol use (see Chapter 11). Adolescents in school settings have reported high satisfaction when allowed to self-select a brief intervention as a secondary prevention.[19] High satisfaction may be evidence of greater engagement. However, adolescent alcohol users themselves report less satisfaction with brief intervention sessions that focus on negative consequences.[19] The most studied brief intervention is motivational interviewing or motivational enhancement therapy. Motivational interviewing purposefully enhances adolescent engagement in treatment by promoting intrinsic motivation to change.

Motivational interviewing

"Motivational interviewing" was coined by Miller[20] as "a client-centered, directive method for enhancing intrinsic motivation to change by exploring and resolving ambivalence." There are five key principles that underlie a motivational interviewing orientation of communication.[21] First, motivational interviewing seeks to understand in a nonjudgmental way the patient's own values and understanding of their problems. Second, motivational interviewing focuses on resolving ambivalence to change by selectively reinforcing the patient's communication. Third, as a method of communication rather than an ordered set of techniques, motivational interviewing enhances a patient's understanding of their priorities and problems rather than asserting the clinician's advice. Fourth, it aligns the patient's innate rational problem-solving to their intrinsic motivation to change. Finally, motivational interviewing ultimately relies on the patient's own set of values to facilitate change.

Miller and Rollnick[22] described the following five communication skills often present in motivational interviewing:

- By *expressing empathy*, the clinician reflects the language used by the patient to engage and understand the patient's point of view.
- By *developing discrepancy*, the clinician responds to conflicting values and priorities in the patient's communication.
- By *avoiding argumentation*, the clinician is selectively reinforcing the patient's positive rationale for change without attending to dissent.
- By *rolling with resistance*, the clinician again is nonconfrontational and allows resistance to pass by without response.
- Finally, by *supporting self-efficacy*, the clinician emphasizes and empowers the patient's own problem resolution as derived from a clearer understanding of the patient's own value system.

Motivational enhancement therapy also involves normative comparisons of alcohol use to current prevalence estimates for peers. For instance, the clinician assesses and presents objectively the individualized patterns of alcohol use, pros and cons of use, alcohol expectancies, social supports, relationship of life goals to alcohol use, costs and benefits of reduced alcohol use, and self-efficacy for resisting use. Often the feedback is given in summary statements during the session. The clinician may wish to provide a personalized binder of this feedback for the adolescent to keep.

Few brief intervention studies using motivational interviewing have specifically addressed alcohol use in high-risk youth.[23–28] These studies all have small sample sizes making it difficult to determine treatment effect. A meta-analysis combining these studies revealed a significant effect, although the effect size was small ($d = 0.241$).[29] Two more recent randomized controlled trials using brief motivational interviewing intervention in an emergency department setting to treat alcohol using youth demonstrated a significant reduction of alcohol use.[30,31] Spirito and colleagues[30] randomized 152 alcohol-positive adolescents aged 13–17 years at an emergency department to a brief motivational interviewing intervention or a control standard care condition with 3-, 6-, and 12-month follow-up. Only adolescents who were screened positive at baseline for significant alcohol problems on the Adolescent Drinking Inventory ($ADI < 15$) had significantly lower drinking frequency and fewer high-volume drinking days if they received the brief motivational interviewing intervention compared to standard care. The overall motivational interviewing intervention group's main effects on alcohol use were not significantly different than the standard care group at any follow-up. A second study by the same group randomized 198 young adults aged 18–24 years to the motivational interviewing intervention or standard care and found a significant treatment effect for reduced drinking and alcohol-related consequences.[31] An earlier study by the same group found a significant reduction for alcohol-related consequences, but no significant difference in alcohol use from a similar intervention among older adolescents aged 18–19 years.[27] Despite some evidence of efficacy for adolescent alcohol use, three randomized, controlled trials of young alcohol users found no significant difference in alcohol reduction for a single session of motivational interviewing compared to a control session.[32,33]

Deterioration of treatment effect over time has been a major concern regarding brief interventions as a stand-alone treatment. An adolescent may experience a "flight into health" after a significant consequence such as a DUI, but maintenance of sobriety often depends on skills that an adolescent cannot acquire in a brief intervention. For example, an initial treatment effect was found at 3 months for reduced alcohol use among 200 substance-using young people randomized to a single-session of motivational interviewing compared to a control group given education and advice.[33] However, the treatment effect was lost at 12-month follow-up.[33] McCambridge and Strang[33] postulated that the initial 3-month treatment effect for alcohol use in the motivational intervention group may have been lost due to "assessment reactivity" in the control group during the more intensive assessment at 3 months, making the treatment effect disappear at 12 months. Poor fidelity among clinicians may be another factor in a second, larger multisite clinical trial of a motivational intervention among substance using youth that found no treatment effect.[33]

Most studies demonstrate an immediate response but then decaying effect for motivational intervention, which suggests that combined treatments are noteworthy. The addition of motivational enhancement therapy to other evidence-based psychosocial treatments may provide a greater engagement and enhances the initiation phase of other psychosocial treatments for adolescent alcohol use disorders. Integrated treatments combining motivational enhancement therapy with CBT and contingency management have been shown to reduce marijuana use in randomized trials for marijuana use disorder in adolescents.[34,35] Further studies focusing on alcohol use that integrate motivational interviewing are needed for adolescents.

Contingency management

Contingency management (CM) reinforcement procedures are based on operant conditioning principles and may be a useful psychosocial treatment strategy for adolescent alcohol use disorders. As mentioned previously, adolescents are difficult to engage in treatment due to a low motivation to abstain from using alcohol. CM provides reinforcing incentives for initiating treatment and maintaining abstinence with vouchers for monetary rewards and social reinforcers. Any detected alcohol use by the adolescent in a CM procedure results in immediate loss of this reinforcement. The essential ingredient for CM is a readily detected, objective measure of abstinence such as a negative urine drug test or a negative Breathalyzer. Three successful case studies of contingency management to treat adolescents with alcohol use disorders have been reported. In Brigham's[36] study, each adolescent could earn 5 points and $1 every day of alcohol abstinence. Points were exchanged for prosocial privileges such as tickets to the movies, or to avoid tasks such as mowing the lawn. Adolescent self-report was the primary measure of alcohol use, and attempts were made to get parents to use the Breathalyzer to detect alcohol use. Although these case studies do not have the systematic controlled approach of research studies, they demonstrate reductions in drinking due to the behavioral reinforcement procedure. A few randomized, controlled studies for CM to treat adolescent cigarette smoking and marijuana use disorders in clinical settings have shown good efficacy.[35,37,38] However, no randomized studies of CM exist for the treatment of adolescent alcohol use disorders.

Combined interventions for adolescent substance use such as CM plus motivational enhancement therapy/CBT as well as CM plus MST have been reported.[7,38] Due to the rapid elimination of alcohol, a major barrier to CM procedures for alcohol use has been the lack of a reliable and valid biological marker with longer detection duration. Often utilizing Breathalyzers at scheduled clinician visits are futile and impractical. Adolescent binge drinking is also sporadic and inconsistent making it more difficult to detect. To address this concern in a very different but difficult population, breath samples were laboriously collected on a random, unpredictable schedule averaging two times per week among 92 homeless alcohol-dependent adults and found to be a useful strategy.[39] While this was useful in adults, the episodic nature of adolescent drinking may render this approach futile. It may be necessary to modify the existing contingency management approaches for the treatment of adolescent alcohol use disorders in clinical practice.

Parents should be reminded that while the incentive has monetary value, actual cash should not be exchanged for the vouchers. The voucher value may be used to purchase actual goods and parents will execute the payment.

A useful modification may be to implement a contingency management protocol for alcohol use as a home intervention to be administered by a parent or guardian. Kamon[40] first described a CM program targeting substance use and conduct problems in youth that uses both clinic-administrated and parent-administrated rewards.[40] The clinic rewarded both the youth who demonstrated abstinence and the parents who participated in their child's treatment compliance. For example, the parents received monetary incentives to bring their youth to appointments. In addition, the program taught parents to administer rewards for alcohol abstinence and problem-free behavior. A recent controlled trial of this program found reduced substance use in adolescents with marijuana use disorders. Adolescents received incentives only if urine drug test, Breathalyzer, and parent(s) and self-reports indicated no substance use including alcohol.[35] This study is significant in that it treated the comorbidity of multiple substances. A suggested modification of this CM procedure tailored to focus on alcohol use follows.

The adolescent and parent(s) after assessment of an alcohol use disorder are presented with the CM protocol as a contractual agreement by the clinician who would coordinate implementation of the procedure. The written agreement would have a detailed schedule of incremental and accumulating voucher-based monetary or social rewards for consecutive negative Breathalyzer readings. The parent is expected to purchase or borrow a personal Breathalyzer (ranging $50–100). Adolescent binge drinking patterns occur mostly during unsupervised time outside school. Therefore, a testing strategy with the Breathalyzer is recommended to be done twice weekly for 12 weeks at the parent's discretion upon the adolescent returning from unsupervised settings at likely times of drinking. The initial negative Breathalyzer is rewarded with a baseline monetary or social value. For example, Stanger and colleagues[35] used a baseline $1.50 voucher value with $1.50 increments for each consecutive negative breath test. They also gave a $10 bonus for each two consecutive negative tests. This paradigm adds up to a potential $570 over a 12-week period, but adolescents in their study averaged $312. A substance-monitoring contract was developed in this study between parents and youth specifying incentives for abstinence or consequences for substance use. Often poor parental support and participation in treatment can pose difficulty for adolescents with alcohol use disorders. In these cases, CM procedures that reward the parents are often helpful. For example, parents may be given chances in a random drawing to win a prize dependent upon their degree of participation. In one study, this method was implemented to enhance parents to fully participate in treatment, administer Breathalyzers and implement the substance-monitoring contract.[41]

Variations on this monetary reward are possible, such as exchange for privileges or abstaining from expected duties. Each consecutive reward for a negative Breathalyzer should be added to the previous one incrementally on the agreed upon schedule. Studies have shown that an increasing magnitude of reinforcement for consecutive abstinences with a complete reset to baseline for a positive drug test produces superior results.[42] For example, if using $2.50 increments with weekly testing after a $5 baseline, then a completely abstinent (perhaps undetected may be more accurate) adolescent will have earned a total of $225 over 12 weeks ($5 for the first negative Breathalyzer, $5 + $2.50 = $7.50 for the second, $7.50 + $2.50 = $10 for the third, etc.). If the adolescent has a positive Breathalyzer at any time during this course, then the schedule resets to baseline ($5). If the adolescent has succeeded, then a maintenance reward for every random assessment by the parent is suggested.

Clinical tailoring is often necessary for adolescent contingency management procedures especially due to cost. Often the family will determine the acceptable monetary contribution, which can be modified by reducing the amount of testing or prize value. Fortunately, adolescents have a stronger preference for small immediate rewards and novelty than adults.[43] Prizes or items solicited from the community can also be a rare privilege (e.g., free movie passes, video games, and admission to amusement park) and are equally efficacious as monetary vouchers in community settings.[41,44] For example, Lott and Jencius[44] demonstrated a successful CM procedure in a community substance abuse treatment program for adolescents that averaged $0.39 per patient per day using a prize drawing bag of colored beads of which 50% had no value, 30% small $1 value, 15% medium $5 value, and 5% large $15 value. It is important that the baseline and potential accumulated value is big enough for the adolescent to engage in treatment. Monetary rewards in the form of gift cards or vouchers are preferred to cash for adolescents who may spend cash on other deviant behaviors, such as drugs. For example, a detailed monetary contribution toward car insurance or a trip to an amusement park may be as valuable and more acceptable to parents. Other examples include working toward expenses for college, a class trip, or a creative privilege exchange system based on parental choices. The incentive must hold enough value in the adolescent's mind to curtail the decision to drink. The CM approach is transportable to various settings and situations and empowers both parents and adolescents.

Summary

Great strides have been made in the development and implementation of treatments for adolescents with alcohol and other drug use disorders. The mainstay treatments for these adolescents are psychosocial, especially since there is no FDA-approved medications for the treatment of adolescents with alcohol dependence. Family therapies have been very successful in this population and tend to involve many systems relevant to the adolescent, including the family, social systems, and the environment. Behavioral therapy and cognitive therapy show promise. The integration of developmental, social, and cognitive factors in CBT sets the stage for identifying problematic behaviors and disrupting the patterns leading to alcohol and other drug use. Brief interventions such as motivational interviewing and motivational enhancement therapy may be attractive to adolescents because of their client-centered approach, and emphasis on empowering the patient in the resolution of the problems that foster alcohol and other drug use. The aforementioned treatments undoubtedly lay the platform for expansion of current treatments, perhaps by combining different types of therapies as well as the development of innovative therapies to address specific needs of the adolescents and their families.

Acknowledgments

The authors wish to acknowledge and thank Ms. Marshelle Grant for her assistance in the manuscript preparation.

References

1. Johnston LD, O'Malley PM, Bachman JG, Schulenberg JE. *Monitoring the Future National Results on Adolescent Drug Use: Overview of Key Findings, 2008.* Bethesda, MD: National Institute on Drug Abuse; 2009.
2. Deas D, Riggs P, Langenbucher J, Goldman M, Brown S. Adolescents are not adults: Developmental considerations in alcohol users. *Alcohol Clin Exp Res* 2000; 24:232–237.
3. Pickerl S, Henggeler S. Multisystematic therapy for adolescent substance abuse and dependence. *Child Adolesc Psychiatry Clin N Am* 1996; 5:201–211.
4. Friedman A. Family therapy vs. parent groups: Effects on adolescent drug abusers. *Am J Fam Ther* 1989; 17:335–347.
5. Barton C, Alexander J. Functional family therapy In: Gurman A, Kniskern D, eds. *Handbook of Family Therapy.* New York: Brunner/Mazel; 1981, pp. 403–443.
6. Lewis RA, Piercy FP, Sprenkle DH, Trepper TS. Family-based interventions for helping drug-abusing adolescents. *J Adolesc Res* 1990; 5:82–95.
7. Henggeler SW, Clingempeel WG, Brondino MJ, Pickrel SG. Four-year follow-up of multisystematic therapy with substance-abusing and substance-dependent juvenile offenders. *J Am Acad Child Adolesc Psychiatry* 2002; 41:868–874.
8. Henggeler SW, Melton GB, Smith LA. Family preservation using multisystemic therapy: An effective alternative to incarcerating serious juvenile offenders. *J Consult Clin Psychol* 1992; 60:953–961.
9. Henggeler SW, Pickerl SG, Brondino MJ. Multisystematic treatment of substance-abusing and dependent delinquents: Outcomes, treatment fidelity, and transportability. *Ment Health Serv Res* 1999; 1:171–184.
10. Joanning H, Quinn Q, Thomas F, Mullen R. Treating adolescent drug abuse: A comparison of family systems therapy, group therapy and family systems therapy, group therapy, and family drug education. *J Marital Fam Ther* 1992; 18:345–356.
11. Latimer WW, Winters KC, D'Zurilla T, Nichols M. Integrated family and cognitive-behavioral therapy for adolescent substance abusers: A state1 efficacy study. *Drug Alcohol Depend* 2003; 71:303–317.

12. Waldron HB, Slesnick N, Brody JL *et al.* Treatment outcomes for adolescent substance abuse at 4- and 7-month assessments. *J Consult Clin Psychol* 2001; 69:802–813.

13. Jacob T, Johnson S. Parenting influences on development of alcohol abuse and dependence. *Alcohol Health Res World* 1997; 21:204–209.

14. D'Amico EJ, Fromme K. Health risk behaviors of adolescent and young adult siblings. *Health Psychol* 1997; 16:426–432.

15. Azrin N, Acierno E, Kogan E, Donahue B, Besalel V, McMahon P. Follow-up results of supportive versus behavioral therapy of illicit drug use. *Behav Res Ther* 1996; 34:41–46.

16. Kaminer Y, Burleson J, Blitz C, Sussman J, Rounsaville B. Psychotherapies for adolescent substance abusers: A pilot study. *J Nerv Ment Dis* 1998; 186:684–690.

17. Kaminer Y, Burleson J, Goldberger R. Cognitive-behavioral coping skills and psychoeducation therapies for adolescent substance abuse. *J Nerv Ment Dis* 2002; 190:737–745.

18. Vasilaki EI, Hosier SG, Cox WM. The efficacy of motivational interviewing as a brief intervention for excessive drinking: A meta-analytic review. *Alcohol Alcohol* 2006; 41:328–335.

19. Kia-Keting M, Brown SA, Schulte MT, Monreal TK. Adolescent satisfaction with brief motivational enhancement for alcohol abuse. *J Behav Health Serv Res* 2009; 36:385–395.

20. Miller WR. Motivational interviewing with problem drinkers. *Behav Psychother* 1983; 11:147–172.

21. Miller WR, Rollnick S. *Motivational Interviewing: Preparing People for Change.* 2nd edn. New York: Guilford Press; 2002.

22. Miller WR, Rollnick S. *Motivational Interviewing: Preparing People to Change Addictive Behavior.* New York: Guilford Press; 1991.

23. Aubrey LL. *Motivational Interviewing with Adolescents Presenting for Outpatient Substance Abuse.* Doctoral dissertation, Albuquerque: University of New Mexico; 1998.

24. Borsari B, Carey KB. Effects of a brief motivational intervention with college student drinkers. *J Consult Clin Psychol* 2000; 68:728–733.

25. Larimer ME, Turner AP, Anderson BK, Fader JS, Kilmer JS, Palmer RS, Cronce JM. Evaluating a brief alcohol intervention with fraternities. *J Stud Alcohol Drugs* 2001; 62:370–380.

26. Marlatt GA, Baer JS, Kivlahan DR *et al.* Screening and brief intervention for high-risk college student drinkers: results from a 2-year follow-up assessment. *J Consult Clin Psychol* 1998; 66:604–615.

27. Monti PM, Colby SM, Barnett NP *et al.* Brief intervention for harm reduction with alcohol-positive older adolescents in a hospital emergency department. *J Consult Clin Psychol* 1999; 67:989–994.

28. Murphy JG, Duchnick JJ, Vuvhinivh RE *et al.* Relative efficacy of a brief motivational intervention for college student drinkers. *Psychol Addict Behav* 2001; 15:373–379.

29. Taite RJ, Hulse GK. A systemic review of the effectiveness of brief interventions with substance using adolescents by type of drug. *Drug Alcohol Rev* 2003; 22:337–346.

30. Spirito A, Monti P, Barnett N, Colby S, Sindelar H, Rohesnow D, Lewander W, Myers M. A randomized clinical trial of a brief motivational intervention for alcohol-positive adolescents treated in an emergency department. *J Pediatr* 2004; 145:396–402.

31. Monti PM, Barnett NP, Colby SM, Gwaltney CJ, Spirito A, Rohsenow DJ, Woolard R. Motivational interviewing vs. feedback only in emergency care for young adult problem drinking. *Addiction* 2007; 102:1234–1243.

32. Peterson P, Baer JS, Wells EA, Ginzler JA, Garrett SB. Short-term effects of a brief motivational intervention to reduce alcohol and drug risk among homeless adolescents. *Psychol Addict Behav* 2006; 20:254–264.

33. McCambridge J, Strang J. The efficacy of single-session motivational interviewing in reducing drug consumption and perceptions of drug-related risk and harm among young people: Results from a multi-site cluster randomized trial. *Addiction* 2004; 99:39–52.
34. Dennis M, Godley SH, Diamond G, Tims FM, Babor T, Donaldson J, Liddle H, Titus JC, Kaminer Y, Webb C, Hamilton N, Funk R. The Cannabis Youth Treatment (CYT) Study: Main findings from two randomized trials. *J Subst Abuse Treat* 2004; 27:197–213.
35. Stanger C, Budney A, Kamon J, Thostensen J. A randomized trial of contingency management for adolescent marijuana abuse and dependence. *Drug Alcohol Depend* 2009; 108:240–247.
36. Brigham SL, Rekers GA, Rosen AC, Swihart JJ, Pfrimmer J, Ferguson L. Contingency management in the treatment of adolescent alcohol drinking problems. *J Psychol* 1981; 109:73–85.
37. Corby EA, Roll JM, Ledgerwood DM, Schuster CR. Contingency management interventions for treating the substance abuse of adolescents: A feasibility study. *Exp Clin Psychopharmacol* 2000; 8:371–376.
38. Krishnan-Sarin S, Duhig AM, McKee SA, McMahon TJ, Liss T, McFetridge A, Cavallo DA. Contingency management for smoking cessation in adolescent smokers. *Exp Clin Psychopharmacol* 2006; 14:306–310.
39. Wong CJ, Diemer K, Webb L et al. *Random Breath Sample Collection to Detect Alcohol Use in Homeless Alcoholics.* Paper present at the College on Problems of Drug Dependence, San Juan, Puerto Rico; 2004.
40. Kamon JL, Budney AJ, Stanger C. A contingency management intervention for adolescent marijuana abuse and conduct problems. *J Am Acad Child Adolesc Psychiatry* 2005; 44:513–521.
41. Petry NM, Marting B, Cooney JL, Kranzler HR. Give them prizes, and they will come: Contingency management for treatment of alcohol dependence. *J Consult Clin Psychol* 2000; 68:250–257.
42. Roll JM, Shoptaw S. Contingency management: Schedule effects. *Psychiatry Res* 2006; 144:91–93.
43. Olson EA, Hooper CJ, Collins P, Luciana M. Adolescents' performance on delay and probability discounting tasks: Contributions of age, intelligence, executive functioning, and self-reported externalizing behavior. *Pers Individ Dif* 2007; 43:1886–1897.
44. Lott DC, Jencius S. Effectiveness of very low-cost contingency management in a community adolescent treatment program. *Drug Alcohol Depend* 2009; 102:162–165.

Chapter 16

Pharmacological approaches to the treatment of alcohol dependence in the young

Bankole A. Johnson

Department of Psychiatry and Neurobehavioral Sciences, University of Virginia, Charlottesville, VA, USA

Key points

- Alcohol dependence is a treatable disorder when efficacious medicines are added to enhance the effects of psychosocial treatment.
- The past decade has seen an expansion of research and knowledge on pharmacotherapy for the treatment of alcohol dependence; however, no pharmacotherapeutic agent has been established as a treatment for alcohol-abusing or -dependent adolescents or emerging adults. Thus, most of what is known has been extrapolated from the adult literature.
- The newer approved medications for adults include acamprosate as well as naltrexone and its intramuscular analog, Vivitrol®. Among the other promising agents, topiramate, ondansetron, and baclofen appear to be the most noteworthy. Additionally, there is published preliminary work showing some utility for acamprosate, disulfiram, ondansetron, and naltrexone in treating alcohol-abusing or -dependent adolescents.
- Presently, research is pursuing the application of ondansetron or naltrexone for the treatment of alcohol-abusing or -dependent emerging adults.
- The current state of the art is to find medications that enhance the efficacy of brief psychosocial treatments, which are the standard treatment for alcohol-abusing or -dependent adolescents and emerging adults.
- An important clinical aspect of treating alcohol-abusing or -dependent adolescents or emerging adults is that a goal of lifelong abstinence might not be adopted by most, thus emphasizing the need for a harm reduction approach as well as appropriate safeguards and procedures for lifetime monitoring.
- As neuroscientific research progresses, it is plausible that unique medication combinations will be tested as treatment agents for alcohol abuse or dependence in adolescents and emerging adults. Intriguingly, pharmacogenetic approaches could be particularly useful because they might provide an approach for early intervention in treating alcohol abuse or dependence, particularly among those who may have a high genetic predisposition to the disease.

Young People and Alcohol: Impact, Policy, Prevention, Treatment, First Edition.
Edited by John B. Saunders and Joseph M. Rey.
© 2011 Blackwell Publishing Ltd. Published 2011 by Blackwell Publishing Ltd.

Alcohol abuse in adolescents or emerging adults, if left untreated, often progresses to alcohol dependence in adulthood, and such individuals appear to be at increased risk of abusing other drugs.[1] It is, therefore, important to treat alcohol-abusing adolescents or emerging adults effectively to prevent progression of the disease to alcoholism with or without comorbid drug dependence in adulthood.[1] Early treatment also may prove to be beneficial as the worsening pathogenesis of alcohol dependence with age can lead to an increased resistance to treatment. These data emphasize the need for more effective treatments for alcohol-dependent adolescents.[1]

The pathogenesis of hazardous drinking or alcohol abuse in adolescents and emerging adults probably involves the same brain neurotransmitters as in alcohol-dependent adults. Notably, the most important pathways involved in the expression of excessive drinking behavior are those associated with modulators of the corticomesolimbic system. More recently, however, there has been growing interest in other neuronal substrates that appear to maintain long-term cravings for alcohol, even after a prolonged period of cessation, thereby triggering a relapse. These pathways have been coined romantically as the "dark side" of addiction. Importantly, medications that are being developed to treat alcohol dependence have been designed to target one or more neurotransmitters within these pathways.[2] For a description of the neuronal basis of alcohol dependence, see Figure 16.1.[2,3]

There has been little research on treatments for alcohol-dependent adolescents or emerging adults beyond psychosocial interventions. Some adolescents may benefit from cognitive behavioral therapy and family-based therapies, but data show that relapse rates still remain high among these groups.[1] In a study of 132 substance-abusing adolescents, Joanning and colleagues[4] showed that the percentage of abstainers was 54% for those who received family system therapy, 28% for those who received adolescent group therapy, and 16% for those who received family drug education. For subjects who received family system therapy, nearly one-half continued to use illicit drugs. In this study, similar to most others, therapy including medication treatment was not included, and Dawes and Johnson[1] have pointed out that bioethical considerations that promote bias against the use of medications have contributed to the lack of pharmacotherapy trials for this population.

Alcohol abuse and dependence in adulthood typically originate in drinking problems that began in adolescence and early adulthood (between 18 and 25 years), a period termed "emerging adulthood." This age range overlaps with the years of attending college. Among emerging adults, binge drinking—consuming more than five and four standard drinks per occasion for men and women, respectively—has been associated with increased risk for progressive alcohol abuse and alcohol dependence, and increased legal, social, and health problems including unwanted pregnancies and the transmission of sexually transmitted diseases such as HIV.[5,6] Indeed, the National Epidemiologic Survey on Alcohol and Related Conditions data show that severe or binge drinking among emerging adults, which peaks at the age of 19 years, is the strongest predictor of a chronic and progressive course of abusing or being dependent on alcohol over the course of a lifetime.[7,8] Finding effective treatment(s) for binge drinking among emerging adults has the largest clinical potential to improve lifetime drinking outcomes and related psychosocial and health problems.

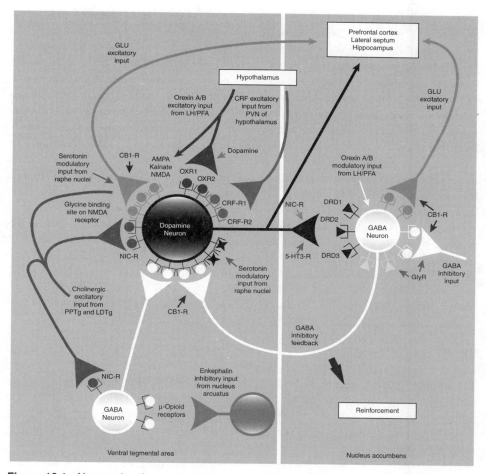

Figure 16.1   Neuronal pathways involved with the reinforcing effects of alcohol and other drugs of abuse. Cholinergic inputs arising from the caudal part of the pedunculopontine tegmental nucleus (PPTg) and laterodorsal tegmental nucleus (LDTg) can stimulate ventral tegmental area dopamine neurons. The ventral tegmental area dopamine neuron projection to the nucleus accumbens and cortex, the critical substrate for the reinforcing effects of drugs of abuse (including alcohol), is modulated by a variety of inhibitory [gamma-aminobutyric acid (GABA) and opioid] and excitatory [nicotinic (NIC-R), glutamate (GLU), and cannabinoid-1 receptor (CB1-R)] inputs. The glutamate pathways include those that express alpha-amino-3-hydroxy-5-methylisoxazole-4-propionic acid (AMPA), kainate, and *N*-methyl-D-aspartate (NMDA) receptors. Serotonin-3 receptors (5-HT3-R) also modulate dopamine release in the nucleus accumbens. The glycine system, orexins, and corticotrophin-releasing factor also are shown. CRF-R1 and CRF-R2: corticotrophin-releasing factor receptors 1 and 2, respectively; DRD1, DRD2, and DRD3: dopamine receptors D1, D2, and D3, respectively; GlyR: glycine receptor; LH/PFA: perifornical region of the lateral hypothalamus; OXR1 and OXR2: orexin receptor types 1 and 2, respectively; PVN: paraventricular nucleus. Adapted and embellished from reference 3 (copyright © 2006, American Medical Association; all rights reserved). Reprinted from reference 2 with permission from *The American Journal of Psychiatry* (copyright © 2010, American Psychiatric Association).

In the past decade, there have been great advancements made in pharmacotherapy for the treatment of alcohol dependence. The U.S. Food and Drug Administration (FDA) has approved oral naltrexone, a derivative depot formulation of injectable naltrexone (Vivitrol), and acamprosate treatment of alcohol dependence in adults of age 18 and older. Research continues to explore which types of alcohol-dependent individual would benefit the most from treatment with naltrexone or acamprosate. In combination, naltrexone and acamprosate have demonstrated efficacy for treating alcohol dependence in one European study,[9] but the same results were not found in a multisite study in the United States.[10] Disulfiram is an aversive agent that does not diminish craving for alcohol but might be effective when given to those who are highly compliant or to those who receive medication under supervision. Exciting research continues as the search for more effective treatments for alcohol dependence is ongoing. Drugs such as topiramate and ondansetron have demonstrated promising results for the treatment of alcohol dependence.

No area of psychiatric research in recent years has received more attention than the problem of severe or binge drinking in emerging adults and college students. In 2002, NIAAA published a report that showed a marginal effect for the usual educational programs at reducing the consequences of severe or binge drinking on campus.[11] Brief motivational interventions that enhance readiness to change, provide feedback on normative drinking patterns, and develop skills and strategies[12] have been the mainstay of treatment in emerging adults or college drinkers to moderate their drinking.

In general, brief motivational interventions for hazardous drinkers have had extensive support as an effective intervention in multiple health care and treatment settings. Meta-analyses have produced consistently positive results.[13,14] Ballesteros *et al.*[15] reviewed 13 carefully selected, randomized controlled trials of brief interventions in primary care and found significant support for the effectiveness of these interventions in primary care settings, with an odds ratio of 1.55. Thus, although brief interventions do reduce the harm of severe or binge drinking, there is much room for improvement, and many continue to drink at hazardous levels.

Among college students, the most well-validated brief intervention has been BASICS—Brief Alcohol Screening and Intervention for College Students.[16] The BASICS program provides personal feedback, motivation, and strategies that enhance normative drinking patterns.[17] In a recent study of motivational interviewing with college students sent to alcohol counseling, both the in-person personal feedback intervention and a control condition of written personal feedback reduced drinking and related problems at the 4-month follow-up. However, at the 15-month follow-up, the in-person brief motivational feedback intervention demonstrated less alcohol use and fewer related problems than the control condition.[18] Thus, there is support for BASICS to moderate college students' drinking. Nevertheless, research with BASICS and other brief interventions shows that the relative therapeutic effect of brief intervention among college students is rather small[19,20]; however, success rates might be better when severe- or binge-drinking college students are mandated to enter a program.[21] Therefore, even though brief motivational interventions, including BASICS, decrease drinking in emerging adults, many remain severe or binge drinkers, with significant immediate or lifetime consequences. Also, the potential for further lapses to heavy drinking, even among those in recovery, remains substantial because of the cultural and social pressure on emerging adults or college students to conform to abnormally high drinking levels, especially on weekends.[22,23] Hence, motivational treatment alone, no matter how potent, might not be sufficient to moderate drinking patterns below hazardous levels among most emerging adults or college students at risk for severe or binge drinking. Therefore, the main thrust of pharmacotherapeutic approaches is to pair a putative therapeutic medication with BASICS or some other brief intervention as a treatment for alcohol-dependent adolescents or emerging adults.

In the past decade, there has been great interest in developing medications to treat alcohol-dependent adolescents and emerging adults. While the neuronal pathogenesis of adolescent or emerging adult alcohol use disorders is likely to be similar to that in the adult,[1] what makes the effects of pharmacotherapy in the developing human more complex is that, throughout adolescence, there are changes in the density and distribution of the serotonin, dopamine, acetylcholine, glutamate, and gamma-aminobutyric acid systems. Indeed, it is thought that the number and density of particular receptors may decline throughout the brain at different rates during adolescence, thereby producing a relative decline in excitatory stimulation to the neocortex.[24]

Clinicians should be aware that when choosing medications for alcohol-dependent adolescents, many factors should be taken into consideration. It is imperative that clinicians weigh the potential risks and benefits of medication with the hazards of continuous alcohol use. In the treatment of adolescents, it also is important to keep neurodevelopmental factors in mind when determining type of medication and when to use and for how long.[1]

Serotonin

Dawes and Johnson[1] highlighted the complex changes that occur in the developing human brain that affect the availability of serotonin (5-HT) receptors and, commensurately, the potential effects of medications that alter 5-HT levels in alcohol-abusing or -dependent adolescents or emerging adults. During adolescence, normal brain development involves structural changes in gray and white matter, reorganization of cortical synapses, and modifications in the level of the 5-HT. In individuals who are vulnerable, removal and reorganization of cortical synapses and changes in neurotransmitter systems are hypothesized to increase the risk for developing alcohol use disorders.[1] This large loss in the number of 5-HT neurons and their reorganization in the neocortex during adolescence[24] have led to the speculation that this relative hyposerotonergic brain is more likely than that of an adult to be involved in impulsive behaviors including hazardous drinking. Thus, putative therapeutic medications with actions at the 5-HT receptor may have different effects in adolescents and emerging adults compared with adults.

Serotonin-3 receptor antagonists

Basic science studies support the role of the serotonin-3 (5-HT$_3$) receptor in mediating alcohol's important neurochemical effects, and medications that antagonize the 5-HT$_3$ receptor antagonists appear to be promising treatment for alcohol dependence. In neurophysiological studies, ethanol potentiates 5-HT$_3$ receptor-mediated ion currents in NCB-20 neuroblastoma cells[25,26] and in human embryonic kidney 293 cells transfected with

5-HT$_3$ receptor antagonist complementary DNA.[27] Serotonin-3 receptor antagonists block these effects.[28] Thus, the 5-HT$_3$ receptor is a site of action for ethanol in the brain.[29,30]

Pharmacobehavioral studies show that many of alcohol's reinforcing effects are mediated by 5-HT$_3$ and dopamine interactions in the corticomesolimbic system.[31–35] 5-HT$_3$ receptor antagonists have three principal effects that demonstrate their ability to modulate ethanol consumption and related behaviors. First, 5-HT$_3$ receptor antagonists suppress hyperlocomotion in the rat induced by dopamine or ethanol injection into the nucleus accumbens.[36] Second, 5-HT$_3$ receptor antagonists inhibit DiMe-C7 (a neurokinin)-induced hyperlocomotion, which also is reduced by the dopamine antagonist, fluphenazine.[37,38] Third, 5-HT$_3$ receptor antagonists reduce ethanol consumption in several animal models and across different species[32,39–48] (cf. reference 49).

Three clinical studies have provided evidence that ondansetron is a promising treatment for alcohol-dependent individuals, particularly those with an early-onset or Type B-like subtype. First, in a 6-week, double-blind, placebo-controlled study of 71 nonseverely alcohol-dependent males, Sellers et al.[50] observed that the 0.5-mg dose but not the 4-mg dose of ondansetron was associated with a nonsignificant trend ($p = 0.06$) toward a reduction in alcohol consumption. Post hoc analysis that eliminated 11 subjects who consumed less than 10 drinks/drinking day rendered the difference in drinking outcomes between the ondansetron 0.5 mg and placebo groups to be significant statistically ($p = 0.001$). Despite the limitations of this initial trial, which included a relatively short treatment period, the inclusion of just males, and the small number of subjects, the results of this study provided general support for ondansetron's promise in treating alcohol dependence. Also, these results showed that ondansetron might exhibit a nonlinear dose–response effect in the treatment of alcohol dependence.

Second, in a large-scale ($N = 321$), 12-week, randomized, double-blind clinical trial in which alcohol-dependent individuals received weekly cognitive behavioral therapy, Johnson et al.[51] showed that ondansetron (1, 4, and 16 μg/kg b.i.d.) was superior to placebo at improving drinking outcomes of those of the early-onset or Type B-like subtype but not the late-onset or Type A-like subtype. The self-reported decreases in alcohol consumption were corroborated by the concomitant reduction in carbohydrate-deficient transferrin level—a biomarker of transient alcohol consumption.

Third, Kranzler et al.[52] provided replication of the results by Johnson et al.[51] by showing that early-onset (Type B-like) alcoholics had a significantly greater improvement in drinking outcomes compared with their late-onset (Type A-like) counterparts following 8 weeks of ondansetron (4 μg/kg b.i.d.) treatment. Intriguingly, these results demonstrate a differential effect of ondansetron treatment by subtype of alcohol-dependent individual. Indeed, the contrast is striking when compared with the effects of selective serotonin reuptake inhibitors on different subtypes of alcohol-dependent individuals as described above. Basically, early onset or Type B-like alcoholics with apparent serotonergic deficiency respond best to a medication that blocks the 5-HT$_3$ receptor, whereas late-onset or Type A-like alcoholics with apparently normal serotonergic function derive the most benefit from a medication that can increase serotonin turnover and function.

One potential disadvantage of subtyping by psychosocial variables is that they might not be stable across all populations (i.e., differences by ethnicity and regions could occur due to different exposure levels to alcohol), and the more complex algorithms for subtyping (e.g., into Type A or B) cannot be carried out prospectively or applied directly to a single individual. Also, because alcoholism is mostly determined by biological factors, the more specific delineation of subtypes that respond to ondansetron would most likely come from an understanding of variations in molecular genetic characteristics. Arguably, a more stable, robust, and generalizable dichotomization of different populations of alcoholics responsive to ondansetron might be achievable using pertinent and specific biomolecular variables.[53]

Johnson has proposed a biomolecular explanation by which polymorphisms in the serotonergic transporter gene may predict drinking behavior, thereby providing a molecular target for the specific administration of ondansetron to particular alcohol-dependent individuals who are likely to respond.[54] Briefly, the key feature of Johnson's molecular hypothesis is that polymorphic variation(s) at the serotonin transporter gene might result in a relative intrasynaptic hyposerotonergic state with consequent upregulation of postsynaptic serotonin receptors.[2] Alcohol-dependent individuals with these polymorphic types may be prone to a heavier and more chronic pattern of drinking,[54,55] perhaps through a counterregulatory mechanism to increase serotonin turnover. Because this attempted counterregulation through increased alcohol consumption can only be partially effective, as further drinking reduces the expression of the serotonin transporter gene further,[54] a vicious cycle is set up. Johnson[56] has proposed that ondansetron treatment may ameliorate heavy or severe drinking in such alcohol-dependent individuals, presumably by blockade of upregulated postsynaptic serotonin receptors. Indeed, the results of a recent clinical trial suggest that ondansetron may have an effect to decrease severe drinking among individuals with specific polymorphisms of the serotonin transporter gene.[57] Obviously, a molecular genetic explanation for this effect, if proven, may enable a pharmacogenetic approach to treatment whereby the appropriate medication can be provided to the particular subtype of alcohol-dependent individual who would benefit the most from such treatment.

This concept also has been expanded to address molecular differences that can result in specific targets to treat hazardous drinking in adolescents.[58] Specifically, in that preliminary study, we found that polymorphic variation at the serotonin transporter gene was associated with the intensity of drinking and the increased likelihood of impulsive behaviors. Furthermore, we also have shown in an 8-week, prospective, open-label trial that ondansetron may reduce craving in adolescents.[59] Due to the promise of these preliminary studies, there are ongoing trials by our group to determine which type of adolescents or emerging adults with specific variation at the serotonin transporter gene responds best to ondansetron.

Intriguingly, ondansetron has shown efficacy in treating alcohol-dependent individuals with social phobia, presumably because of its anxiolytic effects.[60] Since the prevalence of social phobia may be high in adolescents and emerging adults, these results should be investigated and validated in future large-scale clinical trials.

In sum, preclinical data support an important role for 5-HT_3 receptors in mediating alcohol's important reinforcing effects associated with its abuse liability. Ondansetron is a promising medication for the treatment of early-onset or Type B-like alcohol dependence. Molecular variation at the serotonin transporter gene offers a more distinct method to identify alcohol-dependent individuals likely to respond to ondansetron.

The results of such studies, provide support for this approach. Similar studies are ongoing in adolescents and emerging adults. Ondansetron's potential to treat alcohol-dependent individuals with comorbid social phobia, which is relatively common in adolescents and emerging adults, will need validation in larger clinical trials.

Serotonin reuptake inhibitors

For decades, it has been known that pharmacological manipulations that deplete the brain of serotonin decrease the preference for ethanol.[61,62] Using preference paradigms, pharmacological agents that inhibit serotonin reuptake from the synapse reduce the voluntary consumption of ethanol solutions.[63–68] Knockout mice at the serotonin transporter do, however, exhibit a general decrease in ethanol preference and consumption.[69] Thus, there is ample preclinical support for the notion that selective serotonin reuptake inhibitors suppress ethanol consumption in animals.

Although these preclinical studies have shown that selective serotonin reuptake inhibitors can reduce ethanol consumption, the selectivity of this effect on reinforcement as opposed to general consummatory behaviors has been questioned.[70–72] The inhibition of serotonin reuptake function alters food intake and fluid consumption.[73] Specifically, selective serotonin reuptake inhibitors do suppress food intake[74,75] and fluid consumption[73] and decrease palatability.[76] Yet, motivational factors exert some control on the expression of these behaviors.[77] For instance, selective serotonin reuptake inhibitors enhance satiety[70] but selectively reduce preference for certain macronutrients (i.e., sweet items and carbohydrates)[78–80] (cf. references 81 and 82) that increase the palatability and rewarding effects of food.[83–85] Hence, selective serotonin reuptake inhibitors might decrease ethanol consumption via the suppression of nonspecific general consummatory behaviors and specific antireinforcing effects.

Despite the promise of preclinical studies, there is, at present, little support for the proposal that selective serotonin reuptake inhibitors are an efficacious treatment for a heterogeneous group of alcohol-dependent individuals. Initial studies of small sample size reported that selective serotonin reuptake inhibitors can produce short-term (1–4 weeks) decreases in alcohol consumption among problem drinkers.[86–90] Nevertheless, these studies were limited by at least three factors. First, most of the studies were conducted in men, thereby limiting the generalizability of the results to the general population.[86–88] Second, the adjunctive psychosocial treatment, which can decrease the apparent efficacy of the putative therapeutic medication because this too can have an important effect on drinking outcomes, was not standardized. Third, the treatment periods were short; thus, it was not possible to determine whether these initial effects, which could be due to nonspecific factors, would be sustained. Indeed, the problem with studies of short duration that focus on a chronic relapsing disorder such as alcohol dependence was highlighted in a later study by Gorelick and Paredes,[91] who found that there also was an effect for fluoxetine, compared with placebo, to decrease alcohol consumption by about 15% in the first 4 weeks of the trial but not over the entire length of the trial. Also, Naranjo *et al.*[92] did not demonstrate that citalopram (40 mg/day) was superior to placebo in a 12-week treatment trial. Further, neither Kabel and Petty[93] nor Kranzler *et al.*[94] in two separate

12-week studies found fluoxetine (60 mg/day) to be superior to placebo for the treatment of alcohol dependence.

There has been renewed understanding about how the administration of functionally different serotonergic agents can lead to different drinking outcomes among various sub-types of alcoholic (for a review, see Johnson[95]). Adapted from Cloninger's classification scheme,[96] two methods for subtyping alcoholics have been used in these pharmacotherapy studies. Basically, a particular type of alcoholic (i.e., Type A-like or late-onset) charac-terized by a later age of onset of problem drinking (typically over the age of 25 years), a preponderance of psychosocial morbidity, and low familial loading can experience improved drinking outcomes after selective serotonin reuptake inhibitor treatment.

Indeed, it appears that Type A-like or late-onset alcoholics, with presumably more nor-mative serotonin function, have been observed to experience improved drinking outcomes from sertraline both during active treatment[97] and at 6-month follow-up.[98] Also, Chick *et al.*[99] have shown that early-onset or Type B-like alcoholics were more likely to relapse than their late-onset or Type A-like counterparts following fluvoxamine treatment. Thus, at present, selective serotonin reuptake inhibitors appear to be efficacious only in Type A-like or late-onset alcoholics.

Fluoxetine has been reported to be beneficial for the treatment of alcohol-dependent in-dividuals with suicidal tendencies and severe comorbid depression.[100] A recent study did not find that sertraline treatment was more beneficial than placebo in treating depressed men and women with alcohol dependence irrespective of the severity of the depression.[101] In another trial, sertraline was again found not to be beneficial in both men and women for the treatment of comorbid alcohol dependence and depression, although women did have a very slight but not clinically meaningful improvement in depressive symptoms.[102] Notably, it has not been shown that the reduction in dysphoria in depressed alcoholics is associated with concomitant decreases in alcohol consumption.[103,104] Hence, the conclu-sion to be drawn from these studies is that except for a subtype of depressed alcoholic with suicidal tendencies or, perhaps, in women, there is not much evidence to recommend selective serotonin reuptake inhibitors alone over placebo for the treatment of depressed alcoholics. Nevertheless, more recently, it has been shown that the combination of naltrex-one and sertraline appears to be effective treatment for depressed alcoholics[105]; however, further studies are needed to establish this finding.

The results of treating depressed alcoholics with a selective serotonin reuptake inhibitor have not been compelling. In a 12-week trial of adolescents with alcohol use disorders who received a combination of cognitive behavioral therapy and motivational enhancement therapy, Cornelius and colleagues[106] did not find a therapeutic effect of fluoxetine versus placebo to reduce depressive symptoms or drinking. There is, therefore, no support for the use of selective serotonin reuptake inhibitors to treat adolescents with comorbid depression and alcohol dependence.

Sertraline might have some utility in the treatment of alcohol-dependent individu-als whose comorbid posttraumatic stress disorder is associated with early trauma,[107] thereby suggesting that different subtypes might vary in treatment response. Also, there is promise that paroxetine might prove useful in treating alcohol-dependent individuals with social phobia.[108] There is no specific treatment, apart from symptomatic management, for alcohol-dependent individuals with comorbid generalized anxiety disorder.[109]

In sum, despite strong preclinical data that would support the use of selective serotonin reuptake inhibitors as a promising treatment for alcohol dependence, there is no evidence that they are of therapeutic benefit to a heterogeneous group of alcohol-dependent individuals. Notably, however, there is growing confirmation that selective serotonin reuptake inhibitors can improve the drinking outcomes of Type A-like or late-onset alcoholics. Rather than being a cause for discouragement, this finding might: (a) open up the possibility of identifying important biogenetic or pharmacological mechanisms that underlie the alcoholism disease and (b) improve understanding about which type of alcohol-dependent individual can benefit the most from specific serotonergic treatment. Further, there is evidence that providing a selective serotonin reuptake inhibitor to severely depressed alcoholics with suicidal tendencies is of therapeutic benefit. There also is recent preliminary evidence that the combination of naltrexone and sertraline relieves both symptoms in depressed alcoholics. In contrast, in adolescents with comorbid depression and alcohol use disorders, the addition of fluoxetine to a combination of cognitive behavioral therapy and motivational enhancement therapy neither improves the symptoms of depression nor decreases alcohol consumption. More studies are needed to determine whether selective serotonin reuptake inhibitors are efficacious in treating alcohol-dependent individuals with anxiety and related disorders including posttraumatic stress disorder and social phobia.

Serotonin-1A partial receptor agonist

Preclinical studies have suggested that the serotonin-1A partial agonist, buspirone, may be effective at reducing ethanol consumption. Buspirone decreased volitional alcohol consumption from 60% to 30% in macaque monkeys, but there was considerable interindividual variation.[110] In Sprague-Dawley rats, buspirone significantly reduced ethanol intake in animals induced to drink by repeated brainstem injection of tetrahydropapaveroline. In a group of medium alcohol-preferring rats, buspirone (0.0025–0.63 mg/kg) reduced, while buspirone (>2.5 mg/kg) increased, alcohol consumption without affecting water consumption.[40] While buspirone is a partial serotonin-1A agonist, the net effect of its repeated administration is to enhance serotonin function via facilitation of the postsynaptic receptor, which is more sensitive than the autoreceptor, and downregulation of autoreceptor function.[111] Nevertheless, this preclinical evidence would have been strengthened by operant studies examining the dose–response characteristics of buspirone as a function of ethanol concentration.

Buspirone has not been demonstrated to be an efficacious medication for the treatment of alcohol-dependent individuals without comorbidity. In a review of five published trials, buspirone was without a convincing effect in noncomorbid alcoholics; however, alcoholics with comorbid anxiety experienced some benefit.[112,113] Hence, buspirone's anxiolytic effects might translate to those who also are dependent on alcohol.

In sum, there is no current evidence that would suggest a role for buspirone in the treatment of alcohol dependence without comorbid anxiety disorder.

Serotonin-2 receptor antagonist

Preclinical studies have suggested that the serotonin-2 receptor antagonist, ritanserin, can reduce ethanol consumption in animals[114,115] (cf. reference 116). Also, the serotonin-2 antagonists, amperozide[117-120] and FG5974,[121,122] significantly suppress ethanol intake without affecting water consumption. The exact mechanism by which serotonin-2 receptor antagonists might reduce ethanol consumption is unknown. It has, however, been suggested that they might exert their effects by acutely substituting for alcohol's pharmacobehavioral effects by facilitating burst firing in corticomesolimbic dopamine neurons,[123] or by the suppression of dopamine neurotransmission following their chronic administration.

In the clinical setting, ritanserin is not an efficacious treatment for alcohol dependence. In a rigorously conducted, 12-week, multicenter clinical trial ($N = 423$) of ritanserin (2.5 or 5 mg/day) versus placebo as an adjunct to weekly cognitive behavioral therapy, none of the ritanserin doses were superior to placebo.[124] In a later study using similar methodology, ritanserin (2.5, 5.0, or 10.0 mg/day) was not superior to placebo at improving drinking outcomes.[125] Although higher doses of ritanserin might be of therapeutic benefit, testing these doses is precluded by ritanserin's potential to cause dose-dependent prolongation of the QTc interval on the electrocardiogram, thereby increasing the potential for life-threatening cardiac arrhythmias.

In summary, there is no clinical evidence that would support the use of ritanserin as a treatment for alcohol dependence.

Opioids: mu-receptor antagonist—naltrexone

The endogenous opioid system, particularly through its interactions with the corticomesolimbic dopamine system, is involved in the expression of alcohol's reinforcing effects[31,126-131] (Figure 16.2[126,128]). Obviously, opioid receptors also have interactions with other neurotransmitters, including those in the glutamate,[132] gamma-aminobutyric acid,[133] serotonin,[134] cannabinoid,[135] and perhaps glycine[136] systems, that contribute to its effects on ethanol intake.

Even though naltrexone has some affinity for the kappa-opioid receptor,[137] its principal pharmacological effect on alcohol consumption is through blockade of the mu-opioid receptor as mice that lack the mu-opioid receptor do not self-administer alcohol.[138] Further, alcohol intake increases beta-endorphin release in brain regions such as the nucleus accumbens,[139-141] an effect that is blocked by naltrexone.[142] Mu-receptor antagonists, such as naltrexone and naloxone, also suppress ethanol intake across a wide range of animal paradigms[143-153] (cf. references 154 and 156). More recently, there also has been interest in elucidating the role of the hypothalamic–pituitary–adrenocortical axis in stress-induced ethanol consumption and sensitivity and how this might be influenced by naltrexone treatment.[157,158]

Oral naltrexone

In 1994, the FDA approved naltrexone for the treatment of alcohol dependence based on data from two relatively small (total $N = 167$) studies.[159,160] In those studies, recently abstinent, alcohol-dependent individuals who received naltrexone (50 mg/day), compared with their counterparts who got placebo, were less likely to relapse during the treatment

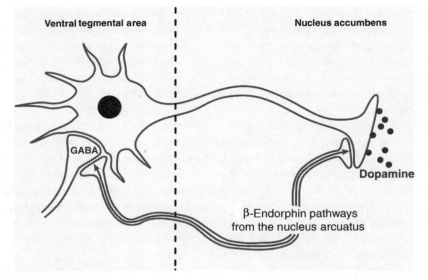

Figure 16.2   Schematic representation of opioid interactions with the corticomesolimbic dopamine reward pathway. Functional activity of beta-endorphin pathways primarily originating from the nucleus arcuatus can lead to increased dopamine release in the nucleus accumbens via two mechanisms. First, beta-endorphins can disinhibit the tonic inhibition of gamma-aminobutyric acid (GABA) neurons on dopamine cells in the ventral tegmental area.[127,129,131] Second, beta-endorphins can stimulate dopamine cells in the nucleus accumbens directly. Both mechanisms may be important for alcohol reward. Alcohol stimulates beta-endorphin release in both the nucleus accumbens and the ventral tegmental area.[126] Mu-receptor antagonists such as naloxone and naltrexone block these central effects of beta-endorphins.[31,126] Embellished from reference 126. Reprinted from reference 128 with kind permission from Springer Science+Business Media.

period of 12 weeks. Nevertheless, 5 months after treatment, the relapse rates for the naltrexone and placebo groups were similar. The anti-alcohol-craving effects that were ascribed to naltrexone were based on three findings. First, individuals with the highest level of baseline craving appeared to benefit the most from naltrexone.[161] Second, abstinent individuals who had received naltrexone had less of an impulse to initiate drinking.[162] Third, even among those who sampled alcohol, less pleasure was derived from the beverage.[163] These earlier studies were limited by the fact that only male veterans were tested in one of the studies,[160] and either there was no biomarker used to corroborate the self-reported data[159] or when the liver enzyme gamma-glutamyl transferase was used as a biomarker the results were not contributory[160]—presumably due to the relative insensitivity of this measure to capture transient drinking patterns.

Notably, in two large meta-analytic studies,[164,165] naltrexone was demonstrated to be efficacious at reducing the risk of relapse among recently abstinent, alcohol-dependent individuals. What has emerged from an examination of these studies is that naltrexone's effect size was small, with a corresponding number needed to treat (i.e., the number of individuals who need to be treated to prevent relapse in a single individual) of 7. An important threat to demonstrating efficacy for naltrexone is not having quite high enough levels of medication compliance. Indeed, in a 3-month follow-up and systematic replication of their study, Volpicelli *et al.*[166] only found a significant effect of naltrexone treatment compared with placebo recipients if the pill-taking rate exceeded 90%; even here, the difference in the percentage of drinking days between the naltrexone and placebo groups was small—3% and 11%, respectively.

Perhaps because of this small effect size, some studies have failed to demonstrate naltrexone's efficacy in treating alcohol dependence. For instance, in the UK collaborative trial led by Chick *et al.*, no overall difference was found between the naltrexone 50 mg/day and placebo groups on any of the endpoint measures; however, when individuals with less than 80% pill-taking compliance were excluded from the analysis, naltrexone was associated with a lower percentage of drinking days compared with placebo—12% versus 20%, respectively.[167,168] With naltrexone treatment, reduced pill-taking compliance is typically the result of adverse events such as nausea that can be reported as significant in up to 15% of trial participants.[169] Therefore, new technologies that aim to improve compliance by delivering naltrexone in depot form might possess a therapeutic advantage to the oral formulation. These technologies are discussed later in this section.

Importantly, the COMBINE study ($N = 1,383$) has served to underscore that naltrexone (100 mg/day) plus medication management to enhance compliance compared with placebo reduced the risk of a heavy drinking day (hazard ratio $= 0.72$; 97.5% CI $= 0.53$–0.98; $p = 0.02$).[10] Uniquely, this study used a higher naltrexone dose (i.e., 100 mg/day vs. 50 mg/day), and the high compliance rate of pill taking—85.4%—improved clinical outcome.

Recently, it has been proposed that individuals with the Asp variant of the OPRM1 gene exhibited preferentially higher relapse prevention rates when receiving naltrexone treatment.[170] As described previously, a similar response to naltrexone treatment on cue-elicited craving was not observed among non-treatment-seeking, alcohol-dependent individuals in a human laboratory study.[171] Further, a recent clinical trial did not find a preferential effect of naltrexone treatment on any of the variants of the OPRM1 gene.[172] Notably, the functional importance of variation in the OPRMI gene is still being elucidated. Although earlier studies in transfected cells suggested that the OPRM1-Asp[40] variant had a threefold higher affinity for beta-endorphin than OPRM1-Asn,[40] which would suggest enhanced function,[173] this has not been corroborated by others.[174,175] Recent in vitro transfection studies have, however, suggested that the G118 allele might be associated with lower OPRM1 protein expression than the A118 allele.[176] A further complication to estimating the general clinical significance of the effects of the Asp[40] allele on pharmacotherapeutic response to naltrexone is that its frequency can vary considerably between populations—from as low as 0.047 in African Americans to 0.154 in European Americans, and as high as 0.485 among those of Asian descent.[177,178] More genetic studies are, therefore, needed to elucidate fully the mechanistic effects of the Asp[40] allele, and to establish whether or not naltrexone response varies by variation at the OPRM1 gene (see Chapter 5). However, certain clinical characteristics have been associated with good clinical response to naltrexone, and these include a family history of alcohol dependence[161,179,180] or strong cravings or urges for alcohol.[180]

In a small ($N = 14$), open-label, 8-week pilot trial of young adults, naltrexone appeared to enhance the antidrinking effects of the brief motivational intervention, BASICS.[181]

A larger-sample, double-blind clinical trial is currently under way to establish whether naltrexone is an efficacious treatment to decrease drinking behavior among adolescents or emerging adults with alcohol use disorders.

Naltrexone's utility compared with placebo as an add-on treatment in alcohol-dependent individuals with comorbid bipolar I or II disorder was investigated recently.[182] All individuals received their concomitant medications prescribed for bipolar disorder prior to study entry, along with standardized cognitive behavioral therapy designed for the treatment of bipolar disorder and substance use at scheduled intervals during treatment.[183] Naltrexone did not differ statistically from placebo on any outcome measure of drinking, and the attrition rate was high—48%.

Naltrexone's utility compared with placebo as a treatment for alcohol dependence and smoking cessation also has been studied recently.[184] In that placebo-controlled study, there was no overall effect of naltrexone on either the consumption of alcohol or smoking. In a subsequent subset analysis confined to heavy drinkers (defined as those with at least one heavy drinking episode during the 2-week preenrollment baseline period), there was an effect of naltrexone to reduce heavy drinking; however, again there was no effect on smoking. Interestingly, there was a significant negative association between quitting smoking and decreasing alcohol consumption, whereby greater success in stopping smoking was correlated with increased amounts of heavy drinking. These results do not provide strong support for the use of naltrexone as a medication for the simultaneous reduction or cessation of alcohol consumption and smoking among individuals comorbid for these conditions.

Depot naltrexone

Depot forms of naltrexone also have been developed for the treatment of alcohol dependence. Of these, the only approved product is Vivitrol (Alkermes, Inc., Cambridge, MA, USA), formerly known as Vivitrex.

In 2004, Johnson et al.[185] published the initial safety, tolerability, and efficacy trial of Vivitrex for treating alcohol dependence. The design of the study was a 16-week randomized, placebo-controlled, double-blind clinical trial. Of the 25 alcohol-dependent individuals who participated in the trial, five of them got placebo and the remainder ($n = 20$) got 400 mg of Vivitrex. Results of that trial showed the safety of Vivitrex, with the most common adverse events being nonspecific abdominal pain, nausea, pain at the injection site, and headaches. None of the placebo recipients dropped out due to adverse events; in contrast, two of those who got Vivitrex discontinued for that reason. Due to the unbalanced design and small subject numbers, any inferences regarding efficacy had to be viewed quite cautiously. Nevertheless, there was a trend for those on Vivitrex, compared with placebo, to have a lower percentage of heavy drinking days—11.7% versus 25.3%. Later, in a large placebo-controlled, double-blind, randomized, multisite, 24-week clinical trial, Garbutt et al.[186] showed that high-dose Vivitrex (380 mg) recipients had a significantly lower percentage of heavy drinking days than those who got placebo (hazard ratio = 0.75; 95% CI = 0.60–0.94; $p = 0.02$). Recipients of low-dose Vivitrex (190 mg) had outcomes similar to those who got placebo. The treatment response signal in the high-dose Vivitrex recipients came from the male participants as the effect of both Vivitrex doses was no different from that in women who took placebo (hazard ratio = 1.23; 95% CI = 0.85–1.78; $p = 0.28$). The lack of efficacy for Vivitrol in women has been ascribed to greater subclinical affective symptoms, less of a family history of alcoholism (which is meant to be associated with good clinical outcomes to naltrexone), more responsiveness to placebo, and more clinical heterogeneity in the sample. In contrast with the premise for developing depot preparations, the dropout rate of 14.1% in the high-dose Vivitrex group was similar to that reported in studies with oral naltrexone. The chosen objective biomarker to corroborate the self-reported data—gamma-glutamyl transferase—did not show a difference between any of the Vivitrex doses and the placebo group. The common reasons for study discontinuation were injection site reactions, headaches, and nausea. Serious adverse events were reported in two participants taking active medication that resulted in an interstitial pneumonia and an allergic-type eosinophilic pneumonia, both of which resolved after medical treatment. Thus, the evidence remains that Vivitrol appears to be efficacious in preventing heavy drinking in men; however, it was approved by the FDA for treatment of both men and women based on the extant literature on naltrexone as a treatment for alcohol dependence. The expected advantage of Vivitrol to increase compliance did not materialize quickly although this might become more manifest in generic treatment settings rather than a closely monitored clinical trial. The potential for hypersensitivity reactions to Vivitrol, while small, does require post-marketing evaluation by the FDA.

Naltrexone: conclusions

In sum, the majority of the data show that naltrexone is an efficacious medication for treating alcohol dependence. The therapeutic treatment effect size is, however, small, and poor pill-taking compliance can be associated with poor clinical outcome. Large-scale, double-blind, clinical studies are needed to establish whether naltrexone is an efficacious treatment for adolescents and emerging adults with alcohol use disorders. Further research is needed to establish whether naltrexone's therapeutic efficacy in treating alcohol dependence differs among individuals who have variants of the OPRM1 gene. Alcohol-dependent individuals with a positive family history for the disease and individuals with strong cravings for alcohol appear to benefit the most from naltrexone treatment. Naltrexone combined with sertraline might be a promising medication for the treatment of alcohol dependence with comorbid depression. Naltrexone does not appear to be efficacious for the contemporaneous reduction or cessation of alcohol consumption and smoking. The naltrexone depot formulation, Vivitrol, is approved for the treatment of alcohol dependence; however, its therapeutic effect appears to predominate in men.

Glutamate

Metabotropic glutamate receptor-5 modulator and N-methyl-ᴅ-aspartate antagonist: acamprosate

Acamprosate's principal neurochemical effect appears to be the modulation of glutamate neurotransmission at metabotropic-5 glutamate receptors.[187] Evidence that acamprosate modulates a novel site of action at metabotropic-5 glutamate receptors comes from the finding that it inhibits the binding and neurotoxic effects of ±-1-aminocyclopentane-*trans*-1,3-dicarboxylic acid.[187]

Acamprosate has been shown to decrease: (a) ethanol consumption in rodents,[188–190] but this effect may not be specific in food-deprived C57BL/6J mice as both ethanol and water were reduced in a schedule-induced polydipsia task[191]; (b) dopamine hyperexcitability in the nucleus accumbens during alcohol withdrawal[192,193]; (c) general neuronal hyperexcitability[194,195]; (d) glutamatergic neurotransmission in alcohol-dependent rats[192,196]; (e) voltage-gated calcium channel activity; and (f) the expression of brain *c-fos*, an immediate early gene associated with alcohol withdrawal.[197,198] Nevertheless, it is acamprosate's ability to suppress alcohol-induced glutamate receptor sensitivity,[199] as well as conditioned cue responses to ethanol in previously dependent animals even after prolonged abstinence,[200–203] that has been linked with its therapeutic effect in humans—dampening negative affect and craving post-abstinence[128,204] (Figure 16.3[128,204,205]).

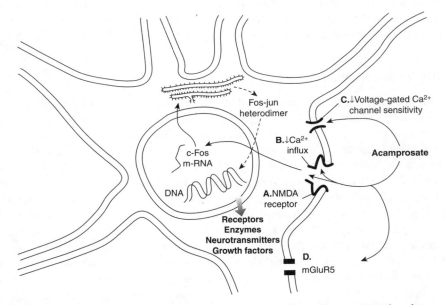

Figure 16.3   Schematic representation of acamprosate's effects. Acamprosate has four principal effects: A, reducing postsynaptic excitatory amino acid neurotransmission at *N*-methyl-D-aspartate (NMDA); B, diminishing Ca^{2+} influx into the cell, which interferes with expression of the immediate early gene *c-fos*; C, decreasing the sensitivity of voltage-gated calcium channels, and D, modulating metabotropic-5 glutamate receptors (mGluR5). mGluR5 are postsynaptic and are coupled to their associated ion channels by a second messenger cascade system (not shown). Also shown in this representation is synthesis of *c-fos* and *c-jun* in the endoplasmic reticulum, which can bind with DNA to alter the transcription of late effector genes. Late effector genes regulate long-term changes in cellular activity such as the function of receptors, enzymes, growth factors, and the production of neurotransmitters. Embellished from reference 204. Adapted from 128 with kind permission from Springer Science+Business Media. Reprinted from reference 204 with permission from Elsevier.

Most of the clinical evidence for the efficacy of acamprosate in the treatment of alcohol dependence comes from a series of European studies. In 2004, Mann *et al.*[206] wrote a meta-analysis of 17 published studies that included 4,087 alcohol-dependent individuals. In that report, continuous abstinence rates at 6 months were greater on acamprosate than for those who got placebo (acamprosate, 36.1%; placebo, 23.4%; relative benefit, 1.47; 95% CI = 1.29–1.69; $p < 0.001$). The overall pooled difference in success rates between acamprosate and placebo was 13.3% (95% CI = 7.8–18.7%), and the number needed to treat was 7.5. Similar results were obtained from another meta-analysis conducted at about the same time.[164] Generally, the effect size of acamprosate is small—0.14 for increasing the percentage of non-heavy drinking days[207] and 0.23 for reducing the relapse to heavy drinking.[208] Early studies also had some methodological problems, including nonstandardization of diagnostic criteria and the psychosocial adjunct to the medication, which were resolved in later trials.

Despite approval by the FDA on July 29, 2004, for the use of acamprosate in the treatment of alcohol dependence, largely based on the data from European studies, the results of studies in the United States have been disappointing. In the US multisite trial by Lipha Pharmaceuticals, Inc., there was no overall clinical evidence that acamprosate was superior to placebo among a heterogeneous cohort of alcohol-dependent individuals; however, post hoc analysis suggested that a subgroup of alcoholics with a treatment goal of abstinence might derive benefit.[209] Further, in 2006, the multisite COMBINE study also failed to find any therapeutic benefit of acamprosate compared with placebo on any drinking outcome measures.[10] Obviously, the findings of these US studies have reduced the enthusiasm for using it by addiction specialists in the United States. Scientifically, these findings do beg the questions as to what type of alcohol-dependent individual benefits the most from acamprosate and why there is an important discrepancy between the results of the US and European studies. From the European studies, acamprosate appears to benefit alcohol-dependent individuals with increased levels of anxiety, physiological dependence, negative family history, late age of onset, and female gender.[210]

There are at least four possible explanations for the discrepancy between the US and European studies. First, the populations sampled differed, with the European, compared with the US, studies having alcohol-dependent individuals with more prolonged drinking histories and alcohol-related neurological and psychosocial impairments. Thus, it is tempting to speculate that European studies might have included individuals with greater neuroplasticity and, therefore, higher response to the ameliorating effects of antigluta-matergic agents such as acamprosate. Second, the US, compared with the European, studies have tended to have higher levels of standardized psychosocial intervention as an adjunct to acamprosate, thereby masking the effect of the medication. Third, the therapeutic effect of acamprosate is small; hence, by chance, some trials can be expected to fail, especially those conducted in a multisite rather than a single-site environment due to the greater heterogeneity and variability of the cohort and research settings. Fourth, it is possible that future research might uncover other important differences between the US and European cohorts to explain the discrepant findings such as potential differences in participants' subtype, stage of the alcoholism disease, or biomolecular constitution.

The efficacy of acamprosate in treating alcohol-dependent adolescents has been examined in preliminary fashion. In a 90-day, double-blind, controlled study ($N = 26$) of alcohol-dependent individuals aged between 16 and 19 years, 7/13 who took acamprosate (1,332 mg daily) versus 2/13 who received a placebo were abstinent at the end of treatment ($p = 0.0076$). The acamprosate-treated group also had a greater mean cumulative abstinence duration than the placebo group—79.8 (SD 37.5) versus 32.8 (19.0) days, respectively; $p = 0.012$.[211] Further double-blind, randomized controlled studies with a more ample sample size are needed to validate these promising results.

In sum, European studies have clearly demonstrated efficacy for acamprosate as a treatment for alcohol dependence. Acamprosate was FDA approved in the United States largely based on the results of the European studies. Acamprosate's therapeutic effect is small, but it is well tolerated, with the most prominent adverse events being diarrhea, nervousness, and fatigue, especially at a relatively high dose (3 g/day). In contrast, studies in the United States have, to date, been unable to find efficacy for acamprosate among a heterogeneous group of alcohol-dependent individuals. The reason for the discrepancy between the results of the US and European studies has not been established. Perhaps, however, this discrepant finding might be due to differences in participants' selection, subtype, stage of the alcoholism disease, or biomolecular constitution that are yet to be determined. Intriguingly, preliminary results presented for the recently completed multisite collaborative European Study—Project Predict—also did not find an effect for acamprosate in the treatment of alcohol dependence.[212] Future studies are needed to delineate more clearly what type of alcohol-dependent individual can benefit from acamprosate treatment. The promising results of a potential effect of acamprosate to increase abstinence in adolescence require validation from large-scale clinical studies.

Alpha-amino-3-hydroxy-5-methylisoxazole-4-propionic acid and kainate glutamate receptor antagonist: topiramate

Topiramate, a sulfamate-substituted fructopyranose derivative, has six important mechanisms of action. Additional to its ability to antagonize alpha-amino-3-hydroxy-5-methylisoxazole-4-propionic acid receptors and kainate glutamate receptors,[213–215] topiramate also facilitates inhibitory gamma-aminobutyric acid-A-mediated currents at nonbenzodiazepine sites on the gamma-aminobutyric acid-A receptor,[216,217] inhibits L-type calcium channels and limits calcium-dependent second messenger systems,[218] reduces activity-dependent depolarization and excitability of voltage-dependent sodium channels,[219] activates potassium conductance,[220] and is a weak inhibitor of carbonic anhydrase isoenzymes, CA-II and CA-IV,[221] which are found in both neuronal and peripheral tissues. In renal tubules, carbonic anhydrase isoenzyme inhibition reduces hydrogen ion secretion and increases secretion of Na^+, K^+, HCO_3^-, and water, thereby enhancing the likelihood of acidosis and renal stone formation.[221,222]

Johnson[223,224] has proposed a neuropharmacological model by which topiramate can decrease alcohol reinforcement and the propensity to drink (Figure 16.4[225]). Nevertheless, few studies on the effects of topiramate on ethanol consumption in animals have been published. An initial animal study had shown complex effects of topiramate on ethanol drinking in C57BL/6 mice. In that study, high-dose (50 mg/kg) but not low-dose (1, 5, and 10 mg/kg) topiramate suppressed ethanol intake 2 hours after it was injected into the animal. Topiramate also decreased saccharin preference, but its ability to suppress

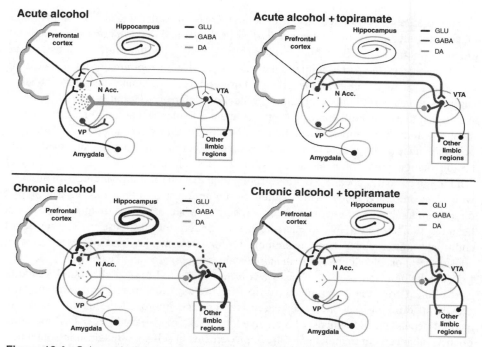

Figure 16.4 Schematic illustration of the hypothesized effects of acute and chronic alcohol, both with and without topiramate, on the corticomesolimbic dopamine (DA) reward circuit.[223] (Upper left) Acute alcohol suppresses the firing rate of ventral tegmental area (VTA) gamma-aminobutyric acid (GABA) neurons, which leads to less suppression of VTA DA neuronal activity. This disinhibition leads to VTA DA neuronal firing and DA release in the nucleus accumbens (N Acc.).[223] (Lower left) With chronic drinking, VTA GABA neurons are hyperexcitable, mainly because of increased glutamatergic input, less GABA tone from the N Acc., and rebound firing of GABA neurons because of their long-term suppression from repeated alcohol ingestion. This leads to VTA DA hypofunction and decreased release (compared with the acute condition) of DA in the N Acc.[223] (Upper right) During acute drinking, the GABAergic influence of topiramate probably predominates, particularly in the N Acc. This leads to greater inhibition of N Acc. DA neurons, and greater GABA tone from the N Acc. to the VTA suppresses VTA DA cell firing. Topiramate concomitantly inhibits the excitatory effects of glutamatergic neurons on DA neurons in the VTA and N Acc. These combined actions of topiramate should lead to profound suppression of DA neuronal activity and DA release in the N Acc. Hence, topiramate reduces the DA-mediated reinforcing effects of acute alcohol.[223] (Lower right) During chronic drinking, the predominant neuronal activity resides with the hyperexcitable state of VTA GABA neurons. Because of GABA-mediated inhibition and glutamatergic blockade of these neurons, topiramate "normalizes" VTA GABA neuronal activity. Although this would, at first, suggest that DA release in the N Acc. would be enhanced, this does not occur, and DA release in the N Acc. is most likely reduced because these N Acc. terminals are contemporaneously inhibited by GABA inhibition and blockade of glutamate (GLU). In the chronic drinker, the antiglutamatergic and L-type calcium channel effects of topiramate to block sensitization might predominate. Hence, topiramate would make it easier for a chronic alcoholic to withdraw from alcohol because rebound DA release would not occur (if drinking were ceased abruptly), and topiramate would aid in relapse prevention because alcohol's reinforcing effects would be decreased.[223] Line weights represent relative strengths of neuronal activity (heavy, medium, and light). The broken line represents decreased tone. VP: ventral pallidum. Reprinted from reference 223 with the permission of John Wiley & Sons, Inc.

ethanol preference was associated with some increase in water intake.[225] Notably, in an elegant, recent animal study, Nguyen *et al.*[226] demonstrated that topiramate can suppress ethanol drinking in C57BL/6 mice; additionally, in contrast with the effects of naltrexone and tiagabine in the same animals, the mice treated with topiramate did not develop any tolerance to its antidrinking effects. Furthermore, topiramate has been shown to suppress ethanol drinking persistently in alcohol-preferring (P) but not Wistar rats.[227] Additional to its ethanol-suppressing effects, there is evidence that topiramate can reduce alcohol withdrawal symptoms in a model of handling-induced convulsions.[228] Hence, the preponderance of the animal literature does support topiramate as a promising medication for the treatment of alcohol dependence. Nevertheless, the effect of topiramate on ethanol drinking in animals appears to be less striking than that on drinking outcomes in humans, which are presented below. This challenges the notion that animal models can predict directly treatment response in humans, especially when a variety of models have not been used or been available to characterize or "fingerprint" response.[229] The results of additional animal experiments examining topiramate's mechanistic effects on ethanol consumption or related behaviors in animals are, therefore, awaited eagerly.

Recently, Johnson *et al.*[230,231] and Ma *et al.*[232] showed in a double-blind, randomized clinical trial that topiramate (up to 300 mg/day), compared with placebo, improved all drinking outcomes, decreased craving, and improved the quality of life of alcohol-dependent individuals who received 12 weeks of weekly brief behavioral compliance enhancement treatment.[233] The improvements in self-reported drinking outcomes were confirmed by plasma gamma-glutamyl transferase, an objective biochemical measure of alcohol consumption.[234] The therapeutic effect size for the primary efficacy variable—percentage of heavy drinking days—was 0.63.

In a 6-week experimental study of 76 heavy drinkers who were not seeking treatment, Miranda *et al.*[235] showed that low- and high-dose topiramate—200 and 300 mg/day, respectively—were significantly better than placebo at decreasing the percentage of heavy drinking days. Furthermore, in a subsequent 17-site ($N = 371$) US trial, topiramate (up to 300 mg/day) was again superior to placebo at improving all self-reported drinking outcomes, gamma-glutamyl transferase level, and some measures of quality of life among alcohol-dependent individuals who received 14 weeks of weekly brief behavioral compliance enhancement treatment.[236,237] Topiramate's therapeutic effect size for the reduction in percentage of heavy drinking days was 0.52, and the number needed to treat was 3.4.[238]

Taken together, these clinical studies provide strong evidence that topiramate is a promising medication for the treatment of alcohol dependence. Encouragingly, topiramate's therapeutic effect size is in the moderate range, and the clinical effects appear to increase with greater length of time on the medication.

Generally, topiramate has a favorable adverse event profile, with most reported symptoms being classified as mild to moderate.[224] The most common adverse events are paresthesia, anorexia, difficulty with memory or concentration, and taste perversion. Slow titration to the ceiling dose (up to 300 mg/day) for 8 weeks is critical to minimizing adverse events and improving tolerability (see Table 16.1[53]); however, about 10% of individuals taking topiramate may experience some cognitive difficulty irrespective of the dose titration schedule.[239] Topiramate use has been linked with acute but rare visual adverse events. As of January 2005, there had been 371 spontaneous reports of myopia,

Table 16.1   Topiramate dose-escalation schedule.

Week	AM dose	PM dose	Total daily dose (mg)
1	0 mg	One 25-mg tablet	25
2	0 mg	Two 25-mg tablets	50
3	One 25-mg tablet	Two 25-mg tablets	75
4	Two 25-mg tablets	Two 25-mg tablets	100
5	Two 25-mg tablets	One 100-mg tablet	150
6	One 100-mg tablet	One 100-mg tablet	200
7	One 100-mg tablet	One 100-mg tablet and two 25-mg tablets	250
8	One 100-mg tablet and two 25-mg tablets	One 100-mg tablet and two 25-mg tablets	300

Reprinted from reference 53 with kind permission from Springer Science+Business Media.

angle-closure glaucoma, or increased intraocular pressure, for a rate of 12.7 reports per 100,000 patient-years of exposure.[205] Usually, the syndrome of acute bilateral myopia associated with secondary angle-closure glaucoma presents as the acute onset of visual blurring, ocular pain, or both. Associated bilateral ophthalmologic findings can include myopia, shallowing of the anterior chamber, conjunctival hyperemia, and raised intraocular pressure. This syndrome resolves within a few days of discontinuing topiramate administration.[224]

Although topiramate has not shown efficacy in the treatment of bipolar disorder,[240] there is an ongoing National Institutes of Health-funded study of its efficacy in the treatment of individuals with comorbid alcohol dependence and bipolar disorder. It is presumed that among individuals whose bipolar disorder is stabilized by concurrent medication prior to the trial, topiramate would have an added effect to improve drinking outcomes. Results of this study are awaited eagerly. Promisingly, another anticonvulsant, valproic acid, has been shown to decrease heavy drinking in alcohol-dependent individuals with bipolar disorder.[241]

As a subgroup analysis of a 12-week double-blind, randomized, controlled trial, the effect of topiramate versus placebo among alcohol-dependent smokers was evaluated.[242] Topiramate recipients were significantly more likely than placebo recipients to become abstinent from smoking (odds ratio = 4.46; 95% CI 1.08–18.39; $p = 0.04$). Using a serum cotinine level of ≤ 28 ng/mL to segregate nonsmokers from smokers, the topiramate group had 4.97 times the odds of being nonsmokers (95% CI 1.1–23.4; $p = 0.04$). The strength of these results showing topiramate's treatment efficacy is bolstered by the fact that smoking cessation was not a goal of the study, and no specific measures, advice or counseling, or therapeutic targets were provided to help the participants quit smoking; thus, the improvements in smoking rate represent a naturalistic change in behavior. Interestingly, cigarette consumption and serum cotinine levels lessened as individuals became more abstinent in the topiramate group. In contrast, increasing abstinence from alcohol was associated with greater consumption of cigarettes and higher serum cotinine levels for the placebo group. These findings provide initial support for the proposal that topiramate may be an efficacious medicine for the simultaneous treatment of alcohol dependence and smoking.

In sum, predicated upon a neuropharmacological conceptual model, there now is strong clinical support for topiramate as a promising medication for the treatment of alcohol dependence. Topiramate's therapeutic effects appear to be robust, with a medium effect size, thereby potentially ushering in a new era of a reliably efficacious medicine for the treatment of alcohol dependence with or without smoking. Intriguingly, although the animal data do provide support for topiramate's antidrinking effects, more research is needed to characterize fully or "fingerprint" the pattern of response. Such preclinical studies should enable us to elucidate more clearly the basic mechanistic processes that underlie topiramate's efficacy as a treatment for alcohol dependence. While it is not yet known whether topiramate will be useful in treating alcohol-dependent individuals with bipolar disorder, another anticonvulsant (i.e., valproic acid) has shown some promise.

Gamma-aminobutyric acid-B receptor agonist: baclofen

Animal studies have demonstrated that the gamma-aminobutyric acid-B receptor agonist, baclofen [beta-(4-chlorophenyl)-gamma-aminobutyric acid], causes decreases in voluntary ethanol intake,[243] the ethanol-deprivation effect,[244,245] and morphine-induced stimulation of ethanol consumption.[246] Clinical trials have bolstered the findings of animal studies that suggest a role for baclofen in treating alcohol dependence. In an open-label, 4-week study, 9 alcohol-dependent men were given baclofen (up to 30 mg/day). Seven of the 9 subjects achieved abstinence, while the other 2 participants improved their self-reported drinking outcomes during the study period, according to self-reports corroborated by family members. Several objective biological markers of alcohol intake also showed significant reductions between the beginning and the end of the study. Furthermore, craving, as measured by median Alcohol Craving Scale scores, decreased in the first study week and remained stable thereafter.[247]

In a 4-week, randomized, placebo-controlled, double-blind clinical trial with 39 alcohol-dependent individuals, 14 of 20 (70%) participants treated with baclofen (up to 30 mg/day) achieved abstinence, compared with 4 of 19 (21.1%) in the placebo group ($p < 0.005$). Baclofen treatment improved significantly drinking outcomes, state anxiety scores, and craving measures. Baclofen generally was well tolerated and had no apparent abuse liability. Adverse events, none of which were serious, consisted of nausea, vertigo, transient sleepiness, and abdominal pain.[248]

Recently, Addolorato and colleagues[249] reported in a randomized, double-blind clinical trial that baclofen was more efficacious than placebo at promoting abstinence in alcohol-dependent individuals with liver cirrhosis. Because baclofen is primarily excreted unchanged in the urine and feces, it might be uniquely suitable for treating alcoholics with compromised hepatic function. Baclofen was well tolerated in this study, with few adverse events.

These findings indicate that baclofen is a promising medication for the treatment of alcohol dependence, particularly among those with compromised hepatic function.

Additional studies of larger sample size and longer duration are awaited to establish the efficacy of baclofen for this indication.

Disulfiram

Disulfiram, an FDA-approved medication, has been used for treating alcoholism since the 1940s and is perhaps still the most widely used such medication in the United States today. Its principal mode of action is as an aversive agent. Disulfiram inhibits aldehyde dehydrogenase and prevents the metabolism of alcohol's primary metabolite, acetaldehyde. In turn, the accumulation of acetaldehyde in the blood causes unpleasant effects to occur if alcohol is ingested; these include sweating, headache, dyspnea, lowered blood pressure, flushing, sympathetic overactivity, palpitations, nausea, and vomiting. The association of these symptoms with drinking discourages further consumption of alcohol.[205,250]

Disulfiram has no significant effect on craving for alcohol. Hence, patients must be highly motivated to maintain disulfiram treatment, whereas those who wish to drink can simply stop taking the medication. The efficacy of disulfiram generally is limited to those who are highly compliant or who receive their medication under supervision—that is, the type of alcohol-dependent individuals who might be likely to abstain on their own, without adjunctive pharmacotherapy. Including a supportive spouse or partner in a disulfiram treatment plan helps to improve outcome.[250,251]

The efficacy of disulfiram in treating alcohol-dependent adolescents has been examined in preliminary fashion. In a 90-day, double-blind, controlled study ($N = 26$) of alcohol-dependent individuals aged between 16 and 19 years, 7/13 who took disulfiram (200 mg daily) versus 2/13 who received a placebo were abstinent at the end of treatment ($p = 0.0063$). The disulfiram-treated group also had a greater mean cumulative abstinence duration than the placebo group—68.5 (SD 37.5) versus 29.7 (19.0) days, respectively; $p = 0.012$.[252] Furthermore, in 2008, De Sousa and De Sousa[253] published results from an open randomized trial comparing disulfiram and naltrexone for relapse prevention in adolescents with alcohol dependence. They found that disulfiram and naltrexone in combination with psychosocial treatment over a 6-month period yielded abstinence rates of 79.31% and 51.72%, respectively. Further double-blind, randomized controlled studies with a more ample sample size are needed to validate these promising results.

Summary

Alcohol dependence is a treatable disorder when efficacious medicines are added to enhance the effects of psychosocial treatment (see Chapter 15). No pharmacotherapeutic agent has, however, been established as a treatment for alcohol-abusing or -dependent adolescents or emerging adults. Thus, most of what is known has been extrapolated from the adult literature.

Several medications have demonstrated efficacy as treatments for alcohol dependence in adults. These include acamprosate, disulfiram, naltrexone (and its depot analog, Vivitrol), and topiramate. Additionally, ondansetron appears to be efficacious in Type B or early-onset alcoholics; however, a clearer demarcation of efficacy is likely to be seen among those with specific subtypes of the serotonin transporter gene. Selective serotonin reuptake inhibitors may be efficacious for the treatment of Type A or late-onset alcoholism, as well as alcoholism associated with suicidal tendencies and depression. In combination with naltrexone, sertraline appears to be efficacious in the treatment of alcoholism with comorbid depression. Promising results also have been seen with the use of baclofen for the treatment of alcohol dependence.

Few pharmacotherapy studies have been done to identify efficacious treatments in adolescents or emerging adults with alcohol dependence or alcohol use disorders. There is, however, promising work that has been conducted with acamprosate, disulfiram, ondansetron, and naltrexone—all of which require validation from large-scale, randomized, controlled double-blind clinical trials.

As neuroscientific research progresses, it is plausible that unique medication combinations will be tested as treatment agents for alcohol abuse or dependence in adolescents and emerging adults. Intriguingly, pharmacogenetic approaches could be particularly useful because they might provide an approach for early intervention in treating alcohol abuse or dependence, particularly among those who may have a high genetic predisposition to the disease.

Acknowledgments

We are grateful to Elsevier for permission to reproduce some text from a recent review article,[205] as well as to Springer Science+Business Media for permission to reproduce some text from a recent book chapter.[53] We also thank Ann Richards and Robert H. Cormier Jr for assistance with manuscript preparation.

References

1. Dawes MA, Johnson BA. Pharmacotherapeutic trials in adolescent alcohol use disorders: Opportunities and challenges. *Alcohol Alcohol* 2004; 39:166–177.
2. Johnson BA. Medication treatment of different types of alcoholism. *Am J Psychiatry* 2010; 167:630–639.
3. Johnson BA. New weapon to curb smoking: No more excuses to delay treatment. *Arch Intern Med* 2006; 166:1547–1550.
4. Joanning H, Quinn W, Thomas F, Mullen R. Treating adolescent substance abuse: A comparison of family systems therapy, group therapy, and family drug education. *J Marital Fam Ther* 1992; 18:345–356.
5. Jennison KM. The short-term effects and unintended long-term consequences of binge drinking in college: A 10-year follow-up study. *Am J Drug Alcohol Abuse* 2004; 30:659–684.
6. Perkins HW. Surveying the damage: A review of research on consequences of alcohol misuse in college populations. *J Stud Alcohol Suppl* 2002; 14:91–100.
7. Hasin DS, Stinson FS, Ogburn E, Grant BF. Prevalence, correlates, disability, and comorbidity of DSM-IV alcohol abuse and dependence in the United States: Results from the National Epidemiologic Survey on Alcohol and Related Conditions. *Arch Gen Psychiatry* 2007; 64:830–842.

8. Grant BF, Dawson DA. Age at onset of alcohol use and its association with DSM-IV alcohol abuse and dependence: Results from the National Longitudinal Alcohol Epidemiologic Survey. *J Subst Abuse* 1997; 9:103–110.

9. Kiefer F, Jahn H, Tarnaske T *et al.* Comparing and combining naltrexone and acamprosate in relapse prevention of alcoholism: A double-blind, placebo-controlled study. *Arch Gen Psychiatry* 2003; 60:92–99.

10. Anton RF, O'Malley SS, Ciraulo DA *et al.* Combined pharmacotherapies and behavioral interventions for alcohol dependence—The COMBINE Study: A randomized controlled trial. *JAMA* 2006; 295:2003–2017.

11. Task Force of the National Advisory Council on Alcohol Abuse and Alcoholism. *How to Reduce High-Risk College Drinking: Use Proven Strategies, Fill Research Gaps. Final report of the Panel on Prevention and Treatment.* Bethesda, MD: U.S. Department of Health and Human Services; 2002.

12. Miller WR, Rollnick S. *Motivational Interviewing: Preparing People to Change Addictive Behavior.* New York: Guilford Press; 1991.

13. Bien TH, Miller WR, Tonigan JS. Brief interventions for alcohol problems: A review. *Addiction* 1993; 88:315–335.

14. Wilk AI, Jensen NM, Havighurst TC. Meta-analysis of randomized control trials addressing brief interventions in heavy alcohol drinkers. *J Gen Intern Med* 1997; 12:274–283.

15. Ballesteros J, Duffy JC, Querejeta I, Ariño J, González-Pinto A. Efficacy of brief interventions for hazardous drinkers in primary care: Systematic review and meta-analyses. *Alcohol Clin Exp Res* 2004; 28:608–618.

16. Dimeff LA, Baer JS, Kivlahan DR, Marlatt GA. *Brief Alcohol Screening and Intervention for College Students (BASICS): A Harm Reduction Approach.* New York: Guilford Press; 1999.

17. Baer JS, Kivlahan DR, Blume AW, McKnight P, Marlatt GA. Brief intervention for heavy-drinking college students: A 4-year follow-up and natural history. *Am J Public Health* 2001; 91:1310–1316.

18. White HR, Mun EY, Pugh L, Morgan TJ. Long-term effects of brief substance use interventions for mandated college students: Sleeper effects of an in-person personal feedback intervention. *Alcohol Clin Exp Res* 2007; 31:1380–1391.

19. Murphy JG, Duchnick JJ, Vuchinich RE *et al.* Relative efficacy of a brief motivational intervention for college student drinkers. *Psychol Addict Behav* 2001; 15:373–379.

20. Carey KB, Carey MP, Maisto SA, Henson JM. Brief motivational interventions for heavy college drinkers: A randomized controlled trial. *J Consult Clin Psychol* 2006; 74:943–954.

21. Fromme K, Corbin W. Prevention of heavy drinking and associated negative consequences among mandated and voluntary college students. *J Consult Clin Psychol* 2004; 72:1038–1049.

22. Kuo M, Wechsler H, Greenberg P, Lee H. The marketing of alcohol to college students: The role of low prices and special promotions. *Am J Prev Med* 2003; 25:204–211.

23. Weitzman ER, Nelson TF, Wechsler H. Taking up binge drinking in college: The influences of person, social group, and environment. *J Adolesc Health* 2003; 32:26–35.

24. Rakic P, Bourgeois JP, Goldman-Rakic PS. Synaptic development of the cerebral cortex: Implications for learning, memory, and mental illness. *Prog Brain Res* 1994; 102:227–243.

25. Lovinger DM, White G. Ethanol potentiation of 5-hydroxytryptamine3 receptor-mediated ion current in neuroblastoma cells and isolated adult mammalian neurons. *Mol Pharmacol* 1991; 40:263–270.

26. Zhou Q, Lovinger DM. Pharmacologic characteristics of potentiation of 5-HT_3 receptors by alcohols and diethyl ether in NCB-20 neuroblastoma cells. *J Pharmacol Exp Ther* 1996; 278:732–740.

27. Lovinger DM, Zhou Q. Alcohols potentiate ion current mediated by recombinant 5-HT₃RA receptors expressed in a mammalian cell line. *Neuropharmacology* 1994; 33:1567–1572.

28. Lovinger DM. Inhibition of 5-HT₃ receptor-mediated ion current by divalent metal cations in NCB-20 neuroblastoma cells. *J Neurophysiol* 1991; 66:1329–1337.

29. Lovinger DM. Ethanol potentiates ion current mediated by 5-HT₃ receptors on neuroblastoma cells and isolated neurons. *Alcohol Alcohol Suppl* 1991; 1:181–185.

30. Lovinger DM. 5-HT₃ receptors and the neural actions of alcohols: An increasingly exciting topic. *Neurochem Int* 1999; 35:125–130.

31. Hemby SE, Johnson BA, Dworkin SI. Neurobiological basis of drug reinforcement. In: Johnson BA, Roache JD, eds. *Drug Addiction and Its Treatment: Nexus of Neuroscience and Behavior.* Philadelphia: Lippincott-Raven; 1997, pp. 137–169.

32. Barnes NM, Sharp T. A review of central 5-HT receptors and their function. *Neuropharmacology* 1999; 38:1083–1152.

33. Johnson BA, Cowen PJ. Alcohol-induced reinforcement: Dopamine and 5-HT₃ receptor interactions in animals and humans. *Drug Dev Res* 1993; 30:153–169.

34. Koob GF. Neural mechanisms of drug reinforcement. *Ann NY Acad Sci* 1992; 654:171–191.

35. Wise RA, Bozarth MA. A psychomotor stimulant theory of addiction. *Psychol Rev* 1987; 94:469–492.

36. Bradbury AJ, Costall B, Domeney AM, Naylor RJ. Laterality of dopamine function and neuroleptic action in the amygdala in the rat. *Neuropharmacology* 1985; 24:1163–1170.

37. Eison AS, Iversen SD, Sandberg BE, Watson SP, Hanley MR, Iversen LL. Substance P analog, DiMe-C7: Evidence for stability in rat brain and prolonged central actions. *Science* 1982; 215:188–190.

38. Hagan RM, Jones BJ, Jordan CC, Tyers MB. Effect of 5-HT₃ receptor antagonists on responses to selective activation of mesolimbic dopaminergic pathways in the rat. *Br J Pharmacol* 1990; 99:227–232.

39. Johnson BA, Campling GM, Griffiths P, Cowen PJ. Attenuation of some alcohol-induced mood changes and the desire to drink by 5-HT₃ receptor blockade: A preliminary study in healthy male volunteers. *Psychopharmacology* 1993; 112:142–144.

40. Meert TF. Effects of various serotonergic agents on alcohol intake and alcohol preference in Wistar rats selected at two different levels of alcohol preference. *Alcohol Alcohol* 1993; 28:157–170.

41. Costall B, Domeney AM, Naylor RJ, Tyers MB. Effects of the 5-HT₃ receptor antagonist, GR38032F, on raised dopaminergic activity in the mesolimbic system of the rat and marmoset brain. *Br J Pharmacol* 1987; 92:881–894.

42. Dyr W, Kostowski W. Evidence that the amygdala is involved in the inhibitory effects of 5-HT₃ receptor antagonists on alcohol drinking in rats. *Alcohol* 1995; 12:387–391.

43. Fadda F, Garau B, Marchei F, Colombo G, Gessa GL. MDL 72222, a selective 5-HT₃ receptor antagonist, suppresses voluntary ethanol consumption in alcohol-preferring rats. *Alcohol Alcohol* 1991; 26:107–110.

44. Hodge CW, Samson HH, Lewis RS, Erickson HL. Specific decreases in ethanol- but not water-reinforced responding produced by the 5-HT₃ antagonist ICS 205–930. *Alcohol* 1993; 10:191–196.

45. McBride WJ, Li TK. Animal models of alcoholism: Neurobiology of high alcohol-drinking behavior in rodents. *Crit Rev Neurobiol* 1998; 12:339–369.

46. Rodd-Henricks ZA, McKinzie DL, Li T-K, Crile RS, Murphy JM, McBride WJ. Intracranial self-administration of ethanol into the posterior VTA of Wistar rats is mediated by 5-HT₃ receptors [abstract]. *Alcohol Clin Exp Res* 1999; 23(Suppl. 5):49A.

47. Sellers EM, Higgins GA, Tompkins DM, Romach MK. Serotonin and alcohol drinking. *NIDA Res Monogr* 1992; 119:141–145.
48. Tomkins DM, Le AD, Sellers EM. Effect of the 5-HT₃ antagonist ondansetron on voluntary ethanol intake in rats and mice maintained on a limited access procedure. *Psychopharmacology* 1995; 117:479–485.
49. Beardsley PM, Lopez OT, Gullikson G, Flynn D. Serotonin 5-HT₃ antagonists fail to affect ethanol self-administration of rats. *Alcohol* 1994; 11:389–395.
50. Sellers EM, Toneatto T, Romach MK, Somer GR, Sobell LC, Sobell MB. Clinical efficacy of the 5-HT₃ antagonist ondansetron in alcohol abuse and dependence. *Alcohol Clin Exp Res* 1994; 18:879–885.
51. Johnson BA, Roache JD, Javors MA *et al.* Ondansetron for reduction of drinking among biologically predisposed alcoholic patients: A randomized controlled trial. *JAMA* 2000; 284:963–971.
52. Kranzler HR, Pierucci-Lagha A, Feinn R, Hernandez-Avila C. Effects of ondansetron in early- versus late-onset alcoholics: A prospective, open-label study. *Alcohol Clin Exp Res* 2003; 27:1150–1155.
53. Johnson BA, Ait-Daoud N. Pharmacotherapy for alcoholism and some related psychiatric and addictive disorders: Scientific basis and clinical findings. In: Johnson BA, ed. *Addiction Medicine: Science and Practice.* New York: Springer Science+Business Media; 2010, pp. 943–980.
54. Johnson BA, Javors MA, Roache JD *et al.* Can serotonin transporter genotype predict serotonergic function, chronicity, and severity of drinking? *Prog Neuropsychopharmacol Biol Psychiatry* 2008; 32:209–216.
55. Seneviratne C, Huang W, Ait-Daoud N, Li MD, Johnson BA. Characterization of a functional polymorphism in the 3′ UTR of SLC6A4 and its association with drinking intensity. *Alcohol Clin Exp Res* 2009; 33:332–339.
56. Johnson BA. Pills for the pharmacogenetic treatment of alcohol dependence. In: the NIAAA-sponsored symposium organized by Willenbring M. Update on genetics and neuroscience. Presentation at the American Society of Addiction Medicine annual meeting, New Orleans, LA; 2009.
57. Johnson BA, Ait-Daoud N, Seneviratne C *et al.* Pharmacogenetic approach at the serotonin transporter gene as a method of reducing the severity of alcohol drinking. *Am J Psychiatry* 2011; 168:(in press).
58. Dawes MA, Roache JD, Javors MA *et al.* Drinking histories in alcohol-use-disordered youth: Preliminary findings on relationships to platelet serotonin transporter expression with genotypes of the serotonin transporter. *J Stud Alcohol Drugs* 2009; 70:899–907.
59. Dawes MA, Johnson BA, Ma JZ, Ait-Daoud N, Thomas SE, Cornelius JR. Reductions in and relations between 'craving' and drinking in a prospective, open-label trial of ondansetron in adolescents with alcohol dependence. *Addict Behav* 2005; 30:1630–1637.
60. Sloan TB, Roache JD, Johnson BA. The role of anxiety in predicting drinking behaviour. *Alcohol Alcohol* 2003; 38:360–363.
61. Myers RD, Veale WL. Alcohol preference in the rat: Reduction following depletion of brain serotonin. *Science* 1968; 160:1469–1471.
62. Nachman M, Lester D, Le Magnen J. Alcohol aversion in the rat: Behavioral assessment of noxious drug effects. *Science* 1970; 168:1244–1246.
63. Daoust M, Chretien P, Moore N, Saligaut C, Lhuintre JP, Boismare F. Isolation and striatal (3H) serotonin uptake: Role in the voluntary intake of ethanol by rats. *Pharmacol Biochem Behav* 1985; 22:205–208.

64. Geller I. Effects of para-chlorophenylalanine and 5-hydroxytryptophan on alcohol intake in the rat. *Pharmacol Biochem Behav* 1973; 1:361–365.
65. Gill K, Amit Z, Koe BK. Treatment with sertraline, a new serotonin uptake inhibitor, reduces voluntary ethanol consumption in rats. *Alcohol* 1988; 5:349–354.
66. Gill K, Filion Y, Amit Z. A further examination of the effects of sertraline on voluntary ethanol consumption. *Alcohol* 1988; 5:355–358.
67. McBride WJ, Murphy JM, Lumeng L, Li TK. Serotonin and ethanol preference. *Recent Dev Alcohol* 1989; 7:187–209.
68. Zabik JE, Binkerd K, Roache JD. Serotonin and ethanol aversion in the rat. In: Naranjo CA, Sellers EM, eds. *Research Advances in New Psychopharmacological Treatments for Alcoholism: Proceedings of the Symposium, Toronto, 4–5 October 1984.* Amsterdam: Excerpta Medica; 1985, pp. 87–105.
69. Boyce-Rustay JM, Wiedholz LM, Millstein RA *et al.* Ethanol-related behaviors in serotonin transporter knockout mice. *Alcohol Clin Exp Res* 2006; 30:1957–1965.
70. Blundell JE. Serotonin and appetite. *Neuropharmacology* 1984; 23:1537–1551.
71. Blundell JE, Latham CJ. Behavioural pharmacology of feeding. In: Silverstone T, ed. *Drugs and Appetite.* London: Academic Press; 1982, pp. 41–80.
72. Maurel S, De Vry J, Schreiber R. Comparison of the effects of the selective serotonin-reuptake inhibitors fluoxetine, paroxetine, citalopram and fluvoxamine in alcohol-preferring cAA rats. *Alcohol* 1999; 17:195–201.
73. Gill K, Amit Z. Serotonin uptake blockers and voluntary alcohol consumption. A review of recent studies. *Recent Dev Alcohol* 1989; 7:225–248.
74. Gottfries CG. Influence of depression and antidepressants on weight. *Acta Psychiatr Scand Suppl* 1981; 290:353–356.
75. Simpson RJ, Lawton DJ, Watt MH, Tiplady B. Effect of zimelidine, a new antidepressant, on appetite and body weight. *Br J Clin Pharmacol* 1981; 11:96–98.
76. Leander JD. Fluoxetine suppresses palatability-induced ingestion. *Psychopharmacology* 1987; 91:285–287.
77. Stellar JR, Stellar E. *The Neurobiology of Motivation and Reward.* New York: Springer-Verlag; 1985.
78. Li ET, Anderson GH. 5-Hydroxytryptamine control of meal to meal composition chosen by rats. *Fed Proc* 1983; 42:542–548.
79. Wurtman JJ, Wurtman RJ. Fenfluramine and fluoxetine spare protein consumption while suppressing caloric intake by rats. *Science* 1977; 198:1178–1180.
80. Wurtman JJ, Wurtman RJ. Drugs that enhance central serotoninergic transmission diminish elective carbohydrate consumption by rats. *Life Sci* 1979; 24:895–903.
81. Heisler LK, Kanarek RB, Gerstein A. Fluoxetine decreases fat and protein intakes but not carbohydrate intake in male rats. *Pharmacol Biochem Behav* 1997; 58:767–773.
82. Heisler LK, Kanarek RB, Homoleski B. Reduction of fat and protein intakes but not carbohydrate intake following acute and chronic fluoxetine in female rats. *Pharmacol Biochem Behav* 1999; 63:377–385.
83. Fantino M. Role of sensory input in the control of food intake. *J Auton Nerv Syst* 1984; 10:347–358.
84. Smith GP. The physiology of the meal. In: Silverstone T, ed. *Drugs and Appetite.* London: Academic Press; 1982.
85. Wise RA, Raptis L. Effects of pre-feeding on food-approach latency and food consumption speed in food deprived rats. *Physiol Behav* 1985; 35:961–963.
86. Naranjo CA, Sellers EM. Serotonin uptake inhibitors attenuate ethanol intake in problem drinkers. *Recent Dev Alcohol* 1989; 7:255–266.

87. Naranjo CA, Sellers EM, Roach CA, Woodley DV, Sanchez-Craig M, Sykora K. Zimelidine-induced variations in alcohol intake by nondepressed heavy drinkers. *Clin Pharmacol Ther* 1984; 35:374–381.
88. Naranjo CA, Sellers EM, Sullivan JT, Woodley DV, Kadlec K, Sykora K. The serotonin uptake inhibitor citalopram attenuates ethanol intake. *Clin Pharmacol Ther* 1987; 41:266–274.
89. Naranjo CA, Kadlec KE, Sanhueza P, Woodley-Remus D, Sellers EM. Fluoxetine differentially alters alcohol intake and other consummatory behaviors in problem drinkers. *Clin Pharmacol Ther* 1990; 47:490–498.
90. Naranjo CA, Poulos CX, Bremner KE, Lanctot KL. Citalopram decreases desirability, liking, and consumption of alcohol in alcohol-dependent drinkers. *Clin Pharmacol Ther* 1992; 51:729–739.
91. Gorelick DA, Paredes A. Effect of fluoxetine on alcohol consumption in male alcoholics. *Alcohol Clin Exp Res* 1992; 16:261–265.
92. Naranjo CA, Bremner KE, Lanctot KL. Effects of citalopram and a brief psycho-social intervention on alcohol intake, dependence and problems. *Addiction* 1995; 90:87–99.
93. Kabel DI, Petty F. A placebo-controlled, double-blind study of fluoxetine in severe alcohol dependence: Adjunctive pharmacotherapy during and after inpatient treatment. *Alcohol Clin Exp Res* 1996; 20:780–784.
94. Kranzler HR, Burleson JA, Korner P *et al.* Placebo-controlled trial of fluoxetine as an adjunct to relapse prevention in alcoholics. *Am J Psychiatry* 1995; 152:391–397.
95. Johnson BA. Serotonergic agents and alcoholism treatment: Rebirth of the subtype concept—an hypothesis. *Alcohol Clin Exp Res* 2000; 24:1597–1601.
96. Cloninger CR. Neurogenetic adaptive mechanisms in alcoholism. *Science* 1987; 236:410–416.
97. Pettinati HM, Volpicelli JR, Kranzler HR, Luck G, Rukstalis MR, Cnaan A. Sertraline treatment for alcohol dependence: Interactive effects of medication and alcoholic subtype. *Alcohol Clin Exp Res* 2000; 24:1041–1049.
98. Dundon W, Lynch KG, Pettinati HM, Lipkin C. Treatment outcomes in type A and B alcohol dependence 6 months after serotonergic pharmacotherapy. *Alcohol Clin Exp Res* 2004; 28:1065–1073.
99. Chick J, Aschauer H, Hornik K, Investigators' Group. Efficacy of fluvoxamine in preventing relapse in alcohol dependence: A one-year, double-blind, placebo-controlled multicentre study with analysis by typology. *Drug Alcohol Depend* 2004; 74:61–70.
100. Cornelius JR, Salloum IM, Ehler JG *et al.* Fluoxetine in depressed alcoholics: A double-blind, placebo-controlled trial. *Arch Gen Psychiatry* 1997; 54:700–705.
101. Kranzler HR, Mueller T, Cornelius J *et al.* Sertraline treatment of co-occurring alcohol dependence and major depression. *J Clin Psychopharmacol* 2006; 26:13–20.
102. Moak DH, Anton RF, Latham PK, Voronin KE, Waid RL, Durazo-Arvizu R. Sertraline and cognitive behavioral therapy for depressed alcoholics: Results of a placebo-controlled trial. *J Clin Psychopharmacol* 2003; 23:553–562.
103. Mason BJ, Kocsis JH, Ritvo EC, Cutler RB. A double-blind, placebo-controlled trial of desipramine for primary alcohol dependence stratified on the presence or absence of major depression. *JAMA* 1996; 275:761–767.
104. McGrath PJ, Nunes EV, Stewart JW *et al.* Imipramine treatment of alcoholics with primary depression: A placebo-controlled clinical trial. *Arch Gen Psychiatry* 1996; 53:232–240.
105. Pettinati HM, Oslin DW, Kampman KM *et al.* A double-blind, placebo-controlled trial combining sertraline and naltrexone for treating co-occurring depression and alcohol dependence. *Am J Psychiatry* 2010; 167:668–675.

106. Cornelius JR, Bukstein OG, Wood DS, Kirisci L, Douaihy A, Clark DB. Double-blind placebo-controlled trial of fluoxetine in adolescents with comorbid major depression and an alcohol use disorder. *Addict Behav* 2009; 34:905–909.

107. Brady KT, Sonne S, Anton RF, Randall CL, Back SE, Simpson K. Sertraline in the treatment of co-occurring alcohol dependence and posttraumatic stress disorder. *Alcohol Clin Exp Res* 2005; 29:395–401.

108. Randall CL, Johnson MR, Thevos AK *et al.* Paroxetine for social anxiety and alcohol use in dual-diagnosed patients. *Depress Anxiety* 2001; 14:255–262.

109. Brady KT. Evidence-based pharmacotherapy for mood and anxiety disorders with concurrent alcoholism. *CNS Spectr* 2008; 13:7–9.

110. Collins DM, Myers RD. Buspirone attenuates volitional alcohol intake in the chronically drinking monkey. *Alcohol* 1987; 4:49–56.

111. Blier P, de Montigny C. Modification of 5-HT neuron properties by sustained administration of the 5-HT$_{1A}$ agonist gepirone: Electrophysiological studies in the rat brain. *Synapse* 1987; 1:470–480.

112. Bruno F. Buspirone in the treatment of alcoholic patients. *Psychopathology* 1989; 22:49–59.

113. Malec TS, Malec EA, Dongier M. Efficacy of buspirone in alcohol dependence: A review. *Alcohol Clin Exp Res* 1996; 20:853–858.

114. Meert TF, Awouters F, Niemegeers CJ, Schellekens KH, Janssen PA. Ritanserin reduces abuse of alcohol, cocaine, and fentanyl in rats. *Pharmacopsychiatry* 1991; 24:159–163.

115. Myers RD, Lankford M, Bjork A. Selective reduction by the 5-HT antagonist amperozide of alcohol preference induced in rats by systemic cyanamide. *Pharmacol Biochem Behav* 1992; 43:661–667.

116. Svensson L, Fahlke C, Hard E, Engel JA. Involvement of the serotonergic system in ethanol intake in the rat. *Alcohol* 1993; 10:219–224.

117. Biggs TA, Myers RD. Naltrexone and amperozide modify chocolate and saccharin drinking in high alcohol-preferring P rats. *Pharmacol Biochem Behav* 1998; 60:407–413.

118. Myers RD, Lankford M. Action of the 5-HT$_{2A}$ antagonist amperozide on alcohol-induced poikilothermia in rats. *Pharmacol Biochem Behav* 1998; 59:91–95.

119. Myers RD, Lankford MF. Suppression of alcohol preference in high alcohol drinking rats: Efficacy of amperozide versus naltrexone. *Neuropsychopharmacology* 1996; 14:139–149.

120. Overstreet DH, McArthur RA, Rezvani AH, Post C. Selective inhibition of alcohol intake in diverse alcohol-preferring rat strains by the 5-HT$_{2A}$ antagonists amperozide and FG 5974. *Alcohol Clin Exp Res* 1997; 21:1448–1454.

121. Lankford MF, Bjork AK, Myers RD. Differential efficacy of serotonergic drugs FG5974, FG5893, and amperozide in reducing alcohol drinking in P rats. *Alcohol* 1996; 13:399–404.

122. Roberts AJ, McArthur RA, Hull EE, Post C, Koob GF. Effects of amperozide, 8-OH-DPAT, and FG 5974 on operant responding for ethanol. *Psychopharmacology* 1998; 137:25–32.

123. Ugedo L, Grenhoff J, Svensson TH. Ritanserin, a 5-HT$_2$ receptor antagonist, activates midbrain dopamine neurons by blocking serotonergic inhibition. *Psychopharmacology* 1989; 98:45–50.

124. Johnson BA, Jasinski DR, Galloway GP *et al.* Ritanserin in the treatment of alcohol dependence—a multi-center clinical trial. *Psychopharmacology* 1996; 128:206–215.

125. Wiesbeck GA, Weijers HG, Chick J, Naranjo CA, Boening J. Ritanserin in relapse prevention in abstinent alcoholics: Results from a placebo-controlled double-blind international multicenter trial. Ritanserin in Alcoholism Work Group. *Alcohol Clin Exp Res* 1999; 23:230–235.

126. Gianoulakis C. Alcohol-seeking behavior. The roles of the hypothalamic–pituitary–adrenal axis and the endogenous opioid system. *Alcohol Health Res World* 1998; 22:202–210.

127. Gysling K, Wang RY. Morphine-induced activation of A10 dopamine neurons in the rat. *Brain Res* 1983; 277:119–127.

128. Johnson BA, Ait-Daoud N. Neuropharmacological treatments for alcoholism: Scientific basis and clinical findings. *Psychopharmacology* 2000; 149:327–344.

129. Johnson SW, North RA. Opioids excite dopamine neurons by hyperpolarization of local interneurons. *J Neurosci* 1992; 12:483–488.

130. Lee YK, Park SW, Kim YK *et al.* Effects of naltrexone on the ethanol-induced changes in the rat central dopaminergic system. *Alcohol Alcohol* 2005; 40:297–301.

131. Matthews RT, German DC. Electrophysiological evidence for excitation of rat ventral tegmental area dopamine neurons by morphine. *Neuroscience* 1984; 11:617–625.

132. Krystal JH, Madonick S, Perry E *et al.* Potentiation of low dose ketamine effects by naltrexone: Potential implications for the pharmacotherapy of alcoholism. *Neuropsychopharmacology* 2006; 31:1793–1800.

133. Foster KL, McKay PF, Seyoum R *et al.* GABA(A) and opioid receptors of the central nucleus of the amygdala selectively regulate ethanol-maintained behaviors. *Neuropsychopharmacology* 2004; 29:269–284.

134. Matsuzawa S, Suzuki T, Misawa M, Nagase H. Roles of 5-HT$_3$ and opioid receptors in the ethanol-induced place preference in rats exposed to conditioned fear stress. *Life Sci* 1999; 64:PL241–PL249.

135. Manzanares J, Ortiz S, Oliva JM, Perez-Rial S, Palomo T. Interactions between cannabinoid and opioid receptor systems in the mediation of ethanol effects. *Alcohol Alcohol* 2005; 40:25–34.

136. Resch GE, Shridharani S, Millington WR, Garris DR, Simpson CW. Glycyl-glutamine in nucleus accumbens reduces ethanol intake in alcohol preferring (P) rats. *Brain Res* 2005; 1058:73–81.

137. Raynor K, Kong H, Chen Y *et al.* Pharmacological characterization of the cloned kappa-, delta-, and mu-opioid receptors. *Mol Pharmacol* 1994; 45:330–334.

138. Roberts AJ, McDonald JS, Heyser CJ *et al.* Mu-opioid receptor knockout mice do not self-administer alcohol. *J Pharmacol Exp Ther* 2000; 293:1002–1008.

139. Marinelli PW, Quirion R, Gianoulakis C. A microdialysis profile of beta-endorphin and catecholamines in the rat nucleus accumbens following alcohol administration. *Psychopharmacology* 2003; 169:60–67.

140. Marinelli PW, Quirion R, Gianoulakis C. An in vivo profile of beta-endorphin release in the arcuate nucleus and nucleus accumbens following exposure to stress or alcohol. *Neuroscience* 2004; 127:777–784.

141. Olive MF, Koenig HN, Nannini MA, Hodge CW. Stimulation of endorphin neurotransmission in the nucleus accumbens by ethanol, cocaine, and amphetamine. *J Neurosci* 2001; 21: RC184; 1–5.

142. Załewska-Kaszubska J, Gorska D, Dyr W, Czarnecka E. Effect of acute administration of ethanol on beta-endorphin plasma level in ethanol preferring and non-preferring rats chronically treated with naltrexone. *Pharmacol Biochem Behav* 2006; 85:155–159.

143. Altshuler HL, Phillips PE, Feinhandler DA. Alteration of ethanol self-administration by naltrexone. *Life Sci* 1980; 26:679–688.

144. DeWitte P. Naloxone reduces alcohol intake in a free-choice procedure even when both drinking bottles contain saccharin sodium or quinine substances. *Neuropsychobiology* 1984; 12:73–77.

145. Froehlich JC, Harts J, Lumeng L, Li TK. Naloxone attenuation of voluntary alcohol consumption. *Alcohol Alcohol* 1987; Suppl 1: 333–337.

146. Froehlich JC, Harts J, Lumeng L, Li TK. Naloxone attenuates voluntary ethanol intake in rats selectively bred for high ethanol preference. *Pharmacol Biochem Behav* 1990; 35:385–390.
147. Froehlich JC, Zweifel M, Harts J, Lumeng L, Li TK. Importance of delta opioid receptors in maintaining high alcohol drinking. *Psychopharmacology* 1991; 103:467–472.
148. Heyser CJ, Moc K, Koob GF. Effects of naltrexone alone and in combination with acamprosate on the alcohol deprivation effect in rats. *Neuropsychopharmacology* 2003; 28:1463–1471.
149. Kamdar NK, Miller SA, Syed YM, Bhayana R, Gupta T, Rhodes JS. Acute effects of naltrexone and GBR 12909 on ethanol drinking-in-the-dark in C57BL/6J mice. *Psychopharmacology* 2007; 192:207–217.
150. Le AD, Poulos CX, Quan B, Chou S. The effects of selective blockade of delta and mu opiate receptors on ethanol consumption by C57B1/6 mice in a restricted access paradigm. *Brain Res* 1993; 630:330–332.
151. Samson HH, Doyle TF. Oral ethanol self-administration in the rat: Effect of naloxone. *Pharmacol Biochem Behav* 1985; 22:91–99.
152. van Ree JM, Kornet M, Goosen C. Neuropeptides and alcohol addiction in monkeys. *EXS* 1994; 71:165–174.
153. Volpicelli JR, Davis MA, Olgin JE. Naltrexone blocks the post-shock increase of ethanol consumption. *Life Sci* 1986; 38:841–847.
154. Berman RF, Lee JA, Olson KL, Goldman MS. Effects of naloxone on ethanol dependence in rats. *Drug Alcohol Depend* 1984; 13:245–254.
155. Juarez J, Eliana Bde T. Alcohol consumption is enhanced after naltrexone treatment. *Alcohol Clin Exp Res* 2007; 31:260–264.
156. Ross D, Hartmann RJ, Geller I. Ethanol preference in the hamster: Effects of morphine sulfate and naltrexone, a long-acting morphine antagonist. *Proc West Pharmacol Soc* 1976; 19:326–330.
157. Kiefer F, Jahn H, Schick M, Wiedemann K. Alcohol self-administration, craving and HPA-axis activity: An intriguing relationship. *Psychopharmacology* 2002; 164:239–240.
158. Williams KL, Broadbear JH, Woods JH. Noncontingent and response-contingent intravenous ethanol attenuates the effect of naltrexone on hypothalamic–pituitary–adrenal activity in rhesus monkeys. *Alcohol Clin Exp Res* 2004; 28:566–571.
159. O'Malley SS, Jaffe AJ, Chang G, Schottenfeld RS, Meyer RE, Rounsaville B. Naltrexone and coping skills therapy for alcohol dependence: A controlled study. *Arch Gen Psychiatry* 1992; 49:881–887.
160. Volpicelli JR, Alterman AI, Hayashida M, O'Brien CP. Naltrexone in the treatment of alcohol dependence. *Arch Gen Psychiatry* 1992; 49:876–880.
161. Jaffe AJ, Rounsaville B, Chang G, Schottenfeld RS, Meyer RE, O'Malley SS. Naltrexone, relapse prevention, and supportive therapy with alcoholics: An analysis of patient treatment matching. *J Consult Clin Psychol* 1996; 64:1044–1053.
162. O'Malley SS, Jaffe AJ, Rode S, Rounsaville BJ. Experience of a "slip" among alcoholics treated with naltrexone or placebo. *Am J Psychiatry* 1996; 153:281–283.
163. Volpicelli JR, Watson NT, King AC, Sherman CE, O'Brien CP. Effect of naltrexone on alcohol "high" in alcoholics. *Am J Psychiatry* 1995; 152:613–615.
164. Bouza C, Angeles M, Munoz A, Amate JM. Efficacy and safety of naltrexone and acamprosate in the treatment of alcohol dependence: A systematic review. *Addiction* 2004; 99:811–828.
165. Srisurapanont M, Jarusuraisin N. Opioid antagonists for alcohol dependence. *Cochrane Database Syst Rev* 2005; 1:CD001867.
166. Volpicelli JR, Rhines KC, Rhines JS, Volpicelli LA, Alterman AI, O'Brien CP. Naltrexone and alcohol dependence: Role of subject compliance. *Arch Gen Psychiatry* 1997; 54:737–742.

167. Litten RZ, Allen JP. Advances in development of medications for alcoholism treatment. *Psychopharmacology* 1998; 139:20–33.
168. Litten RZ, Fertig J. International update: New findings on promising medications. *Alcohol Clin Exp Res* 1996; 20:216A–218A.
169. Croop RS, Faulkner EB, Labriola DF. The safety profile of naltrexone in the treatment of alcoholism. Results from a multicenter usage study. The Naltrexone Usage Study Group. *Arch Gen Psychiatry* 1997; 54:1130–1135.
170. Oslin DW, Berrettini W, Kranzler HR *et al.* A functional polymorphism of the mu-opioid receptor gene is associated with naltrexone response in alcohol-dependent patients. *Neuropsychopharmacology* 2003; 28:1546–1552.
171. McGeary JE, Monti PM, Rohsenow DJ, Tidey J, Swift R, Miranda RJ. Genetic moderators of naltrexone's effects on alcohol cue reactivity. *Alcohol Clin Exp Res* 2006; 30:1288–1296.
172. Gelernter J, Gueorguieva R, Kranzler HR *et al.* Opioid receptor gene (OPRM1, OPRK1, and OPRD1) variants and response to naltrexone treatment for alcohol dependence: Results from the VA Cooperative Study. *Alcohol Clin Exp Res* 2007; 31:555–563.
173. Bond C, LaForge KS, Tian M *et al.* Single-nucleotide polymorphism in the human mu opioid receptor gene alters beta-endorphin binding and activity: Possible implications for opiate addiction. *Proc Natl Acad Sci USA* 1998; 95:9608–9613.
174. Befort K, Filliol D, Décaillot FM, Gavériaux-Ruff C, Hoehe MR, Kieffer BL. A single nucleotide polymorphic mutation in the human mu-opioid receptor severely impairs receptor signaling. *J Biol Chem* 2001; 276:3130–3137.
175. Beyer A, Koch T, Schröder H, Schulz S, Höllt V. Effect of the A118G polymorphism on binding affinity, potency and agonist-mediated endocytosis, desensitization, and resensitization of the human mu-opioid receptor. *J Neurochem* 2004; 89:553–560.
176. Zhang Y, Wang D, Johnson AD, Papp AC, Sadée W. Allelic expression imbalance of human mu opioid receptor (OPRM1) caused by variant A118G. *J Biol Chem* 2005; 280:32618–32624.
177. Zhang H, Luo X, Kranzler HR *et al.* Association between two mu-opioid receptor gene (OPRM1) haplotype blocks and drug or alcohol dependence. *Hum Mol Genet* 2006; 15:807–819.
178. Gelernter J, Kranzler H, Cubells J. Genetics of two mu opioid receptor gene (OPRM1) exon I polymorphisms: Population studies, and allele frequencies in alcohol- and drug-dependent subjects. *Mol Psychiatry* 1999; 4:476–483.
179. King AC, Schluger J, Gunduz M *et al.* Hypothalamic–pituitary–adrenocortical (HPA) axis response and biotransformation of oral naltrexone: Preliminary examination of relationship to family history of alcoholism. *Neuropsychopharmacology* 2002; 26:778–788.
180. Monterosso JR, Flannery BA, Pettinati HM *et al.* Predicting treatment response to naltrexone: The influence of craving and family history. *Am J Addict* 2001; 10:258–268.
181. Leeman RF, Palmer RS, Corbin WR, Romano DM, Meandzija B, O'Malley SS. A pilot study of naltrexone and BASICS for heavy drinking young adults. *Addict Behav* 2008; 33:1048–1054.
182. Sherwood Brown E, Carmody TJ, Schmitz JM *et al.* A randomized, double-blind, placebo-controlled pilot study of naltrexone in outpatients with bipolar disorder and alcohol dependence. *Alcohol Clin Exp Res* 2009; 33:1863–1869.
183. Schmitz JM, Averill P, Sayre S, McCleary P, Moeller FG, Swann A. Cognitive–behavioral treatment of bipolar disorder and substance abuse: A preliminary randomized study. *Addict Disord Their Treat* 2002; 1:17–24.
184. King A, Cao D, Vanier C, Wilcox T. Naltrexone decreases heavy drinking rates in smoking cessation treatment: An exploratory study. *Alcohol Clin Exp Res* 2009; 33:1044–1050.

185. Johnson BA, Ait-Daoud N, Aubin H-J *et al.* A pilot evaluation of the safety and tolerability of repeat dose administration of long-acting injectable naltrexone (Vivitrex®) in patients with alcohol dependence. *Alcohol Clin Exp Res* 2004; 28:1356–1361.

186. Garbutt JC, Kranzler HR, O'Malley SS *et al.* Efficacy and tolerability of long-acting injectable naltrexone for alcohol dependence: A randomized controlled trial. *JAMA* 2005; 293:1617–1625.

187. Harris BR, Prendergast MA, Gibson DA *et al.* Acamprosate inhibits the binding and neurotoxic effects of trans-ACPD, suggesting a novel site of action at metabotropic glutamate receptors. *Alcohol Clin Exp Res* 2002; 26:1779–1793.

188. Boismare F, Daoust M, Moore N *et al.* A homotaurine derivative reduces the voluntary intake of ethanol by rats: Are cerebral GABA receptors involved? *Pharmacol Biochem Behav* 1984; 21:787–789.

189. Czachowski CL, Legg BH, Samson HH. Effects of acamprosate on ethanol-seeking and self-administration in the rat. *Alcohol Clin Exp Res* 2001; 25:344–350.

190. Le Magnen J, Tran G, Durlach J. Lack of effects of Ca-acetyl homotaurine on chronic and acute toxicities of ethanol in rats. *Alcohol* 1987; 4:103–108.

191. Escher T, Mittleman G. Schedule-induced alcohol drinking: Non-selective effects of acamprosate and naltrexone. *Addict Biol* 2006; 11:55–63.

192. Dahchour A, De Witte P, Bolo N *et al.* Central effects of acamprosate. Part 1. Acamprosate blocks the glutamate increase in the nucleus accumbens microdialysate in ethanol withdrawn rats. *Psychiatry Res* 1998; 82:107–114.

193. Rossetti ZL, Carboni S. Ethanol withdrawal is associated with increased extracellular glutamate in the rat striatum. *Eur J Pharmacol* 1995; 283:177–183.

194. Gewiss M, Heidbreder C, Opsomer L, Durbin P, De Witte P. Acamprosate and diazepam differentially modulate alcohol-induced behavioural and cortical alterations in rats following chronic inhalation of ethanol vapour. *Alcohol Alcohol* 1991; 26:129–137.

195. Spanagel R, Putzke J, Stefferl A, Schobitz B, Zieglgansberger W. Acamprosate and alcohol. II. Effects on alcohol withdrawal in the rat. *Eur J Pharmacol* 1996; 305:45–50.

196. Bolo N, Nedelec JF, Muzet M *et al.* Central effects of acamprosate. Part 2. Acamprosate modifies the brain in-vivo proton magnetic resonance spectrum in healthy young male volunteers. *Psychiatry Res* 1998; 82:115–127.

197. Littleton J. Acamprosate in alcohol dependence: How does it work? *Addiction* 1995; 90:1179–1188.

198. Putzke J, Spanagel R, Tolle TR, Zieglgansberger W. The anti-craving drug acamprosate reduces c-fos expression in rats undergoing ethanol withdrawal. *Eur J Pharmacol* 1996; 317:39–48.

199. Krystal JH, Petrakis IL, Krupitsky E, Schutz C, Trevisan L, D'Souza DC. NMDA receptor antagonism and the ethanol intoxication signal: From alcoholism risk to pharmacotherapy. *Ann NY Acad Sci* 2003; 1003:176–184.

200. Sinclair JD, Li TK. Long and short alcohol deprivation: Effects on AA and P alcohol-preferring rats. *Alcohol* 1989; 6:505–509.

201. Spanagel R, Herz A, Shippenberg TS. Opposing tonically active endogenous opioid systems modulate the mesolimbic dopaminergic pathway. *Proc Natl Acad Sci USA* 1992; 89:2046–2050.

202. Spanagel R, Holter SM, Allingham K, Landgraf R, Zieglgansberger W. Acamprosate and alcohol. I. Effects on alcohol intake following alcohol deprivation in the rat. *Eur J Pharmacol* 1996; 305:39–44.

203. Wolffgramm J, Heyne A. From controlled drug intake to loss of control: The irreversible development of drug addiction in the rat. *Behav Brain Res* 1995; 70:77–94.
204. Spanagel R, Zieglgansberger W. Anti-craving compounds for ethanol: New pharmacological tools to study addictive processes. *Trends Pharmacol Sci* 1997; 18:54–59.
205. Johnson BA. Update on neuropharmacological treatments for alcoholism: Scientific basis and clinical findings. *Biochem Pharmacol* 2008; 75:34–56.
206. Mann K, Lehert P, Morgan MY. The efficacy of acamprosate in the maintenance of abstinence in alcohol-dependent individuals: Results of a meta-analysis. *Alcohol Clin Exp Res* 2004; 28:51–63.
207. Kranzler HR, Van Kirk J. Efficacy of naltrexone and acamprosate for alcoholism treatment: A meta-analysis. *Alcohol Clin Exp Res* 2001; 25:1335–1341.
208. Chick J, Lehert P, Landron F, Plinius Maior Society. Does acamprosate improve reduction of drinking as well as aiding abstinence? *J Psychopharmacol* 2003; 17:397–402.
209. Mason BJ, Goodman AM, Chabac S, Lehert P. Effect of oral acamprosate on abstinence in patients with alcohol dependence in a double-blind, placebo-controlled trial: The role of patient motivation. *J Psychiatr Res* 2006; 40:383–393.
210. Verheul R, Lehert P, Geerlings PJ, Koeter MW, van den Brink W. Predictors of acamprosate efficacy: Results from a pooled analysis of seven European trials including 1485 alcohol-dependent patients. *Psychopharmacology* 2005; 178:167–173.
211. Niederhofer H, Staffen W. Acamprosate and its efficacy in treating alcohol dependent adolescents. *Eur Child Adolesc Psychiatry* 2003; 12:144–148.
212. Mann KF, Anton RF (Organizers/Chairs). Towards an individualized treatment in alcohol dependence: Results from the US-COMBINE Study and German PREDICT Study—in honor of past work of Dr. Jack Mendelson. Symposium presented at the 2008 Joint Scientific Meeting of the Research Society on Alcoholism and the International Society for Biomedical Research on Alcoholism, June 29, 2008, Washington, DC. *Alcohol Clin Exp Res* 2008; 32(s1):281A.
213. Gibbs JW, Sombati S, DeLorenzo RJ, Coulter DA. Cellular actions of topiramate: Blockade of kainate-evoked inward currents in cultured hippocampal neurons. *Epilepsia* 2000; 41(Suppl. 1):S10–S16.
214. Gryder DS, Rogawski MA. Selective antagonism of GluR5 kainate-receptor-mediated synaptic currents by topiramate in rat basolateral amygdala neurons. *J Neurosci* 2003; 23:7069–7074.
215. Skradski S, White HS. Topiramate blocks kainate-evoked cobalt influx into cultured neurons. *Epilepsia* 2000; 41(Suppl. 1):S45–S47.
216. White HS, Brown SD, Woodhead JH, Skeen GA, Wolf HH. Topiramate enhances GABA-mediated chloride flux and GABA-evoked chloride currents in murine brain neurons and increases seizure threshold. *Epilepsy Res* 1997; 28:167–179.
217. White HS, Brown SD, Woodhead JH, Skeen GA, Wolf HH. Topiramate modulates GABA-evoked currents in murine cortical neurons by a nonbenzodiazepine mechanism. *Epilepsia* 2000; 41(Suppl. 1):S17–S20.
218. Zhang X, Velumian AA, Jones OT, Carlen PL. Modulation of high-voltage-activated calcium channels in dentate granule cells by topiramate. *Epilepsia* 2000; 41(Suppl. 1):S52–S60.
219. Taverna S, Sancini G, Mantegazza M, Franceschetti S, Avanzini G. Inhibition of transient and persistent Na+ current fractions by the new anticonvulsant topiramate. *J Pharmacol Exp Ther* 1999; 288:960–968.
220. Herrero AI, Del Olmo N, Gonzalez-Escalada JR, Solis JM. Two new actions of topiramate: Inhibition of depolarizing GABA(A)-mediated responses and activation of a potassium conductance. *Neuropharmacology* 2002; 42:210–220.

221. Dodgson SJ, Shank RP, Maryanoff BE. Topiramate as an inhibitor of carbonic anhydrase isoenzymes. *Epilepsia* 2000; 41:S35–S39.
222. Shank RP, Gardocki JF, Streeter AJ, Maryanoff BE. An overview of the preclinical aspects of topiramate: Pharmacology, pharmacokinetics, and mechanism of action. *Epilepsia* 2000; 41(Suppl. 1):S3–S9.
223. Johnson BA. Progress in the development of topiramate for treating alcohol dependence: From a hypothesis to a proof-of-concept study. *Alcohol Clin Exp Res* 2004; 28:1137–1144.
224. Johnson BA. Recent advances in the development of treatments for alcohol and cocaine dependence: Focus on topiramate and other modulators of GABA or glutamate function. *CNS Drugs* 2005; 19:873–896.
225. Gabriel KI, Cunningham CL. Effects of topiramate on ethanol and saccharin consumption and preferences in C57BL/6J mice. *Alcohol Clin Exp Res* 2005; 29:75–80.
226. Nguyen SA, Malcolm R, Middaugh LD. Topiramate reduces ethanol consumption by C57BL/6 mice. *Synapse* 2007; 61:150–156.
227. Breslin FJ, Johnson BA, Lynch WJ. Effect of topiramate treatment on ethanol consumption in rats. *Psychopharmacology* 2010; 207:529–534.
228. Farook JM, Morrell DJ, Lewis B, Littleton JM, Barron S. Topiramate (Topamax) reduces conditioned abstinence behaviours and handling-induced convulsions (HIC) after chronic administration of alcohol in Swiss-Webster mice. *Alcohol Alcohol* 2007; 42:296–300.
229. Johnson BA, Mann K, Willenbring ML *et al.* Challenges and opportunities for medications development in alcoholism: An international perspective on collaborations between academia and industry. *Alcohol Clin Exp Res* 2005; 29:1528–1540.
230. Johnson BA, Ait-Daoud N, Bowden CL *et al.* Oral topiramate for treatment of alcohol dependence: A randomised controlled trial. *Lancet* 2003; 361:1677–1685.
231. Johnson BA, Ait-Daoud N, Akhtar FZ, Ma JZ. Oral topiramate reduces the consequences of drinking and improves the quality of life of alcohol-dependent individuals. *Arch Gen Psychiatry* 2004; 61:905–912.
232. Ma JZ, Ait-Daoud N, Johnson BA. Topiramate reduces the harm of excessive drinking: Implications for public health and primary care. *Addiction* 2006; 101:1561–1568.
233. Johnson BA, DiClemente CC, Ait-Daoud N, Stoks SM. Brief Behavioral Compliance Enhancement Treatment (BBCET) manual. In: Johnson BA, Ruiz P, Galanter M, eds. *Handbook of Clinical Alcoholism Treatment*. Baltimore, MD: Lippincott Williams & Wilkins; 2003, pp. 282–301.
234. Conigrave KM, Degenhardt LJ, Whitfield JB *et al.* CDT, GGT, and AST as markers of alcohol use: The WHO/ISBRA collaborative project. *Alcohol Clin Exp Res* 2002; 26:332–339.
235. Miranda R, Monti P, Swift R *et al.* Effects of topiramate on alcohol cue reactivity and the subjective effects of drinking. Poster presentation at the 45th Annual Meeting of the American College of Neuropsychopharmacology, Hollywood, FL, December 6, 2006.
236. Johnson BA, Rosenthal N, Capece JA *et al.* Topiramate for treating alcohol dependence: A randomized controlled trial. *JAMA* 2007; 298:1641–1651.
237. Johnson BA, Rosenthal N, Capece JA *et al.* Improvement of physical health and quality of life of alcohol-dependent individuals with topiramate treatment. *Arch Intern Med* 2008; 168:1188–1199.
238. Johnson BA, Rosenthal N, Capece JA *et al.* Topiramate for the treatment of alcohol dependence: Results of a multi-site trial. New Research poster presentation at the 160th Annual Meeting of the American Psychiatric Association, San Diego, CA, May 22, 2007.
239. Biton V, Edwards KR, Montouris GD *et al.* Topiramate titration and tolerability. *Ann Pharmacother* 2001; 35:173–179.

240. Vasudev K, Macritchie K, Geddes J, Watson S, Young A. Topiramate for acute affective episodes in bipolar disorder. *Cochrane Database Syst Rev* 2006; 1:CD003384.
241. Salloum IM, Cornelius JR, Daley DC, Kirisci L, Himmelhoch JM, Thase ME. Efficacy of valproate maintenance in patients with bipolar disorder and alcoholism: A double-blind placebo-controlled study. *Arch Gen Psychiatry* 2005; 62:37–45.
242. Johnson BA, Ait-Daoud N, Akhtar FZ, Javors MA. Use of oral topiramate to promote smoking abstinence among alcohol-dependent smokers: A randomized controlled trial. *Arch Intern Med* 2005; 165:1600–1605.
243. Colombo G, Agabio R, Carai MA *et al.* Ability of baclofen in reducing alcohol intake and withdrawal severity. I. Preclinical evidence. *Alcohol Clin Exp Res* 2000; 24:58–66.
244. Colombo G, Serra S, Brunetti G, Vacca G, Carai MA, Gessa GL. Suppression by baclofen of alcohol deprivation effect in Sardinian alcohol-preferring (sP) rats. *Drug Alcohol Depend* 2003; 70:105–108.
245. Quintanilla ME, Perez E, Tampier L. Baclofen reduces ethanol intake in high-alcohol-drinking University of Chile bibulous rats. *Addict Biol* 2008; 13:326–336.
246. Colombo G, Serra S, Vacca G, Gessa GL, Carai MA. Suppression by baclofen of the stimulation of alcohol intake induced by morphine and WIN 55,212-2 in alcohol-preferring rats. *Eur J Pharmacol* 2004; 492:189–193.
247. Addolorato G, Caputo F, Capristo E, Colombo G, Gessa GL, Gasbarrini G. Ability of baclofen in reducing alcohol craving and intake. II. Preliminary clinical evidence. *Alcohol Clin Exp Res* 2000; 24:67–71.
248. Addolorato G, Caputo F, Capristo E *et al.* Baclofen efficacy in reducing alcohol craving and intake: A preliminary double-blind randomized controlled study. *Alcohol Alcohol* 2002; 37:504–508.
249. Addolorato G, Leggio L, Ferrulli A *et al.* Effectiveness and safety of baclofen for maintenance of alcohol abstinence in alcohol-dependent patients with liver cirrhosis: Randomised, double-blind controlled study. *Lancet* 2007; 370:1915–1922.
250. Ait-Daoud N, Johnson BA. Medications for the treatment of alcoholism. In: Johnson BA, Ruiz P, Galanter M, eds. *Handbook of Clinical Alcoholism Treatment*. Baltimore, MD: Lippincott Williams & Wilkins; 2003, pp. 119–130.
251. Anton RF. Pharmacologic approaches to the management of alcoholism. *J Clin Psychiatry* 2001; 62:11–17.
252. Niederhofer H, Staffen W. Comparison of disulfiram and placebo in treatment of alcohol dependence of adolescents. *Drug Alcohol Rev* 2003; 22:295–297.
253. De Sousa A, De Sousa A. An open randomized trial comparing disulfiram and naltrexone in adolescents with alcohol dependence. *J Subst Use* 2008; 13:382–388.

Chapter 17

Alcoholics Anonymous and young people

John F. Kelly and Julie D. Yeterian
Center for Addiction Medicine, Massachusetts General Hospital, Harvard Medical School,
Boston, MA, USA

Key points

- Alcoholics Anonymous (AA) is a free and widely available peer-led, community resource shown to be helpful to individuals with alcohol use disorders exhibiting a broad range of alcohol-related involvement and impairment.
- The mostly adult age composition of most meetings means that young people may face additional barriers to engagement with AA due to developmentally related differences in clinical profile and social contexts.
- Young people make up only a small percentage of AA membership, but designated young persons' meetings are available in most communities where teens and young adults may find a concentrated source of support for recovery.
- Young people treated for alcohol and other drug problems have been shown to attend and benefit from participation in 12-step groups in prospective, controlled, observational studies.
- Young people with greater substance involvement and more severe alcohol and other drug related problems appear most likely to attend and benefit from AA; engagement in groups where at least some other young people are present may potentiate engagement and benefit.
- A number of empirically supported clinical strategies to engage alcohol/drug-dependent persons with 12-step groups have been shown to be effective. Although not explicitly tested among youth samples, these methods might be adapted with sensitivity to developmental factors in order to facilitate youth engagement with these free community resources.

Alcohol has been called the world's favorite drug,[1] and Alcoholics Anonymous (AA) may be the world's favorite approach to dealing with addiction to it.[2] Although most societies provide professional services to treat alcohol and other drug use disorders, many countries also rely on peer-led, community-based mutual-help resources, such as AA, to help shoulder the enormous burden of disease attributable to alcohol.[3] Since being founded in Akron, Ohio in 1935, through a conversation between a newly sober

---

Young People and Alcohol: Impact, Policy, Prevention, Treatment, First Edition.
Edited by John B. Saunders and Joseph M. Rey.
© 2011 Blackwell Publishing Ltd. Published 2011 by Blackwell Publishing Ltd.

alcohol-dependent stockbroker (Bill W) and an alcohol-dependent surgeon (Dr Bob S), the organization has grown exponentially, and currently operates through 55,000 weekly group meetings in almost every community in the US and a further 50,000 groups in other countries.[4] AA initially attracted and catered to the most severe and chronic, middle-aged, alcohol-dependent individuals.[4,5] However, with societal changes since the 1930s in the acceptance of, and access to, alcohol and other drugs among youth, as well as greater knowledge and acceptance of alcohol addiction as a disease, AA increasingly began to receive younger referrals and to engage young people in the program, often before the onset of severe health problems and associated disabilities.[5] However, until recently, little was known empirically about how young people utilize or benefit from AA.

In this chapter, we examine the utility and benefits of AA for young people. We begin by describing how some of the life context and clinical differences between young people and their older adult counterparts may serve as barriers to youth engagement with AA. We then review the available empirical evidence regarding which youth are likely to attend AA, how often they attend, the degree to which they appear to benefit, and why. In the last section, we describe some proven clinical strategies that may be adapted and implemented to systematically facilitate youth engagement with community recovery resources such as AA.

Alcohol use in adolescence and young adulthood

In most cultures, there persists an enduring curiosity and fascination with alcohol use that peaks during adolescence and emerging adulthood. For many young people, consumption of this "forbidden (fermented) fruit" marks an implicit gateway to sophistication, pleasure, and maturity. Experimentation with and the subjective experience of alcohol's intoxicating effects typify the ways in which people discover its dose-response effects. However, there is variable sensitivity to alcohol's effects across individuals, which modulates awareness of intoxication and perceived harm, increasing the risk of severe problems for some. In addition, experimentation with alcohol during the teenage years can be hazardous—sometimes fatal—and early consumption is associated with the onset of alcohol use disorders (AUDs), which can have lifelong ramifications.[6] Despite this, alcohol is the most commonly misused substance among young people. Additionally, late adolescence and emerging adulthood are the developmental periods that confer the highest risk for heavy alcohol use, as well as the onset of AUDs. In the US, for example, 17% of young adults (of ages 18–25) meet DSM-IV criteria for an AUD, as compared to 7% of adolescents (of ages 12–17) and 6% of adults aged 26 or older.[7] Unfortunately, for those young people who develop an AUD during this life stage, peer support for abstinence and recovery is often very limited.

Developmentally related clinical differences between young people and adults

Only about 10% of adults and youth who meet criteria for an AUD report receiving treatment in the past year, with the initial treatment episode typically occurring 8–10 years after the onset of the AUD.[8,9] Those youth who do receive treatment for substance use disorders (SUDs) tend to differ in both qualitative and quantitative aspects of substance use behavior and consequences when compared to adults, although there is marked hetero-geneity across this short age span. For example, teenagers in treatment report less frequent substance use, display fewer dependence symptoms, use multiple substances concurrently, and have fewer medical complications and withdrawal symptoms than adults.[10,11] Ado-lescents entering treatment have also been found to differ from adults in their motivation to stop using alcohol and/or drugs, since they rarely enter treatment due to an intrinsic desire to stop using.[12] Instead, youth often have more extrinsic motivations for treatment entry, in that they are usually coerced into treatment, to a lesser or greater degree, as a result of school, legal, or familial/interpersonal problems.[9,13] Adolescents may also face logistical barriers after treatment at a greater frequency than adults, such as a lack of independent financial resources and transportation to access aftercare or 12-step groups.

Beyond their general clinical differences, young people may face specific, develop-mentally related barriers to AA attendance. While AA has meetings that are specifically geared toward young people and beginners of all ages (www.aa.org), as well as online meetings (www.aa-intergroup.org), young people still make up only a small percentage of overall AA membership, with 2.3% of members under age 21 and 11.3% of ages between 21 and 30.[14] Thus, even if teens are willing and able to attend 12-step groups, the adult composition of most groups may provide a barrier to affiliation and continued attendance. One study revealed that teens who attended AA and Narcotics Anonymous (NA) meetings consisting of a substantial proportion of teenagers had significantly better substance use outcomes 3 months posttreatment than those who attended predominantly adult meetings (see Figure 17.1).[15]

Social contexts are particularly influential in helping to establish and maintain the heavy and frequent patterns of alcohol use that can result in the development of an AUD. Youths' social contexts also play a pivotal role in the successful recovery from AUD. Whereas in adults, the precursors to relapse typically involve negative affect (e.g., depression and anger) and interpersonal conflict (e.g., disagreements or quarrels with a partner or caregiver), among adolescents and young adults, the vast majority of relapse occurs in social contexts where alcohol and other drugs are present.[10] Hence, recovery-specific social resources, such as AA, may provide a rare and concentrated group of supportive peers with whom young people can socialize and, thus, lower the influence of this potent relapse risk.[16] In fact, mobilizing changes in social network ties and social activities appears to be one of the major mechanisms through which AA conveys its beneficial effects on sustaining remission and recovery among adults with AUD.[17,18]

In summary, compared to older adults with alcohol-related problems, young people with alcohol and other drug use disorders, on average, present with a less severely addicted clinical profile. This may serve as a barrier to accessing groups such as AA, which focus on complete abstinence, and advocate intensive involvement in the program, especially early in recovery. Also, the older age composition of most AA meetings may mean that young people could find it difficult to relate to topics that may be of little relevance to them, such as employment, marital, or family concerns. On the other hand, given the high rates of alcohol and other drug use among their same-aged peers in the population, AA (particularly young person's meetings) may provide a unique place for young people to find recovery support, friendships, and opportunities to socialize in low-risk ways. Given these pros and cons, we now review what is known about the extent to which young people

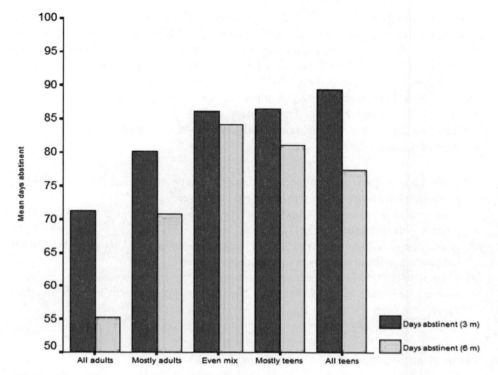

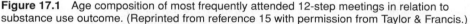

Figure 17.1   Age composition of most frequently attended 12-step meetings in relation to substance use outcome. (Reprinted from reference 15 with permission from Taylor & Francis.)

utilize and benefit from AA, as well as some of the mechanisms through which AA may lead to greater abstinence and recovery rates among young attendees.

Review of the evidence on youth AA participation: benefits and mechanisms

Before presenting the evidence regarding young people's participation in AA, it should be noted that virtually all research in this area to date has been conducted on treated samples, that is, with samples that have been drawn from professional inpatient or outpatient SUD treatment facilities. As it seems that most young people who meet criteria for an AUD do not seek or receive alcohol treatment services of any kind,[9] the young people who do receive treatment, and on whom the vast majority of research on AA involvement has been conducted, may not be representative of the broader population of youth who drink heavily or are dependent on alcohol. Thus, generalizations about the benefits of AA participation for young people who do not also receive professional treatment must be made cautiously.

It should also be noted that the research reported below has typically examined attendance at all types of 12-step meetings (e.g., AA, NA, Cocaine Anonymous (CA)), as opposed to AA alone. Given that all 12-step meetings have the same general format, content, steps, and traditions, this should not pose a problem for interpreting results. However, these studies, except where noted, include young people using all types of substances and who meet criteria for SUDs in general, rather than just those who use mainly alcohol and meet criteria for AUDs only. Thus, this literature review provides a broad overview of participation in 12-step groups by young people exhibiting a broad range of alcohol and other drug-related involvement and impairment.

With these limitations in mind, research regarding young people's involvement in 12-step meetings has shown that:

(a) young people attend 12-step meetings more frequently during and directly following professional treatment, as compared to months or years later;
(b) those treated in inpatient settings seem to attend 12-step meetings at higher rates than those in outpatient settings;
(c) young people with more severe alcohol use profiles are more likely to attend 12-step meetings than those with lower levels of alcohol use;
(d) youth who attend 12-step meetings tend to have better substance use outcomes; and
(e) young people may benefit from AA attendance through different mechanisms than adults (see Table 17.1).

Rates of attendance at 12-step meetings

Two studies of adolescents treated in 12-step-oriented inpatient programs have shown high rates of 12-step meeting attendance immediately following treatment, with declining rates of attendance over time. Kelly, Myers, and Brown[15] found that 72% of adolescent inpatients ($N = 74$) attended at least one 12-step meeting during the first 3 months after discharge, with an average attendance rate of two times per week. During the next 3 months (i.e., 4–6 months postdischarge), the attendance rate dropped to 54%, with average attendance around once per week. In an 8-year follow-up of adolescent inpatients ($N = 166$), rates of 12-step meeting attendance were very high in the first 6 months posttreatment (91% attended at least once, 83% at least monthly, 65% at least weekly), but rates dropped off in the next 6-month period (i.e., 6–12 months posttreatment; 59% attended at least once, 48% at least monthly, 33% at least weekly), and continued to decline steadily across the 8-year follow-up period. By 6–8 years after treatment, only 31% attended at least once, 19% at least monthly, and 6% at least weekly (see Figure 17.2).[16]

In contrast, studies of adolescents treated in outpatient programs have shown lower rates of attendance. For instance, a 3-year follow-up of 357 adolescents in intensive outpatient treatment found that at 1 year postintake, 29% reported having attended *10 or more* 12-step meetings in the past 6 months. At 3 years postintake, this number dropped to 14%, although a total of 19% had gone to at least one 12-step meeting in the prior 6 months.[19] In a 6-month follow-up of 127 adolescents in low intensity outpatient SUD treatment, just over one-quarter of patients (28%) attended at least one 12-step meeting during the 3 months postintake, whereas from 4–6 months postintake, that figure dropped

Table 17.1 Summary of studies of adolescent or young adult 12-step involvement.

Study	N	Age range	Treatment setting	Length of follow-up	Main finding
Alford, Koehler, and Leonard[27]	157	13–19	Inpatient	2 years	84% of those who attended AA/NA regularly were abstinent at 2-year follow-up vs. 31% of those who did not attend AA/NA
Hsieh, Hoffmann, and Hollister[29]	2,317	Adolescent	24 inpatient programs	12 months	AA/NA attendance posttreatment was the most powerful predictor of abstinence at follow-up
Kelly, Myers, and Brown[15]	74	14–18	Inpatient; 12-step model	6 months	Rates of AA attendance were high posttreatment and declined over time Attending meetings with at least some other youth present was associated with greater involvement and better substance use outcomes
Kelly, Brown, Abrantes, Kahler, and Myers[16]	166	13–18	Inpatient; 12-step model	8 years	AA participation consistently predicted abstinence, over and above all other variables related to abstinence
Kelly, Myers, and Rodolico[24]: Two samples	74	14–18	Inpatient	None	Most commonly reported favored aspects of 12-step group participation were a sense of belonging, getting support from others, and gaining hope for recovery
	377	12–21			Common reasons for discontinuing AA were boredom/irrelevance, return to drinking/using, and no perceived need
Chi, Kaskutas, Sterling, Campbell, and Weisner[19]	357	13–18	Intensive outpatient	3 years	12-step participation at 3-year follow-up was associated with abstinence from alcohol and drugs
Kelly, Dow, Yeterian, and Kahler[20]	127	14–19	Low intensity outpatient; cognitive–behavioral	6 month	AA/NA participation predicted abstinence, over and above all other variables related to abstinence
Mason and Luckey[21]	98	18–25	Managed care	None	Compared to older treated adults, young adults attended AA less frequently, were less likely to consider themselves an AA member, and were lower on indices of AA involvement
Delucchi, Matzger, and Weisner[22]	265	18–25	Varied (detox, inpatient, outpatient, n = 88) General population (n = 177)	7 years	Attending AA was associated with less intensive alcohol involvement over the follow-up

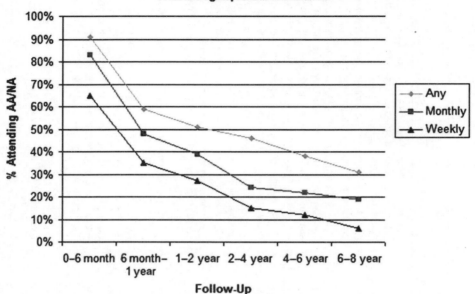

Figure 17.2   Percent of patients attending any, monthly, and weekly AA/NA meetings across 8 years following inpatient treatment. (Reprinted from reference 16 with permission from John Wiley & Sons.)

to just under one-quarter (24%). At intake, less than half (43%) of participants had ever been to a 12-step meeting.[20]

Less research is available on rates of AA attendance among young adults. One study found that among 98 young adults (aged 18–25) currently receiving managed care AUD treatment, 68% reported that they had ever attended an AA meeting.[21] Another study of 270 young adults, drawn from treatment settings and the general population, found that just 35% of the total sample reported having attended AA at baseline.[22] The authors did not break down the attendance rates by treatment status, but it may be reasonable to assume that this overall lower rate was due to the inclusion of a general population subsample, given reports of very low rates of treatment service use (including AA) among those with AUDs in the general population.[9]

Correlates and predictors of 12-step meeting attendance

For inpatient adolescents, AA/NA attendance after discharge has been found to be associated with more severe substance use and higher motivation for abstinence.[23] In addition, seeing oneself as having a problem with alcohol and believing that one could not use substances in moderation (measured at baseline) have been shown to predict AA/NA attendance in the first 6 months after inpatient treatment.[16] Another inpatient adolescent study found that those who had attended AA/NA in the past were more likely to be older, have had prior SUD and/or psychiatric treatment, and have a parent who had attended AA/NA, as compared to those with no prior AA/NA attendance.[24]

Similar themes have emerged in studies of outpatient adolescents. For example, Chi *et al.*[19] found that greater substance use severity at baseline and 1-year follow-up were associated with greater 12-step meeting attendance at 3-year follow-up. Kelly *et al.*[20] found that the baseline predictors of greater 12-step attendance at 3-month follow-up were: (a) less frequent substance use in the 90 days prior to treatment, but greater substance use severity overall; (b) prior substance use treatment and individual therapy; (c) more positive expectations about 12-step attendance; and (d) having an abstinence goal and greater abstinence self-efficacy.

In the young adult sample mentioned above, those who were alcohol dependent were more likely to have attended AA at baseline than those who were problem drinkers (51% vs. 30%). Problem drinkers also had lower ratings of severity than those who were alcohol dependent on a variety of measures.[22]

From this limited research, it may be concluded that, at least for professionally treated youth, those who self-select into 12-step groups: (a) tend to have more severe substance use problems and (b) "fit" with the 12-step model of having an abstinence goal and recognizing and admitting a problem with alcohol. In addition, for these treated individuals, a more extensive history of prior formal treatment for either substance use or mental health issues also seems to be consistently related to 12-step meeting attendance. From a theoretical standpoint, this fits well with the Health Beliefs Model[25] in terms of the construct of "perceived severity." The more severely affected someone perceives himself or herself to be, the more likely they are to seek help for their drinking.

Relationship between 12-step attendance and substance use outcomes

Several correlation studies of adolescents treated in inpatient settings have found that AA/NA attendance following professional treatment is associated with abstinence or lower rates of substance use. For instance, Brown, Mott, and Myers[26] found that youth with more frequent AA/NA attendance had significantly better substance use outcomes during a 12-month follow-up period, with attendees most likely to be abstinent. Alford, Koehler, and Leonard[27] found that, of those who attended 12-step meetings at least once per week (high frequency), 84% were abstinent/essentially abstinent at a 2-year follow-up, compared to only 31% of those who did not attend AA/NA. Of those in the high frequency attendance group, only 13% were still using substances heavily at follow-up, compared to 62% of those who did not attend AA/NA. Similarly, Kennedy and Minami[28] found that, compared to those who did participate in 12-step groups, adolescents who did not participate were substantially more likely to relapse during the 12-month follow-up period. These researchers also found that the relationship between pretreatment severity of drug use and later substance use outcome was moderated by AA/NA participation such that, in general, the most severe cases had the worst outcomes, but those severe patients who attended AA/NA showed similar outcomes to patients who were less severe before treatment. In a large sample ($N = 2,317$) of adolescents from 24 residential programs, AA/NA attendance following treatment was the most powerful predictor of abstinence at 6- and 12-month follow-up.[29] Finally, in the one study that used a young adult sample and that focused specifically on alcohol, not attending AA was associated with more intensive alcohol involvement.[22]

Several studies have shown that the relationship between 12-step group participation and improved substance use outcomes holds even when controlling for variables that also predict better outcomes. For instance, Kelly, Myers, and Brown[30] found that AA/NA participation was uniquely associated with a greater abstinence rate during the 6-month follow-up period after controlling for professional aftercare attendance and substance use frequency at intake. In their 8-year follow-up study, Kelly *et al.*[16] found that after controlling for gender, perceived ability to use alcohol/drugs in moderation and baseline frequency of substance use, as well as percent days abstinent and formal treatment service utilization in each preceding follow-up period, AA/NA participation still independently predicted percent days abstinent across the 8-year follow-up. Above and beyond the other factors associated with abstinence, youth gained nearly two additional days of abstinence for every AA/NA meeting attended.

The two studies that examined AA/NA attendance in outpatient, rather than inpatient, youth have shown similar results. For instance, Chi *et al.*[19] demonstrated that 12-step meeting attendance at 1 year predicted abstinence from alcohol (but not drugs) at 3 years, after controlling for individual characteristics (i.e., demographics, baseline substance use and mental health severity, motivation) and use of SUD and mental health treatment. Kelly *et al.*[20] found that AA/NA attendance independently predicted percent days abstinent both concurrently (i.e., during the same follow-up period) and subsequently (i.e., during the next 3 months) after controlling for baseline percent days abstinent, prior treatment and AA/NA participation, drug abstinence goal and self-efficacy, and concurrent outpatient treatment session attendance.

In summary, the available evidence consistently shows a relationship between 12-step meeting attendance and better substance use outcomes. Studies that have controlled for other pertinent predictors of abstinence have found that AA/NA attendance still predicts abstinence above and beyond these other factors. However, conclusions and derivation of clinical guidelines from the available evidence are limited by the small number of studies, their reliance on treated samples that consist mainly of adolescents, rather than young adults, and their purely observational designs. Whereas a number of clinical trials examining professional 12-step facilitation interventions have been conducted with older adults samples,[31] to our knowledge, there have been no experimental studies of adolescent participation in AA/NA or 12-step facilitation treatment for youth, which prevents cause and effect conclusions. That said, we believe AA and other 12-step groups will be of help to young people with substance dependence and, as we describe later, there are now validated 12-step facilitation methods that can be adapted to help engage young people with AA.

Mechanisms of change: what might explain the relationship between AA and better outcomes?

The study of the mechanisms through which AA participation is associated with better substance use outcomes has emerged as an important area of scientific focus since the United States' Institute of Medicine[32] called for more research on the mechanisms of behavior change within AA. Studies of adults in AA have examined mechanisms such as changes in negative affect,[33] social networks,[34] spirituality,[35] and common processes such as coping, self-efficacy, and motivation.[23,29,36] These have been summarized in detail elsewhere.[17]

Regarding mechanisms of behavior change in samples of youth in AA/NA, three studies have examined factors that could possibly explain the benefits. One study examined several common change processes as potential mediators (i.e., cognitive and behavioral coping, abstinence self-efficacy, and motivation for abstinence) and found that while AA/NA participation increased coping, self-efficacy, and motivation over baseline levels of these variables, only motivation for abstinence mediated the effect of 12-step group attendance on substance use outcome.[29] Another study, based largely on the same sample, examined whether *active involvement* in 12-step groups (e.g., having a sponsor, reading AA/NA literature, engaging in social activities with AA/NA members) was related to greater benefit than *attendance* alone, and which factors explained this relationship.[23] Active involvement in 12-step groups was associated with increased motivation over and above both baseline levels and that attributable to attendance alone, and mediational analyses showed that the observed benefit of involvement on outcome was explained by enhanced motivation during the follow-up period. Thus, increased motivation for abstinence appears to be important in explaining the beneficial effects of 12-step group involvement on substance use outcomes for young people. Causal conclusions from these studies are strengthened by lagged, controlled mediational designs and rigorous analytic methods.[37]

Chi *et al.*[19] also conducted mediational analyses, examining social support and religiosity as mediators of the relationship between 12-step attendance and abstinence. They found that support for reducing substance use from family and friends mediated the relationship between 12-step attendance and abstinence from alcohol and drugs, whereas religiosity (measured by the rate of religious service attendance) mediated the relationship between 12-step attendance and abstinence from drugs, but not alcohol. While this study did not employ a lagged design to examine mediation, findings support results from research with adults that has recently found social network and spirituality factors to mediate the effects of AA on abstinence. While there are many potential mediators at different levels of scale (e.g., social, psychological, neurobiological), it appears that both intrinsic (e.g., motivation) and extrinsic (e.g., social support) factors can at least partially explain the relationship between 12-step attendance and improved substance use outcomes among young people.

Cost–effectiveness of AA participation

While the cost-effectiveness of AA participation has not been examined with adolescent or young adult populations, there is evidence from studies with older adults that more frequent 12-step group participation can reduce the need for more costly professional treatment services and, thus, reduce healthcare costs overall. Two studies compared adult patients initially treated in cognitive–behaviorally oriented inpatient programs to adult patients treated in 12-step-oriented inpatient programs and found that those who received 12-step-oriented treatment attended significantly more 12-step meetings after treatment, whereas those coming from cognitive–behavioral settings utilized more professional inpatient and outpatient services posttreatment.[38,39] Correspondingly, during the 2 years following the index treatment episode, those patients initially treated in 12-step-oriented treatment programs had health care costs that were 30–60% lower than those patients who were initially treated in cognitive–behavioral programs. This translated into savings of approximately $ 2,400–4,700 per patient per year. Importantly, the clinical and demographic profiles of these treated patient groups were similar at treatment intake, as were the psychological and substance use outcomes at follow-up, with the exception that those patients treated in 12-step-oriented treatment were significantly more likely to be abstinent from alcohol and other drugs. These results are compelling and suggest potential health cost offsets attributable to professional 12-step treatments' greater reliance on free peer-led, community 12-step groups, without producing any detriment in mental health functioning and while yielding better substance use outcomes.

The role of clinicians in promoting AA attendance among young clients

A major issue for clinicians treating young people with AUDs is likely to be how to best encourage their young clients to take advantage of free and widely available 12-step recovery resources, in terms of both (a) getting them to attend at all and (b) promoting ongoing attendance and involvement. There are aspects of AA that may make it less appealing or appropriate for younger clients (e.g., admitting a problem, the focus on abstinence, the lack of other young people), especially for those with less severe addiction, who are less motivated to abstain, and who have less extensive treatment histories. Indeed, AA simply may not be a good fit for individuals such as these. Thus, clinicians should make their recommendations strategically to avoid damaging the therapeutic relationship. However, it is likely that young patients who have more severe substance use, are dependent on drugs or alcohol, and/or recognize that they have a problem with alcohol or drugs could benefit from attending AA, so clinicians should be aware of and be able to address AA-related benefits, barriers, and concerns with these clients directly in treatment.

While a recent survey of adolescent SUD treatment centers in the United States found that very few are based solely on a 12-step model (8.6%),[40] it appears that many treatment centers are already incorporating the 12-step program into their professional treatment in other ways, such as linking clients to 12-step meetings at discharge (85%), requiring attendance at 12-step meetings during treatment (49%), and offering 12-step meetings at the treatment center (25%). Thus, the suggestions offered below (see Table 17.2) are ways for clinicians to refine or improve their methods of facilitating 12-step meeting attendance among their younger clients, since many are likely to be already using similar strategies.

As a first step to facilitating clients' attendance, clinicians should educate themselves about AA's basic tenets, format, expectations, and "12 Steps", so as to be as informed as possible when discussing these groups with clients. In order to become familiar with AA, clinicians may choose to read AA literature that is available online, attend "open" meetings (i.e., meetings that are open to the public and not limited to those who are seeking help for an alcohol problem), or talk to clients or other people who have attended AA

Table 17.2 Clinical strategies for promoting AA involvement in young clients.

1. Read AA literature in order to educate yourself about the AA fellowship and 12-step program (e.g., *Living Sober*, *The Big Book* [*Alcoholics Anonymous*]).
2. Attend "open" AA meetings to gain a firsthand understanding of AA and the social climate of the meetings to which you may refer clients.
3. Keep an updated list of local designated young persons' and beginners' meetings.
4. Direct clients to a specific meeting and/or link them with a current AA member.
5. Get parental support for their child's AA attendance (for adolescent clients).
6. Discuss concerns, barriers, and attitudes about AA in session, before and after AA attendance.
7. Start a young person's AA meeting on site.

about their experiences. Additionally, clinicians should seek out and keep an up-to-date list of young persons' and beginners' meetings that are available in the community, to which they may direct their young clients (keeping in mind that beginners' meetings are not specific to young people and can be attended by beginners of all ages). If no such groups are locally available, clinicians should refer their clients to regular all-ages AA meetings, but may need to spend some extra time in session discussing the benefits and drawbacks of attending a group that is likely to consist mainly of older adults. In either case, providing clients with a list of meeting times and locations, and coming to a mutual agreement about a specific one that the client will attend before the next session, is likely to be much more effective at promoting attendance than a vague recommendation to attend. Taking it one step further, clinicians who know other young clients, who attend AA and who offer to act as a contact, can directly link their young clients to these similar-aged contacts, who will likely be able to more directly and accurately address concerns or questions. For adolescent clients under the age of 18, getting the "buy-in" of parents is likely to be important, as parents are often the providers of both permission to attend and transportation to meetings. Some parents of younger adolescents might not want their child to attend AA alone and would feel undermined by a clinician who encouraged their child to attend, so in these cases, having the parent on board would facilitate the adolescent's participation.

It is also important for clinicians to be aware of the perceptions and opinions that their adolescent and young adult clients have about AA, both before and after they attend, and to be able to address these directly. Clinicians should inquire about the perceived barriers to and benefits of AA attendance that their clients possess, and respond to any concerns with information gleaned from research or other young clients. For instance, a qualitative study that asked adolescent inpatients, who had attended 12-step meetings, what they liked best about AA or NA found that the two most common response categories were "a sense of belonging" and "getting support from others". Other perceived benefits included seeing that recovery was possible, catharsis, and learning skills and information (although the fourth most common response was "nothing"). When adolescents who had stopped going to AA/NA were asked why they did so, common responses included boredom, lack of fit/irrelevance, relapse to alcohol or drugs, no perceived need, no longer mandated to attend, and lack of transportation.[24] Clinicians could discuss research such as this with their adolescent/young adult clients, as these issues arise, in order to address concerns and facilitate attendance (e.g., "Having this problem when you are young sometimes feels like you're the only one, but many young people who attend AA actually report that they feel less alone and a greater sense of belonging").

Some young people may be uncomfortable with the themes of spirituality, powerlessness, and personal shortcomings contained within the 12 Steps. In these cases, it can be useful for clinicians to validate that while the steps are worded to reflect these particular themes, they can also be interpreted in ways that make the most sense for a particular individual and in ways that reflect broader, more palatable, meanings. Table 17.3 describes some interpretations of the 12 Steps (based on Kelly and McCrady[41]) that clinicians may find helpful to use in discussing the program with their younger patients.

12-Step facilitation interventions

While these recommendations for facilitating 12-step group attendance among younger clients are based on both common sense and clinical experience, clinicians seeking a structured, manualized, and empirically validated approach might extrapolate procedures from *12-step facilitation therapies* developed and tested with adult SUD populations (e.g., see reference 18). "12-step facilitation" is a professionally delivered intervention wherein the therapist works to educate the patient about AA, and promote his or her active engagement in such groups. It can be implemented in several different ways (see Table 17.4). As mentioned, no studies of 12-step facilitation have been conducted specifically with adolescent or young adult populations, but it is reasonable to think that this form of treatment could be effective with a younger population provided that age-specific concerns and barriers to attendance, such as the ones described above, were incorporated. In the existing adolescent/young adult literature, there are hints that a greater focus on 12-step meetings in professional treatment is associated with more 12-step meeting attendance. For instance, Kelly et al.[20] found a significant correlation between the degree to which adolescents reported that treatment staff encouraged them to attend AA and their actual rates of AA attendance. There are also higher overall rates of AA attendance among young people treated in inpatient programs, which are more likely to be 12-step-oriented, as compared to young people in outpatient treatment. However, findings such as these are confounded with factors such as severity, which is a robust and independent predictor of AA/NA attendance. However, the evidence to date suggests that these free community resources have clinical utility and benefit, and that use of adult-derived 12-step facilitation strategies are likely to result in enhanced attendance and improved outcomes.

Conclusions and recommendations

During its 75-year history, AA has seen dramatic growth in the United States and around the world. While initially attracting only more severely impaired middle-aged and older individuals, the organization has begun to attract increasing numbers of young people, and has begun to publish youth-specific AA literature to cater more effectively to their needs. AA's growing influence in the treatment system, and as a major continuing care referral resource, has produced an increasingly rigorous research agenda to evaluate its

Table 17.3 Interpretation and potential therapeutic outcome of AA's 12-step process.

	AA step	AA theme	Youth-focused interpretation	Therapeutic Outcome
1.	We admitted we were powerless over alcohol, that our lives had become unmanageable.	Honesty	I have got an alcohol/drug problem.	Relief
2.	Came to believe that a power greater than ourselves could restore us to sanity.	Open-mindedness	Help is available; change is possible.	Instillation of hope
3.	Made a decision to turn our will and our lives over to the care of God, as we understood him.	Willingness	Decide to get help.	Self-efficacy
4.	Searching and fearless moral inventory of ourselves.	Self-assessment and appraisal	Take a look at what is bothering you and why.	Insight
5.	Admitted to God, to ourselves, and to another human being the exact nature of our wrongs.	Self-forgiveness	Talk about what is bothering you and why with someone you trust, and who can help you.	Reduced shame and guilt
6.	Were entirely ready to have God remove all these defects of character.	Readiness to change	Start to make the necessary changes.	Cognitive consonance
7.	Humbly asked Him to remove our shortcomings.	Humility	Continue to make the necessary changes.	Cognitive consonance
8.	Made a list of all persons we had harmed, and became willing to make amends to them all.	Taking responsibility and forgiveness of others	Attempt to rectify sources of guilt/shame.	Peace of mind
9.	Made direct amends to such people, whenever possible, except when to do so would injure them or others.	Restitution to others	Talk to those concerned and make amends where necessary.	Peace of mind; self-esteem
10.	Continued to take personal inventory, and when wrong, promptly admitted it.	Emotional balance	Keep on taking a look at yourself and correct mistakes as you go.	Affect- and self-regulation
11.	Sought through prayer and mediation to improve our conscious contact with God, as we understood Him, praying only for knowledge of his will for us and the power to carry it out.	Connectedness and emotional balance	Stay connected, stay mindful.	Awareness; psychological well-being
12.	Have had a spiritual awakening as the result of these steps; we tried to carry this message to alcoholics and to practice these principles in all our affairs.	Helping others achieve recovery	Continue to access help, work on yourself and try to help others.	Self-esteem and mastery

Table 17.4 Ways for clinicians to implement 12-step facilitation strategies.

Method	How it might be implemented	Studies using the approach
Stand-alone treatment	Individual therapy devoted entirely to facilitating AA attendance by promoting an abstinence goal, increasing willingness to use AA as a tool to help achieve abstinence, and monitoring reactions to AA.	Project MATCH Research Group[45]: Compared 12-step facilitation as a stand-alone treatment to CBT and MET.
Integrated with other treatment	Within an existing treatment, such as CBT, incorporating encouragement to attend AA, getting patient to agree to attend specific meetings, and discussing AA literature, meetings, and sponsorship.	Walitzer et al.[46]: Compared treatment as usual (5% of time spent discussing AA), motivational AA facilitation (20% AA related), and directive AA facilitation (38% AA related).
Component of a treatment package	Group education and discussion about AA separate from other treatment, with homework assignments to attend meetings, talk to other AA members outside of sessions, and get a sponsor.	Kaskutas et al.[47]: "Making AA Easier," a group intervention to help encourage participation, minimize resistance, and provide education about AA.
Modular add-on	Assertive linkage to specific groups, review of 12-step program and common concerns, direct connection to current AA members, review of client attendance and experiences.	Timko et al.[48]: Compared standard AA referral to intensive referral.

benefits among adults (see references 42 and 43). During the past 10 years, this focus has begun to include evaluations of youth involvement in such groups, investigations on whether they benefit, and why.[44]

Clinicians working with adolescents and young adults know that younger patients with SUD have specific developmental needs and challenges that distinguish them from their older adult counterparts. In general, they may be less intrinsically motivated for treatment, less likely to have an abstinence goal, and less severe in their substance use, all of which may act as barriers to engagement with 12-step recovery resources. However, research on treated samples has shown that many adolescents and young adults do attend AA, and that beneficial outcomes are consistently related to attendance. Causal conclusions about the effects of AA on substance use outcomes cannot yet be drawn, as no experimental research studies have been conducted with adolescent/young adult samples; but longitudinal studies that control for factors that also predict abstinence have shown that AA attendance predicts abstinence above and beyond these other factors. While AA is not likely to be helpful to every young person, particularly those who do not fit as well with the 12-step model of problem recognition and abstinence orientation, clinicians should encourage their substance dependent or more severely involved patients to at least sample some AA meetings, so that they can take advantage of this free, widely available, and supportive community. Adapting 12-step facilitation methods that have been found effective among older adult samples may be helpful in this regard. AA may be one of the very few concentrated sources of recovery-specific support available to young people during this life stage.

Resources

- For youth, parents, and practitioners: www.aa.org. The official web site of Alcoholics Anonymous, containing information about the program, downloadable literature (including several pamphlets about participation by young people), and links to web sites of local AA chapters.
- For youth and practitioners: www.aagrapevine.org. An archive of articles from the "AA Grapevine" (the international journal for AA), offering firsthand perspectives of AA members about their experiences with the organization. Includes nearly 100 articles written about and by young people in AA, as well as over 100 articles by beginners (a user name and password is required to read archived articles).
- For youth: www.e-aa.org. A resource for online AA meetings (e-mail and chat room format) and discussion forums related to AA, including forums for newcomers and young people. Registration required to participate in online meetings and post to the forums, but no registration required to view forums. Also includes lists of face-to-face AA meetings around the world.
- For youth: www.thecoolspot.gov. An informational site run by NIAAA that contains information on peer pressure and resisting drinking, as well as facts about drinking, rates of alcohol use among teens, and the health and legal risks related to drinking.
- Kelly JF, Myers MG. Adolescents' participation in Alcoholics Anonymous and Narcotics Anonymous: Review, implications, and future directions. *J Psychoactive Drugs* 2007; 39:259–269.
- Kelly JF, Brown SA, Abrantes A, Kahler CW, Myers MG. Social recovery model: An 8-year investigation of adolescent 12-step group involvement following inpatient treatment. *Alcohol Clin Exp Res* 2008; 32:1468–1478.
- Kelly JF, Myers MG, Brown SA. A multivariate process model of adolescent 12-step attendance and substance use outcome following inpatient treatment. *Psychol Addict Behav* 2000; 14:376–389.
- Kelly JF, Myers MG, Brown SA. The effects of age composition of 12-step groups on adolescent 12-step participation and substance use outcome. *J Child Adolesc Subst Abuse* 2005; 15:67–76.
- Kelly JF, Yeterian JD. Mutual-help groups. In: O'Donohue W, Cunningham JR eds. *Evidence-Based Adjunctive Treatments*. New York: Elsevier; 2008, pp. 61–105.

References

1. Edwards G. *Alcohol: The World's Favorite Drug*. New York: St. Martin's Press; 2000.
2. Mäkela K. *Alcoholics Anonymous as a Mutual-Help Movement: A Study in Eight Societies*. Madison, WI: University of Wisconsin Press; 1996.

3. WHO. *The World Health Report 2002. Reducing Risks, Promoting Healthy Life.* Geneva, Switzerland: World Health Organization; 2002.

4. Alcoholics Anonymous. *Alcoholics Anonymous: The Story of How Thousands of Men and Women Have Recovered from Alcoholism,* 4th edn. New York: Alcoholics Anonymous World Services; 2001.

5. Alcoholics Anonymous. *Twelve Steps and Twelve Traditions.* New York: Alcoholics Anonymous World Services; 1953.

6. Grant B, Stinson F, Harford T. Age at onset of alcohol use and DSM-IV alcohol abuse and dependence: A 12-year follow-up. *J Subst Abuse* 2001; 13:493–504.

7. Substance Abuse and Mental Health Services Administration. *Results from the 2008 National Survey on Drug Use and Health: National Findings.* NSDUH Series H-36, HHS Publication No. SMA 09–4434. Rockville, MD: Office of Applied Studies; 2009.

8. Hasin DA, Stinson FS, Ogburn E, Grant BF. Prevalence, correlates, disability, and comorbidity of DSM-IV alcohol abuse and dependence in the United States: Results from the National Epidemiologic Survey on Alcohol and Related Conditions. *Arch Gen Psychiatry* 2007; 64:830–842.

9. Wu L, Pilowsky DJ, Schlenger WE, Hasin D. Alcohol use disorders and the use of treatment services among college-age young adults. *Psychiatr Serv* 2007; 58:192–200.

10. Brown SA. Recovery patterns in adolescent substance abuse. In: Marlatt GA, Baer JS, eds. *Addictive Behaviors Across the Life Span: Prevention, Treatment, and Policy Issues.* Newbury Park, CA: Sage Publications, Inc.; 1993, pp. 161–183.

11. Stewart D, Brown SA. Withdrawal and dependency symptoms among adolescent alcohol and drug abusers. *Addiction* 1995; 90:627–635.

12. Tims FM, Dennis ML, Hamilton N, Buchan BJ, Diamond G. Characteristics and problems of 600 adolescent cannabis abusers in outpatient treatment. *Addiction* 2002; 97:46–57.

13. Brown SA, Vik PW, Creamer VA. Characteristics of relapse following adolescent substance abuse treatment. *Addict Behav* 1989; 14:291–300.

14. Alcoholics Anonymous. *Alcoholics Anonymous 2007 Membership Survey.* New York, NY: Alcoholics Anonymous World Services; 2008.

15. Kelly JF, Myers MG, Brown SA. The effects of age composition of 12-step groups on adolescent 12-step participation and substance use outcome. *J Child Adolesc Subst Abuse* 2005; 15:67–76.

16. Kelly JF, Brown SA, Abrantes A, Kahler CW, Myers MG. Social recovery model: An 8-year investigation of adolescent 12-step group involvement following inpatient treatment. *Alcohol Clin Exp Res* 2008; 32:1468–1478.

17. Kelly JF, Magill M, Stout RL. How do people recover from alcohol dependence? A systematic review of the research on mechanisms of behavior change in Alcoholics Anonymous. *Addict Res Theory* 2009; 17:236–259.

18. Litt MD, Kadden RM, Kabela-Cormier E, Petry NM. Changing network support for drinking: Network support project 2-year follow-up. *J Consult Clin Psychol* 2009; 77:229–242.

19. Chi FW, Kaskutas LA, Sterling S, Campbell CI, Weisner C. Twelve-step affiliation and 3-year substance use outcomes among adolescents: Social support and religious service attendance as potential mediators. *Addiction* 2009; 104:927–939.

20. Kelly JF, Dow SJ, Yeterian JD, Kahler CW. Can 12-step group participation strengthen and extend the benefits of adolescent addiction treatment? A prospective analysis. *Drug Alcohol Depend* 2010; 110 (1–2): 117–125.

21. Mason MJ, Luckey B. Young adults in alcohol–other drug treatment: An understudied population. *Alcohol Treat Q* 2003; 21:17–32.

22. Delucchi K, Matzger H, Weisner C. Alcohol in emerging adulthood: 7-year study of problem and dependent drinkers. *Addict Behav* 2008; 33:134–142.

23. Kelly JF, Myers MG, Brown SA. Do adolescents affiliate with 12-step groups? A multivariate process model of effects. *J Stud Alcohol* 2002; 63:293–304.

24. Kelly JF, Myers MG, Rodolico J. What do adolescents exposed to Alcoholics Anonymous think about 12-step groups? *J Subst Abuse* 2008; 29:53–62.

25. Rosenstock I. Historical origins of the health belief model. *Health Educ Monogr* 1974; 2:328–335.

26. Brown SA, Mott MA, Myers MG. Adolescent alcohol and drug treatment outcome. In: Watson RR, ed. *Drug and Alcohol Abuse Prevention. Drug and Alcohol Abuse Reviews.* Clifton, NJ: Humana Press, Inc; 1990, pp. 373–403.

27. Alford GS, Koehler RA, Leonard J. Alcoholics Anonymous–Narcotics Anonymous model inpatient treatment of chemically dependent adolescents: A 2-year outcome study. *J Stud Alcohol* 1991; 52:118–126.

28. Kennedy BP, Minami M. The Beech hill hospital/outward bound adolescent chemical dependency treatment program. *J Subst Abuse Treat* 1993; 10:395–406.

29. Hsieh S, Hoffmann NG, Hollister CD. The relationship between pre-, during-, post-treatment factors, and adolescent substance abuse behaviors. *Addict Behav* 1998; 23:477–488.

30. Kelly JF, Myers MG, Brown SA. A multivariate process model of adolescent 12-step attendance and substance use outcome following inpatient treatment. *Psychol Addict Behav* 2000; 14:376–389.

31. Kelly JF, Yeterian JD. The role of mutual-help groups in extending the framework of treatment. *Alcohol Res Health*, in press.

32. Institute of Medicine. *Broadening the Base of Treatment for Alcohol Problems.* Washington, DC: National Academy Press; 1990.

33. Kelly J, Stout R, Magill M, Tonigan J, Pagano M. Mechanisms of behavior change in alcoholics anonymous: Does Alcoholics Anonymous lead to better alcohol use outcomes by reducing depression symptoms? *Addiction* 2010; 105:626–636.

34. Bond J, Kaskutas LA, Weisner C. The persistent influence of social networks and alcoholics anonymous on abstinence. *J Stud Alcohol* 2003; 64:579–588.

35. Zemore SE, Kaskutas LA. Helping, spirituality and Alcoholics Anonymous in recovery. *J Stud Alcohol Drugs* 2004; 65:383–391.

36. Morgenstern J, Labouvie E, McCrady BS, Kahler CW, Frey RM. Affiliation with Alcoholics Anonymous after treatment: A study of its therapeutic effects and mechanisms of action. *J Consult Clin Psychol* 1997; 65:768–777.

37. Nock M. Conceptual and design essentials for evaluating mechanisms of change. *Alcohol Clin Exp Res* 2007; 31(Suppl. 10): 4S–12S.

38. Humphreys K, Moos RH. Can encouraging substance abuse patients to participate in self-help groups reduce demand for health care? A quasi-experimental study. *Alcohol Clin Exp Res* 2001; 25:711–716.

39. Humphreys K, Moos RH. Encouraging post-treatment self-help group involvement to reduce demand for continuing care services: Two-year clinical and utilization outcomes. *Alcohol Clin Exp Res* 2007; 31:64–68.

40. Knudsen HK, Ducharme LJ, Roman PM, Johnson JA. Service delivery and use of evidence-based treatment practices in adolescent substance abuse treatment settings: Project report. Robert Wood Johnson Foundation's Substance Abuse Policy Research Program (Grant No. 53130); 2008.

41. Kelly JF, McCrady BS. Twelve-step facilitation in non-specialty settings. In: Galanter M, Kaskutas LA, eds. *Recent Developments in Alcoholism.* New York: Springer; 2008, pp. 325–350.

42. Humphreys K. *Circles of Recovery: Self-Help Organizations for Addictions*. Cambridge, UK: Cambridge University Press; 2004.
43. Kelly JF, Yeterian JD. Mutual-help groups. In: O'Donohue W, Cunningham JR, eds. *Evidence-Based Adjunctive Treatments*. New York: Elsevier; 2008, pp. 61–105.
44. Kelly JF, Myers MG. Adolescents' participation in Alcoholics Anonymous and Narcotics Anonymous: Review, implications, and future directions. *J Psychoactive Drugs* 2007; 39:259–269.
45. Project MATCH Research Group. Matching alcoholism treatment to client heterogeneity: Project MATCH post-treatment drinking outcomes. *J Stud Alcohol* 1997; 58:7–29.
46. Walitzer KS, Derman KH, Barrick C. Facilitating involvement in Alcoholics Anonymous during out-patient treatment: A randomized clinical trial. *Addiction* 2009; 104:391–401.
47. Kaskutas LA, Subbaraman MS, Witbrodt J, Zemore SE. Effectiveness of making Alcoholics Anonymous easier: A group format 12-step facilitation approach. *J Subst Abuse Treat* 2009; 37:228–239.
48. Timko C, DeBenedetti A, Billow R. Intensive referral to 12-step self-help groups and 6-month substance use disorder outcomes. *Addiction* 2006; 101:678–688.

Chapter 18

Epidemiology and management of alcohol misuse comorbid with other disorders

Katherine M. Keyes[1,2] and Deborah S. Hasin[1,2,3]

[1]New York State Psychiatric Institute, New York, NY, USA
[2]Department of Epidemiology, Mailman School of Public Health, Columbia University, New York, NY, USA
[3]Department of Psychiatry, College of Physicians and Surgeons, Columbia University, New York, NY, USA

Key points

- Psychiatric disorders comorbid with substance disorders in adolescence are common, and predict greater adverse outcomes compared to adolescents without comorbid conditions.
- While safe and effective treatments for adolescent substance use disorders are available, treatment uptake is limited and affected by a number of factors such as socioeconomic position of the parents, access, and availability.
- Evidence-based treatments for substance disorders include motivational interviewing, cognitive behavioral therapy, and contingency management. Among adolescents, family therapy, 12-step programs, and therapeutic communities have also been shown to be efficacious.
- Conduct disorder is the most prevalent psychiatric disorder comorbid with substance disorders in adolescence; multisystematic therapy was developed for adolescents confronting comorbid conduct and substance use disorders.
- Attention deficit hyperactivity disorder (ADHD) is commonly seen in adolescents with substance use disorders. Available evidence suggests that minimal improvement in ADHD is seen in adolescents with an active substance disorder; thus, substance disorders should be treated before a rigorous protocol of treatment for ADHD is initiated.
- Mood disorders, including depressive and bipolar disorders, are prevalent among adolescents with a substance use disorder, especially females. A dearth of evidence is available on treatments for comorbid mood and substance use disorders in adolescents.

This chapter will review patterns of and risk factors for alcohol disorder comorbidity with other psychiatric disorders, and discuss evidence-based practices for the treatment of

---

Young People and Alcohol: Impact, Policy, Prevention, Treatment, First Edition.
Edited by John B. Saunders and Joseph M. Rey.
© 2011 Blackwell Publishing Ltd. Published 2011 by Blackwell Publishing Ltd.

alcohol disorders and co-occurring illnesses in adolescence. We begin with an overview of the epidemiology of alcohol disorders in adolescence, with a focus on patterns of comorbidity. Next, we review patterns of treatment seeking among adolescents with alcohol disorders, including barriers to care and recommended treatments for alcohol disorders, both for adults and in adolescence specifically. We then focus our attention on the epidemiology of and specific treatments for alcohol disorder comorbidity with three psychiatric disorders that are among the most common and clinically relevant for alcohol disorders among adolescents: conduct disorder, attention deficit hyperactivity disorder (ADHD), and major depression.

Overview of alcohol abuse/dependence prevalence and comorbidity in adolescence

Psychiatric disorders commonly arise in childhood and adolescence, with community-based studies in the Diagnostic and Statistical Manual of Mental Disorders (DSM) indicating that approximately 25% of adolescents meet criteria for a current disorder.[1-3] Estimates of the prevalence of substance abuse or dependence in adolescents (which includes, but is not limited to, alcohol abuse or dependence) range from 9% to 24% with a median estimate of 4.5% based on a review of 9 community-based samples.[2] Across studies, substance abuse or dependence was the most common psychiatric disorder of those measured. In adolescence, heavy alcohol use is associated with numerous adverse consequences, such as poor academic achievement,[4] victimization, and risky sexual behavior.[5] In the United States, it is estimated that upwards of 40% of adolescent deaths involve alcohol use by the adolescent to some degree.[6,7] In the long term, early onset of alcohol use is associated with the development of chronic alcohol disorders in adulthood,[8,9] which, in turn, is associated with a range of long-term physical and psychological consequences including liver cirrhosis,[10] traffic fatalities,[11] and chronic psychiatric morbidity.[12,13]

Alcohol abuse and dependence commonly co-occur with other psychiatric disorders, a phenomenon we will refer to in this chapter as comorbidity. A meta-analysis of existing literature estimating comorbidity between substance abuse/dependence and other psychiatric disorders in adolescents indicated 13 studies have providing estimates of comorbidity.[2] Conduct, oppositional defiant, and ADHDs are most likely to co-occur with substance abuse/dependence (pooled odds ratios from 8.0 to 7.5), followed by depression (OR = 4.5) and non-ADHD anxiety (OR = 3.0) disorders. Clinical literature indicates that adolescents with a comorbid alcohol and other psychiatric disorder are more likely to be arrested,[14-16] drop out of school,[17,18] and become pregnant.[19,20] While comorbidity increases an adolescent's probability of engaging in a treatment process,[21] these adolescents are also less likely to successfully complete treatment[22] and less likely to remain abstinent from alcohol and other substances.[23-25] Taken together, the available literature indicates that alcohol disorders are unlikely to occur in isolation from other psychiatric conditions, and that such comorbidity is often associated with a higher risk of adverse consequences.

Alcohol treatment in adolescence: patterns and guidelines

General patterns and factors associated with care

Early and effective engagement of adolescents in the treatment process is important to reduce the public health burden and personal morbidity associated with alcohol disorders (see Chapter 11). Table 18.1 provides a heuristic guide developed to match the type of treatment with the level of clinical severity seen in the adolescent patient.[26] While this type of guide has utility in many clinical settings, treatment is only effective when adolescents with alcohol problems are identified, comprehensively assessed, and treatment options are available and accessible.[26] Unfortunately, this combination of factors is rare. Despite the public health burden of psychiatric disorders, including alcohol disorders among adolescents, available data indicate that treatment services are underutilized. Approximately 50% of adolescents with any psychiatric disorder receive some form of mental health treatment. However, the proportion with a substance use disorder who receive treatment is much lower, only 15–25%.[26–31]

Factors associated with receipt of treatment among adolescents are similar to those among adults, and are often conceptualized in the commonly-used Anderson Model of Health Services Utilization in three categories: predisposing, enabling, and need factors.[32,33] Predisposing factors associated with treatment utilization include older age and female gender. Race/ethnicity, consistently a predictor of treatment for many psychiatric disorders,[33–36] is not associated with receiving alcohol treatment in either adolescents[37,37] or adults.[38,36] Enabling factors include socioeconomic position and stability in the home environment. Need factors are among the strongest predictors of treatment entry, with severity of the alcohol disorder a robust risk factor in both adolescents[38,38] and adults.[36,39] Comorbidity also increases the likelihood of treatment utilization.[21]

Psychiatric disorders among adolescents are often identified through the school environment, and the services obtained through the school are the most common route to treatment for children and adolescents with psychiatric disorders. Schools, pediatricians, and juvenile detention centers are frequently considered a "first gate," where adolescents with alcohol and other psychiatric problems are first identified, and where they may be referred for more specialized services.[26] While school-based services are often essential as an initial step to identify children in need of services, available data suggest that students are rarely referred from their school-based services to the necessary specialty treatment or evidence-based practices. Further, the breadth, depth, and quality of services vary widely across schools, making accurate and consistent detection difficult among this population.

Evidence-based behavioral and pharmacological treatments

Evidence-based behavioral treatments for alcohol problems include motivational interviewing (MI), cognitive behavioral therapy (CBT), and contingency management (CM).

- *MI* typically consists of brief (1–12) individual sessions with a trained counselor. Since ambivalence about reducing the target behavior is anticipated as normal, the counselor

Table 18.1 Summary of recommendations for treatment matching for adolescents.

General principles	Client/patient characteristics	Type of intervention/setting	Treatment
• Keep an appropriate level of confidentiality • Assessment of older children and adolescents requires screening about the use of alcohol and other substances of abuse. If positive, conduct a more detailed evaluation • Appropriate toxicology (urine, blood, breath) and testing for biomarkers should be a routine part of the evaluation, and during and after treatment • Treatment should be in the least restrictive setting that is safe and effective	• Screening shows no evidence of current use • Screening shows positive history of use • No or low current use	• Universal • Indicated prevention or early intervention	• Prevention programs (Chapters 7 and 8) • Targeted prevention programs (mostly brief) with individualized feedback and following motivational interviewing principles (Chapters 9 and 10) • Family should be involved whenever possible (e.g., family therapy) (Chapters 14 and 15) • Twelve-step programs (e.g., AA) may be used as a basis for treatment, or combined with other approaches (Chapter 17) • Medication can be used when indicated for the management of craving and withdrawal, and for aversion therapy (Chapter 16) • Adolescents using substances should always be evaluated for comorbid psychiatric disorders (this chapter) • Comorbid conditions should be appropriately treated (this chapter) • Multisystemic therapy (if available) recommended for substance-using adolescents involved in delinquent activities, or with comorbid conduct disorder (this chapter and Chapter 15)
	• Problems resulting from use • Low to moderate use • Able to function in a nonstructured setting • Home environment does not warrant removal from current living situation	• Outpatient	
	• Moderate problems resulting from use • Moderate use • Requires more structured setting • Home environment does not warrant removal from current living situation • Court mandated • Moderate to severe problems resulting from use	• Intensive outpatient • Partial residential ("day treatment") • Multisystemic therapy	
	• Regular current use • Requires more structured setting • Home environment may impact on drug use but does not warrant removal from current living situation • Court mandated		
	• Severe problems resulting from use • Regular current use that may require medical monitoring • Behavior requires structured care and psychiatric management • Home environment is such that adolescent may benefit substantially from being removed • Court mandated	• Inpatient • Residential (e.g., therapeutic community) • Multisystemic therapy	

Modified from American Academy of Child and Adolescent Psychiatry. Practice parameter for the assessment and treatment of children and adolescents with substance use disorders. *J Am Acad Child Adolesc Psychiatry* 2005; 44:609–621 and reference 26.

begins the treatment by eliciting pros and cons of substance use from clients, and then encourages clients to weigh the pros and cons against each other, an activity intended to increase motivation to change. "Change talk", language indicating a commitment to achieving a specified goal, is encouraged by the end of the session if the client appears ready to make such a commitment.[40] Later sessions can focus more on skill-building. Substantial evidence supports the efficacy of MI for the treatment of substance dependence, both in adults and in adolescents.[40,42]

* *CBT* usually requires 12–16 individual sessions with a trained therapist. The approach involves learning to recognize and avoid triggers for substance use, and fostering skills to achieve and maintain abstinence through decision making and social learning as a means of behavioral change. CBT emphasizes a clear sequence of task- and goal-focused treatment sessions that are described for therapists-in-training in CBT manuals.[43–45] The efficacy of CBT has been well documented in adults (see Chapter 15 and reviews and meta-analyses in adults[46,47] and adolescents[47,48]).

* *CM* utilizes the principles of operant conditioning, positively reinforcing behaviors that achieve sobriety goals. These most commonly consist of vouchers that can be redeemed for goods with every biological test confirming abstinence (e.g., urine for drugs, Breathalyzer for alcohol). A large body of research supports the short-term efficacy of CM for the treatment of drug-dependent adults (see review[50] and meta-analysis[51]) and adolescents.[52] Research to date on alcohol has been limited to adults.[53]

Among adults, pharmacological alcohol treatments with a substantial evidence base for efficacy in adults include disulfiram, naltrexone, and acamprosate (see Chapter 16). No contraindications with medications for other psychiatric conditions (e.g., selective serotonin reuptake inhibitors [SSRIs]) have been found. No randomized controlled trials of these medications have been conducted among adolescents. These medications are sometimes used in community treatment settings in conjunction with some form of inter-personal therapy, although the extent of this combined treatment is unknown. Disulfiram, approved for the treatment of alcohol disorders over 50 years ago, is also commonly used for abstinence maintenance. Disulfiram blocks the ability of the liver to metabolize alcohol, causing an unpleasant reaction (e.g., flushing, vomiting, and dizziness) when even small amounts of alcohol are consumed.[54] Thus, disulfiram is extremely effective in maintaining abstinence when taken regularly. The efficacy of naltrexone for reduction in alcohol craving and better long-term abstinence outcomes has been supported by more than 20 randomized clinical trials, both in the United States and in Europe,[55] including the large multisite COMBINE trial in the United States.[56] It was approved by the Food and Drug Administration (FDA) in 1994, and is recommended for use in conjunction with psychosocial therapy. Finally, acamprosate was approved for the treatment of alcohol dependence by the FDA since 2004, and is used for abstinence maintenance. Similarly to naltrexone, the mechanism of action is believed to be reduction in craving for alcohol. A meta-analysis of randomized controlled trials in Europe indicated that six-month continuous treatment using a combination of acamprosate and psychosocial therapy demonstrated higher rates of abstinence compared to placebo.[57] Evidence in the United States, however, has been mixed. While a large multicenter trial of over one thousand recently abstinent individuals with alcohol dependence (COMBINE[56]) demonstrated no benefit of acamprosate compared to placebo in either abstinent or heavy-drinking days, a reanalysis of three other large trials in the United States showed a benefit in time to first drink and percent days abstinent.[58]

Family therapy, 12-step, and therapeutic communities

In addition to the treatment practices outlined above, the three major models of community-based treatment for adolescent alcohol problems, regardless of the presence or extent of comorbidity, are family therapy, 12-step, and therapeutic communities (TCs).[26,59] We briefly describe each of these below before considering specialty services available for adolescents with psychiatric comorbidity more specifically. Note that these treatment models are not mutually exclusive (e.g., TCs often include 12-step involvement on-site). All three models can be integrated into the treatment heuristics defined in Table 18.1, and have common goals of long-term abstinence as well as continuous group therapy and engagement with long-term care; however, each model also has unique aspects that warrant a heuristic demarcation across the models.

Family therapy

Family therapy is a broad rubric that includes multisystemic therapy[60] (discussed in detail in section "Conduct disorder" below), functional family therapy,[61] multidimensional family therapy,[62] and brief strategic family therapy,[63] among others. Family therapies for adolescent substance disorders have received substantial empirical support for short- and long-term success (see reviews[21,64]), and have been shown in randomized experiments to be more effective than peer group therapy[65,66] or individual counseling[67] for the treatment of adolescents.

For family therapy to be a potentially effective treatment model, the family must be interested in engaging in the adolescent's treatment, which may not be the case for some adolescents with alcohol disorders. Within those families for which family treatment is an option, each specific variation on family therapy includes aspects that may or may not apply, given the clinical severity and specifics of each client. For example, functional family therapy focuses on building behavior change within the whole family,[61] developing communication and problem-solving skills to improve familial relations more generally, whereas multidimensional family therapy focuses on direct intervention, at the family and school level, on the factors that are promoting the substance use in the adolescent specifically. Specifics of the client that should be taken into consideration are factors such as the stability of the home environment, and characteristics such as gender; evidence suggests that females may respond better to family-centered therapy, such as functional family therapy, and males to person-centered therapy, such as multidimensional family therapy.[68]

12-Step programs

The 12-step model is the most common type of treatment used by adults and adolescents for alcohol and drug disorders.[69] Meetings are group-based, no cost (often a small donation is suggested but not required), and widely accessible in most US cities and across the world (see Chapter 17). Originated as "Alcoholics Anonymous" by Bill Wilson in 1935 in an effort to solicit help to stop drinking, this peer-based system of treatment has been extended to illicit drugs (e.g., "Narcotics Anonymous," "Cocaine Anonymous," "Methamphetamine Anonymous"), overeating ("Overeaters Anonymous"), and nicotine ("Nicotine Anonymous"), among other substances of abuse. Meetings are organized around twelve "steps" toward recovery, the first of which is admittance of powerlessness over the substance and the last of which is to carry the message of the 12-step philosophy to others and to practice the 12-step principles in everyday life.[70] Developing some form of spirituality is strongly recommended in the 12-step model,[71] although it is not required. The philosophy of the 12 steps also revolves around sharing experiences of addiction and recovery with peers who are also in recovery.

A significant barrier to 12-step participation among adolescents is the lack of youth-friendly meetings;[26,69] adolescents report liking the group dynamics and support of the 12-step model, but the most often cited barrier to continuation is boredom and lack of fit with adolescent-specific problems and lifestyles.[72] Regardless, 12-step meetings remain an important part of almost every treatment plan for both adolescents and adults with substance disorders.

Twelve-step groups do not formally affiliate with professional treatment or organizations, although many members also participate in professional treatment. The anonymous nature of the 12-step model, in conjunction with its philosophy of nonaffiliation with professional organizations, has precluded direct investigation of its effectiveness through randomized trials. However, in a large multisite study of adults, facilitation of 12-step involvement by professionals was shown to be effective in drinking-reduction goals (Project MATCH[73]). Nonrandomized, naturalistic studies have been complicated by large losses to follow-up and the lack of control groups. However, estimates of one- to two-year abstinence are generally around 50%.[74–77] A large cohort study of 12-step-attending adolescents reported that 42% remained abstinent and 23% used alcohol less than monthly.[78] A more recent study of adolescents with excellent follow-up participation demonstrated 50% total abstinence among adolescents in 12-step and Minnesota Model treatment, compared to 28% of those on a waiting list for Minnesota Model treatment who received referrals for treatment services elsewhere.[79] Finally, study of 55 adolescents, comparing 12-step to cognitive behavioral therapy, found greater reductions in self-reported alcohol use among the 12-step group by 12 weeks, though no differences were evident at the six-month follow-up.[80] Taken together, this evidence indicates that 12-step meetings as part of an overall treatment plan may increase the success of adolescent treatment.

Therapeutic communities

Adolescents with the most severe alcohol disorders and/or with the most disordered home environments often find long-term success in a therapeutic community.[81] Therapeutic communities self-sufficiently operate as highly structured environments where the adolescent is expected to perform daily tasks such as chores, schoolwork, and other responsibilities while in a supervised care setting with professional therapists. Lengths of stay vary from 6 months to up to 2 years; in some programs, adolescents live in the therapeutic community, whereas others provide day services only. Differences between therapeutic communities for adults and those for adolescents generally include a shorter stay, a greater focus on education, more involvement from family or key stakeholders (e.g., probation officers, social workers), and less participation of the adolescent in defining the structure of the program itself.[26,81]

Evidence for the effectiveness of therapeutic communities in the treatment of adolescent substance disorders is generally positive in reducing both alcohol and other substance use, though, in general, studies have been small and have lacked control groups.[21,82–84] Adolescents attending therapeutic communities demonstrate reductions in both alcohol consumption and criminal activity, as well as improvements in academic achievement.[85–87] Because of the highly structured environment, therapeutic communities often report high dropout rates; a 2000 review found a 34–90% dropout rate range with a mean of 75% in studies that reported dropout.[21]

Conduct disorder

Epidemiology

On the basis of data from community samples, conduct disorder is estimated to affect approximately 4–10% of adolescents[1,14,88], and is highly comorbid with alcohol disorders in adolescence. A meta-analysis of community samples[2] indicated a mean odds ratio of 8.0, signifying that an adolescent with an alcohol disorder is 8.0 times as likely to have conduct disorder as an adolescent without conduct disorder. Data from clinical samples indicate that approximately 40–60% of substance-abusing adolescents presenting for treatment will also carry a conduct disorder diagnosis.[23,24,89–91] The commonalities characteristically found between conduct disorder symptoms and alcohol/drug use have led researchers to posit the existence of a broad vulnerability to engage in disinhibited behavior, more common in males and distinguished by undersocialized conduct and low levels of dispositional constraint.[92–95]

Alcohol disorders that arise in the presence of conduct disorders often carry more serious consequences for adolescents. Clinical samples indicate that preadolescent conduct disorder symptoms predict greater likelihood of relapse and heavier use among adolescent in inpatient treatment,[23,24,96] and a greater likelihood of recurring violent offenses, aggression, and illicit drug use.[16,97] Adolescents with comorbid conduct disorder and alcohol disorders are at higher risk for adult psychopathology including antisocial personality disorder[15,98] and major depression.[15,98,99] Taken together, conduct disorder is not only common among adolescents with an alcohol disorder but also associated with potentially serious consequences throughout the life course.

Treatment

Multisystematic therapy was developed to specifically treat adolescents with comorbid conduct disorder and substance disorders.[60,100–103] Under the rubric of family therapies discussed previously, multisystematic therapy focuses on adolescents with serious delinquency issues such as repeated juvenile offenders, specifying tailoring interventions that simultaneously address family, school, peer, and neighborhood risk factors. The multi-systematic therapy process involves cognitive-behavioral and behavioral approaches to addressing behavior change within the "social ecology"[101] of an adolescent's environment, while simultaneously empowering caregivers and other supervisors with frequent interaction with the adolescent with resources and skills to effectively deal with problematic behavior. Therapists spend an average of 2–15 hours per week with the adolescent and family, depending on clinical severity. Multisystematic therapy is hypothesized to achieve positive outcomes by improving family relations (e.g., cohesion, functioning, and parental monitoring) while reducing adolescent interaction with delinquent peers.[100] A 2006 randomized controlled trial of juvenile offenders documented that adolescents in a combined drug court/multisystematic therapy group or drug court/multisystematic therapy/contingency management group had greater reductions in alcohol, marijuana, and polysubstance use after one year compared to adolescents in drug court or family court alone.[101] Multisystematic therapy is recommended by the National Institute on Drug Abuse as an evidence-based practice for the treatment of adolescents with comorbid substance disorders and conduct disorder.[104]

Attention deficit hyperactivity disorder

Epidemiology

The prevalence of ADHD in childhood and adolescence is estimated to be approximately 9% in a nationally representative sample of 8–15-year youngsters conducted from 2001 to 2004,[3] which is slightly higher than community-based prevalence estimates from the early 1990s.[105] ADHD is the psychiatric disorder among children and adolescents most likely to be treated, with ADHD cases comprising an estimated 50% of the psychiatric population in childhood.[106] Clinical studies have estimated that approximately 30–50% of those in treatment for substance disorders evidence ADHD,[90,91,107–109] and prospective studies have shown that children with ADHD are at higher risk for the development of substance disorders in adolescence.[110–117] Data from community-based samples indicate that adolescents with substance disorders have approximately 8.0 times the odds of ADHD compared to adolescents without substance disorders.[2]

It should be noted that while ADHD is often comorbid with substance disorders, the relationship seems to be fully explained by the comorbidity between ADHD and conduct disorder. Symptoms of conduct disorders are highly correlated with symptoms of ADHD, and a number of studies from large-scale cohort studies, such as the Christchurch Health and Development Study in New Zealand[114] as well as others,[113,118] have shown that there is no relation between ADHD and later substance use in the absence of conduct disorder symptoms. Nevertheless, clinicians are likely to encounter patients with ADHD and substance disorders on a regular basis, and should be aware of appropriate treatment options.

Treatment

Available evidence suggests that an active alcohol disorder should be treated before ADHD, as minimal improvements in ADHD symptoms are seen when a substance disorder is active in adolescents.[119,120] Treatment of alcohol disorders that are comorbid with ADHD is complicated by the fact that stimulant medications, the most common and effective treatment for ADHD in adolescence (see review[121]), can be abused. The two most common medications for ADHD, methylphenidate and dextroamphetamine, are specified as a schedule II medication by the Drug Enforcement Administration, indicating a substantial likelihood of abuse, especially for adolescents with vulnerability to additive behaviors. However, the counterargument is that adolescents with ADHD do not report the euphoria from stimulants reported by adolescents and adults without ADHD; thus, stimulant medications are often effectively used as part of treatment for ADHD- or substance-abusing adolescents.[121] Nonetheless, the use of stimulants should be carefully considered on a case by case basis, as the risks of prescribing stimulant medication to an adolescent in treatment for an alcohol disorder may outweigh the benefits in some circumstances.[122,123] Atomoxetine, a norepinephrine reuptake inhibitor, is a nonstimulant medication for ADHD approved for use in children, adolescents, and adults.[124] Atomoxetine has less abuse potential compared with traditional stimulant-based ADHD medications; thus, it may be an appropriate treatment choice among adolescents with substance abuse disorders. When such a prescription is made, careful monitoring of nonmedical abuse of the drug, to the extent possible, is needed throughout the treatment.

Little literature exists to evaluate the effect of specific treatments for either ADHD or alcohol disorders in the presence of both diagnoses, though evidence is beginning to accumulate in this area. A randomized controlled trial of the ADHD medication, pemoline, among adolescents with comorbid drug use and conduct disorders indicated reductions in hyperactivity but no effect on substance use including alcohol use,[120,125] but effects among adolescents with alcohol disorders specifically were not assessed and abuse of pemoline was not measured. More promising is the work suggesting that bupropion, an atypical aminoketone antidepressant, may have efficacy in the treatment for ADHD- or substance-disordered adolescents. Bupropion has been shown to be more effective than placebo in treating ADHD symptoms in adolescents,[126,127] and bupropion SR is approved by the FDA to treat nicotine dependence in adults. Several small clinical samples have suggested that bupropion reduces both ADHD symptoms and substance use in adolescents.[128,129] While larger trials with randomized controlled groups are needed, this evidence suggests a promising pathway for the treatment of adolescents with comorbid ADHD and alcohol disorders. Nonpharmacologic treatments with empirically shown benefits for adolescents with comorbid substance disorders and ADHD include CBT[130] and other behaviorally-focused forms of individual therapy.[122,131]

Mood disorders

Epidemiology

Data from national surveys indicate that approximately 20–30% of adolescents, who are either heavy users or dependent on alcohol, evidence major depression,[1,132] and clinical samples indicate that approximately 30–40% of males and up to 70% of females in treatment for an alcohol disorder evidence a history of major depression.[91,133–135]

Adolescent girls are more likely to evidence major depression compared to boys.[135] Similarly to other comorbidities, the presence of major depression predicts a greater likelihood of relapse among adolescents with an alcohol disorder.[136]

It should be noted that epidemiologic studies of adults have documented a high co-occurrence between alcohol disorders and bipolar disorder, with data from the National Comorbidity Study indicating that individuals with alcohol dependence are more than 12 times as likely to evidence bipolar disorder compared to individuals without alcohol dependence.[28] No similar studies have been conducted among children and adolescents; given the growing reported prevalence of bipolar in young age groups, assessment of common comorbidities is essential to continued surveillance and treatment development efforts.

Treatment

Although fluoxetine and escitalopram are the only SSRIs currently approved by the FDA for treating major depression in children and adolescents, off-label use of other SSRIs is common. A controversial black box warning was added in 2004 due to some evidence of an increased risk of self-harming behaviors among adolescents in SSRI-arms of clinical trials.[137] No randomized trials have been conducted to establish the effect of SSRI use on alcohol outcomes among adolescents with comorbid depression and alcohol disorders, although one small open label study has noted reductions in drinking among adolescents using SSRI medications.[138] The dearth of available evidence regarding evidence-based treatments for comorbid alcohol disorders and mood disorders among adolescents has been noted by researchers and clinicians in the field,[123] and remains an evidence gap that is necessary to fill, given the high rates of comorbidity between these disorders.

Conclusion

Alcohol use disorders in adolescence are clinically serious and can potentially have long-lasting adverse consequences. In addition, many adolescents with alcohol disorders have comorbid psychiatric conditions such as ADHD, conduct disorder, and mood disorders, which can complicate treatment options and efficacy. While safe and effective treatments for adolescent alcohol disorders are available, treatment uptake is limited and affected by a number of factors such as socioeconomic position of the parents, access, and availability. The most common treatment models used in adolescence include family therapy, 12-step, and therapeutic communities. The services offered by community-based settings for adolescent alcohol and drug disorders may become more effective if evidence-based treatments are more widely used. The assignment of an adolescent to a particular therapeutic intervention should be based on the clinical severity and the specifics of the home environment. Little empirical evidence is available to assess the efficacy of treatments for comorbid conditions specifically for adolescents, but available evidence suggests that effective treatments are available for adolescents suffering from multiple comorbid conditions. Full clinical assessments early in the intervention process are essential to properly treating adolescents with multiple disorders.

References

1. Kandel DB, Johnson JG, Bird HR *et al.* Psychiatric disorders associated with substance use among children and adolescents: Findings from the Methods for the Epidemiology of Child and Adolescent Mental Disorders (MECA) Study. *J Abnorm Child Psychol* 1997; 25:121–132.
2. Costello EJ, Mustillo S, Keeler G, Angold A. Prevalence of psychiatric disorders in childhood and adolescence. In: Levin BL, Petrila J, Hennessy KD, eds. *Mental Health Services: A Public Health Perspective*. New York: Oxford University Press; 2004.
3. Merikangas KR, He JP, Brody D, Fisher PW, Bourdon K, Koretz DS. Prevalence and treatment of mental disorders among US children in the 2001–2004 NHANES. *Pediatrics* 2009; 125:75–81.
4. Dubow EF, Boxer P, Huesmann LR. Childhood and adolescent predictors of early and middle adulthood alcohol use and problem drinking: The Columbia County Longitudinal Study. *Addiction* 2008; 103(Suppl. 1):36–47.
5. Silverman JG, Raj A, Mucci LA, Hathaway JE. Dating violence against adolescent girls and associated substance use, unhealthy weight control, sexual risk behavior, pregnancy, and suicidality. *JAMA* 2001; 286:572–579.
6. US Department of Health and Human Services. *The Surgeon General's Call to Action To Prevent and Reduce Underage Drinking*. Office of the Surgeon General; 2007.
7. Sinderlar HA, Barnett NP, Spirito A. Adolescent alcohol use and injury. *Minerva Pediatr* 2004; 56:291–309.
8. Hingson RW, Heeren T, Edwards EM. Age at drinking onset, alcohol dependence, and their relation to drug use and dependence, driving under the influence of drugs, and motor-vehicle crash involvement because of drugs. *J Stud Alcohol Drugs* 2008; 69:192–201.
9. Grant BF, Dawson DA. Age at onset of alcohol use and its association with DSM-IV alcohol abuse and dependence: Results from the National Longitudinal Alcohol Epidemiologic Survey. *J Subst Abuse* 1997; 9:103–110.
10. Yoon YH, Yi Y. *Surveillance Report No. 75: Liver Cirrhosis Mortality in the United States, 1970–2003*. Rockville, MD: Division of Biometry and Epidemiology, Alcohol Epidemiologic Data System; August 2006.
11. Chou SP, Dawson DA, Stinson FS *et al.* The prevalence of drinking and driving in the United States, 2001–2002: Results from the national epidemiological survey on alcohol and related conditions. *Drug Alcohol Depend* 2006; 83:137–146.
12. Grant BF, Stinson FS, Dawson DA *et al.* Prevalence and co-occurrence of substance use disorders and independent mood and anxiety disorders: Results from the National Epidemiologic Survey on Alcohol and Related Conditions. *Arch Gen Psychiatry* 2004; 61:807–816.
13. Hasin DS, Stinson FS, Ogburn E, Grant BF. Prevalence, correlates, disability, and comorbidity of DSM-IV alcohol abuse and dependence in the United States: Results from the National Epidemiologic Survey on Alcohol and Related Conditions. *Arch Gen Psychiatry* 2007; 64:830–842.
14. Kazdin AE. *Conduct Disorders in Childhood and Adolescence*. Newbury Park, CA: Sage Publications, Inc; 1987.
15. Robins L, Price RK. Adult disorders predicted by childhood conduct problems: Results from the NIMH epidemiologic catchement area study. *Psychiatry* 1991; 54:116–132.
16. Zhang L, Wieczorek WF, Welte JW. The nexus between alcohol and violent crime. *Alcohol Clin Exp Res* 1997; 21:1264–1271.
17. Crum RM, Ensminger ME, Ro MJ, McCord J. The association of educational achievement and school dropout with risk of alcoholism: A twenty-five-year prospective study of inner-city children. *J Stud Alcohol* 1998; 59:318–326.

18. Wichstrom L. Alcohol intoxication and school dropout. *Drug Alcohol Rev* 1998; 17:413–421.

19. Kessler RC, Berglund PA, Foster CL, Saunders WB, Stang PE, Walters EE. Social consequences of psychiatric disorders, II: Teenage parenthood. *Am J Psychiatry* 1997; 154:1405–1411.

20. Bardone AM, Moffitt TE, Caspi A, Dickson N, Stanton WR, Silva PA. Adult physical health outcomes of adolescent girls with conduct disorder, depression, and anxiety. *J Am Acad Child Adolesc Psychiatry* 1998; 37:594–601.

21. Williams RJ, Chang SY. A comprehensive and comparative review of adolescent substance abuse treatment outcome. *Clin Psychol Sci Prac* 2000; 7:138–166.

22. Adams L, Wallace JL. Residential treatment for the ADHD adolescent substance abuser. *J Child Adolesc Subst Abuse* 1994; 4:35–44.

23. Myers MG, Brown SA, Mott MA. Preadolescent conduct disorder behaviors predict relapse and progression of addiction for adolescent alcohol and drug abusers. *Alcohol Clin Exp Res* 1995; 19:1528–1536.

24. Brown SA, Gleghorn A, Schuckit MA, Myers MG, Mott MA. Conduct disorder among adolescent alcohol and drug abusers. *J Stud Alcohol* 1996; 57:314–324.

25. Moss HB, Kirisci L, Mezzich AC. Psychiatric comorbidity and self-efficacy to resist heavy drinking in alcoholic and nonalcoholic adolescents. *J Stud Alcohol* 1996; 3:204–212.

26. Winters K. Treating adolescents with substance use disorders: An overview of practice issues and treatment outcomes. *Subst Abus* 1999; 20:203–225.

27. Costello EJ, Costello AJ, Edelbrock C *et al.* Psychiatric disorders in pediatric primary care. Prevalence and risk factors. *Arch Gen Psychiatry* 1988; 45:1107–1116.

28. Kessler RC, Walters EE. Epidemiology of DSM-III-R major depression and minor depression among adolescents and young adults in the National Comorbidity Survey. *Depress Anxiety* 1998; 7:3–14.

29. Wu P, Hoven CW, Bird HR *et al.* Depressive and disruptive disorders and mental health service utilization in children and adolescents. *J Am Acad Child Adolesc Psychiatry* 1999; 38:1081–1090; discussion 1090–1082.

30. Angold A, Erkanli A, Farmer EM *et al.* Psychiatric disorder, impairment, and service use in rural African American and white youth. *Arch Gen Psychiatry* 2002; 59:893–901.

31. Canino G, Shrout PE, Rubio-Stipec M *et al.* The DSM-IV rates of child and adolescent disorders in Puerto Rico: Prevalence, correlates, service use, and the effects of impairment. *Arch Gen Psychiatry* 2004; 61:85–93.

32. Andersen RM. Revisiting the behavioral model and access to medical care: Does it matter? *J Health Soc Behav* 1995; 36:1–10.

33. Andersen RM, Davidson PL. Measuring access and trends. In: Andersen RM, Rice TH, Kominski GF, eds. *Changing the US Health Care System*. San Francisco, CA: Jossey-Bass, Inc; 1996.

34. Wang PS, Lane M, Olfson M, Pincus HA, Wells KB, Kessler RC. Twelve-month use of mental health services in the United States: Results from the National Comorbidity Survey Replication. *Arch Gen Psychiatry* 2005; 62:629–640.

35. Hatzenbuehler ML, Keyes KM, Narrow WE, Grant BF, Hasin DS. Racial/ethnic disparities in service utilization for individuals with co-occurring mental health and substance use disorders in the general population: Results from the national epidemiologic survey on alcohol and related conditions. *J Clin Psychiatry* 2008; 69:1112–1121.

36. Keyes KM, Hatzenbuehler ML, Alberti P, Narrow WE, Grant BF, Hasin DS. Service utilization differences for Axis I psychiatric and substance use disorders between white and black adults. *Psychiatr Serv* 2008; 59:893–901.

37. Jainchill N, De Leon G, Yagelka J. Ethnic differences in psychiatric disorders among adolescent substance abusers in treatment. *J Psychopathol Behav Assess* 1997; 19:133–148.
38. Latimer WW, Newcomb M, Winters KC, Stinchfield RD. Adolescent substance abuse treatment outcome: The role of substance abuse problem severity, psychosocial, and treatment factors. *J Consult Clin Psychol* 2000; 68:684–696.
39. Wu P, Hoven CW, Tiet Q, Kovalenko P, Wicks J. Factors associated with adolescent utilization of alcohol treatment services. *Am J Drug Alcohol Abuse* 2002; 28:353–369.
40. Miller WR, Rollnick S. *Motivational Interviewing: Preparing People to Change Addictive Behavior*. New York: Guilford Press; 1991.
41. Dunn C, Deroo L, Rivara FP. The use of brief interventions adapted from motivational interviewing across behavioral domains: A systematic review. *Addiction* 2001; 96:1725–1742.
42. Burke BL, Arkowitz H, Menchola M. The efficacy of motivational interviewing: A meta-analysis of controlled clinical trials. *J Consult Clin Psychol* 2003; 71:843–861.
43. Monti PM, Abrams DB, Kadden RM, Cooney NL. *Treating Alcohol Dependence: A Coping Skills Training Guide in the Treatment of Addictive Behaviors*. New York: Guilford Press; 1989.
44. Carroll KM. *A Cognitive-Behavioral Approach: Treating Cocaine Addiction*. NIH Publication No. 98–4308. Rockville, MD: National Institute on Drug Abuse; 1998.
45. Marlatt GA, Gordon JR. *Relapse Prevention: Maintenance Strategies in the Treatment of Addictive Behaviors*. 2nd edn. New York: Guilford Press; 2005.
46. Irvin JE, Bowers CA, Dunn ME, Wang MC. Efficacy of relapse prevention: A meta-analytic review. *J Consult Clin Psychol* 1999; 67:563–570.
47. Magill M, Ray LA. Cognitive-behavioral treatment with adult alcohol and illicit drug users: A meta-analysis of randomized controlled trials. *J Stud Alcohol Drugs* 2009; 70:516–527.
48. Deas D. Evidence-based treatments for alcohol use disorders in adolescents. *Pediatrics* 2008; 121(Suppl. 4):S348–S354.
49. Tripodi SJ, Bender K, Litschge C, Vaughn MG. Interventions for reducing adolescent alcohol abuse: A meta-analytic review. *Arch Pediatr Adolesc Med* 2010; 164:85–91.
50. Higgins ST, Silverman K. Contingency management. In: Galanter M, Kleber HD, eds. *Textbook of Substance Abuse Treatment*. 4th edn. Wasington, DC: American Psychiatric Press; 2008.
51. Prendergast M, Podus D, Finney J, Greenwell L, Roll J. Contingency management for treatment of substance use disorders: A meta-analysis. *Addiction* 2006; 101:1546–1560.
52. Stanger C, Budney AJ, Kamon JL, Thostensen J. A randomized trial of contingency management for adolescent marijuana abuse and dependence. *Drug Alcohol Depend* 2009; 105:240–247.
53. Petry NM, Martin B, Cooney JL, Kranzler HR. Give them prizes, and they will come: Contingency management for treatment of alcohol dependence. *J Consult Clin Psychol* 2000; 68:250–257.
54. Chick J, Gough K, Falkowski W *et al.* Disulfiram treatment of alcoholism. *Br J Psychiatry* 1992; 161:84–89.
55. Srisurapanont M, Jarusuraisin N. Naltrexone for the treatment of alcoholism: A meta-analysis of randomized controlled trials. *Int J Neuropsychopharmacol* 2005; 8:267–280.
56. Anton RF, O'Malley SS, Ciraulo DA *et al.* Combined pharmacotherapies and behavioral interventions for alcohol dependence: The COMBINE study: A randomized controlled trial. *JAMA* 2006; 295:2003–2017.
57. Mann K, Lehert P, Morgan MY. The efficacy of acamprosate in the maintenance of abstinence in alcohol-dependent individuals: Results of a meta-analysis. *Alcohol Clin Exp Res* 2004; 28:51–63.

58. Kranzler HR, Gage A. Acamprosate efficacy in alcohol-dependent patients: Summary of results from three pivotal trials. *Am J Addict* 2008; 17:70–76.
59. Biglan A, Brennan PA, Foster SL, Holder HD. *Helping Adolescents at Risk: Prevention of Multiple Problem Behaviors*. New York: Guilford Press; 2004.
60. Henggeler SW, Schoenwald SK, Borduin CM, Rowland MD, Cunningham PB. *Multisystematic Treatment of Antisocial Behavior in Children and Adolescents*. New York: Guilford Press; 1998.
61. Alexander J, Barton C, Gordon D, Grotpeter J, Hanson K, Harrison R. *Blueprints for Violence Prevention, Vol. 3: Functional Family Therapy*. Boulder, CO: Center for the Study and Prevention of Violence; 1998.
62. Liddle HA, Dakof GA, Diamond G. Adolescent substance abuse: Multidimensional family therapy in action. In: Kaufman E, Kaufman P, eds. *Family Therapy with Drug and Alcohol Abuse*. Boston, MA: Allyn & Bacon; 1991.
63. Szapocznik J, Henggeler SW. *Breakthroughs in Family Therapy with Drug-Abusing and Problem Youth*. New York: Springer; 1989.
64. Waldron HB, Turner CW. Evidence-based psychosocial treatments for adolescent substance abuse. *J Consult Clin Psychol* 2008; 37:238–261.
65. Joanning H, Quinn W, Thomas F, Mullen R. Treating adolescent drug abuse: A comparison of family systems therapy, group therapy, and family drug education. *J Marital Fam Ther* 1992; 18:345–356.
66. Liddle HA, Dakof GA. Family-based treatment for adolescent drug abuse: State of the science. In: Rahdert E, Czechowicz D, eds. *Adolescent Drug Abuse: Clinical Assessment and Therapeutic Interventions*. Rockville, MD: National Institute on Drug Abuse Research monograph no. 156, DHHS pub. no 95–3908; 1995.
67. Henggeler SW, Bourdin CM, Melton GB *et al.* Effects of multisystemic therapy on drug use and abuse in serious juvenile offenders: A progress report from two outcome studies. *Fam Dynam Addict Q* 1991; 1:40–51.
68. Gross J, McCaul ME. A comparison of drug use and adjustments in urban adolescent children of substance abusers. *Int J Addict* 1990; 25:495–511.
69. Hoffman N, Mee-Lee D, Arrowhead A. Treatment issues in adolescent substance abuse and addictions: Options, outcome, effectiveness, reimbursement, and admission criteria. *Adolesc Med* 1993; 4:371–390.
70. Alcoholics Anonymous. *The Big Book*. 4th edn. New York: Alcoholics Anonymous Word Services, Inc,; 2002. Available at: http://www.aa.org/bigbookonline/en_tableofcnt.cfm. Accessed December 24, 2010.
71. Deas D, Thomas SE. An overview of controlled studies of adolescent substance abuse treatment. *Am J Addict* 2001; 10:178–189.
72. Kelly JF, Myers MG, Rodolico J. What do adolescents exposed to Alcoholics Anonymous think about 12-step groups? *Subst Abus* 2008; 29:53–62.
73. Project Match Research Group. Matching alcoholism treatments to client heterogeneity: Project MATCH posttreatment drinking outcomes. *J Stud Alcohol* 1997; 58:7–29.
74. Brown SA, Vik PW, Creamer VA. Characteristics of relapse following adolescent substance abuse treatment. *Addict Behav* 1989; 14:291–300.
75. Alford GS, Koehler RA, Leonard J. Alcoholics Anonymous–Narcotics Anonymous model inpatient treatment of chemically dependent adolescents: A 2-year outcome study. *J Stud Alcohol* 1991; 52:118–126.
76. Knapp J, Templer D, Cannon WG, Dobson S. Variables associated with success in an adolescent drug treatment program. *Adolescence* 1991; 26:305–317.

77. Richter SS, Brown SA, Mott MA. The impact of social support and self-esteem on adolescent substance abuse treatment outcome. *J Subst Abuse* 1991; 3:371–385.
78. Harrison PA, Hoffman N. *CATOR Report: Adolescent Treatment Completers One Year Later.* St. Paul, MN: CATOR; 1989.
79. Winters KC, Stinchfield RD, Opland E, Weller C, Latimer WW. The effectiveness of the Minnesota Model approach in the treatment of adolescent drug abusers. *Addiction* 2000; 95:601–612.
80. Wells EA, Peterson PL, Gainey RR, Hawkins JD, Catalano RF. Outpatient treatment for cocaine abuse: A controlled comparison of relapse prevention and twelve-step approaches. *Am J Drug Alcohol Abuse* 1994; 20:1–17.
81. Jainchill N, Bhattacharya G, Yagelka J. Therapeutic communities for adolescents. In: Rahdert E, Czechowicz D, eds. *Adolescent Drug Abuse: Clinical Assessment and Therapeutic Interventions.* Rockville, MD: National Institute on Drug Abuse; 1995.
82. Rush TV. Predicting treatment outcome for juvenile and young adult clients in the Pennsylvania substance abuse system. In: Beschner GM, Friedman AS, eds. *Youth Drug Abuse: Problems, Issues, and Treatment.* Lexington, MA: Lexington Books; 1979.
83. Sells SB, Simpson DD. Evaluation of treatment outcome for youths in drug abuse reporting program (DARP): A follow-up study. In: Beschner GM, Friedman AS, eds. *Youth Drug Abuse: Problems, Issues and Treatment.* Lexington, MA: Lexington Books; 1979.
84. De Leon G. *The Therapeutic Community: Study of Effectiveness.* Washington, DC: DHHS Publication No ADM 84–1286; 1984.
85. Jainchill N, Yagelka J, Hawke J. Adolescent admissions to residential drug treatment: HIV risk behaviors pre- and post-treatment. *Psychol Addict Behav* 1999; 13:163–173.
86. Jainchill N, Hawke J, De Leon G, Yagelka J. Adolescents in therapeutic communities: One-year posttreatment outcomes. *J Psychoactive Drugs* 2000; 32:81–94.
87. Jainchill N, Hawke J, Messina M. Post-treatment outcomes among adjudicated adolescent males and females in modified therapeutic community treatment. *Subst Use Misuse* 2005; 40:975–996.
88. Nock MK, Kazdin AE, Hiripi E, Kessler RC. Prevalence, subtypes, and correlates of DSM-IV conduct disorder in the National Comorbidity Sruvey Replication. *Psychol Med* 2006; 36:699–710.
89. DeMilio L. Psychiatric symptoms in adolescent substance abusers. *Am J Psychiatry* 1989; 146:1212–1214.
90. Stowell RJ, Estroff TW. Psychiatric disorders in substance-abusing adolescent inpatients: A pilot study. *J Am Acad Child Adolesc Psychiatry* 1992; 31:1036–1040.
91. Hovens JG, Cantwell DP, Kiriakos R. Psychiatric comorbidity in hospitalized adolescent substance abusers. *J Am Acad Child Adolesc Psychiatry* 1994; 33:476–483.
92. Jessor R, Jessor SL. *Problem Behavior and Psychosocial Development: A Longitudinal Study of Youth.* New York: Academic Press; 1977.
93. Bentler PM, Newcomb MD. Personality, sexual behavior, and drug use revealed through latent variable methods. *Clin Psychol Rev* 1986; 6:363–385.
94. Young SE, Stallings MC, Corley RP, Krauter KS, Hewitt JK. Genetic and environmental influences on behavioral disinhibition. *Am J Med Genet* 2000; 96:684–695.
95. Krueger RF, Hicks BM, Patrick CJ, Carlson SR, Iacono WG, McGue M. Etiologic connections among substance dependence, antisocial behavior, and personality: Modeling the externalizing spectrum. *J Abnorm Psychol* 2002; 111:411–424.
96. Stice E, Myers MG, Brown SA. Relations of delinquency to adolescent substance use and problem use: A prospective study. *Psychol Addict Behav* 1998; 87:205–209.

97. Elliott DS, Huizinga D, Menard S. *Multiple Problem Youth: Delinquency, Substance Use, and Mental Health Problems.* New York: Springer-Verlag; 1989.

98. Pajer KA. What happens to "bad" girls? A review of the adult outcomes of antisocial adolescent girls. *Am J Psychiatry* 1998; 155:862–870.

99. Samuelson YM, Hodgins S, Larsson A, Larm A, Larm P, Tengstrom A. Adolescent antisocial behavior as predictor of adverse outcomes to age 50. *Crim Justice Behav* 2010; 32:158–174.

100. Huey SJ, Henggeler SW, Brondino MJ, Pickrel SG. Mechanisms of change in multisystemic therapy: Reducing delinquent behavior through therapist adherence and improved family functioning. *J Consult Clin Psychol* 2000; 68:451–467.

101. Henggeler SW, Halliday-Boykins CA, Cunningham PB, Randall J, Shapiro SB, Chapman JE. Juvenile drug court: Enhancing outcomes by integrating evidence-based treatments. *J Consult Clin Psychol* 2006; 74:42–54.

102. Henggeler SW, Silverman K, Heil SH. *Contingency Management in Substance Abuse Treatment.* New York: Guilford Press; 2007.

103. Sheidow AJ, Henggeler SW. Multisystematic therapy with substance use adolescents: A synthesis of the research. In: Stevens A, ed. *Crossing Frontiers: International Developments in the Treatment of Drug Dependence.* New York: Springer; 2008.

104. National Institute on Drug Abuse. *Principles of Drug Addiction Treatment: A Research-Based Guide.* NIH Publication No. 99–4180. Available at: http://www.drugabuse.gov/ PODAT/Evidence2.html. 1999.

105. Szatmari P. The epidemiology of attention deficit hyperactivity disorder. In: Weiss G, ed. *Child and Adolescent Psychiatric Clinics of North America.* Philadelphia, PA: W.B. Saunders; 1992.

106. Cantwell DP. Attention deficit disorder: A review of the past 10 years. *J Am Acad Child Adolesc Psychiatry* 1996; 35:978–987.

107. Weiss G. Attention deficit hyperactivity disorder. In: Lewis M, ed. *Child and Adolescent Psychiatry: A Comprehensive Textbook.* 2nd edn. Baltimore: Williams & Wilkins; 1996.

108. Molina BSG, Pelham WE. Substance use, substance abuse, and LD among adolescents with a childhood history of ADHD. *J Learn Disabil* 2001; 34:333–342.

109. Shrier LA, Sion K, Harris MK, Knight JR. Substance use problems and associated psychiatric symptoms among adolescents in primary care. *Pediatrics* 2003; 111:699–705.

110. Klein RG, Mannuzza S. Long-term outcome of hyperactive children: A review. *J Am Acad Child Adolesc Psychiatry* 1991; 30:383–387.

111. Boyle MH, Offord DR, Racine YA, Szatmari P, Fleming JE, Links PS. Predicting substance use in late adolescence: Results from the Ontario Child Health Study follow-up. *Am J Psychiatry* 1992; 149:761–767.

112. Mannuzza S, Klein RG, Bessler A, Malloy P, LaPadula M. Adult outcome of hyperactive boys. Educational achievement, occupational rank, and psychiatric status. *Arch Gen Psychiatry* 1993; 50:565–576.

113. Wilens T, Biederman J. Psychopathology in preadolescent children at high risk for substance abuse: A review of the literature. *Harv Rev Psychiatry* 1993; 1:207–218.

114. Lynskey MT, Fergusson DM. Childhood conduct problems, attention deficit behaviors, and adolescent alcohol, tobacco, and illicit drug use. *J Abnorm Psychol* 1995; 23:281–302.

115. Biederman J, Wilens T, Mick E *et al.* Is ADHD a risk factor for psychoactive substance use disorders? Findings from a four-year prospective follow-up study. *J Am Acad Child Adolesc Psychiatry* 1997; 36:21–29.

116. Milberger S, Biederman J, Faraone SV, Wilens T, Chu MP. Associations between ADHD and psychoactive substance use disorders. Findings from a longitudinal study of high-risk siblings of ADHD children. *Am J Addict* 1997; 6:318–329.

117. Wilens TE, Biederman J, Mick E, Faraone SV, Spencer T. Attention deficit hyperactivity disorder (ADHD) is associated with early onset substance use disorders. *J Nerv Ment Dis* 1997; 185:475–482.
118. Disney ER, Elkins IJ, McGue M, Iacono WG. Effects of ADHD, conduct disorder, and gender on substance use and abuse in adolescence. *Am J Psychiatry* 1999; 156:1515–1521.
119. Riggs PD. Clinical approach to treatment of ADHD in adolescents with substance use disorders and conduct disorder. *J Am Acad Child Adolesc Psychiatry* 1998; 37:331–332.
120. Riggs PD, Hall SK, Mikulich-Gilbertson SK, Lohman M, Kayser A. A randomized controlled trial of pemoline for attention-deficit/hyperactivity disorder in substance-abusing adolescents. *J Am Acad Child Adolesc Psychiatry* 2004; 43:420–429.
121. Goldman LS, Genel M, Bezman RJ, Slanetz PJ. Diagnosis and treatment of attention-deficit/hyperactivity disorder in children and adolescents. Council on Scientific Affairs, American Medical Association. *JAMA* 1998; 279:1100–1107.
122. Brady KT, Halligan P, Malcolm RJ. *Dual Diagnosis*. Washington, DC: The American Psychiatric Press; 1999.
123. Cornelius JR, Clark DB, Bukstein OG, Salloum IM. Treatment of co-occurring alcohol, drug, and psychiatric disorders. *Recent Dev Alcohol* 2005; 17:349–365.
124. Prasad S, Steer C. Switching from neurostimulant therapy to atomoxetine in children and adolescents with attention-deficit hyperactivity disorder: Clinical approaches and review of current available evidence. *Paediatr Drugs* 2008; 10:39–47.
125. Riggs PD, Mikulich SK, Hall SK. Effects of pemoline on ADHD, antisocial behaviors, and substance use in adolescents with conduct disorder and substance use disorder. *Drug Alcohol Depend* 2001; 63:S131.
126. Barrickman LL, Perry PJ, Allen AJ *et al.* Bupropion versus methylphenidate in the treatment of attention-deficit hyperactivity disorder. *J Am Acad Child Adolesc Psychiatry* 1995; 34:649–657.
127. Daviss WB, Bentivoglio P, Racusin R, Brown KM, Bostic JQ, Wiley L. Bupropion sustained release in adolescents with comorbid attention-deficit/hyperactivity disorder and depression. *J Am Acad Child Adolesc Psychiatry* 2001; 40:307–314.
128. Riggs PD, Leon SL, Mikulich SK, Pottle LC. An open trial of bupropion for ADHD in adolescents with substance use disorders and conduct disorder. *J Am Acad Child Adolesc Psychiatry* 1998; 37:1271–1278.
129. Solhkhah R, Wilens TE, Daly J, Prince JB, Van Patten SL, Biederman J. Bupropion SR for the treatment of substance-abusing outpatient adolescents with attention-deficit/hyperactivity disorder and mood disorders. *J Child Adolesc Psychopharmacol* 2005; 15:777–786.
130. McDermott SP, Wilens T. Cognitive therapy for adults with ADHD. In: Brown T, ed. *Subtypes of Attention Deficit Disorders in Children, Adolescents, and Adults*. Washington, DC: The American Psychiatric Press; 2000.
131. Levin FR, Sullivan MA, Donovan SJ. Co-occurring addictive and attention deficit/hyperactivity disorder and eating disorder. In: Graham AW, Schultz TK, Mayo-Smith MF, Ries RK, Wilford BB, eds. *Principles of Addiction Medicine*. 3rd edn. Chevy Chase, MD: American Society of Addiction Medicine, Inc; 2003.
132. Fleming JE, Offord DR. Epidemiology of childhood depressive disorders: A critical review. *J Am Acad Child Adolesc Psychiatry* 1990; 29:571–580.
133. Kashani JH, Keller MB, Solomon N, Reid JC, Mazzola D. Double depression in adolescent substance users. *J Affect Disord* 1985; 8:153–157.
134. Rhode P, Lewinsohn PM, Seeley JR. Psychiatric comorbidity with problematic alcohol use in high school students. *J Am Acad Child Adolesc Psychiatry* 1996; 35:101–109.

135. Clark DB, Pollock N, Bukstein OG, Mezzich AC, Bromberger JT, Donovan JE. Gender and comorbid psychopathology in adolescents with alcohol dependence. *J Am Acad Child Adolesc Psychiatry* 1997; 36:1195–1203.
136. Cornelius JR, Maisto SA, Martin CS *et al*. Major depression associated with earlier alcohol relapse in treated teens with AUD. Addict Behav 2004; 29:1035–1038.
137. Gibbons RD, Brown CH, Hur K *et al*. Early evidence on the effects of regulators' suicidality warnings on SSRI prescriptions and suicide in children and adolescents. *Am J Psychiatry* 2007; 164:1356–1363.
138. Riggs PD, Mikulich SK, Coffman LM, Crowley TJ. Fluoxetine in drug-dependent delinquents with major depression: An open trial. *J Child Adolesc Psychopharmacol* 1997; 7:87–95.

Index

Note: Page numbers with italicized *f*'s, *t*'s, and *b*'s refer to figures, tables, and boxes, respectively.

Young People and Alcohol: Impact, Policy, Prevention, Treatment, First Edition.
Edited by John B. Saunders and Joseph M. Rey.
© 2011 Blackwell Publishing Ltd. Published 2011 by Blackwell Publishing Ltd.